HITCHC

by

FRANÇOIS TRUFFAUT

With the Collaboration of HELEN G. SCOTT

SIMON & SCHUSTER PAPERBACKS
Rockefeller Center
1230 Avenue of the Americas
New York, New York 10020

Copyright © 1983 by François Truffaut and Éditions Ramsay

English language translation copyright © 1984 by François Truffaut

First published in France in 1983 by Éditions Ramsay
under the title Hitchcock/Truffaut

For information about special discounts for bulk purchases,
please contact Simon & Schuster Special Sales:
1-800-456-6798 or business@simonandschuster.com.

Manufactured in the United States of America

50 49 48 47 46 45 44 43 42 41

The Library of Congress has cataloged the hardcover edition as follows:

Truffaut, François.
  Hitchcock.
  Dialogue between Truffaut and Hitchcock.
  Translation of Le cinéma selon Hitchcock.
  Includes index.
  1. Hitchcock, Alfred, 1899–1980.   I. Hitchcock,
Alfred, 1899–1980.   II. Scott, Helen G.   III. Title.
PN1998.A3H573   1984   791.43'0233'0924   84-10686
ISBN-13: 978-0-671-52601-6
ISBN-10:   0-671-52601-4
ISBN-13: 978-0-671-60429-5 (Pbk)
ISBN-10:   0-671-60429-5 (Pbk)

The photographs illustrating this book were published with the kind permission of Alfred Hitchcock (producer), for the film *Number Thirteen*, distributed by W. and F. of London. Michael Balcon (producer), for the films *The White Shadow*, distributed by W. and F. of London and Selznick Distributing Corp. of the U.S.A.; *Woman to Woman*, distributed by W. and F. of London and Selznick Distributing Corp. of the U.S.A.; *Pleasure Garden*, distributed by W. and F. of London and Aywon Independent Distributors of the U.S.A.; *The Mountain Eagle*, distributed by W. and F. of London and Artlee Independent Distributors of the U.S.A.; *The Lodger*, distributed by W. and F. of London and Amer-Anglo Corp. of the U.S.A.; *Downhill*, distributed by W. and F. of London and World Wide Distributors of the U.S.A.; *Easy Virtue*, distributed by W. and F. of London and World Wide Distributors of the U.S.A. John Maxwell, British International Pict. (prod.), for the films: *The Ring*, distributed by Wardour; *The Farmer's Wife*, distributed by Wardour and Ufa Eastern Division of the U.S.A.; *Champagne*, distributed by Wardour; *The Manxman*, distributed by Wardour and Ufa Eastern Division of the U.S.A.; *Blackmail*, distributed by Wardour and Sono Art World Pictures of the U.S.A.; *Juno and the Paycock*, distributed by Wardour and British International of the U.S.A.; *Murder*, distributed by Wardour and British International of the U.S.A.; *The Skin Game*, distributed by Wardour and British International of the U.S.A.; *Rich and Strange*, distributed by Wardour and Powers Pictures of the U.S.A.; *Number Seventeen*, distributed by Wardour. Alfred Hitchcock, British International Pict. (prod.), for the film *Lord Camber's Ladies*, distributed by Wardour. Tom Arnold, Gaumont British production, for the film *Waltzes from Vienna*, distributed by Gaumont Film Distribution, Tom Arnold of the U.S.A. Michael Balcon and Ivor Montagu, G.B. Prod., for the films: *The Man Who Knew Too Much* (1st version), distributed by Gaumont Film Distribution G.B. of the U.S.A.; *The Thirty-nine Steps*, distributed by Gaumont Film Distribution G.B. Productions of the U.S.A.; *Secret Agent*, distributed by Gaumont Film Distribution G.B. Productions of the U.S.A.; *Sabotage*, distributed by Gaumont Film Distribution G.B. Productions of the U.S.A. Edward Black-Gainsborough, Gaumont British Picture for the film *Young and Innocent*, distributed by Gaumont Film Distribution, G.B. Productions of the U.S.A. Edward Black-Gainsborough Picture, for the film *The Lady Vanishes*, distributed by M.G.M. in England and G.B. Productions in the U.S.A. Eric Pommer and Charles Laughton, Mayflower Prod., for the film *Jamaica Inn*, distributed by Associated British, Paramount of the U.S.A. David O. Selznick, for the films *Rebecca*, distributed by United Artists, and *Spellbound*, distributed by United Artists. Walter Wanger, for *Foreign Correspondent*, distributed by United Artists. Harry Edington, for the film *Mr. and Mrs. Smith*, distributed by R.K.O. R.K.O. for the film *Suspicion*, distributed by R.K.O. Frank Lloyd and Jack H. Skirball, for the film *Shadow of a Doubt*, distributed by Universal. Kenneth Macgowan, for the film *Lifeboat*, distributed by 20th Century-Fox. British Ministry of Information, for the films *Bon Voyage* and *Aventure Malgache*. Alfred Hitchcock, for the film *Notorious*, distributed by R.K.O. David O. Selznick, for the film *The Paradine Case*, distributed by Selznick Releasing Organization. Hitchcock and Sidney Bernstein, Transatlantic Picture, for the films: *Rope*, distributed by Warner Brothers; *Under Capricorn*, distributed by Warner Brothers. Alfred Hitchcock, for the films: *Stage Fright*, distributed by Warner Brothers; *Strangers on a Train*, distributed by Warner Brothers; *I Confess*, distributed by Warner Brothers; *Dial M for Murder*, distributed by Warner Brothers; *Rear Window*, distributed by Paramount; *To Catch a Thief*, distributed by Paramount; *The Trouble with Harry*, distributed by Paramount; *The Man Who Knew Too Much* (2nd version), distributed by Paramount; *The Wrong Man*, distributed by Warner Brothers; *Vertigo*, distributed by Paramount; *North by Northwest*, distributed by M.G.M.; *Psycho*, distributed by Paramount; *The Birds*, distributed by Universal; *Marnie*, distributed by Universal; *Torn Curtain*, distributed by Universal. Philippe Halsman, for all the photographs illustrating the conversations of A. Hitchcock and F. Truffaut, © Philippe Halsman 1963.

OCK

REVISED EDITION

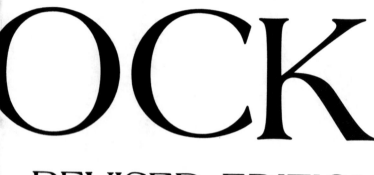

SIMON & SCHUSTER PAPERBACKS

New York   London   Toronto   Sydney

ACKNOWLEDGMENT

We wish to thank all those who helped in conceiving, completing or illustrating this book: Aimée Alexandre, Fanny Ardant, Emmanuele Bernheim, Peter Bogdanovich, René Bonnell, Raymond Cauchetier, Carlos Clarens, Josiane Couëdel, Roger Dagieu, *L'Express*, Odette Ferry, Lucette de Givray, Philippe Halsman, Monique Holveck, Christophe L., Jean-François Lentretien, Lydie Mahias, Madeleine Morgenstern, Christine Pellé, George Perry, Peggy Robertson, Laura Truffaut-Wong, Oliver Vaughan, Alain Venisse, *Cahiers du Cinéma*, Cinémathèque Française, Cinémathèque Royale de Belgique, The Museum of Modern Art, New York, National Film Archive, London.

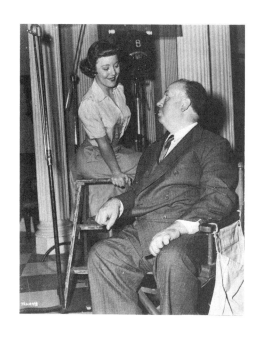

Alfred Hitchcock made
53 films and one daughter.
    I dedicate this book
to Patricia Hitchcock O'Connell

françois
truffaut

CONTENTS

PREFACE TO THE REVISED EDITION

Nowadays, the work of Alfred Hitchcock is admired all over the world. Young people who are just discovering his art through the current rerelease of *Rear Window* and *Vertigo*, or through *North by Northwest*, may assume his prestige has always been recognized, but this is far from being the case.

In the fifties and sixties, Hitchcock was at the height of his creativity and popularity. He was, of course, famous due to the publicity masterminded by producer David O. Selznick during the six or seven years of their collaboration on such films as *Rebecca*, *Notorious*, *Spellbound*, and *The Paradine Case*.

His fame had spread further throughout the world via the television series *Alfred Hitchcock Presents* in the mid-fifties. But American and European critics made him pay for his commercial success by reviewing his work with condescension, and by belittling each new film.

In 1962, while in New York to present *Jules and Jim*, I noticed that every journalist asked me the same question: "Why do the critics of *Cahiers du Cinéma* take Hitchcock so seriously? He's rich and successful, but his movies have no substance." In the course of an interview during which I praised *Rear Window* to the skies, an American critic surprised me by commenting, "You love *Rear Window* because, as a stranger to New York, you know nothing about Greenwich Village." To this absurd statement, I replied, "*Rear Window* is not about Greenwich Village, it is a film about cinema, and I *do* know cinema."

Upon my return to Paris, I was still disturbed by this exchange. From my past career as a critic, in common with all of the young writers from *Cahiers du Cinéma*, I still felt the imperative need to convince. It was obvious that Hitchcock, whose genius for publicity was equalled only by that of Salvador Dali, had in the long run been victimized in American intellectual circles because of his facetious response to interviewers and his deliberate practice of deriding their questions. In examining his films, it was obvious that he had given more thought to the potential of his art than any of his colleagues. It occurred to me that if he would, for the first time, agree to respond seriously to a systematic questionnaire, the resulting document might modify the American critics' approach to Hitchcock.

That is what this book is all about. Patiently prepared with the help of Helen Scott, whose editorial experience was a decisive factor, I dare say that our book achieved this result. At the time it was published, however, a young American film professor predicted: "This book will do more harm to your reputation in America than your worst film." As it happens, Charles Thomas Samuels was mistaken. He committed suicide a year or two later, undoubtedly for other reasons. In fact, from 1968 on, American critics began to take Hitchcock's work more seriously. Today, a movie like *Psycho* is regarded as a classic, and young film buffs have adopted Hitchcock wholeheartedly, without begrudging him his success, wealth, and fame.

While we were recording these talks with Hitchcock in August 1962, the final editing of *The Birds*, his forty-eighth picture, was under way. It took us some four years to transcribe the tapes and gather the photographs. Whenever I met Hitchcock during this period, I would question him in order to update the book I called "the hitchbook." The first edition, therefore, published at the end of 1967, concludes with his fiftieth film, *Torn Curtain*. In the final part of the present edition, there is an additional chapter commenting on *Topaz*, *Frenzy* (his last relative success), *Family Plot*, and, finally, *The Short Night*, a film he was preparing and constantly revising. In truth, his whole entourage was aware that Hitchcock's health and morale had deteriorated to such a point that a fifty-fourth picture was out of the question.

In the case of a man like Hitchcock, who lived only through and for his work, to cease activity was tantamount to a death sentence. He knew it as well as everybody else, and this is why the last four years of his life were so sad.

On May 2, 1980, a few days after his death, a mass was held in a small church on Santa Monica Boulevard in Beverly Hills. One year before, a farewell to Jean Renoir had taken place in the same church. Jean Renoir's coffin had been placed in front of the altar. Family, friends, neighbors, film buffs, and people off the street attended the ceremony. For Hitchcock, it was different. There was no coffin—it had been removed to an unknown destination. The guests, who had been invited by telegram, were checked in at the door by Universal's security men. The police kept the crowds outside at bay.

It was the burial of a timid man who had become intimidating and who, for the first time, was avoiding publicity, since it wouldn't help his work—a man who, since his adolescence, had trained himself to be in control of the situation.

The man was dead, but not the film-maker. For his pictures, made with loving care, an exclusive passion, and deep emotions concealed by exceptional technical mastery, are destined to circulate throughout the world, competing with newer productions, defying the test of time, and confirming Jean Cocteau's image of Marcel Proust: "His work kept on living, like the watches on the wrists of dead soldiers."

FRANÇOIS TRUFFAUT

INTRODUCTION

It all began when we broke the ice.

That happened in the winter of 1955, when Alfred Hitchcock, having completed the location shooting of *To Catch a Thief* on the Côte d'Azur, came to the Saint-Maurice studios, in Joinville, for the post-synchronization of the picture. My friend Claude Chabrol and I decided to go there to interview him for *Cahiers du Cinéma*. Armed with a long list of intricate questions and a borrowed tape recorder, we sallied forth in high spirits.

In Joinville we were directed to a pitch-black auditorium, where a loop showing Cary Grant and Brigitte Auber in a motorboat was being run continuously on the screen. In the darkness we introduced ourselves to Hitchcock, who courteously asked us to wait for him at the studio bar, across the courtyard.

Both movie-crazy, thrilled by our brief preview of Hitchcock's latest work, we emerged into the blinding glare of daylight, literally bursting with excitement. In the heat of our discussion we failed to notice the dark-gray frozen pond in the middle of the courtyard. With a single step forward we went over the ledge, landing on a thin layer of ice, which immediately gave way. Within seconds we were immersed in a pool of freezing water and a state of shock. In a hollow voice I asked Chabrol, "What about the tape recorder?" He replied by slowly raising his left arm to hold the case in mid-air, with the water bleakly oozing out from all sides like a stream of tears.

Staggering around the sloping basin, unable to reach the edge without sliding right back to the center, we were trapped in a situation straight out of a Hitchcock movie. Eventually, with the helping hand of a charitable bystander, we managed to reach firm ground.

A wardrobe mistress who was passing by invited us to follow her to a dressing room where we might take off our clothes and dry out. When we attempted to thank her for her kindness, she said in a businesslike way, "What a way to make a living! Are you extras for *Rififi?*" Upon learning that we were reporters, she lost all interest and told us to clear out.

A few minutes later, still soaking wet and shivering with cold, we made our way to the bar, where Hitchcock awaited us. He merely looked us over and, without a single comment on our appearance, amiably suggested another appointment for that evening at the Hotel Plaza Athénée.

A year later, upon spotting us at one of his Paris press conferences, Hitchcock finally acknowledged the incident by saying, "Gentlemen, every time I see a pair of ice cubes clicking together in a glass of whiskey, I think of you two."

We subsequently learned that he had embellished the story with a twist of his own. According to the Hitchcock version, Chabrol was dressed as a priest and I was wearing a gendarme's uniform when we turned up for the interview.

It was almost a decade after that preliminary aquatic contact that I undertook to approach Hitchcock again with a series of probing questions about his work. What prompted me to emulate Oedipus' consultation of the oracle was that my own efforts as a film-maker, in the years that followed, made me increasingly aware of the exceptional importance of Hitchcock's contribution and of its particular value to all those who work in the screen medium.

The examination of Hitchcock's directorial career, ranging as it does from his silent movies in Great Britain to his current color films in Hollywood, is a richly rewarding source of discovery. In Hitchcock's

work a film-maker is bound to find the answer to many of his own problems, including the most fundamental question of all: how to express oneself by purely visual means.

I am not so much the author as the initiator, or if you prefer, the instigator, of this work on Alfred Hitchcock. The book is essentially a journalistic work, made possible when Alfred Hitchcock agreed to a fifty-hour-long interview.

In 1962 I wrote to Mr. Hitchcock, asking whether he would answer some five hundred questions dealing solely with his career, in chronological order, and suggesting that our discussion deal with the following:

(a) the circumstances attending the inception of each picture;
(b) the preparation and structure of the screenplays;
(c) specific directorial problems on each film;
(d) Hitchcock's own assessment of the commercial and artistic results in relation to his initial expectations for each picture.

Hitchcock cabled his agreement. There now remained one last hurdle, the language barrier, and I turned to my friend Helen Scott, of the French Film Office in New York. An American raised in France, her thorough command of the cinema vocabulary, her sound judgment and exceptional human qualities, made her the ideal accomplice for the project.

We arrived in Hollywood on August 13, Hitchcock's birthday. Every morning he would pick us up at the Beverly Hills Hotel to take us to his office at Univer-

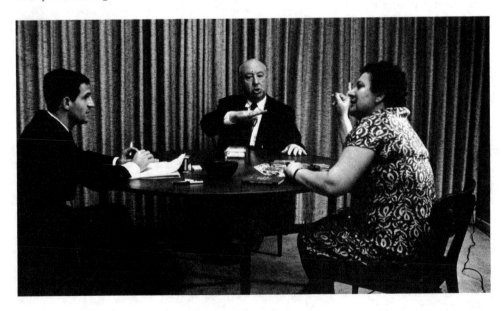

14

sal studios. With each of us wearing a microphone, and a sound engineer in the next room recording our voices, we kept up a running conversation from nine to six every day, achieving something of a track record as we talked our way through lunches.

A witty raconteur, noted for his entertaining interviews, Hitchcock started out true to form, regaling us with a series of amusing anecdotes. It was only on the third day that he became more sober and thoughtful in spelling out the ups and downs of his career. His assessment of the achievements and the failures was genuinely self-critical, and his account of his doubts, frustrations, and hopes was completely sincere.

What emerged, as the talks progressed, was a striking contrast between Hitchcock's public image and his real self. Under the invariably self-possessed and often cynical surface is a deeply vulnerable, sensitive, and emotional man who feels with particular intensity the sensations he communicates to his audience.

The man who excels at filming fear is himself a very fearful person, and I suspect that this trait of his personality has a direct bearing on his success. Throughout his entire career he has felt the need to protect himself from the actors, producers, and technicians who, insofar as their slightest lapse or whim may jeopardize the integrity of his work, all represent as many hazards to a director. How better to defend oneself than to become the director no actor will question, to become one's own producer, and to know more about technique than the technicians?

To stay with the audience, Hitchcock set out to win it over by reawakening all the strong emotions of childhood. In his work the viewer can recapture the tensions and thrills of the games of hide-and-seek or blindman's buff and the terror of those nights when, by a trick of the imagination, a forgotten toy on the dresser gradually acquires a mysterious and threatening shape.

All of this brings us to suspense, which, even among those who acknowledge Hitchcock's mastery of it, is commonly regarded as a minor form of the spectacle, whereas actually it is *the* spectacle in itself.

Suspense is simply the dramatization of a film's narrative material, or, if you will, the most intense presentation possible of dramatic situations. Here's a case in point: A man leaves his home, hails a cab and drives to the station to catch a train. This is a normal scene in an average picture. Now, should

that man happen to look at his watch just as he is getting into the cab and exclaim, "Good God, I shall never make that train!" that entire ride automatically becomes a sequence of pure suspense. Every red light, traffic signal, shift of the gears or touch on the brake, and every cop on the way to the station will intensify its emotional impact.

The manifest clarity and persuasive power of the image are such that it simply will not occur to the viewer to reason: "What's his hurry? Why can't he take the next train?" Thanks to the tension created by the frenzied imagery on the screen, the urgency of the action will never be questioned.

Obviously, this insistence on the dramatization cannot avoid the "arbitrary," and although Hitchcock's art is precisely the ability to impose the "arbitrary," this sometimes leads the die-hards to complain about implausibility. While Hitchcock maintains that he is not concerned with plausibility, the truth is that he is rarely implausible. What he does, in effect, is to hinge the plot around a striking coincidence, which provides him with the master situation. His treatment from then on consists in feeding a maximum of tension and plausibility into the drama, pulling the strings ever tighter as he builds up toward a paroxysm. Then he suddenly lets go, allowing the story to unwind swiftly.

In general the suspense sequences of a film are its "privileged moments," those highlights that linger on in the viewer's memory. But Hitchcock wants each and every scene to be a "privileged moment," and all of his efforts throughout his career have been directed toward achieving pictures that have no gaps or flaws.

It is this determination to compel the audience's uninterrupted attention, to create and then to keep up the emotion, to sustain the tension throughout, that makes Hitchcock's pictures so completely personal and all but inimitable. For it is not only on the crucial passages of the story that he exercises his authority; his single-mindedness of purpose is also reflected in the exposition, the transitions, and all the sequences which in most films are generally inconsequential.

Even an episode that merely serves to bridge two key sequences will never be commonplace, for Hitchcock loathes the "ordinary." For instance, a man who is in trouble with the law—but who we know is innocent—takes his case to a lawyer. This is an everyday situation. As handled by Hitchcock, the lawyer will appear to be skeptical and rather reluctant to become involved. Or he may, as in *The Wrong Man*, agree to go along only after warning his prospective client that he lacks experience in this kind of legal work and may not be the right man for the case.

By introducing this disturbing note, a feeling of apprehension and anxiety has been created that invests this ordinary situation with potential drama.

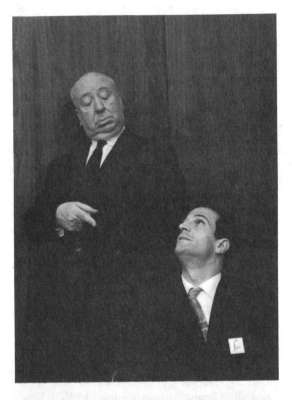

Another illustration of this approach is his out-of-the-ordinary twist to the conventional scene in which a young man is introducing his girl friend to his mother. Naturally, the girl is anxious to please the older woman, who may one day become her mother-in-law. In contrast to her boy friend's relaxed manner, hers is clearly shy and flustered. With the son's introductory ritual fading into the off-screen background, the viewers will see a change come over the woman's expression as she stares at the girl, sizing her up with that purely Hitchcockian look so familiar to cinephiles. The young girl's inner turmoil is indicated by a slight movement of retreat. Here again, by means of a simple look, Hitchcock creates one of those domineering mothers he excels at portraying.

From this point on, all of the family scenes in the picture will be charged with emotion and taut with conflict, with every detail reflecting Hitchcock's determination to keep banality off the screen.

The art of creating suspense is also the art of involving the audience, so that the viewer is actually a participant in the film. In this area of the spectacle, film-making is not a dual interplay between the director and his picture, but a three-way game in which the audience, too, is required to play. In the filmic context, suspense, like Tom Thumb's white pebbles or Little Red Riding-hood's walk through the woods, is a poetic means that serves to heighten the emotions and to make the heart beat faster.

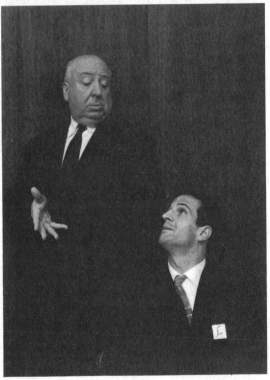

To reproach Hitchcock for specializing in suspense is to accuse him of being the least boring of film-makers; it is also tantamount to blaming a lover who instead of concentrating on his own pleasure insists on sharing it with his partner. The nature of Hitchcock's cinema is to absorb the audience so completely that the Arab viewer will forget to shell his peanuts, the Frenchman will ignore the girl in the next seat, the Italian will suspend his chain smoking, the compulsive cougher will refrain from coughing, and the Swedes will interrupt their love-making in the aisles.

Hitchcock is universally acknowledged to be the

world's foremost technician; even his detractors willingly concede him this title. Yet, isn't it obvious that the choice of a scenario, its construction, and all of its contents are intimately connected to and, in fact, dependent upon that technique? All artists are indignant—and rightly so—at the critical tendency to separate form from content. This procedure is particularly illogical when applied to Hitchcock, who, as Eric Rohmer and Claude Chabrol correctly point out in their book,* is neither a simple storyteller nor an esthete. "Hitchcock," they write, "is one of the greatest inventors of form in the history of cinema. Perhaps the only film-makers who can be compared with him in this respect are Murnau and Eisenstein . . . Here, form does not merely. embellish content, but actually creates it."

The art of film-making is an especially difficult one to master, inasmuch as it calls for multiple and often contradictory talents. The reason why so many brilliant or very talented men have failed in their attempts at directing is that only a mind in which the analytic and synthetic are simultaneously at work can make its way out of the maze of snares inherent in the fragmentation of the shooting, the cutting, and the montage of a film. To a director, the greatest danger of all is that in the course of making his film he may lose control of it. Indeed, this is the most common cause of all fatalities.

Each cut of a picture, lasting from three to ten seconds, is information that is given to the viewer. This information is all too often obscure or downright incomprehensible, either because the director's intentions were vague to begin with or he lacked the competence to convey them clearly.

To those who question whether clarity is all that important, I can only say that it is *the* most important quality in the making of a film. By way of explanation, here is a typical example: "At this point, Balachov, understanding that he had been cheated by Carradine, went to see Benson, proposing that they contact Tolmachef and share the loot between them," etc., etc.

In hundreds of films this dialogue, or a variant thereof, has left you bewildered, or worse, indifferent to the proceedings on the screen. For while the authors know all about Balachov, Carradine, Benson, and Tolmachef, you, the viewer, are utterly confused by virtue of that cardinal rule of cinema:

---

* *Hitchcock*, by Eric Rohmer and Claude Chabrol. Editions Universitaires, Paris, 1957.

Whatever is *said* instead of being *shown* is lost upon the viewer.

Since Hitchcock chooses to express everything by purely visual means, he has no use whatever for Messrs. Balachov, Carradine, Benson, and Tolmachef.

One of the charges frequently leveled at Hitchcock is that the simplification inherent in his emphasis on clarity limits his cinematic range to almost childlike ideas. To my mind, nothing could be further from the truth; on the contrary, because of his unique ability to film the thoughts of his characters and make them perceptible without resorting to dialogue, he is, to my way of thinking, a realistic director.

Hitchcock a realist? In cinema, as on the stage, dialogue serves to express the thoughts of the characters, but we know that in real life the things people say to each other do not necessarily reflect what they actually think and feel. This is especially true of such mundane occasions as dinner and cocktail parties, or of any meeting between casual acquaintances.

If we observe any such gathering, it is clear that the words exchanged between the guests are superficial formalities and quite meaningless, whereas the essential is elsewhere; it is by studying their eyes that we can find out what is truly on their minds.

Let us assume that as an observer at a reception I am looking at Mr. Y as he tells three people all about his recent holiday in Scotland with his wife. By carefully watching his face, I notice he never takes his eyes off Mrs. X's legs. Now, I move over to Mrs. X, who is talking about her children's problems at school, but I notice that she keeps staring at Miss Z, her cold look taking in every detail of the younger woman's elegant appearance.

Obviously, the substance of that scene is not in the dialogue, which is strictly conventional, but in what these people are thinking about. Merely by watching them I have found out that Mr. Y is physically attracted to Mrs. X and that Mrs. X is jealous of Miss Z.

From Hollywood to Cinecitta no film-maker other than Hitchcock can capture the human reality of that scene as faithfully as I have described it. And yet, for the past forty years, each of his pictures features several such scenes in which the rule of counterpoint between dialogue and image achieves a dramatic effect by purely visual means. Hitchcock is almost unique in being able to film directly, that is, without resorting to explanatory dialogue, such intimate emotions as suspicion, jealousy, desire, and envy. And herein lies a paradox: the director who, through the simplicity and clarity of his work, is the most accessible to a universal audience is also the director who excels at filming the most complex and subtle relationships between human beings.

In the United States, the major developments in the art of film direction were achieved between 1908 and 1930, primarily by D. W. Griffith. Most of the masters of the silent screen who were influenced by him, among them Von Stroheim, Eisenstein, Murnau, and Lubitsch, are now dead; others, still alive, are no longer working.

Considering the fact that the Americans who entered the film medium after 1930 have barely scratched the surface of the limitless potential Griffith opened up, I believe it is not an overstatement to conclude that, with the notable exception of Orson Welles, no major visual sensibility has emerged in Hollywood since the advent of sound. If the cinema, by some twist of fate, were to be deprived overnight of the sound track and to become once again the art of silent cinematography that it was between 1895 and 1930, I truly believe most of the directors in the field would be compelled to take up some new line of work. In this sense it would seem as if the only heirs to the Griffith secrets in the Hollywood of 1966 are Howard Hawks, John Ford, and Alfred Hitchcock. One wonders, not without melancholy, whether that legacy will survive when they retire from the screen.

I know that many Americans are surprised that European cinephiles—and the French in particular—regard Alfred Hitchcock as a "film author," in the sense that the term is applied to Ingmar Bergman, Federico Fellini, Luis Bunuel, or Jean-Luc Godard.

When the Americans counter Hitchcock's name by citing others that have enjoyed prestige in Hollywood for the past twenty years, there is clearly a divergence in the viewpoints of the New York critics and their Parisian counterparts.

Among the big Hollywood names, the Oscar "collectors," there are undoubtedly many men of talent. And yet, as they switch from a Biblical opus to a psychological western, or from a war epic to a comedy of manners, how can we look upon them as anything else than simple craftsmen, carrying out instructions, dutifully falling in line with the commercial trends of the day? Why establish any distinction between these motion-picture directors and their counterparts in the theater when, year in and year out, they follow a similar pattern, going from the screen version of a William Inge play to an Irwin Shaw best seller, while working on an adaptation of the latest Tennessee Williams?

Unlike the "film author," who is motivated by the need to introduce his own ideas on life, on people, on money and love into his work, these men are mere show-business specialists, simple technicians. Are they great technicians? Their persistence in limiting themselves to an infinitesimal part of the extraordinary possibilities offered by Hollywood's studios allows for some doubt on this score as well. Of what does their work actually consist?

They set up a scene, place the actors within that setting and then proceed to film the whole of that scene, which is substantially dialogue, in six or eight different ways by varying the shooting angle, from the front, the side, a high shot, and so on. Afterward, they do it over again, this time varying the focus. The next step is to film the whole scene, first using a full shot, then a medium shot, and finally in close-up.

This is not to suggest that the Hollywood greats, as a whole, do not deserve their reputations. To give credit where it is due, most of them have a specialty, something they do exceptionally well. Some excel at getting a superior performance from their stars, while others have a flair for bringing new talent to light. Some directors are brilliant storytellers and others have a remarkable gift for improvisation. Some are excellent at battle scenes and others have a knack with the intimate comedy genre.

If Hitchcock, to my way of thinking, outranks the rest, it is because he is the most complete film-maker of all. He is not merely an expert at some specific aspect of cinema, but an all-round specialist, who excels at every image, each shot, and every scene. He masterminds the construction of the screenplay as well as the photography, the cutting, and the sound track, has creative ideas on everything and can handle anything and is even, as we already know, expert at publicity!

Because he exercises such complete control over all the elements of his films and imprints his personal concepts at each step of the way, Hitchcock has a distinctive style of his own. He is undoubtedly one of the few film-makers on the horizon today whose screen signature can be identified as soon as the picture begins.

The suspense sequences are by no means the only cues to Hitchcock's authorship. His style can be recognized in a scene involving conversation between two people, in his unique way of handling the looks they exchange, and of punctuating their dialogue with silent pauses, by the simplified gestures, and even by the dramatic quality of the frame. Just as unmistakably Hitchcockian is the art of conveying to the viewer that one of the two characters dominates, is in love with, or is jealous of, the other. It is the art of creating a specific dramatic mood without recourse to dialogue, and finally the art of leading us from one emotion to another, at the rhythm of our own sensitivity.

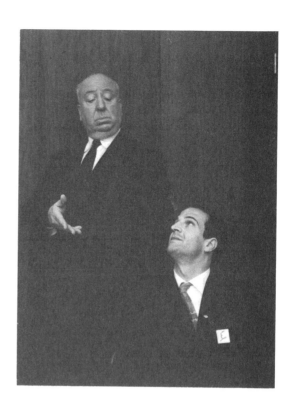

If I apply the term "complete" to Hitchcock's work, it is because I find in it both research and innovation, a sense of the concrete and a sense of the abstract, intense drama as well as a subtle brand of humor. His films are at once commercial and experimental, as universal as William Wyler's *Ben Hur* and as confidential as Kenneth Anger's *Fireworks*.

Psycho is a picture that rallied vast audiences throughout the world; yet, in its savagery and uninhibited license, it goes much further than those daring 16-mm. essays by youthful *avant-garde* film-makers that somehow never get past the censors. Some of the miniatures in *North by Northwest* and many of the special effects in *The Birds* have all the poetic flavor of experimental cinema that Jiri Trnka achieves with his puppets and that Norman McLaren achieves with his four-minute shorts designed directly on film.

When a director undertakes to make a western, he is not necessarily thinking of John Ford, since there are equally fine movies in the genre by Howard Hawks and Raoul Walsh. Yet, if he sets out to make a thriller or a suspense picture, you may be certain that in his heart of hearts he is hoping to live up to one of Hitchcock's masterpieces.

In recent years there have been countless imitations of *Vertigo*, *North by Northwest*, and *Psycho*; whether it is acknowledged or not, there is no doubt that Hitchcock's work has long influenced world cinema.

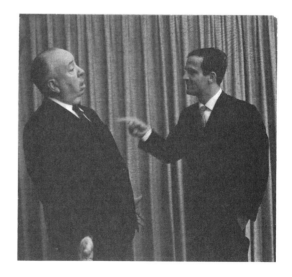

Overt or subconscious, bearing either on the style or the theme, mostly beneficial, occasionally ill-advised, this influence is reflected in the works of film-makers who are vastly different from each other:

Among others, there are Henri Verneuil *(Any Number Can Win)*, Alain Resnais *(Muriel, La Guerre Est Finie)*, Philippe de Broca *(That Man from Rio)*,

Orson Welles (*The Stranger*), Vincente Minnelli (*Undercurrent*), Henri-Georges Clouzot (*Diabolique*), Lee Thompson (*Cape Fear*), René Clément (*Purple Noon, The Day and the Hour*), Mark Robson (*The Prize*), Edward Dmytryk (*Mirage*), Robert Wise (*House on Telegraph Hill, The Haunting*), Ted Tetzlaff (*The Window*), Robert Aldrich (*Baby Jane*), Akira Kurosawa (*High and Low*), William Wyler (*The Collector*), Otto Preminger (*Bunny Lake Is Missing*), Roman Polanski (*Repulsion*), Claude Autant-Lara (*Enough Rope, Over Here*), Ingmar Bergman (*The Virgin Spring*), William Castle (*Homicide*), Claude Chabrol (*The Cousins, The Third Lover, Marie-Chantal contre le Dr. Ka*), Alain Robbe-Grillet (*L'Immortelle*), Paul Paviot (*Portrait Robot*), Richard Quine (*Liaisons Secretes*), Anatole Litvak (*Five Miles to Midnight*), Stanley Donen (*Arabesque, Charade*), André Delvaux (*L'Homme au Crane Rasé*), François Truffaut (*Fahrenheit 451*), not to mention the James Bond series, which is nothing else than a rough caricature of all Hitchcock's work, and of *North by Northwest* in particular.

There is no question here of fatuous admiration, nor am I suggesting that all of Hitchcock's work is perfect and beyond reproach. But inasmuch as his achievements have, until now, been grossly underrated, I feel it is high time Hitchcock was granted the leading position he deserves. Only then can we go on to appraise his work; indeed, his own critical comments in the pages that follow set the tone for such an objective examination.

British critics, who at heart have perhaps never forgiven Hitchcock for his voluntary exile, still marvel —and rightly so—at the youthful, spirited vigor of *The Lady Vanishes*, which he made thirty years ago. But isn't it futile to look back and regret that which must necessarily yield to the passage of time? The ebullient, young Hitchcock of *The Lady Vanishes* could not possibly have captured on film James Stewart's emotions in *Vertigo*, a work of maturity and lyrical commentary on the relation between love and death.

In a critical essay published in *Film Quarterly*, Charles Higham describes Hitchcock as a *"practical joker, a cunning and sophisticated cynic."* He refers to his *"narcissism and its concomitant coldness"* and to his *"pitiless mockery,"* which *"is not a gentle mockery."* According to Higham, Hitchcock has a *"tough contempt for the world"* and his skill *"is most strikingly displayed when he has a destructive comment to make."*

Though he raises an important point, I feel Mr. Higham is definitely mistaken in questioning Hitchcock's sincerity and his serious approach to life. A strong person may be genuinely cynical, whereas in a more sensitive nature, cynicism is merely a front. Von Stroheim used cynicism to cover up his deep sentimentality; in the case of Alfred Hitchcock it is the façade that serves to conceal his pessimism.

Louis-Ferdinand Céline divided people into two categories, the exhibitionists and the voyeurs; Alfred Hitchcock clearly belongs in the latter category. He is not involved in life; he merely contemplates it. In making a film like *Hatari*, Howard Hawks gratifies his dual passion for hunting and for cinema. In the life of Alfred Hitchcock there is but one passion, which was clearly expressed in his reply to a moralizing attack on *Rear Window*. "Nothing," he said, "could have prevented my making that picture, because my love for cinema is stronger than any morality."

While the cinema of Hitchcock is not necessarily exalting, it invariably enriches us, if only through the terrifying lucidity with which it denounces man's desecrations of beauty and purity.

If, in the era of Ingmar Bergman, one accepts the premise that cinema is an art form, on a par with literature, I suggest that Hitchcock belongs—and why classify him at all?—among such artists of anxiety as Kafka, Dostoyevsky, and Poe.

In the light of their own doubts these artists of anxiety can hardly be expected to show us how to live; their mission is simply to share with us the anxieties that haunt them. Consciously or not, this is their way of helping us to understand ourselves, which is, after all, a fundamental purpose of any work of art.

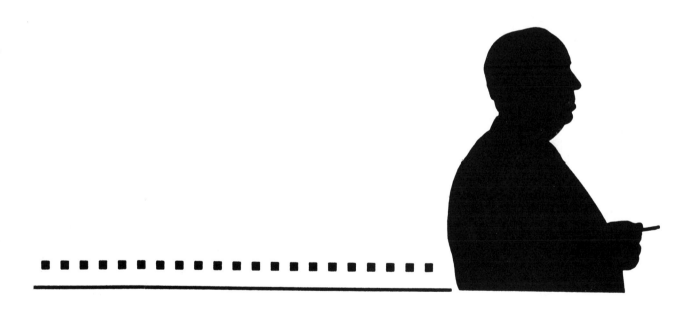

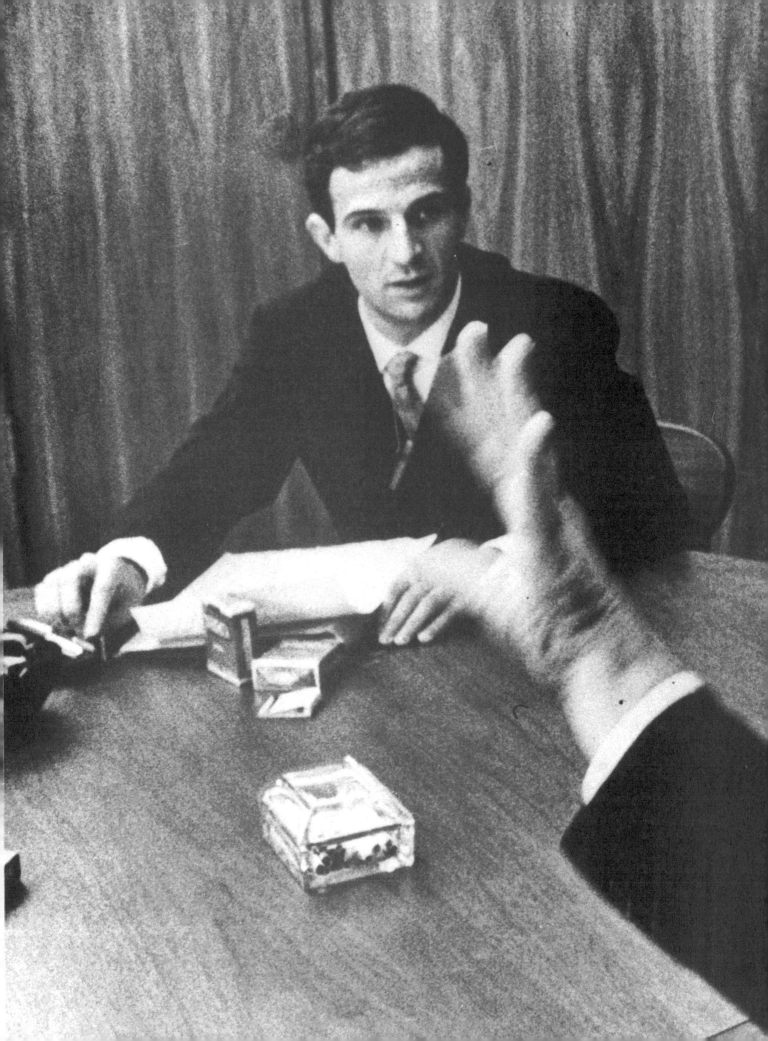

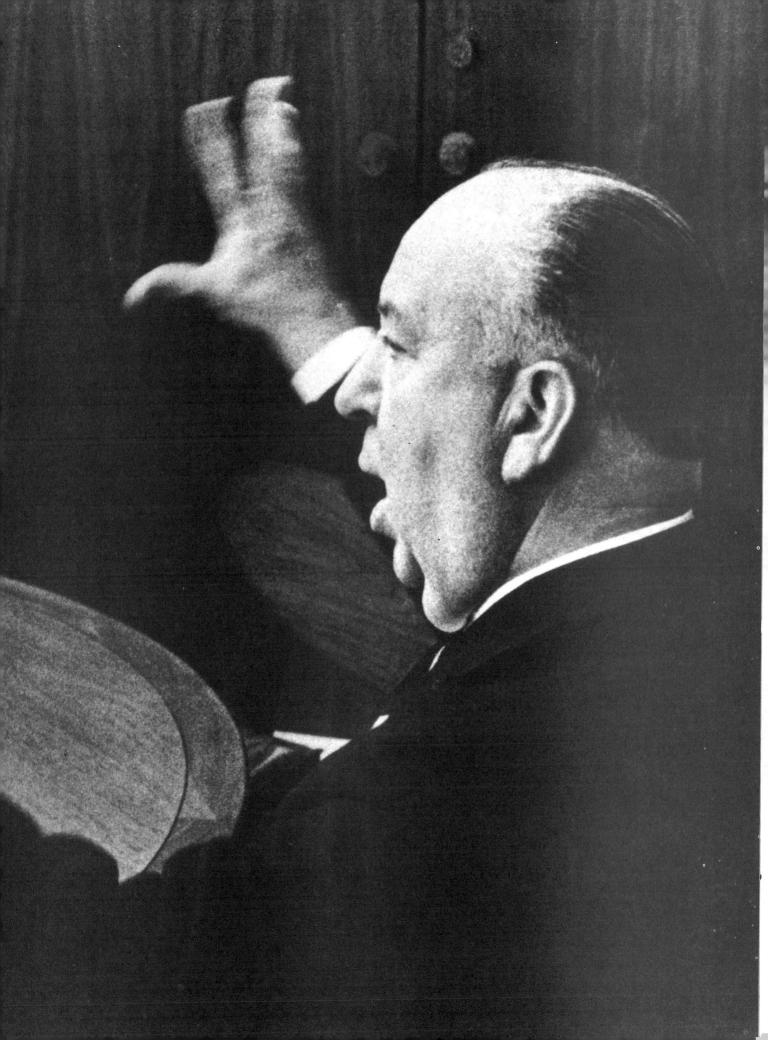

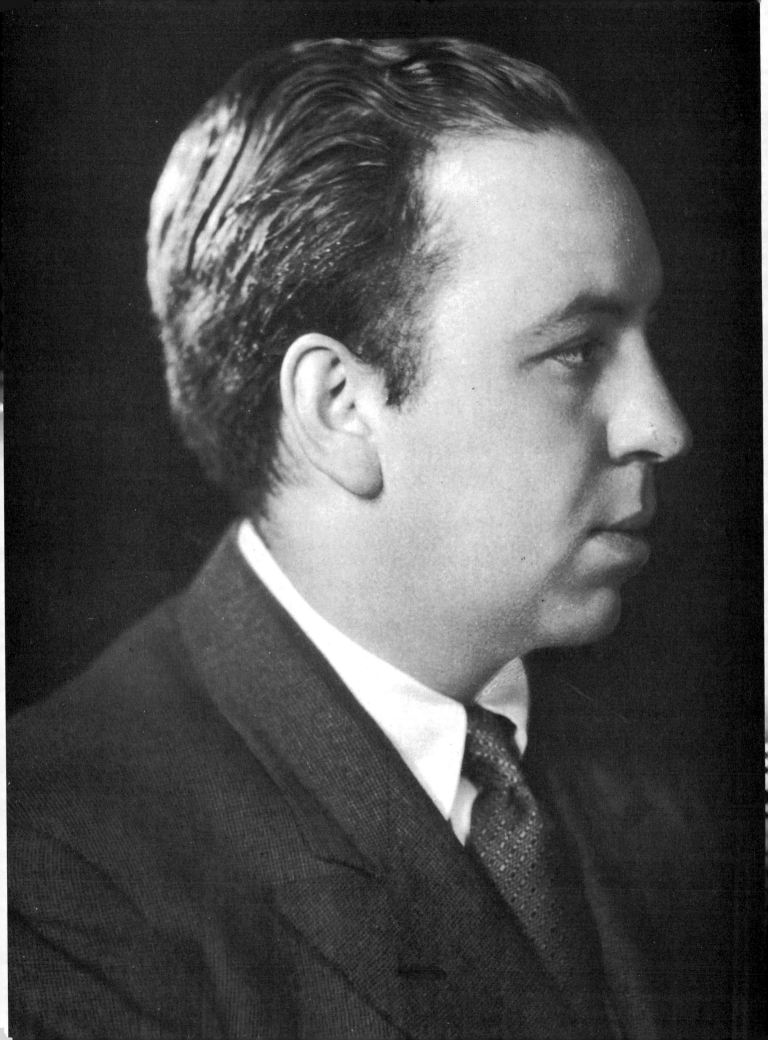

1

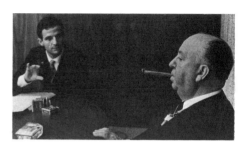

FRANÇOIS TRUFFAUT. Mr. Hitchcock, you were born in London on August 13, 1899. The only thing I know about your childhood is the incident at the police station. Is that a true story?

ALFRED HITCHCOCK. Yes, it is. I must have been about four or five years old. My father sent me to the police station with a note. The chief of police read it and locked me in a cell for five or ten minutes, saying, "This is what we do to naughty boys."

F.T. Why were you being punished?

A.H. I haven't the faintest idea. As a matter of fact, my father used to call me his "little lamb without a spot." I truly cannot imagine what it was I did.

F.T. I've heard that your father was very strict.

A.H. Let's just say he was a rather nervous man. What else can I tell you? Well, my family loved the theater. As I think back upon it, we must have been a rather eccentric little group. At any rate, I was what is known as a well-behaved child. At family gatherings I would sit quietly in a corner, saying nothing. I looked and observed a good deal. I've always been that way and still am. I was anything but expansive. I was a loner—can't remember ever having had a playmate. I played by myself, inventing my own games.

I was put into school very young. At St. Ignatius College, a Jesuit school in London. Ours was a Catholic family and in England, you see, this in itself is an eccentricity. It was probably during

25

this period with the Jesuits that a strong sense of fear developed—moral fear—the fear of being involved in anything evil. I always tried to avoid it. Why? Perhaps out of physical fear. I was terrified of physical punishment. In those days they used a cane made of very hard rubber. I believe the Jesuits still use it. It wasn't done casually, you know; it was rather like the execution of a sentence. They would tell you to step in to see the father when classes were over. He would then solemnly inscribe your name in the register, together with the indication of the punishment to be inflicted, and you spent the whole day waiting for the sentence to be carried out.

F.T.   I've read that you were rather average as a student and that your only strong point was geography.

A.H.   I was usually among the four or five at the top of the class. Never first; second only once or twice, and generally fourth or fifth. They claimed I was rather absent-minded.

F.T.   Wasn't it your ambition, at the time, to become an engineer?

A.H.   Well, little boys are always asked what they want to be when they grow up, and it must be said to my credit that I never wanted to be a policeman. When I said I'd like to become an engineer, my parents took me seriously and they sent me to a specialized school, the School of Engineering and Navigation, where I studied mechanics, electricity, acoustics, and navigation.

F.T.   Then you had scientific leanings?

A.H.   Perhaps. I did acquire some practical knowledge of engineering, the theory of the laws of force and motion, electricity—theoretical and applied. Then I had to make a living, so I went to work with the Henley Telegraph Company. At the same time I was taking courses at the University of London, studying art.
At Henley's I specialized in electric cables. I became a technical estimator when I was about nineteen.

F.T.   Were you interested in motion pictures at the time?

A.H.   Yes, I had been for several years. I was very keen on pictures and the stage and very often went to first nights by myself. From the age of sixteen on I read film journals. Not fan or fun magazines, but always professional and trade papers. And since I was studying art at the University of London, Henley's transferred me to the advertising department, where I was given a chance to draw.

F.T.   What kind of drawings?

A.H.   Designs for advertisements of electric cables. And this work was a first step toward cinema. It helped me to get into the field.

F.T.   Can you remember specifically some of the films that appealed to you at the time?

A.H.   Though I went to the theater very often, I preferred the movies and was more attracted to American films than to the British. I saw the pictures of Chaplin, Griffith, all the Paramount Famous Players pictures, Buster Keaton, Douglas Fairbanks, Mary Pickford, as well as the German films of Decla-Bioscop, the company that preceded UFA. Murnau worked for them.

F.T.   Can you single out a picture that made a special impression?

A.H.   One of Decla-Bioscop's most famous pictures was *Der müde Tod*.

F.T.   Wasn't that directed by Fritz Lang? The British title, I believe, was *Destiny*.

A.H.   I guess so. The leading man, I recall, was Bernhard Goetzke.

F.T.   Did you like Murnau's films?

A.H.   Yes, but they came later. In '23 or '24.

F.T.   What films were being shown in 1920?

A.H.   Well, I remember a *Monsieur Prince*. In England it was called *Whiffles*.

F.T.   You've often been quoted as having said: "Like all directors, I was influenced by Griffith."

A.H.   I especially remember *Intolerance* and *The Birth of a Nation*.

F.T.   How did you happen to go from Henley's to a film company?

A.H.   I read in a trade paper that an American company, Paramount's Famous Players-Lasky, was opening a branch in Islington, London. They were going to build studios there, and they announced a production schedule. Among others, a picture taken from such and such a book. I don't remember the title. While still working at Henley's, I read that book through and then made several drawings that might eventually serve to illustrate the titles.

F.T.   By "titles" you mean the captions that covered the dialogue in silent pictures?

A.H.   That's right. At the time, those titles were illustrated. On each card you had the narrative title, the dialogue, and a small drawing. The most famous of these narrative titles was "Came the dawn." You also had "The next morning . . ." For instance, if the line read: "George was leading a very fast life by this time," I would draw a candle, with a flame at each end, just below the sentence. Very naïve.

F.T.   So you took this initiative and then submitted your work to Famous Players?

A.H.   Exactly. I showed them my drawings and they put me on at once. Later on I became head of the title department. I went to work for the editorial department of the studio. The head of the department had two American writers under him, and when a picture was finished, the head of the editorial department would write the titles or would rewrite those of the original script. Because in those days it was possible to completely alter the meaning of a script through the use of narrative titles and spoken titles.

F.T.   How so?

A.H.   Well, since the actor pretended to speak and the dialogue appeared on the screen right afterward, they could put whatever words they liked in his mouth. Many a bad picture was saved in this way. For instance, if a drama had been poorly filmed and was ridiculous, they would insert comedy titles all the way through and the picture was a great hit. Because, you see, it became a satire. One could really do anything—take the end of a picture and put it at the beginning—anything at all!

F.T.   And this gave you a chance to see the inside of film-making?

A.H.   Yes. At this time I met several American writers and I learned how to write scripts. And sometimes when an extra scene was needed—but not an acting scene—they would let me shoot it. However, the pictures made by Famous Players in England were unsuccessful in America. So the studio became a rental studio for British producers.
Meanwhile, I had read a novel in a magazine, and just as an exercise, I wrote a script based on this story. I knew that an American company had the exclusive world rights to the property, but I did it anyway, since it was merely for practice.
When the British companies took over the Islington studios, I approached them for work and I landed a job as an assistant director.

F.T.   With Michael Balcon?

A.H.   No, not yet. Before that I worked on a picture called *Always Tell Your Wife*, which featured Seymour Hicks, a very well-known London actor. One day he quarreled with the director and said to me, "Let's you and me finish this thing by ourselves." So I helped him and we completed the picture.
Meanwhile, the company formed by Michael Balcon became a tenant at the studios, and I became an assistant director for this new venture. It was the company that Balcon had set up

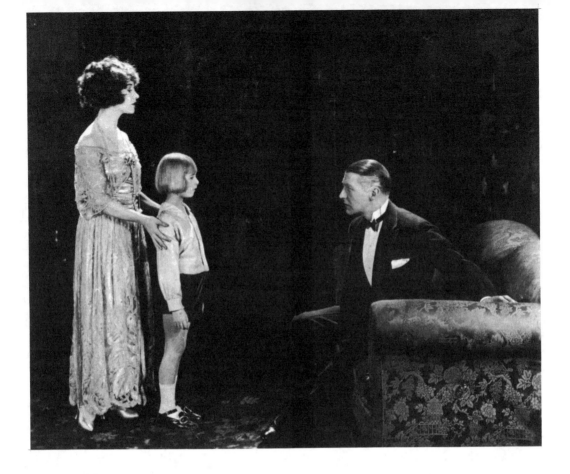

Betty Compson and Clive Brook in *Woman to Woman*.
Set created by Hitchcock for *Woman to Woman*.

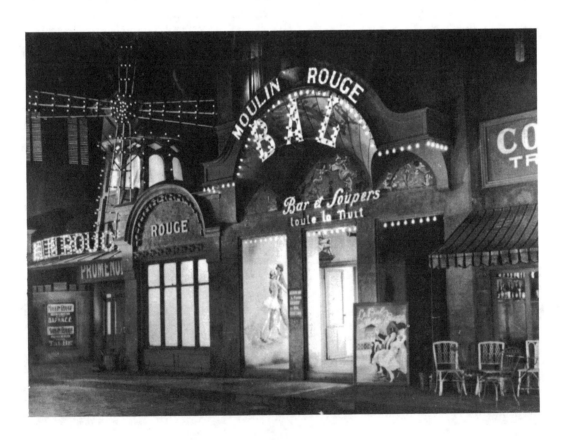

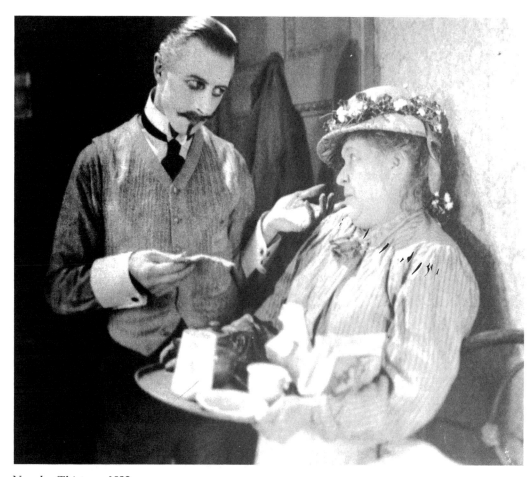

Number Thirteen, 1922.

with Victor Saville and John Freedman. They bought the rights to a play. It was called *Woman to Woman*. Then they said, "Now we need a script," and I said, "I would like to write it."

"You? What have you done?"

I said, "I can show you something." And I showed them the adaptation I'd written as an exercise. They were very impressed and I got the job. That was in 1922.

F.T.   I see. You were then twenty-three. But didn't you direct a little picture called *Number Thirteen* before that time?

A.H.   A two-reeler. It was never completed.

F.T.   Wasn't it a documentary?

A.H.   No. There was a woman working at the studio who had worked with Chaplin. In those days anyone who had worked with Chap-

lin was top drawer: She had written a story and we found a little money. It wasn't very good, really. Aside from which, it was just at this point that the Americans closed their studio.

F.T.   I've never seen *Woman to Woman*. In fact, I don't even know the story.

A.H.   As you said, I was twenty-three at the time, and I'd never been out with a girl in my life. I'd never had a drink in my life. The story was taken from a play that had been a hit in London. It was about a British Army officer in World War I. On leave in Paris he has an affair with a dancer, then he goes back to the front. He is shell-shocked and loses his memory. He returns to England and marries a society woman. And then the dancer turns up with child. Conflict . . . the story ends with the dancer's death.

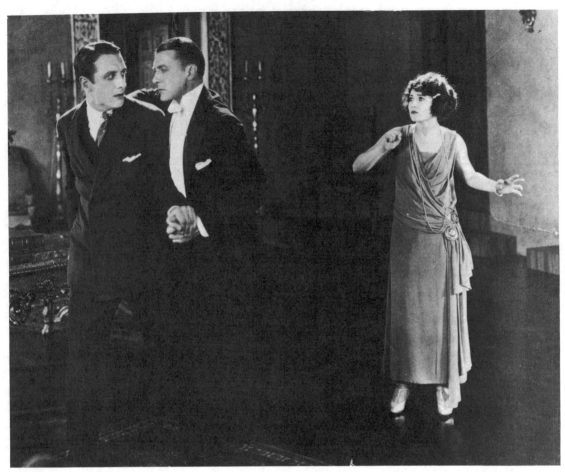

The White Shadow (1923).

F.T.   Graham Cutts directed that picture. You did the adaptation and dialogue, and were assistant director as well?

A.H.   More than that! My friend, the art director, was unable to work on the picture. I volunteered to serve as art director. So I did all of this and also helped on the production. My future wife, Alma Reville, was the editor of the picture as well as the script girl. In those days the script girl and the editor were one and the same person. Today the script girl keeps too many books, as you know. She's a real bookkeeper. It was while working on that picture that I first met my wife.

Then I performed these various functions for several other films. The second was *The White Shadow*, the third was *The Passionate Adventure*, and the fourth was *The Blackguard*. And then there was *The Prude's Fall*.

F.T.   As you recall them now, would you say all of those pictures were about the same, or do you have a preference?

A.H.   *Woman to Woman* was the best of the lot and the most successful. When we made *The Prude's Fall*, the last one of this series, the director took his lady friend along on location. We went to Venice. It was really quite expensive. The director's girl friend apparently didn't approve of any of the locations, so we came back to the studio without shooting a single scene. When the picture was finished, the director told the producer he didn't want me anymore. I've always suspected that someone on the unit had been "political."

F.T.   How long did it take to turn out these pictures?

A.H.   Each one took six weeks.

F.T.   I suppose that one's talent was measured by the ability to make a picture requiring the fewest titles?

A.H.   Exactly.

F.T.   Still, weren't many of the scripts adapted from stage plays?

A.H.   I made a silent film, *The Farmer's Wife*, a play that was all dialogue, but we tried to avoid using titles and, wherever possible, to use the pictorial expression instead. I suppose the only film made without any titles at all was *The Last Laugh*, with Emil Jannings.

F.T.   A great picture, one of Murnau's best.

A.H.   They were making it while I worked at UFA. In that film Murnau even tried to establish a universal language by using a kind of Esperanto. All the street signs, the posters, the shop signs, were in this synthetic language.

F.T.   Well, some of the signs in Emil Jannings' house were in German, but those in the Grand Hotel were in this Esperanto. I imagine you were by then becoming increasingly interested in the technical aspect of film-making, that you were studying . . .

A.H.   I was very much aware of the superiority of the photography in American movies to that of the British films. At eighteen I was studying photography, just as a hobby. I had noticed, for instance, that the Americans always tried to separate the image from the background with backlights, whereas in the British films the image melted into the background. There was no separation, no relief.

––––––––––

F.T.   This brings us to 1925. Following the shooting of *The Prude's Fall*, the director doesn't want you to continue as his assistant. And that's when Michael Balcon suggests that you become a director.

A.H.   Balcon said, "How would you like to direct a picture?" and I answered, "I've never thought about it." And in truth, I had not. I was very happy doing the scripts and the art direction; I hadn't thought of myself as a director. Anyway, Balcon told me that there was a proposal for an Anglo-German picture. Another writer was assigned to the script and I left for Munich. My wife, Alma, was to be my assistant. We weren't married yet, but we weren't living in sin either; we were still very pure.

F.T.   This was *The Pleasure Garden*, from the novel by Oliver Sandys. As I remember it, there was lots of action.*

A.H.   Melodramatic. But there were several interesting scenes in it. I want to tell you something about the shooting, because that was the very first picture I directed, and it was natural for me, I suppose, to have a sense of drama. So, at twenty minutes to eight on Saturday evening, I'm at the station in Munich, ready to leave for the location shooting in Italy. In the station, waiting for the train to start, I'm saying to myself, "This is your first picture." Nowadays, when I leave on location, I have to go with a crew of a hundred and forty people. But then there was only the leading man, Miles Mander; the cameraman, Baron Vintigmilia; and a young girl who was supposed to play a native woman who is drowned. There was also a newsreel cameraman, because we were going to do a ship-departure scene in Genoa. We were going to shoot the ship's departure with one camera on the shore and another on the ship's deck.

––––––––––

* Patsy, a chorus girl at the Pleasure Garden Theater, gets her girl friend Jill a job in the troupe. Jill is engaged to Hugh, who is stationed in the colonies.

Patsy marries Levett, a colleague of Hugh's, and following a honeymoon at Lake Como, Levett also sails for the colonies. Jill, who is having the time of her life in London and enjoying the attentions of other men, keeps on postponing her departure for the islands, where her fiancé awaits her.

But Patsy leaves to join her husband. On her arrival, she discovers him in the arms of a native woman and totally depraved. When she announces her decision to leave him, Levett, in a panic, maneuvers the native woman into drowning, making her death appear a suicide. Then he turns against Patsy, and just as he is about to kill her, he is shot down by the local doctor. Hugh, abandoned by Jill, is drawn to Patsy, and the two embark on a new life together.

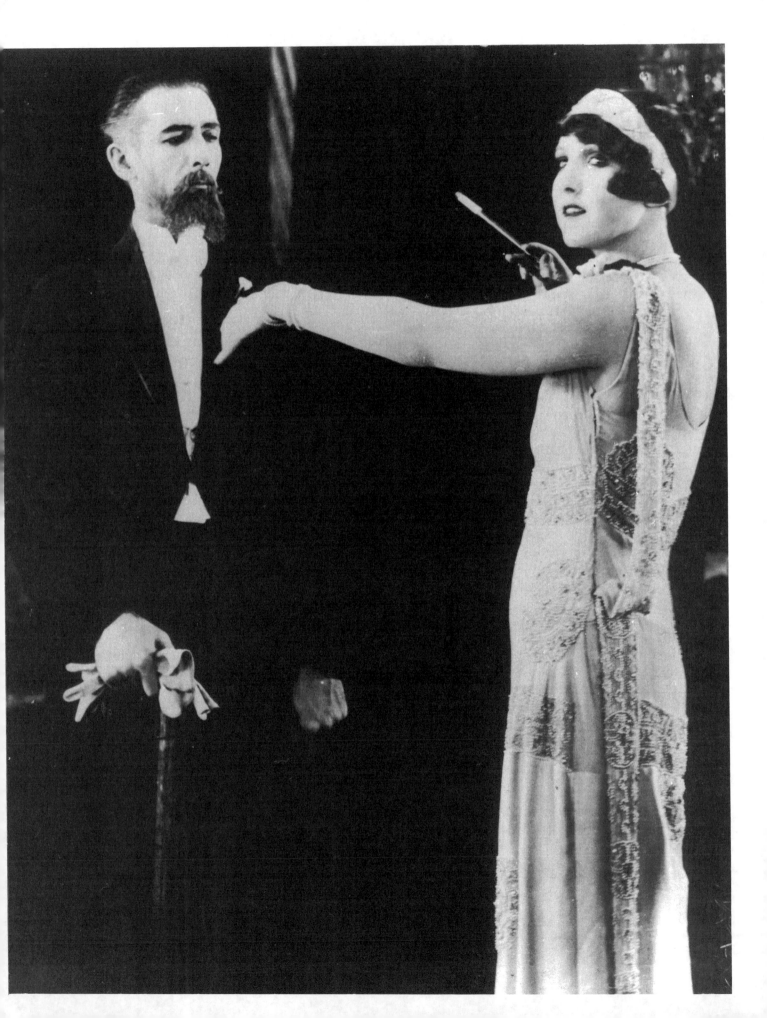

And the ship was going to stop outside the harbor to allow us to get the actors and the newsreel cameraman back to the dock to photograph the characters as they waved their farewells.

The next scene was to be shot in San Remo. This scene has the native girl wading out to sea to commit suicide, and Levett, the villain in the story, is to rush out and make sure the girl is dead, by holding her head underwater. Then he's to bring the body back to shore, saying, "I did my best to save her."

The following scenes take place at Lake Como, in the hotel of the Villa d'Este. Honeymoon, love scenes on the lake, beautiful romance, etc. My wife-to-be is there on the platform at Munich that evening and we are talking together. She's not coming with us. Her job—you know, she's only as tall as that; she was twenty-four then—was to go to Cherbourg by herself to pick up the leading lady, who was coming in from Hollywood. She was Virginia Valli, a very big star at the time, Universal's biggest—and who played Patsy. My fiancée is to pick her up from the *Aquitania* at Cherbourg, take her to Paris, buy her a wardrobe there and then meet us at the Villa d'Este. That's all.

The train is scheduled to leave at eight o'clock.

It is now two minutes to eight. The actor, Miles Mander, says to me, "My God, I've left my makeup case in the taxi," and he runs off.

I shout out after him, "We'll be at the Hotel Bristol, in Genoa. Take the train tomorrow night, because we're shooting on Tuesday." I should remind you that this was on Saturday evening, and we were to arrive in Genoa on Sunday morning to get ready for the shooting.

It's now eight, but the train hasn't left. A few minutes go by. Eight-ten. The train begins to move. And suddenly there's a great row at the barrier and I see Miles Mander leaping over the gate, with three railway officials chasing him down the platform. He had found his make-up case and just manages to hop into the last car.

The first bit of film drama is over, but this is only the beginning!

The train is now on its way. We have no one to handle the accounts and I must take care of them myself. The accounting is more important than the directing. I'm terribly concerned over the money. We are in sleeping cars. As we reach the Austro-Italian border, Vintigmilia says, "Be very careful. We're not to declare the camera. Otherwise, they will charge duty on every lens."

"What do you mean?"

Carmelita Geraghty in *The Pleasure Garden*.

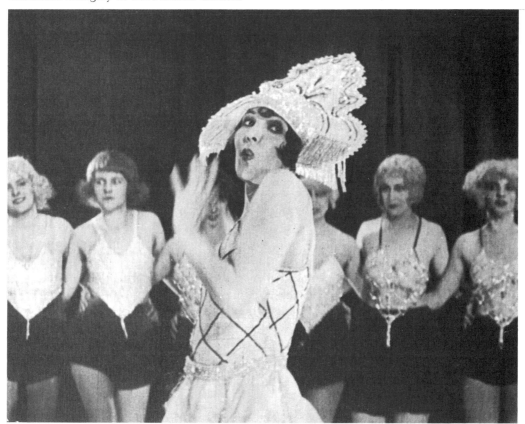

"The German company told us to smuggle the camera through," he tells me. When I ask him where the camera is, he tells me it's under my bunk. As you know, I've always been afraid of policemen and I begin to sweat. And now I am also informed that the ten thousand feet of unexposed stock in our baggage is not to be declared either.

The customs men come into our compartment. Big suspense for me. They don't find the camera, but they discover the film. And since we haven't declared it, they confiscate it.

So we land in Genoa the following morning with no film. And we spend the whole day trying to buy some. On Monday morning I decide to send the newsreel man to Milan to buy some raw stock from Kodak. And I'm still busy with the bookkeeping: lire to marks, marks to pounds —it's all terribly confusing. The cameraman returns at noon, bringing with him twenty pounds' worth of film. And now we are advised that the ten thousand feet of unexposed film that had been confiscated at the border has arrived and I must pay the duty. So I've wasted twenty pounds, a very large amount in our small budget! We have barely enough money left for the shooting of the location scenes.

On Tuesday the boat is scheduled to leave the dock at noon. It's the *Lloyd Prestino*, a large ship that is on its way to South America. We have to rent a tugboat to go out of the harbor. That's another ten pounds. Well, everything is finally settled. But at ten-thirty, when I take out my wallet to tip the tugboat man, I find it's empty. There isn't a sou!

Ten thousand lire gone! I run back to the hotel, look under the bed, everywhere. No sign of the money. I go to the police to report that someone must have entered my room while I was asleep. "It's a good thing I didn't wake up, or I might have been stabbed," I think. I'm very miserable, but the work must go on. And in the excitement of directing my very first scene, I forget all about the loss of the money.

But when the shooting's over, I'm very depressed again. I borrow ten pounds from the cameraman and fifteen from the actor. Since this doesn't cover our needs, I write a letter to London requesting an advance on my salary. I also compose another letter to the German company, in Munich, saying, "I may need a little more money." But I don't dare to mail this request, because they might say, "How do you know you may need more money so early?" So I only mail the letter to London.

Then we go back to the Hotel Bristol, where we're to have lunch before setting out for San Remo. After the meal, I go out in the street. And there is my cameraman, Vintigmilia, with the German girl who is to play the native who throws herself into the sea. With them is the newsreel operator, who has now completed his work and is about to return to Munich. The three of them are standing there, with their heads together, talking very solemnly. I go up to them and say, "Is anything wrong?"

"Yes," they answer. "The girl. She can't go into the water."

I ask, "What do you mean, she can't go into the water?"

And they insist, saying, "That's right, she can't go into the water. You know . . ."

Bewildered, I reply, "No, what do you mean?"

So then and there, on the sidewalk, with people walking back and forth, the two cameramen tell me all about menstruation. I've never heard of it in my life! They go into great detail, and I listen very carefully to what they have to say. When they're through with their explanation, I'm still cross. All I can think about is the money I've wasted in bringing the girl with us, all those lire and marks. Very irritated, I mutter, "Well, why couldn't she have told us about it in Munich, three days ago?"

Anyway, we ship her back with the cameraman and we proceed to Alassio. We manage to find another girl, but this one was somewhat plumper than her ailing predecessor and my leading man was unable to lift her. At each attempt to haul her out of the water, he lets her drop, to the delight of a hundred onlookers, who are howling with laughter. And just as he finally succeeds in carrying her out, a little old lady, who had been quietly gathering sea shells nearby, saunters right across our scene, staring straight into the camera!

Next, we board the train, on our way to the Villa d'Este. And I'm very nervous because Virginia Valli, the Hollywood star, has just arrived. I can't let her know that this is my first picture.

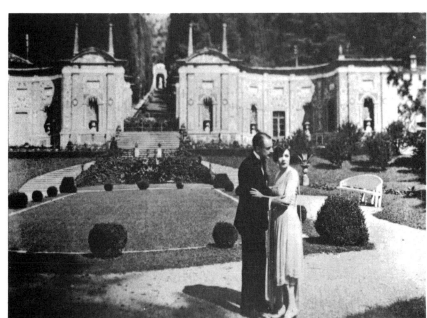

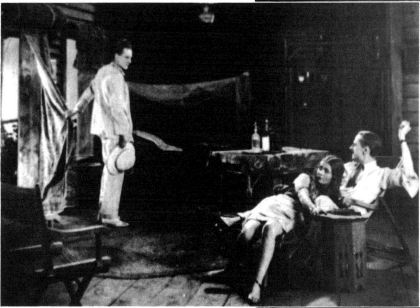

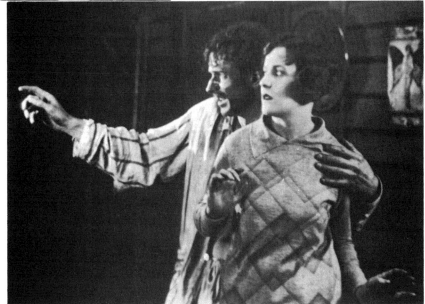

The first thing I say to my fiancée is, "Have you any money?"

"No!"

"But you had enough," I point out.

"Yes, but she brought another actress, Carmelita Geraghty. I tried to take them to the Hotel Westminster on the Rue de la Paix, but they insisted on the Claridge."

So I tell my fiancée all about my troubles. Eventually, we start the shooting and everything works out all right. In those days, of course, we shot moonlight scenes in the sun and we tinted the film blue. After each shot I'd turn back to my fiancée, asking, "Was it all right?"

Only now do I work up the courage to send a cable to Munich saying that we need more money. Meanwhile, I have received the advance on my salary from London. The actor, being a very mean fellow, demands his money back. When I ask him why, he tells me that his tailor insists on being paid. Which wasn't true, you know!

And the suspense continues. I get some money from Munich, but am still fretting over the hotel bill, the rental of motorboats, and all sorts of incidentals. On the night before we're to leave for Munich, I'm terribly nervous. You see, not only don't I want the film star to know it's my first picture, but I don't want her to know that we're short of money either—that we're a very impoverished unit. So I do a really mean thing. I manage to twist the facts and put the whole blame on my fiancée, for bringing the extra girl. "Therefore," I say, "you've got to borrow two hundred dollars from the star."

She tells the star some story and returns with the money, enabling me to pay the hotel bill and buy tickets for our sleepers. We are to change trains at Zurich, in Switzerland, to arrive in Munich the following day. At the station they make me pay for excess baggage because the two American girls have trunks this high! By now we've almost run out of money.

I must begin my scheming again—always those damned accounts! And, as you know, I always make my fiancée do all the dirty work. I tell her to go and ask the two Americans whether they want to have dinner. And to our relief they reply that they won't eat the food on these foreign trains; they have brought sandwiches from the

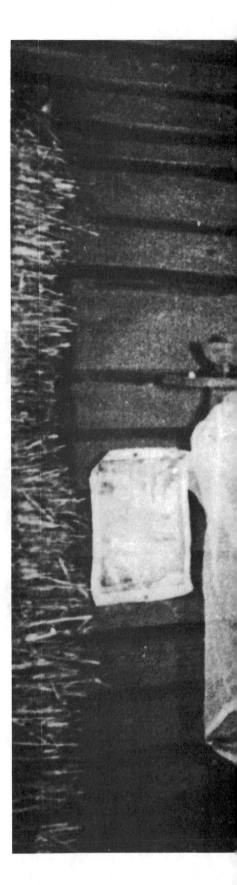

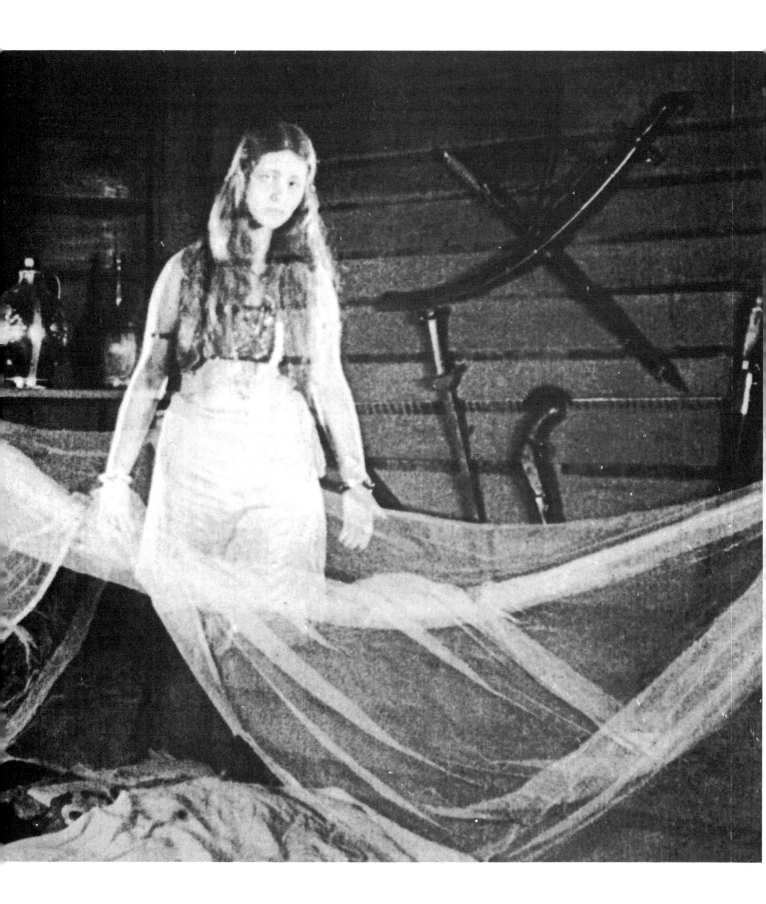

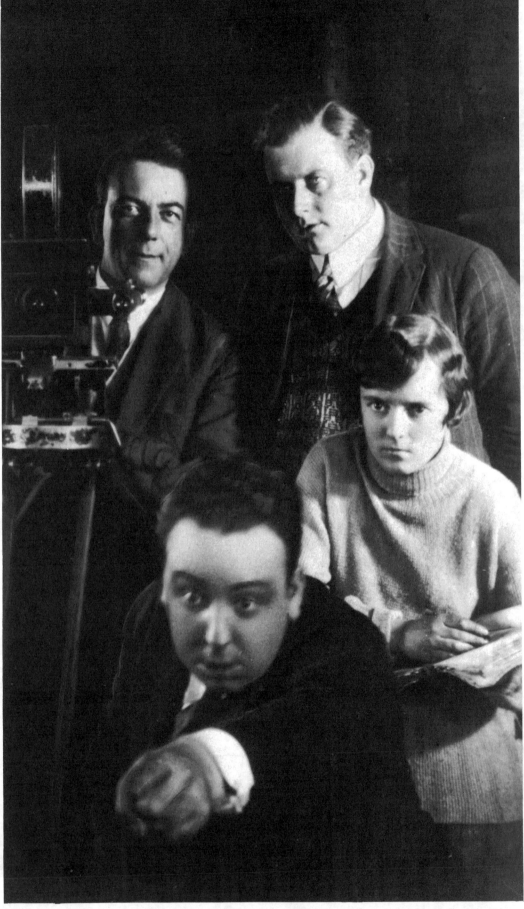

The young man with the mastermind, in full action; behind him, his script-girl and fiancée, Alma Reville.

hotel. This means that the rest of us can afford to have dinner. I go back to my calculations and notice that in transferring lire into Swiss francs there is a loss of a few pennies. The train is late and there is a connection to make in Zurich. At nine P.M. we see a train moving out of the station: it's our train! This means that we will have to spend the night in Zurich. But there's so little money! Just then the train comes to a stop. The suspense is almost more than I can bear. The porters rush up but I wave them away—too expensive—and I start to haul the bags myself. On Swiss trains, as you know, the windows have no frames. The bottom of one of the suitcases hits a window, and there is the loudest noise of falling glass I've ever heard in my life!

A railway official dashes up to us, saying, "Monsieur, this way please."

I'm taken to the office of the stationmaster, where I'm informed that the broken window will cost me thirty-five Swiss francs. So after paying for that I landed in Munich with one pfennig. That was my first location shooting.

F.T. That's quite a story—in fact, it's more exciting than the scenario. But it raises a point I'm curious about. You claim that, at the time, you were ignorant about sexual matters and totally innocent. Yet, in *The Pleasure Garden*, the two girls, Patsy and Jill, really suggest a couple, the one dressed in pajamas, the other wearing a nightgown. In *The Lodger* this same inference is even more explicit, with a little blonde who is shown sitting on the lap of a masculine-looking brunette in a loge. In other words, from your very first pictures on, there is a distinct impression that you were fascinated by the abnormal.

A.H. That may be true, but it didn't go very deep; it was rather superficial. I was quite innocent at the time. The behavior of the two girls in *The Pleasure Garden* was inspired by something that happened when I was assistant director in Berlin in 1924. A highly respectable British family invited me and the director to go out with them. The young girl in the family was the daughter of one of the bosses of UFA. I didn't understand a word of German. After dinner we wound up in a night club where men danced with each other. There were also female

couples. Later on, two German girls, one around nineteen and the other about thirty years old, volunteered to drive us home. The car stopped in front of a hotel and they insisted that we go in. In the hotel room they made several propositions, to which I stolidly replied, "*Nein, nein.*" Then we had several cognacs, and finally the two German girls got into bed. And the young girl in our party, who was a student, put on her glasses to make sure she wouldn't miss anything. It was a *gemütlich* German family soiree.

F.T. I see. At any rate, I take it that the studio work of *The Pleasure Garden* was shot entirely in Germany?

A.H. Yes, in Munich. We showed the finished picture to Michael Balcon, who came over from London to see it.

At the end of the picture there was a scene in which Levett, the heavy, went berserk; he threatened to kill Patsy with a scimitar, and the doctor arrives with a gun. What I did was to have a shot with the gun in the foreground, and we placed the madman and the heroine in the background. The doctor shoots from a distance and the bullet hits the madman. For a moment the shock returns him to sanity. The wild look leaves his face as he turns to the doctor and says in a completely normal manner, "Oh, hello, doctor." Then, noticing that he is bleeding, he says, "Oh," then collapses and dies.

During the showing of this episode, one of the German producers, a very important man, got up and said, "It's impossible. You cannot show a scene like this. It's incredible and it's too brutal." At the end of the screening, Michael Balcon said, "The surprising thing is that technically it doesn't look like a continental picture. It's more like an American film."

Anyway, it got a very good press. The London *Daily Express* ran a headline describing me as the "Young man with a master mind."

F.T. The following year you made your second picture, *The Mountain Eagle*. It was filmed in the studio and on location in the Tyrol.

A.H. It was a very bad movie. The produc-

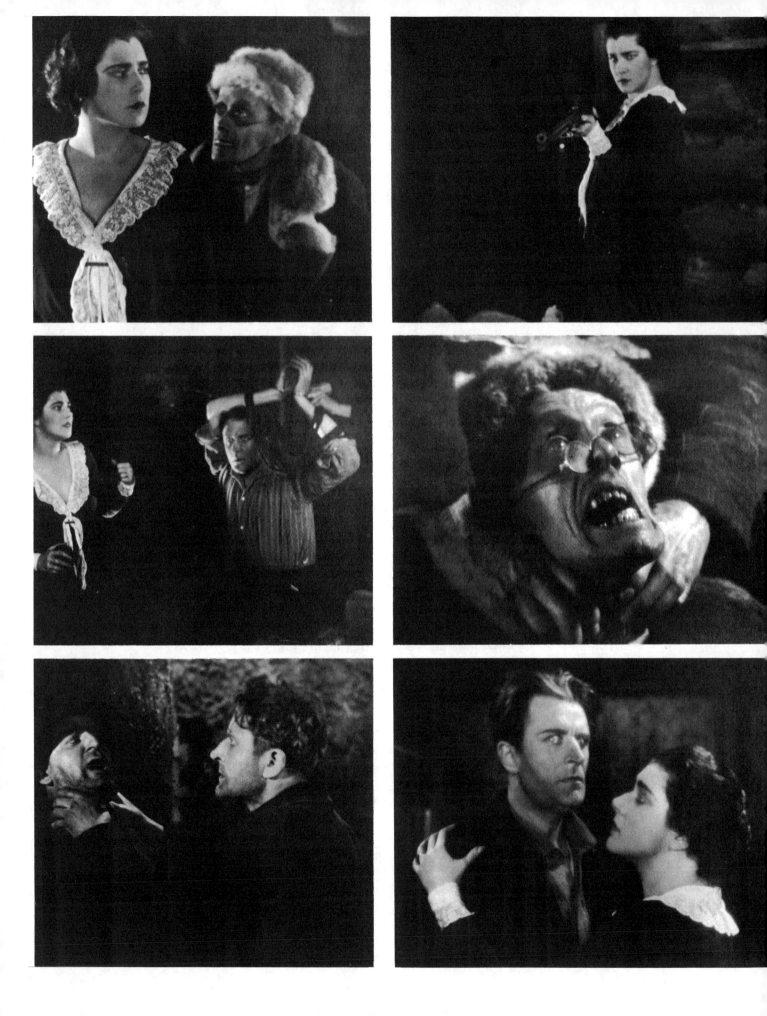

ers were always trying to break into the American market, so they wanted another film star. And so, for the part of the village schoolmistress, they sent me Nita Naldi, the successor to Theda Bara. She had fingernails out to there. Ridiculous!

F.T.   I have the scenario here. The story is about a store manager who is after an innocent young schoolteacher. She takes refuge in the mountains, under the protection of a recluse, whom she eventually marries. Is that right?

A.H.   I'm afraid it is!

These six photos are probably all that remains of *The Mountain Eagle*.

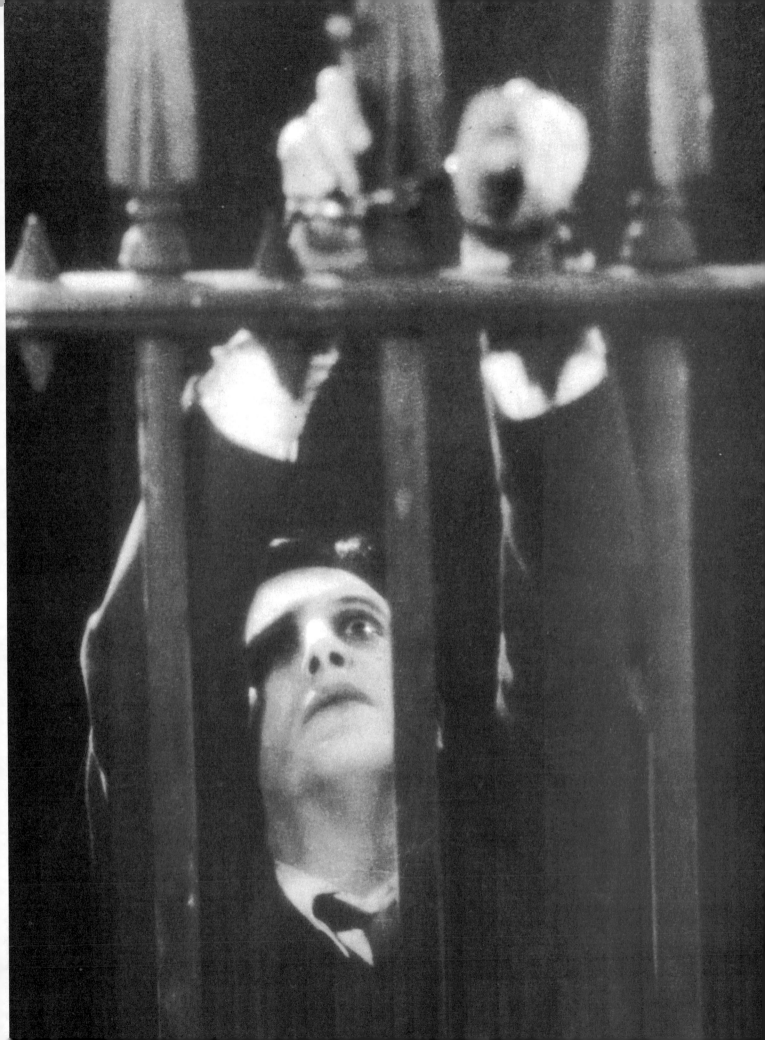

2

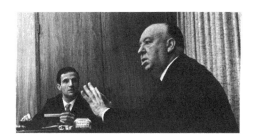

FRANÇOIS TRUFFAUT. *The Lodger,* I believe, was your first important film venture.

ALFRED HITCHCOCK. That's another story. *The Lodger* was the first true "Hitchcock movie." I had seen a play called *Who Is He?*, based on Mrs. Belloc Lowndes's novel *The Lodger.* The action was set in a house that took in roomers and the landlady wondered whether her new boarder was Jack the Ripper or not. I treated it very simply, purely from her point of view. Since then there have been two or three remakes, but they are too elaborate.

F.T. In actual fact, the hero was innocent. He was not Jack the Ripper.

A.H. That was the difficulty. Ivor Novello, the leading man, was a matinee idol in England. He was a very big name at the time. These are

the problems we face with the star system. Very often the story line is jeopardized because a star cannot be a villain.

F.T. I gather that you would have preferred the hero to turn out to be Jack the Ripper?

A.H. Not necessarily. But in a story of this kind I might have liked him to go off in the night, so that we would never really know for sure. But with the hero played by a big star, one can't do that. You have to clearly spell it out in big letters: "He is innocent."

F.T. You know, I am rather surprised that you would consider an ending that failed to provide the public with the answer to its question.

A.H. In this case, if your suspense revolves around the question: "Is he or is he not Jack the

Ripper?" and you reply, "Yes, he *is* Jack the Ripper," you've merely confirmed a suspicion. To me, this is not dramatic. But here, we went in the other direction and showed that he wasn't Jack the Ripper at all.

I ran into the same problem sixteen years later when I made *Suspicion* with Cary Grant. Cary Grant could not be a murderer.

F.T.   Would he have refused?

A.H.   No, not necessarily. But the producers would surely have refused. *The Lodger* is the first picture possibly influenced by my period in Germany. The whole approach to this film was instinctive with me. It was the first time I exercised my style. In truth, you might almost say that *The Lodger* was my first picture.

F.T.   A very good movie which showed great visual inventiveness. I really enjoyed it.

A.H.   As a matter of fact, I took a pure narrative and, for the first time, presented ideas in purely visual terms. We took fifteen minutes of a winter afternoon in London, starting about five-twenty. We opened with the head of a blond girl who is screaming. I remember the way I photographed it. I took a sheet of glass, placed the girl's head on the glass and spread her hair around until it filled the frame. Then we lit the glass from behind so that one would be struck by her light hair. Then we cut to show an electric sign advertising a musical play, *Tonight, Golden Curls*, with the reflection flickering in the water. The girl has drowned. She's hauled out of the water and pulled ashore. The

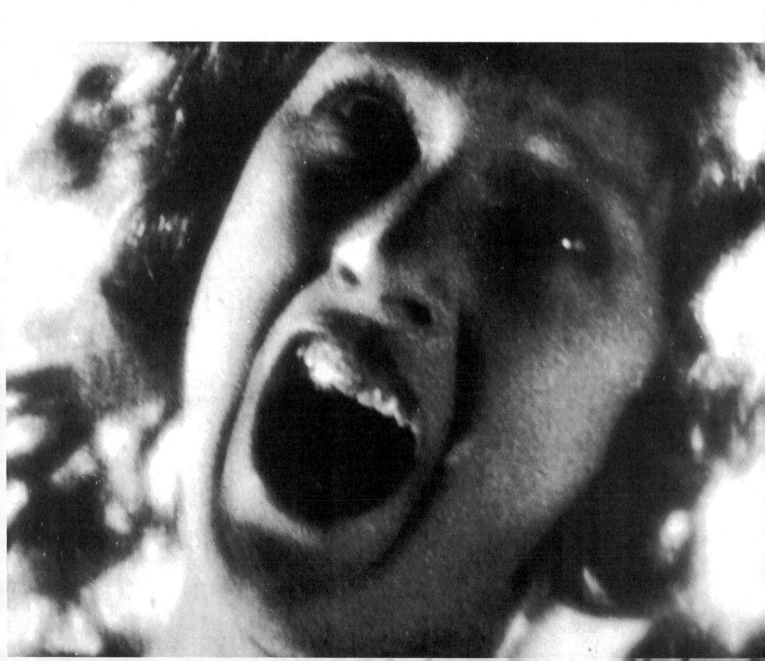

consternation of the bystanders suggests that a murder has been committed. The police arrive on the scene, and then the press. The camera follows one of the newsmen as he moves toward a telephone. He isn't a local reporter, but a wire-service man who is calling his office. And now I proceed to show everything that happens as the news spreads around.

First, the item is typed out on the wire-service machine so that we are able to read a few sentences. Then it is forwarded on the teletypes. People in clubs learn the news. Then there is a radio announcement, with people tuned in to the broadcast. Finally, it is flashed on an electric news sign—you know, like on Times Square. nd each time, we give additional information, ₁ that you learn more about the crime. The ₁ murders only women. Always blondes. He invariably strikes on a Tuesday. How many has he killed to date. Speculation on his motives. He goes around dressed in a black cloak and carries a black bag. What is in that bag?

Through all the different means of communication, the information begins to spread, and finally, the evening papers are out on the street. Now we show the effect on various people. Fair-haired girls are terrified. The brunettes are laughing. Reactions in the beauty parlors or of

people on their way home. Some blondes steal dark curls and put them under their hats.

Lend me your pen a moment. I want to show you a shot, though we were never able to get it right. I showed the back of a small London news van. The back windows are oval. There were two men sitting in the front, the driver and his mate. You see them through the windows—just

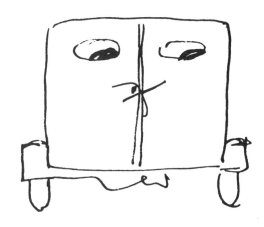

the tops of their heads. And as the van sways from side to side, you have the impression of a face with two eyes and the eyeballs moving. Unfortunately, it didn't work out.

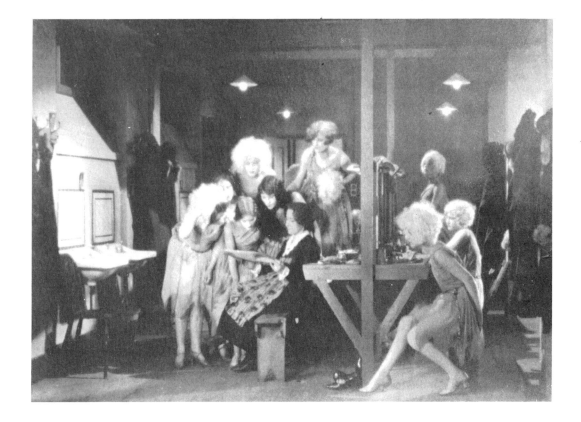

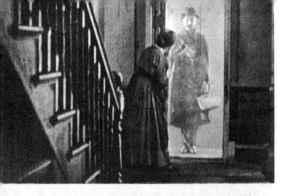

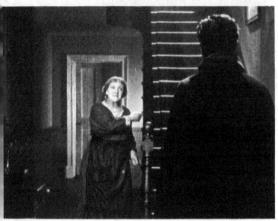

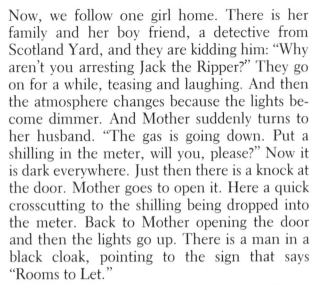

Now, we follow one girl home. There is her family and her boy friend, a detective from Scotland Yard, and they are kidding him: "Why aren't you arresting Jack the Ripper?" They go on for a while, teasing and laughing. And then the atmosphere changes because the lights become dimmer. And Mother suddenly turns to her husband. "The gas is going down. Put a shilling in the meter, will you, please?" Now it is dark everywhere. Just then there is a knock at the door. Mother goes to open it. Here a quick crosscutting to the shilling being dropped into the meter. Back to Mother opening the door and then the lights go up. There is a man in a black cloak, pointing to the sign that says "Rooms to Let."

So I didn't bring the leading man on until fifteen minutes after the beginning of the film. They show him to his room. Now, Father falls off his chair with a loud crash. The new lodger is un-

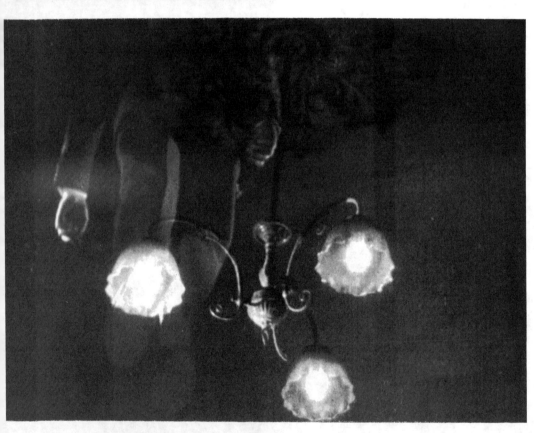

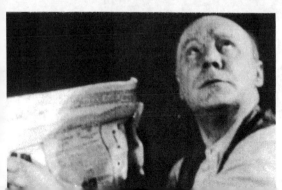

nerved by the noise and this makes him appear suspicious to the others. In his room the man paces up and down. You must remember that we had no sound in those days, so I had a plate-glass floor made through which you could see the lodger moving back and forth, causing the chandelier in the room below to move with him. Naturally, many of these visual devices would be absolutely superfluous today because we would use sound effects instead. The sound of the steps and so on.

F.T.   In any case, in your recent movies, there are far fewer special effects. Nowadays you use an effect only when it's necessary to generate emotion, whereas in the past you seemed to put them in just for the fun of it. I don't imagine you would show someone through a glass floor now.

A.H.   That's the change of style. Today I would simply use the swaying chandelier.

F.T.   I mention this because some people claim that your movies contain a great many gratuitous effects. I believe, on the contrary, that your camerawork is becoming almost invisible. In many pictures the director attempts to provide the Hitchcock touch by placing the camera in an unlikely spot. I have in mind, for example, Lee Thompson, a British director. In one of his so-called Hitchcockian pictures the star goes to fetch something from the refrigerator, and oddly enough, the camera is located *inside* the refrigerator, in the rear. Would you have done it that way?

A.H.   Certainly not. That's like shooting through the fireplace, behind the flames.

F.T.   The finale of *The Lodger*, when the hero is handcuffed, suggests a lynching.

A.H.   Yes. When he tried to climb over the railings. Psychologically, of course, the idea of the handcuffs has deeper implications. Being tied to something . . . it's somewhere in the area of fetishism, isn't it?

F.T.   I don't know, but I have noticed that handcuffs have a way of recurring in your movies.

A.H.   Well, look at the way the newspapers like to show people being taken to jail in hand-cuffs.

F.T.   True. In fact, sometimes they even circle the handcuffs with a white line.

A.H.   I remember one time when they showed the head of the New York Stock Exchange being jailed. He was handcuffed to a Negro. Later on I used that in *The Thirty-nine Steps.*

F.T.   Yes, a man and woman linked to each other. Handcuffs are certainly the most concrete—the most immediate—symbol of the loss of freedom.

A.H.   There's also a sexual connotation, I think. When I visited the Vice Museum in Paris, I noticed there was considerable evidence of sexual aberrations through restraint. You should try to go there sometime. Of course they also have knives, the guillotine, and all sorts of information. Anyway, getting back to the hand-cuffs in *The Lodger*, I think the idea was inspired, to a certain extent, by a German book about a man who spends a whole day in hand-cuffs and tells about all the problems he runs into during that day.

F.T.   Would that be *From Nine to Nine* by Leon Perutz? I believe Murnau was interested in doing a screen version of it around 1927.

A.H.   It might be that one.

F.T.   Is it farfetched to suggest that in the scene where the man in handcuffs is backed up against the railing, you were trying to evoke the figure of Christ?

A.H.   When the people try to lift him and his arms are tied together? Naturally, that thought did occur to me.

F.T.   All of this adds up to the fact that *The Lodger* was really the first Hitchcockian picture, primarily through the theme that recurs in almost all of your later works: a man accused of a crime of which he's innocent.

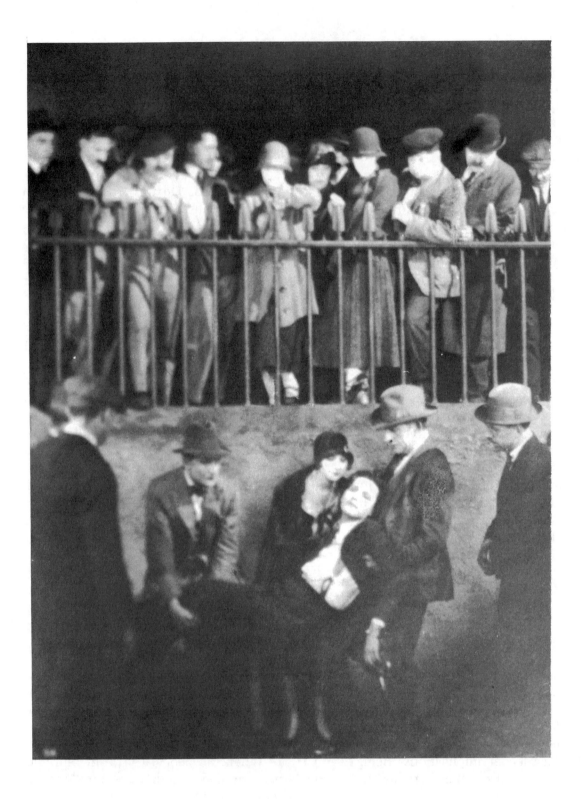

A.H. That's because the theme of the innocent man being accused, I feel, provides the audience with a greater sense of danger. It's easier for them to identify with him than with a guilty man on the run. I always take the audience into account.

F.T. In other words, it's a theme that satisfies the audience's fascination with the clandestine, while also allowing it to identify with the character. Most of your works are about an ordinary man who is involved in an out-of-the-ordinary situation.

48

Wasn't it in *The Lodger* that you made your first personal appearance on the screen?

A.H.   That's right. I was sitting in a newsroom.*

F.T.   Did you do it as a gag? Was it superstition? Or was it simply that there weren't enough extras?

A.H.   It was strictly utilitarian; we had to fill the screen. Later on it became a superstition and eventually a gag. But by now it's a rather troublesome gag, and I'm very careful to show up in the first five minutes so as to let the people look at the rest of the movie with no further distraction.

---

* Alfred Hitchcock can also be recognized in a later sequence of the picture, in which, wearing a cap and leaning against a railing, he is one of the bystanders looking on as Ivor Novello is captured by the police.

F.T.   I understand *The Lodger* was a great hit.

A.H.   It was first shown to the staff of the distribution company and the head of their publicity department. They saw the film and then made their report to the boss: "Impossible to show it. Too bad. The film is terrible." Two days later the big boss came down to the studio to look at it. He arrived at two-thirty. Mrs. Hitchcock and I couldn't bear to wait in the studio to know the results and we walked the streets of London for an hour and a half. Finally, we took a cab and went back. We were hoping our promenade would have a happy ending and that everyone in the studio would be beaming. What they said was: "The boss says it's terrible." And they put the film on the shelf, canceled the bookings that had been made on the basis of Novello's reputation. A few months later they decided to take another look at the picture and

With his back to camera, at extreme right, Alfred Hitchcock during the shooting of *The Lodger*.

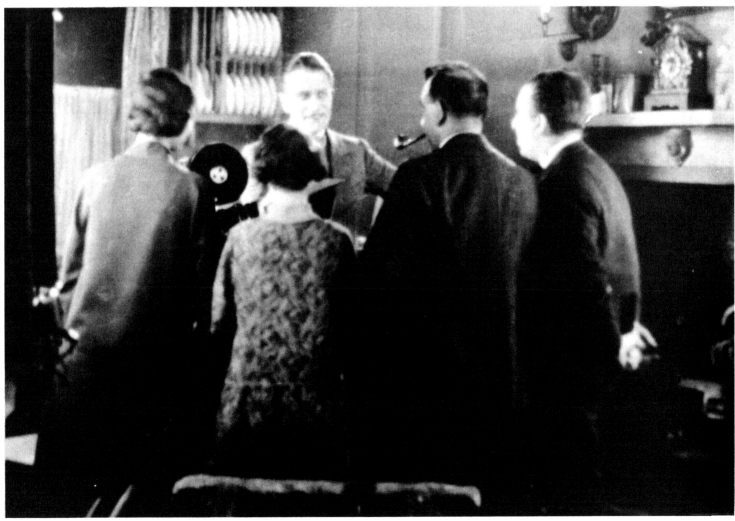

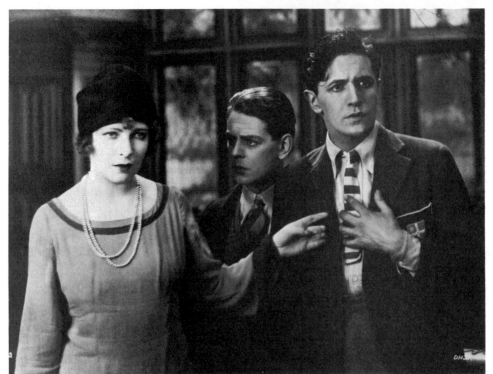

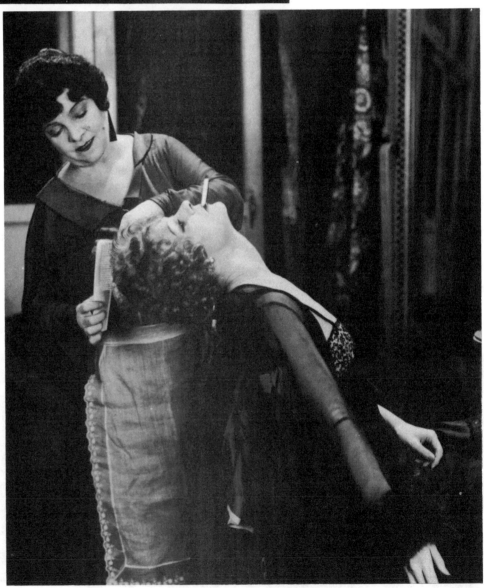

to make some changes. I agreed to make about two. As soon as the picture was shown, it was acclaimed as the greatest British film made up to that date.

F.T. Do you remember what the distributors' objections were?

A.H. I can't remember. I suspect that the director who had had me fired as his assistant was still being "political" against me. I know he told someone, "I don't know what he's shooting. I can't make head nor tail of it!"

F.T. Your next picture, *Downhill*, is about a boy who's accused of a theft in his school. The school authorities expel him, and his father wants nothing more to do with him. As I remember it, he then has an affair with an actress and becomes a professional dancer in Paris. Then, we find him in Marseilles, where he thinks of shipping out to the colonies. Instead, he goes back to London, where his parents, who, in the meantime, have learned he was innocent all along, welcome him with open arms. The action is scattered in all kinds of different places; starting out in a British college, it moves on to Paris and then to Marseilles . . .

A.H. The original play was written that way.

F.T. That's strange. Since it was a play, I would imagine that all the action would be set in the one location, in the college.

A.H. No, no, it was done as a series of sketches. It was a rather poor play. As it happens, the author was Ivor Novello.

F.T. As I remember it, the atmosphere of the school was very meticulously re-created.

A.H. Yes, but the dialogue was pretty dreadful in spots. And just like the transparent ceiling, there was another naïve touch that wouldn't do today. That's when the boy is thrown out of the house by his father. To show the beginning of his downhill journey, I put him on an escalator going down.

F.T. There was a very good scene in a Paris cabaret.

A.H. Yes, there I experimented a bit. I showed a woman seducing a younger man. She is a lady of a certain age, but quite elegant, and he finds her very attractive until daybreak. Then he opens the window and the sun comes in, lighting up the woman's face. In that moment she looks dreadful. And through the open window we show people passing by carrying a coffin.

F.T. There were also some dream sequences.

A.H. I had a chance to experiment in those scenes. At one point I wanted to show that the young man was having hallucinations. He boarded a tiny schooner, and there I had him go down to the fo'c'sle, where the crew slept. At the beginning of his nightmare he was in a dance hall. No dissolve, just straight cutting. He walked over to the side wall and climbed into a bunk. In those days dreams were always dissolves and they were always blurred. Though it was difficult, I tried to embody the dream in the reality, in solid, unblurred images.

F.T. As I recall it, that picture was not particularly successful. The next one was *Easy Virtue*, which I've never seen. According to my notes, it's the story of a woman, Laurita, who becomes notorious when a young artist who is in love with her commits suicide and she divorces her husband, who is a drunkard. Later on she meets the scion of a respectable family, John, who marries her, knowing nothing of her past. But when his mother learns about Laurita's former existence, she forces her son to divorce her. And the picture winds up with Laurita's life in shambles.

A.H. That was taken from a Noel Coward play, and it contained the worst title I've ever written. I'm ashamed to tell you about it, but I will. At the beginning the film shows Laurita during her divorce case. She is very well known and she tells her story to the court. How she married a young man of good family and so

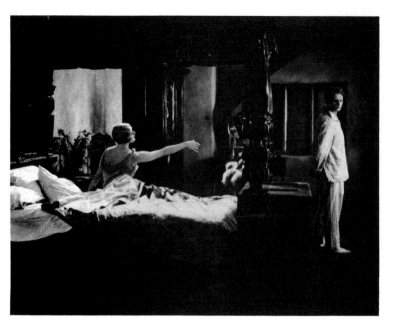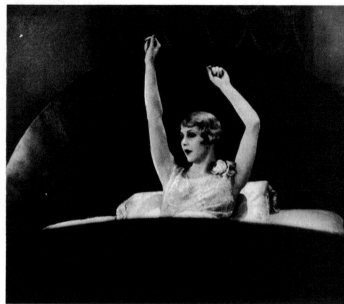

forth. At any rate, her divorce is uncontested and is granted. And the word gets around that the famous Laurita is in the court. The photographers gather outside. Eventually she appears at the courthouse stairs, her arms out, and says, "Shoot, there's nothing left to kill!"

An interesting scene in this picture is when John is proposing marriage to Laurita, and instead of giving him an immediate answer, she says, "I'll call you from my house, around midnight." Next, we show a little watch indicating it is midnight; it's the wrist watch of a switchboard operator who is reading a book. A small light goes on on the board. She puts the plug in and is about to go back to her reading but automatically listens into the earphones. Then, she puts the book down, obviously fascinated by the phone conversation. In other words, I never show either of the two people. You follow what is happening by watching the switchboard operator.

———————

F.T.   I've seen *The Ring*, which came right after that, several times. It isn't a suspense film and has no crime ingredients. It's a story about two prize fighters who are in love with the same woman. I like that picture very much.

A.H.   Yes, that was really an interesting movie. You might say that after *The Lodger*, *The Ring* was the next Hitchcock picture. There were all kinds of innovations in it, and I remember that at the premiere an elaborate montage got a round of applause. It was the first time that had ever happened to me.

There were many things in that picture we wouldn't do today. For instance, there was a little party one evening after a boxing match. The champagne is poured out and it is all bubbly. They drink a toast to the heroine and then discover she isn't there; she's out with another man. And so the champagne goes flat. In those days we were very keen on the little visual touches, sometimes so subtle that they weren't even noticed by the public. You remember that the picture started on the fairgrounds. There was a fighter, played by Carl Brisson, and he was called One-Round Jack.

F.T.   Because he knocked out his opponents in the first round?

A.H.   That's right. And in the crowd, watching the barker, there was an Australian, played by Ian Hunter. As the barker in front of the tent urged the crowd to go in, he had a little flap and could look back over his shoulder to see how

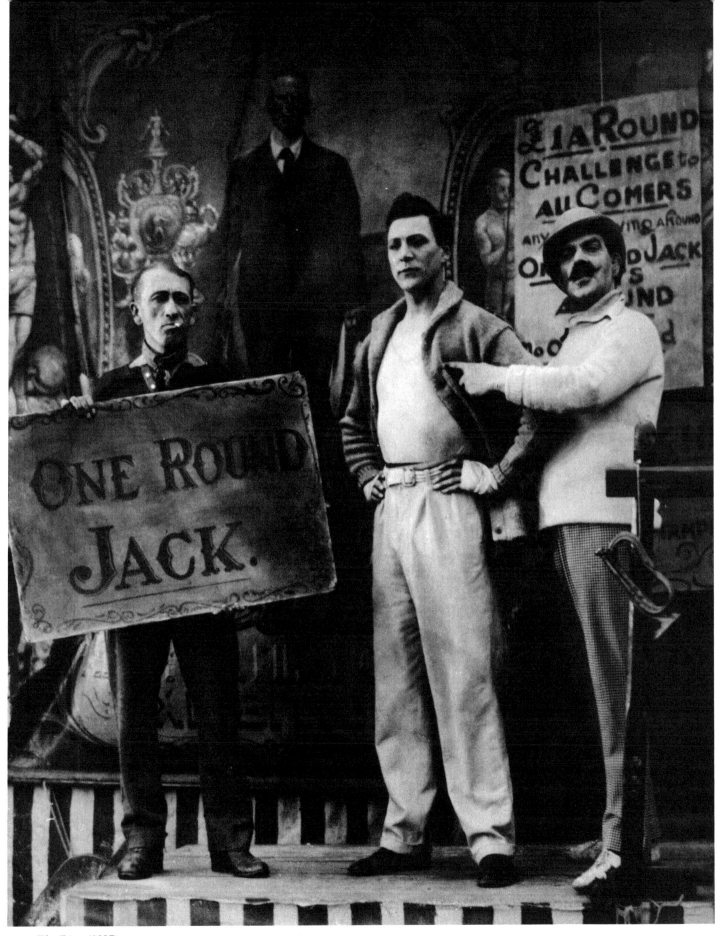

The Ring (1927).

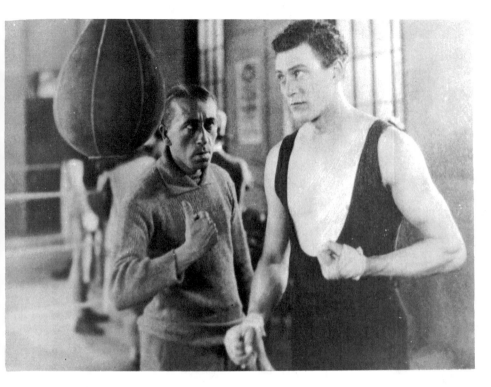

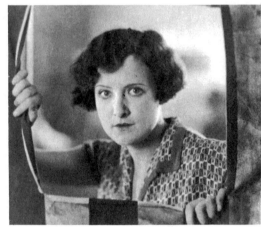

the match was progressing. He used a sign to indicate the round number to the people standing outside. We showed volunteer fighters going into the tent and then coming out holding their jaw. Until Ian Hunter goes in. The seconds were sort of laughing at him and they didn't even bother to hang up his coat. They just held it, thinking that he would never last more than one round. The match started and I showed the expressions of the seconds changing. Then we showed the barker looking in at the match. And at the end of the first round the barker took out the card indicating the round number, which was old and shabby, and they put up number two. It was brand-new! One-Round Jack was so good that they'd never got around to using it before! I think this touch was lost on the audience.

F.T. That was a very nice touch. There were many other visual innovations in the picture. The story was about a triangle, with frequent references to original sin, and I still remember that you used a snakelike bracelet as a symbol in several different ways.*

A.H. These things were noticed by the reviewers and the picture had a *succès d'estime*, but it was not a commercial hit. This is also the film in which I introduced a few notions that were widely adopted later on. For instance, to

---

* After becoming champion, the Australian falls in love with the heroine and presents her with a serpentine bracelet. As they embrace, the girl moves the bracelet high up on her arm, above the elbow. When her fiancé, Jack, arrives on the scene, the girl hastily drops the bracelet down to her wrist, concealing it with her other hand. To embarrass her in front of Jack, the Australian deliberately holds out his hand to say good-by. The girl, intent on concealing the bracelet, fails to respond, and Jack takes this seeming rejection as evidence of her loyalty to him.

In another scene, while the girl and Jack are together near a river, she accidentally drops the bracelet into the water. After retrieving it, Jack asks for an explanation. The Australian, she explains, gave it to her because he didn't want to spend the money won in a fight against his rival on himself. "So, it's really mine," Jack says, taking the bracelet from her and winding it around her finger, like a wedding band.

In this, and several other ways, the sinuous bracelet weaves its way through the theme and winds up being twisted around itself, like a snake. The film's title, *The Ring*, may be taken in its dual sense, referring both to a boxing arena and a wedding band.

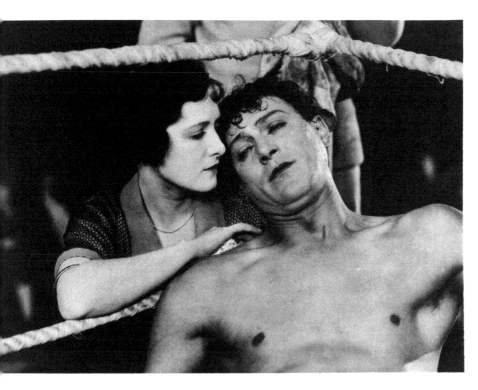

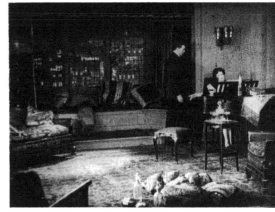

show the progress of a prize fighter's career, we showed large posters on the street, with his name on the bottom. We show different seasons —summer, autumn, winter—and the name is printed in bigger and bigger letters on each of the posters. I took great care to illustrate the changing seasons: blossoming trees for the spring, snow for the winter, and so on.

F.T. Your next picture, *The Farmer's Wife*, was adapted from a light play about a widower who lives on a farm with a housekeeper and is combing the countryside for a new wife. After some disappointing experiences with three matrimonial prospects, he realizes that his housekeeper, who naturally has been secretly in love with him all along, is the ideal choice and so they get married.

A.H. Yes, that was a comedy that ran on the London stage for something like fourteen hundred performances. There was too much dialogue. It was largely a title film.

F.T. As a matter of fact, some of the best scenes were probably the screen additions to the original play. Among the highlights I remember is one sequence in which the servants in the pantry gorge themselves on food intended for the guests at a reception. And Gordon Harker was particularly funny as the old farm hand. I might add that the setting recalls the Murnau films. The photography also suggests the German influence.

A.H. It's possible. When the chief cameraman got sick, I handled the camera myself. I arranged the lighting, but since I wasn't too sure of myself, I sent a test over to the lab. While waiting for the results, we would rehearse the scene. I did what I could, but it wasn't actually very cinematic.

F.T. Just the same, the way in which you handled the adaptation from stage to screen reflects a tenacious effort to create pure cinema. At no time, for instance, is the camera placed

55

where the audience would be if the shooting had been done from the stage, but rather as if the camera had been set up in the wings. The characters never move sideways; they move straight toward the camera, more systematically than in your other pictures. It's filmed like a thriller.

A.H.   What you mean is that the camera is

inside the action. Well, the idea of photographing actions and stories came about with the development of techniques proper to film. The most significant of these, you know, occurred when D. W. Griffith took the camera away from the proscenium arch, where his predecessors used to place it, and moved it as close as possible to the actors. The next major step was when Griffith, improving on the earlier efforts of the

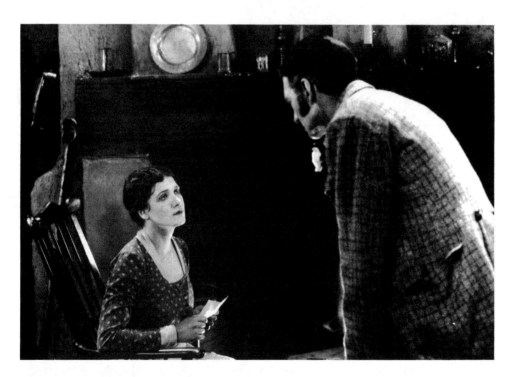

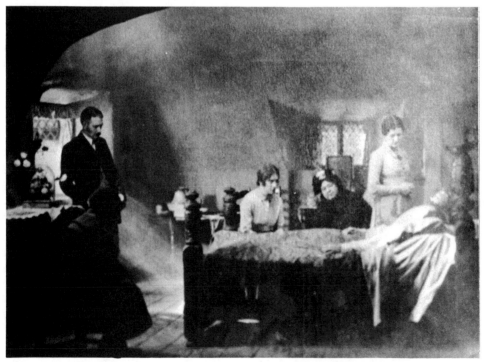

British G. A. Smith and the American Edwin S. Porter, began to get the strips of film together in sequence. This was the beginning of cinematographic rhythm through the use of montage.

I don't remember too much about *The Farmer's Wife*, but I know that filming that play stimulated my wish to express myself in purely cinematic terms.

What comes after *The Farmer's Wife?*

F.T.　The next one was *Champagne*.

A.H.　That was probably the lowest ebb in my output.

F.T.　That's not fair. I enjoyed it. Some of the scenes have the lively quality of the Griffith comedies.

It can be summed up in a few words: A millionaire father objects to the man his daughter is in love with and the girl leaves home and sails to France. To teach her a lesson her father allows her to think he's bankrupt, so that she will have to make her own living. The heroine goes to work in a cabaret, where her job consists of encouraging the clientele to drink the very same champagne to which the family owes its fortune. Eventually, the father, who's had a detective keeping an eye on her all along, realizes that he's gone too far, and he finally agrees to her marriage to the man she loves. That's the story.

A.H.　That's just the trouble. There is no story!

F.T.　I see that you're not very much interested in talking about *Champagne*. Could you just answer one question: Was the film an assignment from the company or was it your own idea?

A.H.　What happened, I think, is that someone said, "Let's do a picture with the title *Champagne*," and I thought of beginning it in a certain way, which was rather old-fashioned and a little like that very old picture of Griffith's, *Way Down East*. The story of a young girl going to the big city.

My idea was to show a girl, working in Reims,

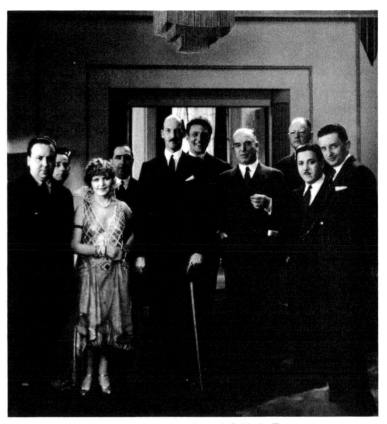

On the set of *Champagne*. From right to left: E. A. Dupont (director of *Variety*), Monty Banks, John Maxwell (producer), Prince Aage, J. Thorpe, Betty Balfour, J. Grossman (studio manager) and Hitchcock.

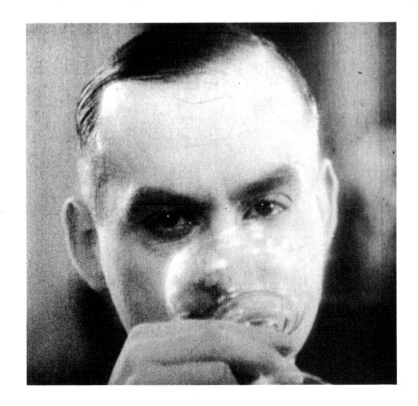

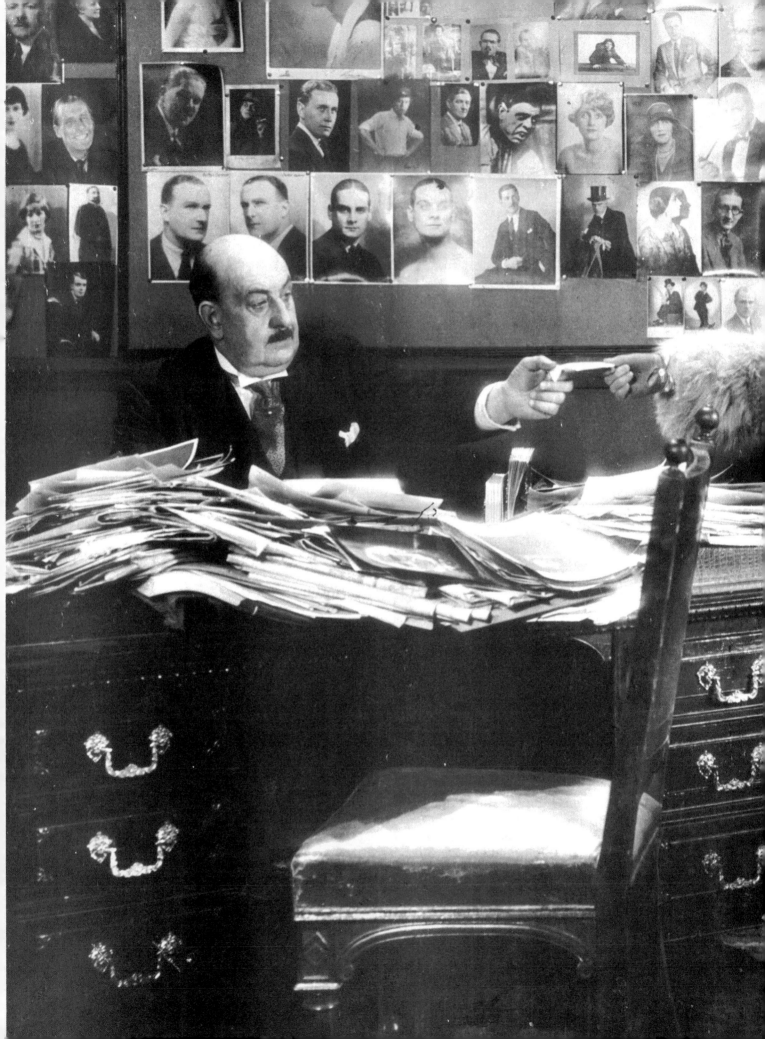

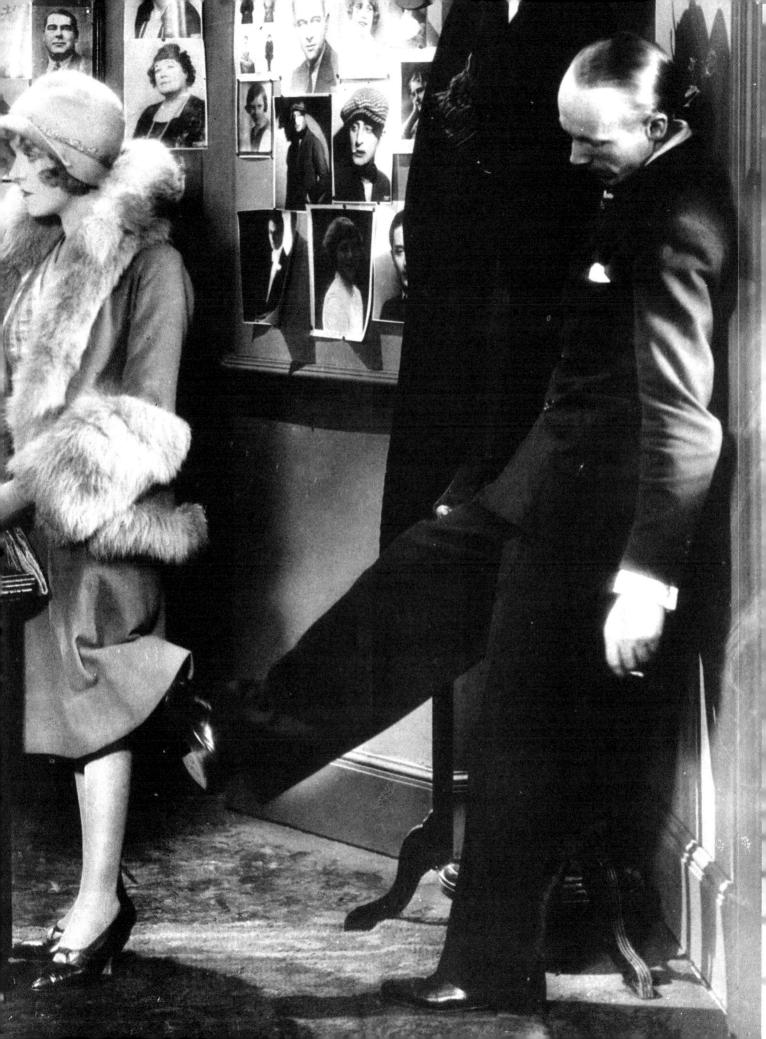

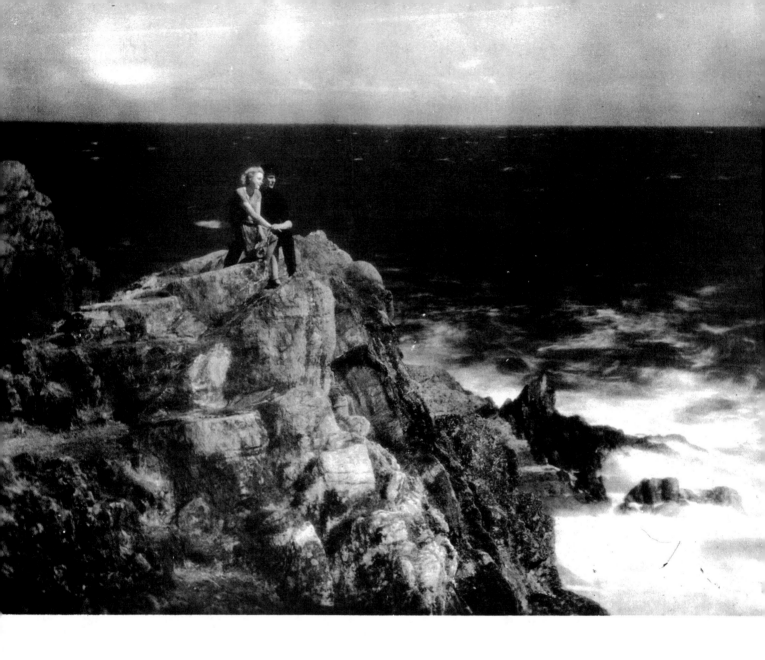

whose job is to nail down the crates of champagne. And always, the champagne is put on the train. She never drinks any—just looks at it. But eventually she would go to the city herself, and she would follow the route of the champagne—the night clubs, the parties. And naturally she would get to drink some. In the end, thoroughly disillusioned, she would return to her old job at Reims, by then hating champagne. I dropped the whole idea—probably because of the moralizing aspect.

F.T.   There were lots of sight gags in the version I saw.

A.H.   The nicest one, I think, was the drunkard who's staggering down the ship's corridor and swaying from side to side when the ship is steady, but when it is rolling like hell and everyone else is having a hard time trying to keep his balance, he walks in a perfectly straight line.

F.T.   I also remember the dish that starts out from the kitchen looking very messy, with everybody putting his filthy fingers in it. As it is carried to the dining room, refining touches are added en route. And what has started out as a revolting-looking mess in the kitchen becomes very elegant and grand by the time it reaches the customer. The picture was full of these humorous inventions.

F.T. *The Manxman*, in contrast with *Champagne*, is a very serious picture.*

A.H. The only point of interest about that movie is that it was my last silent one.

F.T. Another point of interest is that it suggested the talkies. I remember that at one moment the heroine says, "I'm expecting a baby." She articulates the phrase so clearly that one can read her lips. In fact, you dispensed with a title.

A.H. That's true, but it was a very banal picture.

F.T. True, it was fairly humorless, yet the story, in some respects, bears a resemblance to *Under Capricorn* or *I Confess*. One feels you really believed in this film.

A.H. It's not a matter of conviction, but the picture was the adaptation of a very well-known book by Sir Hall Caine. The novel had quite a reputation and it belonged to a tradition. We had to respect that reputation and that tradition. It was not a Hitchcock movie, whereas *Blackmail* . . .

F.T. Before going on to *Blackmail*, which is your first talking picture, I would like a few words on silent films, in general.

---

* The action takes place on the Isle of Man. The plot centers around three characters: Peter, a poor fisherman, and Philip, a lawyer, are both in love with Kate. When Peter's proposal of marriage is rejected by the girl's father on the grounds that he can't support her, he leaves the island, telling Kate he will return for her after he has made a fortune. When they hear a report that Peter has died, Kate discovers that Philip has been in love with her and she admits her feelings for him. But one day Peter unexpectedly turns up again, and Kate, faithful to her promise, marries him. When she gives birth to Philip's child, she realizes she cannot continue living with Peter and asks Philip to run away with her. When he refuses, she attempts suicide. Since suicide is considered a crime on the island, she is summoned before a tribunal, where she and Philip are forced into a public confession. The story winds up with Kate and Philip leaving the isle with their child.

A.H. Well, the silent pictures were the purest form of cinema; the only thing they lacked was the sound of people talking and the noises. But this slight imperfection did not warrant the major changes that sound brought in. In other words, since all that was missing was simply natural sound, there was no need to go to the other extreme and completely abandon the technique of the pure motion picture, the way they did when sound came in.

F.T. I agree. In the final era of silent movies, the great film-makers—in fact, almost the whole of production—had reached something near perfection. The introduction of sound, in a way, jeopardized that perfection. I mean that this was precisely the time when the high screen standards of so many brilliant directors showed up the woeful inadequacy of the others, and the lesser talents were gradually being eliminated from the field. In this sense one might say that mediocrity came back into its own with the advent of sound.

A.H. I agree absolutely. In my opinion, that's true even today. In many of the films now being made, there is very little cinema: they are mostly what I call "photographs of people talking." When we tell a story in cinema, we should resort to dialogue only when it's impossible to do otherwise. I always try first to tell a story in the cinematic way, through a succession of shots and bits of film in between.

It seems unfortunate that with the arrival of sound the motion picture, overnight, assumed a theatrical form. The mobility of the camera doesn't alter this fact. Even though the camera may move along the sidewalk, it's still theater. One result of this is the loss of cinematic style, and another is the loss of fantasy.

In writing a screenplay, it is essential to separate clearly the dialogue from the visual elements and, whenever possible, to rely more on the visual than on the dialogue. Whichever way you choose to stage the action, your main concern is to hold the audience's fullest attention.

Summing it up, one might say that the screen rectangle must be charged with emotion.

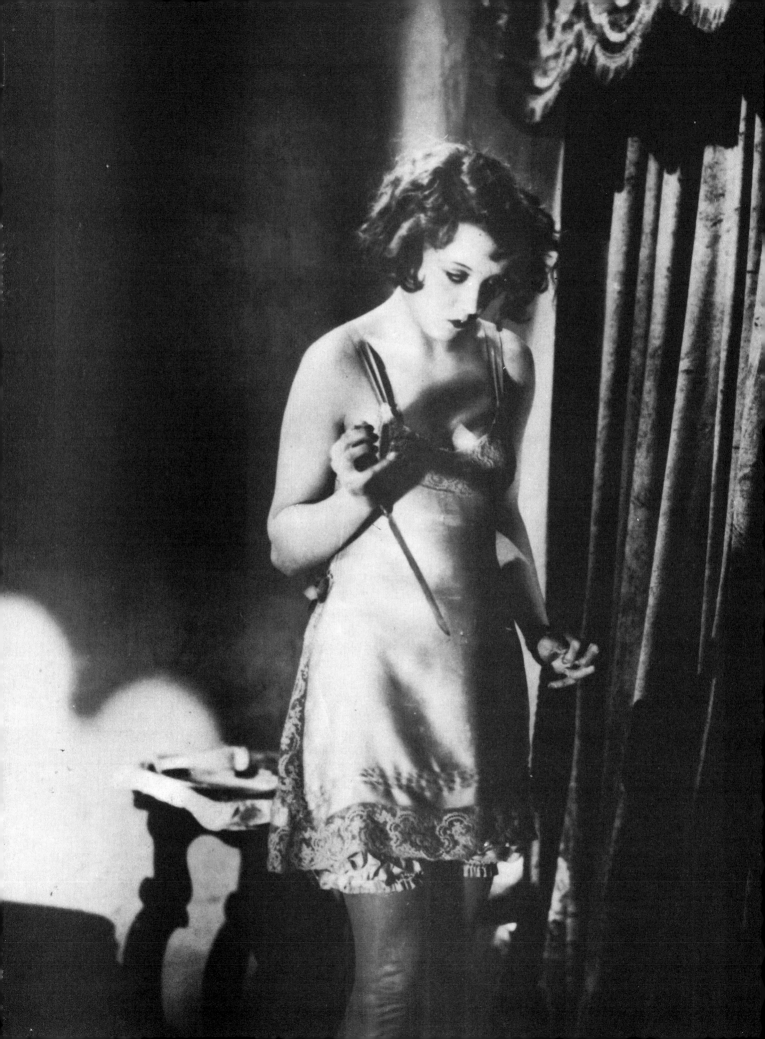

HITCHCOCK'S FIRST SOUND FILM: "BLACKMAIL" ■ THE SHUFTAN PROCESS ■ "JUNO AND THE PAYCOCK" ■ WHY HITCHCOCK WILL NEVER FILM "CRIME AND PUNISHMENT" ■ WHAT IS SUSPENSE? ■ "MURDER" ■ "THE SKIN GAME" ■ "RICH AND STRANGE" ■ TWO INNOCENTS IN PARIS ■ "NUMBER SEVENTEEN" ■ CATS, CATS EVERYWHERE ■ "WALTZES FROM VIENNA" ■ THE LOWEST EBB AND THE COMEBACK ■

3

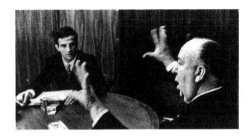

FRANÇOIS TRUFFAUT. This brings us to the end of 1928, when you started your first talking picture, *Blackmail*. Were you satisfied with the screenplay?

ALFRED HITCHCOCK. It was a rather simple story, but I never did it the way I really wanted to. We used the same exposition as for *The Lodger*. In the first reel I show the procedure of an arrest: the detectives go out in the morning; they pick up the man; he has a gun; they take it away and put the handcuffs on. He's taken to the police station, booked, fingerprinted, and questioned. They take a mug shot and lock him up in a cell. And then we come back to the two detectives going to the men's room and washing their hands, just as though they were two office workers. To them it was just the end of a day's work. The younger detective's girl is waiting for him; they go to a restau-

rant, have a row and go their separate ways. She's picked up by an artist who takes her to his place and tries to rape her. She kills him. As it happens, her young man is assigned to the case. He finds a clue, and when he realizes that his girl is involved, he conceals it from his superiors. Then the blackmailer comes into the scene and there's a conflict between him and the girl, with the young detective in between the two. The detective calls the blackmailer's bluff, and the villain stands his ground at first, but in the end he loses his head. There is a chase around the roofs of the British Museum. He falls to his death. Against her boy friend's advice, the girl insists upon going to Scotland Yard to tell them everything. But when she gets there, the clerk turns her over to her young man, who, of course, takes her home.

The ending I originally wanted was different. After the chase and the death of the black-

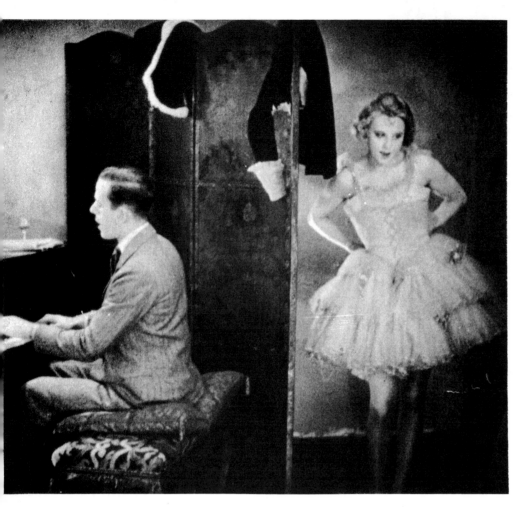
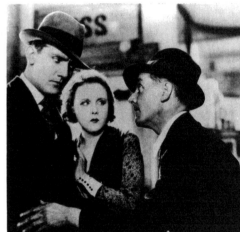

mailer, the girl would have been arrested and the young man would have had to do the same things to her that we saw at the beginning: handcuffs, booking at the police station, and so on. Then he would meet his older partner in the men's room, and the other man, unaware of what had taken place, would say, "Are you going out with your girl tonight?" And he would have answered, "No, I'm going straight home." And the picture would have ended in that way. But the producers claimed it was too depressing.

F.T.   At the cinémathèques there are two versions of *Blackmail*, one silent and the other a sound picture.

A.H.   What happened was that after a good deal of hesitation, the producers decided it would be silent except for the last reel. In those days they would advertise these as "part-sound pictures." But since I suspected the producers might change their minds and eventually want an all-sound picture, I worked it out that way. We utilized the techniques of talkies, but without sound. Then, when the picture was completed, I raised objections to the part-sound version, and they gave me carte blanche to shoot some of the scenes over. The star was Anny Ondra, the German actress, who, naturally, hardly spoke any English. We couldn't dub in the voices then as we do today. So I got around the difficulty by calling on an English actress, Joan Barry, who did the dialogue standing outside the frame, with her own microphone, while Miss Ondra pantomimed the words.

F.T.   I imagine you were searching for sound innovations comparable to the visual ideas you introduced in *The Lodger*.

A.H.   Well, I tried. After the girl has killed the painter, there is a scene showing a breakfast, with her family seated around the table. One of

64

the neighbors is discussing the murder. She says, "What a terrible way to kill a man, with a knife in his back. If I had killed him, I might have struck him over the head with a brick, but I wouldn't use a knife."

And the talk goes on and on, becoming a confusion of vague noises to which the girl no longer listens. Except for the one word, "Knife, knife," which is said over and over again and becomes fainter and fainter. Then suddenly she hears her father's normal, loud voice: "Alice,

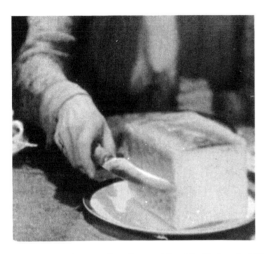

please pass me the bread knife." And Alice has to pick up a knife similar to the one she's used for the killing, while the others go on chattering about the crime.

F.T.　　You used a good many trick shots in the picture, I believe. For instance, the sequence of the chase through the British Museum.

A.H.　　That's right; we used the Shuftan process because there wasn't enough light in the museum to shoot there. You set a mirror at an angle of forty-five degrees and you reflect a full picture of the British Museum in it. The pictures were taken with thirty-minute exposures. We had nine of these pictures, showing various rooms, and we made them into transparencies so that we could backlight them.

Then we scraped the silvering away in the mirror in certain places corresponding to a decor prop we had built on the set. For instance, a doorframe through which one of the characters came in.

The producers knew nothing about the Shuftan process and they might have raised objections, so I did all of this without their knowledge.

F.T.　　In that picture there's one scene that was subsequently used by several other directors of American films. That's the scene in which the painter lures the girl to his apartment with the intention of seducing her and which winds up with his being killed.

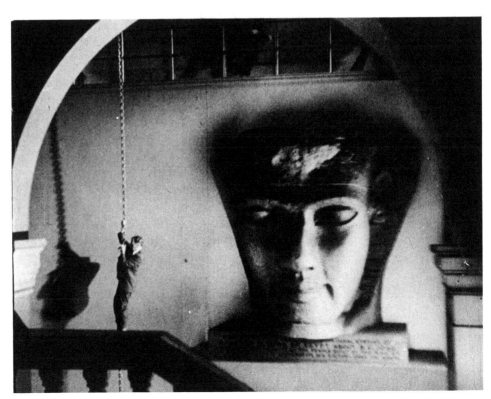

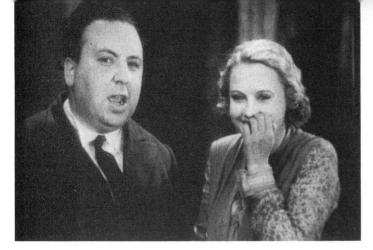

HITCHCOCK: Now, Miss Ondra, we are going to do a sound test. Isn't that what you wanted? Now come right over here.
ONDRA: I don't know what to say. I'm so nervous!

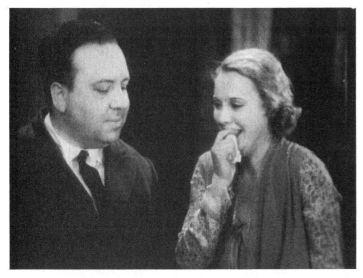

HITCHCOCK: Have you been a good girl?
ONDRA: Oh, no!

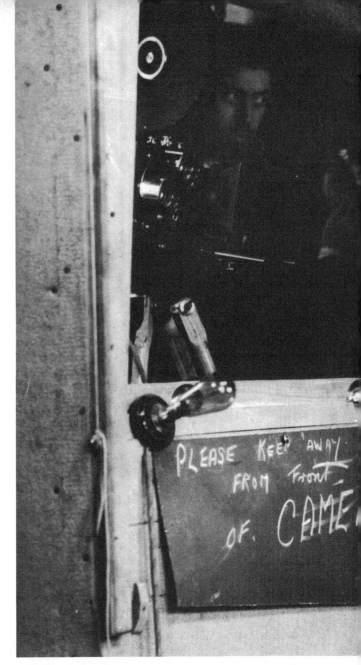

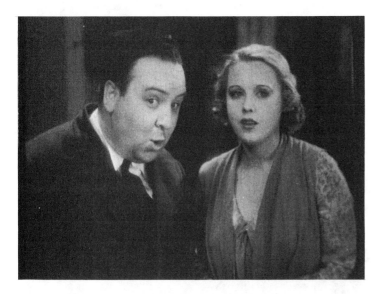

HITCHCOCK: No? Have you slept with men?
ONDRA: No!

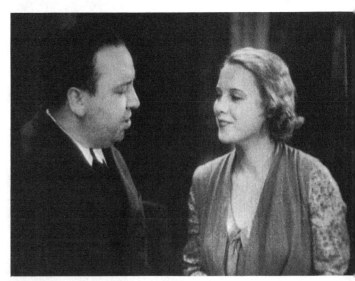

HITCHCOCK: Now come right over here, Miss Ondra, and stand still in your place, or it won't come out right—as the girl said to the soldier.

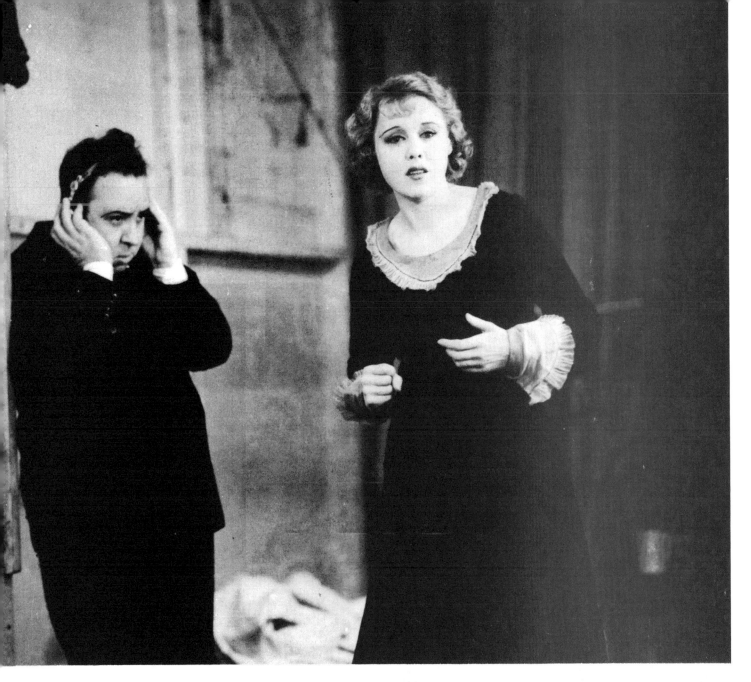

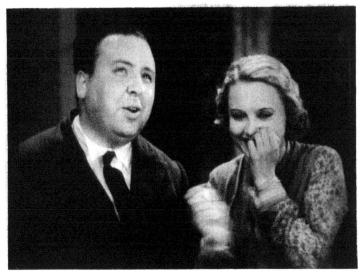

ONDRA: Oh, Hitch, you make me embarrassed!

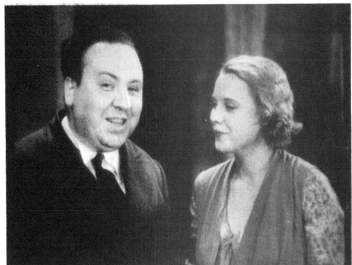

HITCHCOCK: Cut!

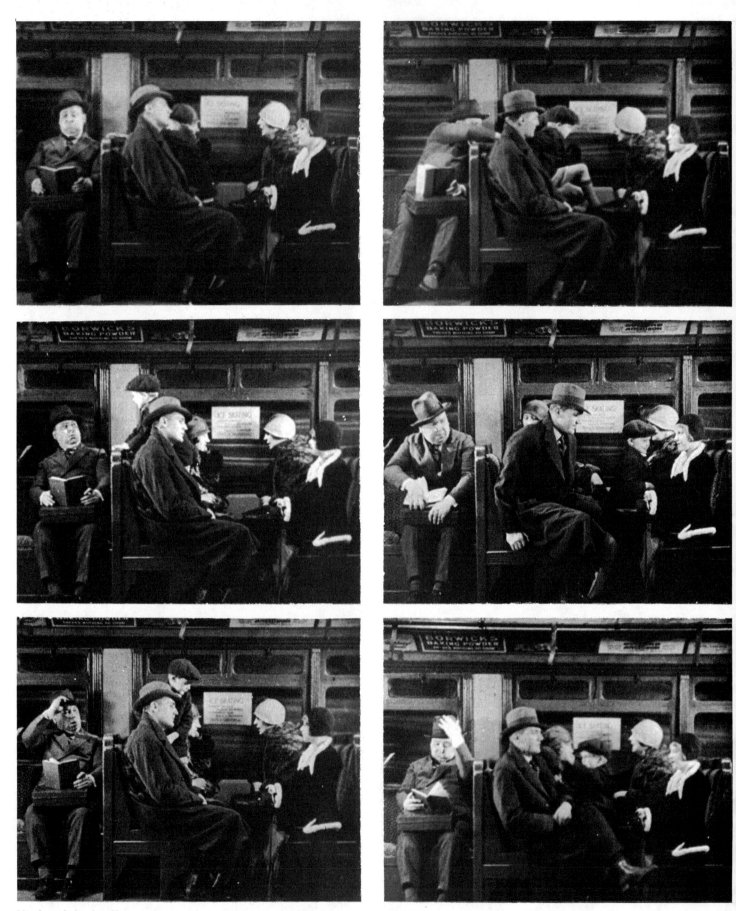

Hitchcock fends off a mischievous brat in *Blackmail* (1929). In the center, the detective hero, played by John Longden.

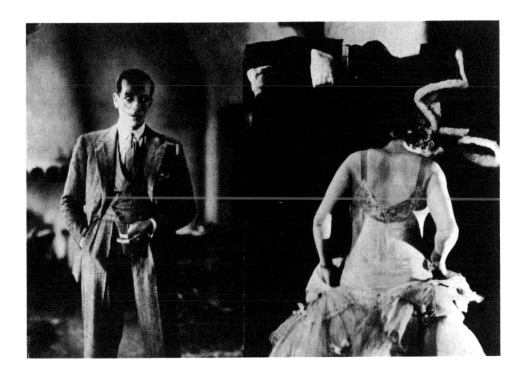

A.H. Of course. I did a funny thing in that scene, a sort of farewell to silent pictures. On the silent screen the villain was generally a man with a mustache. Well, my villain was clean-shaven, but an ironwork chandelier in his studio cast a shadow on his upper lip that suggested an absolutely fierce-looking mustache!

F.T. Then, in 1930, you were asked to direct one or two sequences of the first British musical comedy, a picture entitled *Elstree Calling.*

A.H. Of no interest whatever.

F.T. In that case let's go on to *Juno and the Paycock*, taken from the Sean O'Casey play.*

A.H. *Juno and the Paycock* was made with the Irish Players. I must say that I didn't feel like making the picture because, although I read the play over and over again, I could see no way of narrating it in cinematic form. It's an excellent play, though, and I liked the story, the mood, the characters, and the blend of humor and tragedy very much. As a matter of fact, I had O'Casey in mind when I showed a bum in a café announcing the end of the world in *The Birds*. I photographed the play as imaginatively as possible, but from a creative viewpoint it was not a pleasant experience.

The film got very good notices, but I was actually ashamed, because it had nothing to do with cinema. The critics praised the picture, and I had the feeling I was dishonest, that I had stolen something.

F.T. As a matter of fact, I have here a British review, written by James Agate, which appeared in *The Tatler* in March, 1930. It reads: "*Juno and the Paycock* appears to me to be very nearly a masterpiece. Bravo Mr. Hitchcock! Bravo the Irish Players and Bravo Edward Chapman! This is a magnificent British picture."

But I understand your reaction because it's quite true that critics generally tend to assess a picture on the basis of its literary quality rather than its cinematic value.

Your scruples in relation to O'Casey, no doubt, account for your reluctance to adapt great literary works to the screen. Your own works include a great many adaptations, but mostly they are popular or light entertainment novels,

---

* The story is too long to be properly summed up. It takes place during the Dublin uprising and tells about the eccentric goings on of an impoverished family that's about to inherit some money. The prospect of the inheritance unbalances the head of the family, the self-appointed "Captain" Boyle (the Paycock), whereas his plump wife, Juno, is solid and down to earth. In the end, when it turns out there is no inheritance, the family is disgraced, with the daughter expecting an illegitimate child and the son shot as an informer.

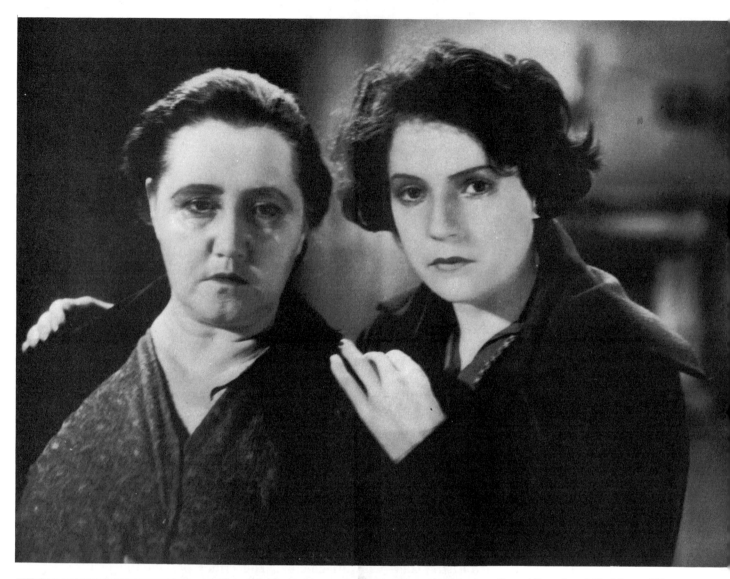

Sara Allgood and Kathleen O'Regan in *Juno and the Paycock*.

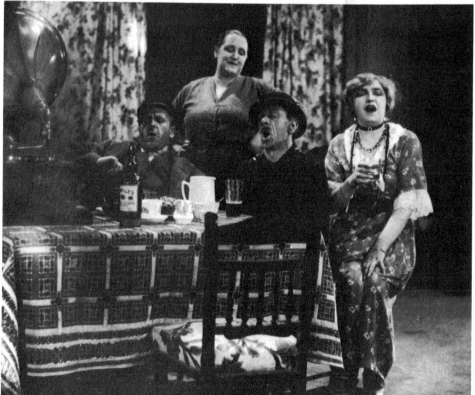

which are so freely refashioned in your own manner that they ultimately become a Hitchcock creation. Many of your admirers would like to see you undertake the screen version of such a major classic as Dostoyevsky's *Crime and Punishment*, for instance.

A.H. Well, I shall never do that, precisely because *Crime and Punishment* is somebody else's achievement. There's been a lot of talk about the way in which Hollywood directors distort literary masterpieces. I'll have no part of that! What I do is to read a story only once, and if I like the basic idea, I just forget all about the book and start to create cinema. Today I would

be unable to tell you the story of Daphne du Maurier's *The Birds*. I read it only once, and very quickly at that. An author takes three or four years to write a fine novel; it's his whole life. Then other people take it over completely. Craftsmen and technicians fiddle around with it and eventually someone winds up as a candidate for an Oscar, while the author is entirely forgotten. I simply can't see that.

F.T. I take it then that you'll never do a screen version of *Crime and Punishment*.

A.H. Even if I did, it probably wouldn't be any good.

Shooting *Juno and the Paycock* (1930). Alma Reville is standing to the side of the fireplace.

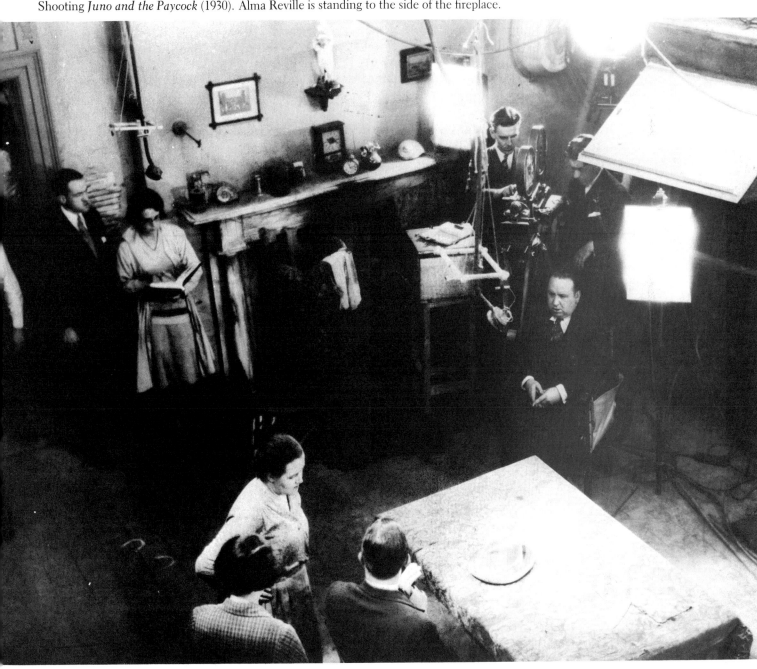

F.T.   Why not?

A.H.   Well, in Dostoyevsky's novel there are many, many words and all of them have a function.

F.T.   That's right. Theoretically, a masterpiece is something that has already found its perfection of form, its definitive form.

A.H.   Exactly, and to really convey that in cinematic terms, substituting the language of the camera for the written word, one would have to make a six- to ten-hour film. Otherwise, it won't be any good.

F.T.   I agree. Moreover, your particular style and the very nature of suspense require a constant play with the flux of time, either by compressing it or, more often, by distending it. Your approach to an adaptation is entirely different from that of most directors.

A.H.   The ability to shorten or lengthen time is a primary requirement in film-making. As you know, there's no relation whatever between real time and filmic time.

F.T.   Of course, that's one of the fundamentals that one learns with one's first picture. For instance, a fast action has to be geared down and stretched out; otherwise, it is almost imperceptible to the viewer. It takes considerable experience and know-how to handle the flux of time properly.

A.H.   This is why I feel it is a mistake to have a novelist adapt his own book for the screen. A dramatist, on the other hand, may be more effective in adapting his own play. But even so, he must face up to a difficulty. In his work for the stage he is called upon to sustain the interest of the audience for three acts. These acts are broken up by two intermissions during which the audience can relax. But for a film one must hold that audience for an uninterrupted two hours or longer.
Even so, a playwright will tend to make a better screenwriter than a novelist because he is used to the building of successive climaxes.

Sequences can never stand still; they must carry the action forward, just as the wheels of a ratchet mountain railway move the train up the slope, cog by cog. A film cannot be compared to a play or a novel. It is closer to a short story, which, as a rule, sustains one idea that culminates when the action has reached the highest point of the dramatic curve.
As you know, a short story is rarely put down in the middle, and in this sense it resembles a film. And it is because of this peculiarity that there must be a steady development of the plot and the creation of gripping situations which must be presented, above all, with visual skill. Now, this brings us to suspense, which is the most powerful means of holding onto the viewer's attention. It can be either the suspense of the situation or the suspense that makes the public ask itself, "What will happen next?"

F.T.   The word "suspense" can be interpreted in several ways. In your interviews you have frequently pointed out the difference between "surprise" and "suspense." But many people are under the impression that suspense is related to fear.

A.H.   There is no relation whatever. Let's go back to the switchboard operator in *Easy Virtue*. She is tuned in to the conversation between the young man and the woman who are discussing marriage and who are not shown on the screen. That switchboard operator is in suspense; she is filled with it. Is the woman on the end of the line going to marry the man whom she called? The switchboard operator is very relieved when the woman finally agrees; her own suspense is over. This is an example of suspense that is not related to fear.

F.T.   Yet the switchboard operator was afraid that the woman would refuse to marry the young man, but, of course, there is no anguish in this kind of fear. Suspense, I take it, is the stretching out of an anticipation.

A.H.   In the usual form of suspense it is indispensable that the public be made perfectly aware of all of the facts involved. Otherwise, there is no suspense.

F.T. No doubt, but isn't it possible to have suspense in connection with hidden danger as well?

A.H. To my way of thinking, mystery is seldom suspenseful. In a whodunit, for instance, there is no suspense, but a sort of intellectual puzzle. The whodunit generates the kind of curiosity that is void of emotion, and emotion is an essential ingredient of suspense.

In the case of the switchboard operator in *Easy Virtue*, the emotion was her wish that the young man be accepted by the woman. In the classical situation of a bombing, it's fear for someone's safety. And that fear depends upon the intensity of the public's identification with the person who is in danger.

I might go further and say that with the old situation of a bombing properly presented, you might have a group of gangsters sitting around a table, a group of villains . . .

F.T. As for instance the bomb that was concealed in a briefcase in the July 20 plot on Hitler's life.

A.H. Yes. And even in that case I don't think the public would say, "Oh, good, they're all going to be blown to bits," but rather, they'll be thinking, "Watch out. There's a bomb!" What it means is that the apprehension of the bomb is more powerful than the feelings of sympathy or dislike for the characters involved. And you would be mistaken in thinking that this is due to the fact that the bomb is an especially frightening object. Let's take another example. A curious person goes into somebody else's room and begins to search through the drawers. Now, you show the person who lives in that room coming up the stairs. Then you go back to the person who is searching, and the public feels like warning him, "Be careful, watch out. Someone's coming up the stairs." Therefore, even if the snooper is not a likable character, the audience will still feel anxiety for him. Of course, when the character is attractive, as for instance Grace Kelly in *Rear Window*, the public's emotion is greatly intensified.

F.T. Yes, that's a good illustration.

A.H. As a matter of fact, I happened to be sitting next to Joseph Cotten's wife at the premiere of *Rear Window*, and during the scene where Grace Kelly is going through the killer's room and he appears in the hall, she was so upset that she turned to her husband and whispered, "Do something, do something!"

F.T. I'd like to have your definition of the difference between "suspense" and "surprise."

A.H. There is a distinct difference between "suspense" and "surprise," and yet many pictures continually confuse the two. I'll explain what I mean.

We are now having a very innocent little chat. Let us suppose that there is a bomb underneath this table between us. Nothing happens, and then all of a sudden, "Boom!" There is an explosion. The public is *surprised*, but prior to this surprise, it has seen an absolutely ordinary scene, of no special consequence. Now, let us take a *suspense* situation. The bomb is underneath the table and the public *knows* it, probably because they have seen the anarchist place it there. The public is *aware* that the bomb is going to explode at one o'clock and there is a clock in the decor. The public can see that it is a quarter to one. In these conditions this same innocuous conversation becomes fascinating because the public is participating in the scene. The audience is longing to warn the characters on the screen: "You shouldn't be talking about such trivial matters. There's a bomb beneath you and it's about to explode!"

In the first case we have given the public fifteen seconds of *surprise* at the moment of the explosion. In the second we have provided them with fifteen minutes of *suspense*. The conclusion is that whenever possible the public must be informed. Except when the surprise is a twist, that is, when the unexpected ending is, in itself, the highlight of the story.

───────────

F.T. Your following picture, *Murder*, was taken from a novel about the theater by Clemence Dane.

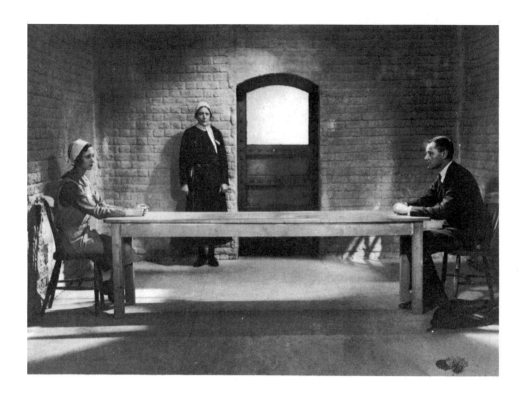

A.H.   That was an interesting picture. Did you see it?

F.T.   Yes, I did. It's about a young actress who's accused of killing one of her friends. She's tried and sentenced to death. Herbert Marshall played the juror who's convinced of her innocence. He conducts an investigation on his own after the trial, and it eventually turns out that the guilty one is none other than the defendant's fiancé.

A.H.   That was one of the rare whodunits I made. I generally avoid this genre because as a rule all of the interest is concentrated in the ending.

F.T.   As in most of the Agatha Christie novels, for instance. There is a laborious investigation, followed by a series of interrogations.

A.H.   That's right. I don't really approve of whodunits because they're rather like a jigsaw or a crossword puzzle. No emotion. You simply wait to find out who committed the murder.
It reminds me of a story about two competing

networks at the time television was in its infancy. One network had advertised a whodunit program. And just before it was to go on the air, an announcer from the rival channel told the audience, "That play on the other network tonight—we can reveal that the butler did it!"

F.T.   Even though *Murder* was a whodunit, I believe you were particularly interested in the filming.

A.H.   Yes, because we did many things that had not been done before. It was Herbert Marshall's first talking part and the role was perfect for him; he turned out to be excellent in the sound medium. Anyway, we had to reveal his inner thoughts, and since I hate to introduce a useless character in a story, I used a stream-of-consciousness monologue. At the time, this was regarded as an extraordinary novelty, although it had been done for ages in the theater, beginning with Shakespeare. But here we adapted the idea to the techniques of sound.
There was a scene in which Herbert Marshall had the radio on while he was shaving and he was listening to some music . . .

F.T. They were playing the Prelude from *Tristan*. That was one of the best scenes.

A.H. Well, I had a thirty-piece orchestra in the studio, behind the bathroom set. You see, it was impossible to add the sound later; the music had to be recorded at the same time, right there on the stage.

I also experimented with improvisations in direct sound. I would explain the meaning of the scene to the actors and suggest that they make up their own dialogue. The result wasn't good; there was too much faltering. They would carefully think over what they were about to say and we didn't get the spontaneity I had hoped for. The timing was wrong and it had no rhythm. I understand that you like improvisation. What's your experience?

F.T. As you say, there is always a danger in giving voice to stammerers. And when people are searching for their words, there is the risk that a scene will turn out twice as long as it

should. So I try for an intermediary formula: When dealing with a key scene I might talk it over with the performers and write it only afterward, using the words of their own vocabulary.

A.H. That's very interesting, but it's probably not too economical, is it?

F.T. In terms of money, footage, and time, the process is by no means economical. But let's get back to *Murder*, which in essence is a thinly disguised story about homosexuality. In the final scene at the circus, the murderer is shown as a transvestite as he confesses he killed the victim because she was about to tell his fiancée all about him, about his special mores. Wasn't that rather risqué at the period?

A.H. Yes, in that sense it was daring. There were also several references to *Hamlet* because we had a play within a play. The presumptive murderer was asked to read the manuscript of a play, and since the script described the killing,

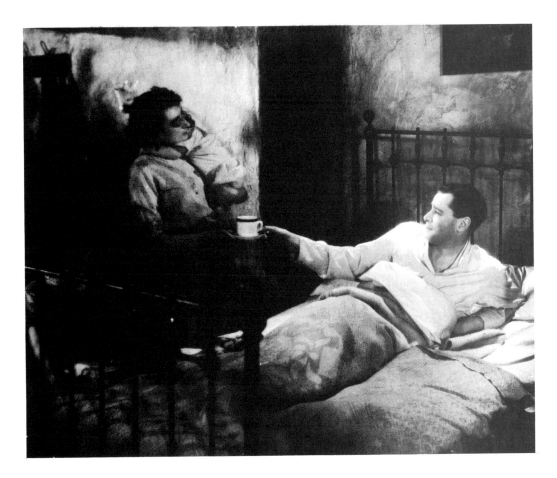

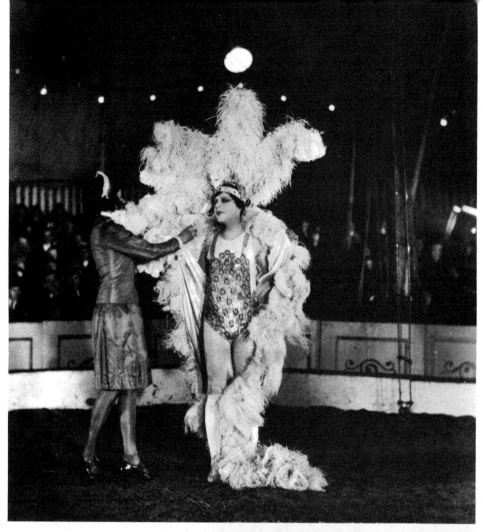

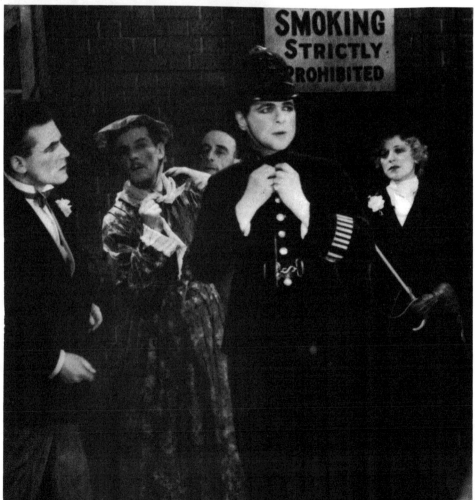

this was a way of tricking him. They watched the man while he was reading out loud to see whether he would show some sign of guilt, just like the king in *Hamlet*. The whole film was about the theater. Another novelty was that *Murder* was my first experience with a bilingual picture. We made the German and English versions simultaneously. I had worked in Germany and had a rough knowledge of the language—just enough to get by. In the English version the hero was Herbert Marshall, and we used a very well-known actor, Alfred Abel, for the German version. Before the shooting, when I went to Berlin to talk over the script, they proposed many changes that I turned down. As it happens, I was wrong. I refused them because I was satisfied with the English version. Besides, we didn't want to shoot two versions that would be too different from each other, for reasons of economy.

Anyway, I returned to London without having altered the script. But as soon as we started to shoot, I realized that I had no ear for the German language. Many touches that were quite funny in the English version were not at all amusing in the German one, as, for instance, the ironic asides on the loss of dignity or on snobbishness. The German actor was ill at ease, and I came to realize that I simply didn't know enough about the German idiom.

I don't mean to discourage you, but this may help you understand why Clair, Duvivier, and Renoir had difficulties in the United States. They aren't familiar enough with the American language and idiom. Strangely enough, a few Germans and Austrians, like Lubitsch and Billy Wilder, managed to adapt themselves to the local climate, and some of the Hungarian directors also succeeded here. It's rather peculiar. My own experience helps me to appreciate what director Michael Curtiz and producer Joe Pasternak were up against when they arrived in California.

F.T. It seems to me, however, that the European directors brought to American motion pictures something that their Hollywood colleagues had failed to provide—namely, a lucid and sometimes critical look at America, which invests many of their pictures with a special interest. You won't find this approach in the works of Hawks or McCarey, whereas the films of Lubitsch, Billy Wilder, Fritz Lang, and many of your own movies often cast perceptive looks at the American way of life. In addition, the European directors also bring over some of their native folklore.

A.H. That's particularly true with respect to humor. For instance, *The Trouble with Harry* is an approach to a strictly British genre, the humor of the macabre. I made that picture to prove that the American public could appreciate British humor, and it went over quite well whenever it reached an audience.

In England one is always running into people who are anti-American although they've never set foot in this country. And I always tell them, "There are no Americans. America is full of foreigners." Take my own household as an example. Our housekeeper is a German from Pomerania. The housekeeper of our country home is Italian and speaks very little English, yet she's an American citizen and she has a big American flag waving over her cottage. Our gardener is a Mexican, and many other gardeners here in Hollywood are Japanese. In the studios you will hear all kinds of different accents around you.

Anyway, to get back to *Murder*, it was an interesting film and was quite successful in London. But it was too sophisticated for the provinces.

F.T. The following picture, *The Skin Game*, was also based on a stage play, I believe. I don't remember it too clearly. It's the story of a fierce rivalry between a landowner and his immediate neighbor, who had made his money in business. The most important scene showed them vying with each other at an auction sale.

A.H. It was taken from the play by John Galsworthy. Edmund Gwenn, who was very famous in London at the time, starred in it. I didn't make it by choice, and there isn't much to be said about it.

F.T. I imagine that the higher budgets, at the advent of the sound era, presented quite a few new problems.

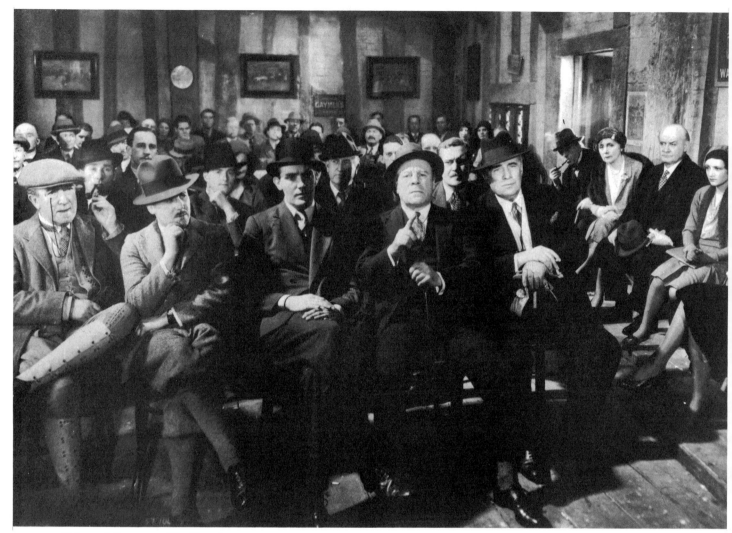

Edmund Gwenn in *The Skin Game*.

A.H.   Exactly. For one thing, since it took more time to make a picture, they were often made in several versions in order to reach an international audience. Therefore each film was much more expensive.

F.T.   There was no dubbing at the time?

A.H.   Not yet. We shot with four cameras and with a single sound track because we couldn't cut sound in those days. That's why when they speak to me about the use of multiple cameras on live television, I say, "That's nothing new. We were already doing it in 1928."

F.T.   Your next picture was *Rich and Strange*, in 1931. I liked that one very much.

A.H.   Yes, it had lots of ideas. The story was about a young couple who won a lot of money and took a trip around the world. Before shooting it, Mrs. Hitchcock and I set out to do some preliminary research on the story. She was writing the script, you know. In the picture I planned to show the young couple in Paris, going to the Folies Bergère and going down during the intermission to see the belly dancing. So we went over to the Folies Bergère. And during the intermission I turned to a young man in a tuxedo and asked him where we could see the belly dancing.
"This way, follow me, please."
So we followed him to the street, and when I appeared surprised, he explained, "It's in the annex." And he put us in a cab.

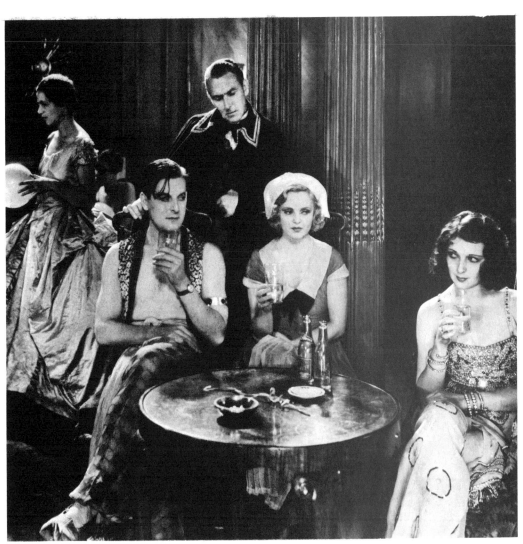

Henry Kendall and Joan Barry in *Rich and Strange*.

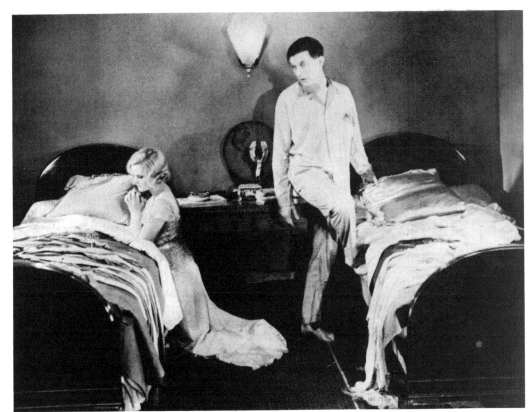

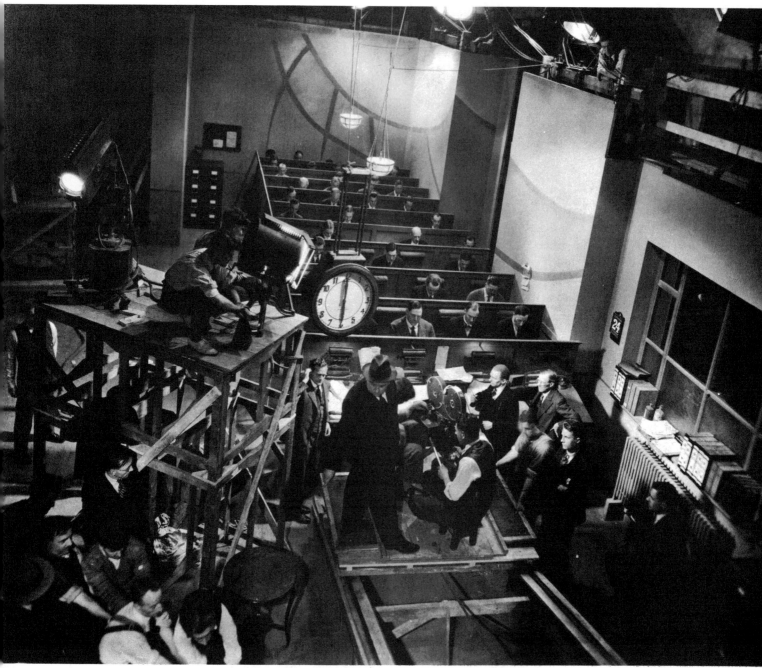

Before leaving to go around the world, one must follow the routine of office life.
Standing near the camera, Hitchcock directs *Rich and Strange*.

I thought there must surely be some mistake. When the cab finally stopped at a door, I said to my wife, "I'll bet he's taking us to a brothel," and asked whether she wanted to go in. We'd never in our lives been in a place like that, but she said, "Yes."

The girls came down. We offered them champagne. In front of my wife, the madam asked me whether I would like one of the young ladies. Well, I've never had anything to do with that sort of woman to this very day! Anyway, we got out of there and went back to the theater. And only then did we realize that we weren't at the Folies Bergère at all but at the Casino de Paris. So we had been behaving exactly like the couple in the book—two innocents abroad!

F.T. How did you plan to use the belly dancing in the film?

A.H. The reason I was interested in the belly dancing is that I wanted to show the heroine looking at a navel that goes round and round and finally dissolves to a spirallike spinning motion.

F.T. Like the main title of *Vertigo?*

A.H. Yes, that's it. In *Rich and Strange* there was a scene in which the young man is swimming with a girl and she stands with her legs astride, saying to him, "I bet you can't swim between my legs."
I shot it in a tank. The boy dives, and when he's about to pass between her legs, she suddenly locks his head between her legs and you see the bubbles rising from his mouth. Finally, she releases him, and as he comes up, gasping for air, he sputters out, "You almost killed me that time," and she answers, "Wouldn't that have been a beautiful death?"
I don't think we could show that today because of censorship.

F.T. I've seen two different prints of that picture, but neither one showed that scene. However, I remember a funny episode that took place aboard a Chinese junk.

A.H. Oh yes! The young couple is in the Far East and the ship on which they are traveling is wrecked. They manage to get off the ship, taking with them a bottle of crème de menthe and the ship's black cat, and they're picked up by a Chinese junk. They huddle up in front of the junk, and after a while the Chinese bring them some food and chopsticks. It's delicious, the best meal they've ever tasted. When it's over, they walk to the rear of the junk and there they see the cat's skin being pinned out to dry. Stunned as well as nauseated, they rush over to the side.

F.T. It was quite a good film, but I believe that the critics were not overly cordial to *Rich and Strange.*

A.H. They felt that the characterizations weren't sufficiently convincing. The actors were all right, but we should have had a stronger cast —in the box-office sense, I mean. I liked the picture; it should have been more successful.

————————

F.T. You made *Number Seventeen* in 1932. I saw the film at the Cinémathèque. It was quite funny, but the story was rather confusing.

A.H. A disaster! But there was a funny incident during the shooting. Part of the film was set in an empty house in which gangsters were hiding out, and there was to be a fair amount of gunplay. It occurred to me that it would be an intriguing idea if we used this house also as a refuge for all the stray cats of the neighborhood. Every time a gun was shot, a hundred cats would run up or down the stairs. These shots were to be separated from the action, for greater facility, in order to play around with the scene in the editing stage.
The camera was set up at the bottom of the stairway. On the morning we were finally all set to shoot the cats, I arrived to find the studio full of people. I asked why there were so many extras. "They're not extras," I was told. "They're the people who own the cats."
We put flat panels all around the bottom of the stairway. Each owner came forward and put his or her cat in the stall and then we were ready to shoot. The cameraman switched his motor on and the prop man fired a gun. All the cats leaped right over the barrier; not one went up the stairs. They were all over the studio. And for the next few hours all you could hear was the owners going around saying, "Pussy, pussy, pussy."
"That's my cat!"
"No, it's mine!"
Eventually, we got them all together again, and this time we had a wire netting put around so that they couldn't run away. Everything was ready. Camera. Bang! This time only three ran up the stairs. All the rest turned and clung desperately to the netting. So I gave it up.

F.T. The picture was based on a novel that

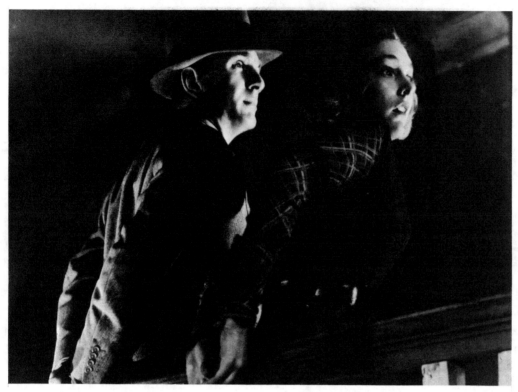

The railing to which the principals of *Number Seventeen* (1932) are attached is about to collapse.

had also been a stage play. Did you choose the story?

A.H.   No, it was bought by the studio and they assigned me to the picture.

F.T.   As movies go, this one was rather short; it ran for about an hour. The first part, inside the house, is probably taken from the play. The second half, as I remember it, was better. There was a long chase sequence, with wonderful miniature models of cars and trains. As a matter of fact, the miniatures in your films are always very handsome. After that you went on to produce *Lord Camber's Ladies*, with Benn W. Levy handling the direction for you, the man who was the author of the dialogue of *Blackmail*.

A.H.   The American companies had contracted to release films that were a hundred per cent British; they were called "quota pictures" and were usually made very cheaply. When British International Pictures took on some of

these films at the Elstree Studios, I agreed to produce one or two. My idea was to turn over the direction to Levy, who was a friend and was quite well known as a playwright. We had a very fine cast, with Gertrude Lawrence, a great star in those days, and Sir Gerald du Maurier, the leading actor of London at the time, and in my opinion, the best actor anywhere. Unfortunately, Mr. Levy turned out to be a very obstinate gentleman. So my handsome gesture, in offering him the direction, blew up in my face. I had two other projects to produce. I wanted to give one of them to John Van Druten, a rather successful playwright, who had written several plays with two characters. I offered him the facilities of shooting the film in the streets of London, with a small crew. Everybody would be paid for a whole year, so that if it rained, he could work in a studio or, if he felt like it, he could lay the whole project aside and start up again when he was ready. He was also offered two very good young actors who would be signed up for a year. In effect, I was offering him a camera in the place of his typewriter.

82

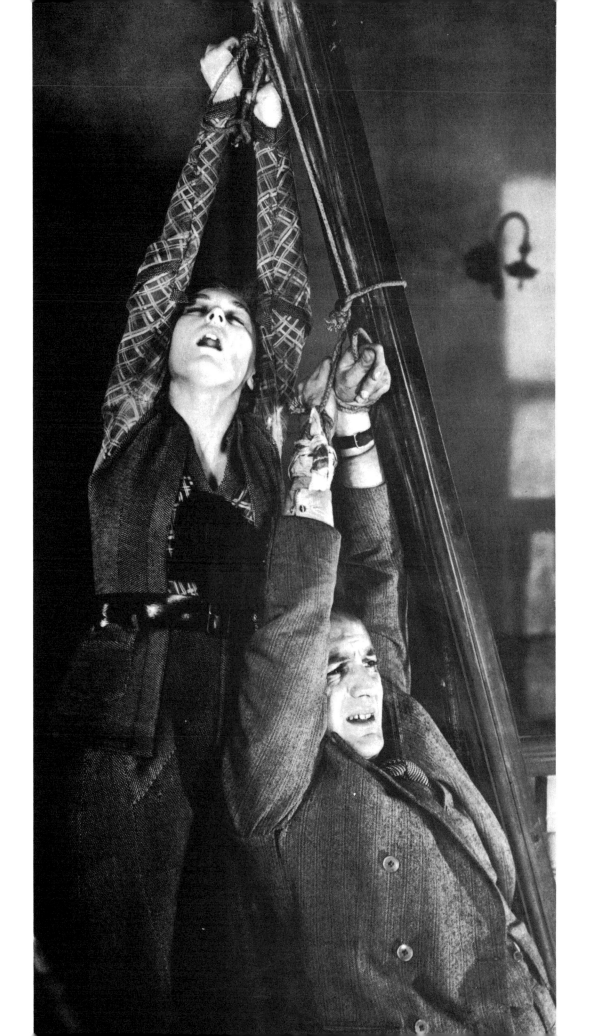

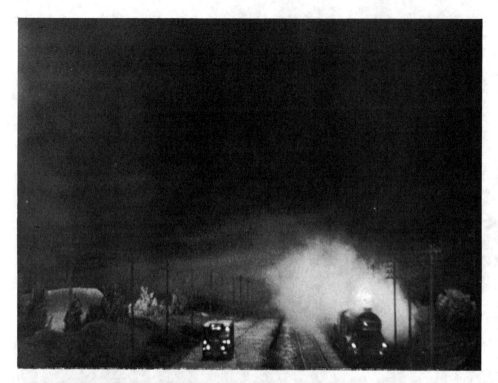

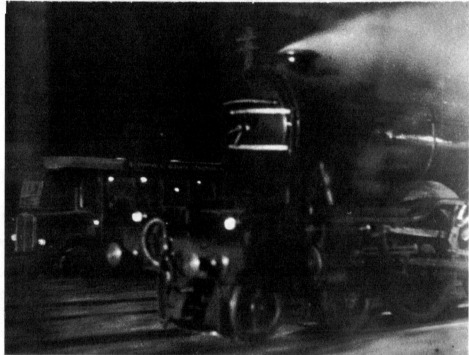

Number Seventeen:
the chase sequence.

Though these were facilities that I had never enjoyed myself, Van Druten turned the proposition down. I was never able to figure out why. Meanwhile, I was also considering a story written by Countess Russell. The story was about a princess who steals away from the court and has two weeks of fun and adventure with a commoner. Does that sound familiar to you?

F.T. Of course. It's *Roman Holiday*.

A.H. Well, we never made it. Then I embarked on a Bulldog Drummond story, with two writers. It was a very good script, and the producer, John Maxwell . . .

F.T.   Maxwell is the man who had produced all of your movies since *The Ring*, in 1927?

A.H.   Yes. Maxwell sent me a letter saying: "It's a brilliant scenario, a tour de force, but I don't want to produce it." I have a hunch that a critic whom I had brought into the studio and recommended as story editor was intriguing against me and the picture. So it was never made. And that was the end of my period with British International Pictures.

F.T.   Which brings us to 1933. Things were not going too well for you at this time. I can't believe *Waltzes from Vienna* was your own choice.

A.H.   It was a musical without music, made very cheaply. It had no relation to my usual work. In fact, at this time my reputation wasn't very good, but luckily I was unaware of this.

Nothing to do with conceit; it was merely an inner conviction that I was a film-maker. I don't ever remember saying to myself, "You're finished; your career is at its lowest ebb." And yet outwardly, to other people, I believe it was.
Rich and Strange had been a disappointment, and *Number Seventeen* reflected a careless approach to my work. There was no careful analysis of what I was doing. Since those days I've learned to be very self-critical, to step back and take a second look. And never to embark on a project unless there's an inner feeling of comfort about it, a conviction that something good will come of it. It's as if you were about to put up a building. You have to see the steel structure first. I'm not talking about the story structure, but about the concept of the film as a whole. If the basic concept is solid, things will work out. What happens to the film, of course, becomes a matter of degree, but there should be no question that the concept is a sound one. My mistake with *Rich and Strange* was my failure to make sure that the two leading players would be attractive to the critics and audience alike. With a story that good, I should not have

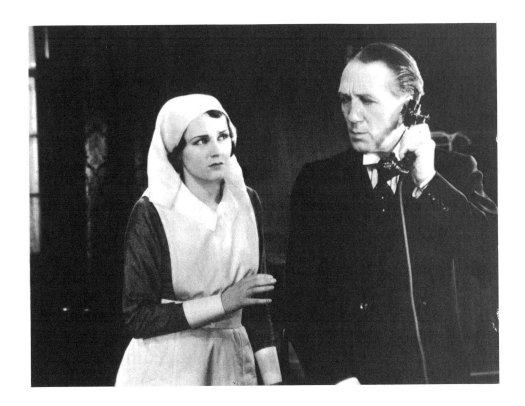

Sir Gerald du Maurier in *Lord Camber's Ladies.*

85

allowed indifferent casting.

While we were shooting *Waltzes from Vienna*, at this low ebb of my career, Michael Balcon came to see me working at the studio. He had given me my first chance to become a director. He said: "What are you doing after this picture?" I said, "I have a script that was written some time ago; it's in a drawer, somewhere." I brought in the scenario; he liked it and offered to buy it. So I went to my former producer, John Maxwell, and bought it from him for two hundred and fifty pounds. I sold it to the new Gaumont-British company, which was headed by Balcon, for five hundred pounds. But I was so ashamed of the hundred per cent profit that I had the sculptor Jacob Epstein do a bust of Balcon with the money. And I presented Balcon with Epstein's bust of him.

F.T. And that was the scenario of *The Man Who Knew Too Much?**

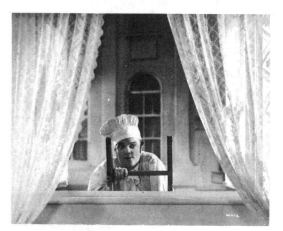

---

* In accordance with the chronological arrangement of these conversations, the above-mentioned picture is the original British version of *The Man Who Knew Too Much*, made in 1934. Twenty-two years later, in 1956, Alfred Hitchcock directed a remake of the picture, co-starring James Stewart and Doris Day.

The cook as voyeur in *Waltzes from Vienna* (1933).

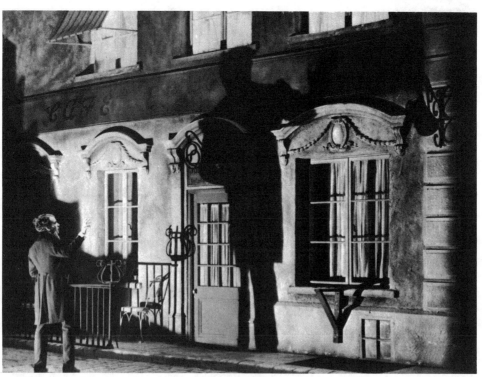

A.H. That's right. It was based on an original Bulldog Drummond story by "Sapper" and adapted by Charles Bennett, with a newspaper columnist, D. B. Wyndham-Lewis, doing the dialogue. So actually, it's to the credit of Michael Balcon that he originally started me as a director and later gave me a second chance. Of course, he was always very possessive of me, and that's why he was very angry, later on, when I left for Hollywood. But before talking about *The Man Who Knew Too Much*, I want to make a point. And that is that whatever happens in the course of your career, your talent is always there. To all appearances, I seemed to have gone into a creative decline in 1933 when I made *Waltzes from Vienna*, which was very bad. And yet the talent must have been there all along since I had already conceived the project for *The Man Who Knew Too Much*, the picture that re-established my creative prestige.

Anyway, to get back to 1934. First, there's a thoroughly sobering self-examination. And now, I'm ready to go to work on *The Man Who Knew Too Much*.

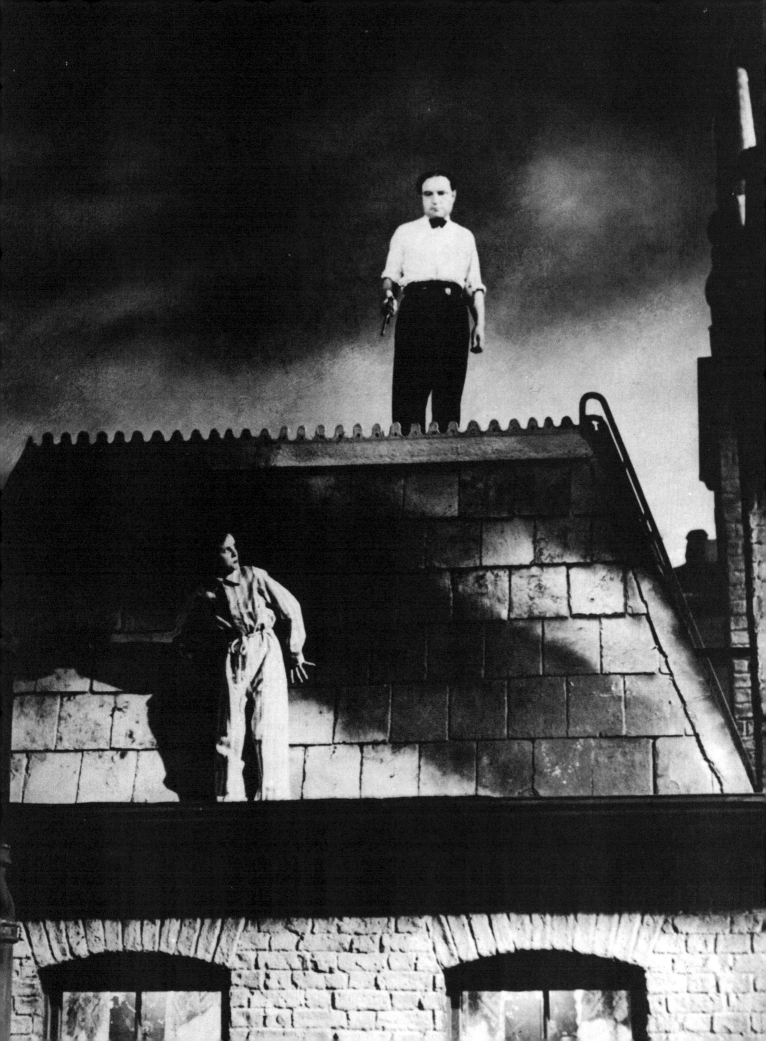

"THE MAN WHO KNEW TOO MUCH" ■ WHEN CHURCHILL WAS CHIEF OF POLICE ■ "M" ■ FROM "THE ONE NOTE MAN" TO THE DEADLY CYMBALS ■ CLARIFICATION AND SIMPLIFICATION ■ "THE THIRTY-NINE STEPS" ■ JOHN BUCHAN'S INFLUENCE ■ UNDERSTATEMENT ■ AN OLD, BAWDY STORY ■ MR. MEMORY ■ SLICE OF LIFE AND SLICE OF CAKE ■ ■ ■ ■ ■ ■ ■ ■ ■ ■ ■ ■ ■ ■ ■ ■

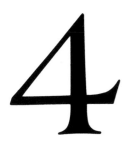

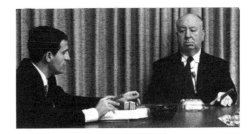

FRANÇOIS TRUFFAUT. *The Man Who Knew Too Much* was your greatest British success and I think it was a big hit in the United States as well.

In the original version the story was about a couple of British tourists traveling in Switzerland with their daughter. They witness the assassination of a Frenchman who, before he dies, tells them about a plot to murder a foreign diplomat in London. To ensure the couple's silence, the spy ring captures the little girl. The couple returns to London to track down the kidnappers, and the mother manages to save the ambassador's life just as he's about to be shot down during a concert at Albert Hall. The picture winds up with the police smoking the spy gang out of their hiding place and the saving of the little girl.

I've read somewhere that it was inspired by a true-life story, an incident in which Winston Churchill was involved at the time he headed the police force.

ALFRED HITCHCOCK. You mean the ending was based on a real-life occurrence. That's true. The incident took place around 1910, I think, and was known as the Sidney Street siege. Some Russian anarchists were holed up in a house and were shooting while the police were trying to get them out of there. It was a very difficult operation so they called out the soldiers. Churchill came down to supervise the operation. That incident was to cause me a lot of trouble with the censors. I'll explain why. You see, the British police don't carry firearms, and during this siege, as I said before, they had to bring out the military. They were even about to call on the artillery when the house caught fire and the anarchists came out. So, when I was shooting the picture, many

89

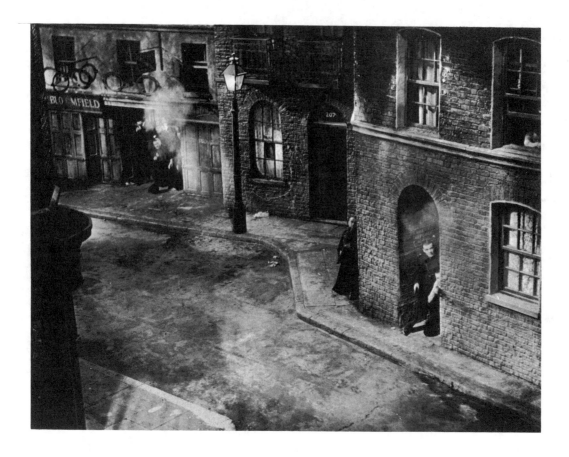

years later, the censors took the view that the incident was a blot on the record of the British police. Yet they wouldn't allow us to show them carrying weapons. When I asked how we were going to get the spies out, the censors suggested that we use water hoses. I did some research and discovered that Winston Churchill himself had made that very suggestion. Finally, the censors agreed to let the police fire some guns, provided I would show them going to a local gunsmith to pick out all sorts of antique weapons. This was to make it perfectly clear that the police are not used to firearms. The whole thing was so ludicrous that I ignored them. Instead, we had a flash showing the arrival of a truck from which rifles were handed out to the police.

F.T.   In the American version of 1956, the picture opens in Marrakech, but in the original the action begins in Switzerland.

A.H.   The picture opens with a scene at St. Moritz, in Switzerland, because that's where I spent my honeymoon with my wife. From our window I could see the skating rink. And it oc-

curred to me that we might start the picture by showing an ice skater tracing numbers—eight—six—zero—two—on the rink. An espionage code, of course. But I dropped the idea.

F.T.   Because you couldn't get the shot?

A.H.   No. It simply had no place in the story. But the point I was trying to make is that from the very outset the contrast between the snowy Alps and the congested streets of London

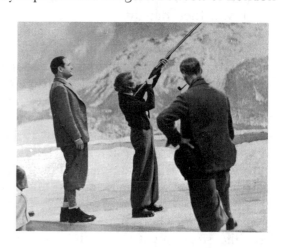

90

was a decisive factor. That visual concept had to be embodied in the film.

F.T. You used Pierre Fresnay in the original and Daniel Gelin in the remake. Why did you want a French actor in that role?

A.H. I didn't especially want a Frenchman; I believe that came from the producer's side. But I did insist on having Peter Lorre. He had just done *M* with Fritz Lang and this was his first British role. He had a very sharp sense of humor. They called him "the walking overcoat" because he went around in a long coat that came down to his feet.

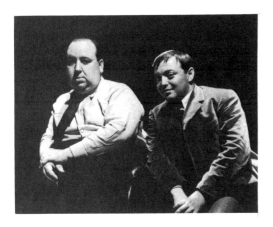

F.T. Had you seen *M*?

A.H. Yes. I don't remember it too well. Wasn't there a whistling man in it?

F.T. Yes, that was Peter Lorre! You must have seen some of the other Fritz Lang films at that time—*The Spy* and *The Testament of Dr. Mabuse.*

A.H. *Mabuse*—that's a long time back. Do you remember, in *The Man Who Knew Too Much*, there's a scene in the dentist's office? At first I had intended to do it in a barbershop, with the hot towels masking the men's faces. But just before the shooting I saw Mervyn LeRoy's *I Am a Fugitive from a Chain Gang*, with Paul Muni, which had a scene just like it. So I transposed it to a dentist's office, and while I was at it, I changed a few other things I didn't like. For instance, at the opening of the film we estab-

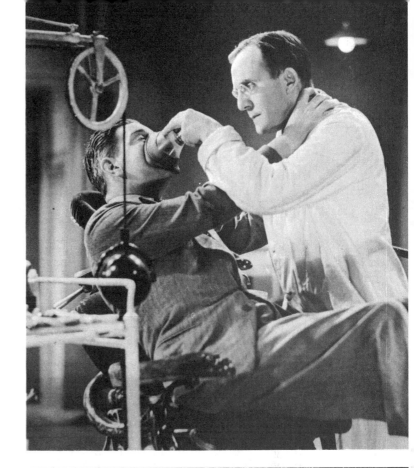

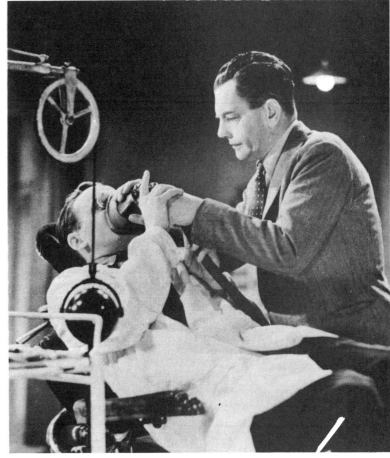

lished the fact that the heroine—the mother of the little girl who's been kidnaped—was a first-rate shot. So the villains were to hypnotize the mother at the chapel. And while she's in a trance, they would take her to Albert Hall, where she would kill the ambassador herself. On thinking it over, I felt that even a crack shot might not aim accurately while in a hypnotic trance. So I dropped it.

F.T.   It's rather interesting that what you did, in fact, was to reverse the idea completely. Instead of shooting the ambassador, the woman actually saves his life by crying out at the right moment.

The situation, as I remember it, has a group of spies planning to assassinate an important foreign statesman. Their plan is to shoot him during the playing of a cantata at a concert in Albert Hall. The killer is to fire at the precise instant when the musical score calls for a clash of cymbals. To make sure of their timing, they rehearse the killing to the sound of a recording of the cantata.

Finally, the concert itself begins, with all the characters in their proper places. And we wait, with rising tension, for that moment when the impassive cymbal player will use his instrument.

A.H.   The idea for the cymbals was inspired by a cartoon, or rather by a comic strip that appeared in a satirical magazine like *Punch*. The drawings showed a man who wakes up in the morning, gets out of bed, goes into the bathroom, gargles, shaves, takes a shower, gets dressed and has his breakfast. Then he puts on his hat and coat, picks up a small leather instrument case and goes out. On the street he gets on a bus that takes him into the city and in front of Albert Hall. He goes in, using the musicians' entrance, takes off his hat and his coat, opens up the case, takes out a small flute. Then, with the other musicians, he traipses onto the large podium and sits down in his place. Eventually, the conductor comes in, gives the signal and the symphony begins. Our little man is sitting there, turning the pages and awaiting his turn. At last the conductor waves the baton in his direction and the little man blows out a single note "Bloop!" When that's over, he puts the flute

back into the case, tiptoes out, puts on his hat and coat and goes out. By now the street is dark. He gets on a bus, arrives home. Supper is ready. He eats, goes up to his room, takes off his clothes, steps into the bathroom, gargles, puts on his pajamas, gets into bed and turns off the lights.

F.T.   It's so good that they've used variants of that idea in several animated cartoons.

A.H.   Probably. They called him "The One Note Man," and the story of that little fellow, waiting to play his one note, gave me the idea of getting a suspense effect from the cymbals.

F.T.   I don't remember how you handled it in the British version, but in the American re-make you took great pains to focus the public's attention upon those cymbals. Right after the main credits the musician is shown waving his cymbals, and there is a superimposed title stating that the clash of cymbals can change the course of an American family's life, or something to that effect. Then, later on, the villains listen to the record of the cantata before going to the concert hall. You have them play the key passage twice over. It's quite precise and very emphatic.

A.H.   We had to do that so that the audience would participate completely. In the audience there are probably many people who don't even know what cymbals are, and so it was necessary not only to show them but even to spell out the word. It was also important that the public be able not only to recognize the sound of the cymbals but to anticipate it in their minds. Knowing what to expect, they wait for it to happen. This conditioning of the viewer is essential to the build-up of suspense.

The reason why the cantata record is played twice is to prevent any confusion in the viewer's mind about the events that are to follow. I've often found that a suspense situation is weakened because the action is not sufficiently clear. For instance, if two actors should happen to be wearing similar suits, the viewer can't tell one from the other; if the location is not clearly established, the viewer may be wondering where

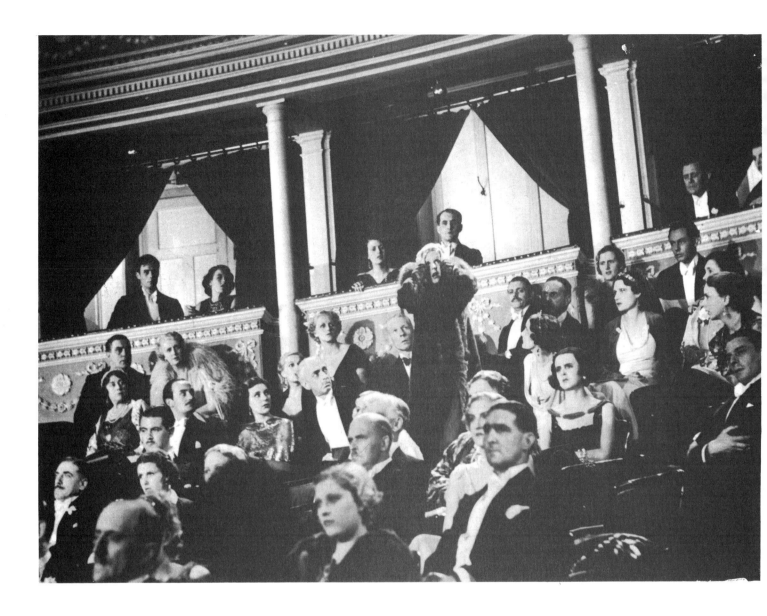

the action is taking place. And if a crucial scene unfolds while he is trying to figure these things out, its emotional impact is dissipated. So it's important to be explicit, to clarify constantly.

F.T.   And just as important as clarification, I think, is the need to simplify. A film director must have a sense of simplification. It seems to me there are two kinds of creative artists: those who simplify, and the others, who might be described as the "complicators." Many fine painters and excellent writers belong to the latter category, but to be successful in the medium of the spectacle, one has to be a "simplifier." Do you agree with that?

A.H.   Oh, absolutely. That's essential, if only because you can't convey an emotion to the public unless you feel it yourself. For instance, you must be able to simplify if only to control the time element. Directors who lose control are concerned with the abstract, and these vague preoccupations prevent them from concentrating on specific problems. They're like a poor speaker who loses his head because he's overly self-conscious and is unable to make a point, or to get to the point.

Incidentally, there is an important difference between the two versions of *The Man Who Knew Too Much*. In the British version the husband remains locked up, so that the wife carries

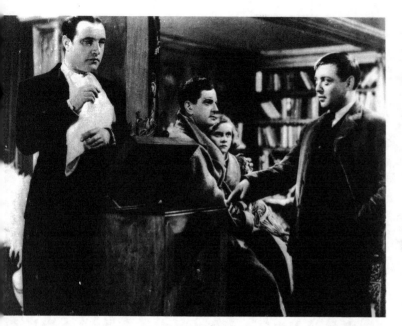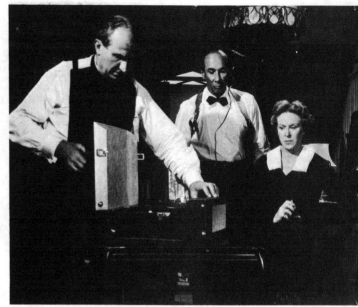

The scene in which the spies listen to the record of the cantata in *The Man Who Knew Too Much*: left, the 1934 version; right, the 1956 version.

the action by herself in Albert Hall and till the end of the picture.

F.T.   The second version was better because the husband's arrival on the scene during the playing of the cantata made it possible to extend the suspense. He sees his wife from a distance, and she explains the situation in sign language, pointing first to the killer and then to the diplomat who is his prospective victim. Stewart must take action, so he tries to make his way to the ambassador's loge. The sequence through the corridors, in which he tries to explain what is happening to the policemen stationed there, who keep on referring him to one of their superiors, is played out in pantomime. That pantomimed performance strengthens the suspense and also points up the irony of the whole situation. The humor is much subtler than in the British version. Another advantage is that instead of interrupting the mood of the sequence, the humor actually heightens the drama.

A.H.   That's true. But aside from this difference the scene in the Albert Hall is quite similar in both versions, don't you agree? The cantata is the same . . .

F.T.   But the second orchestration by Ber-

nard Herrmann is far superior. And isn't this scene longer in the second version? In any case, there's a three-hundred-meter reel that's entirely musical, with no dialogue. All static shots, I think. In the original version the shots were often mobile. There were several panning shots, for instance, when the camera moved from the killer's face to the heroine's, and from hers to the face of the ambassador. In the construction as well as in the rigorous attention to detail, the remake is by far superior to the original.

A.H.   Let's say that the first version is the work of a talented amateur and the second was made by a professional.

———————

F.T.   With the success of *The Man Who Knew Too Much*, I imagine you were given a free hand in the choice of stories. The one you chose was *The Thirty-nine Steps*, about a young Canadian who leaves London and makes his way to Scotland in pursuit of a spy ring that has stabbed a woman to death in his flat. With the police thinking he's committed the murder and the spies out to get him, there are snares and traps wherever he turns. After a series of hair-raising, narrow escapes, the picture winds up

94

with a happy ending. The screenplay was based on a John Buchan novel. He's a writer for whom you have great admiration, I believe.

A.H.   In fact, Buchan was a strong influence a long time before I undertook *The Thirty-nine Steps*, and some of it is reflected in *The Man Who Knew Too Much*. He had written *Greenmantle*, a novel that was probably inspired by the strange personality of Lawrence of Arabia. Korda bought this novel, but he never made the picture. At first I considered this book, but on second thought I chose *The Thirty-nine Steps*, which was a smaller subject. Probably for the very reason we mentioned in connection with Dostoyevsky—my respect for a literary masterpiece.
What I find appealing in Buchan's work is his understatement of highly dramatic ideas.

F.T.   *The Trouble with Harry* has that same quality of understatement.

A.H.   That's right. Understatement is important to me. At any rate, I worked on the scenario with Charles Bennett, and the method I used in those days was to make a treatment complete in every detail, except for the dialogue. I saw it as a film of episodes, and this time I was on my toes. As soon as we were through with one episode, I remember saying, "Here we need a good short story." I made sure the content of every scene was very solid, so that each one would be a little film in itself.
Anyway, despite my admiration for John Buchan, there are several things in the picture that were not in the book. For instance, the scene in which Robert Donat spends the night with the farmer and his wife was inspired by an old story about a South African Boer, a black-bearded man, very austere, with a very young, sex-starved wife. On his birthday she kills a chicken and bakes a chicken pie. It's a very stormy night and she hopes that her husband will be pleased with her surprise. All she gets for her pains is an angry husband, who berates her for killing a chicken without his permission. Hence, a grim birthday celebration. Suddenly there's a knock at the door, and there stands a handsome stranger who has lost his way and requests a night's hospitality. The woman invites him to sit down and offers him some food,

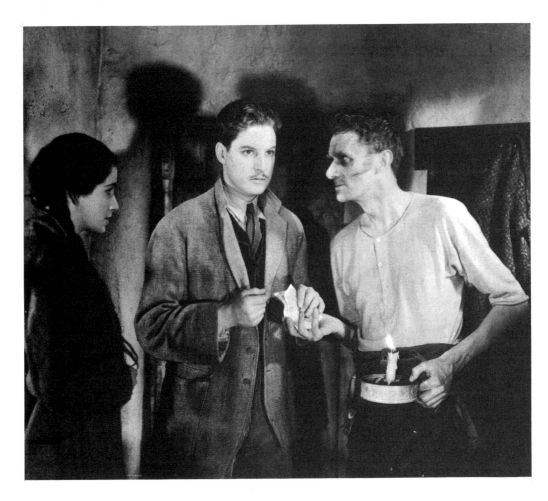

but the farmer, feeling he's eating too much, stops him and says, "Hold on, there. This has got to last us the rest of the week."

The woman is hungrily eying the stranger, wondering how she can get to bed with him. The husband suggests that they put him out in the barn, but the woman objects. Finally, the three of them go to sleep in the great big bed, with the farmer in the middle. The woman is trying to find some way to get rid of her husband, and finally, hearing a noise, she wakes him up, saying, "I think the chickens are out of the coop." The husband goes out to the yard, and the woman shakes the stranger awake, saying, "Come on. Now's your chance." So the stranger gets out of bed and quickly gulps down the rest of the chicken pie.*

F.T. The story is good, but the episode in the picture is better. The mood reminds one of Murnau, probably because of the faces, and also because the characters are at once bound to the earth and to religion. Though that scene is a brief one, the personalities are striking and they emerge forcefully. The prayer sequence is really remarkable. While the husband gives thanks, Robert Donat notices that the newspaper on the table carries his picture. He turns to the woman, who glances down at the picture and then looks at Donat. As their eyes meet, it is clear that she is now aware that he is a wanted man. In reply to her unsmiling, unspoken query, his eyes voice an eloquent appeal. And the farmer, noticing this exchange of looks, clearly suspects a romantic understanding between the two, so he goes outside to watch them through the window.

The whole scene is a beautiful illustration of silent filming, and the characters are admirably well drawn. The husband, for instance, is clearly a fanatic, a man who is possessive, jealous, and excessively puritanical. And this trait of his character has a specific bearing on a subsequent development: the wife gives Donat the farmer's coat, and when he is shot at, his life will be saved because the bullet hits the Bible

---

* The same story was filmed by Carlo-Rim, in 1951, as the sketch on gluttony in the picture *Seven Capital Sins*.

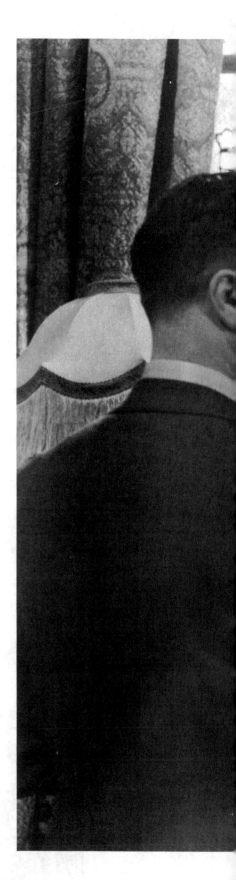

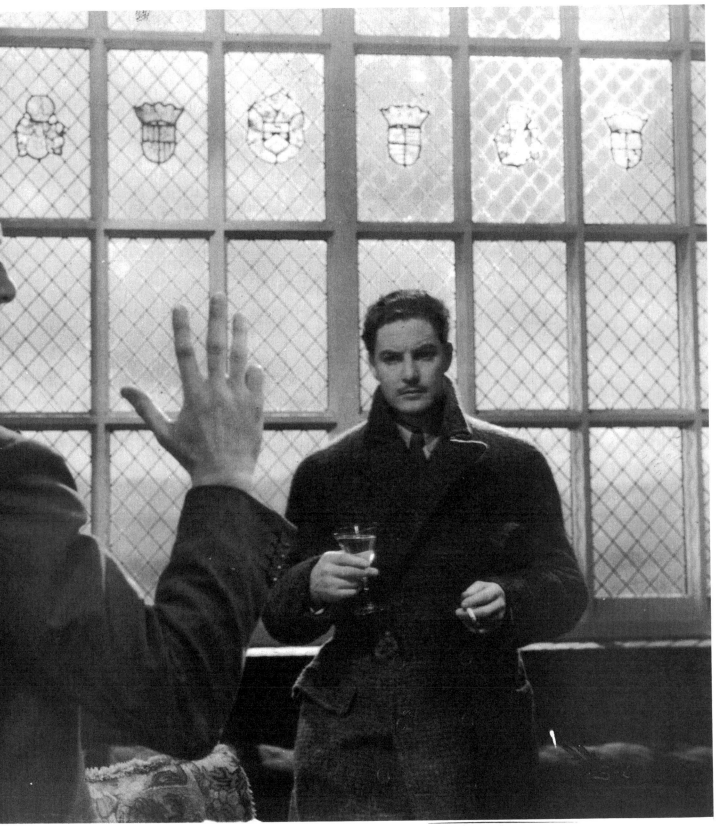

Robert Donat has taken refuge in the mansion of a Scotch nobleman (Godfrey Tearle). He explains to him that he is in pursuit of a master spy who is missing a finger on his left hand. "Are you sure it isn't the right hand?" asks Tearle (*The Thirty-nine Steps*).

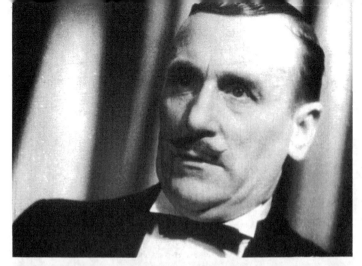

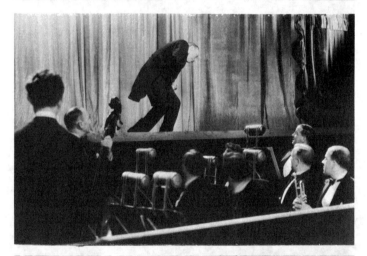

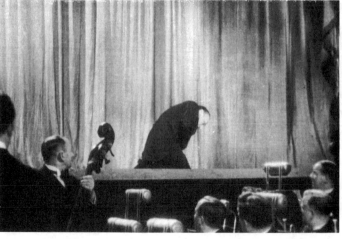

the farmer carried in one of the coat pockets.*

A.H. Yes, that was a nice scene. There was also another interesting character in the film, Mr. Memory. He's based on a true-life music-hall personality called Datas. The audience would ask him questions about major events, like: "When did the *Titanic* sink?" and he would give the correct answer. There were also trick questions. One of them was: "When did Good Friday fall on a Tuesday?" And the answer was: "Good Friday was a horse running at Wolverhampton race track and he fell at the first hurdle on Tuesday, June 21, 1864."

F.T. Mr. Memory was a wonderful character. I particularly liked the way you handled his death, by making him, quite literally, the victim of his professional conscience. When Robert Donat, in the music hall, asks him what the thirty-nine steps are, he can't help blurting out the whole truth about the spy ring, and the ringleader, who's in the audience, shoots him dead. It's this kind of touch that gives so many of your pictures a quality that's extremely satisfying to the mind: a characterization is developed to the limit—until death itself. Within a situation that goes from the picturesque to the pathetic, the incident is handled in the light of a relentless logic that makes the death seem ironic and yet grandiose, almost heroic.

A.H. The whole idea is that the man is doomed by his sense of duty. Mr. Memory *knows* what the thirty-nine steps are, and when he is asked the question, he is *compelled* to give the answer. The schoolteacher in *The Birds* dies for the same reason.

F.T. Recently, I saw *The Thirty-nine Steps* in Brussels, and a few days later in Paris I went to see the remake that was done by Ralph Thomas, with Kenneth More. The remake was poorly directed and rather ridiculous, but the story is so fascinating that the audience was interested anyway.

---

* Fritz Lang's *The Spy*, made in 1928, also showed a book breaking the impact of a bullet, but in the Lang picture the life-saving book was not the Bible.

At times the breakdown followed your own very closely, but even these parts were inferior. And wherever there were changes, they were mostly all wrong. For instance, at the beginning of the movie, when Robert Donat is locked up in a flat in which a woman has been stabbed, he notices from the window two spies pacing back and forth in the street. You showed those spies from *his* viewpoint; the camera was *in* the room and the spies were *outside*, on the sidewalk. They were shown from a distance. But in the remake Ralph Thomas has two or three close shots of the spies in the street. Because of this the scene loses its whole impact; the two men are no longer strange and sinister and there is simply no reason to feel afraid for the hero.

A.H.   It's really too bad; they miss the whole point. It's obvious that you can't change your viewpoint in the midst of a situation of that kind.

F.T.   Incidentally, on reseeing your version of *The Thirty-nine Steps*, I realized that it's approximately at this period that you began to take more liberties with the scenarios, that is, to attach less importance to the credibility of the plot, or at any rate, whenever necessary, to sacrifice plausibility in favor of pure emotion.

A.H.   Yes, that's right!

F.T.   For instance, when Robert Donat is leaving London, on the train, he runs into a series of disturbing incidents. At any rate, that's the way he interprets what he sees. He thinks the two persons sitting opposite him in the train compartment are watching him from behind their papers. And when the train stops at a station, through the window we see a policeman standing at attention and staring straight at the camera. There are indications of danger everywhere; everything is seen as a threat. The deliberate build-up of this mood was a step in the direction of American stylization.

A.H.   Yes, this was a period when there was greater attention to detail than in the past. Whenever I embarked on a new episode, I would say to myself, "The tapestry must be filled here" or "We must fill out the tapestry there."
What I like in *The Thirty-nine Steps* are the swift transitions. Robert Donat decides to go to the police to tell them that the man with the missing finger tried to kill him and how the Bible saved his life, but they don't believe him and suddenly he finds himself in handcuffs. How will he get out of them? The camera moves across the street, and we see Donat, still handcuffed, through the window that is suddenly shattered to bits. A moment later he runs into a Salvation Army parade and he falls in step. Next, he ducks into an alley that leads him straight into a conference hall. Someone says, "Thank heaven, our speaker has arrived," and he is hustled onto a platform where he has to improvise an election speech.
Then there's the girl who doesn't like him because he kissed her on the train. She comes in with two chaps who are supposed to take him to the police station, but who in fact, you will recall, are the spies. And Donat, handcuffed to the girl, manages to escape with her, thanks to a traffic jam caused by a herd of sheep. Still handcuffed to each other, they spend the night in a hotel, and so it goes.
The rapidity of those transitions heightens the excitement. It takes a lot of work to get that kind of effect, but it's well worth the effort. You use one idea after another and eliminate anything that interferes with the swift pace.

F.T.   It's a style that tends to do away with anything that is merely utilitarian, so as to retain only those scenes that are fun to shoot and to watch. It's the kind of cinema that's extremely satisfying to audiences and yet often irritates the critics. While looking at the movie, or after seeing it, they will analyze the script, which, of course, doesn't stand up to logical analysis. So they will single out as weaknesses those aspects that are the very essence of this film genre, as, for instance, a thoroughly casual approach to the plausible.

A.H.   I'm not concerned with plausibility; that's the easiest part of it, so why bother? Do you remember that lengthy scene in *The Birds* in which the people are talking about the birds? In that group there is a woman who is precisely

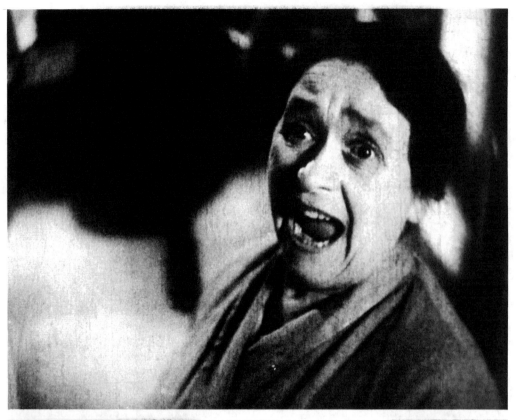

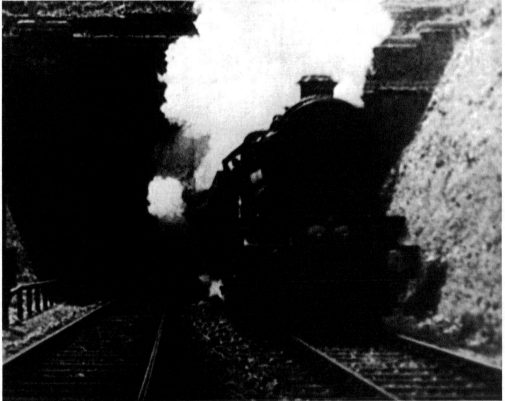

A cleaning woman discovers the body. Her scream dissolves into the whistle of the train carrying Robert Donat on his investigation (*The Thirty-nine Steps*).

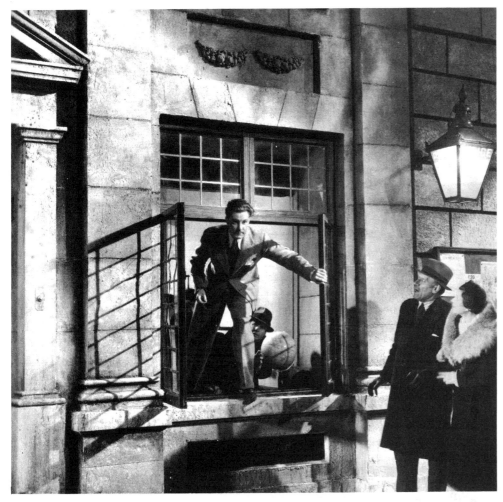

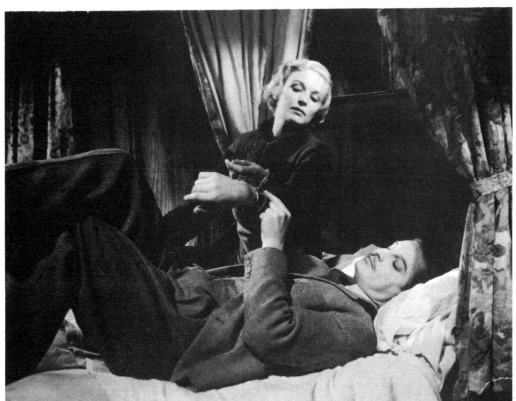

a specialist on the subject of birds, an ornithologist. She happens to be there by pure chance! Naturally, I could have made up three scenes just to give that woman a logical reason for being there, but they would have been completely uninteresting.

F.T.   Not to mention the waste of time for the public!

A.H.   Aside from the waste of time, they make for gaps or flaws in the picture. Let's be logical if you're going to analyze everything in terms of plausibility or credibility, then no fiction script can stand up to that approach, and you wind up doing a documentary.

F.T.   I agree with you that the ultimate of the credible is the documentary. As a matter of fact, the only kind of films that are, as a rule, unanimously endorsed by all the critics are such documentaries as *Naked Island*—pictures that require craftsmanship but no imagination.

A.H.   To insist that a storyteller stick to the facts is just as ridiculous as to demand of a representative painter that he show objects accurately. What's the ultimate in representative painting? Color photography. Don't you agree? There's quite a difference, you see, between the creation of a film and the making of a documentary. In the documentary the basic material has been created by God, whereas in the fiction film the director is the god; he must create life. And in the process of that creation, there are lots of feelings, forms of expression, and viewpoints that have to be juxtaposed. We should have total freedom to do as we like, just so long as it's not dull. A critic who talks to me about plausibility is a dull fellow.

F.T.   It's sometimes said that a critic, by the very nature of his work, is unimaginative, and in a way, that makes sense, since imagination may be a deterrent to his objectivity. Anyway, that lack of imagination might account for a predilection for films that are close to real life. On seeing *The Bicycle Thief*, for instance, he's likely to think this is just the sort of thing he might have written himself, but that thought couldn't possibly occur to him in connection with *North by Northwest*. This being so, he's bound to attribute all kinds of merit to *The Bicycle Thief* and none whatever to *North by Northwest*.

A.H.   Since you mention it, I might tell you that *The New Yorker* critic described that picture as "unconsciously funny." And yet I made *North by Northwest* with tongue in cheek; to me it was one big joke. When Cary Grant was on Mount Rushmore, I would have liked to put him inside Lincoln's nostril and let him have a sneezing fit.
By the way, since we're being so critical of the critics, what line were you in when we met for the first time?

F.T.   I was a film critic. What else?

A.H.   I thought so. You see, when a director has been let down by the critics, when he feels that his work has been passed on too lightly, his only recourse is to seek recognition via the public. Of course, if a film-maker thinks solely in box-office terms, he will wind up doing routine stuff, and that's bad, too. It seems to me that the critics are often responsible for this attitude; they drive a man to make only so-called public-acceptance pictures. Because he can always say to himself, "I don't give a damn about the critics, my films make money." There is a famous saying here in Hollywood: "You can't take a review to the bank!" Some magazines deliberately select critics who don't care about films, but are able to write about them in a condescending way that will amuse the readers. There's an American expression; when something's no good, they say, "It's for the birds!" So I pretty much knew what to expect when *The Birds* opened.

F.T.   Napoleon claimed that the best defense was attack. Wouldn't it have been possible to steal their thunder through some slogan in the advance promotion?

A.H.   It's not worth the effort. I was in London during the Second World War when a picture by John Van Druten opened. It was called *Old Acquaintance*, and it co-starred Bette Davis and Claude Rains. The critics of two London Sunday papers both used the same tag line at the end of their reviews. What do you think it was? "Auld acquaintances should be forgot." In other words, even if the picture had been good, they just couldn't resist that line.

F.T.   Well, in France they do the same whenever a film title ends with the word "*nuit.*" *Les Portes de la Nuit* is automatically labeled *Les Portes de l'Ennui*, and *Marguerite de la Nuit* is invariably referred to as *Marguerite de l'Ennui*. Even if the picture is fascinating, there are bound to be puns around the word "*ennui.*" Incidentally, one play on words I rather like is your own saying: "Some films are slices of life. Mine are slices of cake."

A.H.   I don't want to film a "slice of life" because people can get that at home, in the street, or even in front of the movie theater. They don't have to pay money to see a slice of life. And I avoid out-and-out fantasy because people should be able to identify with the characters. Making a film means, first of all, to tell a story. That story can be an improbable one, but it should never be banal. It must be dramatic and human. What is drama, after all, but life with the dull bits cut out. The next factor is the technique of film-making, and in this connection I am against virtuosity for its own sake. Technique should enrich the action. One doesn't set the camera at a certain angle just because the cameraman happens to be enthusiastic about that spot. The only thing that matters is whether the installation of the camera at a given angle is going to give the scene its maximum impact. The beauty of image and movement, the rhythm and the effects—everything must be subordinated to the purpose.

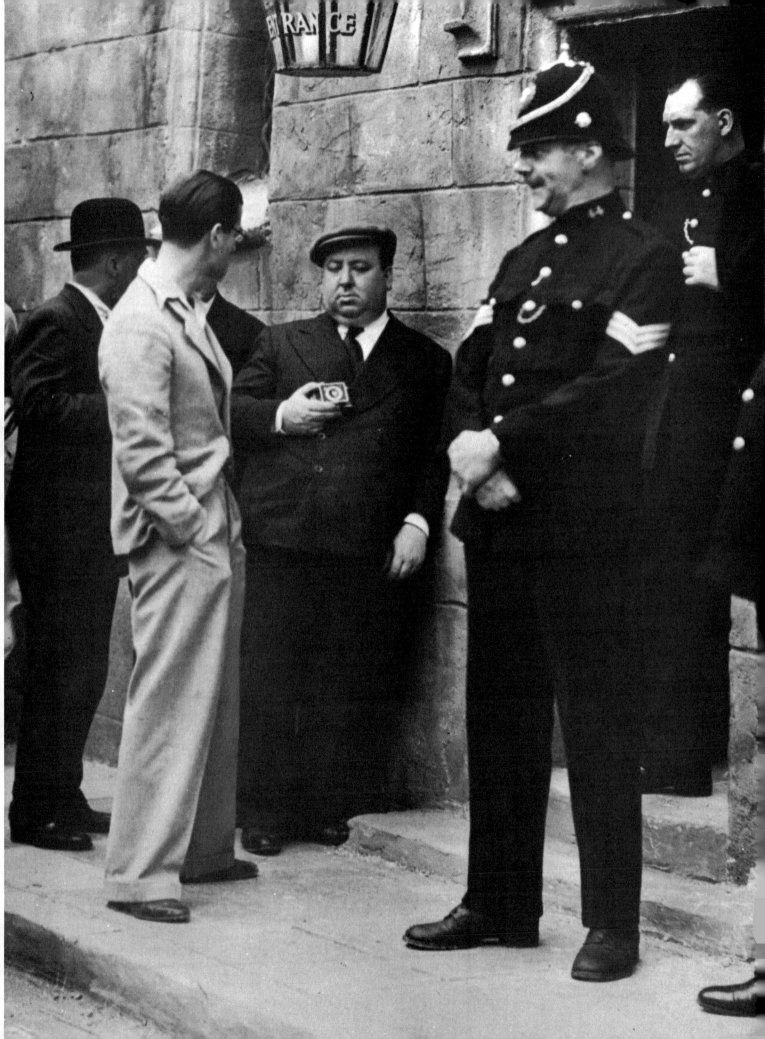

"THE SECRET AGENT" ■ YOU DON'T ALWAYS NEED A HAPPY ENDING ■ WHAT DO THEY HAVE IN SWITZERLAND? ■ "SABOTAGE" ■ THE CHILD AND THE BOMB ■ AN EXAMPLE OF SUSPENSE ■ "THE LADY VANISHES" ■ THE PLAUSIBLES ■ A WIRE FROM DAVID O. SELZNICK ■ THE LAST BRITISH FILM: "JAMAICA INN" ■ SOME CONCLUSIONS ABOUT THE BRITISH PERIOD ■ ■ ■ ■

5

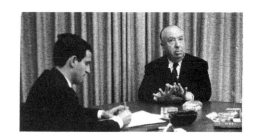

FRANÇOIS TRUFFAUT.   In 1936 you made *The Secret Agent*. John Gielgud played Ashenden, an intelligence agent who is assigned to go to Switzerland to kill a spy and by mistake kills an innocent tourist instead. Robert Young played the real spy, who is accidentally killed at the end of the picture when a train blows up. I only saw the picture once and my recollection of it is not too clear. Wasn't it taken from a Somerset Maugham novel?

ALFRED HITCHCOCK.   It's taken from two of Maugham's Ashenden adventure stories and also from a play by Campbell Dixon that was based on the series. The spy plot is a combination of "The Traitor" and "The Hairless Mexican," and we took the love story from the play. There were lots of ideas in the picture, but it didn't really succeed and I think I know why. In an adventure drama your central figure must have a purpose. That's vital for the progression of the film, and it's also a key factor in audience participation. The public must be rooting for the character; they should almost be helping him to achieve his goal. John Gielgud, the hero of *The Secret Agent*, has an assignment, but the job is distasteful and he is reluctant to do it.

F.T.   You mean his assignment to kill a man.

A.H.   That's right. Therefore, because it's a negative purpose, the film is static—it doesn't move forward. Another thing that's wrong with the picture is that there was too much irony, twists of fate. You may remember that when the hero finally agrees to do the killing, he botches the job by killing the wrong man. From the public's point of view, that was bad.

Opposite, Hitchcock appears as a press photographer outside the court in *Young and Innocent*.

105

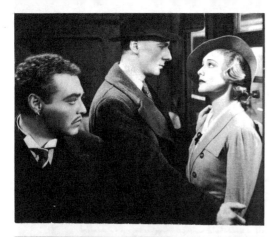

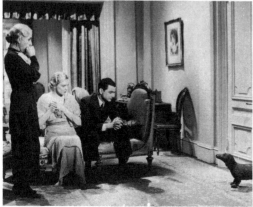

Percy Marmont's dog warns of the death of his master.

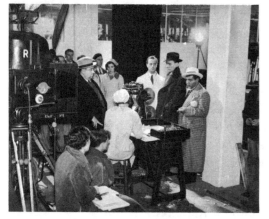

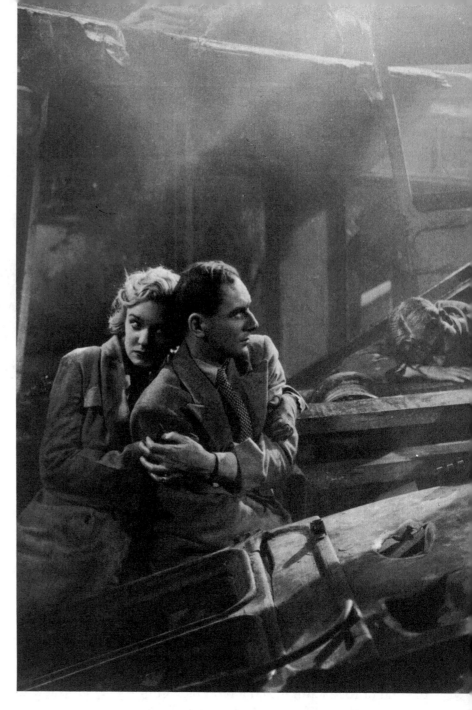

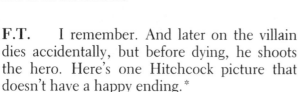

Filming the chase in the chocolate factory.

F.T. I remember. And later on the villain dies accidentally, but before dying, he shoots the hero. Here's one Hitchcock picture that doesn't have a happy ending.*

---

* In fact, I was mistaken on this point. It wasn't the hero who was shot down in the end, but Peter Lorre, who played his accomplice. Alfred Hitchcock apparently forgot that this picture ended in the traditional way. In the light of his interesting comment on happy endings; I'm allowing this excerpt of our conversations to stand as is.—F.T.

A.H. In some cases the happy ending is unnecessary. If you manage to get a solid grip on the audience, they will follow your reasoning. Providing there is sufficient entertainment in the body of the film, people will accept an unhappy ending.

One of the interesting aspects of the picture is that the action takes place in Switzerland. I said to myself, "What do they have in Switzerland?" They have milk chocolate, they have the Alps, they have village dances, and they have lakes.

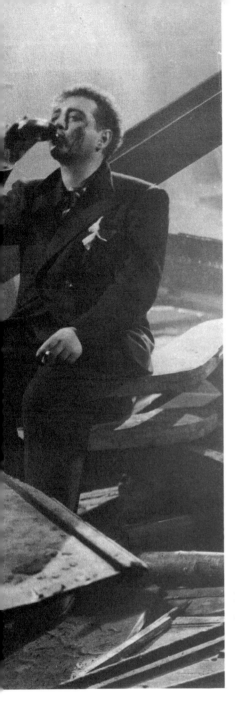

Madeleine Carroll,
John Gielgud,
Robert Young (dead)
and Peter Lorre,
after the train wreck
at the end of
The Secret Agent (1936).

A.H. I use this approach whenever possible, and it doesn't merely apply to the background. Local topographical features can be used dramatically as well. We use lakes for drownings and the Alps to have our characters fall into crevasses.

F.T. I've always enjoyed the way you make dramatic use of your protagonists' professions. In *The Man Who Knew Too Much*, James Stewart plays a doctor, and he behaves like one throughout the whole picture. His line of work is deliberately blended into the action. For instance, before telling Doris Day that their child has been kidnaped, he makes her take a sedative. It's a nice detail. But let's get back to *The Secret Agent*.

In their book about you, Claude Chabrol and Eric Rohmer point out an innovation in this picture that reappears time and again in your later work: the villain is attractive, distinguished, has good manners; he's actually very appealing.

A.H. Certainly. The introduction of the villain is always something of a problem, and this is especially true in melodrama because, even by definition, melodrama is passé and it has to be brought up to date. That's why in *North by Northwest*, where the villainous James Mason is competing with Cary Grant for the affection of Eva Marie Saint, I wanted him to be smooth and distinguished. The difficulty was how we could make him seem threatening at the same time. So what we did was to split this evil character into three people: James Mason, who is attractive and suave; his sinister-looking secretary; and the third spy, who is crude and brutal.

All of these national ingredients were woven into the picture.

F.T. That's why the spies have their headquarters in a chocolate factory! You apply the same principle in *To Catch a Thief*. The action is played out against the background of the Carlton Hotel at Cannes and the flower market in Nice, and the chase sequence is shot on the Grande Corniche.

F.T. It's all the more ingenious in that it justifies the romantic rivalry between Mason and Grant. It also adds the element of homosexual rivalry, with the male secretary clearly jealous of Eva Marie Saint.

Right after *The Secret Agent*, in that same year, in fact, you made *Sabotage*. It's based on a Joseph Conrad novel that happens to be entitled *The Secret Agent*. The coincidence often leads to confusion in your screen credits.

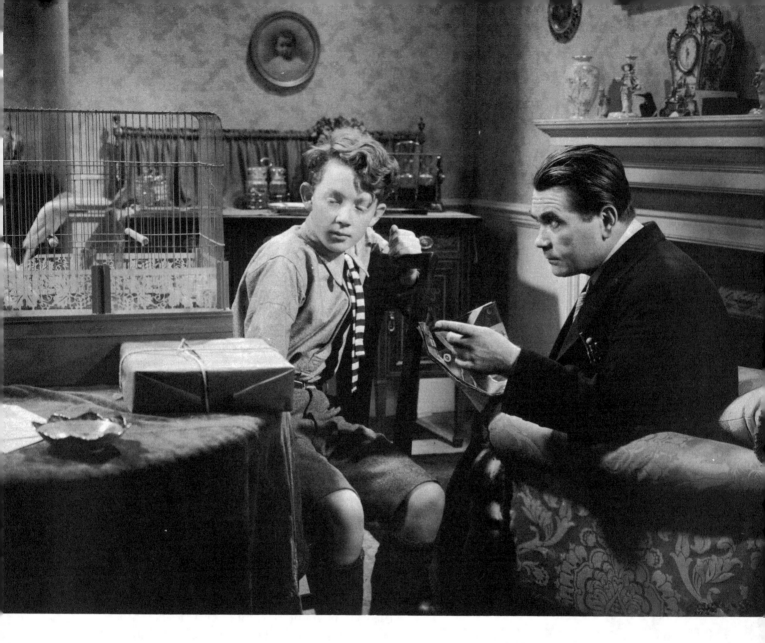

A.H. Well, in America it was called *The Woman Alone*. Have you seen the picture?

F.T. I saw it a little while ago. I must admit that in the light of its reputation, I found it rather disappointing.

However, the exposition is first rate. First, there is a close-up of a dictionary definition of the word "sabotage," then a close-up of an electric light bulb. Next, there's a long shot of a lighted street; then we're back to the light bulb, which suddenly goes out. In the darkened powerhouse someone discovering traces of sand says, "Sabotage!" Back to the street, where a man is peddling lucifer matches. As two nuns pass by, there is the sound of demoniacal laughter. And now, you introduce Oscar Homolka, who is on his way home. In the house he goes over to the sink to wash his hands, and as he rubs them together, a little sand can be seen drifting to the bottom of the washbasin.* The thing that's basically wrong with the whole picture is the char-

---

* Oscar Homolka plays the saboteur, Verloc. He maintains a front as the friendly manager of a small movie house and lives with Sylvia Sidney, his young wife, and her little brother. John Loder is cast as the handsome detective who courts Mrs. Verloc to keep an eye on the theater. One day Verloc, who suspects he's under surveillance, gives the little boy a package, asking him to carry it to the other end of town. It's a time bomb. The boy is delayed and he is killed when the bomb explodes in a bus. When she learns the truth, the wife avenges her brother's death by stabbing Verloc with a knife. Her crime remains undiscovered, thanks to a propitious explosion of the movie house, and the picture winds up with her finding consolation with the detective.

acterization of the detective.

A.H. Well, Robert Donat was supposed to play the detective, but Alexander Korda refused to release him. The actor we got wasn't suitable, and I was forced to rewrite the dialogue during the shooting. But aside from that, I made a serious mistake in having the little boy carry the bomb. A character who unknowingly carries a bomb around as if it were an ordinary package is bound to work up great suspense in the audience. The boy was involved in a situation that got him too much sympathy from the audience, so that when the bomb exploded and he was killed, the public was resentful.
The way to handle it would have been for Homolka to kill the boy deliberately, but without showing that on the screen, and then for the wife to avenge her young brother by killing Homolka.

F.T. Even that solution, I think, might have been resented by the audience. Making a child die in a picture is a rather ticklish matter; it comes close to an abuse of cinematic power.

A.H. I agree with that; it was a grave error on my part.

F.T. At the beginning of the picture you show how a child behaves when he is by himself; he does all sorts of things that are normally forbidden, slyly tasting the food, accidentally breaking a plate and hiding the pieces in a drawer. And by virtue of a dramatic law that favors the adolescent, all of these things endear the boy to us. The same thing is true for the personage of Verloc, but for another reason— probably because Oscar Homolka is plump. Generally speaking, chubby people are regarded as being kindly and rather lovable. And so when the detective begins to flirt with Verloc's wife, the situation is rather distasteful. The audience is *for* Verloc and *against* the detective!

A.H. I agree with you, but that was really a matter of casting. John Loder, who played the detective, simply wasn't the right man for the part.

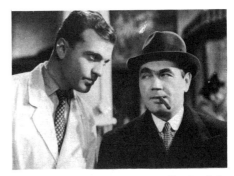

John Loder and Oscar Homolka in *Sabotage* (1936).

F.T. Perhaps, but there's something else I object to here, as well as in some of your other pictures. Wherever you have a romantic relationship between the heroine and the policeman, I find the situation rather hard to swallow —it's contrived. And it's occurred to me that the reason these situations somehow strike a false note is that you are not particularly fond of the police yourself.

A.H. I'm not *against* the police; I'm just afraid of them.

F.T. Aren't we all? Anyway, the fact is that in your pictures the cops always seem to turn up after the event; they never get things straight, and the hero, or hero–villain as the case may be, is always well ahead of them. So that even when the cop is supposed to be "the good guy," or rather, the romantic hero, he's not always as convincing as he should be, perhaps because of your own halfhearted approach.
One instance is the policeman in *Shadow of a Doubt*. Whereas the script requires him to compete, in terms of stature, with Uncle Charlie, he strikes one as being such an ordinary sort of fellow that it somehow spoils the ending for me.

A.H. I see what you're getting at, but I assure you that it's again a matter of casting. This is true of *Sabotage* as well as *Shadow of a Doubt*. In both pictures the roles of the detectives were not sufficiently strong to attract important actors. The real problem is that the names of the actors cast in these parts are listed after the main title.

F.T. What you're saying is that the second-

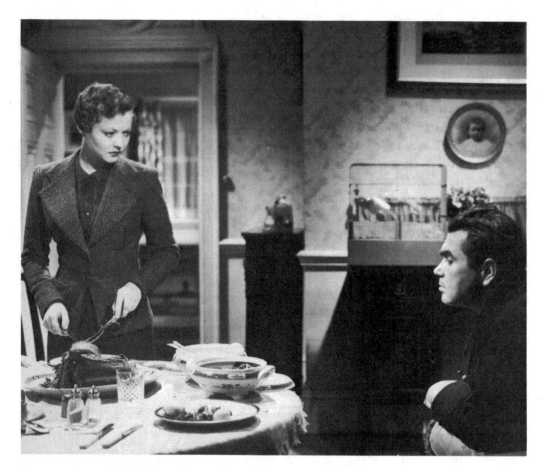

The scene immediately before the murder in *Sabotage*. To follow the cutting of the murder scene, see pages 112–113.

ary characters are more difficult to cast because their parts often call for more acting skill than the starring roles.

A.H.   Exactly.

F.T.   The best scene in *Sabotage* is during the meal, toward the ending, when, following her brother's death, Sylvia Sidney decides to kill Oscar Homolka. Before this there are several visual incidents that evoke the dead child. Then, as she stabs her husband, she utters a little cry of pain, so that the scene almost suggests suicide rather than murder. It's as if Homolka were allowing himself to be killed by Sylvia Sidney. Prosper Mérimée staged Carmen's death on the same dramatic principle, with the victim thrusting her body forward to meet the slayer's fatal stab.

A.H.   We had a problem there. You see, to maintain the public's sympathy for Sylvia Sidney, her husband's death had to be accidental. And to bring this off, it was absolutely essential that the audience identify itself with Sylvia Sidney. Here, we weren't trying to frighten anyone; we had to make the viewer feel like killing a man, and that's a good deal tougher.

This is the way I handled it. When Sylvia Sidney brings the vegetable platter to the table, the knife acts as a magnet; it's almost as if her hand, against her will, is compelled to grab it. The camera frames her hand, then her eyes, moving back and forth between the two until suddenly her look makes it clear that she's become aware of the potential meaning of that knife. At that moment the camera moves back to Verloc, absently chewing his food as on any other day. Then we pan back to the hand and the knife.

The wrong way to go about this scene would have been to have the heroine convey her inner feelings to the audience by her facial expression. I'm against that. In real life, people's faces don't reveal what they think or feel. As a film director I must try to convey this woman's frame of mind to the audience by purely cinematic means.

When the camera is on Verloc, it pans to the knife and then back again to his face. And we realize that he, too, has seen the knife and has suddenly become aware of what it may mean to him. Now the suspense between the two protagonists has been established, and the knife lies there, between them.

Thanks to the camera, the public is now actually living the scene, and if that camera should suddenly become distant and objective, the tension that's been created would be destroyed. Verloc stands up and walks around the table, moving straight toward the camera, so that the spectator in the theater gets the feeling that he must recoil to make way for him. Instinctively, the viewer should be pushing back slightly in his seat to allow Verloc to pass by. Afterward, the camera glides back toward Sylvia Sidney, and then it focuses once more on the central object, that knife. And the scene culminates, as you know, with the killing.

F.T.   The entire scene is utterly convincing! Someone else might have ruined the whole thing merely by changing the angles when Verloc rises to his feet, and placing the camera at the back of the room for a full shot before going back to the close shot. The slightest mistake, like the sharp pulling back of the camera, would dissipate all of that tension.

A.H.   That would ruin the whole scene. Our primary function is to create an emotion and our second job is to sustain that emotion.

When a film has been properly staged, it isn't necessary to rely upon the player's virtuosity or personality for tension and dramatic effects. In my opinion, the chief requisite for an actor is the ability to do nothing well, which is by no means as easy as it sounds. He should be willing to be utilized and wholly integrated into the picture by the director and the camera. He must allow the camera to determine the proper emphasis and the most effective dramatic highlights.

F.T.   This neutrality you expect from your actors is an interesting concept. The point is clearly made in some of your more recent pictures, like *Rear Window* or *Vertigo*. In both films James Stewart isn't required to emote; he simply *looks*—three or four hundred times—and then you show the viewer what he's looking at. That's all. By the way, were you satisfied with Sylvia Sidney?

A.H.   Not entirely. Although I've just told you that the screen player should not emote, I must admit that I found it rather difficult to get any shading into Sylvia Sidney's face, yet on the other hand she had nice understatement.

F.T.   I think she's quite beautiful. Still—and it isn't kind to say this about a woman—she looks a little like Peter Lorre, perhaps because of her eyes. What's your feeling on the whole about *Sabotage*?

A.H.   I would say that it's somewhat sabotaged! Aside from a few scenes, including those we've been talking about, it was a little messy. No clean lines about it. The picture after that was *The Girl Was Young*.

F.T.   You mean *Young and Innocent*?

A.H.   In America it was released as *The Girl Was Young*. It was an attempt to do a chase story with very young people involved. The point of view is that of a young girl who is bewildered when she becomes involved in murder with the police and all the rest. One of the many ways in which we used youth in this picture was to build up a suspense episode around a children's party.

Here again, the younger hero is accused of a crime he hasn't committed. He's on the run and hiding and the girl is helping him, rather reluctantly. She tells him that she's promised to call on her aunt and takes him to the aunt's house, where a children's party is taking place. The kids are playing blindman's buff. The young man and his girl try to get away while auntie is blindman, because if either one of them is caught, they will have to stay. So there's lots of suspense. Auntie nearly catches them, but they

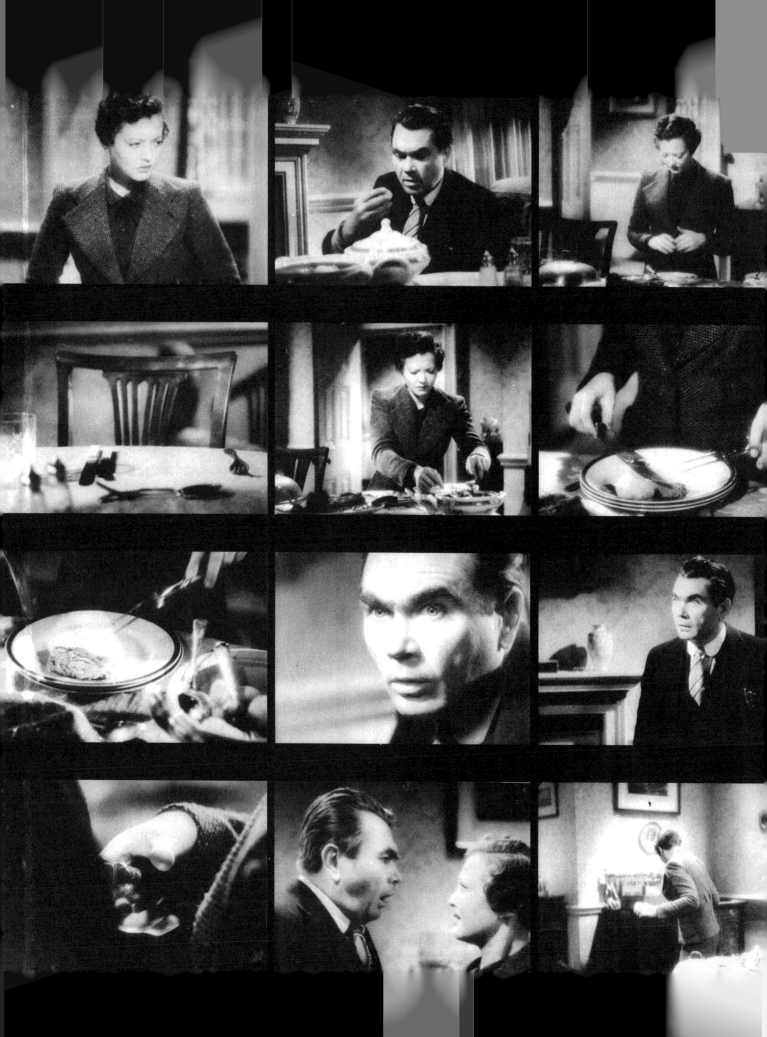

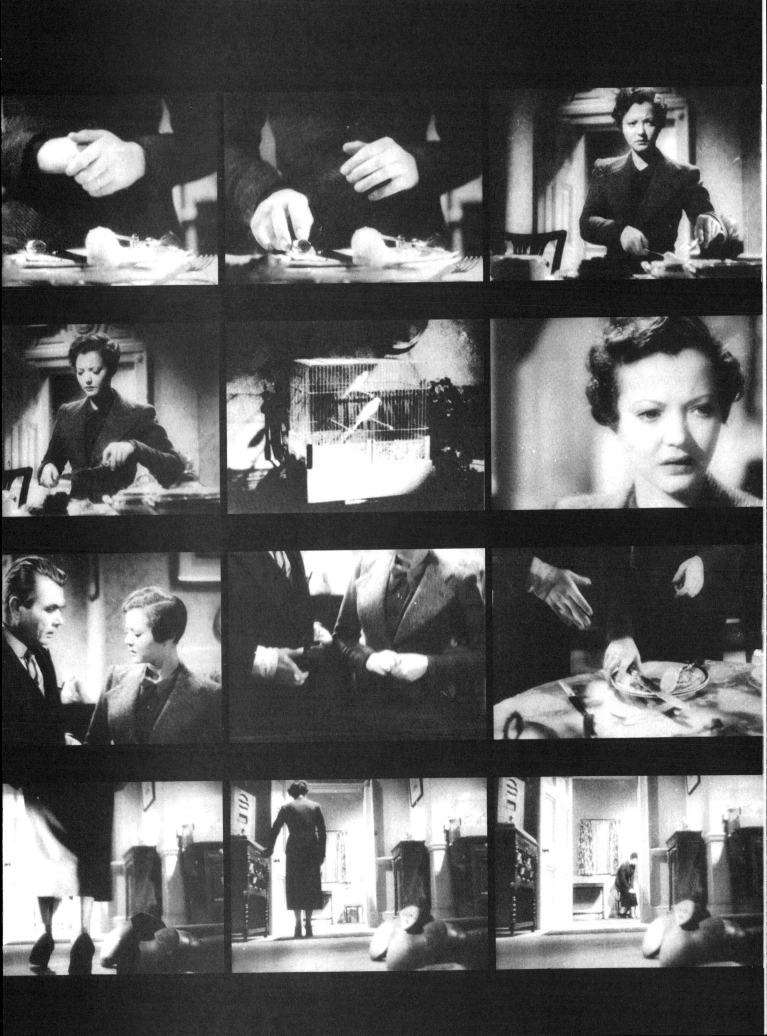

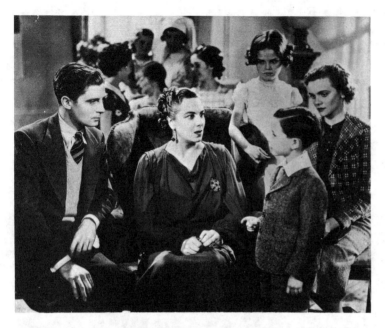

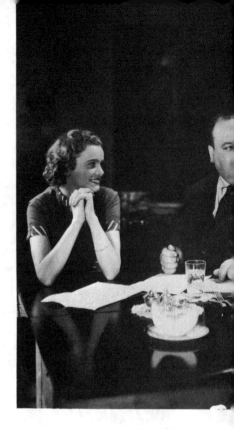

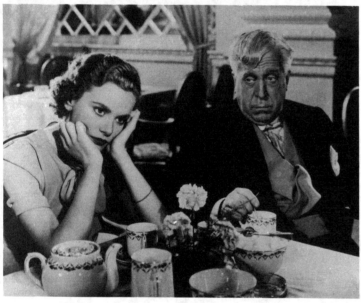

manage to get away.

When the film was released in this country, that was one scene they cut out. It was absurd; that was the essence of the film!

By the way, *Young and Innocent* contains an illustration of that suspense rule by which the audience is provided with information the characters in the picture don't know about. Because of this knowledge, the tension is heightened as the audience tries to figure out what's going to happen next.

Toward the end of the picture the young girl is searching for the murderer, and she discovers an old tramp who has seen the killer and can identify him. The only clue is that the man has a nervous twitch of the eyes.

So the girl dresses up the old tramp in a good suit of clothes and she takes him to this big hotel where a *thé dansant* is in progress. There are lots of people there, and the tramp says, "Isn't it ridiculous to try to spot a pair of twitching eyes in a crowd of this size."

Just then, right on that line of dialogue, I place the camera in the highest position, above the hotel lounge, next to the ceiling, and we dolly it down, right through the lobby, into the big ballroom, and past the dancers, the bandstand, and the musicians, right up to a close-up of the drummer. The musicians are all in blackface, and we stay on the drummer's face until his eyes fill the screen. And then, the eyes twitch. The whole thing was done in one shot.

F.T. That's one of your rules: From the farthest to the nearest, from the smallest to the biggest. . . .

A.H. Yes. At that moment I cut right back to the old man and the girl, still sitting at the other end of the room. Now, the audience has

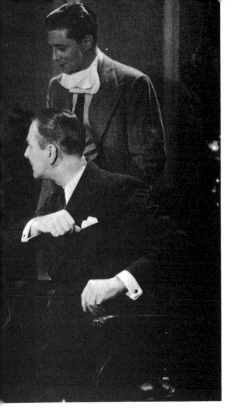

Rehearsing a scene from
Young and Innocent (1937).

the information and the question is: How are this girl and this old boy going to spot the man? A policeman outside sees the girl, who is the daughter of his chief. He goes to the phone. Meanwhile, the band has stopped for a break, and the drummer, having a smoke outside in the alley, sees a group of police hurrying toward the rear entrance of the hotel. Since he's guilty, he quickly ducks back inside, to the bandstand, where the music resumes.

Now the jittery drummer sees the policemen talking to the tramp and the girl at the other end of the ballroom. He thinks they're looking for him, and his nervousness is reflected in the drumbeat, which is out of tune with the rest of the band. The rhythm gets worse and worse. Meanwhile, the tramp, the girl, and the police are preparing to leave through an exit near the bandstand. In fact, the drummer is out of danger, but he doesn't know it. All he can see are those uniforms moving in his direction, and his twitching eyes indicate that he's in a panic. Finally, his beat is so far out of rhythm that the band stops playing and the dancers stop their dancing. And just as the little group is making its way out the door, he falls with a loud crash into his drum.

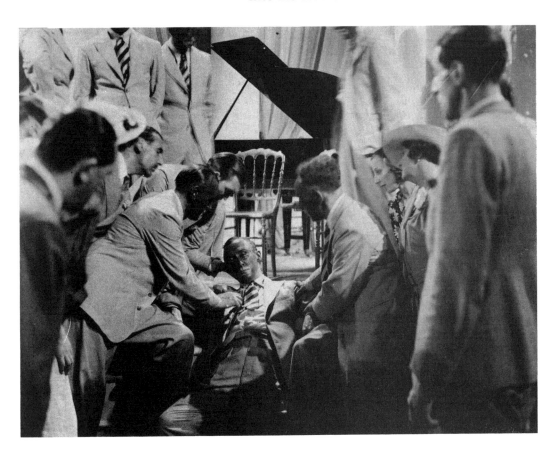

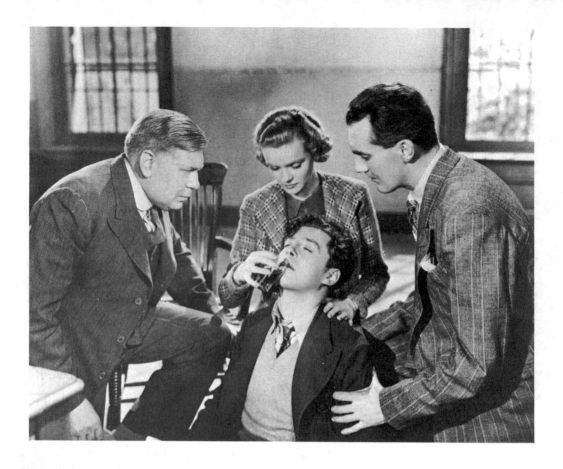

They stop to find out the reason for the commotion, and the girl and the tramp move over to the unconscious man. At the beginning of the story we had established that the heroine is a Girl Scout and an expert on first aid. In fact, she and the hero first got together when he fainted in the police station and she took care of him. So now she volunteers to help the unconscious drummer, and as she leans over him, she notices his twitching eyes. Very quietly she says, "Will someone please get me a wet cloth to wipe his face off," at the same time beckoning the tramp to come over. A waiter hands her the towel; she wipes the man's face clean of its black make-up and looks up at the tramp, who nods and says, "Yes, that's the man."

F.T.   I saw the picture at the Cinémathèque a long time ago, and that scene made such an impression that it's the only one I still remember clearly. Everyone there felt that the track shot of the ballroom was truly remarkable.

A.H.   It took us two days to do that one shot.

F.T.   You used a similar shot in *Notorious*.

Starting with the camera set up high, above the large chandelier, the shot takes in the whole reception hall, to wind up on a frame of the key in Ingrid Bergman's hand.

A.H.   There again we've substituted the language of the camera for dialogue. In *Notorious* that sweeping movement of the camera is making a statement. What it's saying is: "There's a large reception being held in this house, but there is a drama here which no one is aware of, and at the core of that drama is this tiny object, this key."

F.T.   Now let's talk about *The Lady Vanishes*. They show it very often in Paris; sometimes I see it twice in one week. Since I know it by heart, I tell myself each time that I'm going to ignore the plot, to examine the train and see if it's really moving, or to look at the transparencies, or to study the camera movements inside the compartments. But each time I become so absorbed by the characters and the story that

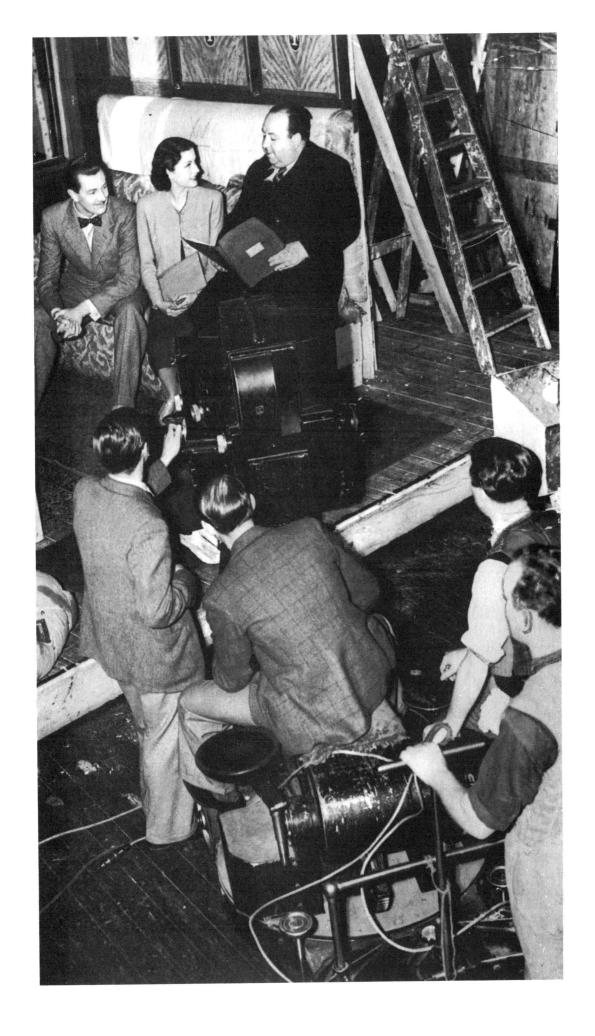

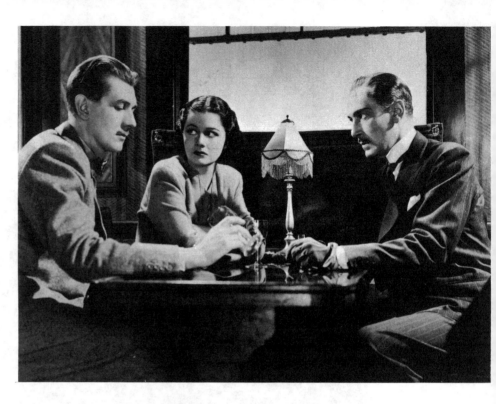

I've yet to figure out the mechanics of that film.*

A.H.   It was made in 1938, on one of the smaller Islington stages, on a set ninety feet long. We used one coach; all the rest were transparencies or miniatures. There are some very interesting technical things in it. For instance, in *The Lady Vanishes*, there was the traditional scene of a drink being doped up. As a rule, that sort of thing is covered by the dialogue.

"Here, drink this."

"No thanks,"

"You really should, you know. It will make you feel better."

---

* In a train on her way home from a vacation in the Balkans, Iris, a young English girl (Margaret Lockwood), becomes acquainted with a charming old lady, Miss Froy (Dame May Whitty). When the old lady mysteriously vanishes during the journey, Iris sets out to find her. To her surprise, all the passengers deny ever having seen the missing woman.

As it happens, the people she turns to are part of a spy ring, and Miss Froy is a counterespionage agent. Iris is mystified and the gang does everything to give her the impression she is losing her mind. Fortunately, a young musician (Michael Redgrave) believes the girl's story and helps her with her search. When the train is shifted to a sidetrack and then besieged by the local agents of the spy ring, Miss Froy, who has been bound and gagged in one of the compartments, manages to contact the young couple before making a clean getaway. The three Britishers will wind up safe and sound in Scotland Yard, where Miss Froy delivers the secret message for which they've all risked their lives—the message, incidentally, turning out to be a few bars of a popular folk song.

"Not now, later . . . You're so kind . . ."

The character takes the glass in his hand, lifts it to his mouth, puts it down, raises it again, then begins to talk before drinking it, and so on. So I said, "Let's not do it that way. We'll try something else."

I had two king-size glasses made, and we photographed part of that scene through the glasses, so that the audience might see the couple all the time, although they didn't touch their drinks until the very end of the scene. Nowadays, I use magnified props in many pictures. It's a good gimmick, isn't it? The giant hand in *Spellbound*, for instance.

F.T.   At the end of the picture, when the doctor's hand holds the revolver in the axis of Ingrid Bergman's silhouette?

A.H.   Yes. There's a simpler way of doing it, and that's to flood a lot of light onto the set so that the lens can be made smaller. We were using George Barnes, a very famous cameraman, who had worked on *Rebecca*, and he said he couldn't stop down because that would be bad for Ingrid's face. The real reason he couldn't do it is that he was a Hollywood-woman cameraman.

I have to digress for a moment to tell you that during the heyday of the great screen sirens, the

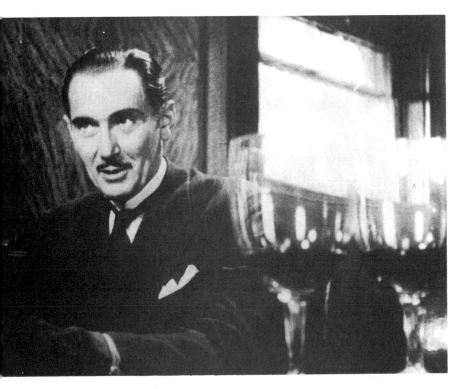

The "giant hand" sequence in *Spell-bound*.

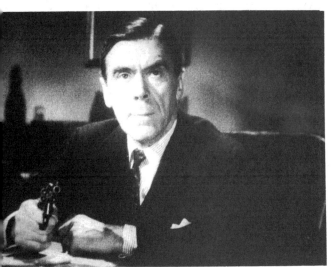

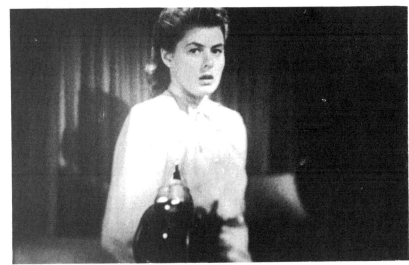

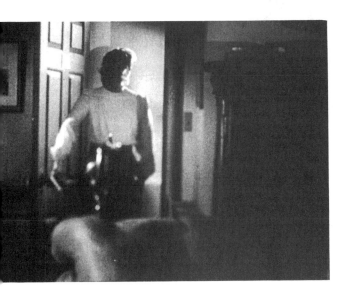

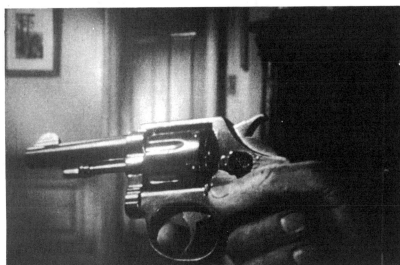

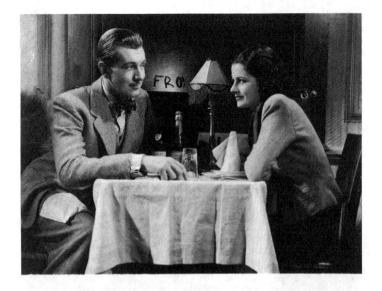

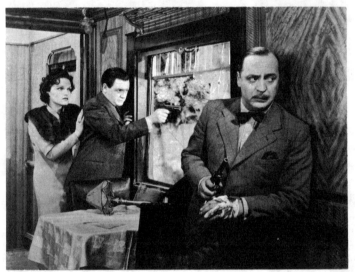

general practice when stars showed signs of aging was to use gauze in front of the lens. Then they found out that the system was flattering to the face but no good at all for the look. So the cameraman would take a cigarette and burn out two holes in the gauze for the eyes. In this way the face was nice, if somewhat hazy, and the eyes sparkled, but of course it meant that the actress couldn't move her head at all. Next, they moved away from gauze to diffusion disks, but there they ran into another problem. A star would tell the cameraman: "My friends say that I must be getting old because you're using diffusion and it shows when my close-ups are cut into the picture." The cameraman would answer: "I can fix that." And it was very simple. All he had to do was to diffuse the rest of the picture, so that when the close-ups were cut in it didn't show.

Anyway, in *Spellbound*, at first I tried to get the shot of the revolver by putting Ingrid Bergman on a screen and by placing the doctor's hand, in focus, close to the screen, but that looked fuzzy. So I wound up using a giant hand again, and a gun four times the natural size.

F.T.   That's right. We see the doctor aiming the gun at Ingrid Bergman. Though she's frightened, she bravely moves toward the door and leaves the room. With the camera now in

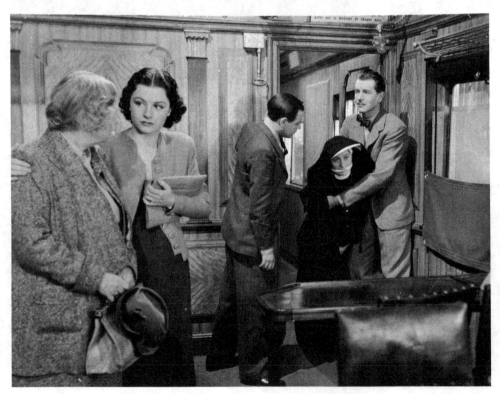

The Lady Vanishes (1938): Top, Margaret Lockwood attempts to convince Michael Redgrave of the existence of the woman who has vanished—Miss Froy. One proof exists: The old lady has written her name on the window. When Margaret Lockwood remembers and starts to show it to Michael Redgrave, the train goes through a tunnel and the writing is mysteriously erased. . . .
Center and bottom, the climax.

the doctor's place, we see him pointing the gun at his head and pulling the trigger, straight into the lens. It's as if he were firing straight at the viewer.

But we seem to have wandered away from *The Lady Vanishes*, which is a first-rate screenplay.

A.H. Yes, by Gilliat and Launder. But let's go back to our old friends, "the plausibles." They might question why a message was entrusted to an elderly lady so helpless that anybody might knock her over. Also, why the counterspies simply didn't send that message by carrier pigeon, and why they had to go through so much trouble to get that old lady on the train, with another woman standing by to change clothes, not to speak of shunting the whole coach away into the woods.

F.T. True. All the more so since the message consists of the first few bars of a little song that she's memorized. It's an absurd idea, but quite delightful!

A.H. It's fantasy, sheer fantasy! Did you know that same story had been filmed three or four times?

F.T. Do you mean there were remakes?

A.H. Not remakes, but the same basic story done in different forms. The whole thing started with an ancient yarn about an old lady who travels to Paris with her daughter in 1880. They go to a hotel and there the mother is taken ill. They call a doctor, and after looking her over, he has a private talk with the hotel manager. Then he tells the girl that her mother needs a certain kind of medicine, and they send her to the other end of Paris in a horse-drawn cab. Four hours later she gets back to the hotel and says, "How is my mother?" and the manager says, "What mother? We don't know you. Who are you?" She says, "My mother's in room so and so." They take her up to the room, which is occupied by new lodgers; everything is different, including the furniture and the wallpaper. I made a half-hour television show on that, and the Rank organization made it into a film with Jean Simmons, called *So Long at the Fair*. It's

supposed to be a true story, and the key to the whole puzzle is that it took place during the great Paris exposition, in the year the Eiffel Tower was completed. Anyway, the women had come from India, and the doctor discovered that the mother had bubonic plague. So it occurred to him that if the news got around, it would drive the crowds who had come for the exposition away from Paris. That's the basic idea of the story.

F.T. That type of story generally starts out in an exciting way, but as a rule, it weakens as it unfolds. Often, by the time it reaches the explanation stage, there's total confusion. But the climax of *The Lady Vanishes* was great and the build-up was very neat.

A.H. Well, it originated with the book by Ethel Lina White, *The Wheel Spins*, and the first script was written by Sidney Gilliat and Frank Launder, a very good team. I made some changes and we added the whole last episode. When the reviews labeled it a Hitchcock picture, Launder and Gilliat decided forthwith to undertake their own producing and directing. Have you seen any of their pictures?

F.T. There was one, *Green for Danger*, that didn't quite come off, and *I See a Dark Stranger*, that was more interesting. But the best one of all wasn't a thriller; it was *The Rake's Progress* with Rex Harrison.
The Lady Vanishes was your next-to-last British picture. I imagine you must have already been contacted by Hollywood at the time. After the successful run of *The Man Who Knew Too Much* in America, there must have been some concrete offers to make pictures there.

A.H. While we were shooting *The Lady Vanishes*, I got a cable from Selznick, asking me to come to Hollywood to direct a picture based on the sinking of the *Titanic*. As soon as I had finished work on *The Lady Vanishes*, I went to America for the first time and stayed there for ten days. That was in August of 1937. I agreed to do the picture about the *Titanic*, but since the contract with Selznick wasn't due to start until April, 1939, I had time to make another British film, and that was *Jamaica Inn*.

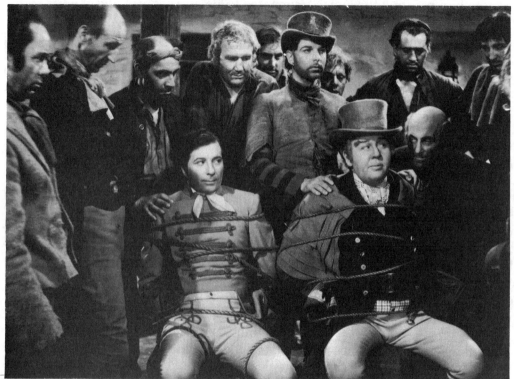
Robert Newton and Charles Laughton tied up.

F.T. Which was produced by Charles Laughton?

A.H. Laughton and Erich Pommer were associated on the production of that one. The novel, as you know, is by Daphne du Maurier, and the first script was written by Clemence Dane, who was a playwright of some note. Then Sidney Gilliat came in and we did the script together. Charles Laughton wanted his part built up, and so he brought in J. B. Priestley for additional dialogue. I had first met Erich Pommer back in 1924, when I was writer and art director in Germany on *The Blackguard*, a picture he had co-produced with Michael Balcon, and I hadn't seen him since that time.

Jamaica Inn was an absurd thing to undertake. If you examine the basic story, you will see that it's a whodunit. At the end of the eighteenth century, Mary, a young Irish girl, goes to Cornwall to live with her Aunt Patience, whose husband, Joss, is an innkeeper. All sorts of things happen in that tavern, which shelters scavengers and wreckers who not only seem to enjoy total immunity, but who are also kept thor-

oughly informed of the movements of ships in the area. Why? Because at the head of this gang of thugs is a highly respectable man—a justice of the peace, no less—who masterminds all of their operations.

It was completely absurd, because logically the judge should have entered the scene only at the end of the adventure. He should have carefully avoided the place and made sure he was never seen in the tavern. Therefore it made no sense to cast Charles Laughton in the key role of the justice of the peace. Realizing how incongruous it was, I was truly discouraged, but the contract had been signed. Finally, I made the picture, and although it became a box-office hit, I'm still unhappy over it.

F.T. But weren't the producers aware of this incongruity?

A.H. Erich Pommer? I'm not sure he understood the English idiom. As for Charles Laughton—well! When we started the picture, he asked me to show him only in close shots because he hadn't yet figured out the manner of his walk. Ten days later he came in and said, "I've found it." It turned out that his step had been inspired by the beat of a little German waltz, and he whistled it for us as he waddled about the room. I can still remember how he did it. Let me show you . . .

F.T.   It's great!

A.H.   Maybe so, but it wasn't serious, and I don't like to work that way. He wasn't really a professional film man.

———————

F.T.   Before embarking on the American phase of your career, I'd like to suggest that we draw a few conclusions about your British achievements, as we did for the silent movies, and talk about the general situation of British cinema. With the passage of time, those of us who have followed your over-all career have the feeling that it was only after your arrival in the United States that you reached your creative peak. It would almost seem as if you were destined to work in Hollywood. Would you agree with that thinking?

A.H.   Let's put it this way: the work in Britain served to develop my natural instinct, and later it enabled me to apply new, offbeat ideas. But the technical know-how, in my opinion, dates back to my work on *The Lodger*. As a matter of fact, the techniques and camera precepts that I learned then have continued to serve me ever since.
For want of a better term, we might label the initial phase the period of the sensation of cinema, and the second phase, the period when the ideas were fertilized.

F.T.   Even so, the fact remains that while you were in England, you dreamed of making American-type pictures, whereas once you got

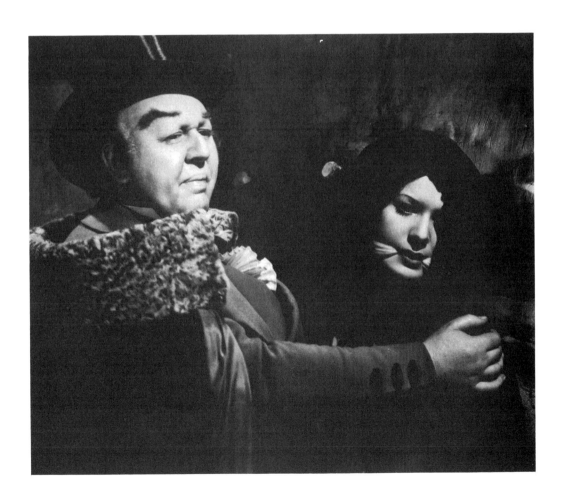

to Hollywood, you never attempted to imitate the British type of film. What I'm trying to get at—and I'm not sure I'm right about this and it's hard to define just what it is—is that there's something about England that's anticinematic.

A.H.   I'm not sure I understand what you're getting at. What do you mean by that?

F.T.   Well, to put it quite bluntly, isn't there a certain incompatibility between the terms "cinema" and "Britain." This may sound far-fetched, but I get the feeling that there are national characteristics—among them, the English countryside, the subdued way of life, the stolid routine—that are antidramatic in a sense. The weather itself is anticinematic. Even British humor—that very understatement on which so many of the good crime comedies are hinged—is somehow a deterrent to strong emotion. It's my feeling that these characteristics worked against your particular style of narration, which is essentially to color the story with fast-moving action and striking incidents. Despite the tongue-in-cheek approach and however vivid, it must be convincing. Above all, it seems to me, these national characteristics are in conflict with plastic stylization and even with the stylization of the actors.

Considering the high intellectual level in England, and in the light of the universal stature of her great writers and poets, isn't it rather curious that in the seventy years since cinema came into being, the only two British film-makers whose works have actually survived the test of time—and space, for that matter—are Charlie Chaplin and Alfred Hitchcock.

We're talking now in the historical context—in terms of the international evolution of movie-making. It goes without saying that there are exceptions to the rule, and we all know that new things are happening on the British film scene today.

A.H.   If you examine the history of the cinema, you will see that the art of film-making was often held in contempt by the intellectuals. That must have been true in France, and it was even truer of the British. No well-bred English person would be seen going into a cinema; it simply wasn't done. You see, England is strongly class-conscious. When Paramount opened the Plaza Theatre in London, a few members of the upper classes began to go to the movies. The management set up four rows of seats in the mezzanine which were very expensive, and they called that section "Millionaires' Row."

Prior to 1925, English films had been very mediocre; they were mostly for local consumption and were made by bourgeois. Then, around 1925–26, certain young university students, mostly from Cambridge, began to take an interest in the cinema, particularly in the Russian films or such foreign pictures as René Clair's *Italian Straw Hat*. Out of this was born the London Film Society, which put on special shows on Sundays for a coterie of intellectuals. Their enthusiasm, somehow, didn't project them into the creative end, but they were film fans, particularly in respect to foreign films.

Even today, foreign films get the largest coverage in the Sunday papers, while the Hollywood product is relegated to the bottom of the page. You must remember also that British intellectuals traditionally spend their holidays on the Continent. They go into the slums of Naples to take pictures of the starving kids. They love to look at the wash hanging out between the tenements, the donkeys in the cobblestone streets. It's all so picturesque!

Today, the young British film-makers are beginning to show that sort of thing in their pictures. The social angle is in fashion. I never thought of it while I was living in England, but when I went back there, after living in America, I noticed all of these differences and I realized that the general attitude in Britain is an insular one. Outside of England, there is a much more universal concept of life, which one gets by talking with people and even by the manner in which they tell a story.

British humor is quite superficial and it's also rather limited. The British press raised violent objections to *Psycho*; there was hardly a critic who had any sense of humor about the picture. Anyway, you have a point. I certainly was deeply entrenched in American cinema. This dates back to the time when I was reading the film trade papers at the age of sixteen. They were full of material on the American pictures, and I used to compare the photography of the English and American films. I wanted to work in the medium, and I succeeded in doing just that by the time I was eighteen. While I was a student in the engineering school, I was drawn to design and then to photography. It never occurred to me to go and offer my services to a British company, yet, as soon as I read that an American company was going to open a studio, I said to myself, "I want to do their titles." So I went to work there; the American actors and writers came in and I learned from them. You might say I had an American training. This doesn't mean that I was a devotee of everything American. But I did regard their movie-making as truly professional and very much in advance of that of the other countries. In actual fact, I started out, in 1921, in an American studio that happened to be located in London and never set foot in a British studio until 1927. In between those years there was an interval in German films. But even when the British came into Islington and gradually took over its studio facilities, the cameras we used were American, the lights were American, and the film we used was Kodak.

Later on I often wondered about the fact that I made no attempt to visit America until 1937; I'm still puzzled about that. I was meeting Americans all the time and was completely familiar with the map of New York. I used to send away for train schedules—that was my hobby—and I knew many of the timetables by heart. Years before I ever came here, I could describe New York, tell you where the theaters and stores were located. When I had a conversation with Americans, they would ask, "When were you over there last?" and I'd answer, "I've never been there at all." Strange, isn't it?

F.T.   It is and it isn't; it might be explained by a mixture of love and pride. You didn't want to come here as a tourist, but as a film director. You didn't want to try to make a picture here; you wanted to be asked to make one. Hollywood or bust!

A.H.   That's true. But I wasn't in the least interested in Hollywood as a place. The only thing I cared about was to get into a studio to work.

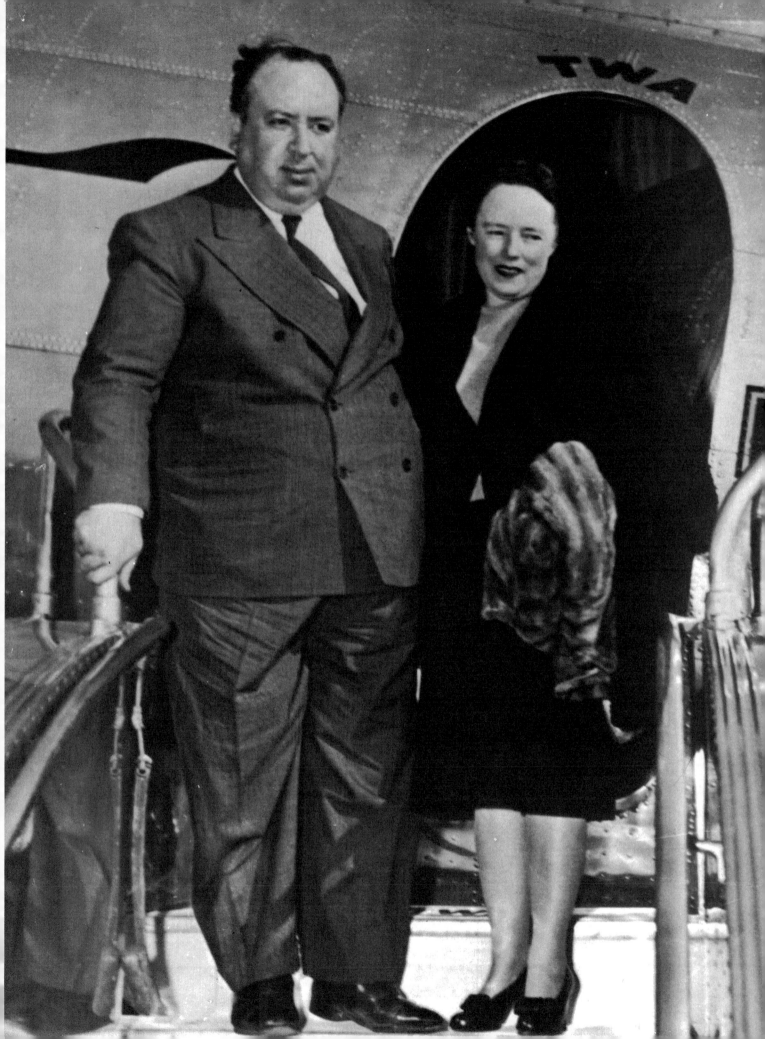

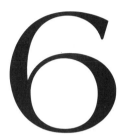

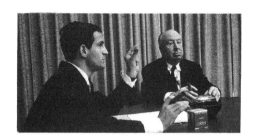

FRANÇOIS TRUFFAUT. I take it, Mr. Hitchcock, that you came to Hollywood expecting to do a film on the *Titanic*, but instead you made *Rebecca*. How did that happen?

ALFRED HITCHCOCK. David O. Selznick informed me that he'd changed his mind and had acquired the rights to *Rebecca*. So I said, "All right, let's switch!"

F.T. I thought you might have had something to do with that switch. Weren't you already interested in filming *Rebecca* before coming here?

A.H. Yes and no. I had an opportunity to buy the rights while I was shooting *The Lady Vanishes*, but the price was too high.

F.T. The name of Joan Harrison appears on the credits of *Rebecca* and on several of your British movies. Did she actually work on the screenplay or was that simply a way of representing you on the credits?

A:H. At one time Joan was a secretary, and as such she would take notes while I worked on a script, with Charles Bennett, for instance. Gradually she learned, became more articulate, and she became a writer.

F.T. Are you satisfied with *Rebecca*?

A.H. Well, it's not a Hitchcock picture; it's a novelette, really. The story is old-fashioned; there was a whole school of feminine literature at the period, and though I'm not against it, the fact is that the story is lacking in humor.

F.T. Maybe so, but it does have the merit

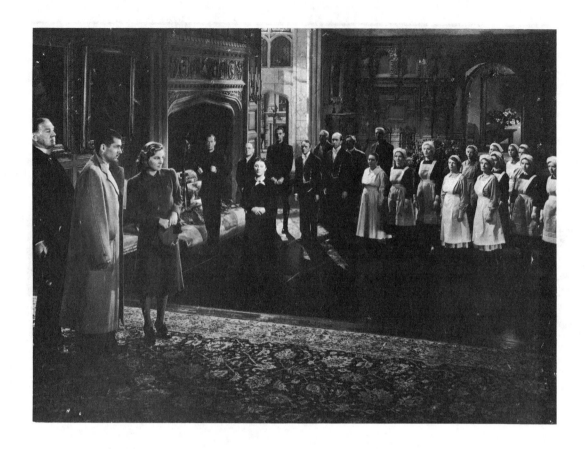

of simplicity. Joan Fontaine, Laurence Olivier, and Judith Anderson were an interesting trio: A young and shy lady's companion miraculously marries the handsome master of Manderley, whose first wife, Rebecca, has died in mysterious circumstances. When they get to the grandiose family mansion, the young bride feels inadequate to her new situation. Increasing her lack of self-confidence is the sinister, domineering housekeeper, Mrs. Danvers, whose obsessive devotion to Rebecca is manifested in active hostility to her new mistress. Then a new investigation into Rebecca's death brings out some unpleasant facts that cause Mrs. Danvers to set fire to the house and commit suicide. With the destruction of Manderley and the death of her tormentor, the heroine's sufferings come to an end.

Anyway, this was your first American project and I imagine you must have felt a little intimidated at the idea of undertaking it.

A.H.   Well, not exactly, because in fact it's a completely British picture: the story, the actors, and the director were all English. I've some-

times wondered what that picture would have been like had it been made in England with the same cast. I'm not sure I would have handled it the same way. The American influence on it is obvious. First, because of Selznick, and then because the screenplay was written by the playwright Robert Sherwood, who gave it a broader viewpoint than it would have had if made in Britain.

F.T.   It's a very romantic theme.

A.H.   Yes, it's romantic. Of course, there's a terrible flaw in the story, which our friends, the plausibles, never picked up. On the night when the boat with Rebecca's body in it is found, a rather unlikely coincidence is revealed: on the very evening she is supposed to have drowned, another woman's body is picked up two miles down the beach. And this enables the hero to identify that second body as his wife's. Why wasn't there an inquest at the time the unknown woman's body was discovered?

F.T.   Yes, that is a coincidence, but the

whole story is so completely dominated by the psychological elements that no one pays any attention to the explanations, particularly since they don't really affect the basic situation. As a matter of fact, I never completely understood the final explanation.

A.H. Well, the explanation is that Rebecca wasn't killed by her husband; she committed suicide because she had cancer.

F.T. Well, I understood that, because it's specifically stated, but what I'm not too clear about is whether the husband himself believes that he is guilty.

A.H. No, he doesn't.

F.T. I see. Was the adaptation faithful to the novel?

A.H. Yes, it follows the novel very faithfully because Selznick had just made *Gone with the Wind*. He had a theory that people who had read the novel would have been very upset if it had been changed on the screen, and he felt this dictum should also apply to *Rebecca*. You probably know the story of the two goats who are eating up cans containing the reels of a film taken from a best seller. And one goat says to the other, "Personally, I prefer the book!"

F.T. There are many variations to that story. I must say that even today, twenty-six years after it was made, *Rebecca* is still very modern, very solid.

A.H. Yes, it has stood up quite well over the years. I don't know why.

F.T. Making that picture, I imagine, was something of a challenge. After all, the novel itself was a rather unlikely one for you; it wasn't a thriller, there was no suspense. It was simply a psychological story, into which you deliberately introduced the element of suspense around the conflict of personalities. The experience, I think, had repercussions on the films that came later. Didn't it inspire you to enrich many of them with the psychological ingredi-

ents you initially discovered in the Daphne du Maurier novel?

A.H. That's true.

F.T. The relationship of the heroine, for instance . . . By the way, what was her name?

A.H. She never had a name.

F.T. . . . anyway, her relationship with the housekeeper, Mrs. Danvers, was something new in your work. And it reappears time and again later on, not only in the scenarios, but even visually: two faces, one dead-still, as if petrified by fear of the other; the victim and the tormentor framed in the same image.

A.H. Precisely. In *Rebecca* I did that very deliberately. Mrs. Danvers was almost never seen walking and was rarely shown in motion. If she entered a room in which the heroine was, what happened is that the girl suddenly heard a sound and there was the ever-present Mrs. Danvers, standing perfectly still by her side. In this way the whole situation was projected from the heroine's point of view; she never knew when

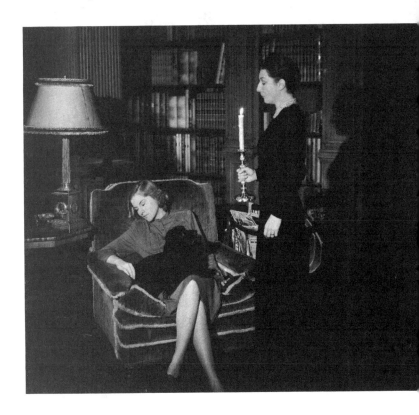

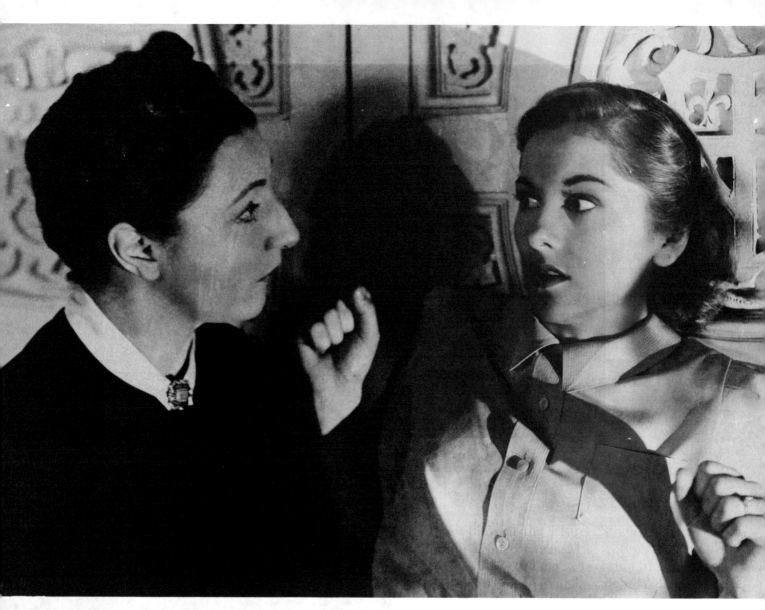

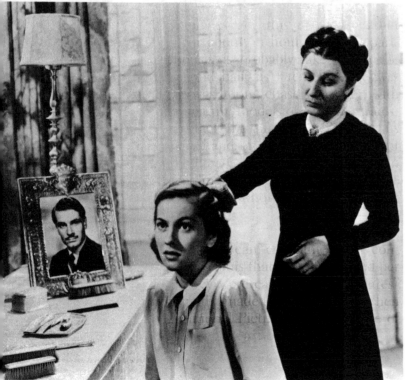

Mrs. Danvers might turn up, and this, in itself, was terrifying. To have shown Mrs. Danvers walking about would have been to humanize her.

F.T. It's an interesting approach that is sometimes used in animated cartoons. Incidentally, you've said that the picture is lacking in humor, but my guess would be that you must have had some fun with the scenario because it's actually the story of a girl who makes one blunder after another. Recently, I saw the picture again, and I couldn't help imagining the working sessions between you and your scriptwriter: "Now, this is the scene of the meal. Shall we have her drop her fork or will she upset her glass? Let's have her break the plate . . ." Anyway, that's the impression I got.

A.H.   That's quite true; it did happen that way and we had a good deal of fun with it.

F.T.   The characterization of the girl recalls the little boy in *Sabotage*. When she breaks a statuette, she furtively hides the pieces in a drawer, although she's the mistress of the estate. Something else: Whenever that home is mentioned, it's as the Manderley mansion or the estate. Whenever it is shown there is an aura of magic about it, with mists, and the musical score heightens that haunting impression.

A.H.   That's right, because in a sense the picture is the story of a house. The house was one of the three key characters of the picture.

F.T.   It's the first one of your pictures that evokes a fairy tale.

A.H.   It is. It's almost a period piece.

F.T.   This fablelike quality is of interest because it recurs in several of your works. It is suggested by the emphasis on the keys to the house, by a closet that no one has the right to open, or by a room that is sealed off.

A.H.   Yes, we were aware of that aspect in our treatment of *Rebecca*. It's quite true that children's fairy tales are often terrifying. Take the Grimms' "Hansel and Gretel," for instance, in which two children shove an old lady into an oven. But I'm not aware of any of my other pictures resembling a fairy tale.

F.T.   Well, it's probably because you're dealing with fear that many of your pictures have that quality. Anything connected with fear takes us back to childhood. All of children's literature is linked to sensations and particularly to fear.

A.H.   You have a point, there. You may remember that the location of the house is never specified in a geographical sense; it's completely isolated. That's also true of the house in *The Birds*. I felt instinctively that the fear would be greater if the house was so isolated that the people in it would have no one to turn to.
In *Rebecca* the mansion is so far away from anything that you don't even know what town it's near. Now, it's entirely possible that this abstraction, which you've described as American stylization, is partly accidental, and to some extent due to the fact that the picture was made in the United States. Let us assume that we'd made *Rebecca* in England. The house would not have been so isolated because we'd have been

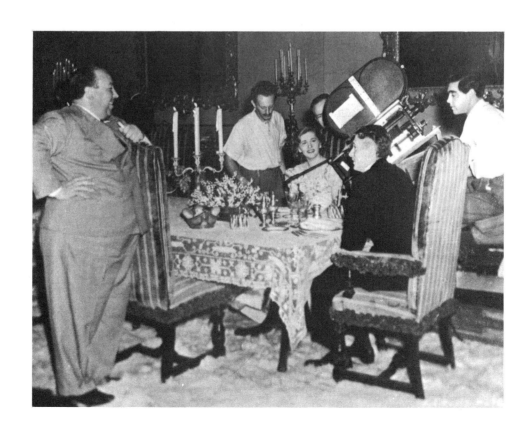

tempted to show the countryside and the lanes leading to the house. But if the scene had been more realistic, and the place of arrival geographically situated, we would have lost the sense of isolation.

F.T.   Were the British critical about the American aspects of *Rebecca?*

A.H.   No, they rather liked the picture.

F.T.   What about the whole mansion, as shown from the outside. Was that a real house or a miniature?

A.H.   We built a miniature. Even the road leading up to the home was a miniature.

F.T.   Plastically speaking, the use of miniatures resembling old woodcuts idealized the film and further strengthened the fairy-tale quality. Actually, the story of *Rebecca* is quite close to "Cinderella."

A.H.   The heroine *is* Cinderella, and Mrs. Danvers is one of the ugly sisters. But it was even closer to Pinero's *His House in Order*. That's a play in which the villain isn't the housekeeper but the sister of the master of the house;

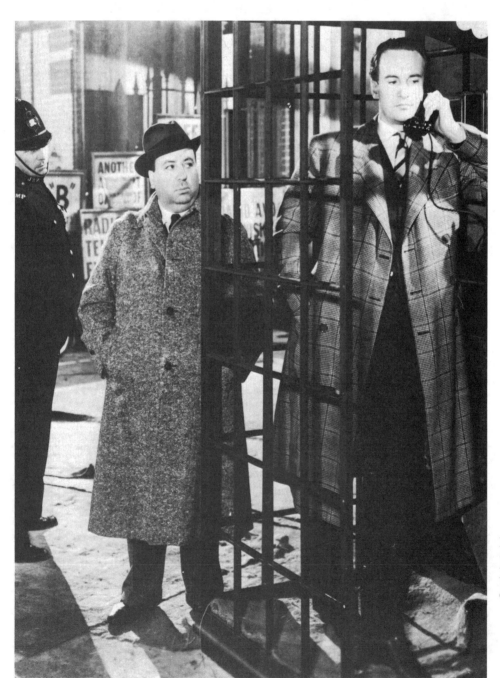

Hitchcock appears in *Rebecca* (1940), passing by the telephone booth being used by George Sanders.

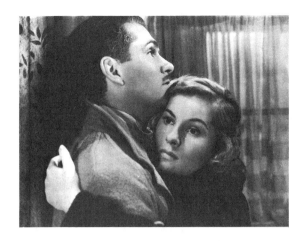

in other words, she's Cinderella's sister-in-law.

F.T. The mechanism of *Rebecca* is remark-able. The sinister momentum is built up solely through references to a dead woman who is never shown. The picture won an Oscar, didn't it?

A.H. Yes, the Academy voted it the best picture of the year.

F.T. I believe that's the only Oscar you've ever won.

A.H. I've never received an Oscar.

F.T. But you just said that *Rebecca* . . .

A.H. The award went to Selznick, the pro-ducer. The directing award that year was given to John Ford for *The Grapes of Wrath*.

F.T. Let's get back to the American film scene. One of the more unfortunate aspects of Hollywood is that film-making is arbitrarily sep-arated into distinct classifications. There are the directors who make what are rated as "A" pic-tures and the others who make the "B" and "C" films. And short of a sensational hit, it appears to be very difficult to switch from one category to another.

A.H. That's right. They stay on one line all the time.

F.T. The point I'm getting at is this: I am rather surprised that after an outstandingly suc-cessful picture like *Rebecca* you would go on to make *Foreign Correspondent*. Though I admire the picture very much, it definitely belongs in the "B" category.

A.H. I can explain that quite easily. Here again, the problem is the casting. In Europe, you see, the thriller, the adventure story is not looked down upon. As a matter of fact, that form of writing is highly respected in England, whereas in America it's definitely regarded as second-rate literature; the approach to the mys-tery genre is entirely different. When I had completed the script of *Foreign Correspondent*, I went to Gary Cooper with it, but because it was a thriller, he turned it down. This attitude was so commonplace when I started to work in Hollywood that I always ended up with the next best—in this instance, with Joel McCrea. Many years later Gary Cooper said to me, "That was a mistake. I should have done it."

F.T. Walter Wanger was the producer of that picture. Did he choose the story?

A.H. Yes. He had always been interested in foreign politics, and he had a book called *Per-sonal History*, written by Vincent Sheean, a very famous foreign correspondent.
But the book was a straight autobiographical ac-count; there was no story, no adventure; there was nothing we could use pictorially. So it be-came an original screenplay by Charles Bennett and myself.

F.T. The story, as I recall it, went some-thing like this: Joel McCrea, an American news-paperman, is assigned to go over to Europe at the beginning of 1939 to assess the threatened outbreak of a world conflict. In London he meets an elderly Dutch diplomat who is carry-ing a secret Allied treaty back to his country. When the Nazis kidnap the Dutch diplomat, the hero goes to Holland to try and find him. Laraine Day plays the young English girl who helps him on his rescue mission, and Herbert Marshall plays her father, a member of the Brit-ish upper class who masquerades as the head of an international pacifist organization, but is, in reality, an agent of the Nazis.

On the day war is declared, the father, who is about to be exposed, manages to get on a plane leaving for America. Joel McCrea and Laraine Day, having completed their mission, are also on the plane. When the Germans attack, the plane crashes into the sea and the father sacrifices himself to save his daughter. The young couple make their way back to London, where the hero resumes his duties with a dramatic broadcast to America about the war that has just begun. So much for the story.

A.H.   As you see, it's in line with my earlier films, the old theme of the innocent bystander who becomes involved in an intrigue.

F.T.   I imagine you were not particularly keen on the choice of Laraine Day as your leading lady.

A.H.   I would have liked to have bigger star names.

F.T.   But Joel McCrea was likable in the role.

A.H.   Yes, except that he was too easygoing.

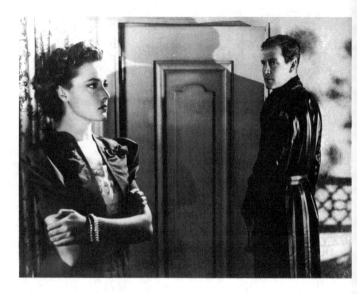

There were lots of ideas in that picture, though.

F.T.   There certainly were. One of them is the windmill scene, which, I understand, was your point of departure for the whole film. Your idea was to show that wings spinning against the direction of the wind might be used to convey a secret message to the planes above.

A.H.   Yes, we started out with the idea of the windmill sequence and also the scene of the murderer escaping through the bobbing um-

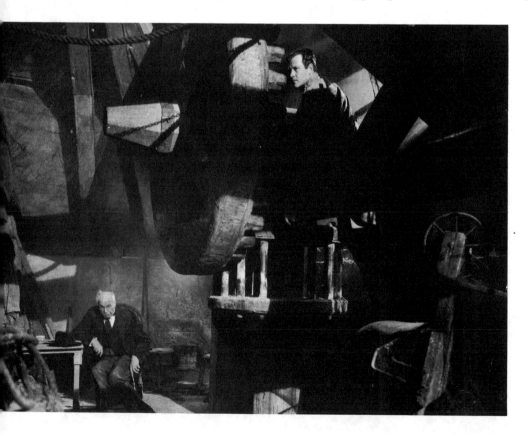

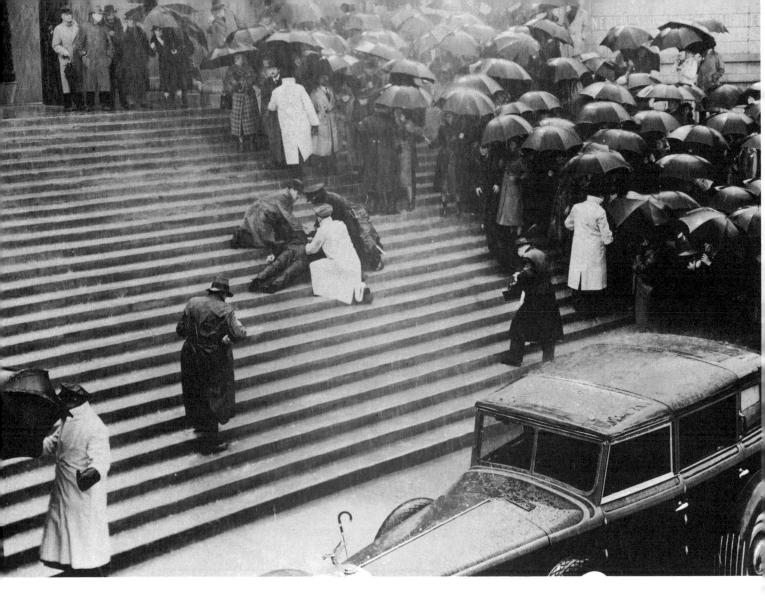

brellas. We were in Holland and so we used windmills and rain.

Had the picture been done in color, I would have worked in a shot I've always dreamed of: a murder in a tulip field. Two characters: the killer, a Jack-the-Ripper type, behind the girl, his victim. As his shadow creeps up on her, she turns and screams. Immediately, we pan down to the struggling feet in the tulip field. We would dolly the camera up to and right into one of the tulips, with the sounds of the struggle in the background. One petal fills the screen, and suddenly a drop of blood splashes all over it. And that would be the end of the killing.

In *Foreign Correspondent* there's one shot so unusual that it's rather surprising that the technicians never bothered to question how it was done. That's when the plane is diving down to-

ward the sea because its engines are crippled. The camera is inside the cabin, above the shoulders of the two pilots who are trying to pull the plane out of the dive. Between them, through the glass cabin window, we can see the ocean coming closer. And then, *without a cut*, the plane hits the ocean and the water rushes in, drowning the two men. That whole thing was done in a *single shot*, without a cut!

F.T.   I suppose the way you did it was to combine some transparencies with streams of real water.

A.H.   I had a transparency screen made of paper, and behind that screen, a water tank. The plane dived, and as soon as the water got close to it, I pressed the button and the water

135

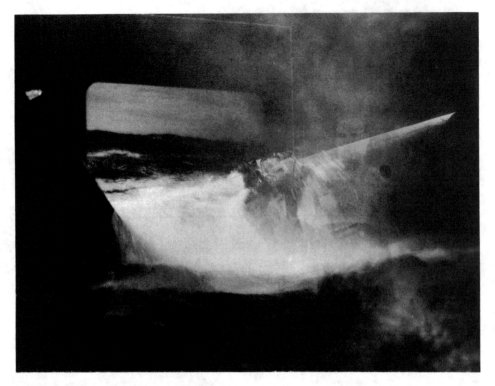

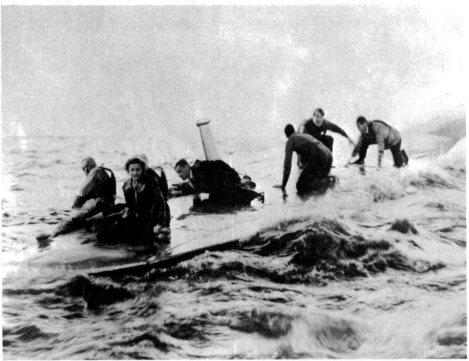

burst through, tearing the screen away. The volume was so great that you never saw the screen.

A little later on there was another tricky shot. Just before the plane sank, we wanted to show one of the wings, with people on it, breaking away from the body of the plane. At the bottom of a large water tank, we installed some rails and we put the airplane on those rails. And we had a branch rail, like on the railways, so that when the wing broke away, it moved off on that branch track. It was all quite elaborate, but we had lots of fun doing it.

F.T. The climax was great.

A.H. A lot of the material for that picture was shot by a second unit on location in London and in Amsterdam. This was in 1940, you see, and the cameraman who went over the first time from London to Amsterdam was torpedoed and lost all his equipment. He had to go over a second time.

F.T. It's been said that Dr. Goebbels enjoyed *Foreign Correspondent* very much.

Van Meer (Albert Basserman), held prisoner, is questioned by the spy Stephen Fisher (Herbert Marshall), whom he thinks is his friend. At the left is Eduardo Ciannelli as Krug. The sympathetic ffolliott, played by George

A.H. Yes, I heard that too; it's possible that he got a print of the film through Switzerland. The picture was pure fantasy, and, as you know, in my fantasies, plausibility is not allowed to rear its ugly head. In *Foreign Correspondent* you have the masculine counterpart of the old lady of *The Lady Vanishes*. Here the secret is in the possession of an elderly gentleman.

F.T. You mean Mr. Van Meer, the man who knows the famous secret clause?

A.H. That secret clause was our "Mac-Guffin." I must tell you what that means.

Sanders, has just arrived in time to prevent old Van Meer from revealing the famous secret clause, but a hand holding a revolver is enough to turn the situation around.

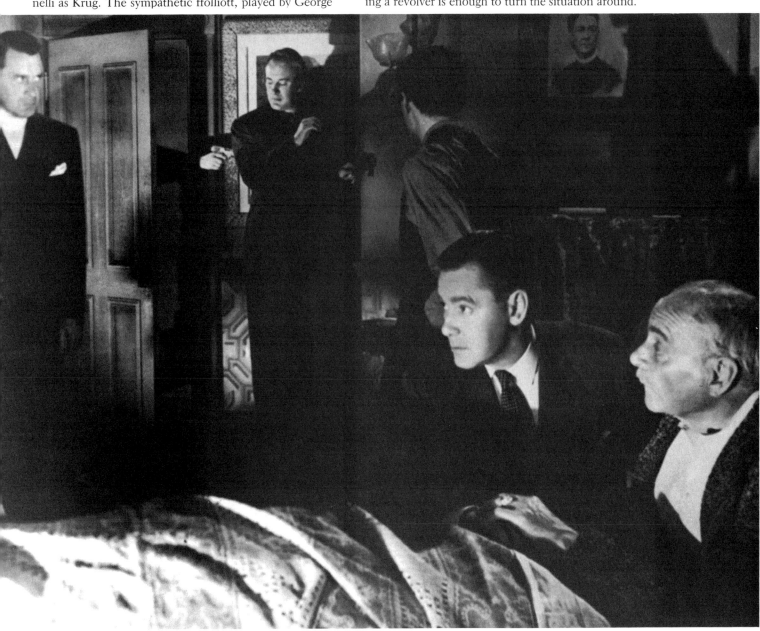

F.T.   Isn't the MacGuffin the pretext for the plot?

A.H.   Well, it's the device, the gimmick, if you will, or the papers the spies are after. I'll tell you about it. Most of Kipling's stories, as you know, were set in India, and they dealt with the fighting between the natives and the British forces on the Afghanistan border. Many of them were spy stories, and they were concerned with the efforts to steal the secret plans out of a fortress. The theft of secret documents was the original MacGuffin. So the "MacGuffin" is the term we use to cover all that sort of thing: to steal plans or documents, or discover a secret, it doesn't matter what it is. And the logicians are wrong in trying to figure out the truth of a MacGuffin, since it's beside the point. The only thing that really matters is that in the picture the plans, documents, or secrets must seem to be of vital importance to the characters. To me, the narrator, they're of no importance whatever.

You may be wondering where the term originated. It might be a Scottish name, taken from a story about two men in a train. One man says, "What's that package up there in the baggage rack?"

And the other answers, "Oh, that's a MacGuffin."

The first one asks, "What's a MacGuffin?"

"Well," the other man says, "it's an apparatus for trapping lions in the Scottish Highlands."

The first man says, "But there are no lions in the Scottish Highlands," and the other one answers, "Well then, that's no MacGuffin!" So you see that a MacGuffin is actually nothing at all.

F.T.   That's funny. A fascinating idea.

A.H.   Another funny thing is that whenever I'm working with a writer who's never been on a Hitchcock project before, he invariably becomes obsessed with the MacGuffin. And, though I keep on explaining that it's not important, the most elaborate schemes are mapped out. For instance in *The Thirty-nine Steps*, what are the spies after? The man with the missing finger? And that woman at the beginning, was she on to some big secret? Is it because she

was getting close to the truth that it became necessary to stab her in the back?

In the early stages of the construction, we felt, and we were all wrong, that since life and death were involved, the pretext had to be a very important one. In our first draft, when Robert Donat arrives in Scotland, he picks up some additional information on his way to the spy's house, possibly by following the spy. He rides to the top of the hill, and looking down, he sees underground plane hangars carved into the side of the mountain, secret hangars, which made the planes safe from bombings. Our original idea was that this MacGuffin should be something big and pictorially striking. Then we went on to work it out in our minds: What does Donat do upon discovering these secret hangars? Will he send off a message to report their locations? And in that case, what countersteps would the spies take?

F.T.   Well, the only way to work that out in the script was to have them blow up the hangars.

A.H.   We thought of that. But how were we going to have them blow up a whole mountain? Anyway, whenever we found ourselves getting terribly involved in this way, we would drop the idea for something very simple.

F.T.   In other words, not only is there no need for the MacGuffin to be important or serious, but it's even preferable that it should turn out to be something as trivial and absurd as the little tune of *The Lady Vanishes*.

A.H.   Exactly. In *The Thirty-nine Steps* the MacGuffin turned out to be the mechanical formula for the construction of an airplane engine. Instead of putting it down on paper, the spies used Mr. Memory's brain to carry it out of the country.

F.T.   If I understand you correctly, whenever a person's life is at stake, the dramatic rule is that concern for his survival must become so intense that, as the action moves forward, the MacGuffin will pretty much be forgotten. But this approach, it seems to me, involves a certain risk, doesn't it? In many films the audience will hiss and jeer at the final explanation, the scene in which the so-called MacGuffin is revealed. But I've noticed that one of your tricks is to dispose of the MacGuffin, not at the end of the picture, but at some point midway in the story, so that there's no need to condense the whole exposé into the finale.

A.H. On the whole, that's correct, but the main thing I've learned over the years is that the MacGuffin is nothing. I'm convinced of this, but I find it very difficult to prove it to others. My best MacGuffin, and by that I mean the emptiest, the most nonexistent, and the most absurd, is the one we used in *North by Northwest*. The picture is about espionage, and the only question that's raised in the story is to find out what the spies are after. Well, during the scene at the Chicago airport, the Central Intelligence man explains the whole situation to Cary Grant, and Grant, referring to the James Mason character, asks, "What does he do?"
The counterintelligence man replies, "Let's just say that he's an importer and exporter."
"But what does he sell?"
"Oh, just government secrets!" is the answer. Here, you see, the MacGuffin has been boiled down to its purest expression: nothing at all!

F.T. That's right, nothing that is specific.

Anyway, all of this clearly shows that you're always fully aware of your intention, and that everything you do is carefully thought out. And yet, these pictures, hinged around a MacGuffin, are the very ones that some of the critics have in mind when they claim that "Hitchcock's got nothing to say." The only answer to that is that a film-maker isn't supposed to *say* things; his job is to *show* them.

A.H. Precisely.

F.T. Right after *Foreign Correspondent*, in 1941, you went on to make a picture that's rather out of line with the rest of your works, since it's your only American comedy. *Mr. and Mrs. Smith* is the classic story about a divorced couple who seem to run into each other after their separation, engage in a certain amount of competition and wind up getting together again.

A.H. That picture was done as a friendly gesture to Carole Lombard. At the time, she was married to Clark Gable, and she asked whether I'd do a picture with her. In a weak moment I accepted, and I more or less followed Norman Krasna's screenplay. Since I really didn't understand the type of people who were portrayed in the film, all I did was to photograph the scenes as written.
There's an amusing little sidelight on that pic-

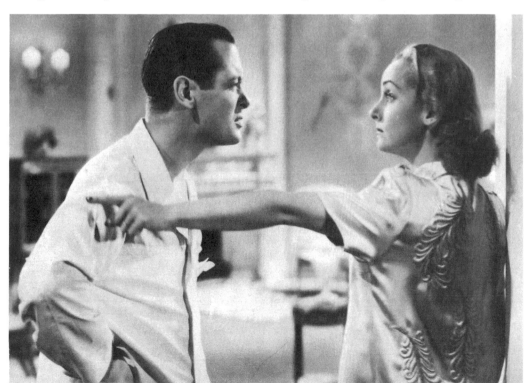

Robert Montgomery
and Carole Lombard
in
Mr. and Mrs. Smith (1941).

ture. A few years prior to my arrival in Hollywood, I had been quoted as saying that all actors are cattle. I'm not quite sure in what context I might have made such a statement. It may have been made in the early days of the talkies in England, when we used actors who were simultaneously performing in stage plays. When they had a matinee, they'd leave the set, I felt, much too early for a matinee, and I suspected they were allowing themselves plenty of time for a very leisurely lunch. And this meant that we had to shoot our scenes at breakneck speed so that the actors could get out on time. I couldn't help feeling that if they'd been really conscientious, they'd have swallowed their sandwich in the cab, on the way to the theater, and get there in time to put on their make-up and go on stage. I had no use for that kind of actor. Another reason for resentment is that I'd sometimes overhear two actresses talking in a restaurant. One would say to the other, "What are you doing now, dear?" and the other one would say, "Oh, I'm filming," in the same tone of voice as if she were saying, "Oh, I'm slumming."

And this raises a grievance I have against those people who come into our industry by way of the theater or as writers and who work in our medium for the money only. I think the worst culprits are the writers, particularly those who are here in Hollywood. Authors come in from New York, get a contract from M-G-M with no specific assignment, and then they say, "What do you want me to write?" Some playwrights sign three-month contracts just in order to spend their winters in California. By the way, how did we get on to this subject?

F.T.   We were talking about your statement that "actors are cattle."

A.H.   Oh yes. Well, what I was leading up to is that when I arrived on the set, the first day of shooting, Carole Lombard had had a corral built, with three sections, and in each one there was a live young cow. Round the neck of each of them there was a white disk tied on with a ribbon, with three names: Carole Lombard, Robert Montgomery, and the name of a third member of the cast, Gene Raymond.

I should add that my comment was a generalization, and Carole Lombard's spectacular repartee was her way of kidding me. She probably agreed with me.

———————

F.T.   This brings us to *Suspicion*, and you might cover a point we skipped. In our talks about *Rebecca* I forgot to ask your opinion of Joan Fontaine. I believe she was an important actress to you.

A.H.   Well, in the preparatory stages of *Rebecca*, Selznick insisted on testing every woman in town, known or unknown, for the lead in the picture. I think he really was trying to repeat the same publicity stunt he pulled in the search for Scarlett O'Hara.

He talked all the big stars in town into doing tests for *Rebecca*. I found it a little embarrassing, myself, testing women who I knew in advance were unsuitable for the part. All the more so since the earlier tests of Joan Fontaine had convinced me that she was the nearest one to our heroine. In the early stages of the actual shooting, I felt that Joan Fontaine was a little self-conscious, but I could see her potential for restrained acting and I felt she could play the character in a quiet, shy manner. At the outset she tended to overdo the shyness, but I felt she would work out all right, and once we got going, she did.

F.T.   In the sense of her physical frailty, she's quite unlike Ingrid Bergman and Grace Kelly.

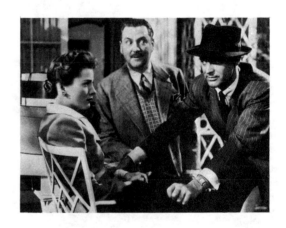

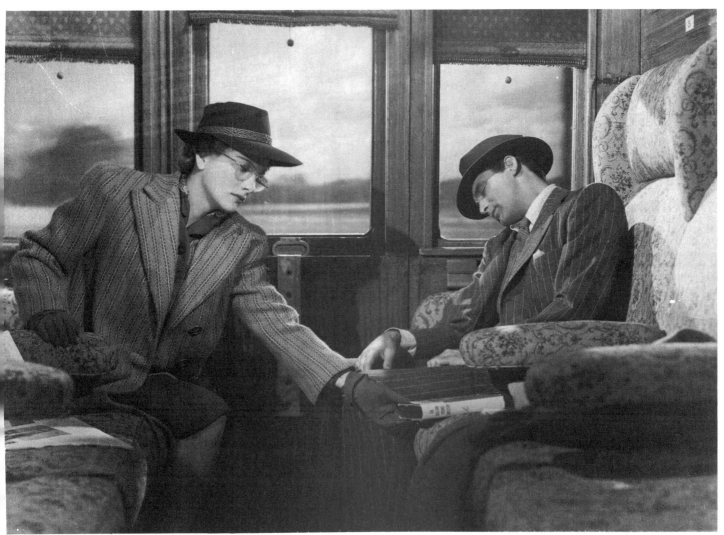

A.H. I think so, too. You might say *Suspicion* was the second English picture I made in Hollywood: the actors, the atmosphere, and the novel on which it's based were all British. The screenwriter was Samson Raphaelson, who'd worked on the early talking pictures of Ernst Lubitsch.

F.T. And with him, the family brain trust, Alma Reville and Joan Harrison.

A.H. The original novel was *Before the Fact*, and the author's—Francis Iles'—real name was A. B. Cox. He sometimes also wrote under the pen name of Anthony Berkeley. I've often wanted to film his first novel, *Malice Aforethought*. The book opens with the sentence: "It was not until several weeks after he had decided to murder his wife that Dr. Bickleigh took any active steps in the matter." The reason I didn't

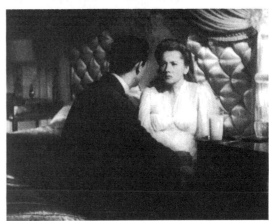

do it is that it requires a mature man in the part. It's hard to find the right actor, perhaps Alec Guinness . . .

F.T. Would you do it with James Stewart?

A.H. James Stewart would never play a killer.

141

F.T. Some of the critics who'd read *Before the Fact* reproach you with having changed the whole thing. The novel is the story of a woman who gradually realizes that she's married a murderer and is so much in love that she finally allows herself to be killed by him. Your picture is about a woman who, upon discovering that her husband is indifferent, a liar, and a spendthrift to boot, begins to imagine he's a killer as well, and suspects him—though, in fact, subsequent events will prove she's wrong—of wanting to murder her.

In our discussions about *The Lodger*, you referred to *Suspicion* and said that the producers would have objected to Cary Grant being the killer. If I understood you correctly, you'd have preferred that he be the guilty one.

A.H. Well, I'm not too pleased with the way *Suspicion* ends. I had something else in mind. The scene I wanted, but it was never shot, was for Cary Grant to bring her a glass of milk that's been poisoned and Joan Fontaine has just finished a letter to her mother: "Dear Mother, I'm desperately in love with him, but I don't want to live because he's a killer. Though I'd rather die, I think society should be protected from him." Then, Cary Grant comes in with the fatal glass and she says, "Will you mail this letter to Mother for me, dear?" She drinks the milk and dies. Fade out and fade in on one short shot: Cary Grant, whistling cheerfully, walks over to the mailbox and pops the letter in.

F.T. That would have been a great twist. I've read the novel and I liked it, but the screenplay's just as good. It is not a compromise; it's actually a different story. The film version, showing a woman who believes her husband is a killer, is less farfetched than the novel, which is about a woman who accepts the fact that her husband is a murderer. It seems to me that the film, in terms of its psychological values, has an edge over the novel because it allows for subtler nuances in the characterizations.

One might even say that Hollywood's unwritten laws and taboos helped to purify *Suspicion* by dedramatizing it, in contrast with routine screen adaptations, which tend to magnify the melodramatic elements. I'm not saying that the

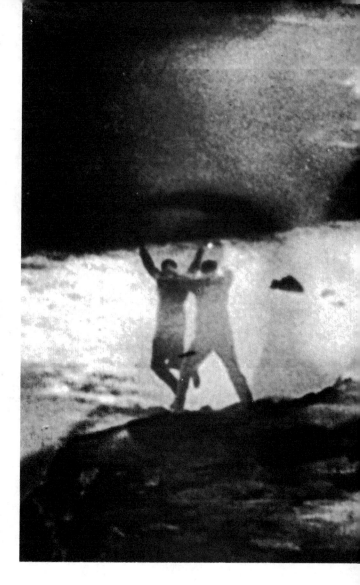

picture is superior to the novel, but I do feel that a novel that followed the story line of your screenplay might have made a better book than *Before the Fact*.

A.H. That may or may not be; I can't say, but I do know that I ran into lots of difficulties on that picture. When it was finished, I spent two weeks in New York, and I had quite a shock when I came back. One of RKO's producers had screened the picture, and he found that many of the scenes gave the impression that Cary Grant was a killer. So he simply went ahead and ordered that all of these indications be deleted; the cut version only ran fifty-five minutes. Fortunately, the head of RKO realized that the result was ludicrous, and they allowed me to put the whole thing back together again.

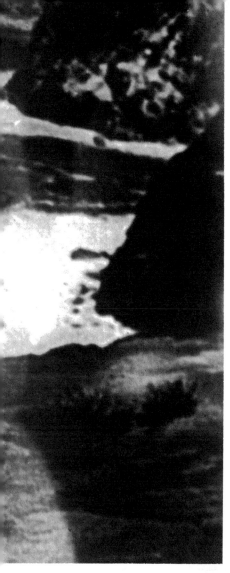

F.T. Aside from that, are you satisfied with *Suspicion?*

A.H. Up to a point. The elegant sitting rooms, the grand staircases, the lavish bedrooms, and so forth, those were the elements that displeased me. We came up against the same problem we had with *Rebecca*, an English setting laid in America. For a story of that kind, I wanted authentic location shots. Another weakness is that the photography was too glossy. By the way, did you like the scene with the glass of milk?

F.T. When Cary Grant takes it upstairs? Yes, it was very good.

A.H. I put a light in the milk.

F.T. You mean a spotlight on it?

A.H. No, I put a light right inside the glass because I wanted it to be luminous. Cary Grant's walking up the stairs and everyone's attention had to be focused on that glass.

F.T. Well, that's just the way it worked out. It was a very effective touch.

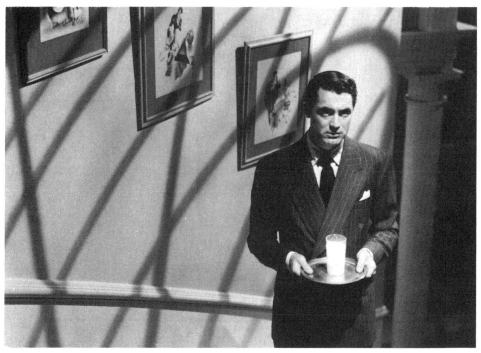

Joan Fontaine thinks
her husband is a murderer.

143

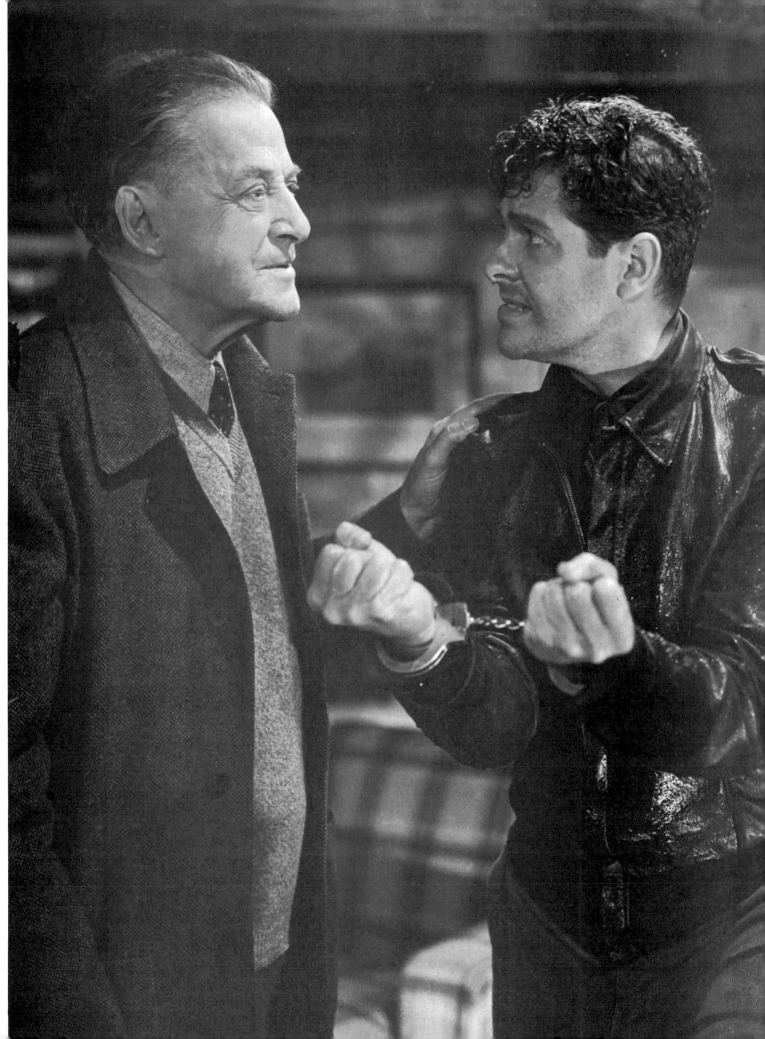

"SABOTAGE" VERSUS "SABOTEUR" ■ A MASS OF IDEAS CLUTTERS UP A PIC-
TURE ■ "SHADOW OF A DOUBT" ■ TRIBUTE TO THORNTON WILDER ■ "THE
MERRY WIDOW" ■ AN IDEALISTIC KILLER ■ "LIFEBOAT" ■ A MICROCOSM OF
WAR ■ LIKE A PACK OF DOGS ■ RETURN TO LONDON ■ MODEST WAR CON-
TRIBUTION: "BON VOYAGE" AND "AVENTURE MALGACHE" ■ ■ ■ ■ ■ ■ ■ ■ ■

7

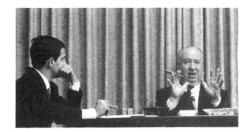

FRANÇOIS TRUFFAUT. Since *Sabo-
teur* is often confused with *Sabotage*, which was
made in Britain six years earlier, let's point out
that *Saboteur* was filmed in Hollywood and New
York in 1942.

A young worker in a munitions factory is wrong-
fully accused of sabotage. He runs away and
meets a girl who at first wants to turn him over
to the police but then decides to help him. The
story, on the whole, is not too different from
most of your manhunt yarns, so that the best
way to recall this one is to mention the finale,
on top of the Statue of Liberty.

ALFRED HITCHCOCK. In several respects *Saboteur* belongs to *The Thirty-nine
Steps*, the *Foreign Correspondent*, and the
North by Northwest kind of film. Here again, we
have a MacGuffin, the handcuffs, and a story
that covers lots of territory, a variety of locales.

A major problem with this sort of film is getting
an actor of stature to play the central figure. I've
learned from experience that whenever the
hero isn't portrayed by a star, the whole picture
suffers, you see, because audiences are far less
concerned about the predicament of a character who's played by someone they don't know.
Robert Cummings played the hero of *Saboteur*;
he's a competent performer, but he belongs to
the light-comedy class of actors. Aside from
that, he has an amusing face, so that even when
he's in desperate straits, his features don't convey any anguish.
I ran into another problem on this picture. I was
on loan by Selznick to an independent producer
releasing through Universal. Without consult-
ing me, they imposed the leading lady on me as
a *fait accompli*. She simply wasn't the right type
for a Hitchcock picture.

145

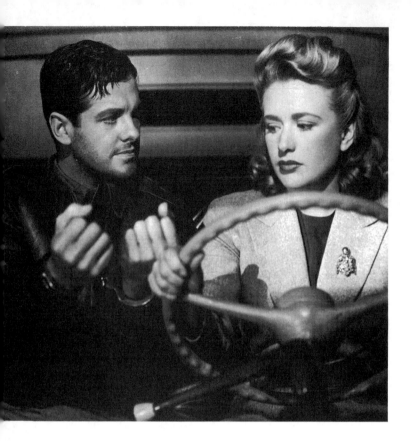

F.T. No doubt that Priscilla Lane is hardly a sophisticated woman. She's too familiar, in fact.

A.H. I was double-crossed on that. The third frustration in connection with this picture

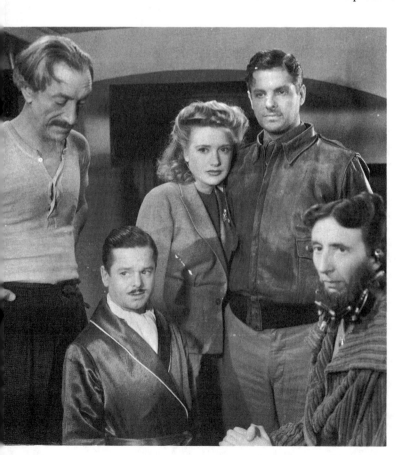

was the casting of the villain. We were in 1941 and there were pro-German elements who called themselves America Firsters and who were, in fact, American Fascists. This was the group I had in mind while writing the scenario, and for the role of the heavy I had thought of a very popular actor, Harry Carey, who generally played the good guy in westerns.

When I approached him his wife was very indignant. She said, "I am shocked that you should dare to offer my husband a part like this. After all, since Will Rogers' death, the youth of America have looked up to my husband!"

So, the loss of that counterpoint element was another disappointment. In the end we wound up with a conventional heavy.

F.T. The other villain, the man who falls from the Statue of Liberty, is quite good. I saw him again in *Limelight*.

A.H. Yes, he's a very fine actor, Norman Lloyd.

F.T. I notice that the producers of the picture are J. Skirball and F. Lloyd. Is that the Frank Lloyd who used to be a film director?

A.H. Yes, that's the man. The famous Dorothy Parker collaborated on the screenplay. Some of her touches, I'm afraid, were missed altogether; they were too subtle. There was the scene of the couple who boarded a train and landed in what turned out to be the car for circus freaks. A midget opens the door, and at first the couple can't see anyone; it's only when they look down that they see the midget. Then there was the bearded lady with her beard done up in curlers for the night. And the row between the thin man and the midget, who was known as "the Major." The Siamese twins who weren't on speaking terms with each other and communicated through a third person had a funny line. One of them says, "I wish you'd tell her to do something about her insomnia. I do nothing but toss and turn all night!"

F.T. Those things came across very well; I remember people roaring with laughter throughout that whole scene.

A.H. One interesting thing: Fry, the real saboteur, in a cab on his way to the Statue of Liberty, looks out of the window on the right and I cut to the hulk of the *Normandie* which was then lying on its side, following the fire in the harbor of New York. I cut back to a close-up of the saboteur, who, after staring at the wreck, turns around with a slightly smug smile on his face. The Navy raised hell with Universal about these three shots because I implied that the *Normandie* had been sabotaged, which was a reflection on their lack of vigilance in guarding it.

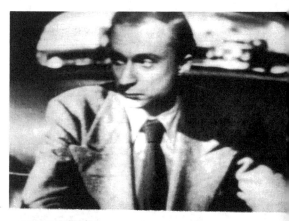

F.T. I noticed the wreckage but hadn't realized it was the *Normandie*. Another interesting touch is the scene of the fight on top of the Statue of Liberty, when the villain is suspended in midair. You have a close-up there of his sleeve that's coming apart at the shoulder seam, and what the scene is saying is that against the towering background of the Statue of Liberty, a life hangs by a mere thread. Here again, there is dramatic force in your way of going from the smallest to the greatest, from the trivial to the all-important.

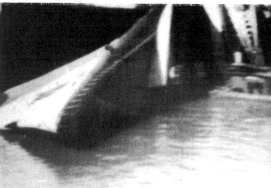

A.H. Yes, I do like to work that into the texture. Still, there's a serious error in this scene. If we'd had the hero instead of the villain hanging in mid-air, the audience's anguish would have been much greater.

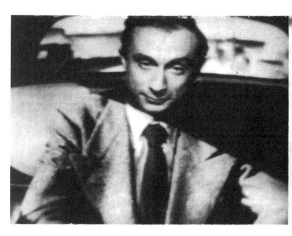

F.T. Probably, but the scene is so powerful that the public can't help being terrified just the

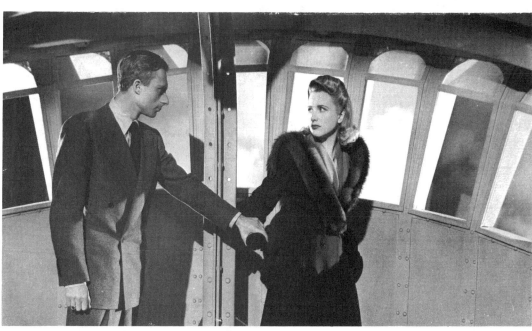

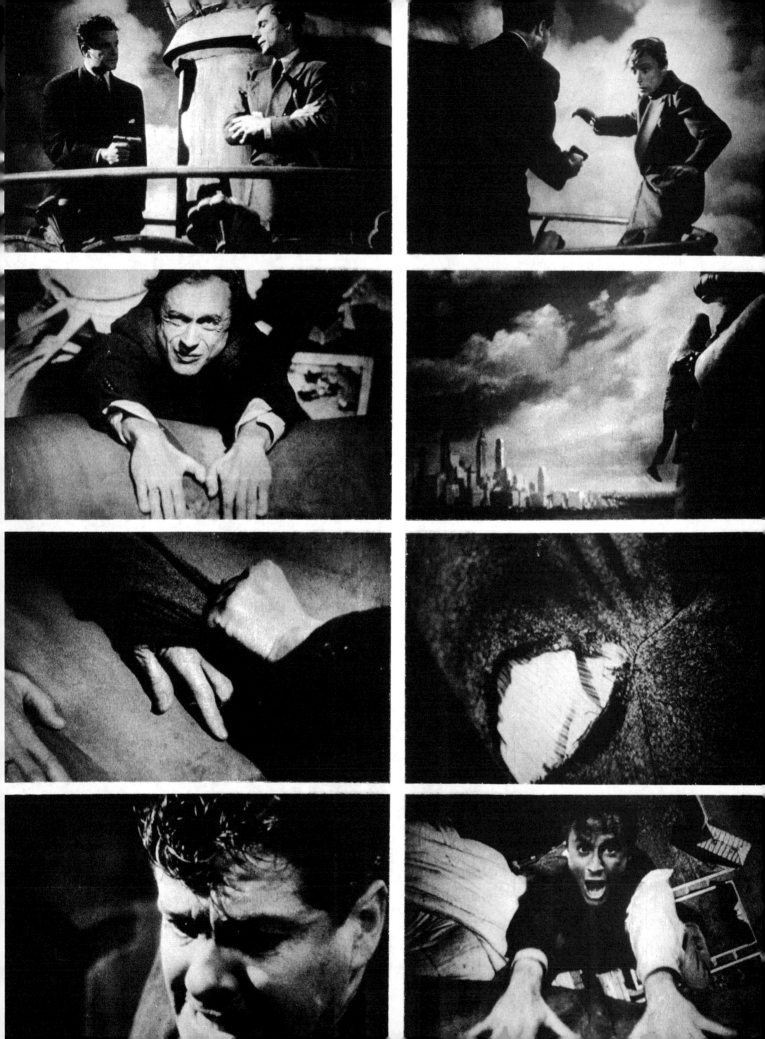

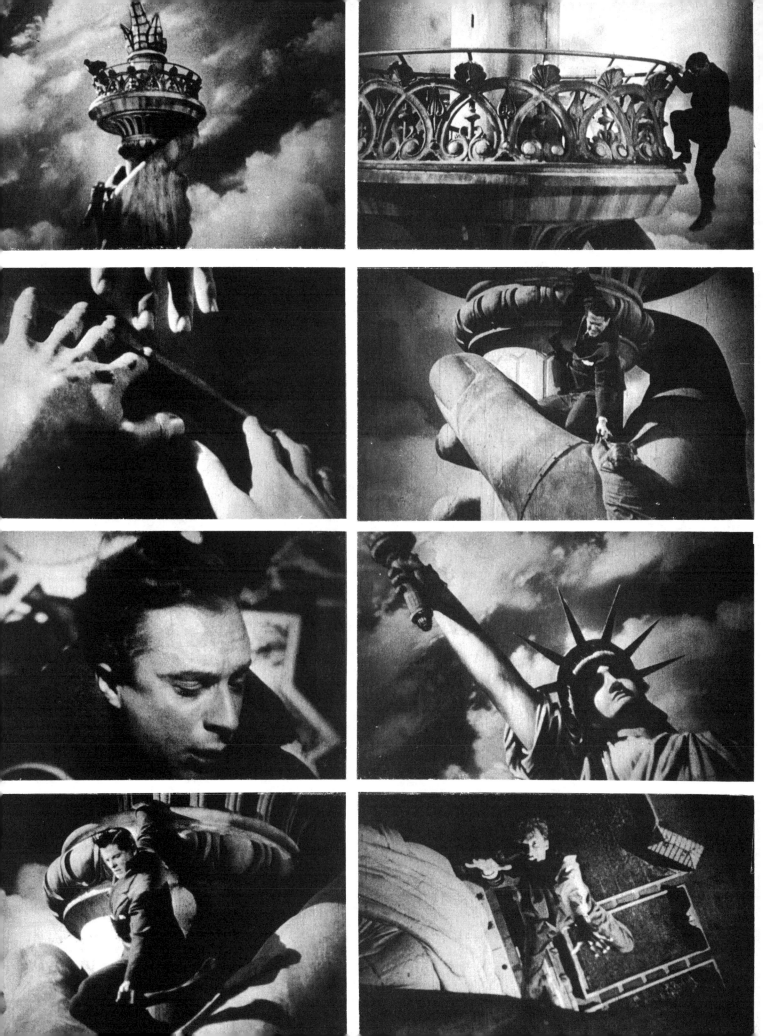

same. Besides, the hero is endangered later on, at the end of that scene, when Priscilla Lane grabs his arm to haul him back to the railing. That bit is the forerunner of one of the final shots of *North by Northwest*, but there the traction idea is enriched and completed by the jump cut of the hauling hands which go directly from the top of Mount Rushmore to the train compartment.

A.H.   Yes, it was far better in *North by Northwest*. And the final shot, immediately following that scene in the sleeping-car, is probably one of the most impudent shots I ever made.

F.T.   When the train goes into the tunnel?

A.H.   Yes. The phallic symbol.

F.T.   All the more important since *North by Northwest*, unlike *Psycho*, is a family-type picture, the kind one takes the kiddies to. In some

respects, *North by Northwest* can be seen as a remake of *Saboteur*.

A.H.   The approach to both pictures was a desire to cover various parts of America in the same way that *The Thirty-nine Steps* traveled across England and Scotland. But *North by Northwest* had a bigger leading man and I managed to embody Mount Rushmore in the action; I'd been wanting to do that for years.

F.T.   In a sense, just as *The Thirty-nine Steps* is regarded as the synthesis of all of your British work, *North by Northwest* can be seen as the compendium of your American pictures.

A.H.   That's true. Anyway, to get back to *Saboteur*, I felt that it was cluttered with too many ideas; there's the hero in handcuffs leaping down from a bridge; the scene of the elderly blind man in the house; the ghost town with the deserted workyards; and the long shot of Boul-

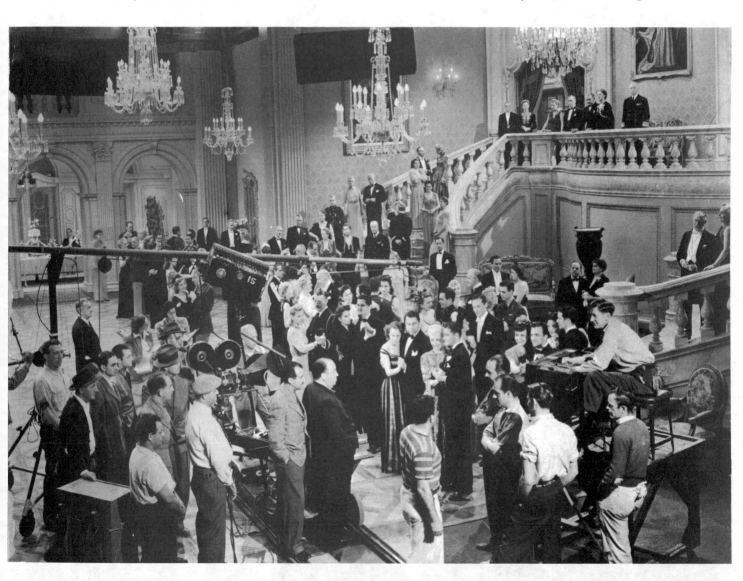

der Dam. I think we covered too much ground.

F.T.   I saw nothing wrong with that. In scenarios of this kind, involving a man who's in danger, the major difficulty is how to deal·with the girl, how to introduce her into a scene, then separate her from the hero, before bringing them back together again.

A.H.   You're quite right; it *is* a major headache.

F.T.   Which accounts for a sort of parallel montage throughout the whole last part of *Saboteur*. The man and girl are locked up separately; each one makes a separate getaway and this alternation of sequences, shifting from the man to the girl, is rather bad for the dramatic curve of the picture. In fact, the strongest scenes are those in which the two are coupled in danger; for instance, the scene in the grand ballroom.

A.H.   I remember asking myself how I could create an impression of a man and a girl being absolutely trapped in a public place. Anyone in that situation would go up to someone and say, "Look, I'm a prisoner here." And the answer would be: "You must be crazy." And yet, if they moved over to any one of the doors or windows, the villains were there waiting for them. To the average person, that situation is so fantastic as to be unbelievable. It was very difficult to find a way of handling it.

F.T.   Yet that concept of a man being more isolated in the middle of a crowd than in a deserted spot recurs in many of your films; your hero is often trapped in a movie house, in a music hall, at a political rally, at an auction sale, in a ballroom, or at a fund-raising event. It sets up a contrast within the scenario, especially when the hero starts out more or less on his own, or in isolated surroundings. Those crowd-filled scenes, I imagine, also are to dispose of the objection: "But the whole thing's idiotic. Why doesn't he call the police, or go up to someone on the street?"

A.H.   Absolutely. You can see what happens in *The Man Who Knew Too Much* when James Stewart goes up to the policemen in the Albert Hall to warn them the ambassador is about to be shot. The policemen simply take him to be a crank.

But looking back on *Saboteur*, I would say that the script lacks discipline. I don't think I exercised a clear, sharp approach to the original construction of the screenplay. There was a mass of ideas, but they weren't sorted out in proper order; they weren't selected with sufficient care. I feel the whole thing should have been pruned and tightly edited long before the actual shooting. It goes to show that a mass of ideas, however good they are, is not sufficient to create a successful picture. They've got to be carefully presented with a constant awareness of the shape of the whole. And this raises a big problem in American film-making, the difficulty of finding a responsible writer who is competent at building and sustaining the fantasy of a story.

———

F.T.   I take it that of all the pictures you've made, *Shadow of a Doubt* is the one you prefer. And yet it gives a rather distorted idea of the Hitchcock touch. I feel that the film which provides the most accurate image of the ensemble of your work, as well as of your style, is *Notorious*.

A.H.   I wouldn't say that *Shadow of a Doubt* is my favorite picture; if I've given that impression, it's probably because I feel that here is something that our friends, the plausibles and logicians, cannot complain about.

F.T.   What about the psychologists?

A.H.   That's right, the psychologists as well! In a sense, it reveals a weakness. On the one hand I claim to dismiss the plausibles, and on the other I'm worried about them. After all, I'm only human! But that impression is also due to my very pleasant memories of working on it with Thornton Wilder. In England I'd always had the collaboration of top stars and the finest writers, but in America things were quite different. I was turned down by many stars and by writers who looked down their noses at the genre I work in. That's why it was so gratifying for me to find out that one of America's most eminent playwrights was willing to work with me and, indeed, that he took the whole thing quite seriously.

F.T.   Did you select Thornton Wilder or did someone suggest him to you?

A.H.   I wanted him. Let's go back a little into the history of the picture. A woman called Margaret MacDonell, who was head of Selznick's story department, had a husband who was a novelist. One day she told me her husband had an idea for a story but he hadn't written it down yet. So we went to lunch at the Brown Derby and they told me the story, which we elaborated together as we were eating. Then I told him to go home and type it up.

In this way we got the skeleton of the story into a nine-page draft that was sent to Thornton Wilder. He came right here, to this studio we are now in, to work on it. We worked together in the morning, and he would work on his own in the afternoon, writing by hand in a school notebook. He never worked consecutively, but jumped about from one scene to another according to his fancy. I might add that the reason I wanted Wilder is that he had written a wonderful play called *Our Town*.

F.T.   I saw Sam Wood's screen version of that play.

A.H.   When the script was finished, Wilder enlisted in the Psychological Warfare Department of the U.S. Army. But I felt there was still something lacking in our screenplay, and I wanted someone who could inject some comedy highlights that would counterpoint the drama. Thornton Wilder had recommended an M-G-M writer, Robert Audrey, but he struck me as being more inclined toward serious drama, so Sally Benson was brought in.*

---

* The story of *Shadow of a Doubt* centers on Charlie Oakley (Joseph Cotten), opening with his arrival in Santa Rosa for a visit with his family. The real purpose of his visit is to elude two investigators who are on his trail. The family, a doting older sister, her husband, and a young, adoring niece (Teresa Wright) who has been named after her uncle, welcomes him with open arms. But gradually the young girl begins to suspect that her beloved uncle may be the mystery man wanted by the police for the killing of several widows.

Her suspicions are shared by a young detective (MacDonald Carey) who enters the household by pretending to be a fact finder for a national poll. Meanwhile, in the East, another suspect is accidentally killed just as the police are about to arrest him, and the inquiry is officially closed.

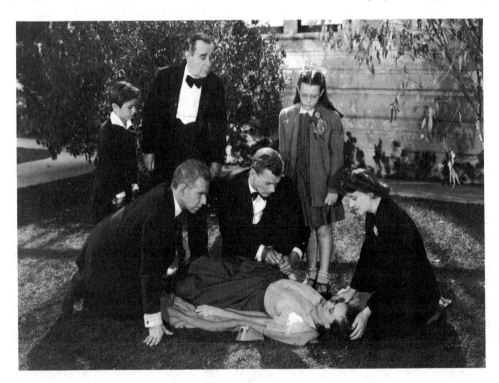

Uncle Charlie busies himself trying to revive his niece, who has been found unconscious in the garage—but he is the one who locked her in there (kneeling, at left, Hume Cronyn).

152

Before the writing, Wilder and I went to great pains to be realistic about the town, the people, and the decor. We chose a town and we went there to search for the right house. We found one, but Wilder felt that it was too big for a bank clerk. Upon investigation it turned out that the man who lived there was in the same financial bracket as our character, so Wilder agreed to use it. But when we came back, two weeks prior to the shooting, the owner was so pleased that his house was going to be in a picture that he had had it completely repainted. So we had to go in and get his permission to paint it dirty again. And when we were through, naturally, we had it done all over again with bright, new colors.

F.T. The acknowledgment to Thornton Wilder in the main credits of *Shadow of a Doubt* is rather unusual.

A.H. It was an emotional gesture; I was touched by his qualities.

F.T. In that case, why didn't you work with him on other screenplays?

A.H. Because he went off to war and I didn't see him for several years after that.

F.T. I was wondering where you got the idea of illustrating the tune of "The Merry Widow" with dancing couples. It's an image that reappears several times.

A.H. I even used it as a background for the credits.

F.T. Was it a stock shot?

A.H. No, I made it up especially for the picture. I can't remember now whether Uncle Charlie is the one who first had the idea of whis-

tling a few bars of "The Merry Widow" or whether it was the girl.

F.T. At first you showed the dancing couples and the air is played by an orchestra. Then the mother hums the opening bars and everyone at the table is trying to remember the title of the song. Joseph Cotten, who's a little disturbed, says that it's the "Blue Danube," and his niece then says, "That's right . . . Oh no, it's The Merry . . ." Whereupon Cotten spills his glass to create a diversion.

A.H. Yes, because it's too close to the truth. It's also another indication of the telepathy between Uncle Charlie and his niece.

F.T. *Psycho* is the only other picture in which your central figure is a villain; the character in *Shadow of a Doubt* even has the public's sympathy, probably because you never actually show him in the act of killing the widows.

A.H. That may be one reason, but aside from that, he's a killer with an ideal; he's one of those murderers who feel that they have a mission to destroy. It's quite possible that those widows deserved what they got, but it certainly wasn't his job to do it. There is a moral judgment in the film. He's destroyed at the end, isn't he? The niece accidentally kills her uncle. What it boils down to is that villains are not all black and heroes are not all white; there are grays everywhere. Uncle Charlie loved his niece, but not as much as she loved him. And yet she *has* to destroy him. To paraphrase Oscar Wilde: "You destroy the thing you love."

F.T. I'm puzzled by one detail of the picture. In the first scene at the station, when the train carrying Uncle Charlie is coming in, there's a heavy cloud of black smoke coming out of the engine's smokestack, and as the train comes close, it darkens the whole station. I have the feeling that this was done deliberately because when the train is leaving the station, at the end of the picture, there's simply a small puff of light smoke.

A.H. That's right; I asked for lots of black

When he becomes aware of his niece's suspicion, Uncle Charlie makes two unsuccessful attempts to kill her in the house. On boarding the train which is to take him back to New York, he tries to push her off the platform. In the ensuing scuffle he falls and is crushed to death by another passing train.

At the funeral the townfolk of Santa Rosa pay their respectful tribute to the dead man. The knowledge of his guilt will remain a secret bond between his young niece and her detective friend.

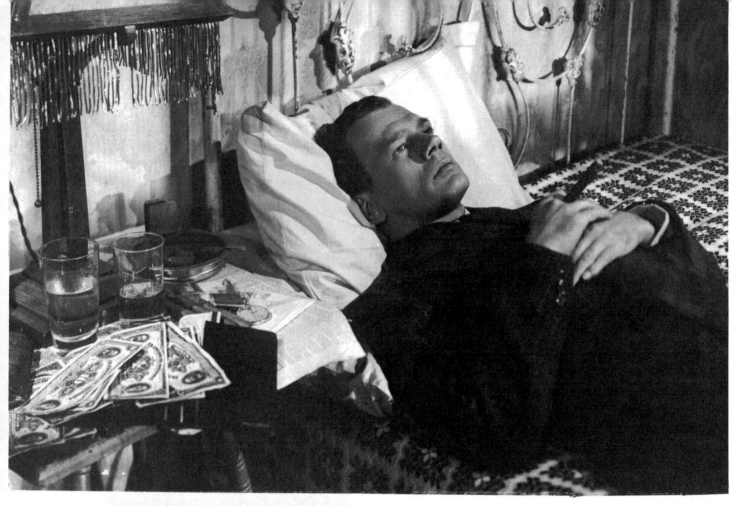

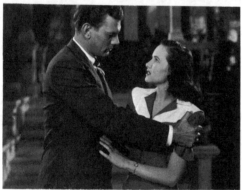

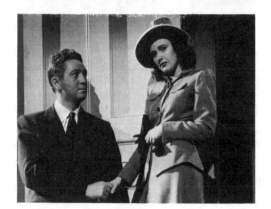

smoke for the first scene. It's one of those ideas for which you go to a lot of trouble, although it's seldom noticed. But here, we were lucky. The position of the sun created a beautiful shadow over the whole station.

F.T.   The black smoke implies that the devil was coming to town.

A.H.   Exactly. There's a similar detail in *The Birds* when Jessica Tandy, in a state of shock after having discovered the farmer's body, takes off in her car. To sustain that emotion, I had them put smoke in the truck's exhaust and we also made the road dusty. It also served to establish a contrast with the peaceful mood of her arrival at the farm. For that scene we had the road slightly dampened and there was no smoke coming out of the truck.

F.T.   With the exception of the detective, the casting is excellent, and I imagine you were very pleased with the performances of Joseph

Cotten and Teresa Wright. Her portrait of a young American girl was outstanding; she had a lovely face, a nice shape, and her way of walking was particularly graceful.

A.H.   Teresa Wright was under contract to Goldwyn and we got her on loan. All the irony of the situation stemmed from her deep love for her uncle.

F.T.   In the final scene the girl and her detective sweetheart are standing in front of the church. From the background we hear the minister's tribute to Uncle Charlie, describing him as an exceptional person. Meanwhile, the girl and the detective are planning their future together, and she makes a rather ambiguous comment, something to the effect that they are the only ones to know the truth.

A.H.   I don't remember the exact wording, but that's the general meaning; the girl will be in love with her Uncle Charlie for the rest of her life.

F.T.   With *Lifeboat* we come to the type of picture that represents a challenge. Wasn't it pretty daring to undertake to shoot a whole film in a lifeboat? *

---

* Played by Tallulah Bankhead, John Hodiak, William Bendix, Walter Slezak, Mary Anderson, Henry Hull, Heather Angel, Hume Cronyn, and Canada Lee, the story of *Lifeboat* is set against the background of World War II.

When a passenger-carrying freighter is torpedoed by a submarine, the group of survivors that manages to make its way to a lifeboat includes a fashion writer, a left-wing crew member, a young Army nurse, a millionaire, a Negro steward, the ship's radio operator, an Englishwoman carrying her dead child, and a seaman with a badly injured leg.

Hit by the explosion, the U-boat is also sinking. A German emerges from the debris and swims over to the lifeboat. The group discusses whether to throw him overboard, but when his skill saves the boat from capsizing, he assumes command of the boat. As the days go by, thirst and hunger have a telling effect and tensions rise among the members of the group. Only the man at the helm is completely self-possessed. He is actually a Nazi naval officer, who is deliberately steering the lifeboat off its course, toward a German supply ship. When the wounded seaman discovers his secret, the Nazi tosses him overboard. The next morning he tells the others that it was a suicide, but guessing the truth, they gang up in a savage attack on the Nazi, beating him to death.

Just as they are reaching the German supply ship, it is sunk by an Allied ship. Almost unbelieving, the survivors watch as the rescuing vessel heads in their direction, bringing with it the assurance that their ordeal is over.

A.H.   That's right, it was a challenge, but it was also because I wanted to prove a theory I had then. Analyzing the psychological pictures that were being turned out, it seemed to me that, visually, eighty per cent of the footage was shot in close-ups or semiclose shots. Most likely it wasn't a conscious thing with most of the directors, but rather an instinctive need to come closer to the action. In a sense this treatment was an anticipation of what was to become the television technique.

F.T.   That's an interesting point. At any rate, you'd always been intrigued by experiments with the unity of space, time, or action. Still, another interesting aspect is that *Lifeboat* is the very opposite of a thriller; it's a film of characterizations. Did the success of *Shadow of a Doubt* have anything to do with your choice of this subject?

A.H.   No, *Shadow of a Doubt* had no bearing on *Lifeboat*, which was solely concerned with the war. It was a microcosm of the war.

F.T.   At one time I was under the impression that *Lifeboat* intended to show that everyone is guilty, that each of us has something to be ashamed of, and that your conclusion meant that no one man is qualified to pass judgment on others. But now I believe that I was mistaken in that interpretation.

A.H.   You were indeed; the concept of the film is quite different. We wanted to show that at that moment there were two world forces confronting each other, the democracies and the Nazis, and while the democracies were completely disorganized, all of the Germans were clearly headed in the same direction. So here was a statement telling the democracies to put their differences aside temporarily and to gather their forces to concentrate on the common enemy, whose strength was precisely derived from a spirit of unity and of determination.

F.T.   It was quite convincing.

A.H.   The seaman, played by John Hodiak,

was practically a Communist, and on the other extreme you had the businessman who was more or less a Fascist. And in the great moments of indecision, no one, not even the Communist, knew just what to do. There was a lot of criticism. The famous columnist Dorothy Thompson gave the picture ten days to get out of town!

F.T.   The picture isn't only psychological; it's also frequently moral. Toward the end, for instance, when the people in the boat want to lynch the German, you show their backs huddled together from a distance. Wasn't it your intent to create a repulsive vision of them?

A.H.   Yes, they're like a pack of dogs.

F.T.   So there's a psychological conflict as well as a moral fable in this picture, with both elements well blended into the dramatic texture so that they never clash.

A.H.   I had assigned John Steinbeck to the screenplay, but his treatment was incomplete and so I brought in MacKinlay Kantor, who worked on it for two weeks. I didn't care for what he had written at all. He said, "Well, that's the best I can do." I thanked him for his efforts and hired another writer, Jo Swerling, who had worked on several films for Frank Capra. When

the screenplay was completed and I was ready to shoot, I discovered that the narrative was rather shapeless. So I went over it again, trying to give a dramatic form to each of the sequences.

F.T.   And you handled that by emphasizing inanimate objects, like Tallulah Bankhead's typewriter, her jewelry, and so on?

A.H.   Yes. One of the things that drew the fire of the American critics is that I had shown a German as being superior to the other characters. But at that time, 1940–41, the French had been defeated, and the Allies were not doing too well. Moreover, the German, who at first claimed to be a simple sailor, was actually a submarine commander; therefore there was every reason for his being better qualified than the others to take over the command of the lifeboat. But the critics apparently felt that a nasty Nazi couldn't be a good sailor.

Anyway, though it wasn't a commercial hit elsewhere, the picture had a good run in New York, perhaps because the technical challenge was enormous. I never let that camera get outside the boat, and there was no music at all; it was very rigorous. Of course, the characterization by Tallulah Bankhead dominated the whole film.

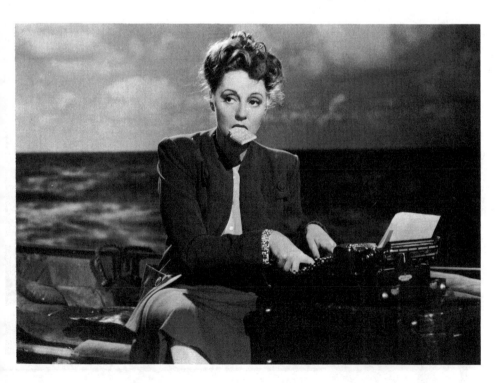

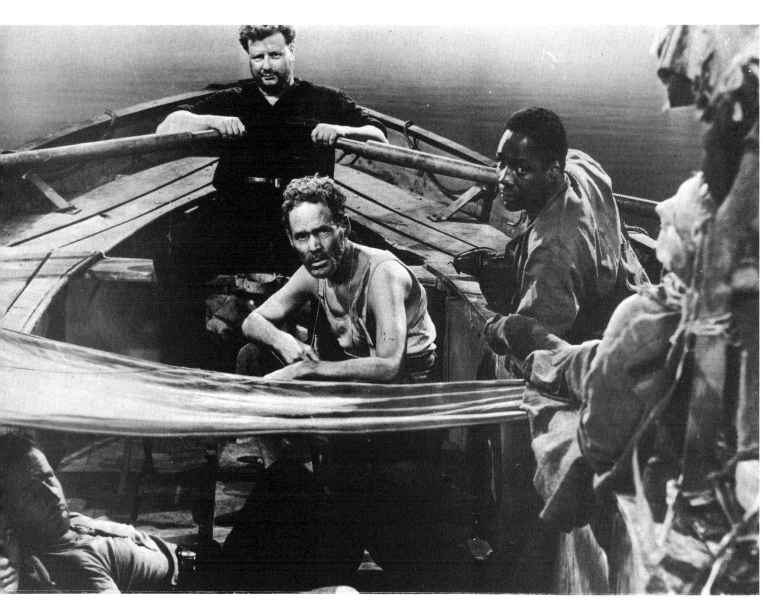

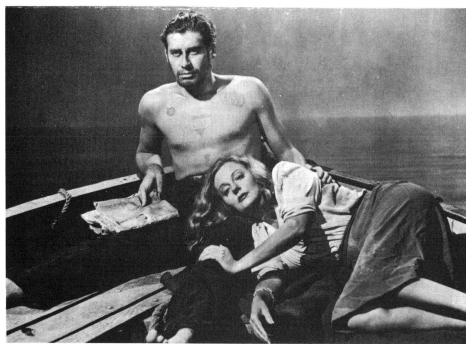

F.T. In a sense, she follows the same route as the heroine of *The Birds*, starting out as a jaded sophisticate and, in the course of her physical ordeal, gradually becoming more natural and humane. Her moral itinerary is punctuated by the discarding of purely material objects. It starts out with the typewriter that falls into the water and winds up with the gold bracelet being used as fish bait when the survivors are starving.

By the way, speaking of objects, I noticed that you used an old newspaper this time as a means of making your ritual appearance.*

A.H. That's my favorite role and I must admit that I had an awful time thinking it up. Usually I play a passer-by, but you can't have a passer-by out on the ocean. I thought of being a dead body floating past the lifeboat, but I was afraid I'd sink. I couldn't play one of the nine survivors, since each had to be played by a competent performer. Finally, I hit on a good idea. At the time, I was on a strenuous diet, painfully working my way from three hundred to two hundred pounds.

So I decided to immortalize my loss and get my bit part by posing for "before" and "after" pictures. These photographs were used in a newspaper ad for an imaginary drug, Reduco, and the viewers saw them—and me—when William

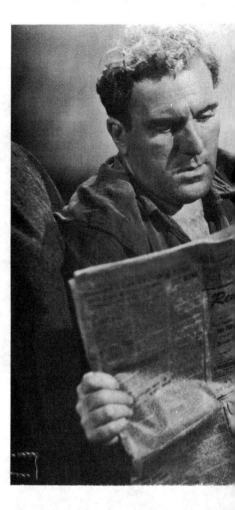

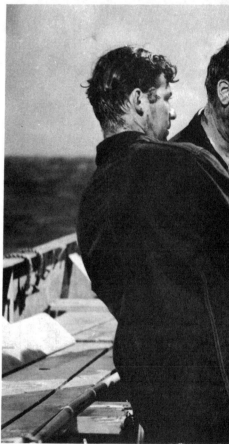

---

* Ever since *The Lodger*, in which he assumed a bit part to "fill the screen," Alfred Hitchcock has appeared in each of his pictures. In *The Lodger* he is seen twice, the first time at a desk in a newsroom and later among a crowd of people watching an arrest. In *Blackmail* he is reading a newspaper in the subway while a little boy is pestering him. In *Murder* and *The Thirty-nine Steps* he is seen passing by in the street. In *Young and Innocent* he is a clumsy photographer outside the courtroom. In *The Lady Vanishes* there is a glimpse of him at a London railroad station, and in *Rebecca* he walks by a telephone booth. In *Shadow of a Doubt* he is a bridge player on the train; in *Spellbound* he was a man coming out of a crowded elevator; in *Notorious* he is one of the party guests drinking champagne. In *The Paradine Case* he carries a cello case, and in *Rope* he crosses the street after the main title. In *Under Capricorn* he listens to a speech, and in *Stage Fright* he turns back in the street to look at Jane Wyman, who is talking to herself. In *Strangers on a Train* he boards a train, carrying a double-bass, and in *I Confess* he is seen crossing the screen at the top of a staircase. In *Dial M for Murder* his image looks out from a college photo album. In *Rear Window* he is winding a clock, and in *To Catch a Thief* he is seated in a bus, next to Cary Grant. In *The Man Who Knew Too Much* he is seen from the back, watching some Arab acrobats. In *Vertigo* and *North by Northwest* he crosses the street, and in *Psycho* he stands on the sidewalk, wearing a wide Texan hat. In *The Birds* he is walking two small dogs, and in *Marnie* he is strolling through the hotel corridor.

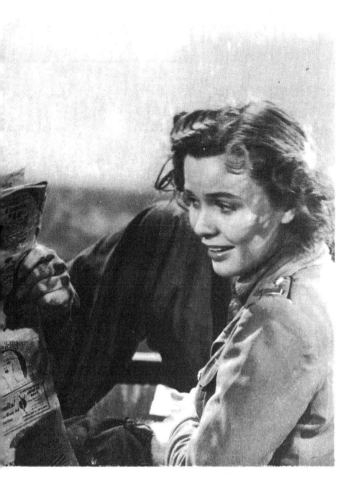

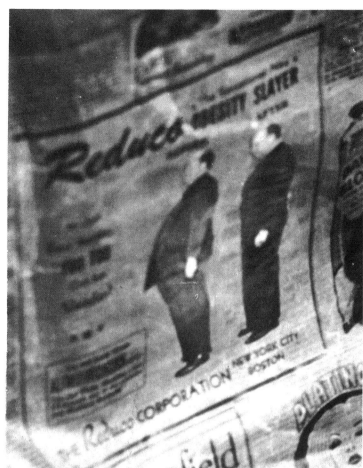

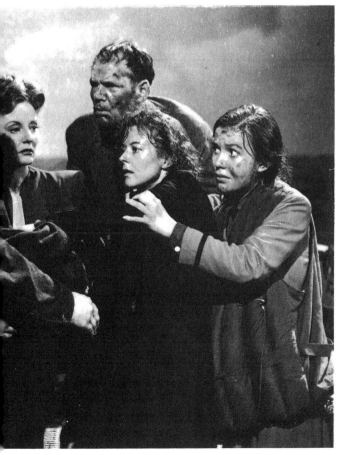

Bendix opened an old newspaper we had put in the boat. The role was a great hit. I was literally submerged by letters from fat people who wanted to know where and how they could get Reduco.

F.T.   Did the critics' harsh reaction to *Lifeboat* have a bearing on your decision to undertake two propaganda shorts for the British Ministry of Information in 1944?

A.H.   Not at all! I felt the need to make a little contribution to the war effort, and I was both overweight and overage for military service. I knew that if I did nothing I'd regret it for the rest of my life; it was important for me to do something and also to get right into the atmosphere of war. Before that, I had discussed my next feature for Selznick; it was to be based on an English novel called *The House of Dr. Edwardes*. Then I took off, but it wasn't too easy to get to England in those days. I flew over in a

159

bomber, sitting on the floor, and when we got halfway across the Atlantic, the plane had to turn back. I took another one two days later. In London my friend Sidney Bernstein was the head of the film section of the British Ministry of Information. It was at his request that I undertook two small films that were tributes to the work of the French Resistance.

F.T.   It seems to me that I saw one of them in Paris toward the end of 1944.

A.H.   That's quite possible because the idea was to show them in parts of France where the Germans were losing ground in order to help the French people appreciate the role of the Resistance. The first short was called *Bon Voyage*. It was a little story about an RAF man who is being escorted out of France through the Resistance channels. His escort was a Polish officer. When he arrives in London, the RAF man is interrogated by an officer of the Free French Forces, who informs him that his Polish escort was really a Gestapo man. Upon that startling revelation, we go through the journey across France all over again, but this time we show all sorts of details that the young RAF man hadn't noticed at first, various indications of the Pole's complicity with the Gestapo detail. At the end

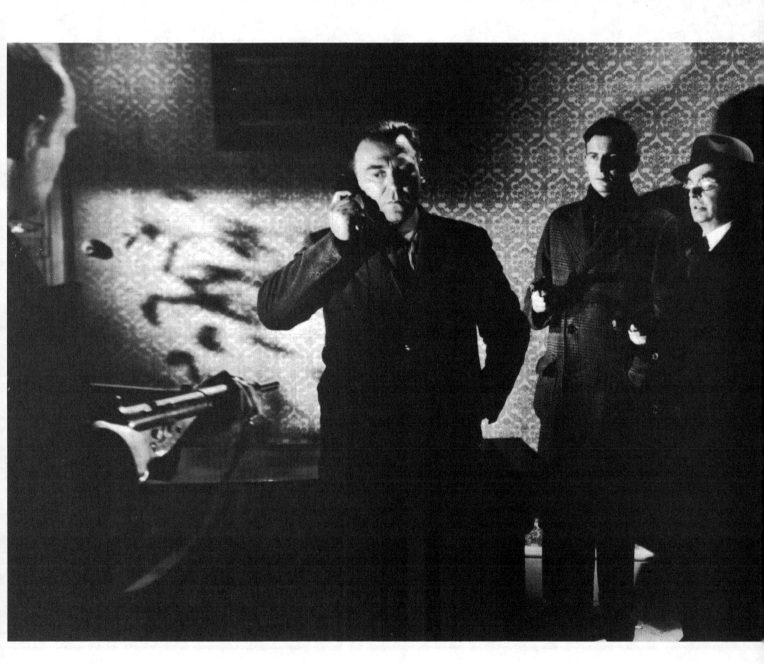

of the story there was a twist showing how the Polish officer had been trapped. At the same time, the RAF man learned that the young French girl who'd helped them, and had spotted the Pole as a spy, had been killed by him.

F.T.   Yes, that's the one I saw.

A.H.   It was a four-reel picture and the Free French forces supplied me with technical advisers. For instance, Claude Dauphin helped us with the dialogue. We used to work on the screenplay in my room at Claridge's, and there was a whole group of French officers, including a certain Commander or Colonel Forestier who never agreed to anything the others suggested. We realized that the Free French were very divided against one another, and these inner conflicts became the subject of the next film, *Aventure Malgache*.

One of the men there was an actor and a lawyer whose Resistance name was Clarousse. He was in his late sixties, but he had lots of energy and he was always at odds with his Free French companions who finally threw him in jail, in Tananarive. It was a true story and Clarousse told it himself. But when it was finished, there was some disagreement about it and I believe they decided not to release it.

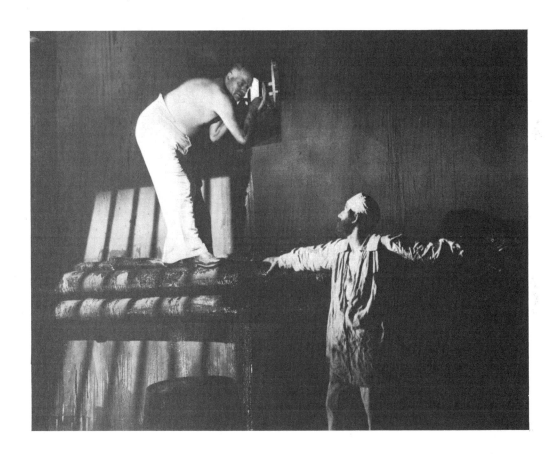

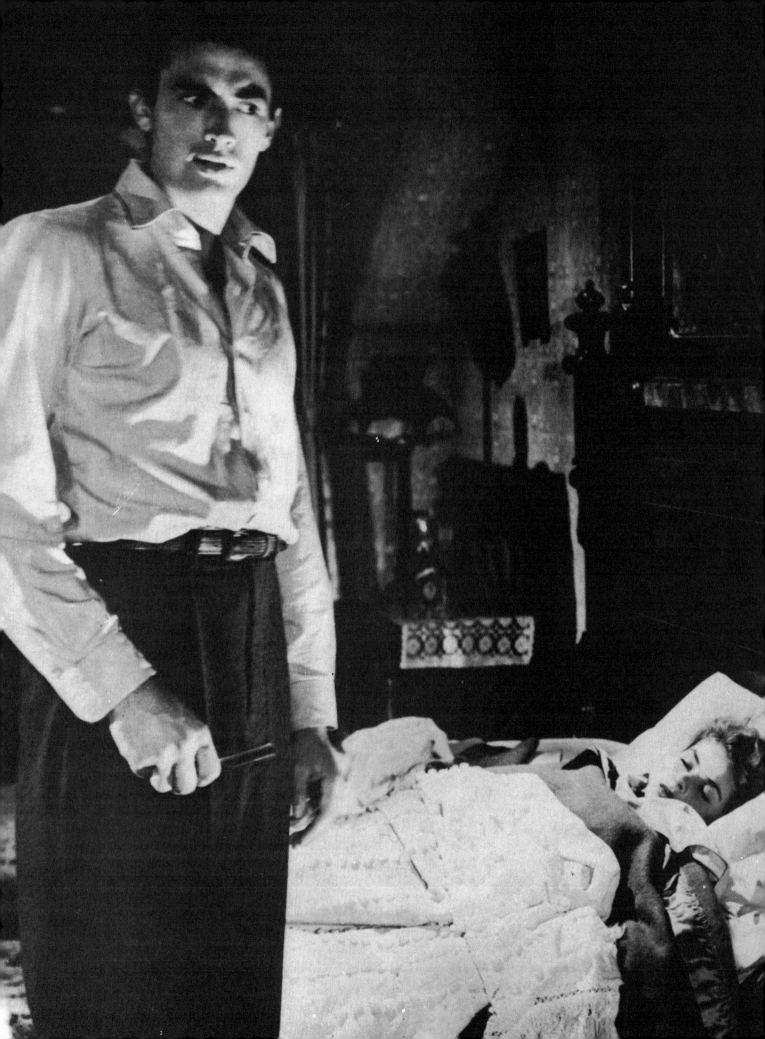

RETURN TO AMERICA ■ "SPELLBOUND" ■ COLLABORATION WITH SALVADOR DALI ■ "NOTORIOUS" ■ "THE SONG OF THE FLAME" ■ THE URANIUM MacGUFFIN ■ UNDER SURVEILLANCE BY THE FBI ■ A FILM ABOUT THE CINEMA ■ "THE PARADINE CASE" ■ CAN GREGORY PECK PLAY A BRITISH LAWYER? ■ AN INTRICATE SHOT ■ HORNY HANDS, LIKE THE DEVIL! ■ ■ ■ ■ ■ ■

8

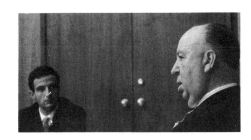

FRANÇOIS TRUFFAUT.　In 1944 you went back to America to make *Spellbound*. I notice among the credits the name of Angus MacPhail. I believe he also worked with you on *Bon Voyage*.

ALFRED HITCHCOCK.　Angus Mac-Phail was the head of Gaumont-British's scenario department. He had been one of those young Cambridge intellectuals who had taken an interest in cinema in the early days. I first met him on the set of *The Lodger*, when we were both working for Gaumont-British. I met him again in London when I went over to do those French shorts, and we outlined the first treatment of *Spellbound* together. But the script wasn't tight enough, it rambled; so when I came back to Hollywood, Ben Hecht was assigned to it. Since he was very keen on psychoanalysis, he turned out to be a very fortunate choice.

F.T.　In the book they've written about you, Eric Rohmer and Claude Chabrol claim you intended *Spellbound* to be a wilder, more extravagant picture. The clinic director, for instance, was to have the Cross of Christ tattooed on his soles so that he trampled it with each step. He also engaged in various forms of black magic.

A.H.　Well, the original novel, *The House of Dr. Edwardes*, was about a madman taking over an insane asylum. It was melodramatic and quite weird. In the book even the orderlies were lunatics and they did some very queer things. But I wanted to do something more sensible, to turn out the first picture on psychoanalysis. So I worked with Ben Hecht, who was in constant touch with prominent psychoanalysts.
I was determined to break with the traditional way of handling dream sequences through a blurred and hazy screen. I asked Selznick if he

163

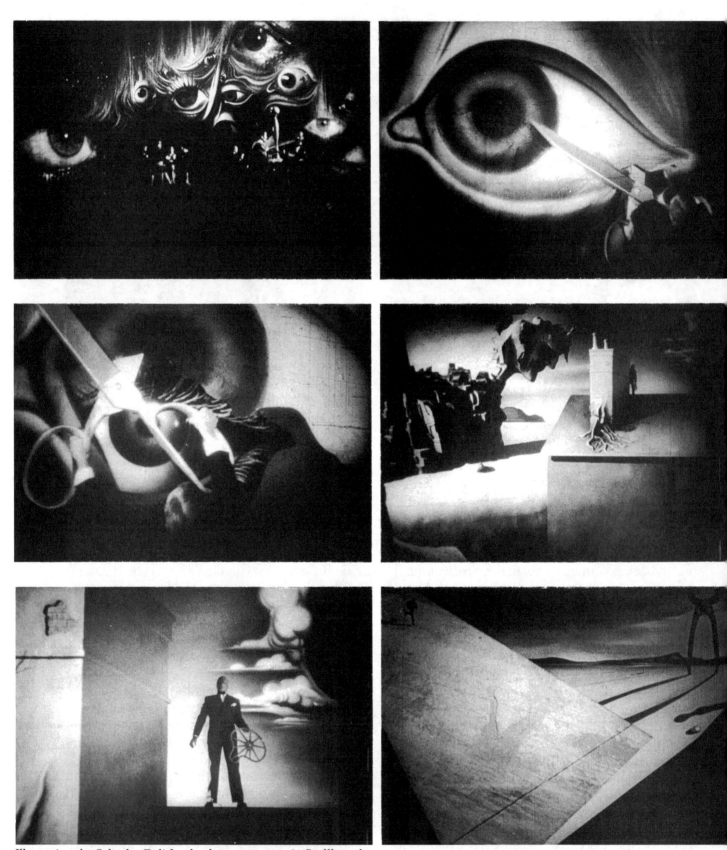

Illustrations by Salvador Dali for the dream sequence in *Spellbound*.

could get Dali to work with us and he agreed, though I think he didn't really understand my reasons for wanting Dali. He probably thought I wanted his collaboration for publicity purposes. The real reason was that I wanted to convey the dreams with great visual sharpness and clarity, sharper than the film itself. I wanted Dali because of the architectural sharpness of his work. Chirico has the same quality, you know, the long shadows, the infinity of distance, and the converging lines of perspective.

But Dali had some strange ideas; he wanted a statue to crack like a shell falling apart, with ants crawling all over it, and underneath, there would be Ingrid Bergman, covered by the ants! It just wasn't possible.

My idea was to shoot the Dali dream scenes in the open air so that the whole thing, photographed in real sunshine, would be terribly sharp. I was very keen on that idea, but the producers were concerned about the expense. So we shot the dream in the studios.

F.T.   Finally, there was a single dream divided into four separate parts. I saw *Spellbound* again recently and I must admit that I didn't care very much for the scenario.*

A.H.   Well, it's just another manhunt story wrapped up in pseudo-psychoanalysis.

F.T.   The peculiar thing is that several of your pictures—among them *Notorious* and *Vertigo*—really look like filmed dreams, and that's why one expects a Hitchcock film on psycho-

analysis to be wildly imaginative—way out! Instead, this turns out to be one of your most sensible pictures, with lots of dialogue. My criticism is that *Spellbound* is rather weak on fantasy, especially in the light of some of your other works.

A.H.   Since psychoanalysis was involved, there was a reluctance to fantasize; we tried to use a logical approach to the man's adventure.

F.T.   I see. Well anyway, there are some very beautiful scenes in the picture. For instance, the one showing the seven doors opening after the kiss, and even the first meeting between Gregory Peck and Ingrid Bergman; that was so clearly love at first sight.

A.H.   Unfortunately, the violins begin to play just then. That was terrible!

F.T.   I also liked the group of shots following Gregory Peck's arrest and the close-ups of In-

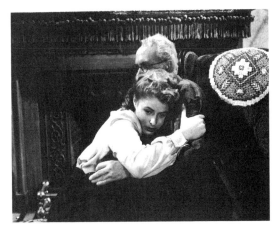

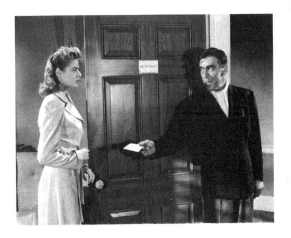

---

* Constance (Ingrid Bergman) is a doctor in an insane asylum. Dr. Murchison (Leo G. Carroll), the asylum director, is about to retire, and the staff is awaiting the arrival of his successor, Dr. Edwardes (Gregory Peck). Constance falls in love with her new chief, but after a while she discovers that he is a mental case who has assumed the identity of Dr. Edwardes. When he becomes aware of his amnesic condition, he is convinced he must have killed the real doctor and he runs away from the clinic. Constance manages to track him down. Since he is wanted by the police, she takes him into hiding, to the home of her former professor (Michael Chekhov), who will be able to analyze the sick man's dreams and the reasons for his guilt complex. The professor finds out that the pseudo-Edwardes has always felt responsible for the accidental death of his younger brother during their childhood and is suffering from shock at having witnessed Dr. Edwardes' death in a similar manner. It turns out that this death was not an accident, but a premeditated murder by Dr. Murchison to save his position. The film winds up with the criminal being exposed and the lovers free to embark on a happy life together.

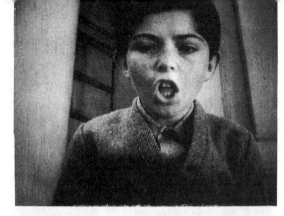

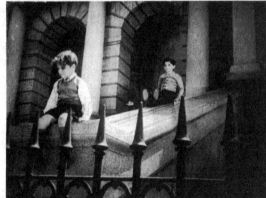

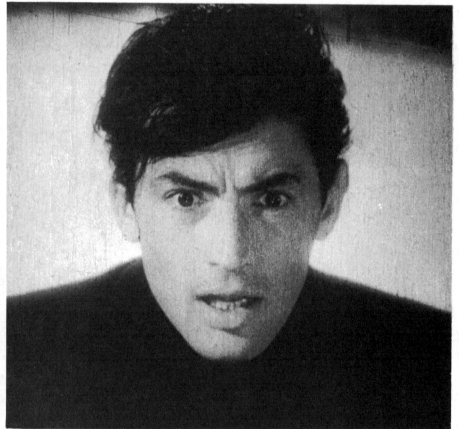

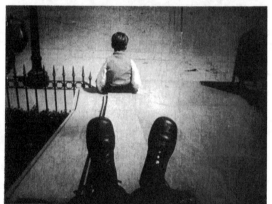

Gregory Peck relives the scene in which he accidentally killed his brother.

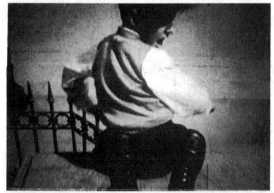

166

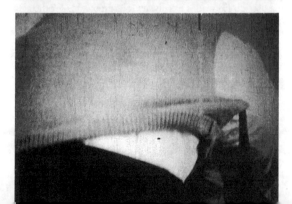

grid Bergman before she begins to cry. On the other hand, the whole sequence in which they take refuge with the elderly professor was of no particular interest. I hope you won't be offended, but I must say I found the picture something of a disappointment.

A.H.   Not at all. The whole thing's too complicated, and I found the explanations toward the end very confusing.

F.T.   Another serious weakness of this film —and this also applies to *The Paradine Case*—is Gregory Peck. Whereas Ingrid Bergman is an extraordinary actress, ideally well suited to your style, Gregory Peck isn't a Hitchcockian actor. He's shallow for one, but the main thing is the lack of expression in his eyes. Even so, I prefer *The Paradine Case* to *Spellbound*. How about you?

A.H.   I don't know. There are several errors in that one as well.

————————

F.T.   I'm impatient to get to *Notorious* because this is truly my favorite Hitchcock picture;

at any rate, it's the one I prefer in the black-and-white group. In my opinion, *Notorious* is the very quintessence of Hitchcock.

A.H.   When I started to work with Ben Hecht on the screenplay for *Notorious*, we were looking for a MacGuffin, and as always, we proceeded by trial and error, going off in several different directions that turned out to be too complex. The basic concept of the story was already on hand. Ingrid Bergman was to play the heroine, and Cary Grant was to portray the FBI man who accompanied her to Latin America, where she was to worm her way into the household of a nest of Nazi spies in order to find out what they were up to. Our original intention had been to bring into the story government officials and police agents and to show groups of German refugees training in secret camps in South America with the aim of setting up an enemy army. But we couldn't figure out what they were going to do with the army once it was organized. So we dropped the whole idea in favor of a MacGuffin that was simpler, but concrete and visual: a sample of uranium concealed in a wine bottle.

At the beginning the producer had given me an old-fashioned story, "The Song of the Flame,"

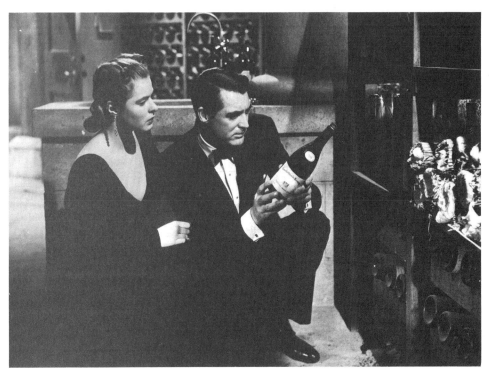

that appeared in *The Saturday Evening Post*. It was the story of a young woman who had fallen in love with the son of a wealthy New York society woman. The girl was troubled about a secret in her past. She felt that her great love would be shattered if ever the young man or his mother found out about it. What was the secret? Well, during the war, the government counterspy service had approached a theatrical impresario to find them a young actress who would act as an agent; her mission was to sleep with a certain spy in order to get hold of some valuable information. The agent had suggested this young girl and she had accepted the assignment. So now, filled with apprehensions about the whole thing, she goes back to her agent and tells him all about her problem, and he, in turn, tells the whole story to the young man's mother. The story winds up with the aristocratic mother saying, "I always hoped that my son would find the right girl, but I never expected him to marry a girl as fine as this!"

So here is the idea for a picture co-starring Ingrid Bergman and Cary Grant, to be directed by Alfred Hitchcock. Well, after talking it over with Ben Hecht, we decide that the idea we'll retain from this story is that the girl is to sleep with a spy in order to get some secret information. Gradually, we develop the story, and now I introduce the MacGuffin: four or five samples of uranium concealed in wine bottles.

The producer said, "What in the name of goodness is that?"

I said, "This is uranium; it's the thing they're going to make an atom bomb with."

And he asked, "What atom bomb?"

This, you must remember, was in 1944, a year before Hiroshima. I had only one clue. A writer friend of mine had told me that scientists were working on a secret project some place in New Mexico. It was so secret that once they went into the plant, they never emerged again. I was also aware that the Germans were conducting experiments with heavy water in Norway. So these clues brought me to the uranium MacGuffin. The producer was skeptical, and he felt it was absurd to use the idea of an atom bomb as the basis for our story. I told him that it wasn't the basis for the story, but only the MacGuffin, and I explained that there was no need to attach too much importance to it.

Finally, I said, "Look, if you don't like uranium, let's make it industrial diamonds, which the Germans need to cut their tools with." And I pointed out that if it had not been a wartime story, we could have hinged our plot on the theft of diamonds, that the gimmick was unimportant.

Well, I failed to convince the producers, and a few weeks later the whole project was sold to RKO. In other words, Ingrid Bergman, Cary Grant, the script, Ben Hecht, and myself, we were sold as a package.

There's something else I should tell you about this uranium MacGuffin. It happened four years after *Notorious* was released. I was sailing on the *Queen Elizabeth*, and I ran into a man called Joseph Hazen, who was an associate of producer Hal Wallis. He said to me, "I've always wanted to find out where you got the idea for the atom bomb a year before Hiroshima. When they offered us the *Notorious* script, we turned it down because we thought it was such a goddamn foolish thing to base a movie on."

There was another incident that took place prior to the shooting of *Notorious*. Ben Hecht and I went over to the California Institute of Technology at Pasadena to meet Dr. Millikan, at that time one of the leading scientists in America. We were shown into his office, and there in a corner was a bust of Einstein. Very impressive. The first question we asked him was: "Dr. Millikan, how large would an atom bomb be?"

He looked at us and said, "You want to have yourselves arrested and have me arrested as well?" Then he spent an hour telling us how impossible our idea was, and he concluded that if only they could harness hydrogen, then that would be something. He thought he had succeeded in convincing us that we were barking up the wrong tree, but I learned later that afterward the FBI had me under surveillance for three months.

To get back to Mr. Hazen on the boat, when he told me how idiotic he had thought our gimmick was, I answered, "Well, all it goes to show is that you were wrong to attach any importance to the MacGuffin. *Notorious* was simply the story of a man in love with a girl who, in the

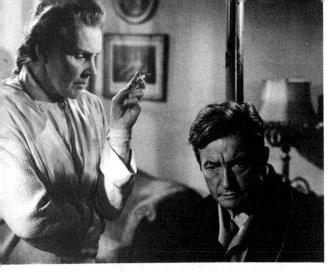

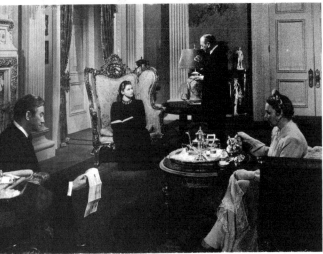

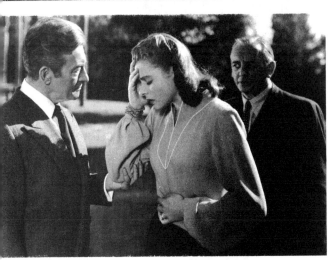

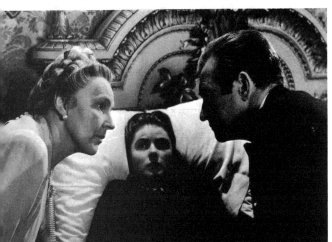

course of her official duties, had to go to bed with another man and even had to marry him. That's the story. That mistake of yours cost you a lot of money, because the movie cost two million dollars to make and grossed eight million dollars for the producers."

F.T.   So it was a big hit. Incidentally, how did *Spellbound* fare, in terms of dollars and cents?

A.H.   *Spellbound* was less expensive; it cost us about a million and a half dollars to make, and it brought in seven million to the producer.

F.T.   I'm awfully pleased to see that *Notorious* is re-released time and again all over the world. Despite a lapse of twenty years it's still a remarkably modern picture, with very few scenes and an exceptionally pure story line. In the sense that it gets a maximum effect from a minimum of elements, it's really a model of scenario construction.* All of the suspense scenes hinge around two objects, always the same, namely the key and the fake wine bottle. The sentimental angle is the simplest in the world:

---

* In America, at the end of the war, a Nazi agent is sentenced to jail. His daughter, Alicia (Ingrid Bergman), who was never involved in his activities, leads a fast life. One day a government agent named Devlin (Cary Grant) approaches her with a request that she undertake a secret mission. She accepts and they go to Rio together. They fall in love, but Devlin is wary of the former playgirl and maintains a certain distance between them. Alicia's assignment is to establish contact with Sebastian (Claude Rains), a former friend of her father's, who harbors in his home a group of prominent Nazi refugees in Brazil. Alicia succeeds in establishing contact and becomes a regular visitor to Sebastian's home. He falls in love with her and proposes marriage. She hopes Devlin will object, but when he fails to do so, she accepts the offer.

Despite the hostility of her rather terrifying mother-in-law, Alicia is now the new mistress of the Nazi household, with instructions from her employers to get hold of the keys to the cellar which Sebastian always carries with him. During a large reception Alicia and Devlin explore the cellar and discover uranium concealed in fake wine bottles.

The next morning Sebastian, aware that his bride is an American agent, begins to administer poison to Alicia, with the help of his mother. The aim is to conceal his blunder from their Nazi entourage by arranging for what will appear to be a death from natural causes.

Eventually, Devlin, alarmed at the lack of news from Alicia, forces his way into Sebastian's household and finds Alicia critically ill.

After telling her of his love, he lifts her out of bed and carries her downstairs and through the foyer, into his car, with Sebastian looking on helplessly, unable to raise the alarm. As the car drives off, Sebastian fearfully turns back to face the circle of his compatriots, which closes ominously about him.

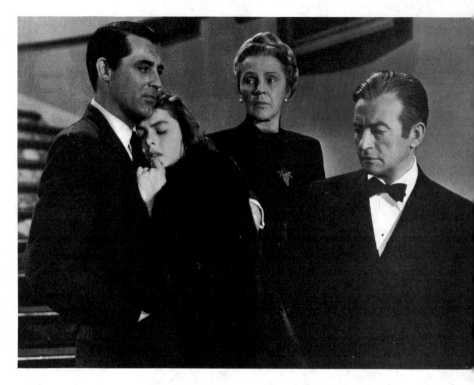

At the end of *Notorious* (1946), Cary Grant rescues Ingrid Bergman while her husband, Claude Rains, watches, unable to say anything, paralysed by the presence of other spies who are going to ask him for an explanation. At far right, planning the famous zoom-in on the key in Ingrid Bergman's hand.

two men in love with the same woman. It seems to me that of all of your pictures this is the one in which one feels the most perfect correlation between what you are aiming at and what appears on the screen. I don't know whether you were already drawing detailed sketches of each shot, but to the eye, the ensemble is as precise as an animated cartoon. Of all its qualities, the outstanding achievement is perhaps that in *Notorious* you have at once a maximum of stylization and a maximum of simplicity.

A.H.   I'm pleased you should mention that, because we did try for simplicity. As a rule, there's a good deal of violence in movies dealing with espionage, and here we tried to avoid that. We used a method of killing that was quite simple; it was as commonplace as the real-life killings you read about in newspaper stories. Claude Rains and his mother try to kill Ingrid Bergman by poisoning her very slowly with arsenic. Isn't that the conventional method for disposing of someone without being caught? Usually, when film spies are trying to get rid of someone, they don't take so many precautions; they shoot a man down or they take him for a ride in some isolated spot and then simulate an accident by hurling the car down from a high

cliff. Here, there was an attempt to make the spies behave with reasonable evil.

F.T.   That's true; the villains are human and even vulnerable. They're frightening and yet we sense that they, too, are afraid.

A.H.   That was the approach we used throughout the entire film. Do you remember the scene in which Ingrid Bergman, after having carried out her instructions to become friendly with Claude Rains, meets Cary Grant to report to him? In speaking of Claude Rains, she says, "He wants to marry me." Now that's a simple statement and the dialogue is quite ordinary, but that scene is photographed in a way that belies that simplicity. There are only two people in the frame, Cary Grant and Ingrid Bergman, and the whole scene hinges on that sentence: "He wants to marry me." The impression is that it calls for some sort of sentimental suspense around whether she's going to allow Claude Rains to marry her or not. But we didn't do that because the answer to that question is beside the point. It has nothing to do with the scene; the public can simply assume that the marriage will take place. I deliberately left what appears to be the important emotional factor

170

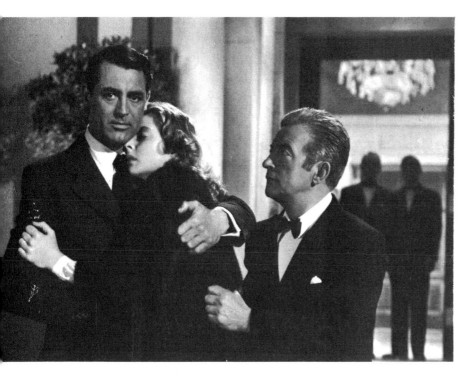

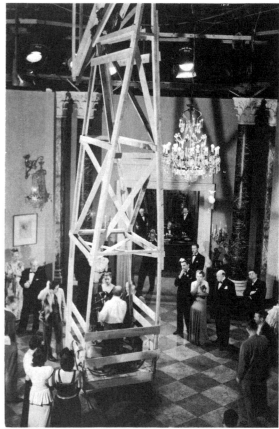

aside. You see, the question isn't whether Ingrid will or will not marry Claude Rains. The thing that really matters is that, against all expectations, the man she's spying on has just asked her to marry him.

F.T. If I understand you correctly, the important thing in this scene isn't Ingrid Bergman's reply to the proposal, but the fact that such a proposal has been made.

A.H. That's it.

F.T. It's also interesting in that the proposal comes as a sort of bombshell. Somehow, one doesn't expect the subject of marriage to crop up in a story about spies.
Something else that impressed me—and you deal with it again in *Under Capricorn*—is the imperceptible transition from one form of intoxication to another, going from liquor to poison. In the scene where Cary Grant and Ingrid Bergman are seated together on a bench, she's beginning to feel the effects of the arsenic, but he assumes she's gone back to her drinking and he's rather contemptuous. There's real dramatic impact in this misunderstanding.

A.H. I felt it important to graduate this poisoning in the most normal manner possible; I didn't want it to look wild or melodramatic. In a sense, it's almost a transference of emotion.
The story of *Notorious* is the old conflict between love and duty. Cary Grant's job—and it's a rather ironic situation—is to push Ingrid Bergman into Claude Rains's bed. One can hardly blame him for seeming bitter throughout the story, whereas Claude Rains is a rather appealing figure, both because his confidence is being betrayed and because his love for Ingrid Bergman is probably deeper than Cary Grant's. All of these elements of psychological drama have been woven into the spy story.

F.T. Ted Tetzlaff's photography is excellent.

A.H. In the early stages of the film, we were doing the scene of Ingrid Bergman and Cary Grant driving in the car; she's a little drunk and she's driving too fast. We were working in the studios, with transparencies. On the transpar-

171

ency screen we showed a motorcycle cop in the background; he's getting gradually closer to the car, and just as he goes out of the frame, on the right side, I cut to a cross angle and continue the scene, with the motorcycle cop inside the studio this time, showing him as he pulls up to them and stops the car.

When Tetzlaff announced he was all set to shoot, I said, "Don't you think it would be a good idea to have a little light on the side, sweeping across the backs of their necks, to represent the motorcycle headlights that are shown on the transparency screen?"

He had never done anything like that, and he was not too pleased that I should draw his attention to it. And he said, "Getting a bit technical, aren't you, Pop?"

A little incident came up while we were making the picture that was rather sad. We needed to use a house in Beverly Hills to represent the exterior of the big spy house in Rio. The head of the location department sent a minor member of his staff to show me the house they'd selected, a very quiet, little man who said to me, "Mr. Hitchcock, will this house do?" That little man was the same man to whom I originally submitted my titles at Famous Players-Lasky when I was starting out in 1920.

F.T.   That's awful.

A.H.   Yes, it took me a little while to recognize him; when I did I felt terrible.

F.T.   Did you show him you knew who he was?

A.H.   No, I didn't. That's one of the occupational tragedies of this industry. When I was shooting *The Thirty-nine Steps*, there were some odd, extra shots to be done, and in order to speed up the production, the producer offered to get someone to do it. When I asked him whom he had in mind, he answered, "Graham Cutts."

I said, "No, I won't have it. I used to work for him; I did the writing on *Woman to Woman* for him. How can I have him come on as my assistant?"

And he answered, "Well, if you won't use him,

you'll be doing him out of a job and he really needs the money."

So I finally agreed, but it's a terrible thing, don't you think so?

F.T.   It is, indeed. But, getting back to *Notorious*, I wanted to say that a key factor in the picture's success is probably the perfect casting: Cary Grant, Ingrid Bergman, Claude Rains, and Leopoldine Konstantin. With Robert Walker and Joseph Cotten, Claude Rains was undoubtedly your best villain. He was extremely human. It's rather touching: the small man in love with a taller woman. . . .

A.H.   Yes, Claude Rains and Ingrid Bergman made a nice couple, but in the close shots the difference between them was so marked that if I wanted them both in a frame, I had to stand Claude Rains on a box. On one occasion we wanted to show them both coming from a distance, with the camera panning from him to Bergman. Well, we couldn't have any boxes out there on the floor, so what I did was to have a plank of wood gradually rising as he walked toward the camera.

F.T.   Working these snags out can be pretty funny, especially when you're shooting in CinemaScope, because there, for each separate shot, you've got to have the chandeliers, the paintings, and all wall installations brought down, while at the same time, the beds, tables and chairs, and anything else that happens to be on the floor, have to be raised. For a visitor who accidentally wanders in on the set, it's truly a ridiculous sight. It's often occurred to me that one might make a first-rate comedy on the making of a movie.

A.H.   It's a pretty good idea, and the way I'd do it is to have everything take place inside a film studio. But the drama would not be in front of the camera, but off the set, between takes. The stars in the picture would be minor characters and the real heroes would be the extras. In this way you'd get a wonderful counterpoint between the banal story being filmed and the real drama that takes place off stage. You might have a great feud between the cameraman and one of the electricians, so that when the cameraman sits down on the crane, it rises to the rigging loft, and the two men take a few minutes out to swap insults. Of course, you'd have satirical elements in the background of the whole thing.

F.T. We had a picture along those lines in France, Jacques Prévert's *The Lovers of Verona*, which was directed by André Cayatte. But there seems to be a general impression that backstage stories don't make box-office hits.

A.H. It depends on the way they're handled. They made a movie here called *What Price Hollywood?* that was a big success, and *A Star Is Born*, which was very good.

F.T. That's true, and there's also *Singin' in the Rain*, which had some wonderful gags on the early days of talking pictures.

———

F.T. *The Paradine Case* scenario is credited to Selznick himself, with the adaptation by Mrs. Hitchcock—Alma Reville—of a novel by Robert Hichens.*

A.H. Robert Hichens also wrote *The Garden of Allah, Bella Donna*, and many other novels; he was famous in the early part of this century. Mrs. Hitchcock and I did the original script, which Selznick wanted for budget purposes. Then I recommended James Bridie, a Scottish playwright who had a big reputation in

England as well. He was in his early sixties and a very independent man. Selznick brought him to New York, but when he wasn't met at the airport, he took the first plane back to London. He worked on the script in England and sent it over to us; the arrangement wasn't too successful. But Selznick wanted to do the adaptation himself; that's the way he did things in those days. He would write a scene and send it down to the set every other day—a very poor method of work.

Let's go over some of the more apparent flaws of that picture. First of all, I don't think that Gregory Peck can properly represent an English lawyer.

F.T. Whom would you have chosen?

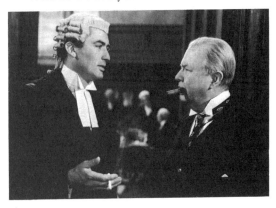

A.H. I would have brought in Laurence Olivier. I also considered Ronald Colman for the part. For a while we hoped we might get Greta Garbo to make her comeback in the role of the wife. But the worst flaw in the casting was assigning Louis Jourdan to play the groom. After all, the story of *The Paradine Case* is about the degradation of a gentleman who becomes enamored of his client, a woman who is not only a murderess, but also a nymphomaniac. And that degradation reaches its climactic point when he's forced to confront the heroine with one of her lovers, who is a groom. But that groom should have been a manure-smelling stable hand, a man who really reeked of manure. Unfortunately, Selznick had already signed up Alida Valli—he thought she was going to be another Bergman—and he also had Louis Jourdan under contract, so I had to use them, and this miscasting was very detrimental to the story.

———

* Mrs. Paradine (Alida Valli), a beautiful woman of questionable past, is accused of having murdered her blind husband. Her defense lawyer, Keane (Gregory Peck), married to a lovely wife (Ann Todd), falls deeply in love with his client and is convinced of her innocence. Before the trial he learns that Mrs. Paradine had been the mistress of the groom (Louis Jourdan).

The trial opens with Judge Harnfield (Charles Laughton), who is resentful over his unsuccessful attempt to become Mrs. Keane's lover, openly hostile to the defense lawyer.

The groom takes the witness stand. Under Keane's merciless badgering he accuses his mistress of the crime and later commits suicide. In open court the grief-stricken Mrs. Paradine discloses that her attorney is in love with her and defiantly confesses her guilt.

Stunned by this double blow, Keane walks out on the trial. His career has been shattered, but his wife's steadfast loyalty is a hopeful omen for the future.

Aside from that, I myself was never too clear as to how the murder was committed, because it was complicated by people crossing from one room to another, up and down a corridor. I never truly understood the geography of that house or how she managed the killing. What interested me in this picture was to take a person like Mrs. Paradine, to put her in the hands of the police, to have her submit to all their formalities, and to say to her maid, as she was leaving her home between the two inspectors, "I don't think I shall be back for dinner." And then to show her spending the night in a cell, from which, in fact, she will never emerge. There is an echo of that situation in *The Wrong Man*.

It may be an expression of my own fear, but I've always felt the drama of a situation in which a normal person is suddenly deprived of freedom and incarcerated with hardened criminals. There's nothing to it when a habitual law-breaker, like a drunk, is involved, but I am intrigued by the contrast in shading when it happens to a person of a certain social standing.

F.T.   The contrast is very well pointed up by a little incident that takes place when she gets to the prison. A prison matron runs her fingers through the woman's hair to make sure she isn't concealing anything. It seems to me that Ann Todd, in the role of the lawyer's wife, was also an unfortunate choice.

A.H.   She was too coldly written, I'm afraid.

F.T.   Actually, the best characters in the picture are some of the secondary figures. I'm referring to Charles Laughton, who plays the judge, and Ethel Barrymore's performance as his wife. They have a wonderful scene together, toward the end of the picture, when Ethel Barrymore indicates her compassion for Alida Valli while Charles Laughton shows no mercy whatever.

At another point in the picture there's a scene between him and Ann Todd to show that he's a lustful man. First, there's the look in his eyes, with the camera then traveling over to Ann Todd's bare shoulders. Now, in front of her husband and his wife, he walks over to the

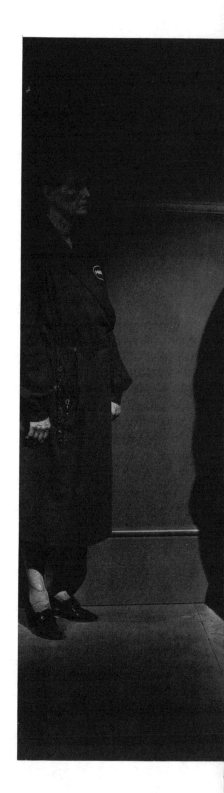

couch, sits down next to her and coolly puts his hand on top of hers. This little episode is handled discreetly, yet the impact is outrageous.

A.H.   Very much so. All the elements of the conflict were presented in the first part in order

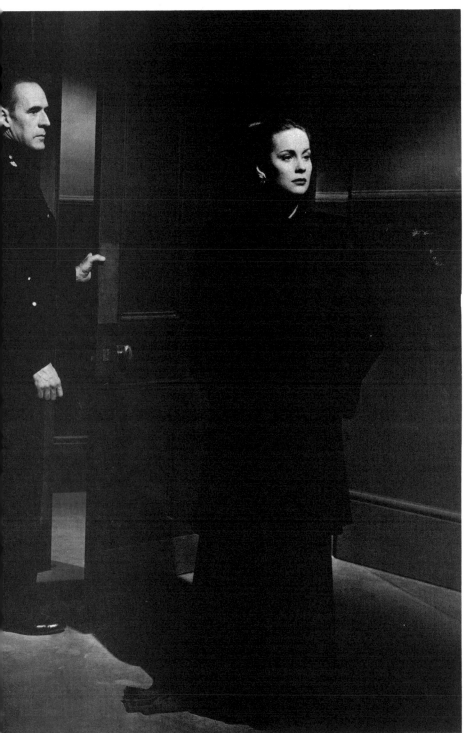

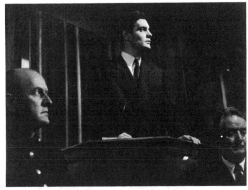

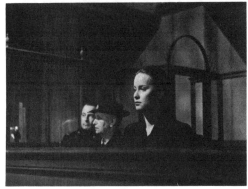

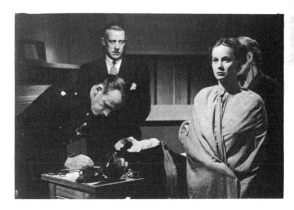

to let the trial get off to an exciting start. There is an interesting shot in the courtroom when Louis Jourdan is called in to give evidence; he comes into the courtroom and must pass behind Alida Valli. She's turning her back to him, but we wanted to give the impression that she senses his presence—not that she guesses he's there—that she actually can feel him behind her, as if she could smell him. We had to do that in two takes. The camera is on Alida Valli's face, and in the background you see Louis Jourdan coming down to the witness

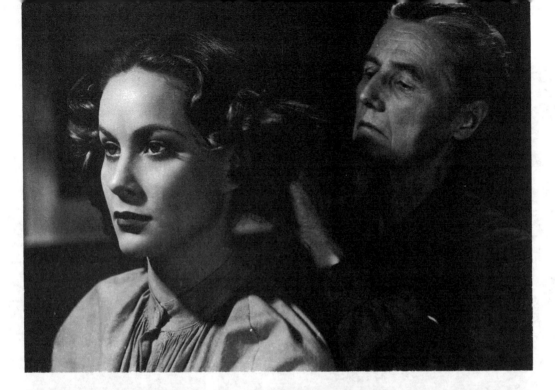

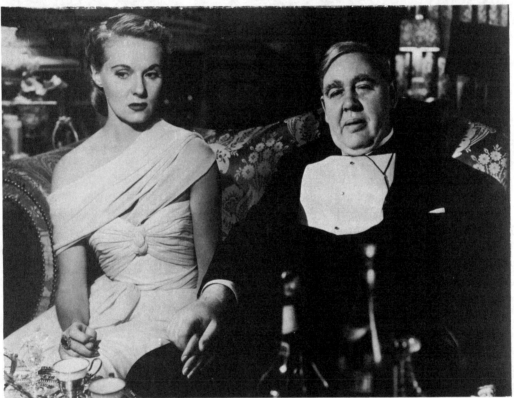

box. First, I photographed the scene without her; the camera panned him all around, at a two-hundred-degree turn, from the door to the witness box. Then, I photographed her in the foreground; we sat her in front of the screen, on a twisting stool, so that we might have the re-

volving effect, and when the camera went off her to go back to Louis Jourdan, she was pulled off the screen. It was quite complicated, but it was very interesting to work that out.

F.T.   Of course the highlight of the trial is

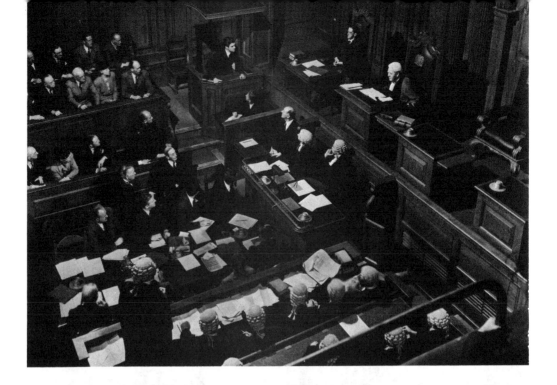

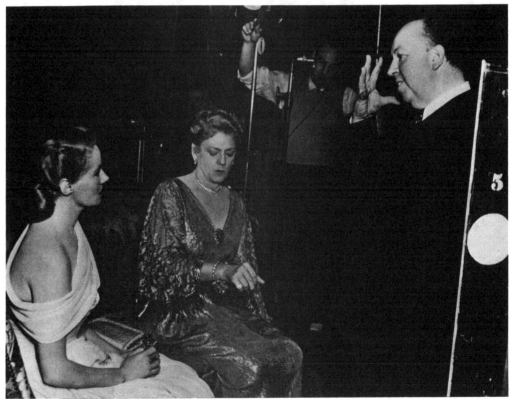

Hitchcock is probably explaining to Ann Todd the reaction of Charles Laughton upon seeing her bare shoulder.

that very high shot showing Gregory Peck as he's leaving the courtroom when he gives up his client's defense. I agree with you that Laurence Olivier would have been far better suited for that part. Whom did you have in mind for the character played by Louis Jourdan?

A.H. Robert Newton.

F.T. I see what you mean. He would have been perfect as a rough character.

A.H. With horny hands, like the devil!

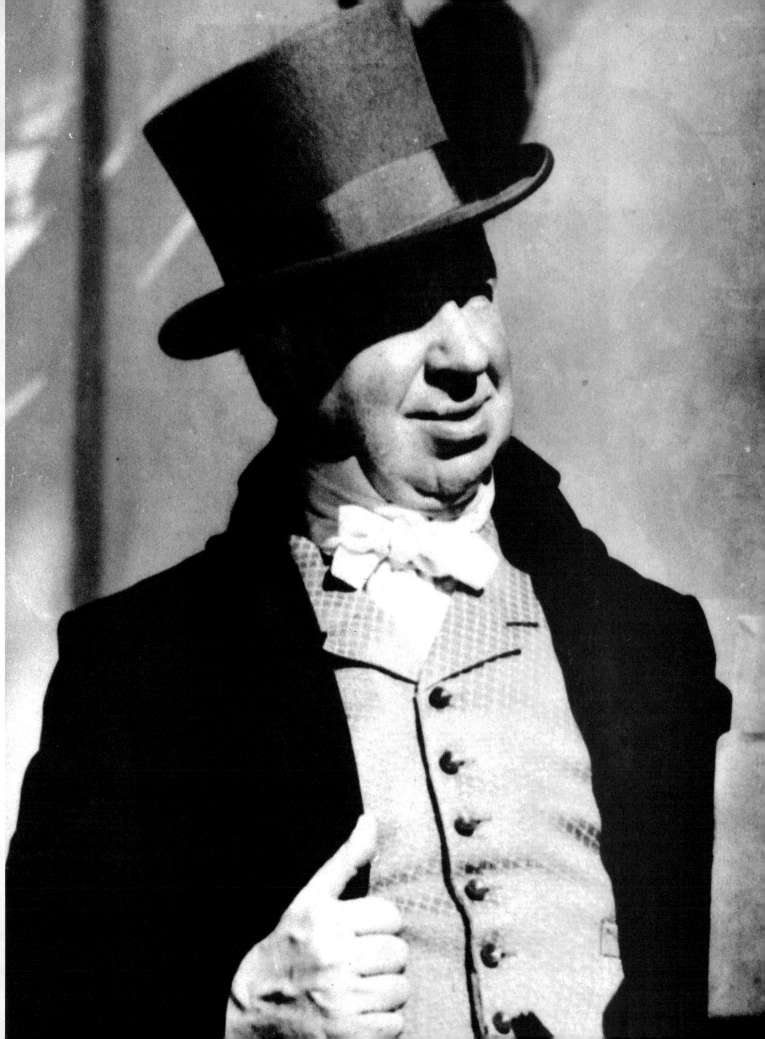

"ROPE": FROM 7:30 to 9:15 IN ONE SHOT ■ CLOUDS OF SPUN GLASS ■ COLORS AND SHADOWS ■ WALLS THAT FADE AWAY ■ FILMS MUST BE CUT ■ HOW TO MAKE NOISES RISE FROM THE STREET ■ "UNDER CAPRICORN" ■ INFANTIL-ISM AND OTHER ERRORS IN JUDGMENT ■ RUN FOR COVER! ■ "INGRID, IT'S ONLY A MOVIE!" ■ "STAGE FRIGHT" ■ THE FLASHBACK THAT LIED ■ THE BETTER THE VILLAIN, THE BETTER THE PICTURE ■ ■ ■ ■ ■ ■ ■ ■ ■ ■ ■ ■ ■

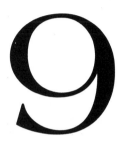

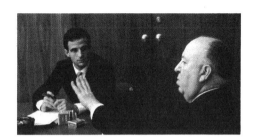

FRANÇOIS TRUFFAUT. *Rope* was made in 1948. In several respects this picture is a milestone in your career. For one thing, you produced it; for another, it was your first color film; and finally, it represented an enormous technical challenge. Is the screenplay very different from Patrick Hamilton's stage play? *

ALFRED HITCHCOCK. No, not really. Arthur Laurents did the screenplay and Hume Cronyn worked with me on the adaptation. The dialogue was partly from the original play and partly by Laurents.

I undertook *Rope* as a stunt; that's the only way I can describe it. I really don't know how I came to indulge in it.

The stage drama was played out in the actual time of the story; the action is continuous from the moment the curtain goes up until it comes down again. I asked myself whether it was technically possible to film it in the same way. The only way to achieve that, I found, would be to handle the shooting in the same continuous action, with no break in the telling of a story that begins at seven-thirty and ends at nine-fifteen. And I got this crazy idea to do it in a single

---

* Since Alfred Hitchcock deals solely with the technical aspects of *Rope*, a brief description of the story is sufficient for our purposes. All of the action takes place on a summer evening in a New York apartment. Two young homosexuals (John Dall and Farley Granger) strangle a college friend just for the thrill of it and conceal his body in a chest in the very room in which his parents and fiancée are expected for a cocktail party. Among the guests is their former college professor (James Stewart). As the party is in progress, their attempt to impress their mentor leads them to disclose bits of truth which he eventually pieces together. Before the evening is over, he will discover the body and turn the two young men over to the police.

---

* Alfred Hitchcock's description of *Rope* as a stunt calls for an explanation to those readers who are unfamiliar with shooting

---

Opposite, Hitchcock appears in *Under Capricorn*.   179

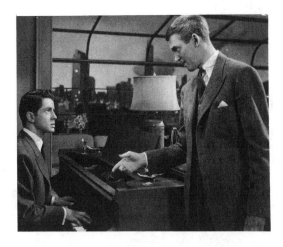

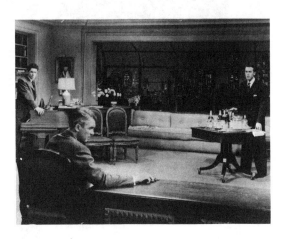

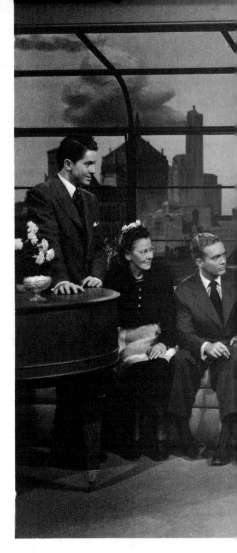

When I look back, I realize that it was quite nonsensical because I was breaking with my own theories on the importance of cutting and montage for the visual narration of a story. On the other hand, this film was, in a sense, precut. The mobility of the camera and the movement of the players closely followed my usual cutting practice. In other words, I maintained the rule of varying the size of the image in relation to its emotional importance within a given episode. Naturally, we went to a lot of trouble to achieve

techniques. As a rule, a film sequence is divided into shots that last between five to fifteen seconds. A film that runs an hour and a half will average six hundred shots. Occasionally—and this is particularly true of the highly precut Hitchcock pictures—there may be as many as a thousand shots; there were thirteen hundred and sixty shots in *The Birds*.

In *Rope* each shot runs to ten minutes, that is, the entire film roll in the camera magazine, and is referred to as a ten-minute take. In the history of cinema this is the only instance in which an entire film has been shot with no interruption for the different camera setups.

this, and the difficulties went beyond our problems with the camera. Since the action starts in broad daylight and ends by nightfall, we had to deal with the gradual darkening of the background by altering the flow of light between seven-thirty and nine-fifteen. To maintain that continuous action, with no dissolves and no time lapses, there were other technical snags to overcome, among them, how to reload the camera at the end of each reel without interrupting the scene. We handled that by having a figure pass in front of the camera, blacking out the action very briefly while we changed from one camera to the other. In that way we'd end on a close-up of someone's jacket, and at the beginning of the next reel, we'd open with the same close-up of the same character.

F.T.   Aside from all of this, I imagine that the fact that you were using color for the first

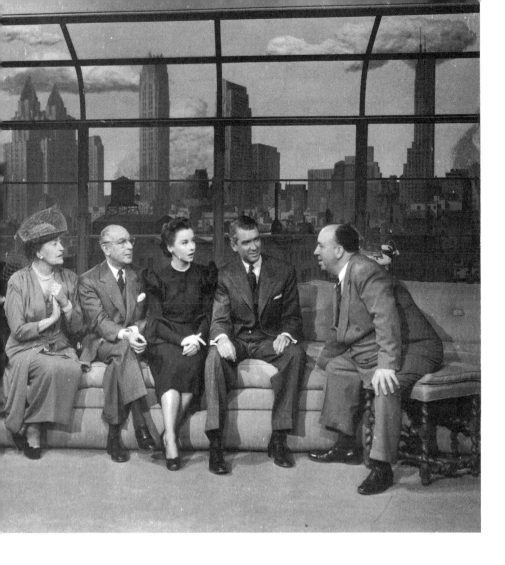

time must have added to your difficulties.

A.H.   Yes. Because I was determined to reduce the color to a minimum. We had built the set of an apartment, consisting of a living room, a hallway, and a section of a kitchen. The picture overlooked the New York skyline, and we had that background made up in a semicircular pattern, so that the camera might swing around the room. To show that in proper perspective, that background was three times the size of the apartment decor itself. And between the set and the skyscrapers, we had some cloud formations made of spun glass. Each cloud was separate and mobile; some were hung on invisible wires and others were on stands, and they were also set in a semicircular pattern. We had a special working plan designed for the clouds, and between reels they were shifted from left to right. They were never actually shown in motion, but

you must remember that the camera wasn't always on the window, so whenever we changed the reels, the stagehands would shift each cloud into the position designated on our working plan. And as soon as a cloud reached the edge of the horizon, it would be taken off and another one would appear in view of the window at the other side.

F.T.   What about the problems with the color?

A.H.   Toward the last four or five reels, in other words, by sunset, I realized that the orange in the sun was far too strong, and on account of that we did the last five reels all over again. We now have to digress a little to talk about color.
The average cameraman is a very fine technician. He can make a woman look beautiful; he

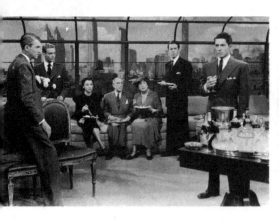 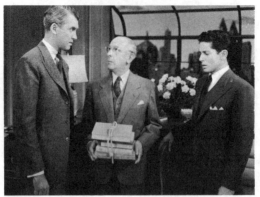 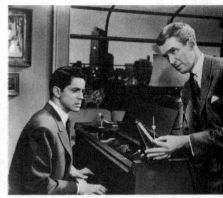

can create natural lighting that is effective without being exaggerated. But there is often a problem that stems purely from the cameraman's artistic taste. Does he have a sense of color and does he use good taste in his choice of colors? Now, the cameraman who handled the lighting on *Rope* simply said to himself, "Well, it's just another sunset." Obviously, he hadn't looked at one for a long time, if ever at all, and what he did was completely unacceptable; it was like a lurid postcard.

Joseph Valentine, who photographed *Rope*, had also worked on *Shadow of a Doubt*. When I saw the initial rushes, my first feeling was that things show up much more in color than in black and white. And I discovered that it was the general practice to use the same lighting for color as for black and white. Now, as I've already told you, I especially admired the approach to lighting used by the Americans in 1920 because it overcame the two-dimensional nature of the image by separating the actor from the background through the use of backlights—they call them liners—to detach him from his setting.

Now in color there is no need for this, unless the actor should happen to be dressed in the

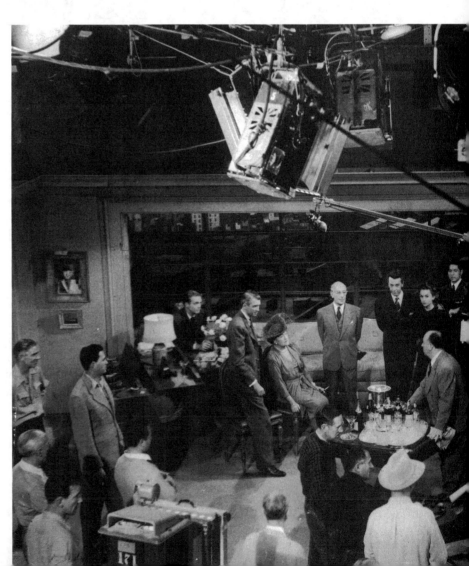

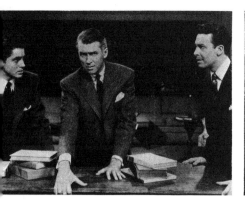 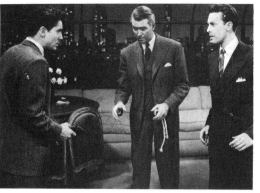

Lending some books to the father of his victim, John Dall ties them with the cord he used to kill his friend.

same color as the background, but that's highly improbable. It sounds elementary, doesn't it, and yet that's the tradition, and it's quite hard to break away from it. Surely, now that we work in color, we shouldn't be made aware of the source of the studio lighting. And yet, in many pictures, you will find people walking through the supposedly dingy corridors between the stage and dressing rooms of a theater, and because the scene is lighted by studio arc lamps, their shadows on the wall are black as coal. You just can't help wondering where those lights could possibly be coming from.

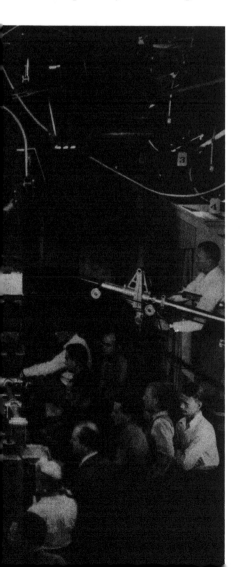

I truly believe that the problem of the lighting in color films has not yet been solved. I tried for the first time to change the style of color lighting in *Torn Curtain*. Jack Warren, who was on *Rebecca* and *Spellbound* with me, is the cameraman who cooperated.

We must bear in mind that, fundamentally, there's no such thing as color; in fact, there's no such thing as a face, because until the light hits it, it is nonexistent. After all, one of the first things I learned in the School of Art was that there is no such thing as a line; there's only the light and the shade. On my first day in school I did a drawing; it was quite a good drawing, but because I was drawing with lines, it was totally incorrect and the error was immediately pointed out to me.

Going back to *Rope*, there's a little sidelight. After four or five days the cameraman went off "sick." So I wound up with a Technicolor consultant, and he completed the job with the help of the chief electrician.

F.T. What about the problems of a mobile camera?

A.H. Well, the technique of the camera movements was worked out, in its slightest details, well beforehand. We used a dolly and we mapped out our course through tiny numbers all over the floor, which served as guide marks. All the dollyman had to do was to get his camera on position Number One or Number Two at a given cue of the dialogue, then dolly over to the next number. When we went from one room into another, the wall of the hallway or of the living room would swing back on silent rails. And the furniture was mounted on rollers so that we could push it aside as the camera

183

passed. It was an amazing thing to see a shot taken.

F.T. What is truly remarkable is that all of this was done so silently that you were able to make a direct sound track. For a European, particularly if he works in Rome or Paris, that's almost inconceivable.

A.H. They'd never done it in Hollywood either! To do it, we had a special floor made. The opening scene, you will recall, shows two young fellows strangling a man and putting his body into a chest. There was some dialogue. Then there is more dialogue as they go into the dining room and then to the kitchen. Walls are being moved and lights are being raised and lowered. I was so scared that something would go wrong that I couldn't even look during the first take. For eight minutes of consecutive shooting everything went very smoothly. Then the camera panned around as the two killers walked back toward the chest, and there, right in camera focus, was an electrician standing by the window! So the first take was ruined.

F.T. That raises a point I'm curious about. How many takes were there for each reel that was completed? In other words, how many takes were interrupted and how many did you complete?

A.H. Well, there were ten days of rehearsal with the cameras, the actors, and the lighting. Then there were eighteen days of shooting, including the nine days in which we did the retakes because of that orange sun I told you about.

F.T. Eighteen days of shooting. That would mean that the work on six of those days was totally useless. Were you ever able to complete two whole reels in a single day?

A.H. No, I don't think so.

F.T. In any case, I don't agree that *Rope* should be dismissed as a foolish experiment, particularly when you look at it in the context of your whole career: a director is tempted by the dream of linking all of a film's components into a single, continuous action. In this sense, it's a positive step in your evolution. Nevertheless, weighing the pros and cons—and the practices of all the great directors who have considered the question seem to bear this out—it is true that the classical cutting techniques dating back to D. W. Griffith have stood the test of time and still prevail today. Don't you agree?

A.H. No doubt about it; films must be cut. As an experiment, *Rope* may be forgiven, but it was definitely a mistake when I insisted on applying the same techniques to *Under Capricorn*.

F.T. Before winding up our discussion of *Rope*, one remarkable aspect is the painstaking quest for realism. The sound track of that picture is fantastically realistic, in particular, toward the end, when James Stewart opens the window to fire a shot in the night and one hears the noises gradually rising from the street.

A.H. You put it very correctly when you referred to the rise of the noises from the street. As a matter of fact, to get that effect, I made them put the microphone six stories high and I gathered a group of people below on the sidewalk and had them talk about the shots. As for the police siren, they told me they had one in the sound library. I asked them, "How are you going to give the impression of distance?" and they answered, "We'll make it soft at first, and then we'll bring it up loud." But I didn't want it done that way. I made them get an ambulance with a siren. We placed a microphone at the studio gate and sent the ambulance two miles away and that's the way we made the sound track.

F.T. *Rope* was the first film you produced. Was it financially rewarding?

A.H. Yes, that part was all right, and it had good notices. It cost about a million and a half dollars to make because so many things in it were being done for the first time. James Stewart was paid three hundred thousand dollars. M-G-M bought the rights a little while ago and they reissued the picture.

F.T. After *Rope* you made your second pic-

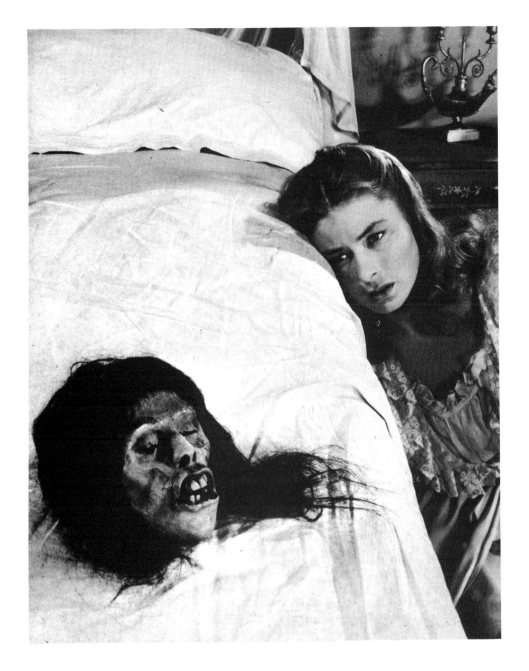

ture as an independent producer, and that was *Under Capricorn*. In France there was and still is some confusion around that movie. It turned out to be a financial disaster, and you are reported to be sorry you ever undertook it. Yet many of your admirers regard it as your very best work. Wasn't it taken from a British novel that you liked?

A.H.   I had no special admiration for the novel, and I don't think I would have made the picture if it hadn't been for Ingrid Bergman. At that time she was the biggest star in America and all the American producers were competing for her services, and I must admit that I made

the mistake of thinking that to get Bergman would be a tremendous feat; it was a victory over the rest of the industry, you see. That was bad thinking, and my behavior was almost infantile. Because even if the presence of Bergman represented a commercial asset, it made the whole thing so costly that there was no point to it. Had I examined the whole thing more carefully from the commercial angle, I would not have spent two and a half million dollars on the picture. At the time that was a lot of money, you see.

In 1949 I was regarded as a specialist in the suspense and thriller genre, but *Under Capricorn* fitted into neither one of these categories. In fact, *The Hollywood Reporter* commented on it

185

by saying that one "had to wait a hundred and five minutes for the first thrill of the picture."* Anyway, I looked upon Bergman as a feather in my cap. We were making it with our own production company and all I could think about was: "Here I am, Hitchcock, the onetime English director, returning to London with the biggest star of the day." I was literally intoxicated at the thought of the cameras and flashbulbs that would be directed at Bergman and myself at the London airport. All of these externals seemed to be terribly important. I can only say now that I was being stupid and juvenile.

My second mistake was to ask my friend Hume Cronyn to do the script with me; I wanted him because he's a very articulate man who knows how to voice his ideas. But as a scriptwriter he hadn't really sufficient experience.

Still another error was calling upon James Bridie to help with the scenario. He was a semi-intellectual playwright and not in my opinion a very thorough craftsman. On thinking it over later on, I realized that he always had very good first and second acts, but he never succeeded in ending his plays. I still remember one of our working sessions on the script. The man and wife had separated after a series of terrible quarrels, and I asked Bridie, "How are we going to bring them together again?" He said, "Oh, let them just apologize to each other and say, 'I'm sorry, it was all a mistake.' "

F.T.   It is true, even to an admirer of the picture, that the last fifteen minutes are rather weak; the denouement is too contrived. . . .

A.H.   That's what I mean. At any rate, I'm

---

* The action of *Under Capricorn* is set in Sydney, Australia, in 1830. The governor's nephew, Charles Adare (Michael Wilding), newly arrived from England, is invited to dinner by Sam Flusky (Joseph Cotten), a former convict who is now the wealthy husband of Charles's cousin, Henrietta (Ingrid Bergman).

There, he finds himself in a strange household. Henrietta has become an alcoholic. The shrewish housekeeper, Milly (Margaret Leighton), who is secretly in love with her master, terrorizes the young woman. Charles undertakes to restore his cousin's self-confidence and subsequently falls in love with her.

At a brilliant ball the jealous husband, inflamed by the housekeeper's Iagolike intrigues, provokes a row in which Adare is wounded. Henrietta then admits to her cousin that she is guilty of the crime for which her husband had been convicted.

The confession leads Adare to renounce his love, but before leaving the country, he discovers that Milly has been administering slow poison to her mistress and succeeds in exposing her.

trying to give you a clear picture of my proper confusion at the time and of how wrong I was. For a director there should be no question on this one matter: Whenever you feel yourself entering an area of doubt or vagueness, whether it be in respect to the writer, the subject matter, or whatever it is, you've got to run for cover. When you feel you're at a loss, you must go for the tried and true!

F.T.   What do you mean by "to run for cover" behind the "tried and true"? Do you mean that when you have doubts about something it's best to fall back on elements that have already been tested?

A.H.   You've got to use an approach you're completely sure of. I mean literally, that whenever there is confusion or doubt in your mind, the first thing to do is to recover your bearings. Any guide or explorer will tell you that. When they realize they're lost, or they've taken the wrong road, they won't take a short cut through the forest, nor do they rely on their instincts to set them back in the right direction. What they do is to carefully go back over the whole road until they've found their starting point, or the point at which they took the wrong turn.

F.T.   Well, isn't that true of *Under Capricorn*? You have a domineering housekeeper, gradual intoxication, a skeleton in the closet, an admission of guilt . . . all of those ingredients had been used in *Rebecca* and in *Notorious*.

A.H.   That's right, but, you see, those elements would have remained in the picture anyway if I'd had a good professional, like Ben Hecht, writing the script for me.

F.T.   I see. I'll grant you that the picture was too talky, but even so, the dialogue was quite poetic. And if *Under Capricorn* wasn't a good movie, it was certainly a beautiful one.

A.H.   I would have liked it to have been a success, even outside of commercial considerations. With all the enthusiasm we invested in that picture, it was a shame that it didn't amount to anything. I was also ashamed that

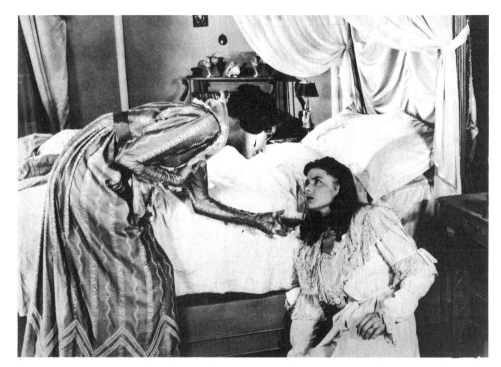

Ingrid Bergman and I—as director–producer—took such large salaries. Perhaps I shouldn't have taken anything at all, but it didn't seem fair at the time for Bergman to be taking so much money and for me to work for nothing.

F.T.   Did the film lose a lot of money?

A.H.   Yes, it did, and the bank that financed it reclaimed the picture. But now it's going to be re-released throughout the world and also probably on American television.

F.T.   The picture is so romantic that it's surprising it wasn't more of a commercial hit. It's true, of course, that it's also rather gloomy and morbid, with all of the characters feeling guilty about something and the over-all nightmarish climate of the action. Even so, the outstanding aspect of the picture is that it perfects upon many of the elements you had used in your past work. For instance, the tyrannical housekeeper in *Under Capricorn* might be the daughter of *Rebecca*'s domineering Mrs. Danvers, but Milly is far more terrifying.

A.H.   I thought so too, but the British critics said it was terrible to take a lovely actress like Margaret Leighton and make her into an un-sympathetic character. And, at a press conference, one London newspaperman said, "I don't see why you had to bring Mr. Joseph Cotten from America when we have such a fine British actor as Kieron Moore."

F.T.   Oh no! The casting was perfect and the acting was first-rate.

A.H.   I'm not so sure. Remember, *Under Capricorn* was again the lady-and-groom story. Henrietta fell in love with the groom, and when Joseph Cotten was shipped to Australia as a convict, she followed him there. The main element is that she degraded herself for the sake of her love. Cotten wasn't the right type; Burt Lancaster would have been better.

F.T.   You were concerned with contrast—the same problem as in *The Paradine Case*. Anyway, even if this picture was a flop, it can't be put in the same class with *Jamaica Inn*. To anyone who sees *Under Capricorn*, it is clear you believed in it, that you like the story—just as you believed in *Vertigo*.

A.H.   Well, it's true that I liked the story, but not as much as *Vertigo*. As I say, *Under Capricorn* was made for Ingrid Bergman, and I

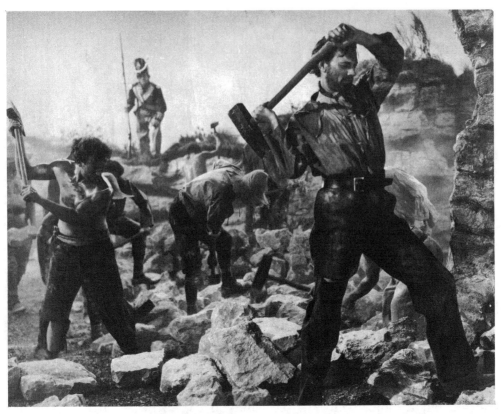

Joseph Cotten at forced labor in a scene that was cut.

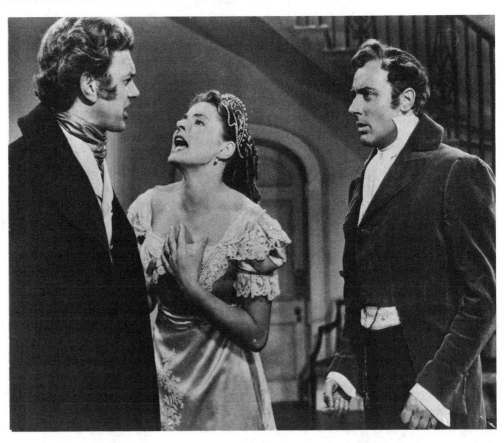

thought this was a story for a woman. But if I'd been thinking clearly, I'd never have tackled a costume picture. You'll notice I've never done any since that time. Besides, there wasn't enough humor in the film. If I were to make another picture in Australia today, I'd have a policeman hop into the pocket of a kangaroo and yell, "Follow that car!"

F.T. Another interesting aspect of *Under Capricorn* is its technique. Like in *Rope*, there are several shots that run from six to eight minutes; in fact, these are more complex since they switch from the ground floor to the floor above.

A.H. Well, we didn't have too much trouble with that, but the fluidity of the camera was probably a mistake, because the easy flow emphasized the fact that the picture wasn't a thriller. But Ingrid Bergman got angry with me one evening because of those long shots. And, since I never lose my temper and I hate arguments, I walked out of the room while her back was turned to me. I went home, and later on someone called to inform me that she hadn't noticed my departure and was still complaining twenty minutes after I'd gone.

F.T. I remember talking to her in Paris later on, and she had harrowing memories of the way large pieces of the decor would vanish into thin air during those long shots.

A.H. That's right. She didn't like that method of work, and since I can't stand arguments, I would say to her, "Ingrid, it's only a movie!" You see, she only wanted to appear in masterpieces. How on earth can anyone know whether a picture is going to turn out to be a masterpiece or not? When she was pleased with a picture she'd just finished, she would think, "What can I do after this one?" Except for *Joan of Arc*, she could never conceive of anything that was grand enough; that's very foolish!
The desire to do something big and, when that's successful, to go on to something else even bigger is like the little boy who's blowing up a balloon and all of a sudden it goes Boom! right in his face. I never reason that way. I might say to myself, "*Psycho* will be a nice little picture to

do." I never think, "I'm going to shoot a picture that will bring in fifteen million dollars"; that idea never enters my mind. In those days I used to tell Bergman, "Go out and play a secretary. It might turn out to be a *big* picture about a *little* secretary." But no! She's got to play the greatest woman in history, Joan of Arc.
Even today we still argue about these things. In spite of her beauty she wants to play mothers because she's over forty-five. What will she play when she's eighty-two years old?

F.T. Grandmothers, I guess!

F.T. While *Under Capricorn* seems a perfectly logical picture for you, it seems to me that *Stage Fright*, which you made right afterward in London, added little or nothing to your prestige. It's simply another one of those little British crime movies in the Agatha Christie tradition. Besides, you claim you disapprove of whodunits. . . .

A.H. That's true, but the aspect that intrigued me is that it was a story about the theater. What specifically appealed to me was the idea that the girl who dreams of becoming an actress will be led by circumstances to play a real-life role by posing as someone else in order to smoke out a criminal. You wonder why I chose that particular story? Well, the book had just come out and several of the reviewers had mentioned that it might make a good Hitchcock picture. And I, like an idiot, believed them!
I did one thing in that picture that I never should have done; I put in a flashback that was a lie.

F.T. Yes, and the French critics were particularly critical of that.

A.H. Strangely enough, in movies, people never object if a man is shown telling a lie. And it's also acceptable, when a character tells a story about the past, for the flashback to show it as if it were taking place in the present. So why is it that we can't tell a lie through a flashback?

F.T. In this picture it isn't as simple as that.

Richard Todd, who's running away from the police, gets into Jane Wyman's car which rolls off at top speed. She says to him, "Now that we've lost the police, could you tell me what this is all about?" Then Richard Todd proceeds to explain, and his story makes up the flashback. He tells her how—and, mind you, this is the way we see it on the screen—Marlene Dietrich had turned up at his house in a bloodstained dress and in a state of near hysteria to ask for his help. Now, since Todd is reporting on something Marlene Dietrich has supposedly told him about, the narration is all the more indirect. Anyway, as told by Todd to Jane Wyman, Marlene Dietrich's story is that she has just killed her husband and wants Todd to help her to de-

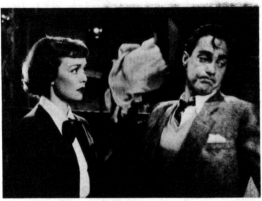

Richard Todd, the cowardly villain of *Stage Fright* (1950), with Jane Wyman.

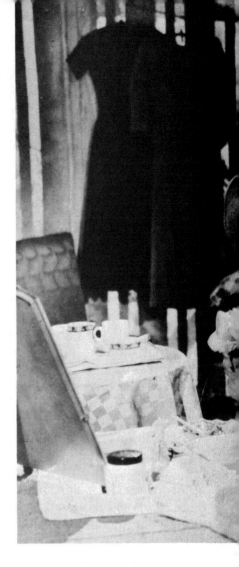

stroy some incriminating bit of evidence. He goes on to explain that the reason for which he is now under suspicion is that he was seen at the scene of the crime when he went there to remove the damaging evidence. Then, at the end of the picture, we learn that Todd has lied to Jane Wyman, to Marlene Dietrich, and to the police, that he is the real killer. Therefore, since the flashback is divided into three parts, it would seem as if he's lied three times.

A.H. I agree that the whole thing was very indirect.

F.T. Anyway, the first three reels are the best part of the picture.

A.H. Perhaps, but I had lots of fun with the theater-benefit garden party.

F.T. Yes, that was funny, but I didn't care for Alastair Sim in the role of Jane Wyman's colorful father. I objected to the actor as well as to the character.

A.H. Here again is the trouble with shooting a film in England. They all tell you, "He's one of our best actors; you've got to have him in your picture." It's that old local and national feeling, that insular mentality again. Aside from that, I had lots of problems with Jane Wyman.

F.T. It occurred to me that you might have chosen her because of her resemblance to your daughter, Patricia Hitchcock. As a matter of fact, I got the impression that the whole film was somehow a paternal, a family, picture.

A.H. Not exactly! I ran into great difficulties with Jane. In her disguise as a lady's maid, she

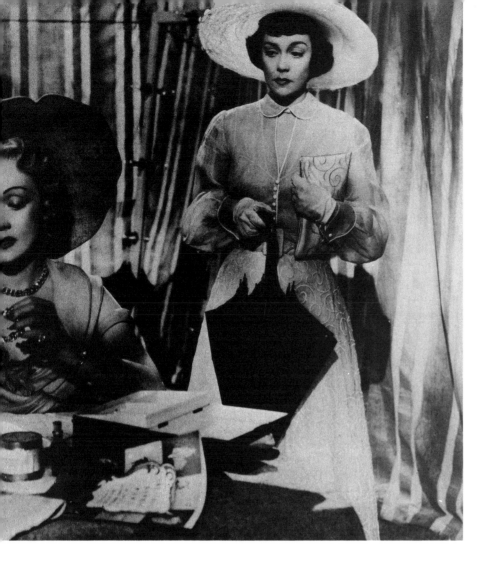

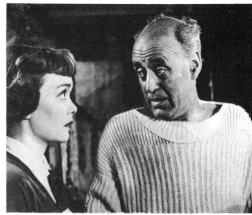

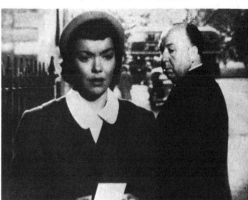

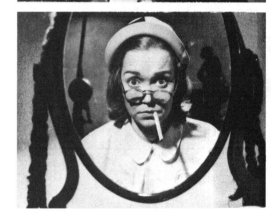

should have been rather unglamorous; after all, she was supposed to be impersonating an unattractive maid. But every time she saw the rushes and how she looked alongside Marlene Dietrich, she would burst into tears. She couldn't accept the idea of her face being in character, while Dietrich looked so glamorous, so she kept improving her appearance every day and that's how she failed to maintain the character.

F.T. Applying the yardstick you used a few days ago, it seems to me that the reason for which the story is of no interest is that none of the people in it are ever in real danger.

A.H. I became aware of that before the shooting was completed, but by then it was too late to do anything about it. Why are none of the people ever in danger? Because we're telling a story in which the villains themselves are

afraid. The great weakness of the picture is that it breaks an unwritten law: The more successful the villain, the more successful the picture. That's a cardinal rule, and in this picture the villain was a flop!

F.T. The better the villain, the better the picture . . . that's an excellent formula! It's true that the reason why *Notorious*, *Shadow of a Doubt*, and *Strangers on a Train* were so great is that Claude Rains, Joseph Cotten, and Robert Walker were your three best villains.

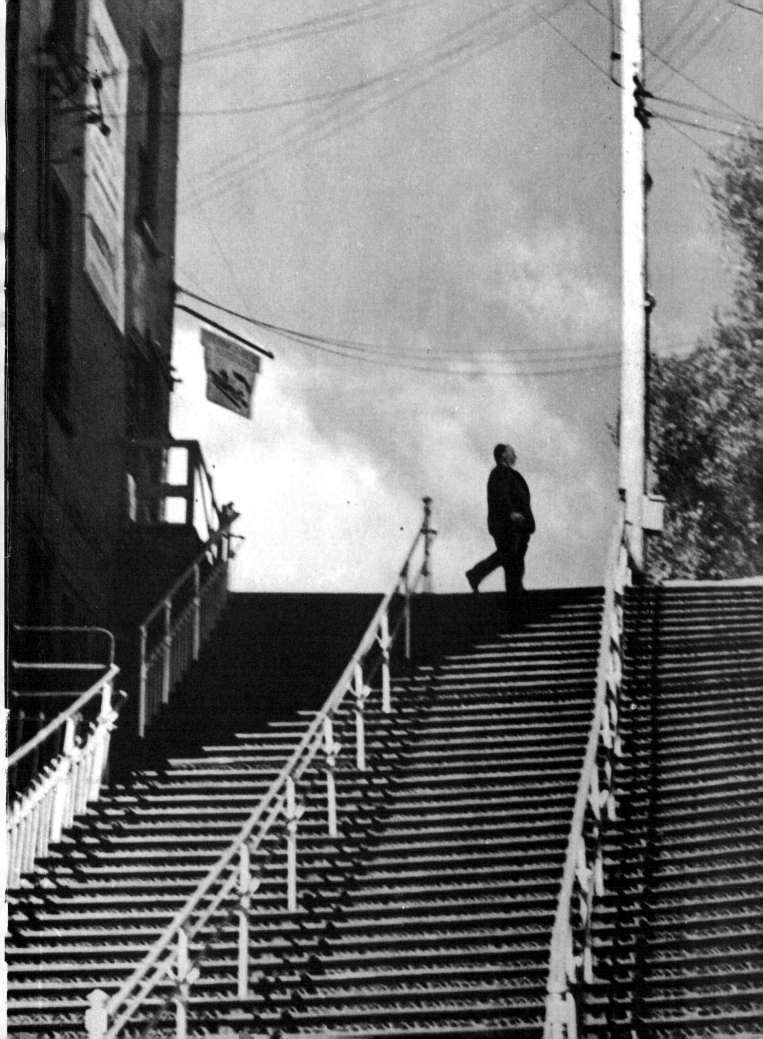

SPECTACULAR COMEBACK VIA "STRANGERS ON A TRAIN" ■ A MONOPOLY ON THE SUSPENSE GENRE ■ THE LITTLE MAN WHO CRAWLED ■ A BITCHY WIFE ■ "I CONFESS" ■ A "BARBARIC SOPHISTICATE" ■ THE SANCTITY OF CONFESSION ■ EXPERIENCE ALONE IS NOT ENOUGH ■ FEAR OF THE POLICE ■ STORY OF A "MÉNAGE À TROIS" ■

10

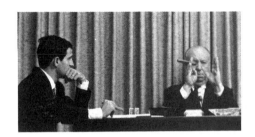

FRANÇOIS TRUFFAUT. Well, this brings us to 1950, when your situation is anything but brilliant. It's very much the same as in 1933, when, right after *Waltzes from Vienna*, your prestige was re-established by *The Man Who Knew Too Much*. Now again, the consecutive failures of *Under Capricorn* and *Stage Fright* will be followed by a spectacular comeback via *Strangers on a Train*.

ALFRED HITCHCOCK. You might say that I again applied that old "run for cover" rule. For your information, *Strangers on a Train* wasn't an assignment, but a novel that I selected myself. I felt this was the right kind of material for me to work with.

F.T. I've read it; it's a good novel, but there must have been lots of problems in adapting it

to the screen.

A.H. There were—and that raises another point. Whenever I collaborate with a writer who, like myself, specializes in mystery, thriller, or suspense, things don't seem to work out too well.

F.T. You're referring to Raymond Chandler?

A.H. Right; our association didn't work out at all. We'd sit together and I would say, "Why not do it this way?" and he'd answer, "Well, if you can puzzle it out, what do you need me for?" The work he did was no good and I ended up with Czenzi Ormonde, a woman writer who was one of Ben Hecht's assistants. When I completed the treatment, the head of Warner's tried

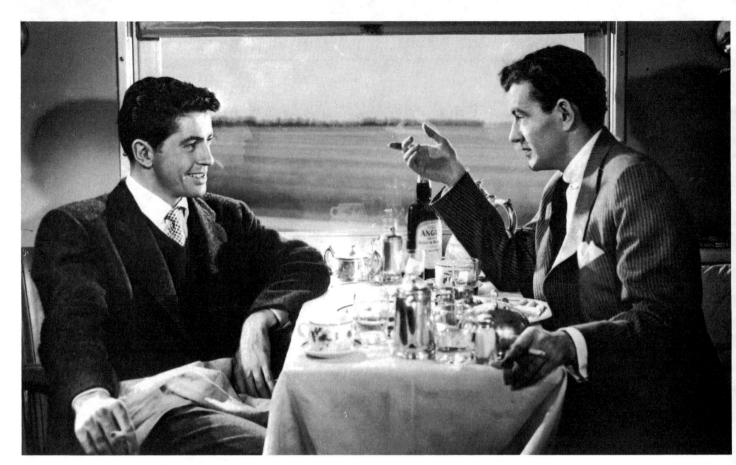

The beginning of *Strangers on a Train*—
the meeting of Guy and Bruno (Farley Granger and Robert Walker).

to find someone to do the dialogue, and very few writers would touch it. None of them thought it was any good.*

---

* On a train, Guy (Farley Granger), a champion tennis player, is approached by Bruno (Robert Walker), a fellow passenger who is a fan of his. Bruno, who seems to know all about Guy's personal life, proposes a friendly arrangement for an exchange of killings: Bruno will get rid of Guy's wife, who refuses to give him the divorce he wants in order to get remarried, if Guy, in return, will murder Bruno's overstrict father. Guy indignantly rejects the insane proposal, but Bruno, disregarding the rebuff, proceeds with his part of the plan, strangling Guy's wife to death in an amusement park.

When the police question Guy, he is unable to provide a solid alibi. Because of his fame and his engagement to a prominent senator's daughter, they decide to keep him under discreet observation.

Bruno contacts Guy, demanding that he now carry out his part of the so-called bargain. Guy is evasive, but his guilty knowledge of the criminal's identity makes his behavior increasingly suspicious to the police.

To get even for what he regards as a failure to honor their contract, Bruno decides to compromise Guy by placing the tennis player's lighter at the scene of the crime. Guy, who is scheduled to play an important match that day, must race against time to catch up with Bruno before he can carry out his threat.

The picture ends with Bruno crushed to death by a runaway carrousel and the discovery of evidence clearly establishing Guy's innocence.

F.T.   I'm not at all surprised; it's often occurred to me that had I read the story, the chances are I wouldn't have cared for it. Here is a case where you really have to see the picture. As a matter of fact, I think that the same story made by someone else wouldn't have been any good at all. Particularly when you consider the many Hitchcock emulators whose attempts at the thriller genre have been disastrous.

A.H.   It's been my good fortune to have something of a monopoly on the genre: nobody else seems to take much interest in the rules for that form.

F.T.   What rules?

A.H.   I'm talking about the rules of suspense. That's why I've more or less had the field to myself. Selznick claimed I was the only director whom he could trust completely, but when I worked for him, he complained about what he called my "goddamn jigsaw cutting." I used to

194

shoot the one piece of film in such a way that no one else could put the pieces together properly; the only way they could be edited was to follow exactly what I had in mind in the shooting stages. Selznick comes from the school of film-makers who like to have lots of footage to play around with in the cutting room. Working as I do, you're sure that no one in the studio is going to take over and ruin your film. That's the reason I won out in the argument over *Suspicion*.

F.T.   One senses that control in your pictures; it's obvious that each shot has been made in a specific way, from a specific angle, and to run for a specific length of time. The only exceptions, possibly, are courtroom scenes or scenes that require crowds.

A.H.   That's inevitable, it can't be helped. That's what happened with the tennis match in *Strangers on a Train*, and it shows the risk in overshooting material. There's too much footage for you to handle by yourself; you turn it over to the cutter to sort it out, but you never know what's been left unused. That's the risk.

F.T.   One of the best things in *Strangers on a Train* is the exposition, with the follow shots on feet going one way and then the other. There are also the crisscrossing rails. There's a sort of symbolic effect in the way they meet and separate, and that's also true of the direction arrows in *I Confess*. You often open your pictures on a symbolic note.

A.H.   The direction arrows exist in Quebec; they use them to indicate one-way streets. The shots of the rails in *Strangers on a Train* were the logical extension of the motif with the feet. Practically, I couldn't have done anything else.

F.T.   Why not?

A.H.   The camera practically grazed the rails because it couldn't be raised; you see, I didn't want to go higher until the feet of Farley Granger and Robert Walker bump together in the railroad car.

F.T.   That's what I mean. That accidental collision of the two men's feet is the point of departure for their whole relationship, and the concept is sustained by deliberately refraining from showing their faces up to that point. In the same light the separating rails suggest the idea of divergent courses—two different ways of life.

A.H.   Naturally, there is that as well. Isn't it a fascinating design? One could study it forever.

F.T.   In several of your pictures, I've noticed, you will enhance a surprise situation with an additional twist; in other words—and I'm not thinking only of *Psycho*—you will use a bit of trickery to create a small suspenseful diversion so that the surprise that comes immediately afterward is even more startling.

A.H.   What do you have in mind?

F.T.   Well, in *Strangers on a Train*, Farley Granger agrees to kill Robert Walker's father, although, in fact, he really intends to warn the old man against his son. So Granger breaks into the house at night; the father's room is upstairs. Now, if he simply tiptoed up the staircase, the public would try to figure out what's going to happen next, and they might even guess that upstairs Granger will find Bruno instead of his father. So you dispose of that anticipation by creating a suspenseful diversion in the form of a huge dog in the middle of the staircase. In this way the question becomes: Will the dog let Farley Granger get by without biting him or won't he? Isn't that right?

A.H.   Yes, in that scene we first have a *suspense* effect, through the threatening dog, and later on we have a *surprise* effect when the person in the room turns out to be Robert Walker instead of his father. I remember we went to a lot of trouble getting that dog to lick Farley Granger's hand.

F.T.   I believe you used a trick shot there. Isn't the image slowed down?

A.H.   Yes, I think that's so.

F.T.   One of the most remarkable aspects of

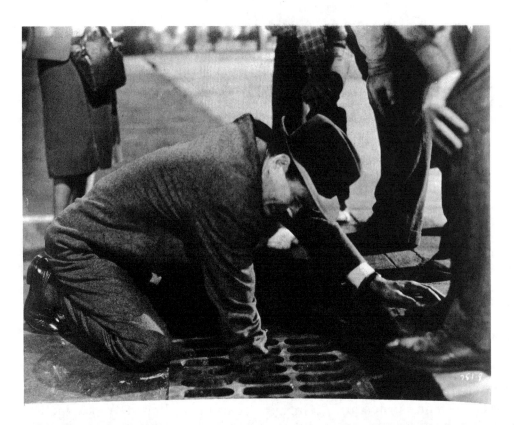

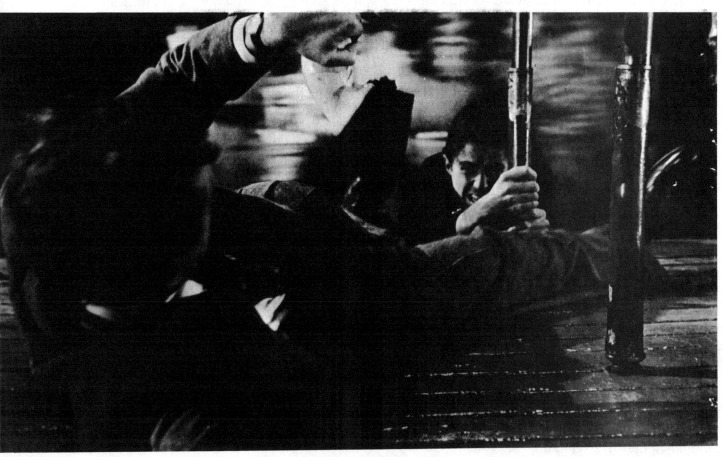

the picture is the bold manipulation of time, the way in which it's contracted and dilated. First, there's Farley Granger's frantic haste to win his tennis match, and then Robert Walker's panic when he accidentally drops Granger's lighter in a manhole. In both these scenes, time is tightly compressed—like a lemon. Then, after Walker gets to the island, you let go, because he can't proceed with his plan to frame Granger in broad daylight. So when he asks one of the men in the amusement park, "At what time does it get dark around here?" everything is decompressed. Real-life time takes over while he waits for nightfall. That dramatic play with time is really stunning.

On the other hand, I have some reservations on the final scene, when the carrousel runs amok, though I understand the reason for it. I guess you needed a paroxysm, is that it?

A.H.   That's true. After so many colorful parts, it seems to me it would have been poor form not to have, at this point, what musicians refer to as a coda. But my hands still sweat when I think of that scene today. You know, that little man actually crawled under that spinning carrousel. If he'd raised his head by an inch, he'd have been killed. I'll never do anything like that again.

F.T.   But when the carrousel breaks . . .

A.H.   That was a miniature blown up on a big screen. The big difficulty with that scene was that the screen had to be angled differently for each shot. We had to move the projector every time the angle changed because many of the shots of the merry-go-round were low camera setups. We spent a lot of time setting the screen in line with the camera lens. Anyway, for the carrousel breakdown we used a miniature blown up on a big screen and we put live people in front of the screen.

F.T.   There's a certain resemblance between the situations of the heroes of *Strangers on a Train* and *A Place in the Sun*. I couldn't help wondering whether the Patricia Highsmith novel was influenced by Theodore Dreiser's *An American Tragedy*.

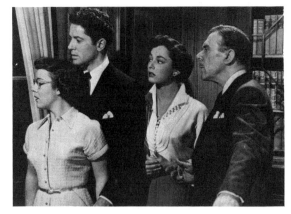

From left to right: Patricia Hitchcock, Farley Granger, Ruth Roman and Leo G. Carroll.

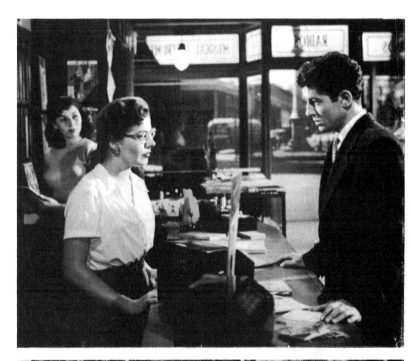

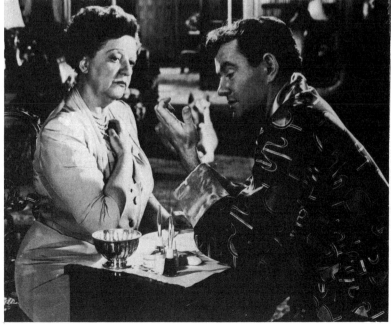

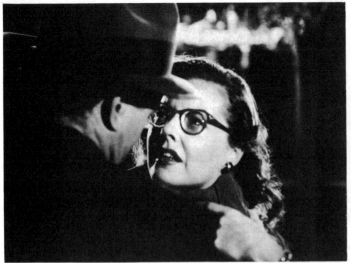

Bruno, pretending to strangle a society lady, is troubled by Patricia Hitchcock's glasses.

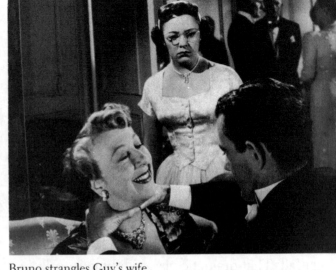

Bruno strangles Guy's wife.

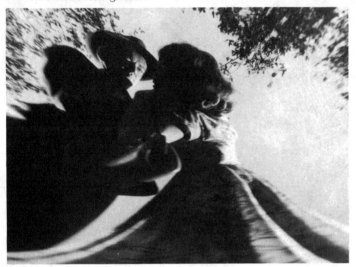

He begins to strangle the woman in earnest.

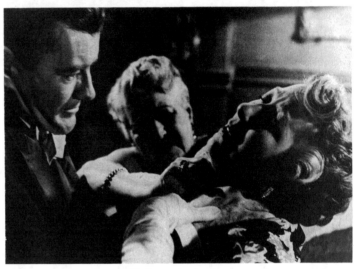

The murder is reflected in the victim's glasses.

A.H. It's quite possible. As I see it, the flaws of *Strangers on a Train* were the ineffectiveness of the two main actors and the weakness of the final script. If the writing of the dialogue had been better, we'd have had stronger characterizations. The great problem with this type of picture, you see, is that your main characters sometimes tend to become mere figures.

F.T. Algebraic figures? You've just raised what I believe is the key dilemma for all directors: a strong film situation involving dull characters, or else the characters are subtle, but the situation in which they move is a static one. All your movies, I think, are hinged on strong situations, and *Strangers on a Train* is actually

mapped out like a diagram. This degree of stylization is so exciting to the mind and to the eye that it's fascinating even to a mass audience.

A.H. I was quite pleased with the over-all form of the film and with the secondary characters. I particularly liked the woman who was murdered; you know, the bitchy wife who worked in a record shop; Bruno's mother was good, too—she was just as crazy as her son.

F.T. The only flaw, to my mind, is the film's leading lady, Ruth Roman.

A.H. Well, she was Warner Brothers' leading lady, and I had to take her on because I had no other actors from that company. But I must say that I wasn't too pleased with Farley Granger; he's a good actor, but I would have liked to see William Holden in the part because he's stronger. In this kind of story the stronger the hero, the more effective the situation.

F.T.   Yet, since Granger was appealing in *Rope* and not particularly appealing in *Strangers on a Train*, I assumed this was intentional, that you meant him to be seen as an opportunistic playboy. By contrast, Robert Walker gives a rather poetic portrayal; he's undoubtedly more attractive. There is a distinct impression that you preferred the villain.

A.H.   Of course, no doubt about it.

F.T.   In many of your pictures—and *Strangers on a Train* is a case in point—there are, aside from coincidences and implausibles, many elements that are arbitrary and unjustified. And yet, in the light of a cinematic logic that is strictly personal, you impose them in such a way that once they're on the screen, these are the very elements that become the film's strong points.

A.H.   The cinematic logic is to follow the rules of suspense. Here we have one of those stories that automatically bring on that old complaint: "But why didn't he tell the police all about it?" Don't forget that we've clearly established the reasons for which he can't go to the police.

F.T.   There can be no argument about that. This picture, just like *Shadow of a Doubt*, is systematically built around the figure "two." Here again, both characters might very well have had the same name. Whether it's Guy or Bruno, it's obviously a single personality split in two.

A.H.   That's right. Though Bruno has killed Guy's wife, for Guy, it's just as if he had committed the murder himself. As for Bruno, he's clearly a psychopath.

———————————

F.T.   I understand you're not too happy with your next picture, *I Confess*. The scenario be-

longs pretty much to the same family as that of *Strangers on a Train*. In fact, almost all of your films center on an interchangeable killing, with one character who has committed the crime and another who might just as well have been guilty of it. I know that you were rather surprised when the French critics pointed this out to you in 1953, and yet it is a fact that almost all of your films actually tell the same story. *I Confess* is another variation on the same motif, and I'm curious to know how the original, a rather mediocre play called *Nos Deux Consciences*, and written by Paul Anthelme in 1902, reached you in the first place.

A.H.   Louis Verneuil sold it to me.

F.T.   I suppose he told you the story before you bought the property?

A.H.   Yes, he did.

F.T.   Well, he told it to you because he thought it would appeal to you, isn't that so?

A.H.   I imagine it is.

F.T.   Louis Verneuil might have tried to promote one of his own plays or he might have told you about any one of the many others he knows about. What I'm trying to bring out is that the story he happened to single out closely resembles your other films.

A.H.   What he said was: "I've got a story in mind that might interest you." Most of the material submitted to me is generally all wrong for me. An agent will say, "I've got a property that's ideal for you," and generally, it turns out to be a gangster story, something about professional criminals, or a whodunit, the kind of material I never touch. Anyway, Verneuil came along with this play, and I guess he must have done a good sales job, because I bought it! Now, when I buy a story, that doesn't mean I'm taking on the theme as well. They tell me the story, and if the subject is suitable and the situation lends itself to what I want, the theme of the film will be worked out later on.

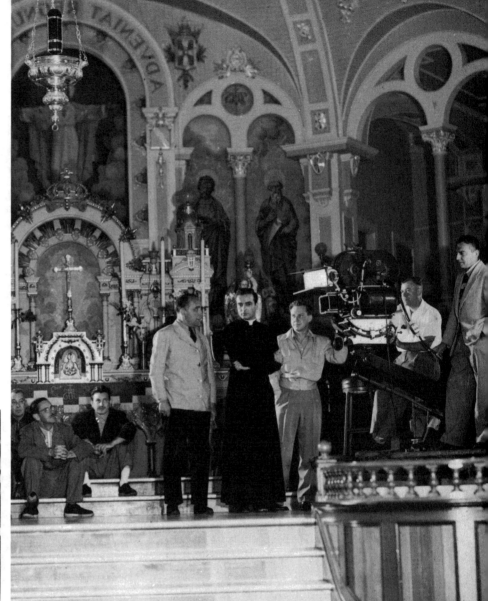

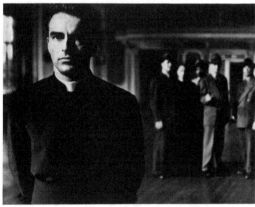

F.T. That's a rather peculiar approach, but since it works, I guess it's logical. You must have run into some ticklish problems in trying to reconcile the criminal and religious elements in the screenplay.*

---

* Caught in the act of stealing, Otto Keller (Otto E. Hasse), a German refugee who is the sexton of a church in Quebec, murders his victim, a lawyer named Vilette. Afterward, Keller confesses his crime to Father Michael (Montgomery Clift).

As it happens, Father Michael was being blackmailed by Vilette over a love affair prior to his ordination as a priest and Keller had worn a cassock during the crime. These coincidences, together with the fact that Father Michael is unable to provide an alibi for the night of the crime, add up to a strong web of circumstantial evidence against him.

When the police suspicions lead to an indictment and then to his trial, Father Michael, bound by his holy vows on the inviolability of confession, makes no move to clear himself. He will be

A.H. As a matter of fact, it was difficult, and the final result was rather heavy-handed. The whole treatment was lacking in humor and subtlety. I don't mean that the film itself should have been humorous, but my own approach should have been more ironic, as in *Psycho*—a serious story told with tongue in cheek.

F.T. That's an interesting distinction because it's generally misunderstood by the critics.

acquitted by virtue of reasonable doubt, but the hostile courtroom crowd reviles him. The truth comes out when Keller's wife turns against him. As he attempts to escape, the police shoot him down, and the killer, before dying, makes his final confession to Father Michael.

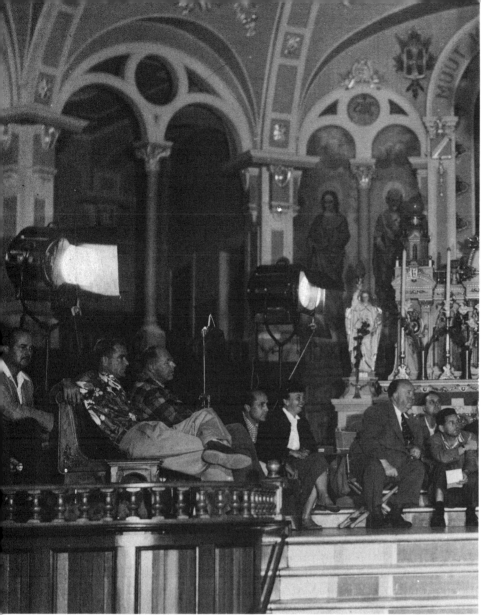

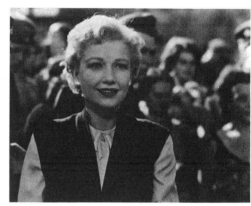

When the content of a film is funny, they will go along with you, but when you handle a serious subject in a humorous way, they don't always see what you're driving at. *The Birds* is a case in point: The material is serious but your approach to it is ironic.

A.H.   As a matter of fact, whenever we're working out a screenplay, we'll often say, "Now, wouldn't this be a funny way to kill him off?"

F.T.   That's why, in your films, the potent elements are neither solemn nor offensive. Of course, to enjoy making terrifying films is bound to suggest a form of intellectual sadism, and yet

it can also be quite wholesome.*

A.H.   I think so, too. A mother sometimes demonstrates her love for her baby by playing a game that consists of frightening the infant with gestures and sounds like "Boo, brr . . ." The baby may be scared, but it will laugh and wave, and as soon as it can talk, it will call for more. One English newspaperwoman said that *Psycho*

---

* During a Hollywood press conference in 1947, Alfred Hitchcock stated: "I aim to provide the public with beneficial shocks. Civilization has become so protective that we're no longer able to get our goose bumps instinctively. The only way to remove the numbness and revive our moral equilibrium is to use artificial means to bring about the shock. The best way to achieve that, it seems to me, is through a movie."

was the film of a "barbaric sophisticate." Who knows, she may be right.

F.T. In any case, it's an interesting definition.

A.H. And probably true at that. If *Psycho* had been intended as a serious picture, it would have been shown as a clinical case with no mystery or suspense. The material would have been used as the documentation of a case history. We've already mentioned that total plausibility and authenticity merely add up to a documentary. In the mystery and suspense genre, a tongue-in-cheek approach is indispensable. I feel that both *I Confess* and *The Wrong Man* suffer from a lack of humor. The only question then is whether one should always have a sense of humor in dealing with a serious subject. It seems to me that some of my British films were too light and some of my American movies have been too heavy-handed, but it's the most difficult thing in the world to control that so as to get just the right dosage. It's only after the picture's done that one can judge that properly. Do you feel that there's a connection between my Jesuit upbringing and the heavy-handedness of *I Confess?*

F.T. Not necessarily. I attributed that to the austerity of the Canadian climate, which is further weighted down by the Teutonic gravity of Otto Keller and his wife.

A.H. Yes, there is a certain off balance there, and we run into it every time a story takes place in a mixed ethnic community: Britishers with Americans or else Americans with French Canadians. It's also true for pictures that are filmed in a foreign country when all the characters are English-speaking; I've never been able to get used to that.
Aside from that, I didn't want Anne Baxter to play the feminine lead; I wanted Anita Bjork, who had played *Miss Julie.* However, Warner Brothers decided against her, sent Anita Bjork back to her fiords, and I was informed by a phone call that Anne Baxter had been assigned to the picture. I met her for the first time a week before the shooting, in the dining room of Quebec's Hotel Château Frontenac. When you compare Anita Bjork and Anne Baxter, wouldn't you say that was a pretty awkward substitution?

F.T. Yes, I would agree on that, but I must say that Montgomery Clift was truly remarkable. Throughout the picture his attitude as well as his expression is consistent. He has an air of total dignity at all times, and it's only through

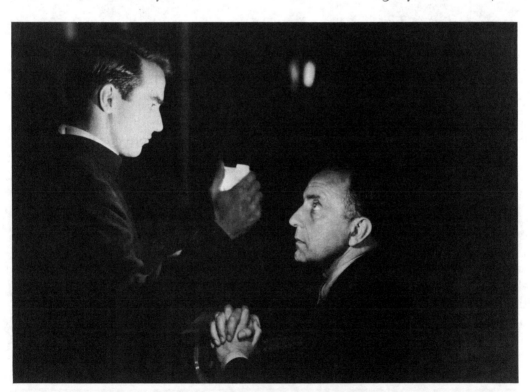

his eyes that we sense his bewilderment at all the things that are happening to him.

The picture, once again, is on the theme of the transference of guilt, which, in this case, is reinforced by religion and an absolute concept of confession. From the moment that Montgomery Clift accepts Otto Keller's confession of the crime, it's as if he himself had become a party to it. And that's the way Keller sees it.

A.H.   I think that's a fundamental fact: Any priest who receives the confession of any killer becomes an accessory after the fact.

F.T.   Certainly, but the trouble, I think, is that the public doesn't realize that. People like the picture, they're absorbed in it, but they keep on hoping that Clift will speak up, which, of course, is a misconception. I feel sure that you didn't expect that sort of reaction.

A.H.   I agree with you. What's more, aside from the public, there were many of the critics who apparently felt that for a priest to guard a secret at the risk of his own life was absurd.

F.T.   I don't think that's what shocked them, but rather the extraordinary coincidence at the beginning.

A.H.   Do you mean when the killer puts on the priest's robe?

F.T.   No, that's the postulate. The coincidence I have in mind is about Vilette, the victim. Isn't it a rather formidable coincidence that the murderer who has killed him in order to rob him should happen to confess his crime to the very priest who was being blackmailed by the dead man?

A.H.   Yes, I suppose so.

F.T.   I think this is the coincidence that really disturbs our friends, the plausibilists. It's not merely an unlikely situation, it's an exceptional situation. In fact, it's the height of the exceptional.

A.H.   Let's say it comes under the heading of an old-fashioned plot. And while we're on the subject, I should like to ask you a question. Why has it become old-fashioned to tell a story, to use a plot? I believe that there are no more plots in the recent French films.

F.T.   Well, that isn't systematic, it's simply a trend that reflects the evolution of the public, the impact of television, and the increasing use of documentary and press materials in the entertainment field. All of these factors have a bearing on the current attitude toward fiction; people seem to be moving away from that form and to be rather leery of the old patterns.

A.H.   In other words, the trend away from the plot is due to the progress in communications? Well, that's possible. I feel that way myself, and nowadays I'd prefer to build a film around a situation rather than a plot.

———————

F.T.   We were talking about *I Confess*, and I should like to get back to it. We agreed that the public was irritated with the plot because they kept on hoping that Montgomery Clift would speak up. Would you consider that a weakness of the screenplay?

A.H.   It certainly is a disadvantage. If the basic idea is not acceptable to the public, it compromises the whole picture. And this brings up another generalization: To put a situation into a film simply because you yourself can vouch for its authenticity, either because you've experienced it or because you've heard of it, simply isn't good enough. You may feel sure of yourself because you can always say, "This is true, I've seen it." You can argue as much as you like, but the public or critics still won't accept it. So we have to go along with the idea that truth is stranger than fiction. Suppose you were to introduce a miser or a recluse like one of the Collier brothers in a picture. After all, they were real, I knew someone just like that, yet I could never put him in a picture because no matter how much I insist that such a character exists, the public will remain skeptical because they don't know him.

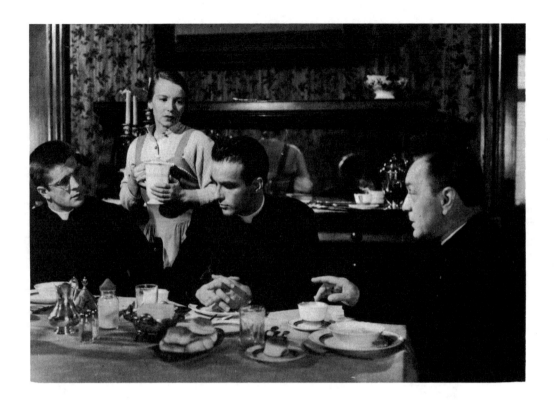

F.T.   In other words, your own knowledge or experience of out-of-the-way things can merely serve to suggest a similar idea, one that can be worked into a film so that it will be accepted.

A.H.   That's the trouble with *I Confess.* We Catholics know that a priest cannot disclose the secret of the confessional, but the Protestants, the atheists, and the agnostics all say, "Ridiculous! No man would remain silent and sacrifice his life for such a thing."

F.T.   Then would you say that the basic concept of the film was wrong?

A.H.   That's right; we shouldn't have made the picture.

F.T.   Just the same, there are some very good things in it. One of them is the way Montgomery Clift is always seen walking; it's a forward motion that shapes the whole film. It also concretizes the concept of his integrity. The scene at the breakfast table is especially Hitchcockian. Otto Keller's wife, serving coffee to all the priests, keeps on passing back and forth behind Montgomery Clift, while she's trying to figure out what he plans to do. The dialogue between the priests is completely innocuous. It's only through the image that one understands that the essential of the scene is happening between the woman and Montgomery Clift. I don't know of any other director who can successfully convey that, or who even tries to.

A.H.   You mean the sound track says one thing while the image says something else? That's a fundamental of film direction. Isn't it exactly the way it is in real life? People don't always express their inner thoughts to one another; a conversation may be quite trivial, but often the eyes will reveal what a person really thinks or feels.

F.T.   Yes, in this sense, your film-making is definitely realistic.
By the way, the turning point in Otto Keller's attitude is when he instructs his wife not to clean up the bloodstained cassock. At that moment he relinquishes any claim to being a naïve and deeply religious man: he is deliberately trying to destroy his confessor and benefactor; he's become diabolic and evil.

A.H. That's the idea. Up to that point he had behaved in good faith.

F.T. Brian Aherne's characterization as the prosecutor was quite interesting. The first time we see him, he's playfully balancing a knife and fork on a glass; the next time he's lying on the floor, balancing a glass of water on his forehead. I had the feeling that both incidents were re-

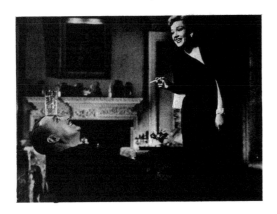

lated to the idea of equilibrium, that they were put there to suggest that in his scale of values, justice was merely a parlor game.

A.H. Yes, that's the general idea. You may recall that in *Murder* I showed the defense attorney and the district attorney having lunch together during the trial recess. In *The Paradine Case* the judge, who has just sentenced Alida Valli to death by hanging, is having a quiet meal at home with his wife. You feel like saying to him, "Tell me, your Honor, what do you think about when you go home after having sentenced a woman to death?" And Charles Laughton's cold, unruffled manner suggests that his answer to such a question would be: "I simply don't think about it!" Another illustration of the same idea is the way the two inspectors in *Blackmail*, after locking the prisoner in his cell, go to the men's room to wash their hands, just like any two office workers. As a matter of fact, I do the same thing. When I shoot a terrifying scene of *Psycho* or *The Birds*, I don't go home to have nightmares all night long. It's simply another day's work; I've done my best and that's all there is to it. In fact, although I'm very serious during the shooting, I might even feel like laughing

about those things afterward. And that's something that bothers me because, at the same time, I can't help imagining how it would feel to be in the victim's place. We come back again to my eternal fear of the police. I've always felt a complete identification with the feelings of a person who's arrested, taken to the police station in a police van and who, through the bars of the moving vehicle, can see people going to the theater, coming out of a bar, and enjoying the comforts of everyday living; I can even picture the driver joking with his police partner, and I feel terrible about it.

F.T. Yes, but what appealed to me in those two instances of equilibrium I mentioned is that they're related to the concept of the scale of justice. And since your pictures are very elaborate throughout . . .

A.H. They're elaborate in an oblique way; yes, they are.

F.T. They're so elaborate that it's difficult to believe that these things just happen to be in your films. If so, they must be credited to a powerful cinematic instinct. Here's another instance of what I mean: When Montgomery Clift leaves the courtroom, he is surrounded by a hostile crowd of people in a lynching mood. And just behind Clift, next to Otto Keller's lovely wife, who is obviously upset, we see a fat and repulsive woman eating an apple and looking on with an expression of malevolent curiosity.

A.H. That's absolutely right; I especially worked that woman in there; I even showed her how to eat that apple.

F.T. Well, what I'm trying to bring out is that these elaborate details are generally overlooked by the public because all the attention is focused on the major characters in the scene. Therefore, you put them in for your own satisfaction and, of course, for the sake of enriching the film.

A.H. Well, we have to do those things; we fill the whole tapestry, and that's why people

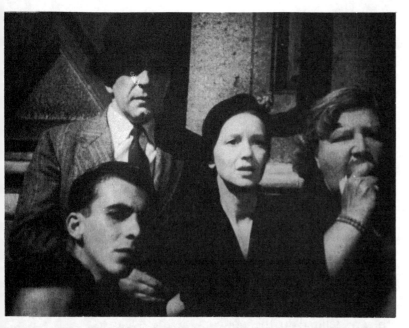

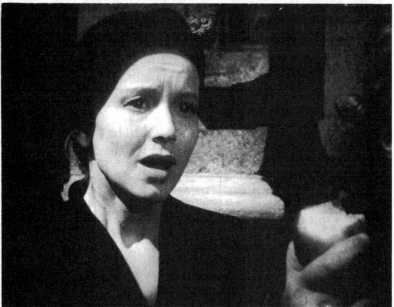

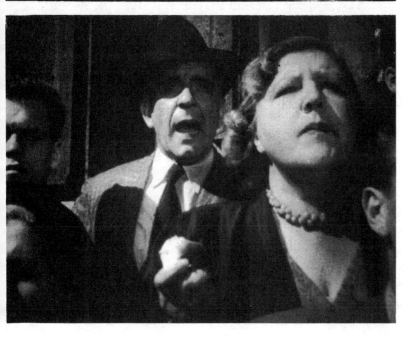

often feel they have to see the picture several times to take in all of these details. Even if some of them appear to be a waste of effort, they strengthen a picture. That's why, when these films are reissued several years later, they stand up so well; they're never out of date.

F.T. In *I Confess*, Montgomery Clift is cleared by the court of the charges against him. In this picture, as well as in several others, including *Vertigo*, although the defendant has been legally cleared, he will remain under a cloud because someone in the court may disapprove of the verdict.

A.H. That's very often the case when the circumstantial evidence is insufficient to warrant a conviction. In the courts of Scotland there's an additional verdict: Not proven.

F.T. In France the expression is: Acquittal by benefit of the doubt.

A.H. There was a very famous trial that took place around 1890, and I often thought it might make a good picture, but since *Jules and Jim*, I've decided to drop it. You see, it also involves a *ménage à trois*. It's a true story. An elderly husband and his young wife, Mr. and Mrs. Bartlett, had a living arrangement in which Reverend Dyson, the local parson, his smoking jacket, and his slippers were part of the same household. The husband would go off to work and the parson would sit and read poetry to the wife, with her head in his lap. To me there was a comical connotation, and I wanted to shoot a scene showing the parson making violent love to the young woman while the husband, sitting in his rocking chair and smoking his pipe, looked on. I would have shown him smoking very contentedly; from time to time he would pull away at his pipe, making little noises that sound like kisses. Anyway, let me tell you the rest of the story.
One day, when the parson was out, the husband told his wife that he wanted to share her favors. Her answer was something like, "Nothing doing. You gave me to him and I can't go back to you now." Anyway, eventually, the husband, Mr. Bartlett, died of chloroform poisoning.

Mrs. Bartlett and Reverend Dyson were arrested for the murder.

Dyson told the police how Mrs. Bartlett, a very small and pretty young woman, had asked him to buy two bottles of chloroform, and the empty bottles were found. The autopsy showed that Mr. Bartlett had died in a recumbent position and that his stomach had been burned while he was in that position. This meant that he could not have absorbed the chloroform while standing up, and that's the only thing they were able to establish.

The whole trial hinged on that point, with the medical experts trying to speculate on the manner of the victim's death, but they were never able to reach a definite conclusion. It was established that Mr. Bartlett couldn't possibly have been asleep while they poured the chloroform down his mouth because swallowing is a voluntary action. Besides, had they poured the chloroform in while he was asleep, it would have gone into his windpipe, and his lungs were clear. Still, there was clear evidence that the man had not committed suicide. The verdict of *I Confess* was inspired by the verdict handed down in that case. The jury said that although there were strong suspicions against Mrs. Bartlett, since there was no proof as to how the chloroform had been administered, she was declared "not guilty."

There must have been a good deal of sympathy for the defendant because the verdict was greeted with a roar of applause in the courtroom. And that evening, when Mrs. Bartlett and her lawyer went to the theater, the public gave them a standing ovation as they came in.

There's an interesting footnote to the case. Several books were written on it, and one very famous British pathologist wrote an article which said that "now that Mrs. Bartlett has her freedom, we feel that, in the interests of science, she should tell us how she did it."

F.T. To what do you attribute the sympathy of the jurors and of the general public for Mrs. Bartlett?

A.H. It seems that she hadn't married for love and that the marriage, in fact, was arranged for her. It was believed that she was the illegitimate daughter of an important British statesman and she was married off at the age of fifteen or sixteen, and then, right after the wedding, she was shipped off to complete her schooling. Anyway, in respect to the film, I must admit that the only reason the idea appealed to me was the scene I described to you: the husband puffing away contentedly at his pipe!

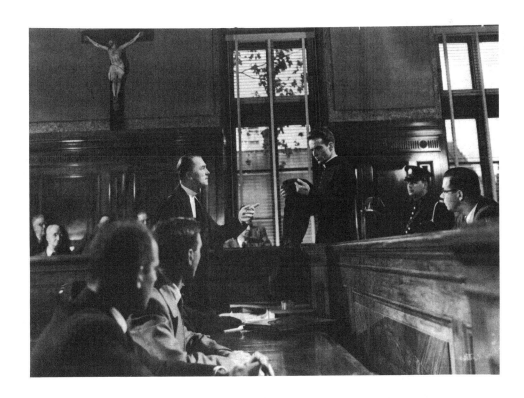

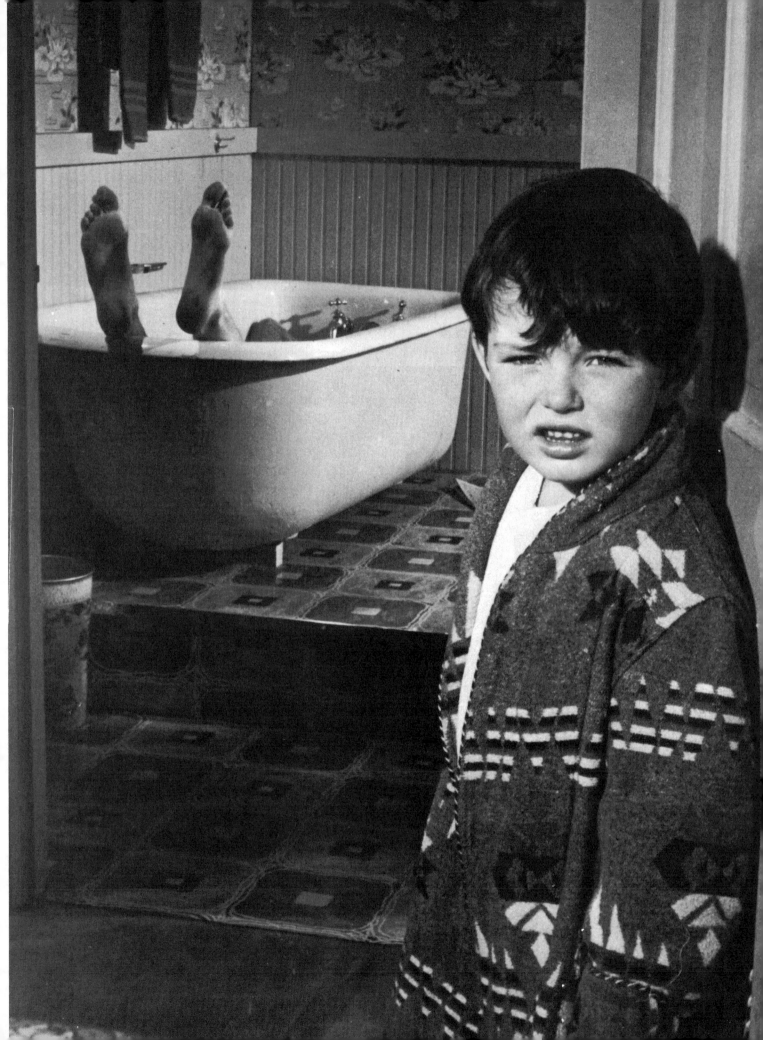

"DIAL M FOR MURDER" ▪ FILMING IN 3-D ▪ THE THEATER CONFINES THE ACTION ▪ "REAR WINDOW" ▪ THE KULESHOV EXPERIMENT ▪ WE ARE ALL VOYEURS ▪ DEATH OF A SMALL DOG ▪ THE SIZE OF THE IMAGE HAS A DRAMATIC PURPOSE ▪ THE SURPRISE KISS VERSUS THE SUSPENSE KISS ▪ THE PATRICK MAHON CASE AND THE DR. CRIPPEN CASE ▪ "TO CATCH A THIEF" ▪ SEX ON THE SCREEN ▪ "THE TROUBLE WITH HARRY" ▪ THE HUMOR OF UNDERSTATEMENT ▪ "THE MAN WHO KNEW TOO MUCH" ▪ A KNIFE IN THE BACK ▪ THE CLASH OF CYMBALS ▪

11

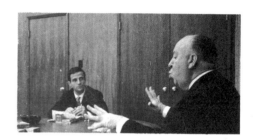

FRANÇOIS TRUFFAUT. Now, we come to 1953, the year in which you made *Dial M for Murder.*

ALFRED HITCHCOCK. There isn't very much we can say about that one, is there?

F.T. I'm not so sure about that. Would you say this picture was made because it happened to be convenient?

A.H. I was running for cover again. I had a contract with Warner's at the time and was working on a scenario called *The Bramble Bush.* It was the story of a man who stole another man's passport without knowing that the passport owner was wanted for murder. I worked on that for a while, but it wasn't any good. Just then I found out that Warner's had bought the rights to the Broadway stage hit *Dial M for Mur-*

der. I immediately said I'd take it because that was coasting, playing it safe.*

F.T. It was filmed very quickly, wasn't it?

A.H. In thirty-six days.

F.T. An interesting aspect is that the pic-

---

* A tennis player (Ray Milland), with no money of his own, is concerned over his wealthy wife's (Grace Kelly) interest in novelist Robert Cummings. He decides to murder her and blackmails an adventurer with a criminal record (Anthony Dawson) into becoming his active accomplice. The carefully worked-out plan calls for Dawson to strangle the wife at home while Milland establishes an alibi by being at a club during the killing.

But things go awry when the young woman unexpectedly manages to get out of the stranglehold. In the ensuing struggle she kills her attacker. Concealing his disappointment, the husband makes the best of the circumstances and comforts his distraught wife. But his overcooperative manner arouses the suspicions of a sharp police inspector who, with the help of the wife and her novelist friend, sets up a trap. The stratagem works and the picture winds up with the husband exposed as the author of the almost-perfect crime.

Opposite, young Jerry Mathers in *The Trouble with Harry.*

ture was shot in 3-D. In France, unfortunately, we only saw the flat version because the theater managers were too lazy to make the necessary arrangements for the distribution of Polaroid spectacles to the audiences.

A.H.   The impression of relief was especially in the low-angle shots. I had them make a pit so that the camera could be at floor level. Aside from that there were very few effects directly in relief.

F.T.   Among the objects projected in depth were a lamp, a flower vase, and particularly the scissors.

A.H.   Yes, when Grace Kelly is looking for a weapon to defend herself. There was another shot of the keyhole and that's all.

F.T.   Was the picture very faithful to the play?

A.H.   Yes. I've got a theory on the way they make pictures based on stage plays; they did it with silent pictures, too. Many film-makers would take a stage play and say, "I'm going to make this into a film." Then they would begin to "open it up." In other words, on the stage it was all confined to one set, and the idea was to do something that would take it away from the confined stage setting.

F.T.   In France we call that "ventilating the play."

A.H.   Well, that whole operation boils down

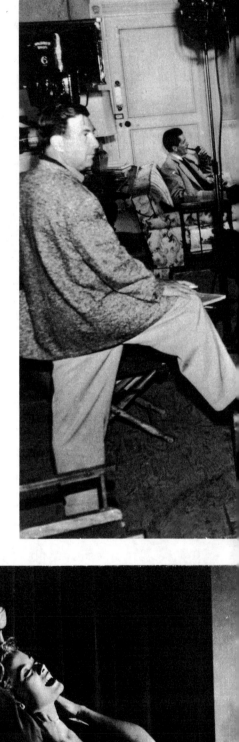

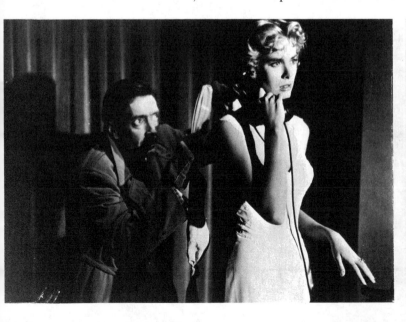

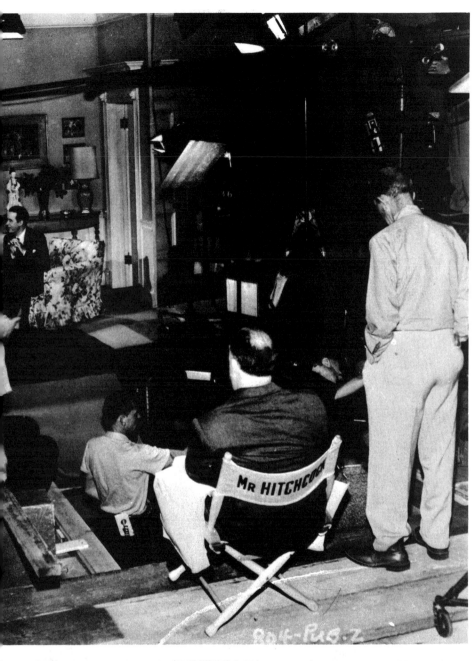

Grace Kelly succeeds in stabbing Anthony Dawson in the back with a pair of scissors after he tries to strangle her.

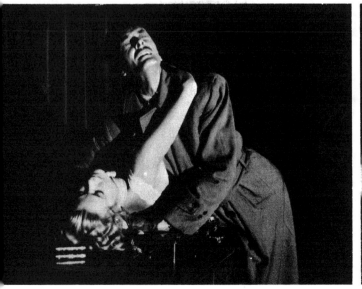

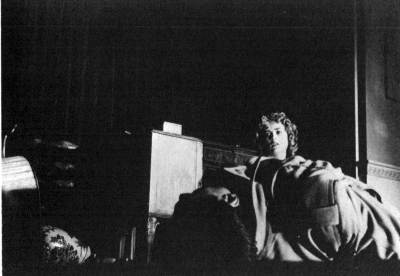

to very little. Let's say that in the play one of the characters arrives in a cab. In the film they will show the arrival of the cab, the person getting out and paying the driver, coming up the stairs, knocking at the door and then coming into the room, and this serves to introduce the long scene that takes place in the room. Sometimes, if a stage character has mentioned something about a trip, the film will show the journey in a flashback. This technique overlooks the fact that the basic quality of any play is precisely its confinement within the proscenium.

F.T.   As a matter of fact, that concentration is the most difficult thing to work out in a stage dramatization. And more often than not in the process of being transposed to the screen, the dramatic effectiveness of a play will be dissipated.

A.H.   Well, this is where the film-makers often go wrong, and what they get is simply some dull footage that's been added to the play artificially. Whereas in *Dial M for Murder*, I did my best to avoid going outside. It happened only two or three times, when the inspector had to verify something, and then, very briefly. I even had the floor made of real tiles so as to get the sound of the footsteps. In other words, what I did was to emphasize the theatrical aspects.

F.T.   The effort at stage realism was even

apparent in the sound track, which, in this respect, was far superior to *Juno and the Paycock* and to *Rope*.

A.H.   Definitely.

F.T.   And this would also explain why the trial was shown simply through a series of close-ups on Grace Kelly's face against a natural background and with color lights revolving behind her, rather than to show the whole courtroom.

A.H.   This way was more intimate, you see, so that the unity of emotion was maintained. If I'd had a courtroom built, people would have started to cough restlessly, thinking, "Now they're starting a second picture."
We did an interesting color experiment with Grace Kelly's clothing. I dressed her in very gay and bright colors at the beginning of the picture, and as the plot thickened, her clothes became gradually more somber.

F.T.   Before dropping *Dial M for Murder*, and particularly since we've discussed it as a minor effort, I should mention that this is one of the pictures I see over and over again. I enjoy it more every time I see it.
Basically, it's a dialogue picture, but the cutting, the rhythm, and the direction of the players are so polished that one listens to each sentence religiously. It isn't all that easy to command the

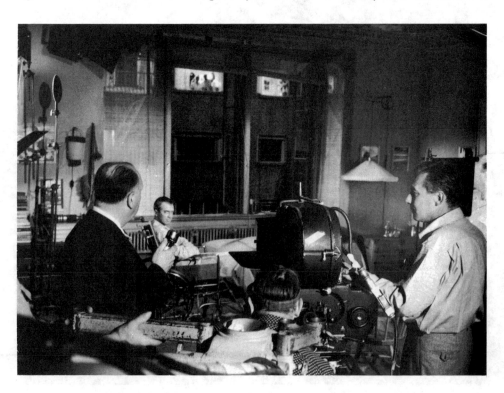

audience's undivided attention for a continuous dialogue. I suspect that here again the real achievement is that something very difficult has been carried out in a way that makes it seem quite easy.

And speaking of facility, I'm aware that it's easier to reply to criticism than to praise, but just the same, I would appreciate your comments.

A.H.   I just did my job, using cinematic means to narrate a story taken from a stage play. All of the action in *Dial M for Murder* takes place in a living room, but that doesn't matter. I could just as well have shot the whole film in a telephone booth. Let's imagine there's a couple in that booth. Their hands are touching, their lips meet, and accidentally one of them leans against the receiver, knocking it off the hook. Now, while they're unaware of it, the phone operator can listen in on their intimate conversation. The drama has taken a step forward. For

the audience, looking at the images, it should be the same as reading the opening paragraphs of a novel or hearing the expositional dialogue of the stage play. You might say that a filmmaker can use a telephone booth pretty much in the same way a novelist uses a blank piece of paper.

———

F.T.   My two favorite Hitchcock pictures are *Notorious* and the one we are going to talk about now, *Rear Window*. I know it's based on a Cornell Woolrich short story, but I've never read it.

A.H.   It dealt with an invalid who was confined to his room. I think there was a man to look after him, but who wasn't there all the time. The story described all the things the invalid saw from his window and showed how his

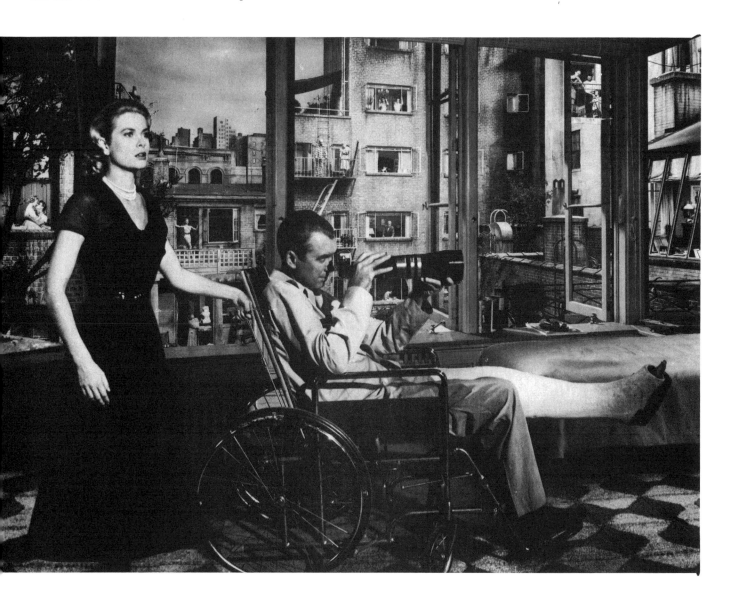

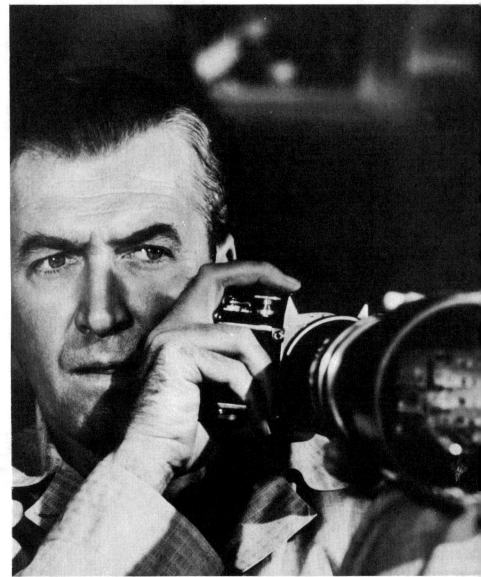

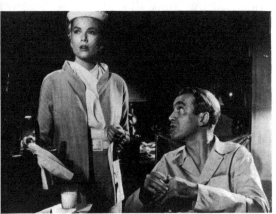

life came to be threatened. If I remember it correctly, it climaxes with the killer taking a shot at the man from the other side of the yard, but the invalid manages to grab a bust of Beethoven and hold it up in front of the window so that Beethoven gets the bullet!

F.T.　I imagine that the story appealed to you primarily because it represented a technical challenge: a whole film from the viewpoint of one man, and embodied in a single, large set.*

A.H.　Absolutely. It was a possibility of doing a purely cinematic film. You have an immobilized man looking out. That's one part of the film. The second part shows what he sees and the third part shows how he reacts. This is actually the purest expression of a cinematic idea. Pudovkin dealt with this, as you know. In one of his books on the art of montage, he describes an experiment by his teacher, Kuleshov. You see a close-up of the Russian actor Ivan Mosjoukine. This is immediately followed by a shot of a dead baby. Back to Mosjoukine again and you

---

* A news photographer (James Stewart), confined to a wheelchair by a broken leg, gazes idly at the behavior of the neighbors across the courtyard of his Greenwich Village apartment. His observations lead him to suspect that one of the neighbors (Raymond Burr) has murdered his wife, but he is unable to convince his fiancée (Grace Kelly) and his detective friend (Wendell Corey)

that he is right. Eventually, when Stewart's fiancée discovers incriminating evidence confirming his suspicions, the killer discovers he is being watched and tries to kill the photographer. The snooper is saved in the nick of time, though his second leg is broken in the course of the rescue operation.

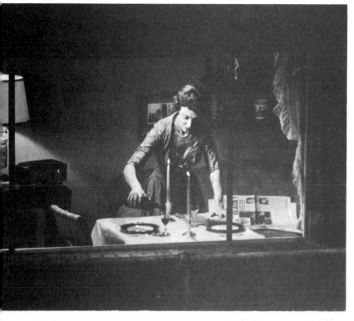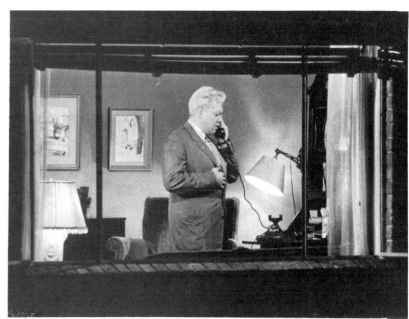

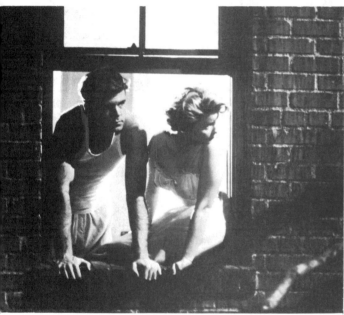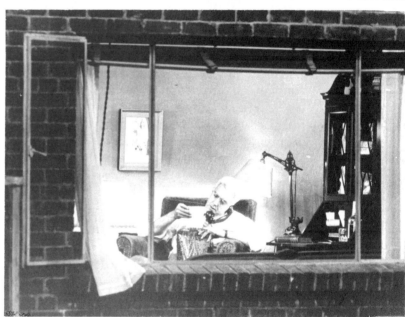

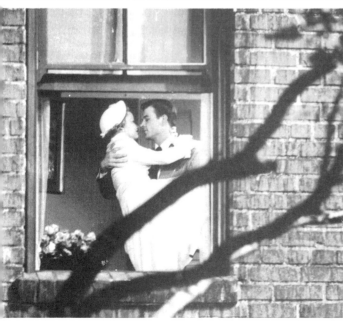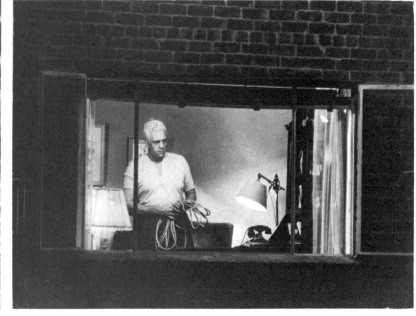

read compassion on his face. Then you take away the dead baby and you show a plate of soup, and now, when you go back to Mosjoukine, he looks hungry. Yet, in both cases, they used the same shot of the actor; his face was exactly the same.

In the same way, let's take a close-up of Stewart looking out of the window at a little dog that's being lowered in a basket. Back to Stewart, who has a kindly smile. But if in the place of the little dog you show a half-naked girl exercising in front of her open window, and you go back to a smiling Stewart again, this time he's seen as a dirty old man!

F.T. Would you say that. Stewart was merely curious?

A.H. He's a real Peeping Tom. In fact, Miss Lejeune, the critic of the London *Observer*, complained about that. She made some comment to the effect that *Rear Window* was a horrible film because the hero spent all of his time peeping out of the window. What's so horrible about that? Sure, he's a snooper, but aren't we all?

F.T. We're all voyeurs to some extent, if only when we see an intimate film. And James Stewart is exactly in the position of a spectator looking at a movie.

A.H. I'll bet you that nine out of ten people, if they see a woman across the courtyard undressing for bed, or even a man puttering around in his room, will stay and look; no one turns away and says, "It's none of my business." They could pull down their blinds, but they never do; they stand there and look out.

F.T. My guess is that at the outset your interest in the picture was purely technical, but in working on the script, you began to attach more importance to the story itself. Intentionally or not, that back yard conveys an image of the world.

A.H. It shows every kind of human behavior—a real index of individual behavior. The picture would have been very dull if we hadn't done that. What you see across the way is a group of little stories that, as you say, mirror a small universe.

F.T. All of the stories have a common denominator in that they involve some aspect of love. James Stewart's problem is that he doesn't want to marry Grace Kelly. Everything he sees across the way has a bearing on love and marriage. There is the lonely woman with no husband or lover, the newlyweds who make love all day long, the bachelor musician who drinks, the little dancer whom all the men are after, the childless couple who dote on their little dog, and, of course, the married couple who are always at each other's throat, until the wife's mysterious disappearance.

A.H. The symmetry is the same as in *Shadow of a Doubt*. On one side of the yard you have the Stewart–Kelly couple, with him immobilized by his leg in a cast, while she can move about freely. And on the other side there is a sick woman who's confined to her bed, while the husband comes and goes.

One of the things I was unhappy about in *Rear Window* was the music. Do you know Franz Waxman?

F.T. Didn't he do the musical score for several Humphrey Bogart movies?

A.H. Yes, and he also did the score for *Rebecca*. You remember that one of the characters in the yard was a musician. Well, I wanted to show how a popular song is composed by gradually developing it throughout the film until, in the final scene, it is played on a recording with a full orchestral accompaniment. Well, it didn't work out the way I wanted it to, and I was quite disappointed.

F.T. Well, that notion is conveyed in the final part of the picture when the old maid, who's about to commit suicide, changes her mind after hearing the musician play the completed song. And isn't it at the same moment, as he's listening to the music, that James Stewart realizes that he's in love with Grace Kelly? Another potent scene is the one in which the childless couple learn that their little dog has

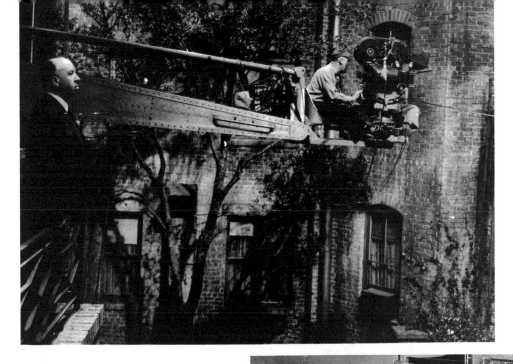

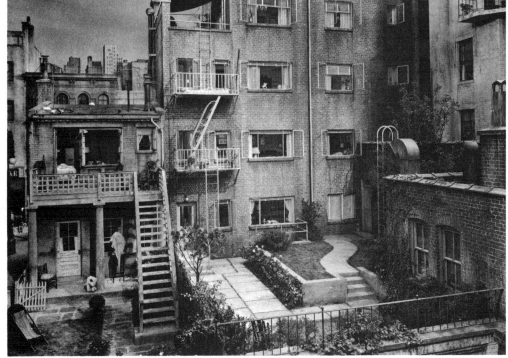

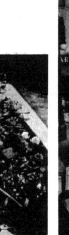

been killed. The thing that's so good about it is that their reaction is deliberately disproportionate. There's a great hue and cry . . . it's handled as if the death of a child were involved.

A.H. Of course, that little dog was their only child. At the end of the scene you notice that everyone's at his window looking down into the yard except for the suspected killer, who's smoking in the dark.

F.T. This, incidentally, is the only moment at which the film changes its point of view. By simply taking the camera outside of Stewart's apartment, the whole scene becomes entirely objective.

A.H. That's right, that was the only such scene.

F.T. Isn't this another illustration of one of

217

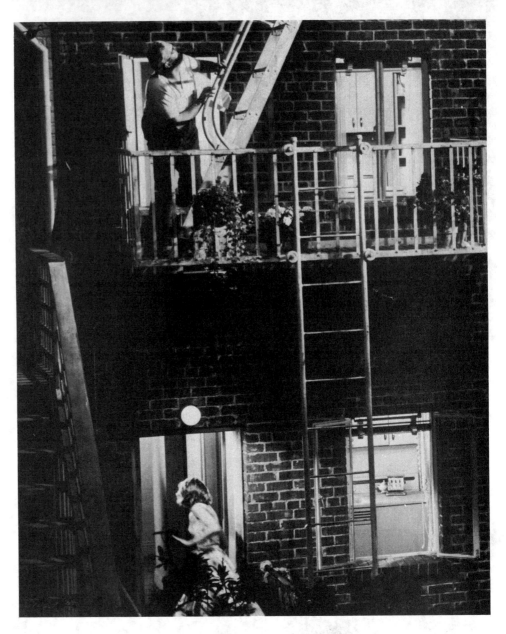

your working rules, which consists of not giving an over-all view of the setting until a scene reaches its dramatic peak? For instance, in *The Paradine Case* fifty minutes of action inside the courtroom are climaxed when a humiliated Gregory Peck walks out on the case. Only then, with the camera showing his departure from a distance, do you give a full view of the courtroom. And again, in *Rear Window* the first time you show the whole courtyard is when the woman begins to scream over the death of her dog and the neighbors all rush to their windows to see what's happening.

A.H.   Absolutely. The size of the image is used for dramatic purposes, and not merely to establish the background.

Just the other day I was doing a television show and there was a scene in which a man came into a police station to give himself up. I had a close shot of the man coming in, the door closing behind him, and the man walking up to the desk; I didn't show the whole set. They asked me, "Aren't you going to show the whole thing so that people know we're in a police station?" I said, "Why bother? The sergeant has three stripes on his arm right next to the camera, and that's enough to get that idea across. Why should we waste a long shot that may be useful at a dramatic moment?"

F.T.   That concept of waste, of saving the image for future use, is an interesting one. Something else: At the end of *Rear Window*,

218

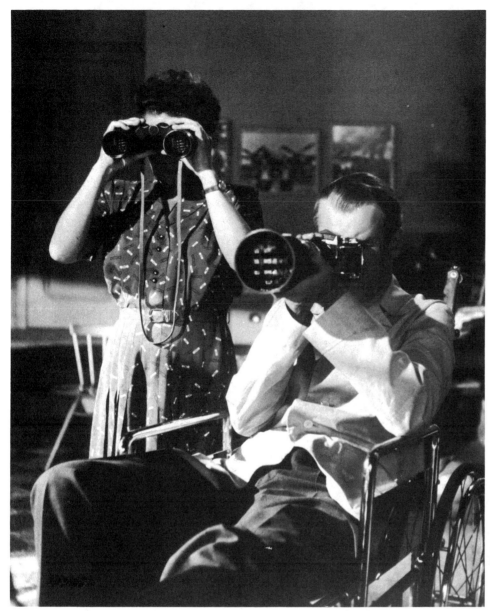

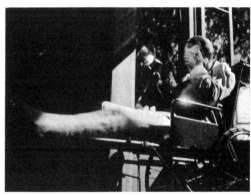

when the killer comes into Stewart's room, he says to him, "What do you want of me?" And Stewart doesn't answer because, in fact, his actions are unjustified; they're motivated by sheer curiosity.

A.H.   That's right, and he deserves what's happening to him!

F.T.   Still, he will defend himself by blinding the killer with his flashbulbs.

A.H.   Those flashes take us back to the mechanics of *The Secret Agent*. You remember, in Switzerland they have the Alps, lakes, and chocolate. Now, here we have a photographer who uses his camera equipment to pry into the back yard, and when he defends himself, he also

uses his professional equipment, the flashbulbs. I make it a rule to exploit elements that are connected with a character or a location; I would feel that I'd been remiss if I hadn't made maximum use of those elements.

F.T.   In this respect the exposition of the film is truly remarkable. You open up with the perspiring face of James Stewart; you move on to his leg in a cast, and then, on a nearby table, there is the broken camera, a stack of magazines, and, on the wall, there are pictures of racing cars as they topple over on the track. Through that single opening camera movement we have learned where we are, who the principal character is, all about his work, and even how it caused his accident.

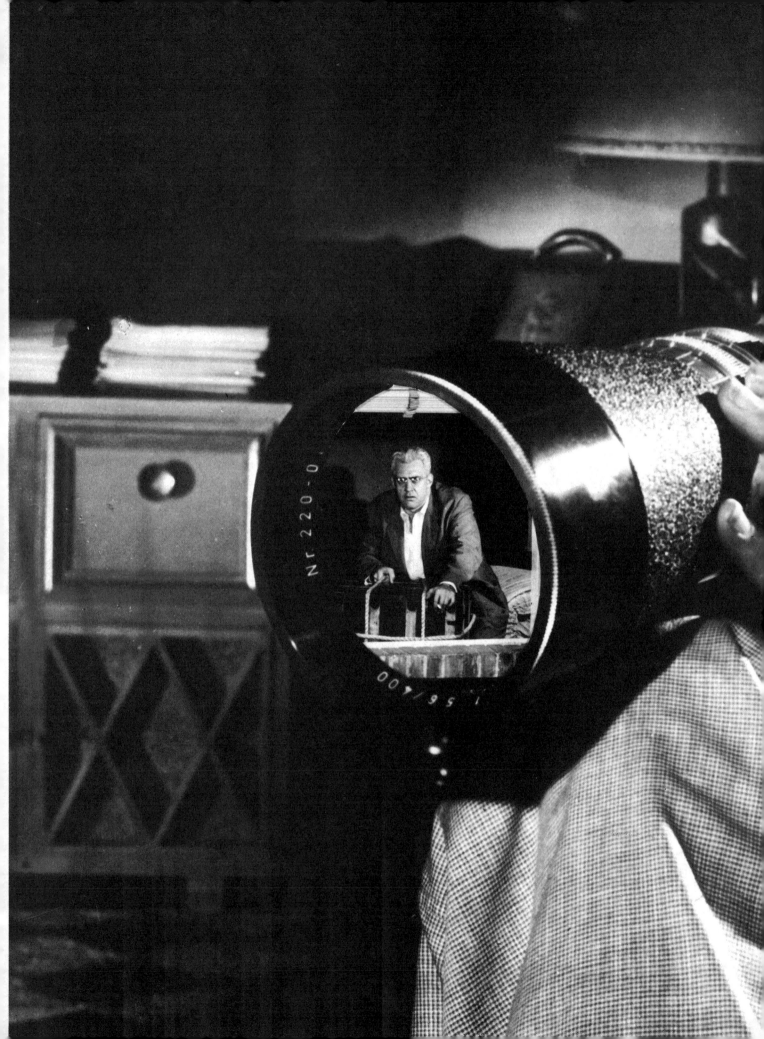

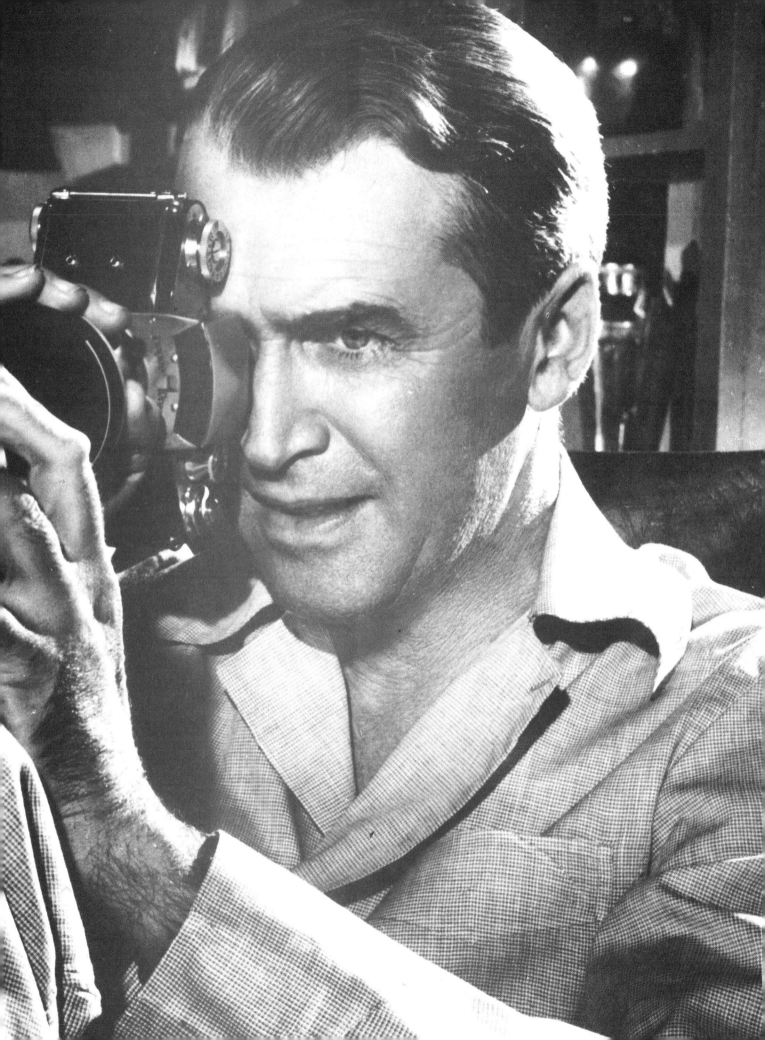

A.H. That's simply using cinematic means to relate a story. It's a great deal more interesting than if we had someone asking Stewart, "How did you happen to break your leg?" and Stewart answering, "As I was taking a picture of a motorcar race, a wheel fell off one of the speeding cars and smashed into me." That would be the average scene. To me, one of the cardinal sins for a script-writer, when he runs into some difficulty, is to say, "We can cover that by a line of dialogue." Dialogue should simply be a sound among other sounds, just something that comes out of the mouths of people whose eyes tell the story in visual terms.

F.T. Something else I've noticed is the way you dispense with the build-up to a love scene. Here, James Stewart is alone at home, and all of a sudden the face of Grace Kelly comes into the frame and they are kissing each other. Why do you do it that way?

A.H. Because I want to get right to the important point without wasting any time. Here it's the surprise kiss. In another case there might be a suspense kiss, and that would be completely different.

F.T. Both in *Rear Window* and *To Catch a Thief* the kiss is a process shot. Not the kiss itself, but the approach to the faces is jerky, as if you had double-printed that frame in the cutting room.

A.H. Not at all. These are puslations that I get by shaking the camera by hand or dollying backward and forward, or sometimes by doing both. One scene I meant to shoot for *The Birds*, but didn't, was a love scene in which the two heads would have started apart, to gradually come together. I was going to try to get a very quick pan from one face to the other by whipping the camera. I would have whipped from one head to the other, and as the two faces got closer to each other, the whipping would decrease until it became a slight vibration. I must try it sometime!

F.T. To my mind, *Rear Window* is probably your very best screenplay in all respects: the construction, the unity of inspiration, the wealth of details.

A.H. I was feeling very creative at the time, the batteries were well charged. John Michael Hayes is a radio writer and he wrote the dialogue. The killing presented something of a problem, so I used two news stories from the British press. One was the Patrick Mahon case and the other was the case of Dr. Crippen. In the Mahon case the man killed a girl in a bungalow on the seafront of southern England. He cut up the body and threw it, piece by piece, out of a train window. But he didn't know what to do with the head, and that's where I got the idea of having them look for the victim's head in *Rear Window*. What Patrick Mahon did was to put the head in the fireplace and light the fire. Then something happened that may sound phony but is absolutely true. Like in a stage play, just as he put the head in the fire, a thunderstorm came on, with lightning and thunder. Somehow, the heat of the fire made the eyes open wide, as if they were staring at Mahon. He ran out to the beach screaming, with the storm pouring down on him, and didn't get back until several hours later. By that time the fire had burned the head.

Several years later one of the four chief inspectors of Scotland Yard came to see me. He had handled the investigation after Mahon's arrest, and he told me they'd had a problem in getting hold of that head; they only found traces of it, but not the head itself. He knew the head had been burned, but he needed to have some indication of the time at which it was put in the fire and how long it had taken to burn. So he went down to the butcher shop, bought a sheep's head and burned it in the same fireplace.

In all cases involving mutilation, you see, the biggest problem for the police is to locate the head.

Now, Dr. Crippen lived in London. He murdered his wife and cut her up. When people noticed his wife had disappeared, he gave the customary explanation: "She's gone to California." But Crippen made a crucial blunder that turned out to be his undoing. He allowed his secretary to wear some of his wife's jewelry, and this started the neighbors talking. Scotland Yard was brought in, and Inspector Dew went down to question Dr. Crippen, who gave a fairly plausible account of his wife's absence, insisting that she had gone to live in California. Inspector Dew had more or less given up, but when he went back for some formality, Dr. Crippen ran away with the secretary. Naturally, there was a big hue and cry, and a description of the missing couple was sent out to all ships at sea. This was when they were just beginning to use radios on ships.

Now, if I may, I'll jump aboard the steamship *Montrose*, going from Antwerp to Montreal, to give you the ship captain's version of the sequel to this story.

The captain had noticed among his passengers a Mr. Robinson and his young son; he had also noticed that the father was particularly affectionate toward the boy. So, being a snooping man—he might have been in *Rear Window*—he noticed that Master Robinson's hat, bought in Antwerp, was full of paper to make it fit. He also noticed that the boy's pants were held together at the waist by a safety pin. According to the description he had received, Dr. Crippen wore a false top and bottom plate of teeth and there was a mark on his nose where he wore gold-rimmed glasses. The captain verified that Mr. Robinson had just such a mark. One evening the captain invited Mr. Robinson to his table and told him a joke so that he would laugh out loud, and he found that the man really had false teeth.

At this point the captain wired a message stating that he believed the wanted couple was on his ship. While that message was being transmitted, Dr. Crippen happened to walk by the radio cabin, and on hearing the spluttering of the keys, he said to the captain, "The wireless is a wonderful invention, isn't it?"

Anyway, upon receiving the message, Inspector Dew got on a fast ship of the Canadian Pacific Line, and he reached the St. Lawrence River at a place called Father Point. He boarded the *Montrose* and walked up to Mr. Robinson, saying, "Good morning, Dr. Crippen." He brought them back. Crippen was hanged and the girl got off.

F.T.   So that's what gave you the idea for the jewelry scene with Grace Kelly?

A.H.   Yes, the scene with the wedding ring. If the wife had really gone on a trip, she'd have taken her wedding ring with her.

F.T.   One of the things I enjoyed in the film was the dual significance of that wedding ring. Grace Kelly wants to get married but James Stewart doesn't see it that way. She breaks into the killer's apartment to search for evidence and she finds the wedding ring. She puts it on her finger and waves her hand behind her back so that James Stewart, looking over from the other side of the yard with his spyglasses, can see it. To Grace Kelly, that ring is a double victory: not only is it the evidence she was looking for, but who knows, it may inspire Stewart to propose to her. After all, she's already got the ring!

A.H.   Exactly. That was an ironic touch.

F.T.   I was still a working critic the first time I saw *Rear Window*, and I remember writing that the picture was very gloomy, rather pessimistic, and quite evil. But now I don't see it in that light at all; in fact, I feel it has a rather compassionate approach. What Stewart sees from his window is not horrible but simply a display of human weaknesses and people in pursuit of happiness. Is that the way you look at it?

A.H.   Definitely.

F.T.   *To Catch a Thief* was the first film you shot on location in France. What do you think of the picture on the whole?

A.H.   It was a lightweight story.

F.T.   Along the lines of the Arsène Lupin stories. Cary Grant played "The Cat," a former high-class American thief who has retired on the Côte d'Azur. When the area is hit by a wave of jewel robberies, he is the logical suspect, both because of his police record and his expert skills. To resume his peaceful existence, he uses these skills to conduct his own investigation. Along the way he finds love, in the person of Grace

223

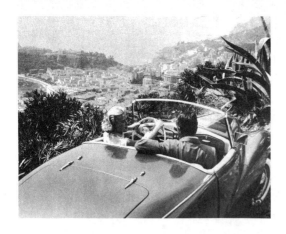

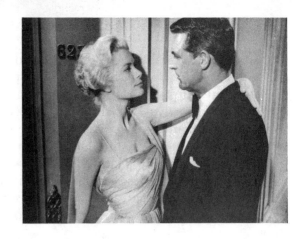

Kelly, and in the end, it turns out that the guilty party is a "she-cat."

A.H.   It wasn't meant to be taken seriously. The only interesting footnote I can add is that since I hate royal-blue skies, I tried to get rid of the Technicolor blue for the night scenes. So we shot with a green filter to get the dark slate blue, the real color of night, but it still didn't come out as I wanted it.

F.T.   Like several of the others, the plot hinges around a transference of guilt, with the difference being that here the villain turns out to be a girl.

A.H.   Brigitte Auber played that role. I had seen a Julien Duvivier picture called *Sous le Ciel de Paris* in which she played a country girl who'd come to live in the city. I chose her because the personage had to be sturdy enough to climb all over the villa roofs. At the time, I wasn't aware that between films Brigitte Auber worked as an acrobat. That turned out to be a happy coincidence.

F.T.   This is the picture that aroused the press's interest in your concept of movie heroines. You stated several times that Grace Kelly especially appealed to you because her sex appeal is "indirect."

A.H.   Sex on the screen should be suspenseful, I feel. If sex is too blatant or obvious, there's no suspense. You know why I favor sophisticated blondes in my films? We're after the drawing-room type, the real ladies, who become whores once they're in the bedroom. Poor Mar-

ilyn Monroe had sex written all over her face, and Brigitte Bardot isn't very subtle either.

F.T.   In other words, what intrigues you is the paradox between the inner fire and the cool surface.

A.H.   Definitely, I think the most interesting women, sexually, are the English women. I feel that the English women, the Swedes, the northern Germans, and Scandinavians are a great deal more exciting than the Latin, the Italian, and the French women. Sex should not be advertised. An English girl, looking like a schoolteacher, is apt to get into a cab with you and, to your surprise, she'll probably pull a man's pants open.

F.T.   I appreciate your viewpoint, but I doubt whether the majority of the public shares your tastes in this matter. I think the male audience prefers a highly carnal woman. The very fact that Jane Russell, Marilyn Monroe, Sophia Loren, and Brigitte Bardot became stars, despite the many flops in which they appeared, seems to bear this out. The majority of the public, it seems to me, prefers the kind of sensuality that's blatant.

A.H.   That may well be true, but you yourself admit that those actresses generally make bad films. Do you know why? Because without the element of *surprise* the scenes become meaningless. There's no possibility to *discover* sex. Look at the opening of *To Catch a Thief*. I deliberately photographed Grace Kelly ice-cold and I kept cutting to her profile, looking classical, beautiful, and very distant. And then, when

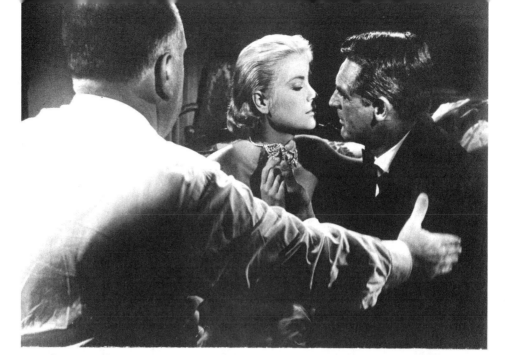

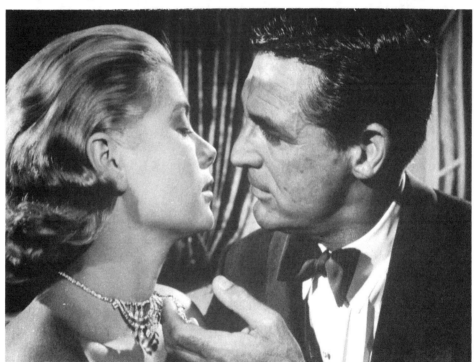

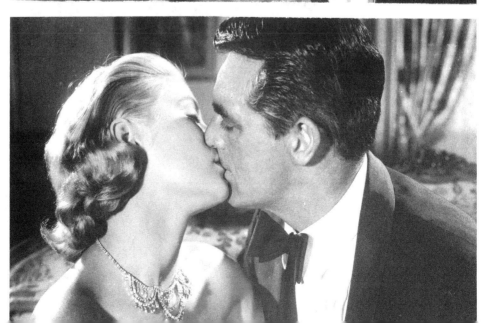

Cary Grant accompanies her to the door of her hotel room, what does she do? She thrusts her lips right up to his mouth.

F.T.   I'm willing to grant that you manage to impose that concept of icy sexuality on the screen, but I still feel the audience prefers the kind of sex that's obvious and tangible.

A.H.   Maybe so. Anyway, when the picture is over, the public's pretty satisfied with it.

F.T.   I'm not overlooking that, but my guess is that this is one aspect of your pictures that's probably more satisfying to the feminine viewers than to the male audience.

A.H.   I'd like to point out that it's generally the woman who has the final say on which picture a couple is going to see. In fact, it's generally the woman who will decide, later on, whether it was a good or a bad picture. On condition that it's not displayed by a person of their own sex, women will not object to vulgarity on the screen. Anyway, to build up Grace Kelly, in each picture between *Dial M for Murder* and *To Catch a Thief* we made her role a more interesting one.

Since *To Catch a Thief* is in a rather nostalgic mood, I didn't want to wind up with a completely happy ending. That's why I put in that scene by the tree, when Cary Grant agrees to marry Grace Kelly. It turns out that the mother-in-law will come and live with them, so the final note is pretty grim.

F.T.   After that you made a very unusual picture, *The Trouble with Harry*. In Paris it opened in a very small theater on the Champs-Elysées. It was expected to run no more than a week or two, but it played to packed houses for half a year. I was never able to figure out whether it was entertaining to Parisians or whether the audience was made up entirely of British and American tourists. I believe it wasn't too successful in other parts of the world.*

A.H.   I chose that novel and was given a free hand with it. When it was finished, the distributors didn't know how to exploit it. It needed special handling. They felt it was too special, but I didn't see it that way.

It's taken from a British novel by Jack Trevor Story and I didn't change it very much. To my

---

* In the rural countryside of Vermont on a fall day, three shots are heard. A little boy playing in the woods discovers the body of a man who, upon investigation, turns out to be Harry. Several people in the community, among them his former wife, Jennifer (Shirley MacLaine), have motives for killing Harry; and others, including an abstract painter (John Forsythe), a retired sea captain (Edmund Gwenn), and an old maid and a nearsighted doctor, believe they may be responsible for his accidental death. Adding to the confusion, Harry keeps showing up in all the splendor of *rigor mortis* at the most embarrassing moments. Eventually, it turns out that Harry has simply died of natural causes and the community resumes its uneventful ways. But for the abstract painter, who has fallen under the spell of Jennifer's very concrete charm, life may never again be the same.

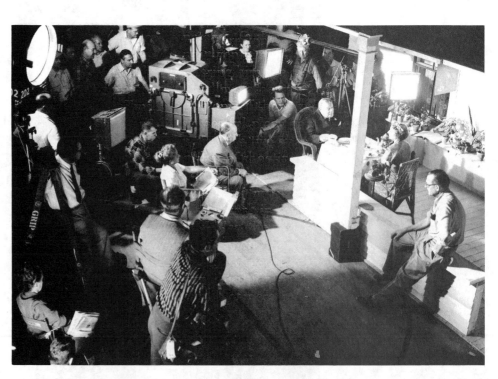

The Trouble with Harry. The year is 1954. Since 1922, Alma Hitchcock, seated at the bottom and to the left, has kept a discreet but attentive eye on her husband's work.

226

taste, the humor is quite rich. One of the best lines is when old Edmund Gwenn is dragging the body along for the first time and a woman comes up to him on the hill and says, "What seems to be the trouble, Captain?" To me that's terribly funny; that's the spirit of the whole story.

F.T.   I understand that you're especially fond of this picture.

A.H.   I've always been interested in establishing a contrast, in going against the traditional and in breaking away from clichés. With *Harry* I took melodrama out of the pitch-black night and brought it out in the sunshine. It's as if I had set up a murder alongside a rustling brook and spilled a drop of blood in the clear water. These contrasts establish a counterpoint; they elevate the commonplace in life to a higher level.

F.T.   I must say you successfully demonstrate how horrible or terrifying things—elements that might easily become morbid or sordid—can be filmed in such a way that they're never repulsive. Very often, they're even fascinating.
Toward the end of the picture each of the characters has the chance to make a wish, and since Shirley MacLaine whispers her request into someone's ear, there's no way of knowing exactly what it is, but one guesses it must be some-

thing very special. Then, at the very end, we find out that what she wanted was a double bed. That wasn't in the book, was it?

A.H.   No. John Michael Hayes put that in.

F.T.   That little touch creates a sort of suspenseful question mark that heightens the interest of the final reel.

A.H.   It's the equivalent of the crescendo or the coda in my other pictures. We did the same sort of thing at the end of *Lifeboat* and *Rope*. *The Trouble with Harry* was Shirley MacLaine's first picture. She was very good in it and she made out very well afterward. The young man, John Forsythe, now very popular in television, had the lead in one of my first hour shows.

F.T.   The whole humor of the picture hinges on a single device: an attitude of disconcerting nonchalance. The characters discuss the corpse as casually as if they were talking about a pack of cigarettes.

A.H.   That's the idea. Nothing amuses me so much as understatement.

F.T.   We've already talked about the differences between the British version of *The Man Who Knew Too Much** and the American re-

---

* See page 89.

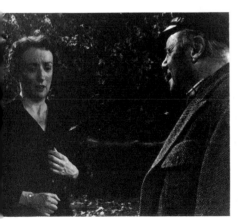

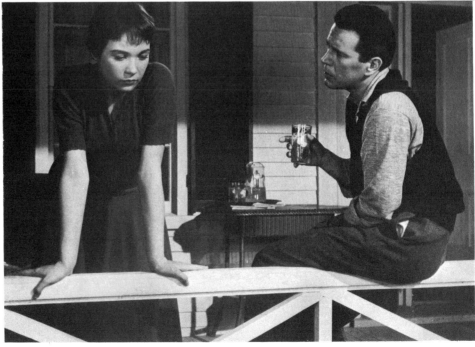

make. One of those differences is, of course, James Stewart's performance in the remake. He's a fine actor and you certainly bring out his best points. It might seem as if Cary Grant and James Stewart were interchangeable in your work, but you actually use each one in a different way. With Cary Grant the picture is more humorous, and with James Stewart the emphasis is on emotion.

A.H.   Naturally. Despite the similarities, they're really quite different from each other. In *The Man Who Knew Too Much*, James Stewart portrayed an earnest and quiet man. Cary Grant couldn't have done it that way. If I'd used him in the picture, the character would have been altogether different.

F.T.   You went to some trouble, I notice, to avoid mention of a specific country; that might raise censorship problems. Whereas the original version starts out in Switzerland, the second one opens in Morocco, and it's never clearly stated whether the diplomat who's slated to be assassinated represents one of the people's democracies or not.

A.H.   Of course, I didn't want to commit myself to any country; we simply indicated that by killing the ambassador, the spies hoped to embarrass the British Government. One thing that bothered me, though, was the choice of an actor to play the ambassador. You simply can't trust the casting department's judgment. I suspect when you ask them for someone to play an elevator boy, they take out a big register and open it up to the letter "E," and then they call in every actor who's ever played an elevator boy.

F.T.   Is that the way they do it?

A.H.   That's exactly how they work. When I was in London I asked for a man to play the ambassador, and they sent me a lot of small men with little beards. I'd ask them, "What have you played?" One man would tell me, "I was the prime minister in such and such a picture," and another would say, "I had the role of the chargé d'affaires in such and such a picture." Finally, I told the casting department to stop sending me ambassadors. I asked them to send someone down to a newspaper morgue and bring me back a picture of all of the ambassadors stationed in London at the time. Well, I looked at the pictures and not one of them had a beard!

F.T.   The man you chose was awfully good —completely bald, with a look of bland innocence that's almost childlike.

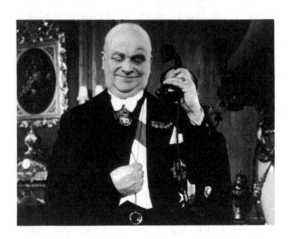

A.H.   He was a very prominent stage actor in Copenhagen.

F.T.   Let's get back to the opening of the picture, in Marrakech. In the original version Pierre Fresnay was shot down, but in this one Daniel Gelin is stabbed in the back.

A.H.   That knife in his back comes from an idea I'd had a long time ago and I managed to use part of it in this picture.
The idea was to show a ship from India sailing into the London docks, with a crew that was three-fourths Indian. One of the sailors was being chased by the police and he'd managed to get on a bus that was going to St. Paul's Cathedral on Sunday morning. He gets up into what's called the Whispering Gallery. The police are up there and he runs to one side while the police run around the other way. Then, just as they nearly catch up with him, he jumps over and falls in front of the altar. The service is interrupted as the congregation rises and the choir stops its singing. Everyone rushes over to the fallen man's body, and when they turn it

over, they discover a knife in his back. Then someone touches his face and the black comes off, showing white streaks. It turns out he wasn't a real Indian.

F.T.   That part—the white streaks on the face—is in the picture, when Daniel Gelin is killed . . .

A.H.   Yes, but I never completed the idea. It would have been interesting to work out the puzzle of how a man being chased by the police can get stabbed in the back after he jumps down.

F.T.   That's an intriguing thought, and the dyed face is a nice touch. But there's something strange in that scene. When James Stewart raises his hand after touching Daniel Gelin's blackened face, there's a blue stain on it. It's rather mystifying.

A.H.   Well, that's another idea that wasn't completed. At the beginning of that chase se-

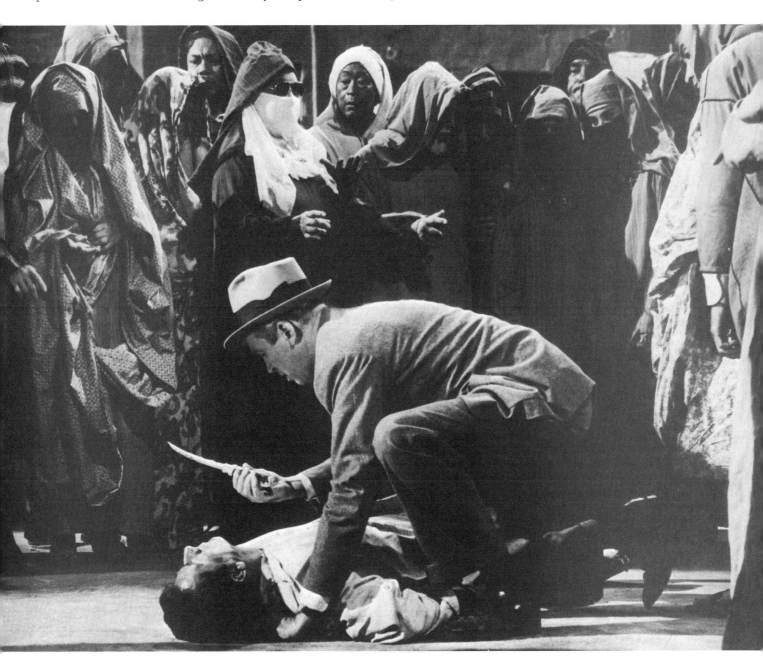

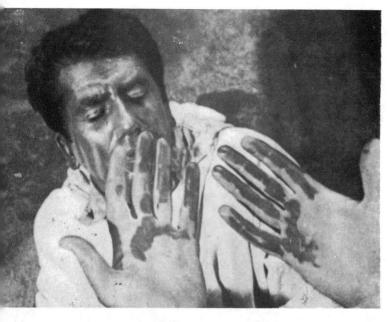
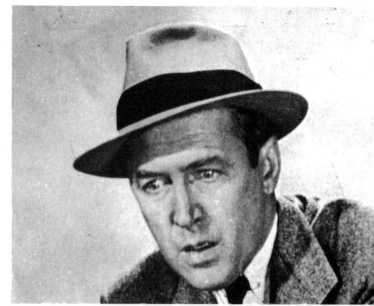
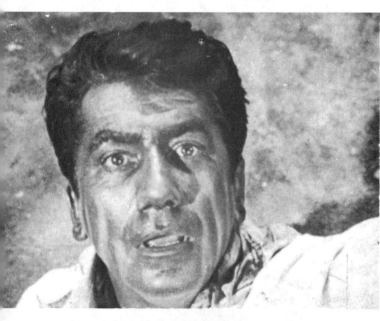
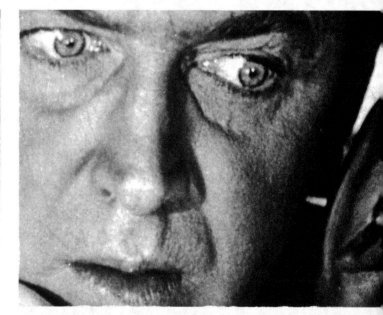
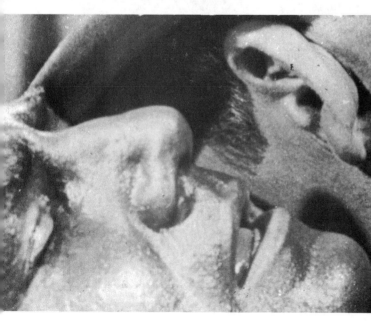
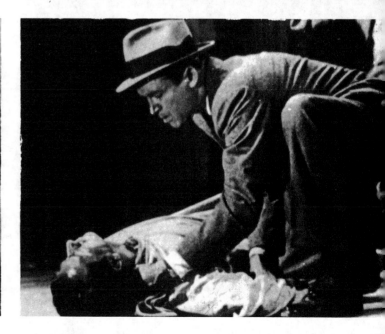

quence with Daniel Gelin in Marrakech, there was to be a scene in the market place in which Daniel Gelin would collide with some men who were dyeing wool. As he passed by, his foot and his robe would have dipped into the blue dye so that he leaves a blue trail in his footsteps as he runs away. It's a variant on the old trail of blood, but instead of following a red trail, the pursuers would be following a blue one.

F.T. It's also a variant on Tom Thumb and the little white stones he drops along his path. We've already discussed some of the differences between the Albert Hall scenes in the 1934 British version and the 1956 American version. The second one is superior by far.

A.H. Yes, I believe we went over that when we were talking about the first version. I can't help feeling that ideally, for that scene to have maximum effect, all of the viewers should be able to read a musical score.*

F.T. Why is that?

---

* The reader will recall that the spy who's been assigned to kill the diplomat during the Albert Hall concert has been instructed to fire precisely at the moment the score calls for the unique clash of cymbals so that the noise will drown out the sound of the fatal crack.

A.H. I went to great pains to make sure that everyone would clearly understand the role of the cymbals, but do you remember the moment when the camera sweeps over to the cymbalist's musical score?

F.T. Yes, you had a panning shot right across the bar of notes.

A.H. During that shot the camera travels over all those silent passages to close in on the single note the cymbalist is supposed to play. Wouldn't the suspense have been stronger if people could actually read that score?

F.T. Naturally, that would have been ideal. In the original version the cymbalist's face isn't shown, but I notice this omission was corrected in the remake. By the way, the musician looks a little like you.

A.H. Just a coincidence!

F.T. He's completely impassive.

A.H. Well, that impassivity was extremely important since the man is unaware that he is the instrument of death. He doesn't know it, but in fact, he's the real killer.

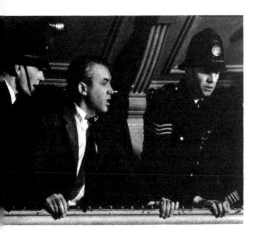

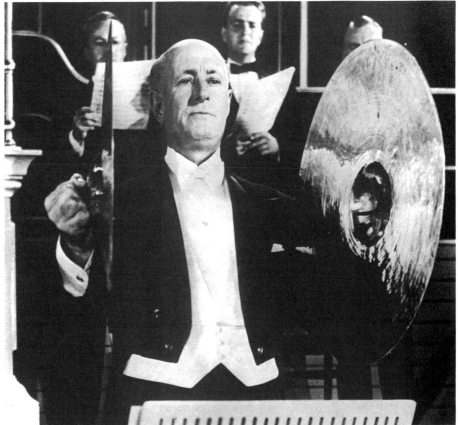

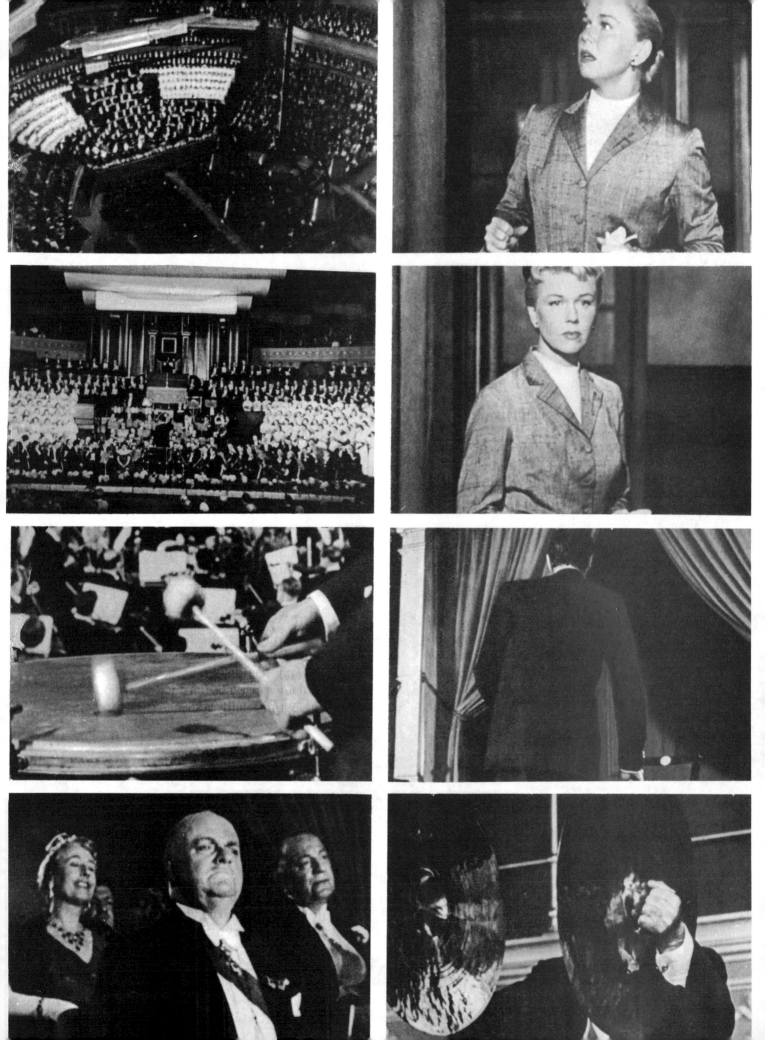

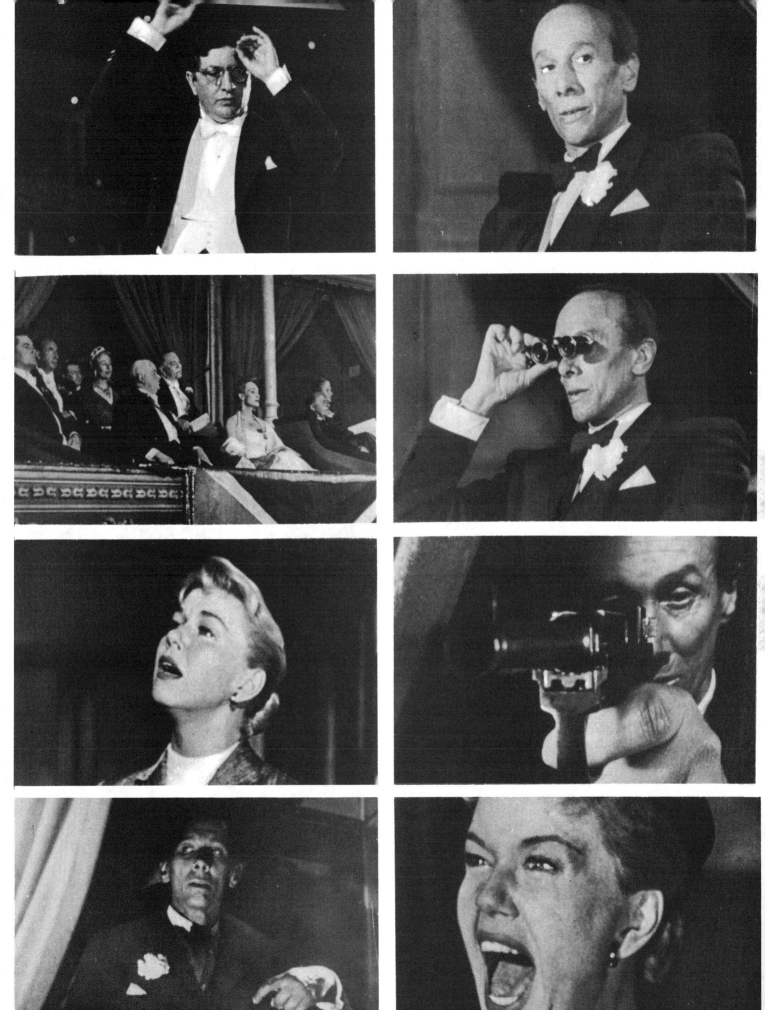

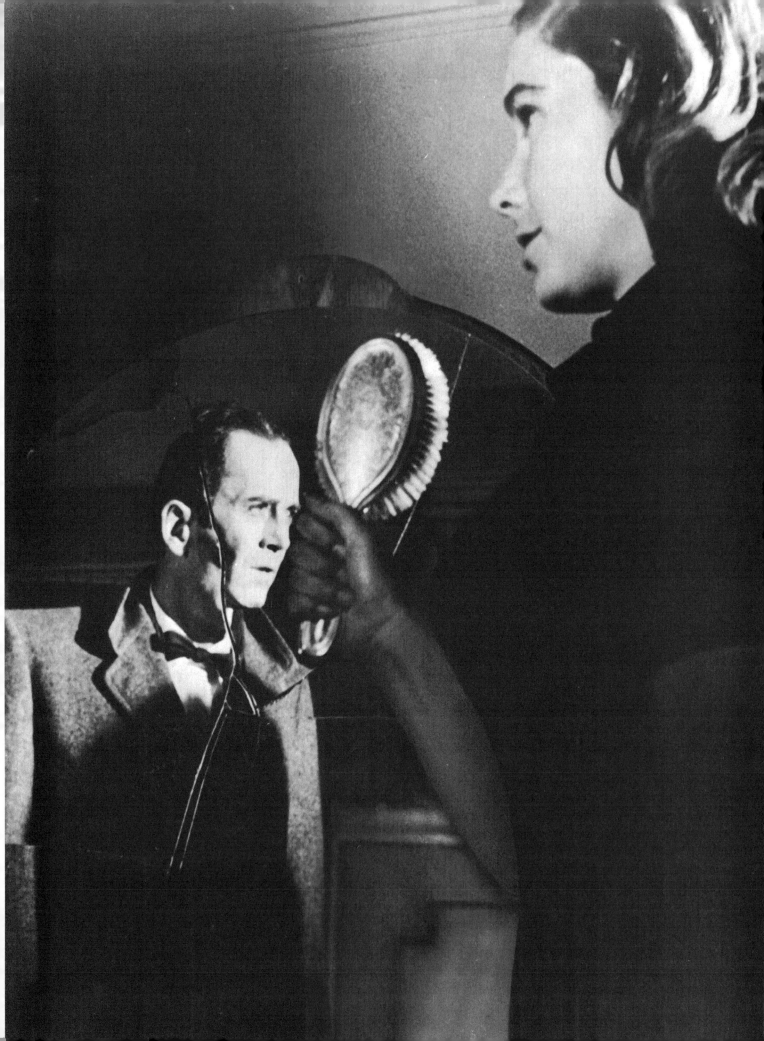

"THE WRONG MAN" ■ ABSOLUTE AUTHENTICITY ■ "VERTIGO" ■ THE USUAL ALTERNATIVES: SUSPENSE OR SURPRISE ■ NECROPHILIA ■ KIM NOVAK ON THE SET ■ TWO PROJECTS THAT WERE NEVER FILMED ■ A POLITICAL SUSPENSE MOVIE ■ "NORTH BY NORTHWEST" ■ THE IMPORTANCE OF PHOTOGRAPHIC DOCUMENTATION ■ DEALING WITH TIME AND SPACE ■ THE PRACTICE OF THE ABSURD ■ THE BODY THAT CAME FROM NOWHERE ■ ■ ■

12

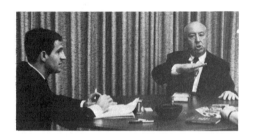

FRANÇOIS TRUFFAUT. After that you went on to make *The Wrong Man*, which is a fairly faithful account of a real-life news story.

ALFRED HITCHCOCK. The screenplay was based on a story I read in *Life* magazine. In 1952, I think, a musician at New York's Stork Club went home at two o'clock in the morning. In front of his door he was met by two men who hauled him off to different places, like saloons, and asked various people there, "Is this the man?" Anyway, he was arrested and charged with a holdup. Though he was completely innocent, he had to stand trial, and eventually, as a result of all the trouble, his wife lost her mind and was put in an insane asylum.

She's probably still there. One of the jurors at the trial was so convinced of the man's guilt that, while the defense lawyer was cross-questioning a witness for the prosecution, he got up and said, "Your Honor, is it absolutely neces-

sary for us to go through all this?" As a result of this violation of the ritual, they had to declare a mistrial. Meanwhile, the police caught the real thief before the new trial opened.

I thought the story would make an interesting picture if all the events were shown from the viewpoint of the innocent man, describing his suffering as a result of a crime committed by someone else. What makes the whole ordeal even more dreadful is that when he protests his innocence, all the people around him are very nice about it, saying, "Yes, of course!"

F.T. I can see why it appealed to you: a concrete, real-life illustration of your favorite theme—the man convicted of a crime committed by someone else, with all the circumstantial evidence working against him.

I'm curious to know to what degree your film is authentic; in other words, where and why you found it necessary to depart from the truth.

235

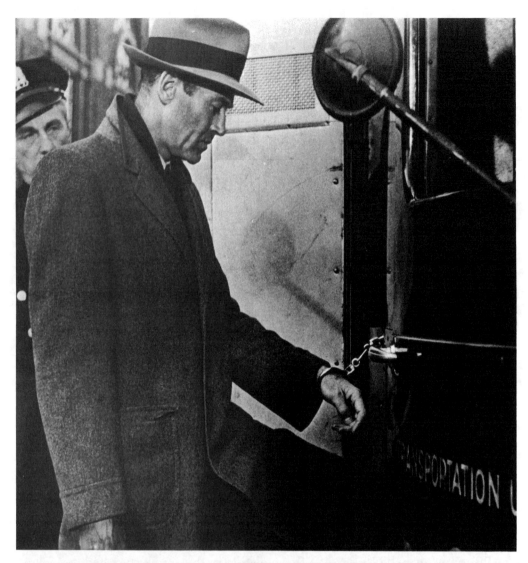

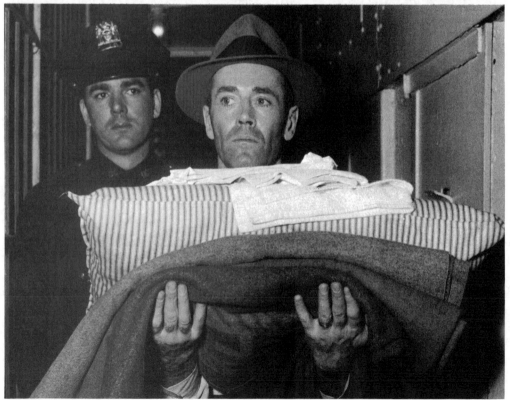

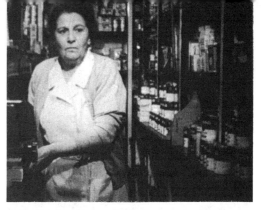

A.H. That's a good question because in the course of shooting that picture I learned a great deal. For instance, for the sake of authenticity everything was minutely reconstructed with the people who were actually involved in that drama. We even used some of them in some of the episodes and, wherever possible, relatively unknown actors. We shot on the locations where the events really took place. Inside the prison we observed how the inmates handle their bedding and their clothes; then we found an empty cell for Fonda and we made him handle these routines exactly as the real inmates had done. We also used the actual psychiatric rest home to which the wife was sent and had the actual doctors playing themselves.

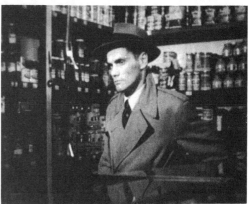

But here's an instance of what we learn by shooting a film in which all the scenes are authentically reconstructed. At the end, the real guilty party is captured while he's trying to hold up a delicatessen, through the courage of the lady owner. I imagined that the way to do that scene was to have the man go into the store, take out his gun and demand the contents of the cash drawer. The lady would manage in some way to sound the alarm, or there might be a struggle of some kind in which the thief was pinned down. Well, what really took place— and this is the way we did it in the picture—is that the man walked into the shop and asked the lady for some frankfurters and some ham. As she passed him to get behind the counter, he held his gun in his pocket and aimed it at her.

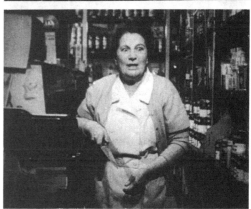

The woman had in her hand a large knife to cut the ham with. Without losing her nerve, she pointed the point of the knife against his stomach, and as he stood there, taken aback, she stamped her foot twice on the floor. The man, rather worried, said, "Take it easy, lady." But the woman, remaining surprisingly calm, didn't budge an inch and didn't say a word. The man was so taken aback by her *sang-froid* that he couldn't think of what to do next. All of a sudden the woman's husband, warned by her stamping, came up from the cellar and grabbed the thief by the shoulders to push him into a corner of the shop against the food shelves while his wife called the police. The thief, thoroughly scared, began to whine: "Let me go. My wife and kids are waiting for me." I loved that line; it's the sort of thing you wouldn't dream of

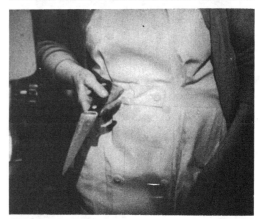

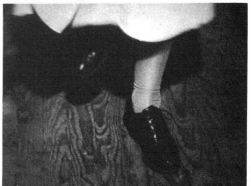

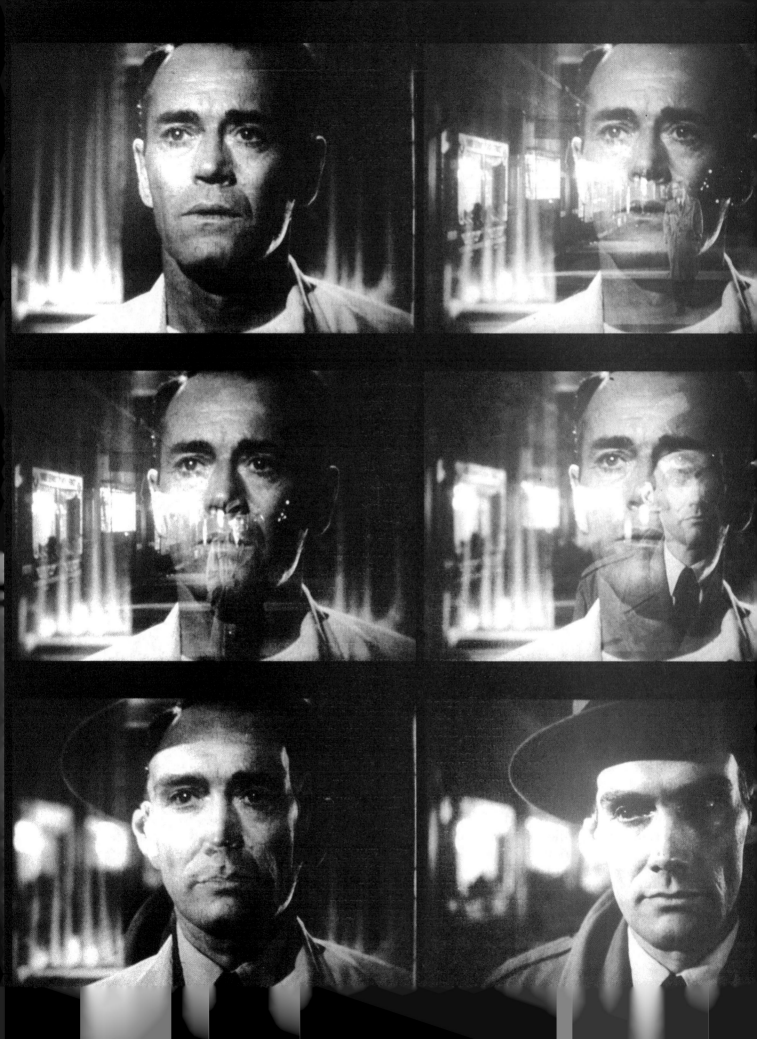

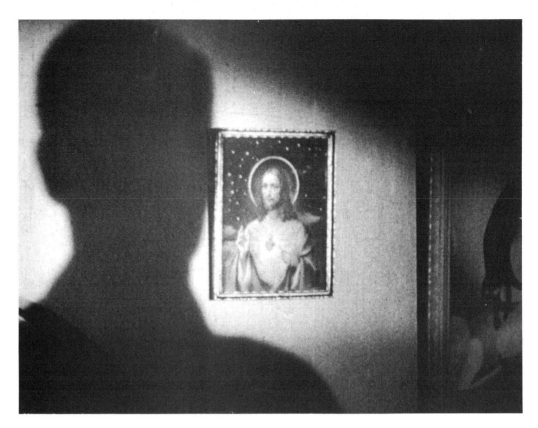

writing into a scenario, and even if it occurred to you, you simply wouldn't dare use it.

F.T. Of course, truth is stranger than fiction. But even so, it's obvious that you had to dramatize the story. In what way did you do that?

A.H. Naturally, that was the problem. For instance, I tried to dramatize the discovery of the real culprit. We showed Henry Fonda murmuring a prayer in front of a holy picture, and from him we dissolved to the real culprit and superimposed his face over Fonda's.

Then again, to the contrary of such pictures as *Boomerang* or *Northside 777*, in which the whole thing is shown through the investigator who is working on the outside to get the innocent man in jail released, my picture is made from the viewpoint of the prisoner himself. From the very outset, when he's arrested, he's seated in the car between the two detectives. There's a close-up of his face, and as he looks to the left, we see the solid profile of his guard from his viewpoint. Then he turns to the right, and we see his other guard lighting a cigar; he looks straight ahead, and in the mirror he sees the driver of the car observing him. The car

starts off and he looks back at his house. At the corner of the block is the bar he usually goes to, with some little girls playing in front of it. As they pass a parked car, he sees that the young woman inside is turning on the radio. Everything in the outside world is taking place normally, as if nothing out of the ordinary had happened, and yet he himself is a prisoner inside the car.

The whole approach is subjective. For instance, they've slipped on a pair of handcuffs to link him to another prisoner. During the journey between the station house and the prison, there are different men guarding him, but since he's ashamed, he keeps his head down, staring at his shoes, so we never show the guards. From time to time one of the handcuffs is opened, and we see a different wrist. In the same way, during the whole trip, we only show the guards' feet, their lower legs, the floor, and the bottom parts of the doors.

F.T. I noticed all of that painstaking detail, but I can't help wondering whether you're fully satisfied with the end result. In other words, do you feel *The Wrong Man* lived up to your usual standards?

A.H. Well, that faithfulness to the original

239

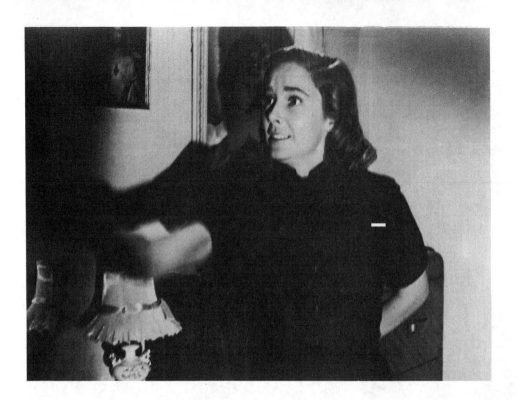

story resulted in some deficiencies in the film's construction. The first weakness was the long interruption in the man's story in order to show how the wife was gradually losing her mind. By the time we got to the trial, it had become anticlimactic. Then, the trial ended abruptly, as it did in real life. It's possible I was too concerned with veracity to take sufficient dramatic license.

F.T. The main trouble, I think, is that your style, which has found its perfection in the fiction area, happens to be in total conflict with the esthetics of the documentary and that contradiction is apparent throughout the picture. Faces, looks, and gestures have been stylized, whereas reality can never be stylized. Wouldn't you agree that the dramatization of authentic events actually served to detract from their reality?

A.H. You've got to remember that *The Wrong Man* was being made as a commercial picture.

F.T. Naturally. And yet I can't help feeling that the picture might have been more commercial had it been directed by another film-maker —someone less talented, less painstaking . . . someone who wouldn't have bothered with the dramatic rules concerning audience participa-

tion, or who didn't even know about them. It would have been an entirely different picture, of course, handled in a purely objective way, like a documentary. I hope you don't mind my saying these things.

A.H. Not at all. It isn't that I disagree with you, but I do feel that it's rather a difficult thing to analyze. What it amounts to, according to your reasoning, is that when you have to tell a story of truly major human importance, it would have to be filmed without actors.

F.T. Not necessarily. Henry Fonda was perfect, very natural and just as authentic as any man on the street. The real problem is with the direction. You're trying to make the public identify with Fonda, but when he goes into his cell, for instance, you show the walls spinning in front of the camera. That's an antirealistic effect. I feel it would have been a good deal more convincing if you had simply shown Henry Fonda sitting on a stool in the cell.

A.H. Maybe so, but wouldn't that be rather dull?

F.T. Frankly, I don't think so, because this case history has a dramatic strength of its own. It should have been done in a very objective

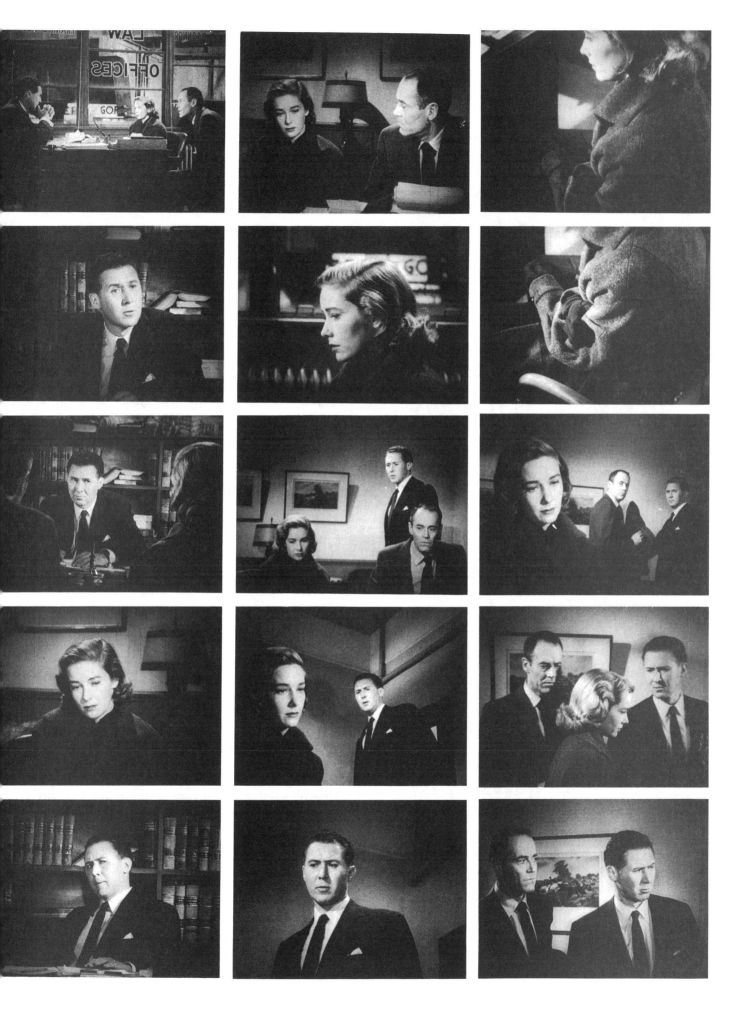

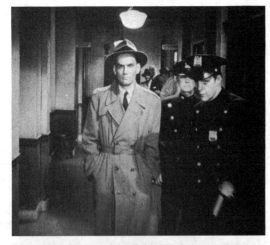

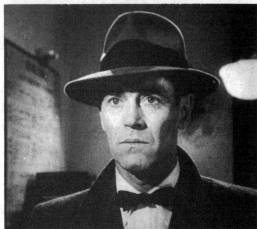

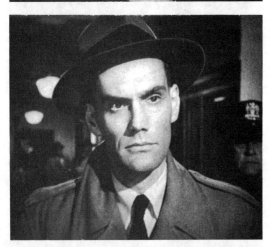

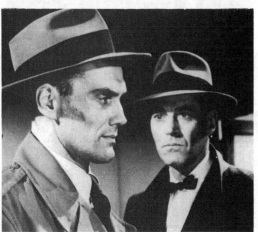

way, with the camera always at normal level, like a documentary; it should have been handled like a newsreel reportage.

A.H.   It seems to me that you want me to work for the art houses.

F.T.   Of course not. I hope you'll forgive my insistence on this point. The scenes inspired by the true-life cases of Dr. Crippen and Patrick Mahon were very successfully integrated into *Rear Window*, but I sincerely believe the kind of material that is a hundred per cent authentic isn't suitable for your style.

A.H.   Let's just say it wasn't my kind of picture. But the industry was in a crisis at the time, and since I'd done a lot of work for Warner Brothers, I made this picture for them without taking any salary for my work. It was their property.

F.T.   I'd like to point out that my objections to this picture are based on your own viewpoint. You've convinced me that the best Hitchcock films are the ones that are the most popular with the audience. That's exactly as it should be, since the public's reaction is an essential component of your work.
Still, I should mention that I liked some of *The Wrong Man* scenes very much. In particular, the second scene in the lawyer's office. Previously there was a scene there in which Henry Fonda appeared to be very disheartened, while Vera Miles was so lively and talkative that she rather annoyed the lawyer. In the second scene Henry Fonda is more confident and eloquent than the first time and the lawyer seems to be more optimistic as well. On the other hand, Vera Miles is now completely apathetic; she hardly listens to what they are saying. And because Henry Fonda sees her every day, he doesn't seem to be aware of the change in his wife, but the lawyer is obviously surprised and disturbed by what's happened to her. As he rises from his desk to walk around the office behind the couple, his face shows what he's thinking. It's obvious that he believes his client's wife is losing her mind. Although the dialogue is perfectly innocuous, all of this comes through very

clearly. It's a superb instance of a purely cinematic scene, a specifically Hitchcockian scene. But I must point out that here you departed from the faithful reconstruction of the real story to return to the fiction form.

A.H.   Well, let's file *The Wrong Man* among the indifferent Hitchcocks.

F.T.   That's not what I was getting at. I hoped you might defend the picture.

A.H.   Impossible, I don't feel that strongly about it. But I did fancy the opening of the picture because of my own fear of the police. I also liked the part where the real culprit is discovered just as Fonda is praying. Yes, I liked that ironic coincidence.

———————

F.T.   *Vertigo* is taken from the Boileau–Narcejac novel *D'Entre les Morts*, which was especially written so that you might do a screen version of it.

A.H.   No, it wasn't. The novel was out before we acquired the rights to the property.

F.T.   Just the same, that book was especially written for you.

A.H.   Do you really think so? What if I hadn't bought it?

F.T.   In that case it would have been bought by some French director, on account of the success of *Diabolique*. As a matter of fact, Boileau and Narcejac did four or five novels on that theory. When they found out that you had been interested in acquiring the rights to *Diabolique*, they went to work and wrote *D'Entre les Morts*, which Paramount bought for you. Can you tell me what it was about this book that specially appealed to you? *

———————

* Scottie Ferguson (James Stewart), who, due to acrophobia (fear of heights), has resigned from the San Francisco police force, is asked by Gavin Elster (Tom Helmore), a former friend, to shadow his wife, Madeleine (Kim Novak), whom he describes as a suicidal neurotic.

A.H.   I was intrigued by the hero's attempts to re-create the image of a dead woman through another one who's alive.

As you know, the story is divided into two parts. The first part goes up to Madeleine's death, when she falls from the steeple, and the second part opens with the hero's meeting with Judy, a brunette who looks just like Madeleine. In the book it's at the beginning of that second part that the hero meets Judy and tries to get her to look like Madeleine, and it's only at the very end that both he and the reader discover that Madeleine and Judy are one and the same girl. That's the final surprise twist.

In the screenplay we used a different approach. At the beginning of the second part, when Stewart meets the brunette, the truth about Judy's identity is disclosed, but *only* to the viewer. Though Stewart isn't aware of it yet, the viewers already know that Judy isn't just a girl who looks like Madeleine, but that she *is* Madeleine! Everyone around me was against this change; they all felt that the revelation should be saved for the end of the picture. I put myself in the place of a child whose mother is telling him a story. When there's a pause in her narration, the child always says, "What comes next, Mommy?" Well, I felt that the second part of the novel was written as if nothing came next, whereas in my formula, the little boy, *knowing* that Madeleine and Judy are the same person, would then ask, "And Stewart doesn't know it, does he? What will he do when he finds out about it?"

———————

The former detective gradually falls deeply in love with the woman he is trailing. He saves her life when she attempts to drown herself but, because of his phobia, is unable to prevent her death when, some time later, she throws herself from the top of a church steeple. Overwhelmed by guilt feelings, Scottie has a nervous breakdown. With the help of an old girl friend, Midge (Barbara Bel Geddes), he returns to a normal life.

One day, on the street, he encounters the living image of his dead love, who claims she is Judy Barton and maintains she has never seen him, or heard of Madeleine. He is attracted to the girl but puzzled by the uncanny resemblance. The truth is that Judy *is* Madeleine, who, at the time of their former meeting, was not Elster's wife but his mistress. Her supposed death was part of a carefully planned hoax to get rid of the real wife, with the two accomplices staging the killing in such a way that the helpless detective would swear he has witnessed Mrs. Elster's suicide.

When Scottie finally becomes suspicious, in an attempt to make Judy confess, he takes her back to the tower and forces himself to accompany her to the top, only to see the terrified young woman accidentally trip and this time really fall to her death.

In other words, we're back to our usual alternatives: Do we want suspense or surprise? We followed the book up to a certain point. At first Stewart thinks Judy may be Madeleine; then he resigns himself to the fact that she isn't, on condition that Judy will agree to resemble Madeleine in every respect. But now we give the public the truth about the hoax so that our suspense will hinge around the question of how Stewart is going to react when he discovers that Judy and Madeleine are actually the same person.

That's the main line of thought. But there's an additional point of interest in the screenplay. You will remember that Judy resisted the idea of being made to look like Madeleine. In the book she was simply reluctant to change her appearance, with no justification for her attitude. Whereas in the film, the girl's reason for fighting off the changes is that she would eventually be unmasked. So much for the plot.

To put it plainly, the man wants to go to bed with a woman who's dead; he is indulging in a form of necrophilia.

F.T. Those scenes in which James Stewart takes Judy to the dress shop to buy a suit just like the one Madeleine wore, and the way in which he makes her try on shoes, are among the best. He's like a maniac.

A.H. That's the basic situation in this picture. Cinematically, all of Stewart's efforts to re-create the dead woman are shown in such a way that he seems to be trying to undress her, instead of the other way around. What I liked best is when the girl came back after having had her hair dyed blond. James Stewart is disappointed because she hasn't put her hair up in a bun. What this really means is that the girl has almost stripped, but she still won't take her knickers off. When he insists, she says, "All right!" and goes into the bathroom while he waits outside. What Stewart is really waiting for is for the woman to emerge totally naked this time, and ready for love.

F.T. That didn't occur to me, but the close-up on Stewart's face as he's waiting for her to come out of the bathroom is wonderful; he's almost got tears in his eyes.

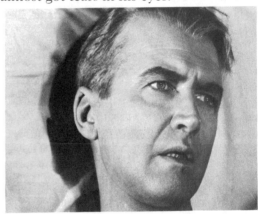

A.H. At the beginning of the picture, when James Stewart follows Madeleine to the cemetery, we gave her a dreamlike, mysterious quality by shooting through a fog filter. That gave us a green effect, like fog over the bright sunshine. Then, later on, when Stewart first meets

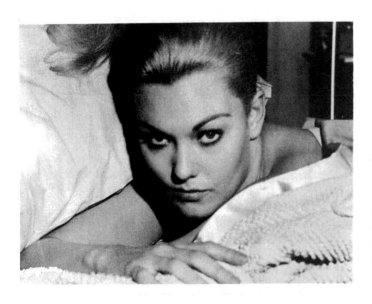

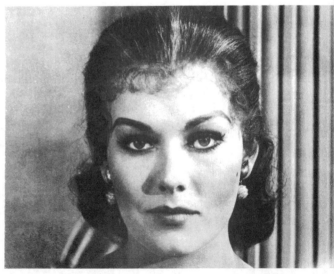

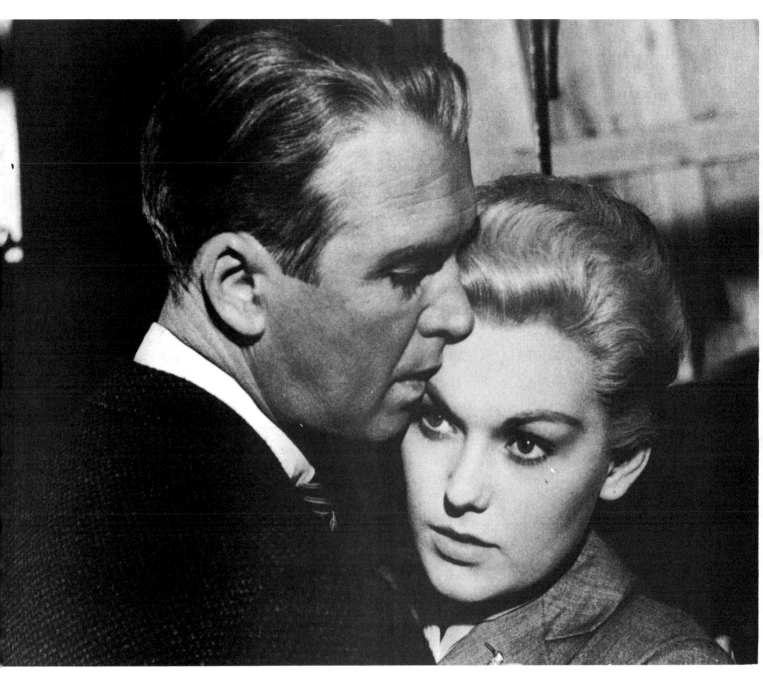

Judy, I decided to make her live at the Empire Hotel in Post Street because it has a green neon sign flashing continually outside the window. So when the girl emerges from the bathroom, that green light gives her the same subtle, ghostlike quality. After focusing on Stewart, who's staring at her, we go back to the girl, but now we slip that soft effect away to indicate that Stewart's come back to reality. Temporarily dazed by the vision of his beloved Madeleine come back from the dead, Stewart comes to his senses when he spots the locket. In a flash he realizes that Judy's been tricking him right along.

F.T.   The whole erotic aspect of the picture is fascinating. I remember another scene, at the beginning, when Stewart hauled Kim Novak out of the water. He takes her to his place, where we find her asleep in his bed. As she gradually comes to, there's an implication, though it's not specifically stated, that he's probably taken the girl's clothes off and has seen her in

245

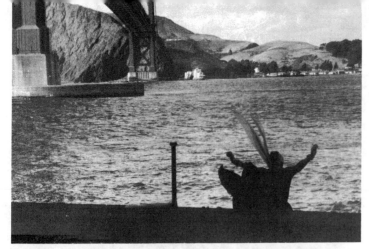

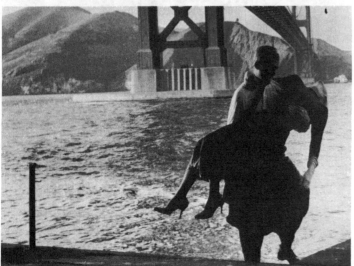

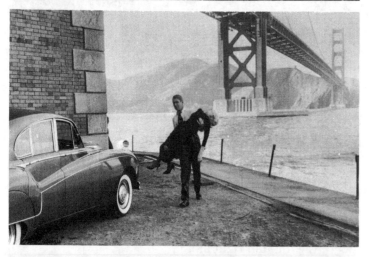

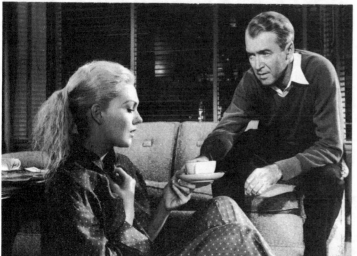

the nude. The rest of that scene is superb, as Kim Novak walks around with her toes sticking out of his bathrobe and then settles down by the fire, with Stewart pacing back and forth behind her.

Vertigo unfolds at a deliberate pace, with a contemplative rhythm that contrasts sharply with your other pictures, which are mostly based on swift motion and sudden transitions.

A.H. That's perfectly natural since we're telling the story from the viewpoint of a man who's in an emotional crisis.

Did you notice the distortion when Stewart looks down the tower stairway? Do you know how we did that?

F.T. Wasn't that a track-out combined with a forward zoom?

A.H. That's it. When Joan Fontaine fainted at the inquest in *Rebecca*, I wanted to show how she felt that everything was moving far away from her before she toppled over. I always remember one night at the Chelsea Arts Ball at Albert Hall in London when I got terribly drunk and I had the sensation that everything was going far away from me. I tried to get that into *Rebecca*, but they couldn't do it. The viewpoint must be fixed, you see, while the perspective is changed as it stretches lengthwise. I thought about the problem for fifteen years. By the time we got to *Vertigo*, we solved it by using the dolly and zoom simultaneously. I asked how much it would cost, and they told me it would cost fifty thousand dollars. When I asked why, they said, "Because to put the camera at the top of the stairs we have to have a big apparatus to lift it, counterweight it, and hold it up in space."

I said, "There are no characters in this scene; it's simply a viewpoint. Why can't we make a miniature of the stairway and lay it on its side, then take our shot by pulling away from it? We can use a tracking shot and a zoom flat on the ground." So that's the way we did it, and it only cost us nineteen thousand dollars.

F.T. As much as that? I feel that you really like *Vertigo.*

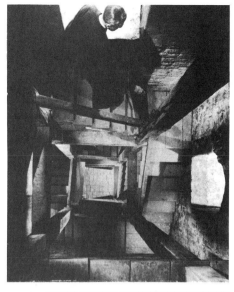

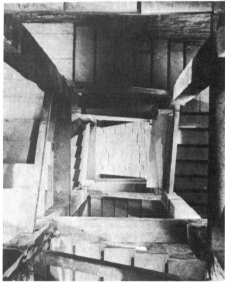

A.H. I suppose so. One of our whimsies when a picture isn't doing too well is to blame it on the faulty exploitation. So let's live up to the tradition and say they just didn't handle the sales properly! Do you know that I had Vera Miles in mind for *Vertigo*, and we had done the whole wardrobe and the final tests with her?

F.T. Didn't Paramount want her?

A.H. Paramount was perfectly willing to have her, but she became pregnant just before the part that was going to turn her into a star. After that I lost interest; I couldn't get the rhythm going with her again.

F.T. I take it, from some of your interviews, that you weren't too happy with Kim Novak, but I thought she was perfect for the picture. There was a passive, animal quality about her that was exactly right for the part.

A.H. Miss Novak arrived on the set with all sorts of preconceived notions that I couldn't possibly go along with. You know, I don't like to argue with a performer on the set; there's no reason to bring the electricians in on our troubles. I went to Kim Novak's dressing room and told her about the dresses and hairdos that I had

A.H. One of the things that bothers me is a flaw in the story. The husband was planning to throw his wife down from the top of the tower. But how could he know that James Stewart wouldn't make it up those stairs? Because he became dizzy? How could he be sure of that!

F.T. That's true, but I saw it as one of those assumptions you felt people would accept. I understand that the picture was neither a hit nor a failure.

A.H. It has made money by now.

F.T. In your terms, wouldn't that be considered a flop?

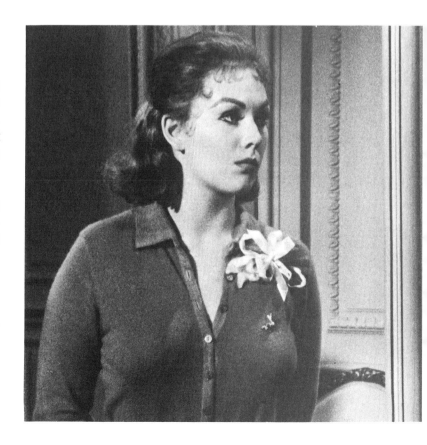

been planning for several months. I also explained that the story was of less importance to me than the over-all visual impact on the screen, once the picture is completed.

F.T. It seems to me these unpleasant formalities make you unfair in assessing the whole picture. I can assure you that those who admire *Vertigo* like Kim Novak in it. Very few American actresses are quite as carnal on the screen. When you see Judy walking on the street, the tawny hair and make-up convey an animal-like sensuality. That quality is accentuated, I suppose, by the fact that she wears no brassière.

A.H. That's right, she doesn't wear a brassière. As a matter of fact, she's particularly proud of that!

F.T. Before shooting *North by Northwest* I believe you worked on a project about a shipwreck and then dropped it. Is that right?

A.H. That was *The Wreck of the Mary Deare*. I went to work on that with Ernest Lehman and we found it wasn't going to be any good. It belongs to the type of story that's very hard to lick. There's a very famous legend called "the Mystery of the Marie Celeste." Do you know it? It's supposed to have happened in the middle of the nineteenth century, when a ship was discovered, in full sail, in the Atlantic. People who boarded the ship found the lifeboats, the galley stove was still hot, and there were the remnants of a meal, but no sign of life.
Why is it that we can't lick this type of story? Because it's too strong to begin with. There's so much mystery from the very outset that the attempt to explain it is bound to be terribly laborious. The rest of the story never quite lives up to the beginning.

F.T. I see what you mean.

A.H. Anyway, a writer called Hammond Innes had written a novel, *The Wreck of the Mary Deare*, about a cargo boat that is sailing along the English Channel with only one man aboard who's stoking coal into the furnace. Two sailors from a salvage vessel that's passing by

manage to board the ship. Anyway, you have a beautiful setup in that mystery ship with a single man on board. But as soon as you go into the explanations, the whole thing becomes very trite, and the public is apt to wonder why you didn't show the events that led up to this point. It's really like picking out the climax of a story and putting it at the beginning. Since I was committed to Metro to do that picture, I told them that the story wouldn't work out and suggested we do something else. So that's how, starting at zero, we went on to do *North by Northwest*.
When you're involved in a project and you see it isn't going to work out, the wisest thing is to simply throw the whole thing away.

F.T. To my knowledge, you've done just that several times. Wasn't there supposed to be a picture on Africa?

A.H. I'd bought a story called *Flamingo Feather*, written by a South African author who was also a diplomat. His name is Laurens van der Post. It was the story of mysterious happenings in South Africa today. A lot of people were involved; it was hinged around a secret compound in which large numbers of natives were being trained under Russian command. I went to South Africa to do some advance research on the shooting, and I found out that there was no chance of getting the fifty thousand Africans we needed. I said, "Well, how did they make *King Solomon's Mines?*" They told me they'd only used a few hundred natives on that, and the costumes had been sent over from Hollywood. Apparently they don't make those costumes in Africa. Then I asked again why we couldn't get fifty thousand Africans, and I was told that the natives work on the pineapple plantations and at many other jobs and the work couldn't be stopped for a movie. When I wanted to look over the terrain, they showed me the Valley of a Thousand Hills in Natal. I said, "We can get the same scenery sixty miles north of Los Angeles." It was all so confusing that I dropped the whole idea.

F.T. Were the political aspects of such a film a factor in your decision to give it up?

A.H.   I suppose so.

F.T.   You generally avoid any politics in your films.

A.H.   It's just that the public doesn't care for films on politics. How else would you account for the fact that most of the pictures dealing with the politics of the Iron Curtain are failures? The same applies to films about domestic politics.

F.T.   Isn't it because they're mostly propaganda films, and rather naïve ones at that?

A.H.   Yet there've been quite a few pictures on East and West Berlin. Carol Reed made one called *The Man Between*; Kazan made *Man on a Tightrope*, and Fox produced a picture with Gregory Peck, which involved a businessman's son captured by the East Germans. I can't remember the name. Then there was *The Big Lift*, with Montgomery Clift. None of them has been really successful.

F.T.   It's possible that people don't like the mélange of reality and fiction. The best might be a straightforward documentary.

A.H.   You know, I have an idea for a really good Cold War suspense movie. An American, speaking Russian fluently, is parachuted into Russia, and the little man who looks after him on the plane accidentally falls through the opening, so that the two men come down together on the one parachute. The first one not only speaks fluent Russian; he also has the necessary papers and could be taken for a Russian citizen, while the little man with him has no papers and doesn't speak a word of Russian. This is the point of departure from the story. Every second would be suspenseful.

F.T.   One solution might be for the Russian-speaking man to pass the other one off as his deaf-mute kid brother.

A.H.   Yes, that could be done at times, but the real value of this situation is that it enables you to do the whole dialogue in Russian all the way through, with the other man constantly asking, "What did they say? What did they do?" His real purpose, you see, would be to serve as the means of narration.

F.T.   It would be fun to work that out.

A.H.   But they'll never allow us to do it!

———————

F.T.   We've already mentioned *North by Northwest* several times in the course of these talks, and you seem to·agree with me that just as *The Thirty-nine Steps* may be regarded as the compendium of your work in Britain, *North by Northwest* is the picture that epitomizes the whole of your work in America. It's always difficult to sum up all the ups and downs in stories in a few words, but this one is almost impossible.*

A.H.   That brings up an amusing sidelight of the shooting. You may remember that during the first part all sorts of things happen to the hero with such bewildering rapidity that he doesn't know what it's all about. Anyway, Cary Grant came up to me and said, "It's a terrible script. We've already done a third of the picture and I still can't make head or tail of it."

F.T.   He felt the story was too confusing?

A.H.   Yes, but without realizing it he was using a line of his own dialogue.

F.T.   By the way, I meant to ask you whether you ever introduce useless dialogue in a scene, knowing in advance that people won't

---

* Here, then, is the broad outline, rather than the synopsis, of *North by Northwest*. The hero of the story is an imaginary agent created by a U.S. intelligence agency. Though he doesn't exist, he has been given an identity via the name Kaplan, a suite in a luxurious New York hotel, and a set of fine clothes. When an enemy espionage group mistakenly identifies advertising executive Cary Grant as Kaplan, he becomes a target for pursuit and is trapped in a web of circumstances so incredible that he cannot turn to the police. The harrowing nightmare is compounded by his perplexity over the confusing behavior of Eva Marie Saint, who works with the spies. After a series of adventures alternating between the ludicrous and the terrifying, the spies are exposed and the mystery is cleared up. Eva Marie Saint turns out to be an undercover agent for the U.S., and the picture winds up on a romantic note for the hero and the lovely adventuress.

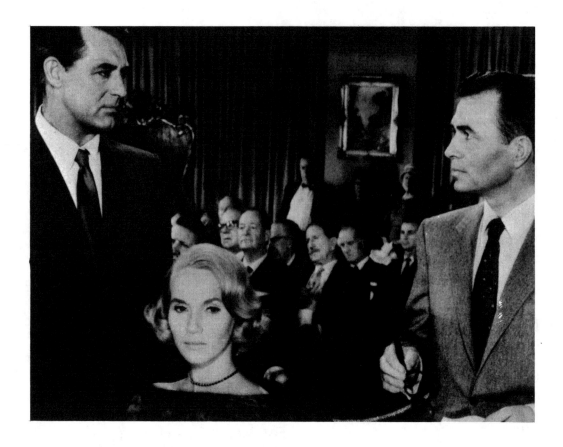

pay any attention to it?

A.H.   Why should we do that, for heaven's sake?

F.T.   Well, either to allow the audience a breather between two moments of tension or else to sum up the situation for the benefit of those viewers who may have missed the beginning of the picture.

A.H.   That practice goes back to the Griffith era. At some midway point of the picture he'd insert a few lines of narrative titles summing up everything that preceded, for the benefit of the late-comers.

F.T.   You have the equivalent of that in the second third of *North by Northwest*. There's a dialogue scene at the airport in which Cary Grant tells Leo G. Carroll, the counterintelligence man, everything that's happened to him since the beginning of the picture.

A.H.   That scene has a dual function.

Firstly, it clarifies and sums up the sequence of events for the audience, and, secondly, Cary Grant's account is the cue for the counterintelligence agent to fill him in on some of the missing elements of these mystifying events.

F.T.   Yes, but we don't know what he's saying because his voice is drowned out by the roar of the plane propellers.

A.H.   It wasn't necessary for that to be heard because the public already had the information.

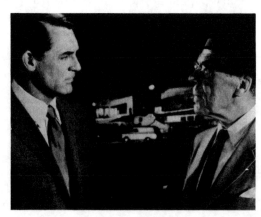

250

The facts had been brought out in a previous scene, when the counterespionage men decide that to help Cary Grant might arouse the suspicion of the spies.

F.T. Of course, I remember now. The deafening sound of the planes also serves another purpose: it makes us lose all notion of time. The counterintelligence man spends thirty seconds in telling Cary Grant a story that, in reality, would take him, at the very least, three minutes to tell.

A.H. Exactly, this is part of the play with time. In this picture nothing was left to chance, and that's why, when it was over, I took a very firm stand. I'd never worked for M-G-M before, and when it was edited, they put on a lot of pressure to have me eliminate a whole sequence at the end of the picture. I refused.

F.T. Which sequence was that?

A.H. Right after the scene in that cafeteria where people look at Mount Rushmore through a telescope. You remember that Eva Marie Saint takes a shot at Cary Grant. Actually, she only pretends to kill him in order to save his life. Well, in the next sequence he's taken to the woods to meet the girl.

F.T. When the two cars come together? But isn't that a key scene?

A.H. It's indispensable because it's truly their first meeting since Cary Grant has learned that she is James Mason's mistress, and this is the scene in which he finds out she is working for Central Intelligence. My contract had been drawn up by MCA, my agents, and when I read it over, I found that, although I hadn't asked for it, they'd put in a clause giving me complete artistic control of the picture, regardless of production time, cost or anything. So I was able to say politely, "I'm very sorry, but this sequence must remain in the picture."

———

F.T. It seems to me that there were many trick shots in that picture, lots of them almost invisible, and also many special effects, like miniatures and fake sets.

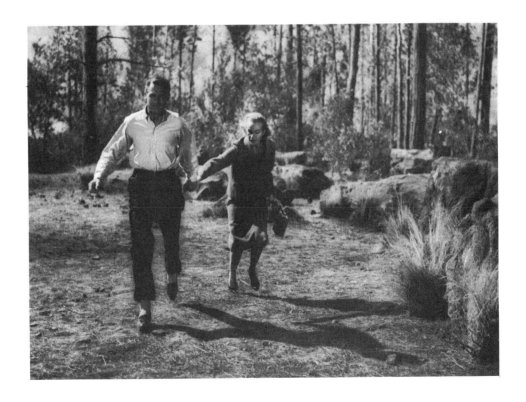

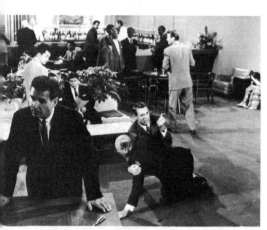

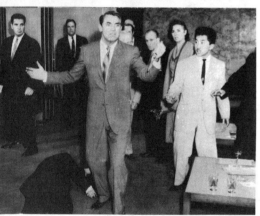

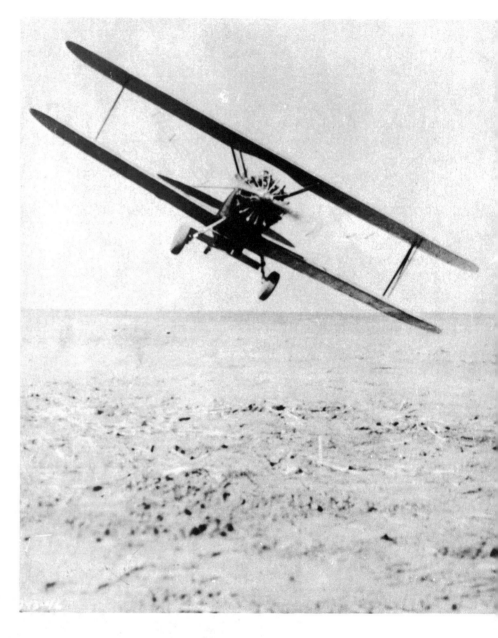

A.H.   We had an exact copy made up of the United Nations lobby. You see, someone had used that setting for a film called *The Glass Wall*, and after that Dag Hammarskjöld prohibited any shooting of fiction films on the premises.

Just the same, while the guards were looking for our equipment, we shot one scene of Cary Grant coming into the building by using a concealed camera. We'd been told we couldn't even do any photography, so we concealed the camera in the back of a truck and in that way we got enough footage for the background. Then we got a still photographer to get permission to take some colored stills inside, and I walked around with him, as if I was a visitor, whispering, "Take that shot from there. And now, another one from the roof down." We used those color photographs to reconstitute the settings in our studios.

The place where the man is stabbed in the back is in the delegates' lounge, but to maintain the prestige of the United Nations, we called it the "public lounge" in the picture, and this also explains how the man with the knife could get in there. Anyway, the locale was very accurately

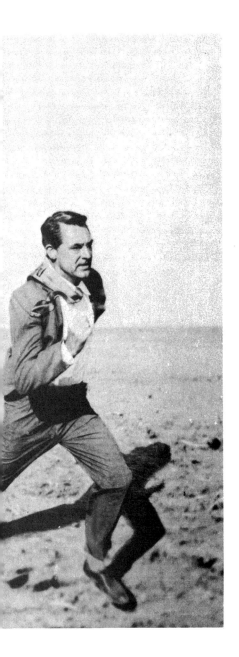

reconstructed. I'm very concerned about the authenticity of settings and furnishings. When we can't shoot in the actual settings, I'm for taking research photographs of everything.

When we were preparing to shoot *Vertigo*, in which James Stewart plays an educated detective who's retired from the police force, I sent a photographer to San Francisco. His assignment was to dig up some retired detectives, preferably college graduates, and to take pictures of their apartments.

The same for *The Birds*. In order to get the characters right, I had every inhabitant of Bodega Bay—man, woman, and child—photo-

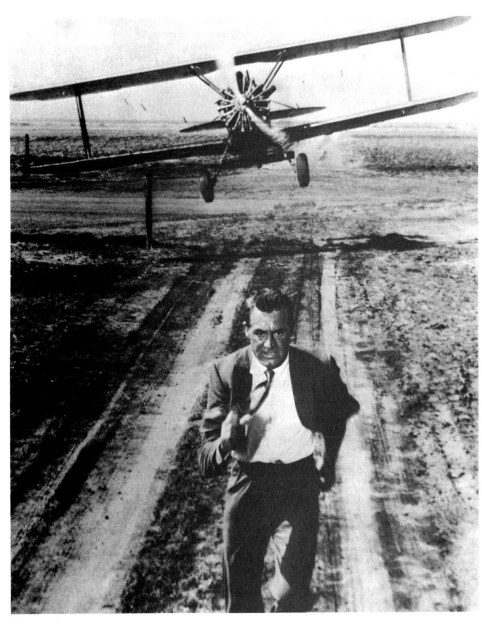

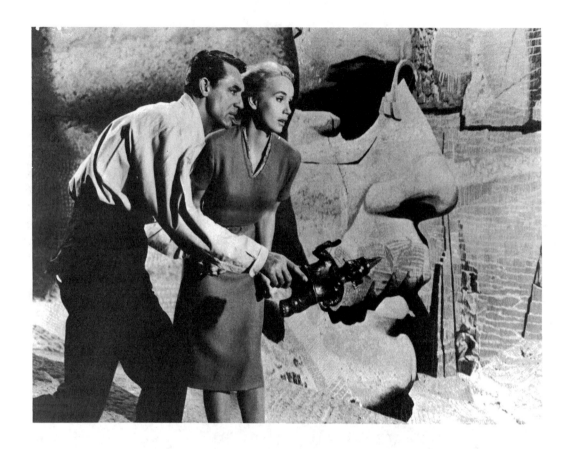

graphed for the costume department. The restaurant is an exact copy of the one up there. The home of the schoolteacher is a combination of a schoolteacher's house in San Francisco and the home of a schoolteacher in Bodega Bay. I covered it both ways because, as you may remember, the schoolteacher in that picture works in Bodega Bay but she comes from San Francisco.

The house of the farmer who's killed by the birds is an exact replica of an existing farm up there: the same entrance, the same halls, the same rooms, the same kitchen. Even the scenery of the mountain that is shown outside the window of the corridor is completely accurate.

The house that's used at the end of *North by Northwest* is the miniature of a house by Frank Lloyd Wright that's shown from a distance. We built part of it for the scene in which Cary Grant circles around it.

F.T. I'd like to talk about that long sequence with Cary Grant in the cornfields which starts long before the plane appears overhead. The scene is completely silent for some seven minutes; it's a real tour de force. In *The Man Who Knew Too Much* there is a ten-minute scene showing the concert at Albert Hall with no dialogue, but that scene is sustained by the cantata music and by the anticipation of an incident we're expecting. I believe the old way of handling this sort of thing was to accelerate the montage by using shorter and shorter cuts, whereas in *North by Northwest* all of the shots are of equal duration.

A.H. Here you're not dealing with time but with space. The length of the shots was to indicate the various distances that a man had to run for cover and, more than that, to show that there was no cover to run to. This kind of scene can't be wholly subjective because it would go by in a flash. It's necessary to show the approaching plane, even before Cary Grant spots it, because if the shot is too fast, the plane is in and out of the frame too quickly for the viewer to realize what's happening. We have the same thing in *The Birds* when Tippi Hedren is attacked in the boat. If the gulls are made to fly in and out of the picture in a flash, the audience

254

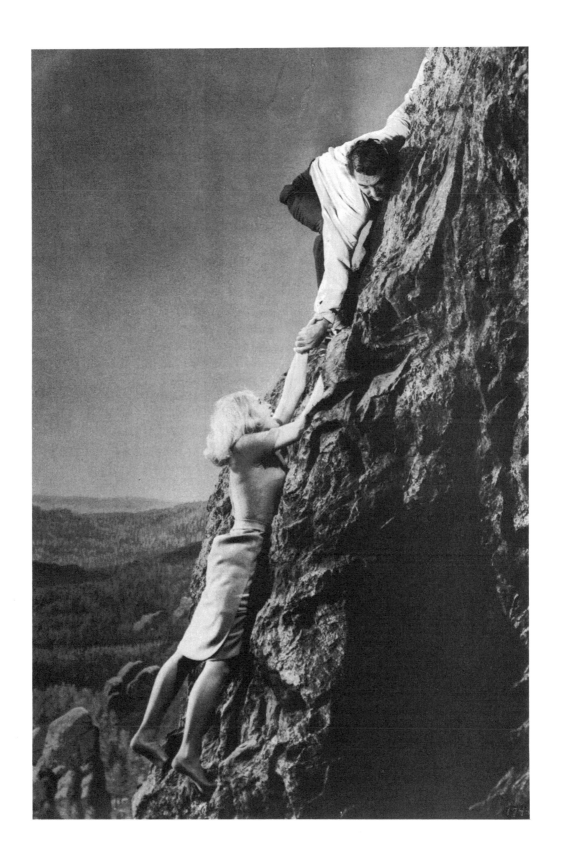

might think it's just a piece of paper that flew into her face. By doing that scene subjectively, you show the girl in the boat, you see her watching the dockside, and suddenly something hits her head. But that's still too fast. So you have to break the rule of the point of view. You deliberately abandon the subjective angle and go to an objective viewpoint, by showing the gull before it strikes, so that the audience might be fully aware of what is happening.

And we apply that same rule in *North by Northwest*, so as to prepare the public for the threat of the plane dive.

F.T.   I believe the accelerated tempo is used in many pictures to get around a technical difficulty or to patch things together in the cutting room. Frequently, when the director hasn't shot sufficient footage, the editor makes do by using the outtakes of various shots and editing them as short takes, but it's never really satisfactory. They often use that technique, for instance, to show someone being run over by a car.

A.H.   You mean that everything happens too quickly.

F.T.   In most pictures, yes.

A.H.   I had a car accident, as the basis for a trial, in one of my recent television shows. What I did was to use five shots of people witnessing the incident before I showed the accident itself. Or rather, I showed five people as they heard the sound of it. Then I filmed the end of the accident, just as the man hits the ground after his motorcycle has turned over and the offending car is speeding away. These are moments when you have to stop time, to stretch it out.

F.T.   I see. Now, let's go back to the scene in the cornfield. The most appealing aspect of that sequence with the plane is that it's totally gratuitous—it's a scene that's been drained of all plausibility or even significance. Cinema, approached in this way, becomes a truly abstract art, like music. And here it's precisely that gratuity, which you're often criticized for, that gives the scene all of its interest and strength. It's deliberately emphasized by the dialogue, when the farmer, who's about to get into the bus, points to the oncoming plane and says to Cary Grant, "Look, here comes a crop-dusting plane." And then he adds, "That's funny, there are no crops to be dusted!" And he's right, of course; that's the whole point: there's nothing to be sprayed! How can anyone object to gratuity when it's so clearly deliberate—it's planned incongruity? It's obvious that the fantasy of the absurd is a key ingredient of your film-making formula.

A.H.   The fact is I practice absurdity quite religiously!

F.T.   Since that scene doesn't serve to move the action forward, it's the kind of concept that would simply never occur to a screenwriter; only a director could dream up an idea like that!

A.H.   I'll tell you how the idea came about. I found I was faced with the old cliché situation: the man who is put on the spot, probably to be shot. Now, how is this usually done? A dark night at a narrow intersection of the city. The waiting victim standing in a pool of light under the street lamp. The cobbles are "washed with the recent rains." A close-up of a black cat slinking along against the wall of a house. A shot of a window, with a furtive face pulling back the curtain to look out. The slow approach of a black limousine, et cetera, et cetera. Now, what was the antithesis of a scene like this? No darkness, no pool of light, no mysterious figures in windows. Just nothing. Just bright sunshine and a blank, open countryside with barely a house or tree in which any lurking menaces could hide.

You'll remember my theory about using chocolate in Switzerland and windmills in Holland. Well, in that spirit, as well as because of my feeling for free fantasy, I thought up a scene for *North by Northwest*, but we never actually made it. It occurred to me that we were moving in a northwesterly direction from New York, and one of the stops on the way was Detroit, where they make Ford automobiles. Have you ever seen an assembly line?

F.T.   No, I never have.

A.H.   They're absolutely fantastic. Anyway, I wanted to have a long dialogue scene between Cary Grant and one of the factory workers as they walk along the assembly line. They might, for instance, be talking about one of the foremen. Behind them a car is being assembled, piece by piece. Finally, the car they've seen being put together from a simple nut and bolt is complete, with gas and oil, and all ready to drive off the line. The two men look at it and say, "Isn't it wonderful!" Then they open the door to the car and out drops a corpse!

F.T.   That's a great idea!

A.H.   Where has the body come from? Not from the car, obviously, since they've seen it start at zero! The corpse falls out of nowhere, you see! And the body might be that of the foreman the two fellows had been discussing.

F.T.   That's a perfect example of absolute nothingness! Why did you drop the idea? Is it because it would have made the scene too long?

A.H.   It wasn't a question of time. The real problem was that we couldn't integrate the idea into the story. Even a gratuitous scene must have some justification for being there, you know!

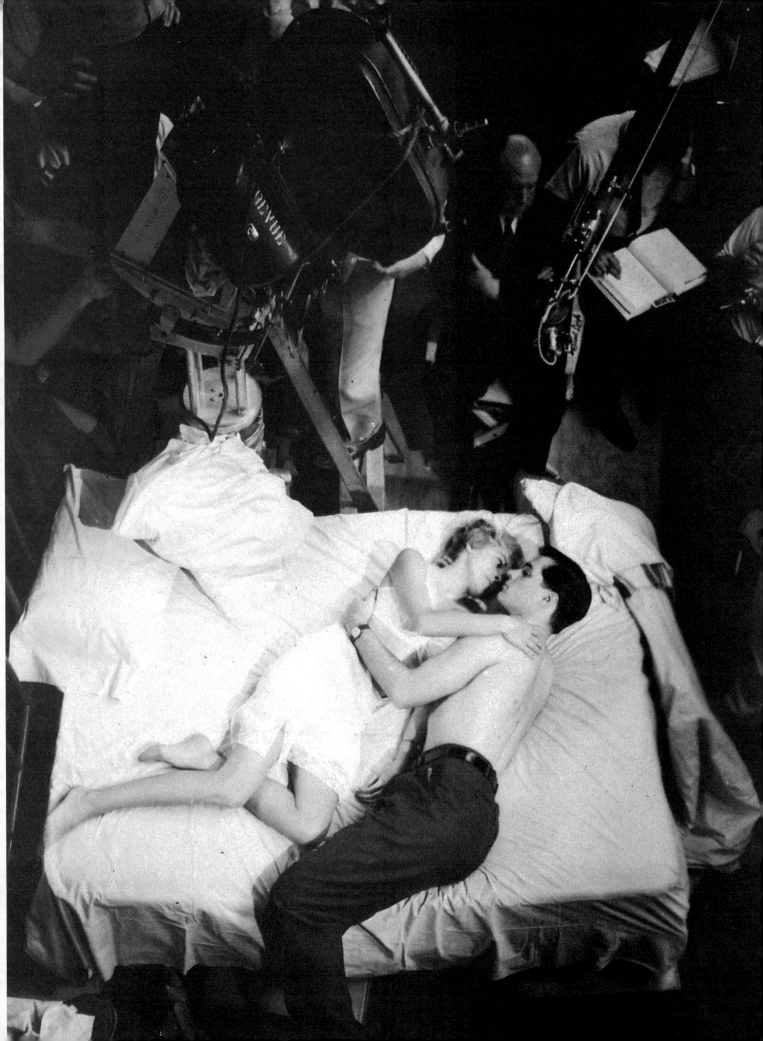

13

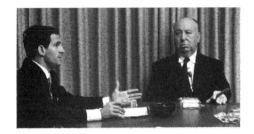

FRANÇOIS TRUFFAUT. Mr. Hitchcock, this morning you mentioned that you had had a bad night and indicated that you were probably disturbed by all of the memories that our talks have been stirring up these past several days. In the course of our conversations we've gone into the dreamlike quality of many of your films, among them *Notorious*, *Vertigo*, and *Psycho*. I'd like to ask whether you dream a lot.

ALFRED HITCHCOCK. Not too much . . . sometimes . . . and my dreams are very reasonable.
In one of my dreams I was standing on Sunset Boulevard, where the trees are, and I was waiting for a Yellow Cab to take me to lunch. But no Yellow Cab came by; all the automobiles that drove by me were of 1916 vintage. And I said to myself, "It's no good standing here waiting for a Yellow Cab because this is a 1916 dream!" So I walked to lunch instead.

F.T. Did you really dream this, or is it a joke?

A.H. No, it's not a gag; I really had a dream like that!

F.T. It's almost a period dream! But would you say that dreams have a bearing on your work?

A.H. Daydreams, probably.

F.T. It may be an expression of the unconscious, and that takes us back once more to fairy tales. By depicting the isolated man who's surrounded by all sorts of hostile elements, and

259

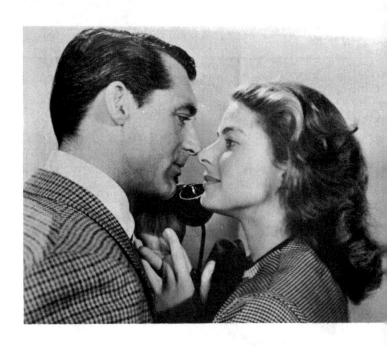

perhaps without even meaning to, you enter the realm of the dream world, which is also a world of solitude and of danger.

A.H.   That's probably me, within myself.

F.T.   It must be, because the logic of your pictures, which is sometimes decried by the critics, is rather like the logic of dreams. *Strangers on a Train* and *North by Northwest*, for instance, are made up of a series of strange forms that follow the pattern of a nightmare.

A.H.   This may be due to the fact that I'm never satisfied with the ordinary. I'm ill at ease with it.

F.T.   That's very evident. A Hitchcock picture that didn't involve death or the abnormal is practically inconceivable. I believe you film emotions you feel very deeply—fear, for instance.

A.H.   Absolutely, I'm full of fears and I do my best to avoid difficulties and any kind of complications. I like everything around me to be clear as crystal and completely calm. I don't want clouds overhead. I get a feeling of inner peace from a well-organized desk. When I take a bath, I put everything neatly back in place. You wouldn't even know I'd been in the bathroom. My passion for orderliness goes hand in hand with a strong revulsion toward complications.

F.T.   That accounts for the way you protect yourself. Any eventual problem of direction is resolved beforehand by your minute predesigned sketches that lessen the risks and prevent trouble later on. Jacques Becker used to say, "Alfred Hitchcock is undoubtedly the director who gets the least surprises when he looks at the rushes."

A.H.   That's right. I've always dreamed of the day I wouldn't have to see the rushes at all! And since we're back to dreams, I'd like to digress a moment to tell you a little story.
There was a movie writer who always seemed to have his best ideas in the middle of the night, and when he woke up in the morning, he never remembered them. So one day the man had a brilliant idea. He said to himself, "I'll put a paper and pencil beside my bed, and when I get the idea, I'll write it down." So he went to bed and, sure enough, in the middle of the night he awoke with a terrific idea. He wrote it down and went back to sleep. When he awoke the next morning, he'd forgotten the whole thing, but all of a sudden, as he was shaving, he thought to himself, "Oh God, I had a terrific idea again last night, and now I've forgotten it. But wait, I had my paper and pencil; that's right, I wrote it down!" So he rushed into the bedroom and

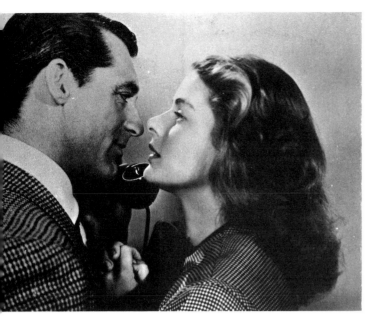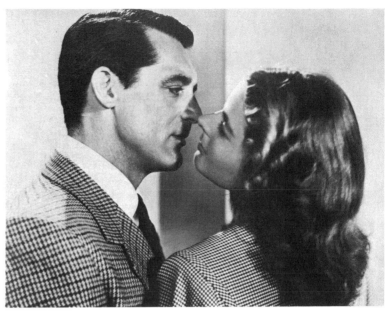

picked up the note and read what he'd written: "Boy meets girl!"

F.T.   That *is* funny.

A.H.   There's some truth to the story, you see, because you have what seems to be a really great idea in the middle of the night, but when you think it over in the cold light of dawn, it's pretty awful!

F.T.   I see we're not getting anywhere with this discussion on the impact of dreams on your work. At any rate, you don't seem to be too interested in this angle.

A.H.   One thing for sure: I never have any erotic dreams!

F.T.   And yet love and even eroticism play important roles in your work. We haven't talked about that yet. After *Notorious* you were regarded not only as the master of suspense, but also as an expert on physical love on the screen.

A.H.   I suppose there is a physical aspect to the love scenes of *Notorious*. You're probably thinking of the kissing scene between Ingrid Bergman and Cary Grant.

F.T.   As I remember it, the publicity blurbs described it as "the longest kiss in screen history."

A.H.   As a matter of fact, the actors hated doing it. They felt terribly uncomfortable at the way in which they had to cling to each other. I said, "I don't care how you feel; the only thing that matters is the way it's going to look on the screen."

F.T.   I imagine the reader will want to know why these two professionals were so ill at ease during this scene. To be specific, there was a close-up on their two faces together as they moved across the whole set. The problem for them was how to walk across, glued to each other in that way, while the only thing that concerned you was to show their two faces together on the screen.

A.H.   Exactly. I conceived that scene in terms of the participants' desire not to interrupt the romantic moment. It was essential not to break up the mood, the dramatic atmosphere. Had they broken apart, all of the emotion would have been dissipated. And, of course, they had to be in action; they had to go over to the phone that was ringing and keep on embracing throughout the whole call and then they had to get over to the door. I felt it was indispensable that they should not separate, and I also felt that the public, represented by the camera, was the third party to this embrace. The public was being given the great privilege of embracing Cary Grant and Ingrid Bergman together. It was

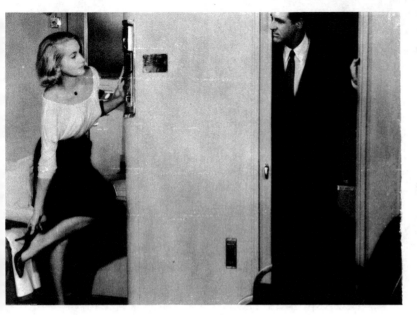 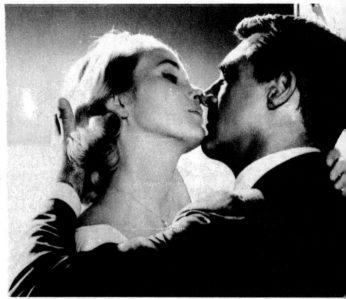

a kind of temporary *ménage à trois.*

The idea not to break up that romantic moment was inspired by the memory of something I witnessed in France several years earlier.

I was on the train going from Boulogne to Paris and we were moving slowly through the small town of Etaples. It was on a Sunday afternoon. As we were passing a large, red brick factory, I saw a young couple against the wall. The boy was urinating against the wall and the girl never let go of his arm. She'd look down at what he was doing, then look at the scenery around them, then back again at the boy. I felt this was true love at work.

F.T.   Ideally, two lovers should never separate.

A.H.   Quite. It was the memory of that incident that gave me an exact idea of the effect I was after with the kissing scene in *Notorious.*

F.T.   Your mention of the actors' irritation when they don't understand what the director is aiming at raises an interesting point. Many directors, I think, will shoot a scene within the context of the whole setting rather than solely in the context of that frame, which ultimately is what appears on the screen. I often think of that, especially when I look at your pictures, which makes me realize that great cinema, pure cinema, can stem from an establishing shot that

may seem completely absurd to the cast as well as to the crew.

A.H.   Absolutely. For instance . . .

F.T.   The long kissing scene in *Notorious* is one illustration; another is the embrace between Cary Grant and Eva Marie Saint in the train coach in *North by Northwest.* Their bodies glide along the panel, making two complete turns as they kiss each other. On the screen it's absolutely perfect, yet it must have seemed completely illogical during the shooting.

A.H.   Yes, they rotate against the wall. There, again, we applied the same rule of not separating the couple. There's just so much one can do with a love scene. Something I wish I could work out is a love scene with two people on each side of the room. It's impossible, I suppose, because the only way to suggest love would be to have them exposing themselves to each other, with the man opening his fly and the girl lifting her skirt, and the dialogue in counterpoint. Something like: "What are we going to have for supper tonight?" But I suppose that would come under the heading of out-and-out exhibitionism. Anyway, we used that counterpoint dialogue in *Notorious,* where they talk about a chicken dinner and who is going to wash the dishes, while they're kissing.

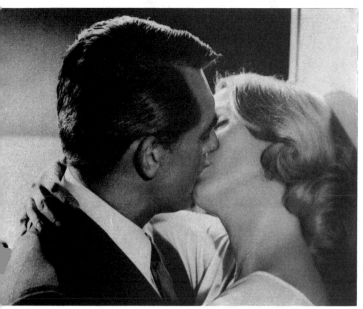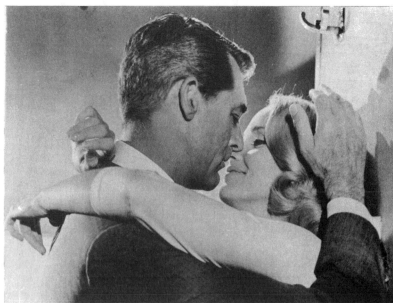

F.T. Can we go back a little? I think that I interrupted you just as you were about to say something about the realism of the frame and the mood on the set.

A.H. Well, I agree with you that many directors are conscious of the over-all atmosphere on the set, whereas they should be concerned only with what's going to come up on the screen. As you know, I never look into the view finder, but the cameraman knows very well that I don't want to have any air or space around the actors and that he must follow the sketches exactly as they are designed for each scene. There's no need to be concerned over the space in front of the camera if you bear in mind that for the final image we can take a pair of scissors to eliminate the unnecessary space.

Another aspect of the same problem is that space should not be wasted, because it can be used for dramatic effect. For instance, in *The Birds*, when the birds attack the barricaded house and Melanie is cringing back on the sofa, I kept the camera back and used the space to show the nothingness from which she's shrinking. When I went back to her, I varied that by placing the camera high to convey the impression of the fear that's rising in her. After that, there was another movement, high up and around her. But the space at the beginning was of key importance to the scene. If I'd started, at the outset, right next to the girl, we'd have the

feeling that she was recoiling in front of some danger that she could see but the public could not. And I wanted to establish just the contrary, to show that there was nothing off screen. Therefore, all of that space had a specific meaning.

Some directors will place their actors in the decor and then they'll set the camera at a distance, which depends simply on whether the actor happens to be seated, standing, or lying down. That, to me, seems to be pretty woolly thinking. It's never precise and it certainly doesn't express anything.

F.T. In other words, to inject realism into a given film frame, a director must allow for a certain amount of unreality in the space immediately surrounding that frame. For instance, the close-up of a kiss between two supposedly standing figures might be obtained by having the two actors kneeling on a kitchen table.

A.H. That's one way of doing it. And we might even raise that table some nine inches to have it come into the frame. Do you want to show a man standing behind a table? Well, the closer you get to him, the higher you must raise the table if you want to keep it inside the image. Anyhow, many directors overlook these things and they hold their camera too far away to keep that table inside the image. They think that everything on the screen will look just the way

263

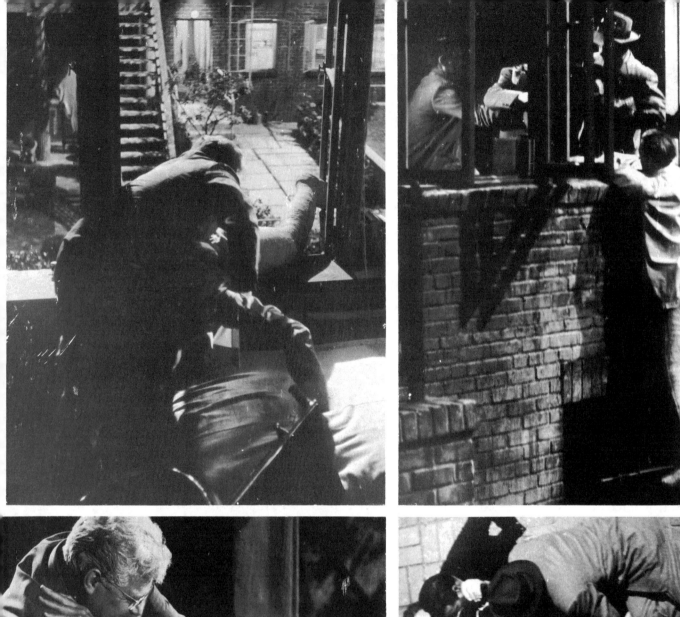

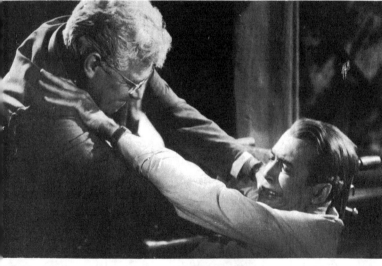

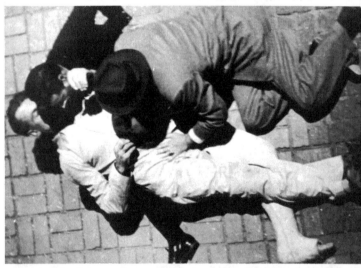

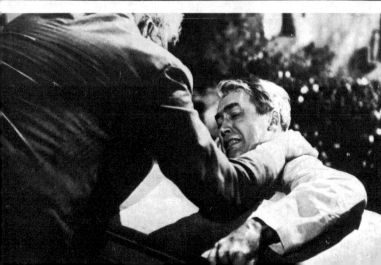

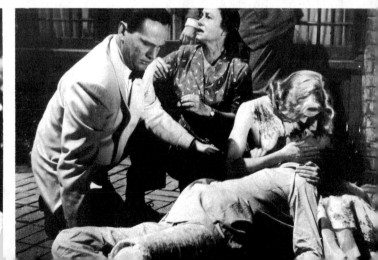

it looks on the set. It's ridiculous!

You've raised a very important point here, a point that's fundamental. The placing of the images on the screen, in terms of what you're expressing, should never be dealt with in a factual manner. Never! You can get anything you want through the proper use of cinematic techniques, which enable you to work out any image you need. There's no justification for a short cut and no reason to settle for a compromise between the image you wanted and the image you get. One of the reasons most films aren't sufficiently rigorous is that so few people in the industry know anything about imagery.

F.T.   The term "imagery" is particularly appropriate, because what we're saying is that it isn't necessary to photograph something violent in order to convey the feeling of violence, but rather to film that which gives the impression of violence.

This is demonstrated in one of the opening scenes of *North by Northwest*, in which the villains in a drawing room begin to manhandle Cary Grant. If you examine that scene in slow motion, on the small screen of the cutting room, you will see that the villains aren't doing anything at all to Cary Grant. But when projected on theater screens, that succession of quick frames and the little bobbing movements of the camera create an impression of brutality and violence.

A.H.   There's a much better illustration in *Rear Window* when the man comes into the room to throw James Stewart out of the window. At first I had filmed the whole thing completely realistically. It was a weak scene; it wasn't impressive. So I did a close-up of a waving hand, a close-up of Stewart's face and another one of his legs; then I intercut all of this in proper rhythm and the final effect was just right.

Now let's take a real-life analogy. If you stand close to a train as it's speeding through a station, you feel it; it almost knocks you down. But if you look at the same train from a distance of some two miles, you don't feel anything at all. In the same way, if you're going to show two men fighting with each other, you're not going to get very much by simply photographing that fight. More often than not the photographic

reality is not realistic. The only way to do it is to get into the fight and make the public feel it. In that way you achieve true realism.

F.T.   One method of unrealistic shooting to get a realitic effect is to set the decor behind the actors into motion.

A.H.   That's one way to do it, but it isn't a rule. It would entirely depend upon the movements of the actors. As for myself, I'm quite satisfied to let the pieces of film create the motion. For instance, in *Sabotage*, when the little boy is in the bus and he's got the bomb at his side, I cut to that bomb from a different angle every time I showed it. I did that to give the bomb a vitality of its own, to animate it. If I'd shown it constantly from the same angle, the public would have become used to the package: "Oh well, it's only a package, after all." But what I was saying was: "Be careful! Watch out!"

F.T.   To get back to that train you mentioned a while back, in *North by Northwest*, there's a scene in which the action takes place inside the train, but you show the whole of the train from the outside. To do that you didn't set your camera on the outside, in the fields, but you attached it to the train so that it was entirely dependent on it.

A.H.   Planting the camera in the countryside to shoot a passing train would merely give us the viewpoint of a cow watching a train go by. I tried to keep the public inside the train, *with* the train. Whenever it went into a curve, we took a longshot from one of the train windows. The way we did that was to put three cameras on the rear platform of the *Twentieth Century Limited*, and we went over the exact journey of the film at the same time of the day. One of our cameras was used for the long shots of the train in the curves, while the two others were used for background footage.

F.T.   In your technique everything is subordinated to the dramatic impact; the camera, in fact, accompanies the characters almost like an escort.

A.H.   While we're on the subject of the camera flow and of cutting from one shot to another, I'd like to mention what I regard as a fundamental rule: When a character who has been seated stands up to walk around a room, I

Opposite, the excitement of this sequence from *Rear Window* is heightened by Hitchcock's editing.

will never change the angle or move the camera back. I always start the movement on the close-up, the same size close-up I used while he was seated.

In most pictures, when two people are seen talking together, you have a close-up on one of them, then a close-up on the other, then you move back and forth again, and suddenly the camera jumps back for a long shot, to show one of the characters rising to walk around. It's wrong to handle it that way.

F.T.   Yes, because that technique *precedes* the action instead of *accompanying* it. It allows the public to guess that one of the characters is about to stand up, or whatever. In other words, the camera should never anticipate what's about to follow.

A.H.   Exactly, because that dissipates the emotion and I'm convinced that's wrong. If a character moves around and you want to retain the emotion on his face, the only way to do that is to travel the close-up.

————

F.T.   Before talking about *Psycho* I would like to ask whether you have any theory in respect to the opening scene of your pictures. Some of them start out with an act of violence; others simply indicate the locale.

A.H.   It all depends on what the purpose is. The opening of *The Birds* is an attempt to suggest the normal, complacent, everyday life in San Francisco. Sometimes I simply use a title to indicate that we're in Phoenix or in San Francisco. It's too easy, I know, but it's economical. I'm torn between the need for economy and the wish to present a locale, even when it's a familiar one, with more subtlety. After all, it's no problem at all to present Paris with the Eiffel Tower in the background, or London with Big Ben on the horizon.

F.T.   In pictures that don't open up with violence, you almost invariably apply the same rule of exposition: From the farthest to the nearest. You show the city, then a building in the city, a room in that building. That's the way *Psycho* begins. *

A.H.   In the opening of *Psycho* I wanted to say that we were in Phoenix, and we even spelled out the day and the time, but I only did that to lead up to a very important fact: that it was two–forty-three in the afternoon and this is the only time the poor girl has to go to bed with her lover. It suggests that she's spent her whole lunch hour with him.

F.T.   It's a nice touch because it establishes at once that this is an illicit affair.

A.H.   It also allows the viewer to become a Peeping Tom.

F.T.   Jean Douchet, a French film critic, made a witty comment on that scene. He wrote that since John Gavin is stripped to his waist, but Janet Leigh wears a brassière, the scene is only satisfying to one half of the audience.

A.H.   In truth, Janet Leigh should not have been wearing a brassière. I can see nothing im-

————

* Marion (Janet Leigh) and her lover, Sam (John Gavin), lack the necessary funds to settle down to married life. When her employer gives her forty thousand dollars to be deposited to his account in the bank, she steals the money and leaves Phoenix. That night she stops at a run-down motel. The young owner, Norman Bates (Anthony Perkins), becomes friendly and tells her that he lives in the brooding Victorian mansion nearby with his mother, a sick and apparently difficult woman.

As Marion is taking a shower before retiring for the night, the old lady suddenly appears in the bathroom and stabs her to death. Minutes later Norman appears, and though apparently grief-stricken, he proceeds to wipe away the bloodstains from the bathroom and to haul Marion's body and her possessions to her car trunk. He then drives the car to a nearby pond and stands by as the muddy waters swallow up all the evidence of the crime.

Three people undertake to trace the missing young woman: her sister, Lila (Vera Miles), Sam, and Arbogast (Martin Balsam), an insurance detective who has been assigned to find the money. Arbogast's investigation leads him to the motel, where Norman speaks to him but arouses his suspicions when he refuses to allow him to meet his mother. The detective calls Sam and Lila to tell them of his suspicions, then steals back into the house to speak to the old lady. He makes his way to the first floor, and as he reaches the landing, he is stabbed to death, his inert body toppling down the stairs.

Lila and Sam now learn from the local sheriff that Norman Bates's mother has been dead and buried for the past eight years. They go to the motel, and when Lila attempts to search the house, she has a narrow escape from death. In the ensuing struggle Norman is revealed as a schizophrenic, leading a dual existence, and who, when impersonating his dead mother, is also a homicidal maniac.

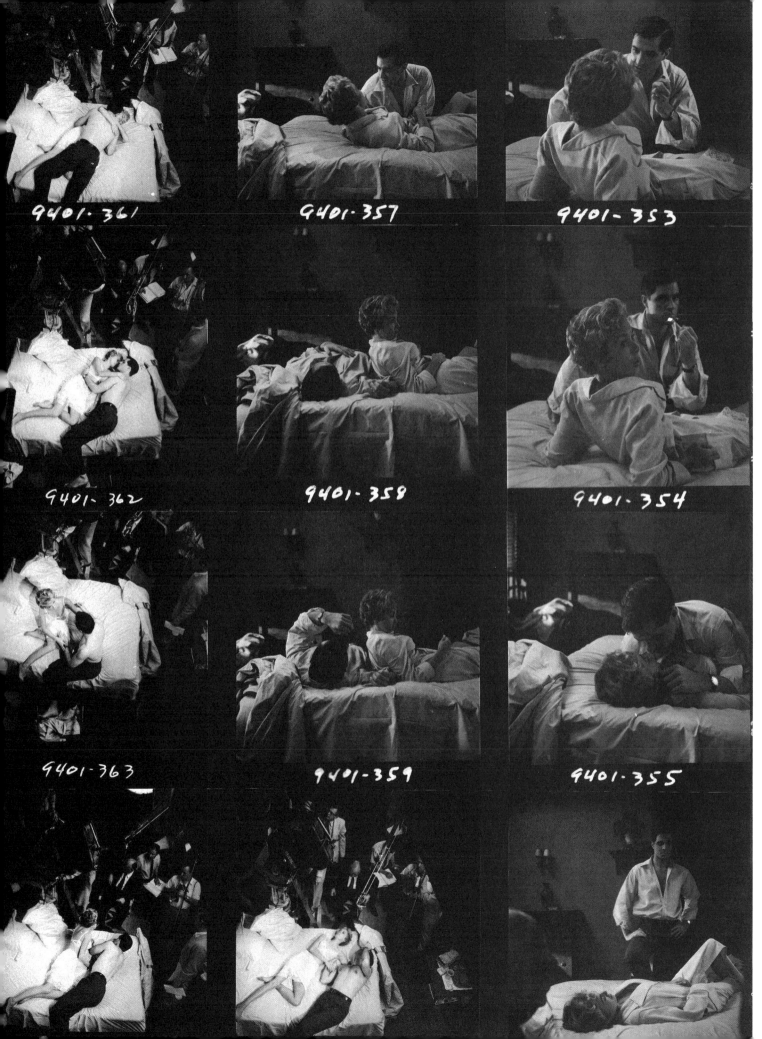

9401-361 9401-357 9401-353

9401-362 9401-358 9401-354

9401-363 9401-359 9401-355

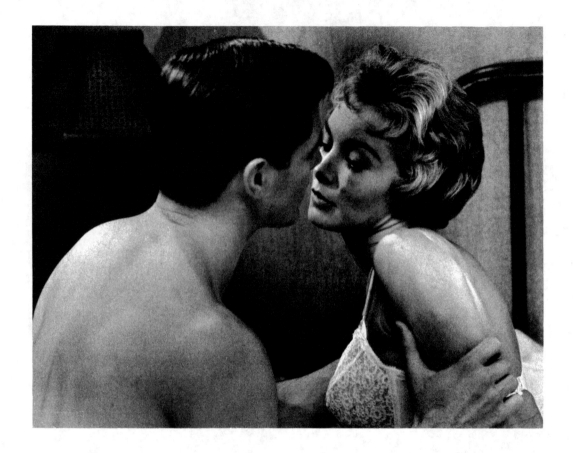

moral about that scene and I get no special kick out of it. But the scene would have been more interesting if the girl's bare breasts had been rubbing against the man's chest.

F.T.   I noticed that throughout the whole picture you tried to throw out red herrings to the viewers, and it occurred to me that the reason for that erotic opening was to mislead them again. The sex angle was raised so that later on the audience would think that Anthony Perkins is merely a voyeur. If I'm not mistaken, out of your fifty works, this is the only film showing a woman in a brassière.

A.H.   Well, one of the reasons for which I wanted to do the scene in that way was that the audiences are changing. It seems to me that the straightforward kissing scene would be looked down at by the younger viewers; they'd feel it was silly. I know that they themselves behave as John Gavin and Janet Leigh did. I think that nowadays you have to show them the way they themselves behave most of the time. Besides, I

also wanted to give a visual impression of despair and solitude in that scene.

F.T.   Yes, it occurred to me that *Psycho* was oriented toward a new generation of filmgoers. There were many things in that picture that you'd never done in your earlier films.

A.H.   Absolutely. In fact, that's also true in a technical sense for *The Birds*.

F.T.   I've read the novel from which *Psycho* was taken, and one of the things that bothered me is that it cheats. For instance, there are passages like this: "Norman sat down beside his mother and they began a conversation." Now, since she doesn't exist, that's obviously misleading, whereas the film narration is rigorously worked out to eliminate these discrepancies. What was it that attracted you to the novel?

A.H.   I think that the thing that appealed to me and made me decide to do the picture was the suddenness of the murder in the shower,

268

coming, as it were, out of the blue. That was about all.

F.T.　The killing is pretty much like a rape. I believe the novel was based on a newspaper story.

A.H.　It was the story of a man who kept his mother's body in his house, somewhere in Wisconsin.

F.T.　In *Psycho* there's a whole arsenal of terror, which you generally avoid: the ghostly house . . .

A.H.　The mysterious atmosphere is, to some extent, quite accidental. For instance, the actual locale of the events is in northern California, where that type of house is very common. They're either called "California Gothic," or, when they're particularly awful, they're called "California gingerbread." I did not set out to reconstruct an old-fashioned Universal horror-picture atmosphere. I simply wanted to be accurate, and there is no question but that both the house and the motel are authentic reproductions of the real thing. I chose that house and motel because I realized that if I had taken an ordinary low bungalow the effect wouldn't have been the same. I felt that type of architecture would help the atmosphere of the yarn.

F.T.　I must say that the architectural contrast between the vertical house and the horizontal motel is quite pleasing to the eye.

A.H.　Definitely, that's our composition: a vertical block and a horizontal block.

F.T.　In that whole picture there isn't a single character with whom a viewer might identify.

A.H.　It wasn't necessary. Even so, the audience was probably sorry for the poor girl at the time of her death. In fact, the first part of the story was a red herring. That was deliberate, you see, to detract the viewer's attention in order to heighten the murder. We purposely made that beginning on the long side, with the bit about the theft and her escape, in order to get the audience absorbed with the question of whether she would or would not be caught. Even that business about the forty thousand dollars was milked to the very end so that the public might wonder what's going to happen to the money.

You know that the public always likes to be one jump ahead of the story; they like to feel they know what's coming next. So you deliberately play upon this fact to control their thoughts. The more we go into the details of the girl's journey, the more the audience becomes absorbed in her flight. That's why so much is made of the motorcycle cop and the change of cars. When Anthony Perkins tells the girl of his life in the motel, and they exchange views, you still play upon the girl's problem. It seems as if she's decided to go back to Phoenix and give the money back, and it's possible that the public anticipates by thinking, "Ah, this young man is influencing her to change her mind." You turn the viewer in one direction and then in another; you keep him as far as possible from what's actually going to happen.

In the average production, Janet Leigh would have been given the other role. She would have played the sister who's investigating. It's rather unusual to kill the star in the first third of the film. I purposely killed the star so as to make the killing even more unexpected. As a matter of fact, that's why I insisted that the audiences be kept out of the theaters once the picture had started, because the late-comers would have been waiting to see Janet Leigh after she has disappeared from the screen action.

Psycho has a very interesting construction and that game with the audience was fascinating. I was directing the viewers. You might say I was playing them, like an organ.

F.T.　I admired that picture enormously, but I felt a letdown during the two scenes with the sheriff.

A.H.　The sheriff's intervention comes under the heading of what we have discussed many times before: "Why don't they go to the police?" I've always replied, "They don't go to the police because it's dull." Here is a perfect

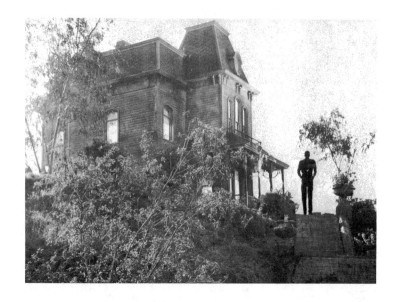

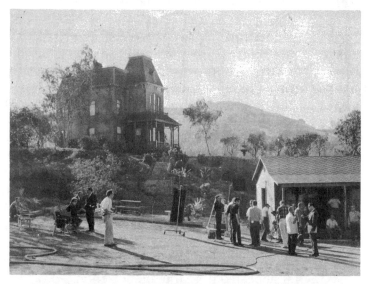

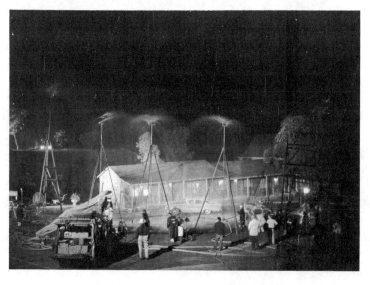

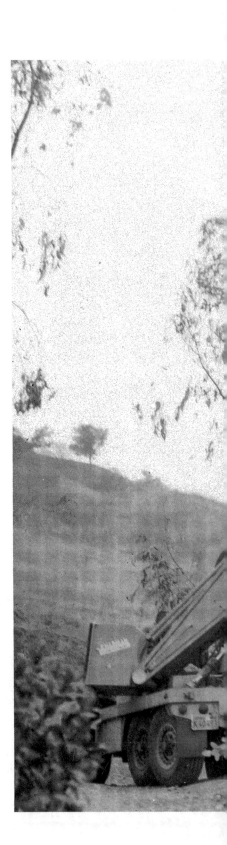

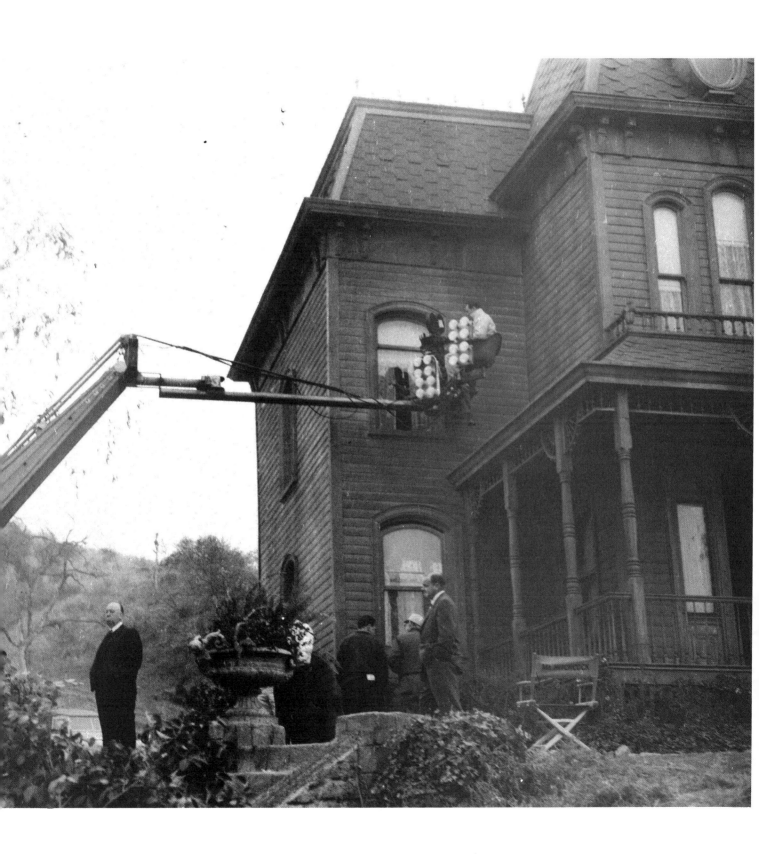

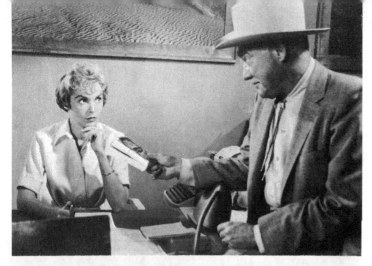

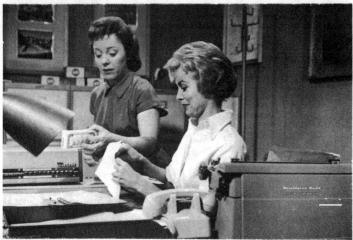

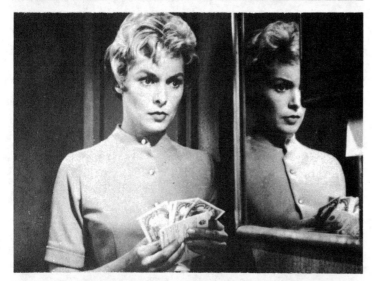

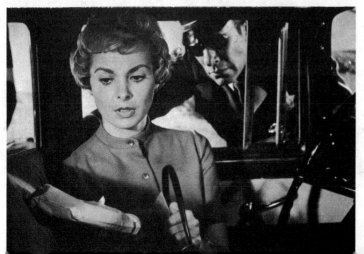

example of what happens when they go to the police.

F.T. Still, the action picks up again almost immediately after that. One intriguing aspect is the way the picture makes the viewer constantly switch loyalties. At the beginning he hopes that Janet Leigh won't be caught. The murder is very shocking, but as soon as Perkins wipes away the traces of the killing, we begin to side with him, to hope that he won't be found out. Later on, when we learn from the sheriff that Perkins' mother has been dead for eight years, we again change sides and are against Perkins, but this time, it's sheer curiosity. The viewer's emotions are not exactly wholesome.

A.H. This brings us back to the emotions of Peeping Tom audiences. We had some of that in *Dial M for Murder*.

F.T. That's right. When Milland was late in phoning his wife and the killer looked as if he might walk out of the apartment without killing Grace Kelly. The audience reaction there was to hope he'd hang on for another few minutes.

A.H. It's a general rule. Earlier, we talked about the fact that when a burglar goes into a room, all the time he's going through the drawers, the public is generally anxious for him. When Perkins is looking at the car sinking in the pond, even though he's burying a body, when the car stops sinking for a moment, the public is thinking, "I hope it goes all the way down!" It's a natural instinct.

F.T. But in most of your films the audience reaction is more innocent because they are concerned for a man who is wrongly suspected of a crime. Whereas in *Psycho* one begins by being scared for a girl who's a thief, and later on one is scared for a killer, and, finally, when one learns that this killer has a secret, one hopes he will be caught just in order to get the full story!

A.H. I doubt whether the identification is that close.

F.T. It isn't necessarily identification, but

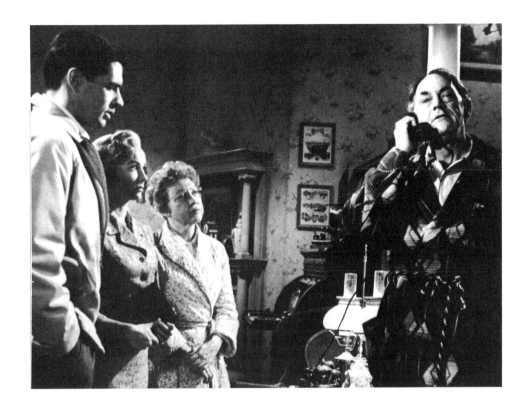

the viewer becomes attached to Perkins because of the care with which he wipes away all the traces of his crime. It's tantamount to admiring someone for a job well done.

I understand that in addition to the main titles, Saul Bass also did some sketches for the picture.

A.H. He did only one scene, but I didn't use his montage. He was supposed to do the titles, but since he was interested in the picture, I let him lay out the sequence of the detective going up the stairs, just before he is stabbed. One day during the shooting I came down with a temperature, and since I couldn't come to the studio, I told the cameraman and my assistant that they could use Saul Bass's drawings. Only the part showing him going up the stairs, before the killing. There was a shot of his hand on the rail, and of feet seen in profile, going up through the bars of the balustrade. When I looked at the rushes of the scene, I found it was no good, and that was an interesting revelation for me, because as that sequence was cut, it wasn't an innocent person but a sinister man who was going up those stairs. Those cuts would have been perfectly all right if they were showing a killer,

but they were in conflict with the whole spirit of the scene.

Bear in mind that we had gone to a lot of trouble to prepare the audience for this scene: we had established a mystery woman in the house; we had established the fact that this mystery woman had come down and slashed a woman to pieces under her shower. All the elements that would convey suspense to the detective's journey upstairs had gone before and we therefore needed a simple statement. We needed to show a staircase and a man going up that staircase in a very simple way.

F.T. I suppose that the original rushes of that scene helped you to determine just the right expression. In French we would say that "he arrived like a flower," which implies, of course, that he was ready to be plucked.

A.H. It wasn't exactly impassivity; it was more like complacency. Anyway, I used a single shot of Arbogast coming up the stairs, and when he got to the top step, I deliberately placed the camera very high for two reasons. The first was so that I could shoot down on top of the

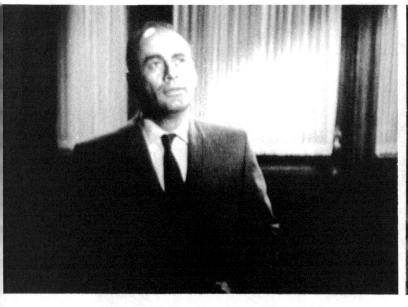
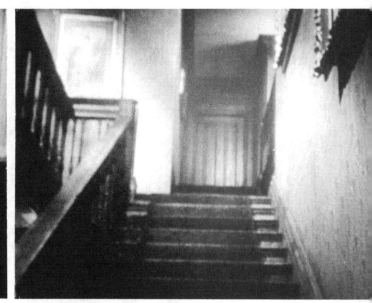
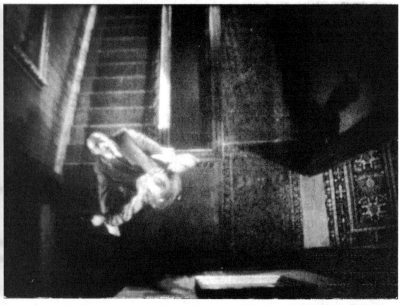
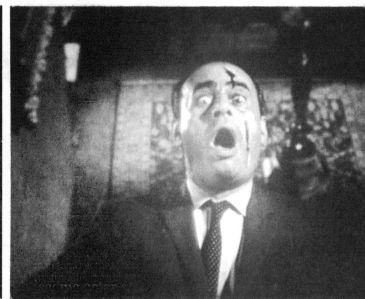
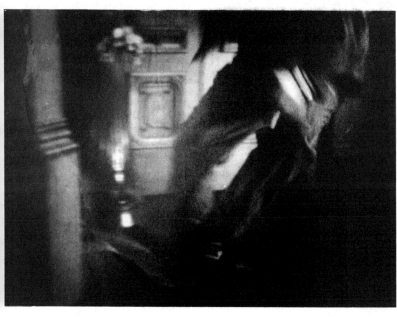
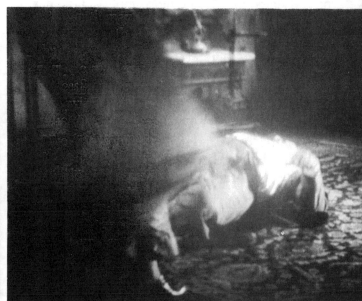

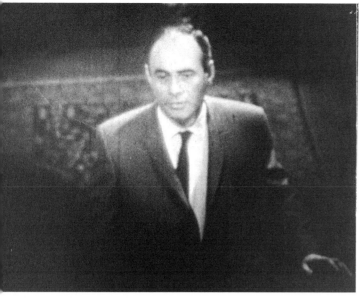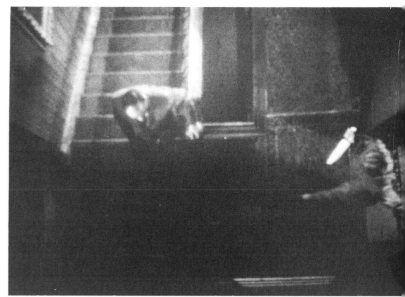

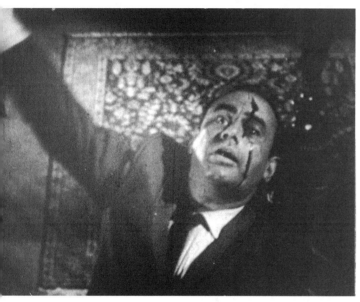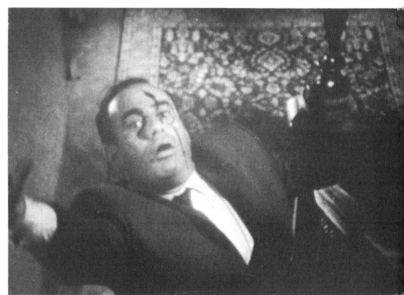

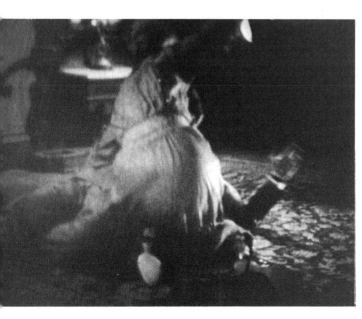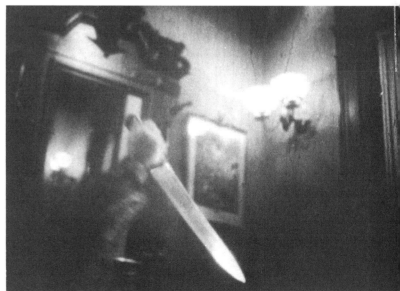

mother, because if I'd shown her back, it might have looked as if I was deliberately concealing her face and the audience would have been leery. I used that high angle in order not to give the impression that I was trying to avoid showing her.

But the main reason for raising the camera so high was to get the contrast between the long shot and the close-up of the big head as the knife came down at him. It was like music, you see, the high shot with the violins, and suddenly the big head with the brass instruments clashing. In the high shot the mother dashes out and I cut into the movement of the knife sweeping down. Then I went over to the close-up on Arbogast. We put a plastic tube on his face with hemoglobin, and as the knife came up to it, we pulled a string releasing the blood on his face down the line we had traced in advance. Then he fell back on the stairway.

F.T. I was rather intrigued by that fall backward. He doesn't actually fall. His feet aren't shown, but the feeling one gets is that he's going down the stairs backward, brushing each step with the tip of his foot, like a dancer.

A.H. That's the impression we were after. Do you know how we got that?

F.T. I realize you wanted to stretch out the action, but I don't know how you did it.

A.H. We did it by process. First I did a separate dolly shot down the stairway, without the man. Then we sat him in a special chair in which he was in a fixed position in front of the transparency screen showing the stairs. Then we shot the chair, and Arbogast simply threw his arms up, waving them as if he'd lost his balance.

F.T. It's extremely effective. Later on in the picture you use another very high shot to show Perkins taking his mother to the cellar.

A.H. I raised the camera when Perkins was going upstairs. He goes into the room and we don't see him, but we hear him say, "Mother, I've got to take you down to the cellar. They're

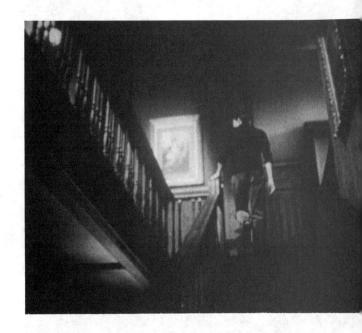

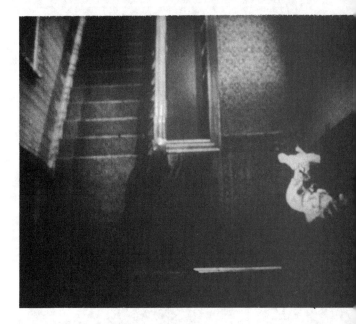

snooping around." And then you see him take her down to the cellar. I didn't want to cut, when he carries her down, to a high shot because the audience would have been suspicious as to why the camera has suddenly jumped away. So I had a hanging camera follow Perkins up the stairs, and when he went into the room I continued going up without a cut. As the camera got up on top of the door, the camera turned and looked back down the stairs again. Meanwhile, I had an argument take place between the son and his mother to distract the

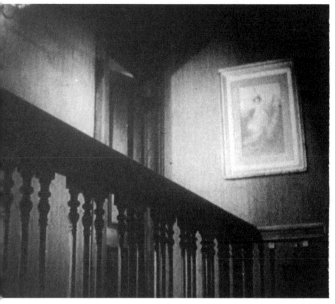

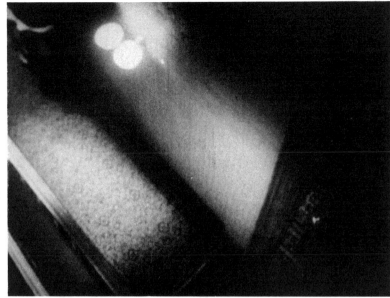

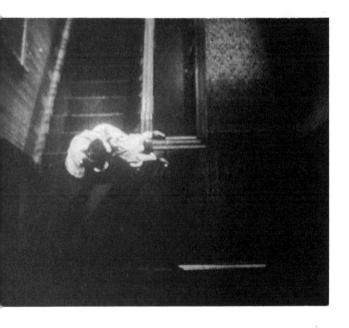

audience and take their minds off what the camera was doing. In this way the camera was above Perkins again as he carried his mother down and the public hadn't noticed a thing. It was rather exciting to use the camera to deceive the audience.

F.T. The stabbing of Janet Leigh was very well done also.

A.H. It took us seven days to shoot that scene, and there were seventy camera setups for forty-five seconds of footage. We had a torso specially made up for that scene, with the blood that was supposed to spurt away from the knife, but I didn't use it. I used a live girl instead, a naked model who stood in for Janet Leigh. We only showed Miss Leigh's hands, shoulders, and head. All the rest was the stand-in. Naturally, the knife never touched the body; it was all done in the montage. I shot some of it in slow motion so as to cover the breasts. The slow shots were not accelerated later on because they were inserted in the montage so as to give an impression of normal speed.

F.T. It's an exceptionally violent scene.

A.H. This is the most violent scene of the picture. As the film unfolds, there is less violence because the harrowing memory of this initial killing carries over to the suspenseful passages that come later.

F.T. Yet, even better than the killing, in the sense of its harmony, is the scene in which Perkins handles the mop and broom to clean away any traces of the crime. The whole construction of the picture suggests a sort of scale of the abnormal. First there is a scene of adultery, then a theft, then one crime followed by another, and, finally, psychopathy. Each passage puts us on a higher note of the scale. Isn't that so?

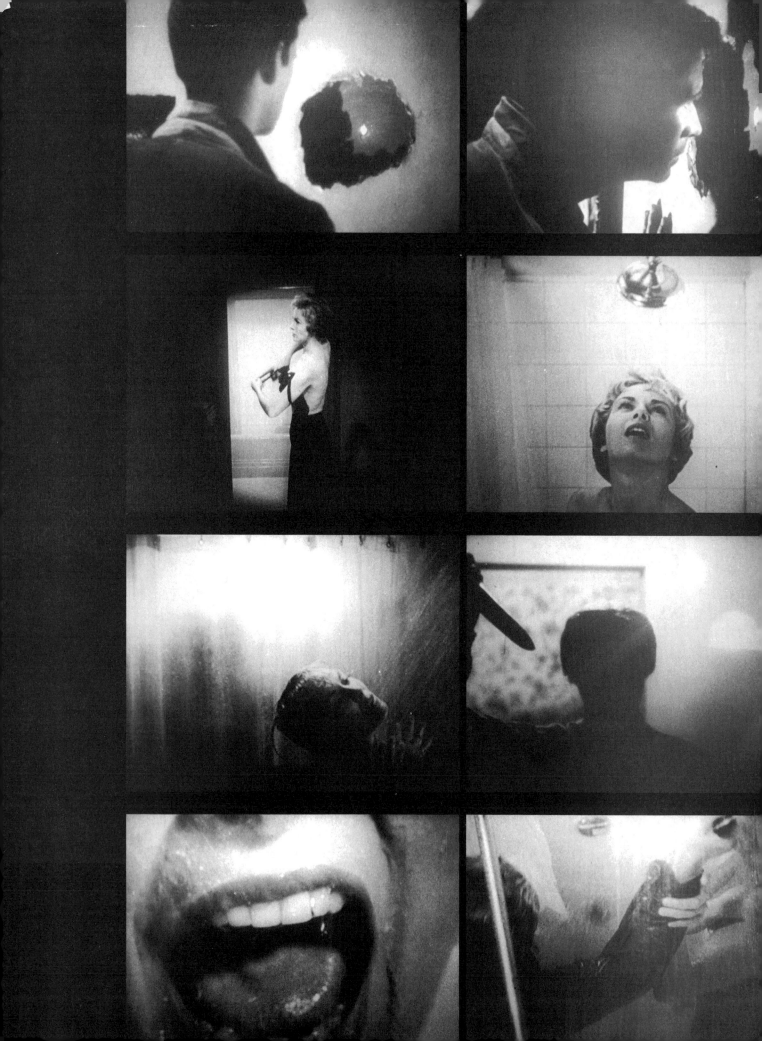

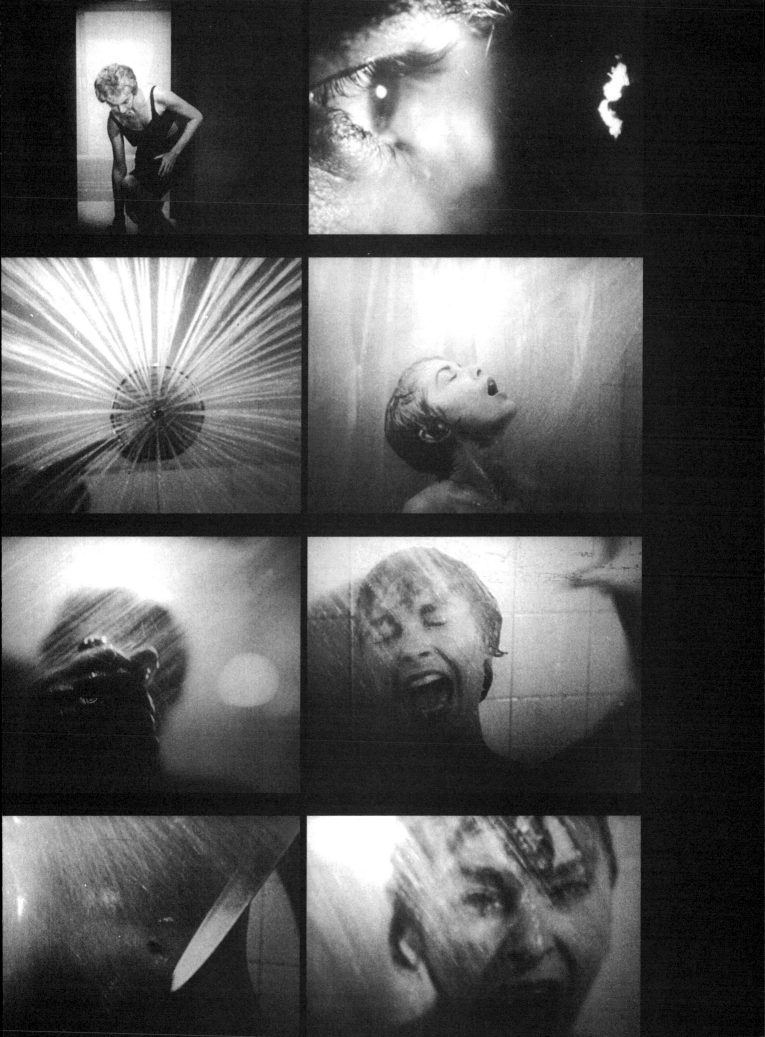

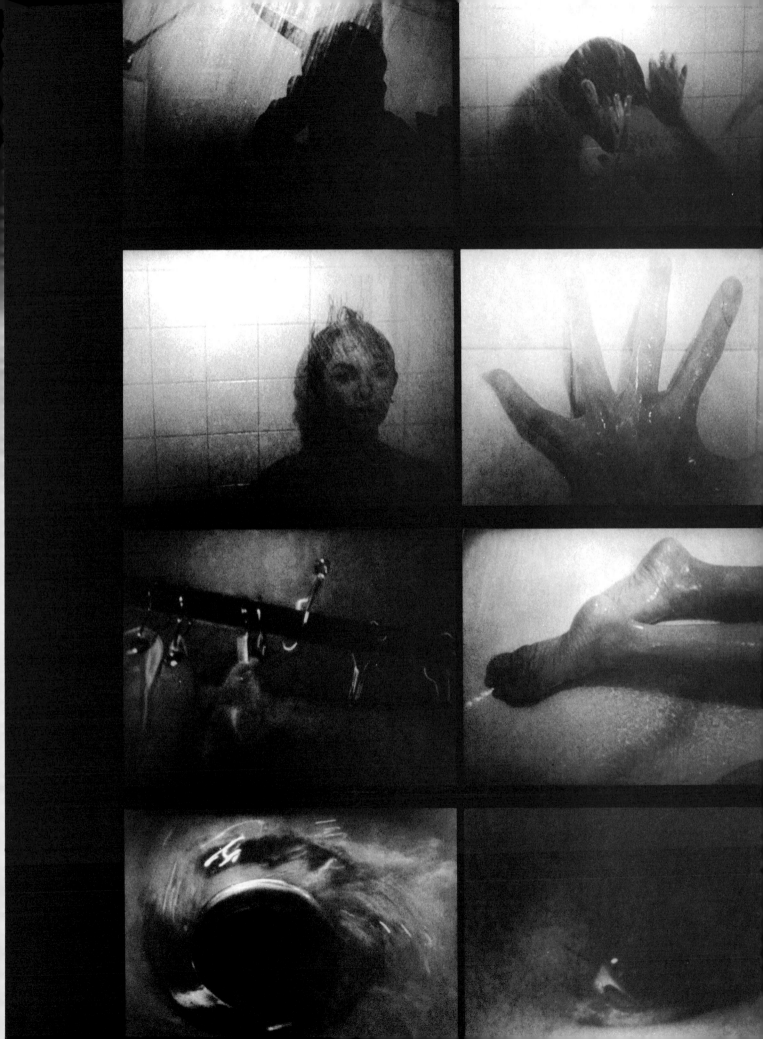

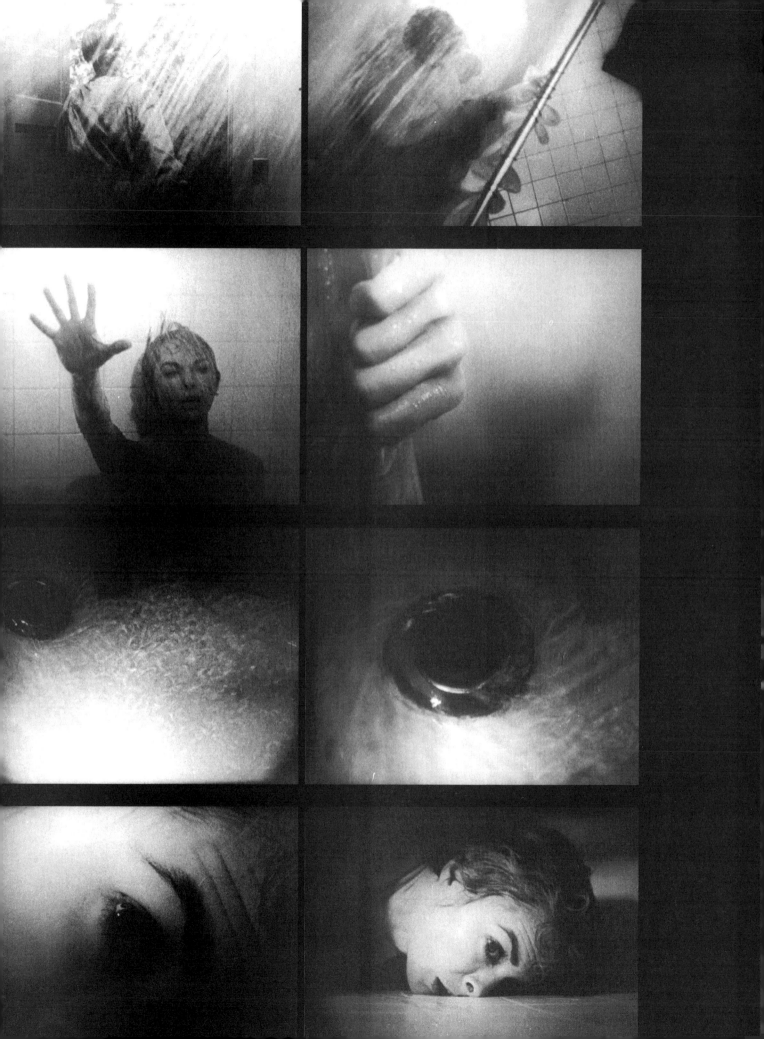

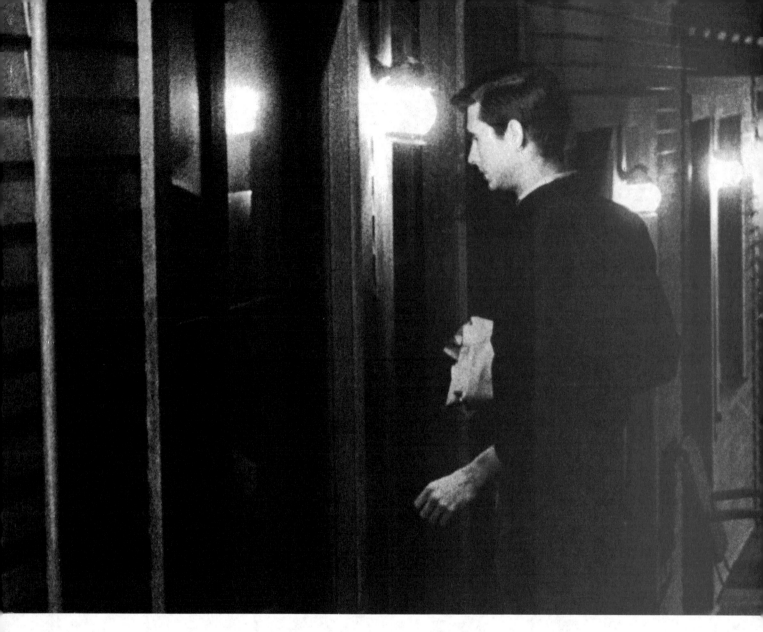

A.H. I suppose so, but you know that to me Janet Leigh is playing the role of a perfectly ordinary bourgeoise.

F.T. But she does lead us in the direction of the abnormal, toward Perkins and his stuffed birds.

A.H. I was quite intrigued with them: they were like symbols. Obviously Perkins is interested in taxidermy since he'd filled his own mother with sawdust. But the owl, for instance, has another connotation. Owls belong to the night world; they are watchers, and this appeals to Perkins' masochism. He knows the birds and he knows that they're watching him all the time.

He can see his own guilt reflected in their knowing eyes.

F.T. Would you say that *Psycho* is an experimental film?

A.H. Possibly. My main satisfaction is that the film had an effect on the audiences, and I consider that very important. I don't care about the subject matter; I don't care about the acting; but I do care about the pieces of film and the photography and the sound track and all of the technical ingredients that made the audience scream. I feel it's tremendously satisfying for us to be able to use the cinematic art to achieve something of a mass emotion. And with *Psycho* we most definitely achieved this. It wasn't a

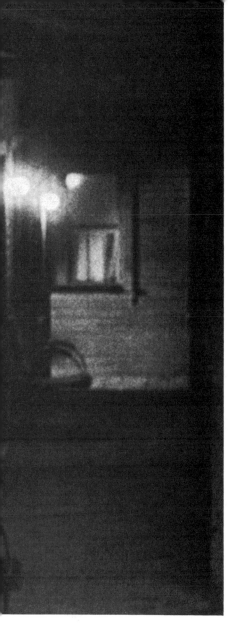

message that stirred the audiences, nor was it a great performance or their enjoyment of the novel. They were aroused by pure film.

F.T.   Yes, that's true.

A.H.   That's why I take pride in the fact that *Psycho*, more than any of my other pictures, is a film that belongs to film-makers, to you and me. I can't get a real appreciation of the picture in the terms we're using now. People will say, "It was a terrible film to make. The subject was horrible, the people were small, there were no characters in it." I know all of this, but I also know that the construction of the story and the way in which it was told caused audiences all over the world to react and become emotional.

F.T.   Yes, emotional and even physical.

A.H.   Emotional. I don't care whether it looked like a small or a large picture. I didn't start off to make an important movie. I thought I could have fun with this subject and this situation. The picture cost eight hundred thousand dollars. It was an experiment in this sense: Could I make a feature film under the same conditions as a television show? I used a complete television unit to shoot it very quickly. The only place where I digressed was when I slowed down the murder scene, the cleaning-up scene, and the other scenes that indicated anything that required time. All of the rest was handled in the same way that they do it in television.

F.T.   I know that you produced *Psycho* yourself. How did you make out with it?

A.H.   *Psycho* cost us no more than eight hundred thousand dollars to make. It has grossed some fifteen million dollars to date.

F.T.   That's fantastic! Would you say this was your greatest hit to date?

A.H.   Yes. And that's what I'd like you to do —a picture that would gross millions of dollars throughout the world! It's an area of film-making in which it's more important for you to be pleased with the technique than with the content. It's the kind of picture in which the camera takes over. Of course, since critics are more concerned with the scenario, it won't necessarily get you the best notices, but you have to design your film just as Shakespeare did his plays—for an audience.

F.T.   That reminds me that *Psycho* is particularly universal because it's a half-silent movie; there are at least two reels with no dialogue at all. And that also simplified all the problems of subtitling and dubbing.

A.H.   Do you know that in Thailand they use no subtitles or dubbing? They shut off the sound and a man stands somewhere near the screen and interprets all the roles, using different voices.

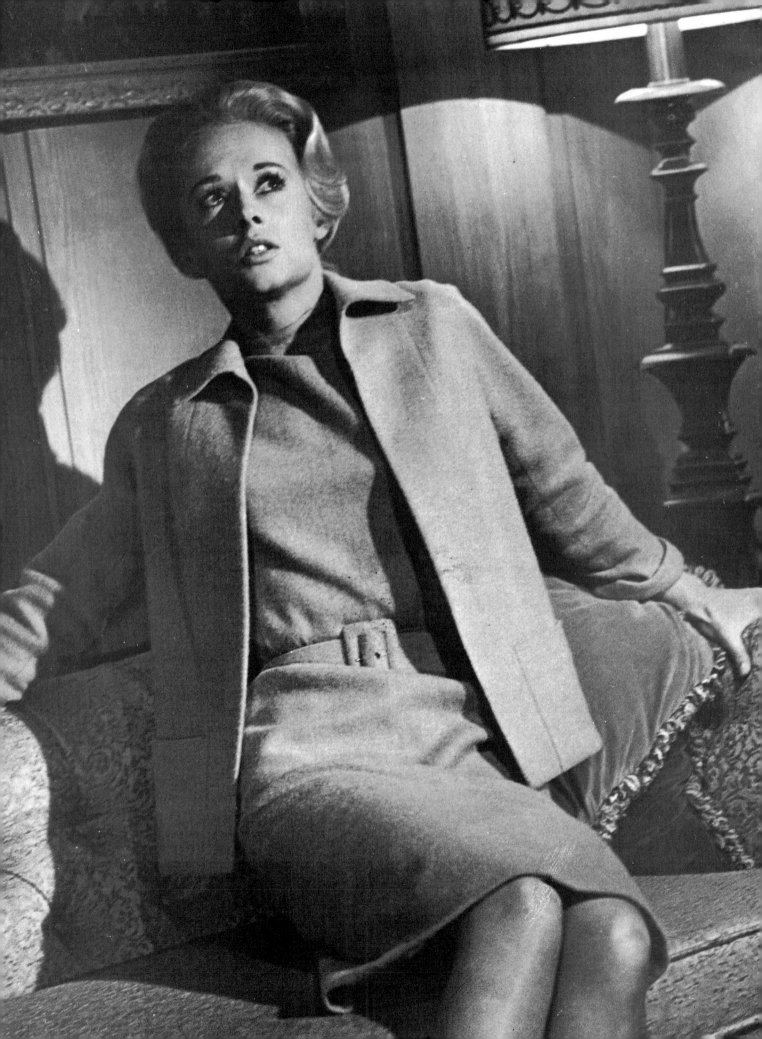

14

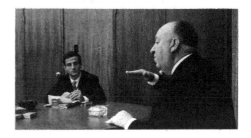

FRANÇOIS TRUFFAUT. I'm curious to find out whether you discovered Daphne du Maurier's *The Birds* before or after publication.

ALFRED HITCHCOCK. Afterward. Actually, it was in one of those "Alfred Hitchcock Presents" books. I found out that there had been attempts to do *The Birds* on radio and television, but they weren't successful.

F.T. Did you investigate before taking on the project to make sure that the technical problems with the birds could be handled?

A.H. Absolutely not! I didn't even give it a thought. I said, "This is the job. Let's get on with it." But I think that if the story had involved vultures, or birds of prey, I might not have wanted it. The basic appeal to me is that it had to do with ordinary, everyday birds. Do you see what I mean?

F.T. Well, it was a chance to apply your old rule of going from the smallest to the biggest, in the intellectual as well as in the plastic sense. What will you do for an encore to the gentle little sparrows that gouge men's eyes out? How about a picture about flowers with a deadly scent?

A.H. We might do better than that with man-eating flowers.

F.T. Since 1945, it's the atom bomb that has represented the ultimate threat to mankind, so it's rather disconcerting to suggest that the end of the world might be brought about by thousands of birds. . . .

A.H. That's reflected in the skeptical atti-

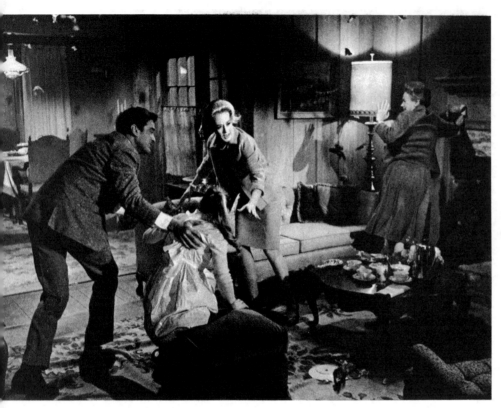

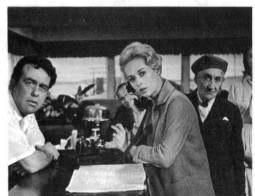

tude of the ornithologist. The old lady is a re-actionary, or at any rate she's too conservative to admit that the birds might be responsible for such a catastrophe.

F.T. I'm glad you didn't give a specific reason for the attacks. It is clearly a speculation, a fantasy.*

---

* Melanie Daniels (Tippi Hedren), a wealthy, snobbish playgirl, meets Mitch Brenner (Rod Taylor), a young lawyer, in a San Francisco bird shop. Despite his sarcastic attitude, she is attracted to him and travels to Bodega Bay to take two small lovebirds as a birthday present to his little sister, Cathy.

As she nears the dock in a rented motorboat, a sea gull swoops down at her, gashing her forehead. Melanie decides to stay, spending the night with Annie Hayworth (Suzanne Pleshette), the local schoolteacher. Annie warns Melanie that Mitch's mother, Mrs. Brenner, is jealous and possessive with her son.

The next day, at Cathy's outdoor birthday party, the gulls swoop down on the picnicking children and that evening hundreds of sparrows come swooping down the chimney, flying all around the house and causing considerable damage. The following morning Mrs. Brenner goes to visit a farmer nearby and finds him dead, with his eyes gouged out. That afternoon, when Melanie discovers an alarming assembly of crows gathering outside the schoolhouse, she and Annie organize the children's escape. As Melanie escorts them down the road, Annie is trapped behind and sacrifices her life in order to save Cathy. Meanwhile, Melanie and the children take refuge in a restaurant as the birds attack the town's business section, causing a fire in the gasoline station.

A.H. That's the way I saw it.

F.T. I understand that Daphne du Maurier's inspiration for a massive attack by the birds was inspired by a real-life incident.

A.H. Yes, these things do happen from time to time and they're generally due to a bird disease, a form of rabies. But it would have been too horrible to put that in a picture, don't you think?

F.T. I don't know about that, but I'm sure it wouldn't have been anywhere near as fascinating to look at.

Melanie's courage during these trials inspires Mitch's love and his mother's approval of their romance.

That evening Melanie and the Brenners board up the windows of their home just in time to protect themselves from the enraged birds which dive suicidally against the house, tear at the shingles and gnaw at the doors to get at the people inside. After peace returns, Melanie, hearing a sound upstairs, goes up to the attic to investigate. There she finds herself in a room full of birds which attack her savagely. Finally rescued by Mitch, the girl is in a state of shock. Taking advantage of a momentary lull, Mitch decides to flee. Between the house and the garage and as far as the eye can see, thousands of birds wait in ominous array as the little group emerges from the battered house and moves slowly toward the car.

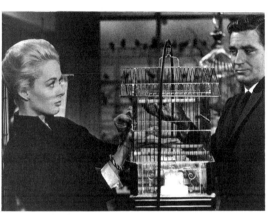

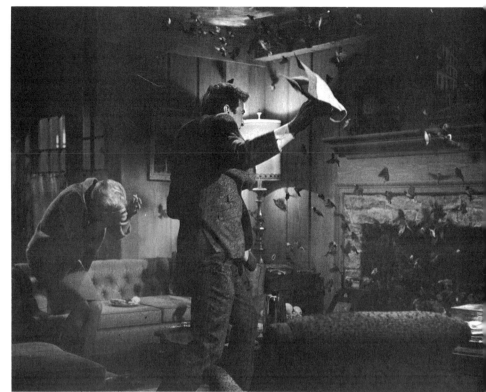

A.H. While I was shooting in Bodega Bay, there was an item in a San Francisco paper about crows attacking some young lambs, and, of all places, right in the same locality where we were working. I met a farmer who told me how the crows swooped down to kill his young lambs. That's where I got the idea for the gouged-out eyes of the dead man.

The picture opens with our two principal characters in San Francisco, and then I take them to Bodega Bay. The house and farm we built ourselves. We made an exact copy of the existing houses. There was an old Russian farm built around 1849. There were many Russians living on the coast at the time, and there's even a town called Sebastopol some twelve miles northeast of Bodega Bay. When the Russians owned Alaska, they used to come down the coast to hunt seals.

F.T. One distinct disadvantage in your kind of films is that however much people enjoy them, they hate to admit that they've been taken in. Their admiration is often mitigated by a tinge of resentment. It's as if they begrudged you the pleasure you give them.

A.H. Of course. They come to the theater and they sit down and say, "All right. Now, show me!" And they want to be one jump ahead of the action: "I know what's going to happen." So, I have to take up the challenge: "Oh, you know what's going to happen. Well, we'll just see about that!" With *The Birds* I made sure that the public would not be able to anticipate from one scene to another.

F.T. This happens to be one picture, I think, in which the public doesn't try to anticipate. They merely suspect that the attacks by the birds are going to become increasingly serious. The first part is an entirely normal picture with psychological overtones, and it is only at the end of each scene that some clue hints at the potential menace of the birds.

A.H. I had to do it that way because the public's curiosity was bound to be aroused by the articles in the press and the reviews, as well as by the word-of-mouth talk about the picture. I didn't want the public to become too impatient about the birds, because that would distract them from the personal story of the two central characters. Those references at the end of each scene were my way of saying, "Just be patient. They're coming soon."

You know, there's a lot of detail in this movie; it's absolutely essential because these little nuances enrich the over-all impact and strengthen the picture.

At the beginning of the film we show Rod Taylor in the bird shop. He catches the canary that has escaped from its cage, and after putting it back, he says to Tippi Hedren, "I'm putting you back in your gilded cage, Melanie Daniels." I added that sentence during the shooting because I felt it added to her characterization as a wealthy, shallow playgirl. And later on, when the gulls attack the village, Melanie Daniels takes refuge in a glass telephone booth and I show her as a bird in a cage. This time it isn't a gilded cage, but a cage of misery, and it's also the beginning of her ordeal by fire, so to speak. It's a reversal of the age-old conflict between men and birds. Here the human beings are in cages and the birds are on the outside. When I shoot something like that, I hardly think the public is likely to notice it.

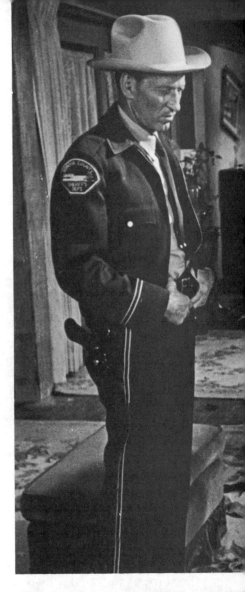

F.T.   Even though that metaphor wasn't obvious—to me, at any rate—this is truly a remarkably powerful scene. It was very ingenious to have that dialogue in the opening scene in the bird shop about the lovebirds because later on the whole film revolves around hate-filled birds. Throughout the picture the lovebirds were used in various ways to punctuate the irony of the content.

A.H.   Aside from the touches of irony, that was necessary because love is going to survive the whole ordeal. At the end of the picture the little girl asks, "Can I take my lovebirds along?" That little couple of lovebirds lends an optimistic note to the theme.

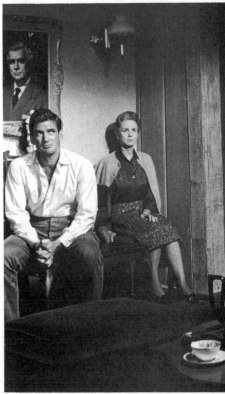

F.T.   They convey a double meaning to several scenes, including one with the mother and another with the schoolteacher.

A.H.   It all goes to show that with a little effort even the word "love" can be made to sound ominous.

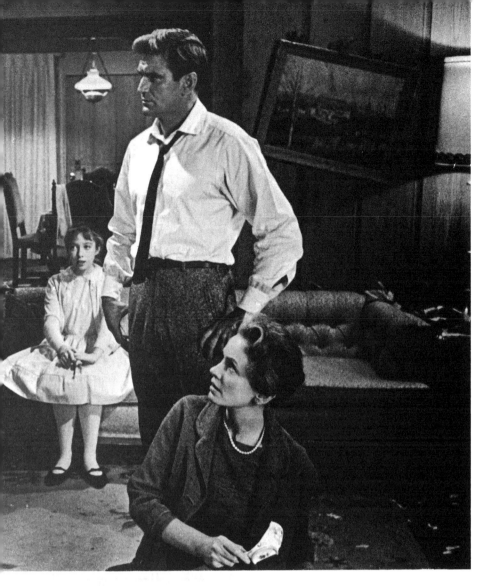

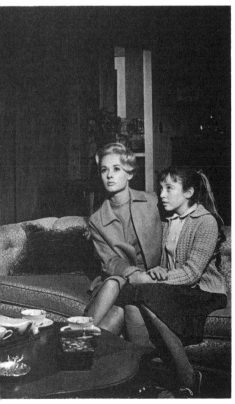

F.T. The story construction follows the three basic rules of classic tragedy: unity of place, of time, and of action. All of the action takes place within two days' time in Bodega Bay. The birds are seen in ever growing numbers and they become increasingly dangerous as the action progresses. It must have been a difficult script, but the story really works.

A.H. I can tell you the emotions I went through. I've always boasted that I never look at a script while I'm shooting. I know the whole film by heart. I've always been afraid of improvising on the set because, although one might have the time to get a new idea, there isn't sufficient time in the studio to examine the value of such an idea. There are too many crew people around. That's overhead, and I'm very conscientious about not wasting production money. I could never work like those directors who have the whole crew stand by while they sit down to think things out. I could never do that. But I was quite tense and this is unusual for me because as a rule I have a lot of fun during the shooting. When I went home to my wife at night, I was still tense and upset.

Something happened that was altogether new in my experience: I began to study the scenario as we went along, and I saw that there were weaknesses in it. This emotional siege I went through served to bring out an additional creative sense in me.

I began to improvise. For instance, the whole scene of the outside attack on the house by birds that are not seen was done spontaneously, right on the set. I'd almost never done anything like that before, but I made up my mind and quickly designed the movements of the people inside the room. I decided that the mother and the little girl would dart around to search for shelter. There was no place to run for cover, so I made them move about in contradictory directions, a little like rats scurrying into corners.

I deliberately shot Melanie Daniels from a distance because I wanted to make it clear that she was recoiling from nothing at all. What could she be drawing back from? She cringes back into the sofa and she doesn't even know what she's recoiling from.

Because I was so keyed up all of this came very easily and very quickly. Then I began to have doubts about other passages of the movie. After the initial attack on the room, when the sparrows came down through the chimney, the sheriff came to the house to talk it over with Mitch. He's a skeptical man who doesn't believe the evidence of his own eyes: "The sparrows came down through this chimney? Well, what makes you think they were out to attack you?" I studied the scene and found that the treatment was too old-fashioned, so I changed the whole thing. I decided to show the mother through Melanie's eyes. The scene begins with the whole group of characters, the sheriff, Mitch, the mother, and Melanie, in the background, and the whole scene that follows is a transfer from the objective viewpoint to a subjective viewpoint. The sheriff says, "It's a sparrow all right!" And from the group of static figures the mother's figure detaches itself and her moving figure bends down. That downward movement now generates interest in the girl and the scene is now going to become her point of view. Melanie looks at the mother and the camera now photographs Jessica Tandy going around the room, in different positions, to pick up the broken teacups, to straighten the picture and to jump back when the bird falls out of its frame. The reverse cuts of Melanie, as she looks at the mother going back and forth, subtly indicate what she's thinking. Her eyes and gestures indicate an increasing concern over the mother's strange behavior and for the mother herself. The vision of the reality belongs to the girl, even when she crosses the room to say to Mitch, "I think I'd better stay the night." To go up to Mitch she has to walk across the room, but even as she's walking, I keep a big close-up on her because her concern and her interest demand that we retain the same size of image on the screen. If I were to cut and drop back to a looser figure, her concern would be diminished as well.

The size of the image is very important to the emotion, particularly when you're using that image to have the audience identify with it. In this scene, which is intended to suggest that Mitch's mother is cracking up, Melanie represents the public.

Another improvisation is the mother driving up to the farm, going into the house and calling the farmer before noticing the wrecked room and discovering the farmer's body. While we were shooting that, I said to myself, "This doesn't make sense." She calls the farmer and he doesn't answer. Well, a woman in that position wouldn't push it any farther; she'd walk out of the house. So that's how I got the idea to keep her there by having her notice the five broken teacups hanging from the hooks.

F.T. And the viewer, who has just seen the broken china after the birds' attack on Brenner's home, guesses what has happened at the same time that she does. It's purely visual and immensely effective.

You've mentioned some last-minute improvisations in *The Birds*. Did you shoot any scenes

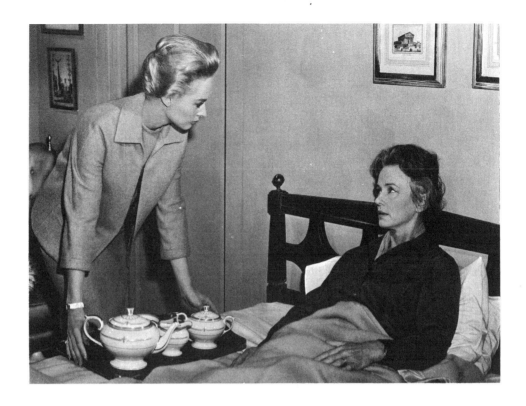

that were eliminated subsequently in the editing stage?

A.H. Only one or two things after the discovery of the farmer's body. First, there was a love scene between the girl and the man that was eliminated. It took place after the mother went off to take the little girl to school. Melanie goes down, puts on her fur coat and sees the man burning the birds in the distance. She wanders off in his direction; she obviously wants to be with him. When he is through with his job of burning the birds, I showed him coming toward her and you can read on her face her desire to receive him. Then, suddenly, he turns around and goes into the house. What's wrong? She's disappointed and I put that in to stress that Melanie's really keen on Mitch. A few minutes later he emerges from the house again and says, "I've put a clean shirt on because the other one smelled of birds."
Then we continued that scene in a light comedy note, with their speculations as to why the birds

were behaving in that way. They joked about the fact that the birds have a leader, that he's a sparrow perched on a platform addressing all the birds and saying to them, "Birds of the world, unite. You've nothing to lose but your feathers."

F.T. Birds of a feather . . .

A.H. The scene became more serious, winding up with a kiss. Then we went on to show the mother driving back from the farm, terribly agitated. She rolls up just as the couple is exchanging another kiss, and I put a slight wince in her expression. One doesn't, at the time, know for sure whether that's because she's seen them in that embrace, but subsequent developments will indicate that was the reason.
Now, since that love scene was suppressed, the dialogue in the following scene between the mother and Melanie is slightly different from what it was originally.
The point I was trying to make is that this

woman, though she was so terribly distressed about having seen the farmer with his eyes gouged out, was still a possessive mother. Her love for her son still dominated all of her other emotions.

F.T. Well then, why did you drop the scene?

A.H. Because I felt that the love interlude slowed down the story. Right along I was concerned about the fact that the word-of-mouth rumors would make the public impatient. I was worried about the audience sitting through this part of the picture and thinking to itself, "Come on. Where are the birds? Let's get on with it." This is why we have an isolated attack on Melanie by a sea gull, why I was careful to put a dead bird outside the schoolteacher's house at night, and also why we put the birds on the wires when the girl drives away from the house in the evening. All of this was my way of saying to the audience, "Don't worry, they're coming. The birds are on their way!" Anyway, I felt that a prolonged love scene at that point might have irritated the public.

F.T. By the way, the first time I saw the picture I had some reservations about the scene in the village café. It seemed too long, maybe because it wasn't exactly essential to the story.

A.H. That scene doesn't necessarily add anything, but I felt that after the attack of the birds on the children at the birthday party, the small birds coming down the chimney, and the attack of the crows outside the school, we should give the audience a rest before going back to horror. That scene in the restaurant is a breather that allows for a few laughs. The character of the drunk is straight out of an O'Casey play, and the elderly lady ornithologist is pretty interesting. In truth, you are right. The scene is a little on the long side, but I feel that if the audience is absorbed in it, it is automatically shortened. I've always measured the length or brevity of a scene by the degree of interest it holds for the public. If they're completely ab-

sorbed, it's a short scene; if they're bored, the scene is bound to be too long.

F.T. The scene in which Melanie Daniels is waiting for the children outside the school illustrates your secret formula for suspense. There's a long, silent wait, during which you build up the mood with great authority, almost imperiously. It's all in the style of cutting: never obvious, always tremendously effective and completely unique.

A.H. Well, let's examine that scene where the girl sits and waits while the crows are gathering behind her. Inside the schoolroom the teacher is saying to the children, "Now, you're going to walk out and when I tell you to run, you'll run!" I carry that scene as far as the door and then I cut back to the birds alone, all of them, and I stay with them, without cutting, for probably half a minute. And you begin to wonder: "What's happening to the children? Where are they?" Eventually, you hear the feet of the children running, while all the birds rise and you see them going over the top of the schoolhouse roof before coming down at the children. Now, the old technique for getting suspense into that scene would have been a cross-cutting of the children down the steps and then back to the waiting crows. Then backward and forward again. But that's an old-fashioned method. That's why, when the girl is waiting outside, smoking a cigarette, I stayed with her for fifty feet of film. And when she turns around to look, she sees all the crows at once.

F.T. The scene of the fire in the gasoline station is really thrilling. That unexpected high shot gives the impression the whole thing's being shown from the viewpoint of the gulls.

A.H. I did that high shot for three reasons. The first was intended to show the beginning of the gulls' descent on the town. The second was to show the exact topography of Bodega Bay, with the town, the sea, the coast, and the gas station on fire, in one single image. The third reason is that I didn't want to waste a lot of footage on showing the elaborate operation of

292

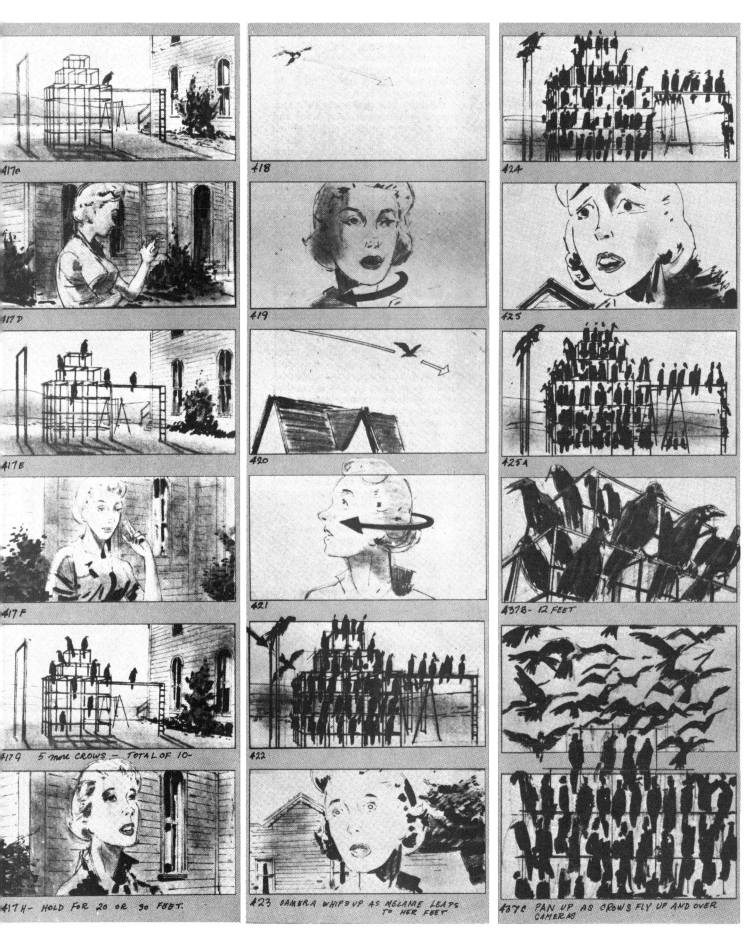

Reproduction of a storyboard (a sequence of sketches designed before shooting). Melanie becomes aware of the gathering crows behind her.

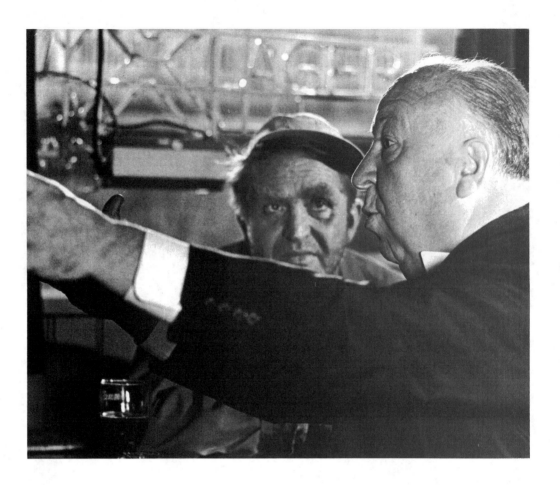

the firemen extinguishing the fire. You can do a lot of things very quickly by getting away from something.

That's a rule that applies whenever you have to deal with something that's confusing or just plain dull and you want to avoid going into all those details. For instance, when the attendant is hurt by one of the gulls and everyone rushes over to help him, we watch that from a distance, from inside the restaurant, through the eyes of Melanie Daniels. In fact, the people who ran over to help the attendant should have picked him up much faster, but I needed more time to create some suspense in connection with the trail of gasoline that's spreading all over the street. In another case I might have done the opposite, and we might have kept away from a slow action to cut down the length of time.

F.T.   In other words, you solve the problem of time by manipulating the space.

A.H.   That's right. We've already talked about the fact that film can be used either to contract time or to extend it at will, in accordance with our needs.

F.T.   I'm curious about that gull that flies across the screen to swoop down upon the garage attendant. How was it possible to direct a bird with such accuracy?

A.H.   That was a live gull thrown from a very high platform off screen. It was trained to go from one place to another by flying just above the man's head. He's an expert on movements and he overplayed his reactions to give the impression that he'd been hit by the gull.

F.T.   Like those fake blows they use in fight scenes?

A.H.   Exactly. Do you think I was right to have the teacher killed off?

F.T. The killing isn't shown on the screen; the viewer doesn't see her until she's dead. As a matter of fact, I was curious about your reason for doing away with her.

A.H. I felt that in the light of what the birds were doing to the town, she was doomed. Besides, she sacrificed herself to protect the sister of the man she loves. It's her final gesture.
In the original script she was in Mitch's home until the end of the picture, and she was the one who went up to the attic and was the victim of that last attack. I decided against that because since Tippi Hedren was the chief character, it was she who had to go through the final ordeal.

F.T. We certainly would be doing an injustice to *The Birds* if we failed to mention the sound track. There's no music, of course, but the bird sounds are worked out like a real musical score. I have in mind, for instance, the scene of the bird attack on the house, which is carried solely by sound.

A.H. We had a problem when we were shooting that scene to get the actors inside the besieged house to respond properly because we didn't yet have the sounds of the wings and the noises made by the birds. I had a drummer put on the set, with a small side drum and a mike

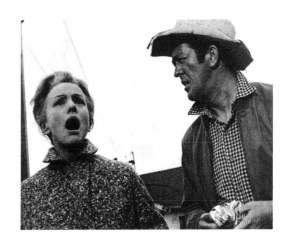

with a loudspeaker. Whenever the actors played their scene, there was a loud drum roll to help them react.
Then I asked Bernard Herrmann to supervise the whole sound track.* When musicians compose a score, or orchestrate, they make sounds rather than music. We used only sounds for the whole of the picture. There was no music.

F.T. When Jessica Tandy discovers the farmer's body, she opens her mouth as if to scream, but we hear nothing. Wasn't that done to emphasize the sound track at this point?

---

* Bernard Herrmann created and directed the musical score for all the Hitchcock pictures since *The Trouble with Harry* in 1955. Prior to that he created the score for Orson Welles's first two films, *Citizen Kane* in 1940 and *The Magnificent Ambersons* in 1942.

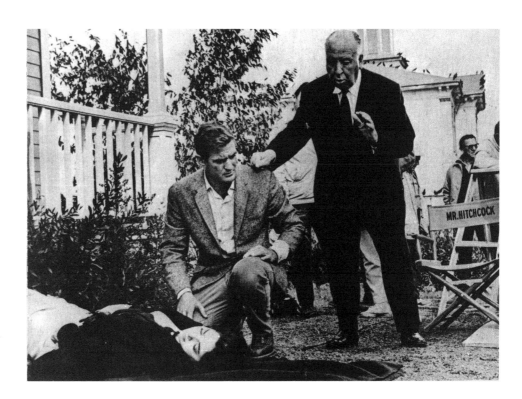

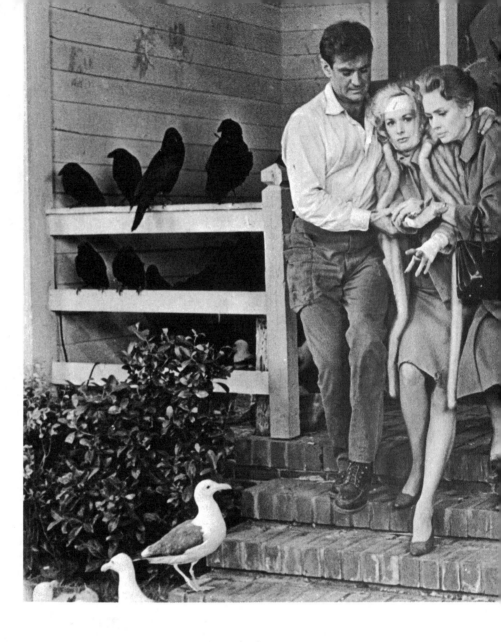

A.H.   The sound track was vital just there; we had the sound of her footsteps running down the passage, with almost an echo. The interesting thing in the sound is the difference between the footsteps inside the house and on the outside. Did you notice that I had her run from the distance and then went to a close-up when she's paralyzed with fear and inarticulate? There's silence at that point. Then, as she goes off again, the sound of the steps will match the size of the image. It grows louder right up to the moment she gets into the truck, and then the screech of the truck engine starting off conveys her anguish. We were really experimenting there by taking real sounds and then stylizing them so that we derived more drama from them than we normally would.

For the arrival of the truck, I had the road watered down so that no dust would rise because I wanted that dust to have a dramatic function when she drives away.

F.T.   I remember that very clearly. In addition to the dust you even had the smoke from the exhaust pipe.

A.H.   The reason we went to all that trouble is that the truck, seen from a distance like that, moving at a tremendous speed, expresses the frantic nature of the mother's moves. In the

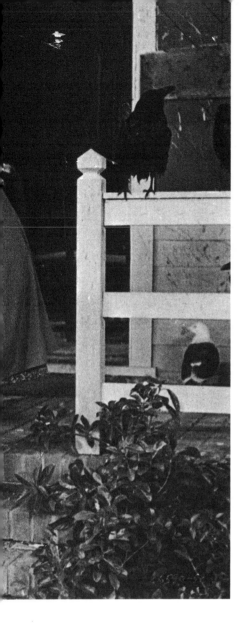

previous scene we had shown that the woman was going through a violent emotion, and when she gets into the truck, we showed that this was an emotional truck. Not only by the image, but also through the sound that sustains the emotion. It's not only the sound of the engine you hear, but something that's like a cry. It's as though the truck were shrieking.

F.T. As a matter of fact, the sound in all your pictures is very elaborate and always dramatic. Quite often the sound does not correspond to the image on the screen, but may extend and intensify a previous scene. There are several instances of this technique.

A.H. After a picture is cut, I dictate what amounts to a real sound script to a secretary. We run every reel off and I indicate all the places where sounds should be heard. Until now we've worked with natural sounds, but now, thanks to electronic sound, I'm not only going to indicate the sound we want but also the style and the nature of each sound.

For instance, when Melanie is locked up in the attic with the murderous birds, we inserted the natural sounds of wings, but we stylized them so as to create greater intensity. We wanted to get a menacing wave of vibration rather than a single level. There was a variation of the noise, an assimilation of the unequal noise of the wings. Of course, I took the dramatic license of not having the birds scream at all.

To describe a sound accurately, one has to imagine its equivalent in dialogue. What I wanted to get in that attack is as if the birds were telling Melanie, "Now, we've got you where we want you. Here we come. We don't have to scream in triumph or in anger. This is going to be a silent murder." That's what the birds were saying, and we got the technicians to achieve that effect through electronic sound.

For the final scene, in which Rod Taylor opens the door of the house for the first time and finds the birds assembled there, as far as the eye can see, I asked for a silence, but not just any kind of silence. I wanted an electronic silence, a sort of monotonous low hum that might suggest the sound of the sea in the distance. It was a strange, artificial sound, which in the language of the birds might be saying, "We're not ready to attack you yet, but we're getting ready. We're like an engine that's purring and we may start off at any moment." All of this was suggested by a sound that's so low that you can't be sure whether you're actually hearing it or only imagining it.

F.T. According to a newspaper story I read, Peter Lorre once played a joke on you by sending you some fifty canaries when you were sailing on a boat and you got even with him by sending him daily wires, giving him news of the birds, one by one. *The Birds* reminded me of

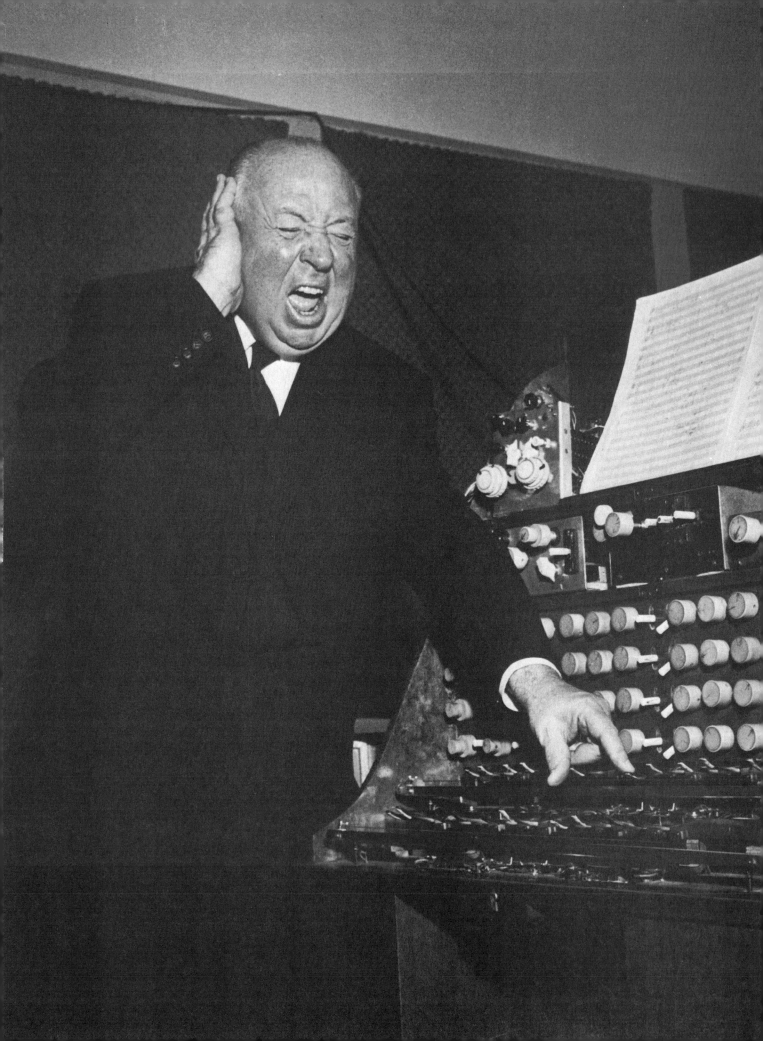

that story, and I'd like to know whether it is true or whether it's just another press canard.

A.H.   No, it isn't true. They credit me with many jokes that have no basis in fact, but I do have a weakness for practical jokes and have played quite a few in my time. Once, we were at a party in a restaurant with some twelve guests to celebrate my wife's birthday. I hired an aristocratic-looking elderly dowager and we put her at the place of honor. Then, I ignored her completely. The guests came in, and when they saw the nice old lady sitting alone at the big table, each one asked me, "Who's the old lady?" and I answered, "I don't know." The waiters were in on the gag, and when anyone asked them, "But what did she say? Didn't anyone speak to her?" the waiters said, "The lady told us that she was a guest of Mr. Hitchcock's." And whenever I was asked about it, I maintained that I hadn't the slightest idea who she was. People were becoming increasingly curious. That's all they could think about. Then, when we were in the middle of our dinner, one writer suddenly banged his fist on the table and said, "It's a gag!" And while all the guests were looking at the old lady to see whether it was true, the writer turned to a young man who'd been brought along by one of the guests and said, "I bet you're a gag, too!"

I've always wanted to carry that joke a little further. I'd like to hire a woman of that type for a dinner and introduce her to the guests as an elderly aunt of mine. The so-called aunt would say, "Can I have a drink?" And in front of everyone, I would say, "Absolutely not. You know how you are when you drink. No drinks for you." So the old lady would wander off into a corner, looking very pathetic. All the guests would be quite uncomfortable. Later on Auntie would come over again, with soulful eyes, and I would say very sharply, "It's no good looking at me like that. Besides, you're embarrassing everybody." And the old lady would simply whimper and then begin to cry softly, while the guests wouldn't know where to look and really would feel they were in the way. Then I'd say, "Look here, you're ruining our whole party. That's enough. You'd better go back to your room."

The only reason I never pulled that joke is that I'm afraid someone might hit me.

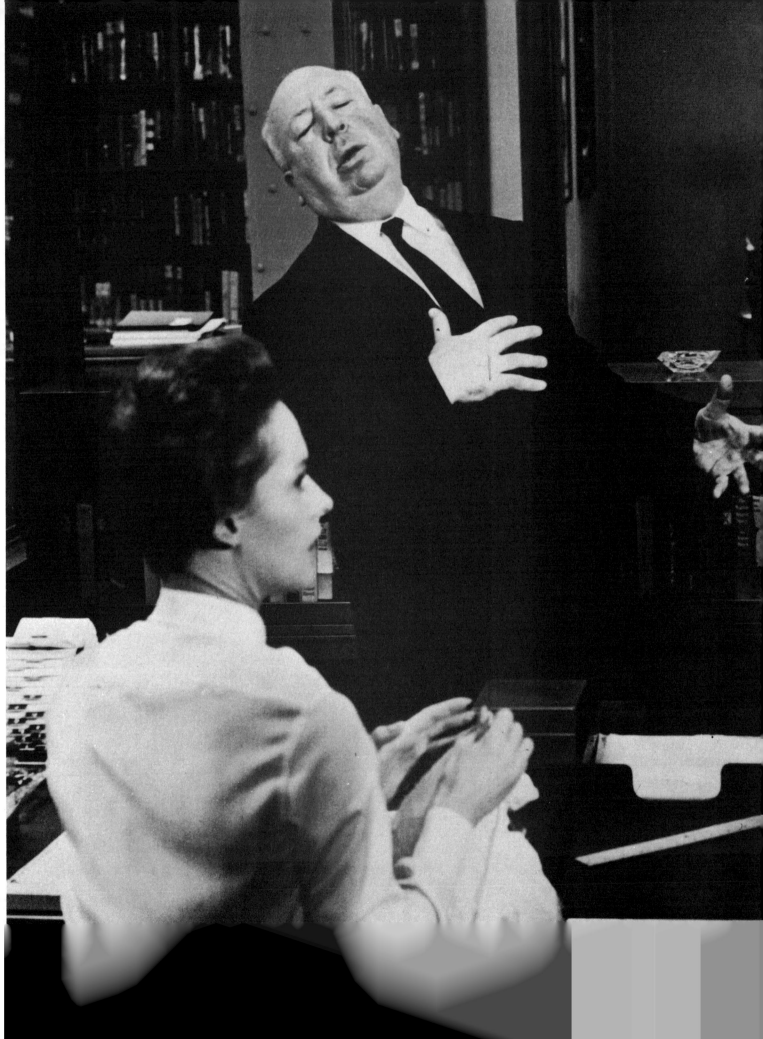

"MARNIE" ■ A FETISHIST LOVE ■ "THE THREE HOSTAGES," "MARY ROSE," AND "R.R.R.R." ■ "TORN CURTAIN" ■ THE BUS IS THE VILLAIN ■ THE SCENE IN THE FACTORY ■ EVERY FILM IS A BRAND-NEW EXPERIENCE ■ THE RISING CURVE ■ THE SITUATION FILM VERSUS THE CHARACTER FILM ■ "I ONLY READ THE LONDON 'TIMES'" ■ A STRICTLY VISUAL MIND ■ HITCHCOCK A CATHOLIC FILM-MAKER? ■ A DREAM FOR THE FUTURE: A FILM SHOWING TWENTY-FOUR HOURS IN THE LIFE OF A CITY ■

15

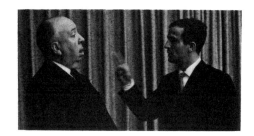

FRANÇOIS TRUFFAUT.   Now, we come to *Marnie*. Long before it was actually made, there was some talk that it might mark Grace Kelly's comeback to the screen. It's taken from a Winston Graham novel, and I'd like to know which aspect of the book made you decide to do the film.

ALFRED HITCHCOCK.   The fetish idea. A man wants to go to bed with a thief because she is a thief, just like other men have a yen for a Chinese or a colored woman. Unfortunately, this concept doesn't come across on the screen. It's not as effective as *Vertigo*, where Jimmy Stewart's feeling for Kim Novak was clearly a fetishist love. To put it bluntly, we'd have had to have Sean Connery catching the girl robbing the safe and show that he felt like jumping at her and raping her on the spot.

F.T.   Why is *Marnie*'s hero so attracted to

the girl? Is it that she depends on him because he knows her secret and can turn her over to the police, or is it simply that he finds it exciting to go to bed with a thief?

A.H.   It's both of those things. Absolutely.

F.T.   I notice one contradiction within the film: Sean Connery is very good and he has a sort of animal-like quality that fits in perfectly with the sex angle of the story. Yet neither the script nor the dialogue ever really touches on this angle, and Mark Rutland is presented to the viewer simply as a protective character. Only by watching his face very closely can one sense your intention to lead the script into a less conventional direction.*

---

* Marnie (Tippi Hedren) is a thief. Her *modus operandi* is to change her identity as soon as she has committed a successful robbery and then move on to another job. Though Mark Rutland

Opposite, Hitchcock demonstrates how Tippi Hedren should faint when she makes a red ink spot on her blouse.

301

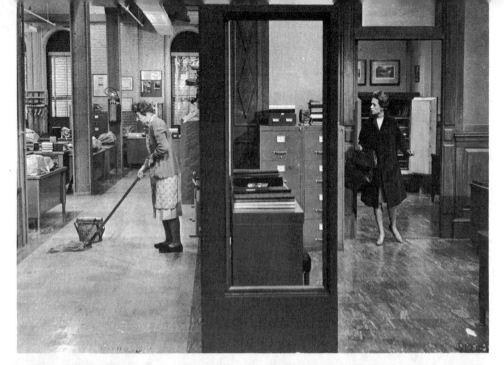

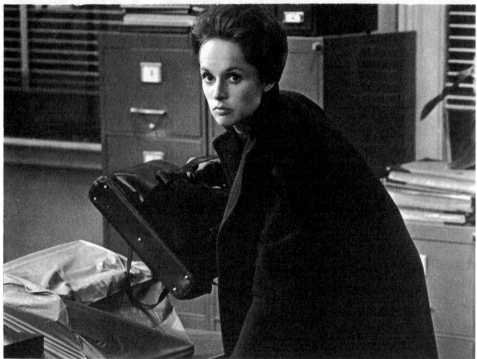

(Sean Connery), the head of an important firm, recognizes her from a previous encounter, he says nothing and hires her as a secretary-bookkeeper. He is clearly attracted to the girl, but she ignores his attentions and soon disappears with the contents of the company safe.

Mark discovers the theft, replaces the stolen money and manages to track Marnie down. Instead of turning her over to the police, he takes her back to Philadelphia and marries her. The girl has no choice but to accept him, but the shipboard honeymoon turns out to be a disaster as Mark learns that his bride is frigid. When he takes her by force, she attempts to commit suicide.

Subject to terrifying nightmares, Marnie is a profoundly neurotic girl, and her kleptomania is obviously a form of compensation for her frigidity. When Mark learns that she has lied in claiming to be an orphan, he hires a detective who locates the girl's mother in Baltimore.

Meanwhile, Marnie makes another attempt to rob the Rutland safe. Mark catches her in the act. Determined to discover the key to her deep-rooted neurosis, he forces his wife to accompany him to Baltimore, where he will try to pry from her mother the secret of her childhood.

Eventually, the puritanical mother breaks down and confesses that she had been a prostitute. When Marnie was a five-year-old child, she killed a sailor with a poker to protect her mother from his molestation. Marnie has, until this day, no memory of the tragedy.

Now that the truth is out in the open, it is clear that Marnie, with the help of her understanding husband, will eventually recover from the secret guilt feelings that have tormented her for years.

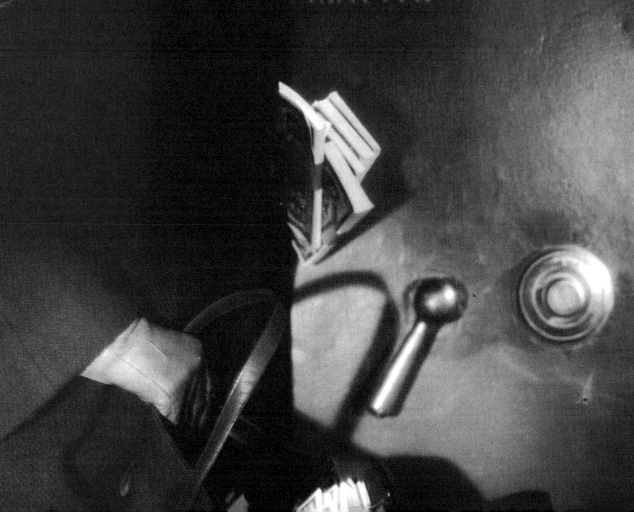

A.H. That's true, but remember that I established at the outset that Mark had spotted Marnie. When he learns that she's robbed the safe, he says, "Oh yes, the girl with the pretty legs . . ." In one of my early British pictures, *Murder*, I used the stream-of-consciousness technique. If I'd used that technique, we might have heard Sean Connery saying to himself, "I hope she hurries up and does the robbery so that I can catch her at it and possess her!" In this way we would have had a double suspense. We still would have played Marnie from Mark's point of view, and we'd have shown his satisfaction as he watches the girl in the act of stealing. I actually thought of constructing the story in that way. I would have shown the man looking at—in fact, secretly watching—a real robbery. Then, he would have followed the thief, would have grabbed Marnie and made out he had just happened on her. He would have taken her by force, while pretending to be outraged. But you can't really put these things on the screen. The public would reject them. They would say, "Oh no, that's not right. I don't believe it!"

F.T. It's a pity, because that story would have been fascinating. I like *Marnie* very much as it is, but I feel that it's difficult for the public, because of the atmosphere, which is stifling, a little like a nightmare.

A.H. In America they've re-released it as a double feature with *The Birds*. It's doing very well at the box office.

F.T. For all the pieces to fit, it seems to me, the picture would have had to run for three hours. As it is, there is nothing redundant in the story; in fact, on many points, one would like to know more.

A.H. That's true. I was forced to simplify the whole psychoanalysis aspect of it. In the novel, you know, Marnie agrees to see the psychiatrist every week, as a concession to her husband. In the book her attempts to conceal her past and her real life added up to some very good passages—both funny and tragic. But in the picture we had to telescope all of that into a single scene, with the husband doing the analysis himself.

F.T. Yes, right after one of her nightmares. That was one of the highlights of the film.

A.H. What really bothered me about *Marnie* were all the secondary characters. I had the feeling that I didn't know these people, the family in the background. Mark's father, for instance. And I wasn't convinced that Sean Connery was a Philadelphia gentleman. You know, if you want to reduce *Marnie* to its lowest common denominator, it is the story of the prince and the beggar girl. In a story of this kind

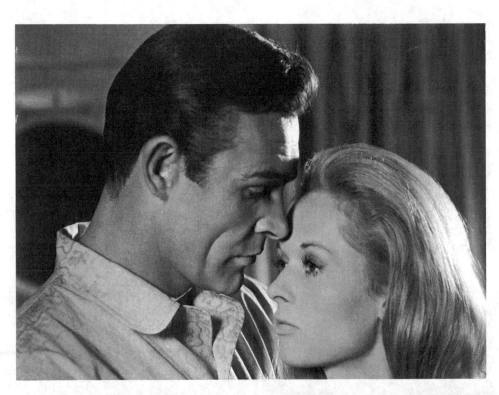

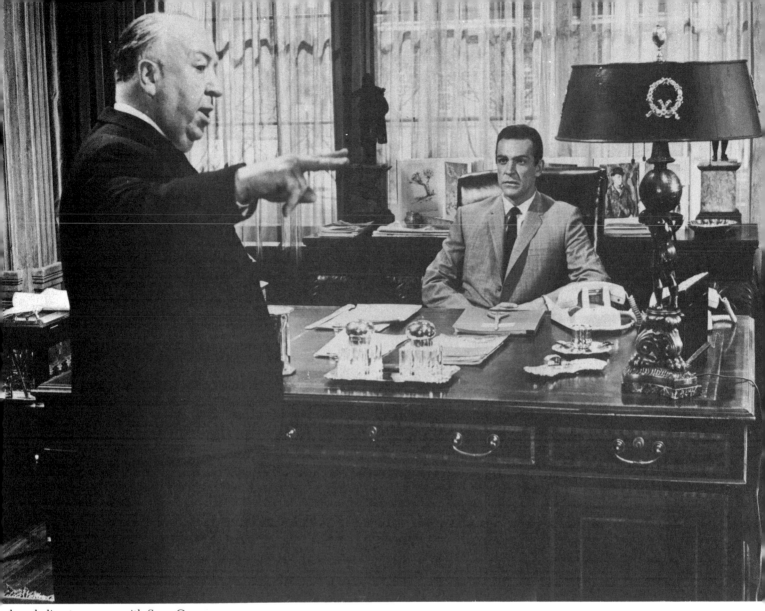

chcock directs a scene with Sean Connery.

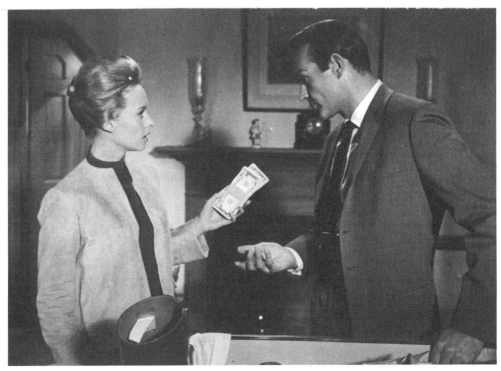

you need a real gentleman, a more elegant man than what we had.

F.T.   Someone like Laurence Olivier in *Rebecca?*

A.H.   Exactly. That's the way you heighten the fetishist concept. I ran into the same trouble on *The Paradine Case.*

F.T.   Claude Chabrol refers to it as the "temptation of self-destruction," and you describe it as "degradation for love." Apparently it's a dramatic motif that appeals to you very strongly, and I hope that someday you can work it out to your satisfaction.

A.H.   I doubt it, because it's the kind of story that is linked to the class consciousness that prevailed thirty years back. After all, today a princess can marry a photographer and no one lifts an eyebrow.

F.T.   In your original treatment there was a wonderful idea, but you dropped it. You wanted to have a love scene that would mark Marnie's release from her sexual inhibitions, a scene that would take place in the presence of other people.

A.H.   Yes, I remember that. In that treatment she went to see her mother and found the house full of neighbors: her mother had just died. That's where the big love scene would have taken place, to be interrupted by the arrival of the police who came to arrest Marnie. I dropped the whole thing because we ran into the inevitable cliché, with the man saying to the woman who's being taken away to prison, "I'll be waiting for you when you come out."

F.T.   So you decided to eliminate the police, and we infer that Marnie is not being harassed because Mark has reimbursed her various victims for their losses. As a matter of fact, it's my impression that the public never has the feeling that Marnie's in danger of being arrested. At no time does one get the feeling that she is a hunted woman or in any real danger.
There was a similar phenomenon in *Spell-*

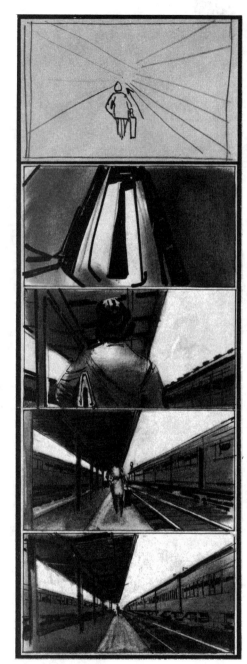

Storyboard for the opening scene of *Marnie.*

bound. Two mysteries of essentially different nature are blended together: a moral–psychological problem: What has this character, Gregory Peck or Tippi Hedren, done in his or her childhood? and a material problem: Will the police catch up with the character or not?

A.H.   I'm sorry, but it seems to me that the threat of a jail sentence is also a moral motive.

306

F.T.   No doubt, but I still feel that a police inquiry and a psychological investigation don't add up to a clear picture. The viewer isn't sure whether he's rooting for the character to discover the key to his neurosis or for him to get away from the police. Aside from that, the trouble with handling both these actions simultaneously is that the police hunt must move quickly, whereas the psychological investigation requires time to be properly developed.

A.H.   That's true. In the construction of *Marnie* I was bothered by the long period between the time she got her job at Rutland's and the time she committed the robbery. Between the two, all we had was Mark on the make for the girl. That just wasn't enough.

We often run into the problem of the logic of time. You feel you must show a certain amount of preparation; yet that preparation can become dull. We're so anxious not to drag it out that we can't fill it with entertaining details that would make it more interesting.

There was a similar problem in *Rear Window*, you know, where a long time went by before James Stewart began to look suspiciously at the man across the courtyard.

F.T.   Yes. You used the first day for the exposition of the story. But I found that very interesting.

A.H.   Well, that's because Grace Kelly was so nice to look at and the dialogue was pretty good.

F.T.   After *Marnie* there were reports of three film projects that have apparently been delayed or dropped. The press mentic _ _ *The Three Hostages*, from the John Buchan novel; *Mary Rose*, based on the play by Sir James Barrie; and an original screenplay entitled *R.R.R.R.*

A.H.   That's right. I worked on those three projects. Let's begin with *The Three Hostages*. The novel is full of typical Buchan situations and very close to another book of his, *The Thirty-nine Steps*. The central figure is the same character, Richard Hannay. *The Three Hostages* was published in 1924. It tells how the govern-ment is about to round up a gang of secret enemies of the British Empire, who Buchan implies are Bolsheviks. These secret enemies, knowing that they are to be arrested at a specific date, kidnap three children whose parents are among the important people in the country. Richard Hannay's job is to find out where the three hostages are hidden and to get them back.

He gets his first clue before leaving London when he meets Medina, a most elegant gentleman, with a touch of the Oriental about him, a connoisseur of wines, a confidant of prime ministers. Medina invites Hannay to his house and offers to help him. Gradually Hannay realizes that while his host is talking, he is actually trying to hypnotize him, and he allows him to believe the hypnosis has taken effect. A few days later he goes back to see Medina. Someone else is present, and to show the accomplice that he has Hannay in his power, Medina says, "Hannay, go on your hands and knees like a dog. Now go over to that small table and bring back that paper knife between your teeth." Of course, it was a very suspenseful and amusing scene, since Hannay actually has all his wits about him.

Nevertheless, through this, Hannay is able to pick up the clues that will lead him to the first hostage, a nineteen-year-old young man interned on an island in Norway; then, to the second, a girl he locates in a low dive in London. I forget where he found the third one, but the point is that each of them had been kidnaped by hypnotism.

Now, the reason I dropped the project is that I feel you cannot put hypnotism on the screen and expect it to hold water. It is a condition too remote from the audience's own experiences. In the same way, it's impossible to put an illusionist on the screen, because the public knows instinctively, through the tricks they have seen in films, how the director went about it. They will say, "Oh well, he stopped the reel and then took her out of the box!" It's the same thing for hypnotism. And visually speaking, there would be no difference between someone who is really hypnotized and someone who's pretending.

F.T.   I believe you had already dropped the concept of a kidnaping through hypnotism in the original version of *The Man Who Knew Too Much.*

A.H. That's right, I did. In fact, though the first screenplay of *The Man Who Knew Too Much* was taken from a Bulldog Drummond story, it was influenced by my reading of Buchan. Now, *Mary Rose,* the second project, is a little like a science-fiction story. I still haven't definitely dropped the idea of making it. A few years back it might have seemed that the story would be too irrational for the public. But since then the public's been exposed to these twilight-zone stories, especially on television.

The play starts out with a young soldier coming into an empty house where he and the housekeeper talk about the past. He tells her he was a member of the family that lived there. And here we have a flashback that takes us back thirty years. We see a family in an everyday atmosphere, and a young Navy lieutenant who is there to ask Mary Rose's parents for her hand in marriage.

The mother and father look at each other in a strange way, and when Mary Rose is out of the room, they say to the young man, "When she was eleven years of age, we went for a holiday to an island in northern Scotland. There, she disappeared for four days. When she came back, she had no awareness of the passage of time and no knowledge of her disappearance." The parents add: "We have never told her about this, and you may marry her, but do not mention it to her."

Now there is a lapse of several years, and Mary Rose, who has a two-and-a-half-year-old child, says to her husband; "I want to go on a delayed honeymoon. I'd like to go back to the island where I went as a little girl." The husband is upset, naturally, but he agrees.

The second act of the play takes place on the island. A young boatman who is studying for the ministry at Aberdeen University is piloting them on a boat and telling them about the local folklore. He mentions that on the island a little boy was once spirited away and a little girl was missing for four days.

They go fishing and the boatman shows the husband how to catch the trout and cook them on the hot stones. Meanwhile, Mary Rose sud-

denly hears celestial voices, like Debussy's *Sirènes,* you know. She starts to move toward them, the wind rises, and presently she is gone. There is a silence, the wind stops, and the husband starts searching for Mary Rose. He is frantic; he calls out, but she has disappeared. And that's the end of the second act.

The final act takes us back to the same family twenty-five years later. Mary Rose has been forgotten; the parents are quite old and the husband is now a middle-aged, paunchy man. The phone rings. It's the boatman, now a minister, who has just found Mary Rose on the island, unchanged. She returns to her family and is bewildered at being confronted with these old people. When she asks to see her little son, they tell her he ran away to sea when he was sixteen. The shock of the whole thing kills her—a heart attack.

Now, we go back to the soldier in the empty house—at the beginning of the story. Mary Rose appears through the door, like a ghost. They have a very natural conversation, and the scene becomes quite pathetic when she tells him that she is waiting and has been waiting for a long time. He asks, "What are you waiting for?" and she says, "I don't know. I've forgotten." She talks rather like a child. Then, suddenly, you hear the voices through the windows and a big, powerful light. Mary Rose gets up and walks toward the light, vanishing out of sight, and that's the end of the play.

F.T. It's quite interesting.

A.H. You should make the picture. You would do it better. It's not really Hitchcock material. What bothers me is the ghost. If I were to make the film, I would put the girl in a dark-gray dress and I would put a neon tube of light inside, around the bottom of the dress, so that the light would only hit the heroine. Whenever she moved, there would be no shadow on the wall, only a blue light. You'd have to create the impression of photographing a presence rather than a body. At times she would appear very small in the image, at times very big. She wouldn't be a solid lump, you see, but rather like a sensation. In this way you lose the feeling of real space and time. You should be feeling that you are in the presence of an ephemeral thing, you see.

F.T.   It's a lovely subject. Also a sad one.

A.H.   Yes, very sad. Because the real theme is: If the dead were to come back, what would you do with them?

F.T.   Your third project is an original screenplay, which you assigned to the writing team of Age and Scarpelli, the writers of *Big Deal on Madonna Street*.

A.H.   That one I've just now abandoned. Definitely. It was the story of an Italian who immigrates to America. He starts out as an elevator boy in a big hotel and eventually becomes the general manager. He brings his family over from Sicily. It turns out they are a gang of thieves, and he has to try to prevent them from stealing a collection of precious coins that are on display in the hotel.
I dropped the project because it seemed to be shapeless. Aside from that, you know that Italians are very slipshod in matters of story construction. They just ramble on.

F.T.   So you just dropped these three projects and you went to work on *Torn Curtain*. Where did you get the idea for this picture? *

A.H.   I got the idea from the disappearance of the two British diplomats, Burgess and MacLean, who deserted their country and went to Russia. I said to myself, "What did Mrs. MacLean think of the whole thing?"
So, you see, the first third of the film is more or less from a woman's point of view, until we have the dramatic showdown between the young couple in the hotel room in Berlin.
From here on I take Paul Newman's point of

---

* An American atomic scientist (Paul Newman) pretends to be a defector so as to get a secret scientific formula from Professor Lindt in Leipzig. A first setback occurs when his fiancée (Julie Andrews) decides to follow him to East Germany; the second is when he is forced to take part in the killing of a bodyguard who has discovered his secret mission. Following an exciting series of adventures while he is on the run, he will eventually manage to secure the secret formula and to leave East Germany with his fiancée.

view. And I show the unpremeditated murder in which he is forced to take a hand and then his efforts to get to Professor Lindt to learn his secret formula before the crime catches up with him. Then, the last part of the film is the couple's escape. As you see, the picture is clearly divided into three sections. The story worked out very naturally in that way, and its movement follows the logical geographical course. To make sure it was exact, before starting the scenario, I made the same trip as the characters. I went to Copenhagen, then, via a Rumanian airline, over to East Berlin, to Leipzig, then to East Berlin again, and finally to Sweden.

F.T.   True, the three-part division is clear, and I must admit I like the picture best from the second third on. The first part didn't move me. It's my feeling that the public guesses the developments well ahead of Julie Andrews and even before the key information is given out.

A.H.   I agree with you on that. From the moment when Newman tells Julie Andrews, "You go back to New York; I'll go back to Sweden," the public cannot fully believe him because we've allowed them to see other cues to his strange behavior. Nevertheless, all that had to be accurately worked out because you've got to be fair to the audience who will be seeing the film more than once. The picture's got to be able to stand up to a double check.
Of course, when the girl learns that her fiancé has booked a reservation for East Berlin and she says, "But that's behind the Iron Curtain," the audience is already ahead of us. But I don't think it matters because what they're really concerned with at this point is to see the effect on the girl—how she is going to react.

F.T.   So far, so good, but I can't go along with what comes next. The girl believes her fiancé to be a traitor long after everyone in the audience has already figured out the truth.

A.H.   No doubt, but I preferred to start the story on a note of "misterioso" so as to avoid the beginning I've used in the past and which has now become a cliché; the man who has been given a mission. I just didn't want to repeat that

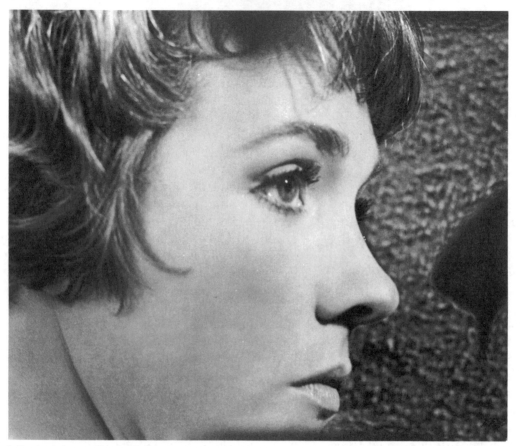

Julie Andrews as Sarah Sherman.

Paul Newman and Ludwig Donath.

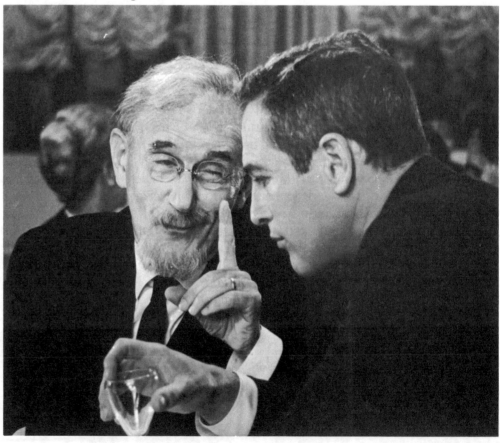

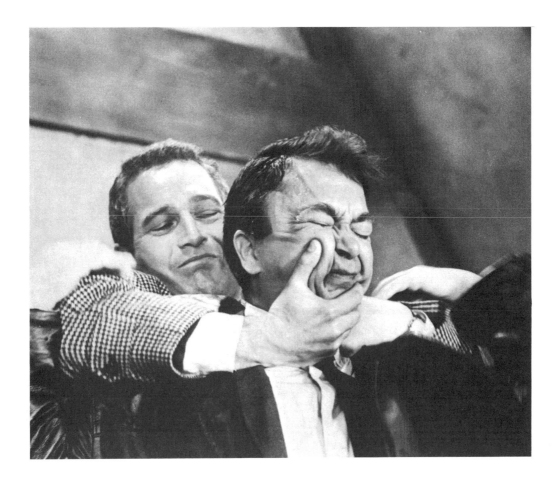

scene again. You have it in every one of the Bond pictures. A man says, "007, you go there. Bring back the gun, or do this or that." So I did that scene anyway, but instead of playing it at the beginning, I brought it in as a surprise in the middle of the film. It's the discussion with the farmer on the tractor, just before the murder.

F.T. The strongest scene, of course, is Gromek's killing on the farm; it's the one that grips the audience the most. Since it is played without music, it is very realistic and also very savage.

A.H. In doing that long killing scene, my first thought again was to avoid the cliché. In every picture somebody gets killed and it goes very quickly. They are stabbed or shot, and the killer never even stops to look and see whether the victim is really dead or not. And I thought it was time to show that it was very difficult, very painful, and it takes a very long time to kill a man. The public is aware that this must be a silent killing because of the presence of the taxi

driver on the farm. Firing a shot is out of the question. In line with our old principle, the killing has to be carried out by means suggested by the locale and the characters. We are in a farmhouse and the farmer's wife is doing the killing. So we use household objects: the kettle full of soup, a carving knife, a shovel, and, finally, the gas oven.

F.T. The height of realism was when the blade of the knife broke against Gromek's throat! There are several remarkable things in that murder sequence: the series of quick shots of Gromek's hand poking at Newman's jacket in a threatening way, the woman hitting out at Gromek's legs with the shovel, and then Gromek's fingers waving around before he finally subsides, with his head in the gas oven.
Going back to the script, I noticed two important changes in the film. One was the elimination of a scene in the factory between Berlin and Leipzig, and the other was the simplification of the sequence in the bus. In the script that was a very elaborate sequence, full of vivid detail.

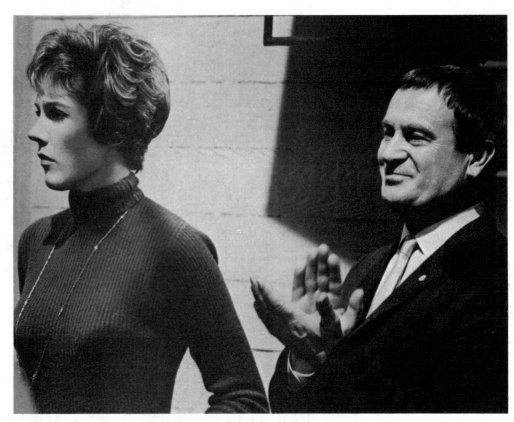

Julie Andrews and Rick Traeger in *Torn Curtain*.

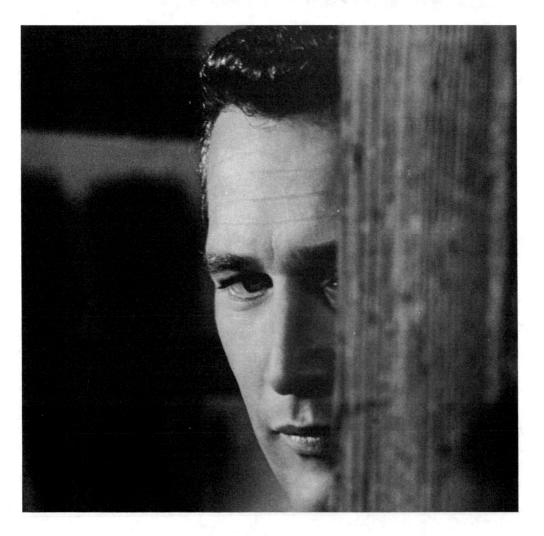

A.H. I had to compress the episode of the bus because if I had allowed it to drag out, I could not have sustained the tension. Remember, it's a scene in which time is compressed to create the illusion of a long journey. I directed that whole scene by imagining the bus to be a character of the film. We have a good bus, which is going to help our couple to escape. And a few hundred yards behind them is the bad bus, which is threatening the good one. But I'm not happy with the technical quality of the transparencies for that scene. For economy reasons I had the background plates shot by German cameramen, but we should have sent an American crew over.

F.T. Couldn't those transparency plates have been filmed on American highways?

A.H. No, because at the end of that sequence we show them coming into the city. We needed the real trolleys and all those genuine details. Aside from that, what did you think of the photography?

F.T. It's very good.

A.H. You know, it represented a drastic change for me. The lighting projected against big white surfaces. We shot the whole film through a gray gauze. The actors kept on asking, "Where are the lights?" We almost attained the ideal, you know, shooting with natural lights.

F.T. What about the factory scene?* Did you drop it before or after the shooting?

A.H. Afterward. I shot it. It's quite effective; in fact, very good. I dropped it from the final version because the film was too long. Aside

_____

* This scene takes place, following Gromek's killing at the farmhouse, in a factory that marks a stopover on the trip between East Berlin and Leipzig. In the canteen Professor Armstrong (Paul Newman) is startled to meet a foreman who bears an uncanny resemblance to Gromek. The man is Gromek's brother. After introducing himself as such to the American visitor, Gromek Two takes hold of a kitchen knife that looks just like the one his brother's been killed with in the previous episode and begins to slice a sausage. Armstrong is understandably very upset when the man says to him, "My brother loves this kind of sausage. Would you be kind enough to give it to him in Leipzig?"

from that, I wasn't too happy with the way Paul Newman played it. As you know, he's a "method" actor, and he found it hard to just give me one of those neutral looks I needed to cut from his point of view. Instead of simply looking toward Gromek's brother, toward the knife or the sausage, he played the scene in the "method" style, with emotion, and he was always turning away. Well, I fixed it somehow in the cutting, but finally I dropped the scene. Aside from the length of the picture, the reason I cut that scene out was also because I remembered the trouble I'd had with *The Secret Agent*. I made that picture in England thirty years ago and it was a flop. Do you remember the reason why? Because the central figure had to commit a killing he didn't want to do, and the public couldn't identify with a hero who was so reluctant to carry out his mission. So I felt that with *Torn Curtain* I would be falling into this trap again through that factory scene.

Anyway, the actor who played Gromek was very good. I had him completely transformed for the brother's role. His hair was white; he had a mustache and wore glasses. The people on the set objected: "But he doesn't look like the other one anymore." They all felt that the public should be under the impression that he was the twin of the dead man. I told them, "That's idiotic. If you turn Gromek Two into the spitting image of Gromek One, the public will just think they're seeing the same man!" You see how people think in stereotype terms?

Anyway, it was a good scene. I'll have that piece sent to Paris.

F.T. Really?

A.H. Yes, I'll give you that piece of film, if you like.

F.T. Thank you very much! I'll look at it and then turn it over to Henri Langlois for the Cinémathèque Française.

_____

F.T. Mr. Hitchcock, there's a systematic pattern that runs throughout all of your work. From the very beginning you have consistently chosen to limit yourself to those film elements that are visually inspiring or that have a dramatic potential. As a matter of fact, during our talks you've referred again and again to the need to "charge the screen with emotion" or to "fill the whole tapestry."

By systematically eliminating what you call "flaws" or "gaps" from your scenarios and by continually improving on the original texture, you have built up a stock of dramatic material that is clearly your own. Whether you're aware of it or not, this filtering process generally serves to express personal concepts that are supplementary to the action; it's as if you were instinctively imposing your own ideas on all your themes. Do you see what I mean?

A.H.   Well, experience tells you a lot. I'm aware that you and many other critics feel that all of my films resemble one another. But to me, strangely enough, every film is a brand-new thing.

F.T.   In your work there's a consistent effort to tackle new experiences. It seems to me that once you get a cinematic idea, you never let go of it until you're entirely satisfied—even if it takes several pictures to work it out successfully.

A.H.   I see what you mean. It's possible that I sometimes go back subconsciously, if only to run for cover. But I've never sunk low enough to say to myself, "I think I'll copy what I did in such and such a film."

F.T.   No, you've surely never done that. And on those rare occasions when you made such pictures as *Waltzes from Vienna* or *Mr. and Mrs. Smith*, which are not in your genre, you dismissed them as an out-and-out waste of time.

A.H.   I agree.

F.T.   Well then, your evolution does follow a systematic pattern of constant amelioration from film to film. If you're not sure an idea has been properly carried out in one picture, you'll work it out in the next one. Only when you're completely satisfied with the result do you go on to tackle something else.

Hitchcock's least favorite motion picture—*Waltzes from Vienna* (1933).

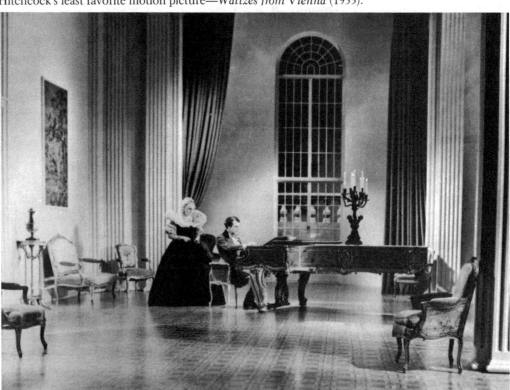

A.H.   Naturally, I expect to go forward, to advance with each picture, but to what degree I will succeed, I don't know.

I might add that I always feel comfortable about a project when I can tell the story in a very simple way, from beginning to end, in a fairly abbreviated version. I like to imagine a young woman who has been to see the movie and goes home very satisfied with what she's seen.

Her mother asks her, "How was the movie?"

And she answers, "It was very good."

The mother says, "What was it about?"

And the girl replies, "Well, it was about a young woman who so and so and so . . ."

Well, I feel that before undertaking to shoot a movie, one should be able to do just that, to satisfy oneself that it can be narrated just as clearly, the whole cycle.

F.T.   That's the main thing—to complete the cycle. This is the biggest problem, particularly for beginners. It's so easy to go astray that one often feels the completed picture has no relation to what was originally intended. So that it's only after friends and critics who see the first screenings talk about it in the same terms we used before it was shot—only then do we know —that despite the mistakes and waste the essential is still there. In other words, it's when somebody else uses your own words about the basic concept that you see you've succeeded in conveying to the screen the ideas that prompted you to undertake this picture instead of something else.

A.H.   That's exactly what I mean. I'm often troubled by the dilemma of whether I should cling to what I call the rising curve of the story, or whether I shouldn't experiment more through a looser form of narrative.

F.T.   I believe you're right to hang on to that rising curve. For you, it works very successfully.

A.H.   For instance, I personally would have been a little bothered by the shape of your film *Jules and Jim* because it doesn't automatically rise in that way. At one point, when one of the characters jumps out of a window, the story stops. Then a title reading "Some time later"

flashes across the screen, and the action is picked up again in a movie house showing a newsreel on the burning of books. Then, one of the characters says, "Look, our friend's down there in the front row." The three of them get together outside the movie house and the story starts again. Now, that may be good and correct in its way, but in the genre of the suspense story, it would be absolutely inadmissible.

F.T.   I absolutely agree with you and not only in the context of suspense. One should not systematically subordinate everything to the characters. In any film there comes a moment when the story must have the priority. You're quite right; one should not compromise the dramatic curve.

A.H.   I note the distinction you make between situation films and character films. I've often wondered whether I could do a suspense story within a looser film, in a form that's not so tight.

F.T.   It's risky, but it might be interesting to try it. It seems to me you have already experimented along these lines.

A.H.   Well, the story of *Marnie* is looser because it is carried by the characters, but we still had the rising curve of interest because of the basic question: When will the girl be found out? That's one question, and the other one is: What's the matter with this girl; why won't she go to bed with her husband? In a sense it's a psychological mystery.

F.T.   While you deal with out-of-the-way subjects, most of the things you film are very personal to you, somewhat like obsessions. I'm not suggesting that you live in murder and sex, but I imagine that when you open up a newspaper you start out with the crime stories.

A.H.   As a matter of fact, I don't read about crime in newspapers. The only newspaper I read is the London *Times*, which is rather dry but has lots of humorous items. A few years ago the *Times* carried an item under the heading: "Fish Sent to Prison." I read the story and it turned out that someone had donated a small tropical aquarium to the women's prison in London. But the heading amused me. I read the paper for that sort of thing.

F.T.   Do you also read magazines and novels?

A.H.   I don't read novels, or any fiction. I would say that most of my reading consists of contemporary biographies and books on travel. I can't read fiction because if I did I would instinctively be asking myself, "Will this make a movie or not?" I'm not interested in literary style, except perhaps when I read Somerset Maugham, whom I admire for the simplicity of his style. I don't like literature that is flowery and where the main attraction is the turn of a phrase. My mind is strictly visual, and when I read an elaborate description of a city street or of the countryside, I'm impatient with it. I'd rather show it myself with a camera.

F.T.   I wonder whether you know *Night of the Hunter*, the only picture Charles Laughton ever directed?

A.H.   No, I never saw it.

F.T.   Well, in that picture there was a very good idea that reminded me of your films. Robert Mitchum plays the preacher of one of those secret, strange religious sects. The word "love" was tattooed on one of his hands and the word "hate" on the other. His sermon consisted in a sort of pathetic struggle between the two hands. It was quite effective. When I saw that, it occurred to me that your pictures also describe the conflict between good and evil. It's shown in a great variety of ways—some of them quite powerful—and yet it's always simplified, just like that fight between the two hands. Do you agree?

A.H.   I would say so. The other day we mentioned a slogan: The better the villain, the better the picture. We might turn that around and say "The stronger the evil, the stronger the film."

F.T.   How do you feel about being labeled a Catholic artist?

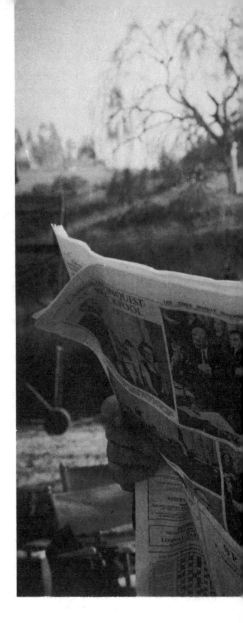

A.H.   That's a rather difficult question, and I'm not sure I can give you a precise answer. I come from a Catholic family and I had a strict, religious upbringing. My wife converted to Catholicism before our marriage. I don't think I can be labeled a Catholic artist, but it may be that one's early upbringing influences a man's life and guides his instinct.

For instance, in several films—and though this seemed, at the time, to be accidental—there were Catholic churches and not Baptist or Lutheran churches. For *Vertigo* I needed a church with a tower, so naturally I looked around for an old church. The only churches of that kind in California are the Catholic missions. On the face of it, it might seem that I deliberately chose to show a Catholic church, but, in reality, the

316

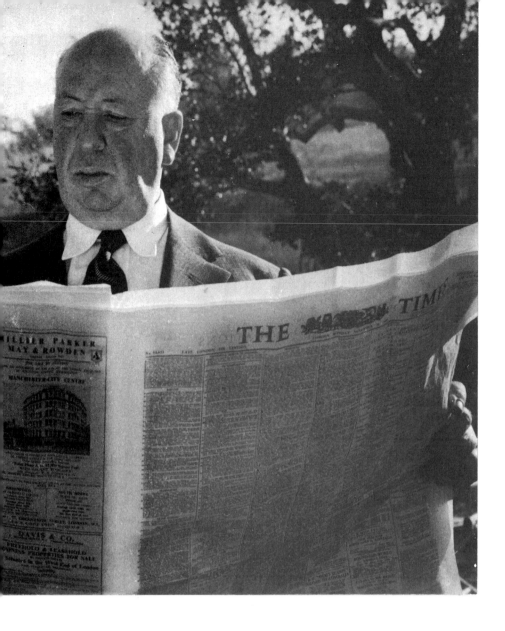

idea originated with the Boileau–Narcejac novel. I simply couldn't see anyone jumping from the tower of a modern Protestant church. I am definitely not anti-religious; perhaps I'm sometimes neglectful.

F.T.   I have no preconceived notions on this and I'm not trying to put words in your mouth, but it seems unlikely to me that anyone but a Catholic would have handled Henry Fonda's prayer scene as you did in *The Wrong Man*.

A.H.   That may be, but on the other hand, you should bear in mind that this was an Italian family. You remember, in Switzerland they have milk chocolate and lakes; in Italy . . .

F.T.   In Italy they have the Pope! I forgot that Henry Fonda was portraying an Italian in the picture. But even so, most of your work is strongly permeated by the concept of the original sin, and of man's guilt.

A.H.   How can you say a thing like that when in fact we always have the theme of the innocent man who is constantly in danger, although he isn't guilty?

F.T.   While your hero is generally innocent of the crime for which he's under suspicion, he is generally guilty of intentions before the fact. For instance, let us take the character of James Stewart in *Rear Window*. Curiosity isn't merely

317

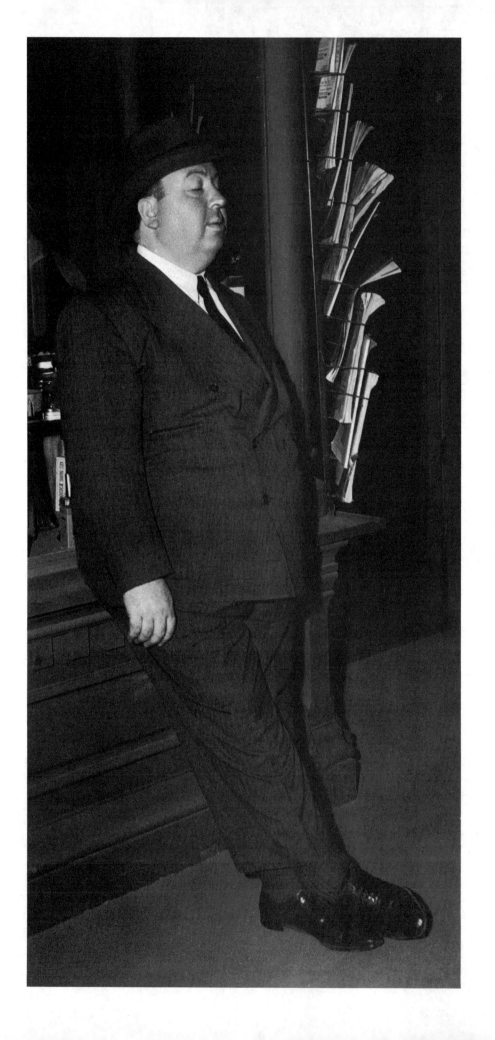

a nasty personality trait; in the eyes of the Church it's actually a sin.

A.H. That's true, and I agree with you. You remember that a reviewer said it was a horrible film because of the Peeping Tom character. Now, if anyone had mentioned that to me before I embarked on that picture, it certainly wouldn't have kept me from going ahead with it, because my love of film is far more important to me than any considerations of morality.

F.T. Well, in my opinion, that reviewer is wrong, because *Rear Window* is anything but an indulgent film. The morality in this picture is simply its lucidity. We've already mentioned that scene in which the killer comes up to James Stewart to ask him, "What do you want of me?" In nine out of ten films you've made—in forty-five of your fifty pictures—you've had tandem confrontations of good and evil characters. The mood grows increasingly oppressive, until someone finally decides to talk up, to turn himself in, or to confess. This is the composite portrait, or the mechanism, that runs through all of your works. Whether by means of a crime plot or not is beside the point; the fact is that for the past forty years you've consistently filmed moral dilemmas.

A.H. That's quite true, and I've often wondered why I've never been interested in pure stories of everyday conflict. I think it may be because, pictorially speaking, they're dull.

F.T. Exactly. It might be said that the texture of your films is made up of three elements: fear, sex, and death. These are not daytime preoccupations, like in films that deal with unemployment, racism, poverty, or in the many pictures on everyday love conflicts between men and women. They are nighttime anxieties, therefore, metaphysical anxieties.

A.H. Well, isn't the main thing that they be connected with life? There might be another reason, and that is that I'm not a writer. I could do a whole script by myself, but I'm too lazy to do that, or too preoccupied in other directions. That's why I bring other writers in. But I sup-

pose that the films with suspense and atmosphere are, to some degree, my creations as a writer. I don't think I'm really any good at stories that are completely written by someone else. I think I told you how I suffered with *Juno and the Paycock*, how helpless I felt at not being able to do something to Sean O'Casey's story. I kept looking at it and studying it. It was an entity of its own, written by Sean O'Casey, and all I could do about it was to cast it and direct the players.

For me to take someone else's script and merely photograph it in my own way simply isn't enough. For better or for worse, I must do the whole thing myself. And yet, in a way, one has to be terribly careful that one doesn't run out of story ideas. Like any artist who paints or writes, I suppose I'm limited to a certain field. Not that I'm comparing myself to him, but old Rouault was content with judges, clowns, a few women, and Christ on the Cross. That constituted his life's work. Cézanne was content with a few still lifes and a few scenes in the forest. But how long can a film-maker go on painting the same picture?

Yet I feel there's still a lot to be done. The phase I'm going through at this time is to try to correct a major weakness in my work in respect to the thin characterizations within the suspense stories. It's not so simple, because when you work with strong characters, they seem to take you where they want to go. I'm like the old lady with the Boy Scouts who're trying to help her across the street: "But that's not where I want to go!" This has always been a conflict with me because I require certain effects. I'm drawn by the wish to put intriguing settings in my pictures, like the motorcar on the Ford assembly line. You might call it a bastard form of writing, an inverted way of arriving at one's goal. Let's take *North by Northwest*, which isn't based on a novel. When I start on the idea of a film like that, I see the whole film, not merely a particular place or scene, but its direction from beginning to end. Aside from that, I may not have the vaguest idea of what the picture will be about.

F.T. As I see it, Mr. Hitchcock, your approach is anti-literary and purely cinematic. Emptiness has a magnetic appeal for you; you see it as a challenge. The movie house is empty; you must fill it. The screen is empty, and you are impelled to fill it. Your point of departure is not the content but the container. You see the film as a receptacle to be filled to the brim with cinematic ideas or, in your own terms, to be "charged with emotion."

A.H. That's about the size of it. Sometimes a film project starts with a very vague idea. One idea, for instance, is that I'd like to do twenty-four hours in the life of a city, and I can see the whole picture from beginning to end. It's full of incidents, full of backgrounds, a complete cyclic movement. It starts out at five A.M., at daybreak, with a fly crawling on the nose of a tramp lying in a doorway. Then, the early stirrings of life in the city. I'd like to try to do an anthology on food, showing its arrival in the city, its distribution, the selling, buying by people, the cooking, the various ways in which it's consumed. What happens to it in various hotels; how it's fixed up and absorbed. And, gradually, the end of the film would show the sewers, and the garbage being dumped out into the ocean. So there's a cycle, beginning with the gleaming fresh vegetables and ending with the mess that's poured into the sewers. Thematically, the cycle would show what people do to good things. Your theme might almost be the rottenness of humanity. You could take it through the whole city, look at everything, film everything, and show all of that.

F.T. That story is a perfect illustration of your approach to a film. You start by spelling out all the imagery and the eventual sensations; from there on, the over-all theme will emerge by itself. It could be a fascinating picture.

A.H. There are lots of ways in which to do that film, but who's going to write it? It would have to be funny, and it would also require a romantic element. You might get ten films in one. I tried it several years ago and asked a writer to do something with the idea, but it didn't work out.

F.T. I suppose the whole picture would fol-low the one character as he goes from one end of the city to the other.

A.H. That is the problem. What can we hang the theme on? Of course, there are several possibilities: the man on the run, the newspaper reporter, or a young couple from the country discovering the city for the first time. But these are all too trite. It's an enormous task, yet I feel the need to do this picture. Strangely enough, when you do a big, modern story, the public doesn't appreciate its size. But if you should take that same story in the Roman period, it is acknowledged as an enormously important picture. The tragedy is that the public accepts modernity without being awed by it. And yet they're impressed by the Roman temples because they know they had to be built on the sets. What is *Cleopatra*, after all, but a little story like *Roman Holiday* which is about a modern princess in everyday clothes.

Of course, one doesn't make a picture like this merely for the first row in the balcony or for a few seats on the aisle. It would have to be geared toward two thousand seats in the theater. Because cinema is the greatest known mass medium there is in the world and the most powerful. If you've designed a picture correctly, in terms of its emotional impact, the Japanese audience should scream at the same time as the Indian audience. To a film-maker, this is always the challenge.

A novel may lose a lot of its interest in the translated version, and a play that's beautifully acted out on opening night may become shapeless during the rest of the run, but a film travels all over the world. Assuming that it loses fifteen per cent of its impact when it's subtitled and ten per cent when it's well dubbed, the image remains intact, even when the projection is faulty. It's *your* work that's being shown—nothing can alter that—and you're expressing yourself in the same terms everywhere.

Hitchcock was not allergic to publicity. Here, he poses disguised as a woman for a major American magazine. Photograph by Maxwell Coplan.

The Man Behind the Body

by John D. Weaver

■ Alfred Hitchcock, like Charles Dickens, has created a popular body of work so distinctive that his name has passed into the language. A hundred years after Dickensian characters had young Queen Victoria's subjects cliff-hanging from one installment to the next, their great-grandchildren streamed into the London cinemas to surrender themselves to a Hitchcockian world of spies and saboteurs, assassins and black-mailers. This shadowy, stylized realm has been ruled for forty years by a calm, ample creature of habit who has made his bundle frightening film audiences while living the orderly nine-to-six life of a civil servant.

He awakens each morning at the same time (seven A.M.) in the same house to the same wife (they were married in 1926). He drinks a cup of tea before break-fast, slips into one of his six identical blue suits and leaves for the office. At six-thirty, after nine hours of cunningly contrived murder and mayhem, he comes home to eat dinner in his remodeled kitchen, help his wife with the dishes, and then read (biography and romantic novels) and watch television. Somewhere between nine-thirty and ten o'clock, his two miniature Sealyhams asleep beside him, he dozes off in front of the television screen.

"Television," he says, "was made for that purpose."

Hitchcock's comfortable, unostentatious house faces the fifteenth fairway of the Bel-Air Country Club, which provides a pleasant suggestion of the English countryside without putting him to any expense or bother, except when a sliced drive sends a ball into Mrs. Hitchcock's azaleas. There is no swimming pool (Hitchcock abhors any form of avoidable exertion), but the wine cellar contains an awesome assortment of estate-bottled vintages from the Médoc and the Côte-d'Or, some so venerable as to be only of historic interest. "I'm a Burgundy man myself," Hitchcock says, and, quite in character, he has sunk more money into renovating his kitchen than he originally spent in buying the house.

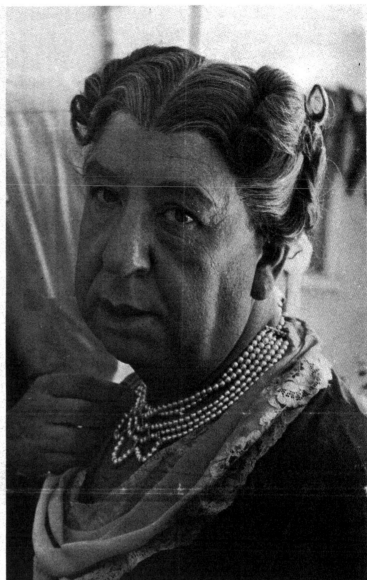

PHOTOGRAPH BY MAXWELL COPLAN

The complex world

of Alfred Hitchcock

includes murder,

mayhem and

artful disguises

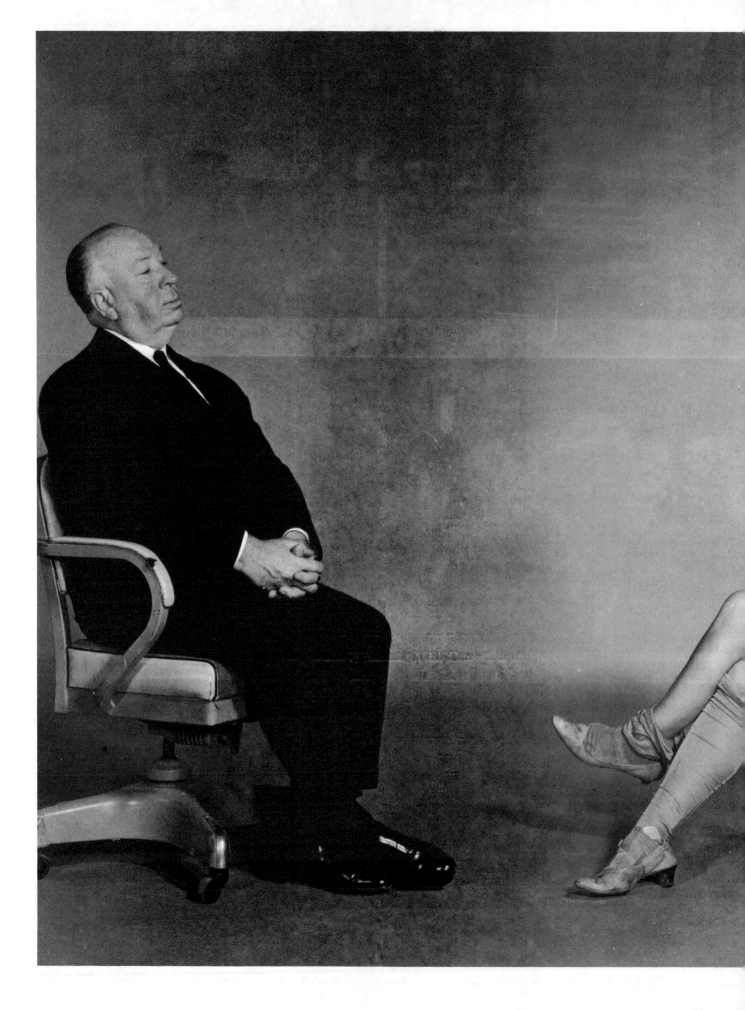

16

At the time we recorded these talks with him, Hitchcock was at the peak of his creative powers. During the previous ten years, he had made eleven movies, among them *Strangers on a Train, Rear Window, The Man Who Knew Too Much, Vertigo, North by Northwest,* and *Psycho.*

Following the termination of his contract with David O. Selznick, he became his own producer, and even acquired the rights to several of his negatives, which is rare in Hollywood.

Starting with *The Birds,* all of his subsequent films were made under the auspices of Universal, the company of Lew Wasserman, his former MCA agent and closest friend. He also became one of the five major stockholders of that company. In exchange for a large number of stocks, he gave Universal-MCA the rights to some two hundred hours of television programs he had produced and supervised over a period of ten years.

In 1962, the major problem for Alfred Hitchcock was the disappearance of his star performers. James Stewart was too old to play the lead in one of his pictures; in private, Hitchcock attributed the commercial failure of *Vertigo* to Stewart's aging appearance. At the same time, despite the success of *North by Northwest,* Cary Grant had voluntarily abandoned his film career in order to leave his fans with a seductive image of his screen personality. In fact, he turned down the male lead in *The Birds,* and Rod Taylor, an actor who was competent but who lacked charisma, was finally cast in the role.

The problem with actresses was even more serious, for the motto "cherchez la femme" was a strain running throughout Hitchcock's work.

323

DOMENICA DEL CORRIERE

Anno 64 - N. 26 - L. 50   Settimanale del CORRIERE DELLA SERA   1 Luglio 1962

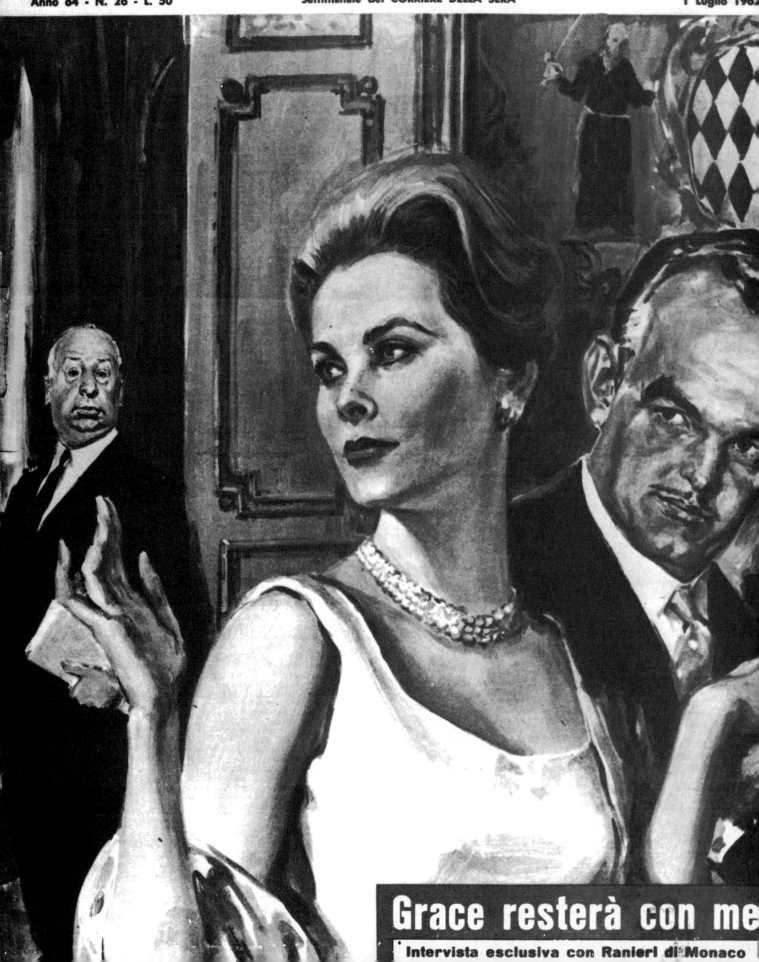

Grace resterà con me

Intervista esclusiva con Ranieri di Monaco

Though he never forgave Ingrid Bergman for having left him for Rossellini, Hitchcock harbored no resentment toward Grace Kelly. One reason was that Prince Rainier was not a film director; another was that the former cockney lad was rather awed by the title of Princess the beautiful Philadelphia society girl acquired when she left Hollywood for the cliffs of Monaco.

But while he bore no grudge against Grace Kelly, he undoubtedly had regrets, and hoped to retrieve her for *Marnie*, a film based on a novel by Winston Graham to which he had acquired the rights especially for Grace Kelly. The deal was almost set: Grace Kelly was genuinely tempted, and Prince Rainier, who was very fond of Hitchcock, seemed to favor the project. However, General de Gaulle, irritated by the fiscal advantages that the Principality granted to French businessmen, launched an attack threatening Monaco's privileged status. In order to maintain his links with France, the Prince was forced to compromise and to make concessions that would alter the frivolous image of his Principality. In the process, Grace Kelly had no choice but to definitively abandon the cinema.

A film lovingly conceived for one actress, and finally enacted by another—the history of cinema is full of these painful disappointments and betrayals. Renoir wanted Catherine Hessling for the title role of *La Chienne*, but it was Janie Marèze who starred in the film. It was Miriam Hopkins, and not Claudette Colbert, who was slated to star in *Bluebeard's Eighth Wife*. *Stromboli* was originally written for Anna Magnani, but the starring role went to Ingrid Bergman. The title role of *The Barefoot Contessa* was inspired by Linda Darnell, but was eventually played by Ava Gardner. In her biography, Doris Day recalls that she was distressed by Hitchcock's taciturnity during the shooting of *The Man Who Knew Too Much*. She was convinced that she had been cast merely because she was a singer, and that Hitchcock would have preferred Grace Kelly in the part. In this she was perhaps mistaken, for at the end of the shooting, Hitchcock told her, "I said nothing because you gave a good performance. If it had been otherwise, I would most certainly have said something."

On the other hand, *Vertigo* was undoubtedly a film in which the leading lady was cast as a substitute for the one Hitchcock had in mind initially. The actress we see on the screen is a substitute, and the change enhances the appeal of the movie, since this substitution is the main theme of the picture: A man who is still in love with a woman he believes to be dead attempts to re-create the image of the dead woman when he meets up with a girl who is her look-alike.

The irony of the situation was pointed up during a tribute to Hitchcock I attended in New York in 1974. Seated next to Grace Kelly, and viewing the scene in which James Stewart urges Kim Novak to put her hair up in a bun, I realized that *Vertigo* was even more intriguing in light of the fact that the director had compelled a substitute to imitate the actress he had initially chosen for the role.

Thus, in the early sixties, Hitchcock missed the stars. Hitchcock needed them more than other directors because his cinema was based not on characters but on situations. He hated useless scenes, the kind that can easily be dropped during the editing because they do not serve to move the action forward. He was not a man for digressions, or for those petty details that "ring true." In his films, one never sees an actor attempt a superfluous gesture, like smoothing down his hair or sneezing. If the actor is framed in a full shot, his silhouette must be impeccable; if he is filmed from the waist up, his hands will not appear at the bottom of the frame. Because of this, the lifelike impact of a Hitchcock movie is based on a personality previously acquired by the actor in films by other directors. James Stewart brought the warmth of John Ford to Hitchcock films, and Cary Grant brings to them the charm he displays in his comedies on marital infidelity.

Yet the immense success of *Psycho*—which was listed in second place at the box office for 1960, just behind *Ben Hur*—reassured Hitchcock on his ability to captivate a *mass* audience with a *small* film. He was, therefore, confident when he undertook the shooting of *The Birds* in 1962.

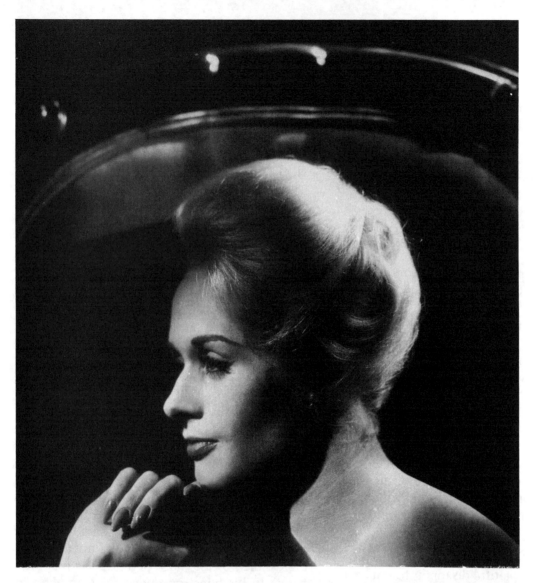

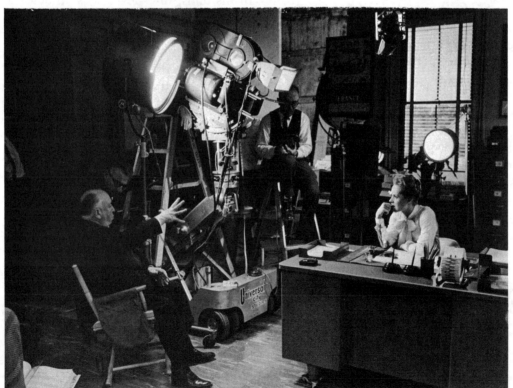

Nevertheless, it was precisely at the time when Hitchcock had finally achieved full recognition, via a series of homages, that his luck changed.

North by Northwest, which he defined as "a drama about a man on the run," had been plagiarized, botched and caricatured—in particular by the James Bond films. Hitchcock felt he had to renounce the film genre he had built up for thirty years, since *The Thirty-nine Steps*, and this meant he would avoid big-budget pictures. *The Birds* was several years in advance of the fad for catastrophe films. Because of the special effects, it was nevertheless fairly costly, but not as successful as it deserved to be. The following picture, *Marnie*, was a fascinating film, but a box-office flop, and belongs in the category known as the "great flawed films."

Parenthetically, I want to define what I mean by a "great flawed film." It is simply a masterpiece that has aborted, an ambitious project weakened by some errors in the making: a fine screenplay that is "unshootable," an inadequate cast, a shooting contaminated by hatred or blinded by love, or an inordinate gap between the original intention and the final execution. This notion of "great flawed films" can apply only to the works of a great director—one who has demonstrated that in other circumstances he can achieve perfection. In an overall view of his achievements, a true cinephile may, on occasion, prefer such a director's "great flawed film" to one of his acknowledged masterpieces —thereby preferring, for example, *A King in New York* to *The Gold Rush*, or *The Rules of the Game* to *Grand Illusion*. If one accepts the concept that a perfect execution often conceals the film-maker's intentions, one must admit that the "great flawed film" may reveal more vividly the picture's raison d'être.

I might also point out that, while the masterpiece does not necessarily arouse the viewer's emotions, the "great flawed film" frequently does—which accounts for the fact that the latter is more apt to become what the American critics call a "cult film" than is the masterpiece.

I would add that the "great flawed film" is often harmed by an excess of sincerity. Paradoxically, this sincerity makes it clearer to the aficionados, but more obscure to the general public, which has been conditioned to absorb mixtures that give priority to gimmicks rather than to straightforward confessions. In my opinion, *Marnie* belongs to that bizarre category of "great flawed films" which is often underrated by the critics.

I am convinced that Hitchcock was never the same after *Marnie*, and that its failure cost him a considerable amount of his self-confidence. This was not so much due to the financial failure of the film (he had had others), but rather to the failure of his professional and personal relationship with Tippi Hedren, whom he discovered through a television commercial. In casting Tippi Hedren in two of his films, he entertained the notion of transforming her into another Grace Kelly.

It is important to recall that after the shooting of *The Birds*, and before giving Tippi Hedren her second chance in *Marnie*, Hitchcock made a series of film tests of several beautiful women, among them many prominent European models.

It is also useful to read Donald Spoto's biography *The Dark Side of Genius*, as well as David Freeman's piece "The Last Days of Alfred Hitchcock" (*Esquire*, April 1982), for details on the disastrous falling-out between Hitchcock and Tippi Hedren, and on Hitchcock's decline following *Family Plot* and during the writing of *The Short Night*. Some commentators have reproached both writers for publicizing the most pathetic moments of the old age of a great man. My own judgment is less severe: Having known Hitchcock socially and professionally only in the final years of his life, these two young men had no reason to feel grateful or friendly to him. From the viewpoint of cinema historians, the case of Alfred Hitchcock—both the man and his work—is so rewarding and complex that we can predict that before the end of this century, there will be as many books written about him as there are now about Marcel Proust.

Hitchcock was not much of a letter writer, but thanks to the 6,000 miles that separated us, we remained in regular contact through a correspondence that enables me to quote him in the final phases of his life.

Throughout this book, it is obvious that Hitchcock was always lucid and self-critical with respect to his own work, provided the film under discussion had been made in the distant past, and had been compensated for by a more recent success. I, in turn, respected this very natural sensitivity in a man who was otherwise neither proud nor vain. That is why I avoided the critical comments on *Marnie* and *Torn Curtain* that I might have made if either one of these films had been made long before our conversations.

In any case, I am convinced that Hitchcock was not satisfied with any of the films he made after *Psycho*.

In the mid-sixties, Hollywood was going through a crisis due to the great strides made by television. American pictures were losing their international impact to such a degree that several major companies set out to finance small European productions in their countries of origin, in order to release them with the Hollywood output on the European marketplace. At the same time, the American majors merged their European outlets: Paramount with Universal and Warner with Columbia, while M-G-M halted its production.

Disappointed by the box-office failure of *Torn Curtain*, Hitchcock found himself without a film project for the first time in years. In addition, as already stated, he had already lost some of his self-confidence after *Marnie*. This accounts for the fact that in shooting *Torn Curtain* he allowed the studio to influence him, first in the choice of the two stars, Paul Newman and Julie Andrews, and—much more seriously—in dropping one of his oldest collaborators—composer Bernard Herrmann. Was Hitchcock so unfair as to attribute the impression of gloom that overshadows *Marnie* to Herrmann? Herrmann's removal is a flagrant injustice, since it is a matter of record that his contributions to *The Man Who Knew Too Much*, *North by Northwest*, and *Psycho* had greatly enhanced the success of these films. Herrmann had written and directed a score of some fifty minutes for *Torn Curtain*. Its beauty, consistent with his talent, can be appreciated today, since it was eventually made into a record in London. What happened?

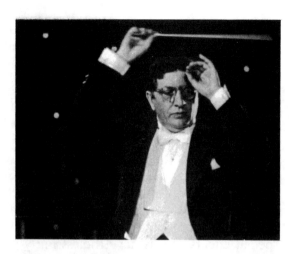

The studio—one always refers to "the studio" when speaking of an aberrant decision—did not like Bernard Herrmann's musical score for *Torn Curtain*, and though it had been recorded, "they" succeeded in convincing Hitchcock to discard it. We must bear in mind here that in 1966, in Hollywood and elsewhere, it was the practice of the film industry to favor scores that would sell as popular records—the kind of film music that could be danced to in discotheques. In this sort of game, Herrmann, a disciple of Wagner and Stravinsky, was bound to be a loser.

Another important name was missing from the credits of *Torn Curtain*: Robert Burks, who, except for *Psycho*, had been the director of photography for all of Hitchcock's films since *Strangers on a Train*. Not only was Hitchcock not responsible for the end of this collaboration, but he was still sincerely missing Burks, since the previous year in the burning of his house.

Deprived of his favorite stars, his director of photography, his composer and his chief editor, Hitchcock felt that he was embarking on a new phase of his career, and that it would be a rough one.

In 1967, at a time when there had been no announcement of a new Hitchcock project in the trade press, he wrote me:

I am, at present, preparing a new picture. It has no title, but deals with a psychopathic murderer of young women. It is roughly based on an English crime case. It is a purely realistic story, and the central figure is a young man who has some kind of relationship with his mother.

The thing that interests me about the story is the fact that after the first murder you know that when he meets the second girl, her life is in danger and you wonder when death will come. The third girl is a young police woman who has been "set up" to trap him. So this third segment of the film is also quite suspenseful, because you are wondering how soon he will find out that this is an attempt to trap him.

I have brought over an English playwright named Benn W. Levy. The last time I worked with him was in 1929, when he did the dialogue for the first English talking picture, *Blackmail*. He has been writing plays on and off over the years with varying degrees of success.

I'm going to treat this film quite realistically and, if possible, use as many real interiors as I can. . . .

—excerpt from a letter dated April 6, 1967

A few weeks later, Hitchcock mailed me the screenplay, which he had titled *Frenzy* (but which should not be confused with the film he made four years later under the same title). As I recall, this initial *Frenzy* had a good plot, but also a disadvantage in that it had too many points in common with *Psycho*, and I suppose this is the reason why Hitchcock finally dropped it.

It was at this time that Hitchcock, who had always had the strength to reject projects he deemed inadequate*—especially during the period he was under contract to Selznick—allowed Universal's front office to persuade him to adapt a novel which the studio had just purchased at a very high price.

Topaz was a spy novel. Its only merits were that it was based on a true story (the presence of a Communist agent in the entourage of General de Gaulle) and that it was a best-seller in Amer-

---

* In 1961, when Rouben Mamoulian was fired from the shooting of *Cleopatra*, Walter Wanger and Darryl F. Zanuck had called upon Hitchcock "as the only director capable of saving the production." Hitchcock refused and went on to shoot *The Birds*. Joseph L. Mankiewicz took over the shooting of *Cleopatra* and went down in the ensuing shipwreck.

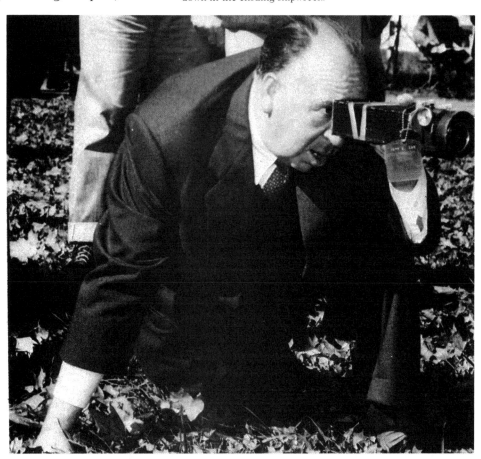

ica. In France, the book had been banned by the Gaullist censorship, but one could acquire a French version published in Canada, under the counter, as during the Occupation.

Unfortunately, the story of *Topaz* involved too many locations, too many conversations, and too many characters. The contract for the literary rights specified that the author of the voluminous novel would write the screenplay. This resulted in a considerable waste of time before Hitchcock was finally allowed to call upon his friend Samuel Taylor, who did the best he could with the screenplay.

While in Paris, where he was shooting some of the exterior scenes for *Topaz*, Hitchcock implied some of his doubts and reservations about the picture in an interview with Pierre Billard of *L'Express*. "For me," he said, "a film is ninety-nine percent finished with the screenplay. Sometimes, I'd prefer not to have to shoot it. You conceive the film you want and after that everything goes to pieces. The actors you had in mind are not available, you can't get a proper cast. I dream of an I.B.M. machine in which I'd insert the screenplay at one end and the film

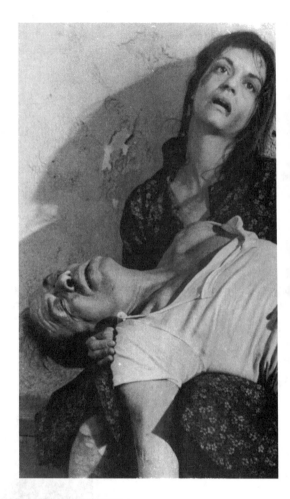

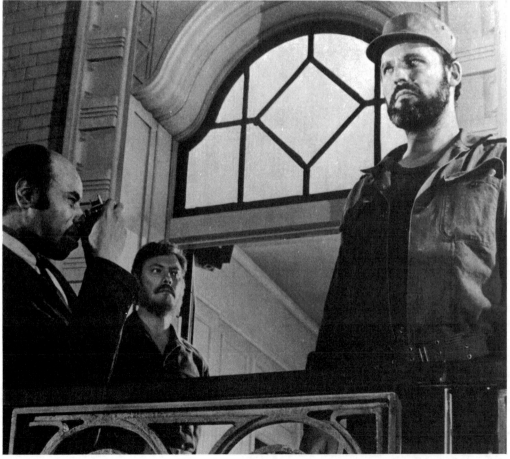

would emerge at the other end, completed, and in color."

Hitchcock had always avoided politics in his pictures, but *Topaz* was deliberately anti-Communist and included several very sarcastic segments on Fidel Castro's entourage. There were even scenes of Cuban policemen torturing members of the opposition. When *L'Express* asked him, "Do you regard yourself as a liberal?", Hitchcock answered, "I think I am in every sense of the term. I was recently asked whether I was a Democrat. I answered that I was a Democrat, but in respect to my money, I am a Republican. I am not a hypocrite."

In contrast to *Torn Curtain*, in which the joint salaries of Paul Newman and Julie Andrews amounted to more than half the film's total budget, *Topaz* had no major stars. Its cast was made up of competent American, French, Scandinavian and Hispanic actors. The French cast included Philippe Noiret, Michel Piccoli, Michel Subor, Dany Robin, and young Claude Jade, who could pass for an illegitimate daughter of Grace Kelly.

An actor of limited ability, Frederick Stafford, although credible as a secret agent, lacked plausibility as the father of the young girl. Impeccable in his virile physique, he was an obvious substitute for Sean Connery. In fact, before shooting *Marnie*, Hitchcock had tried to sign Sean Connery for two or three pictures, but though Connery wanted to get away from the image of James Bond, he refused to commit himself for more than one picture.

The key to the *Topaz* plot is, as I said earlier, the unmasking of a Soviet spy in the entourage of General de Gaulle, with Michel Piccoli portraying the spy. The screenplay winds up with Piccoli, aware that he is about to be discovered, deliberately allowing himself to be killed by Frederick Stafford in the course of a gun duel. The scene was shot in the awesome setting of an empty stadium near Paris. During a sneak preview in Los Angeles, this scene provoked hoots of laughter from a youthful American audience. Hitchcock went back to Paris to reshoot the scene with a few variations. Back in Hollywood, at another sneak preview, there was once

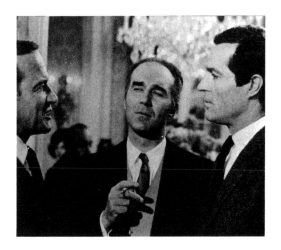

again a scornful reaction to the modified scene, but now Piccoli and Stafford were no longer available. Hitchcock finally discarded the duel scene, but he resented the early reactions to it. He claimed that young Americans had become so materialistic and cynical that they could not accept the concept of chivalrous behavior. It was beyond their understanding that a traitor to his country should accept a gun duel in which he would allow himself to be killed.

In any case, he was under pressure, and for the first time in his long career Hitchcock could not think of an ending to his film. He eventually settled for a purely formal solution which, I suspect, was influenced by a picture that was enjoying a huge success at the time, Costa-Gavras' *Z*. In the final part of *Topaz*, there is a series of shots and close-ups of the film's characters, homogenized by a spirited musical score, with the rhythm of the image and sound track announcing that the conclusion is near. Nevertheless, Hitchcock insisted upon letting the viewer know that Piccoli has finally committed suicide—*but how*, when all the footage shot at the stadium was deemed worthless? Hitchcock resorted to a crude finagling, a solution of despair. Any director who has torn his hair out in front of the moviola because he requires a scene that he has not shot is bound to sympathize with this dilemma. As the film unfolds, the public has seen the exterior of Piccoli's home, a sort of bachelor apartment facing the courtyard on the ground floor of a town house located somewhere in the 17th arrondissement. Now, the scene Hitchcock needs would show Piccoli going home after be-

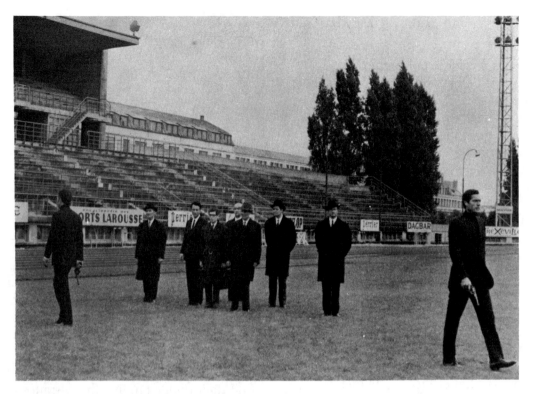

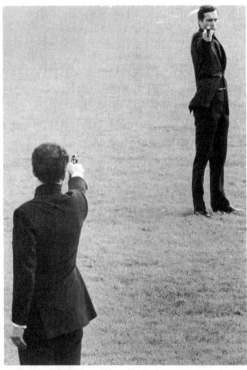

enters his house and shoots himself as soon as the door closes behind him.

Unfortunately, throughout the entire film, we have never once seen Piccoli going home. At the beginning of the picture we see him in his dressing gown, welcoming his mistress, Dany Robin. As she leaves the house, she runs into Philippe Noiret, who is about to call on Piccoli. Therefore, the only piece of film Hitchcock possessed to convey his idea—that of Piccoli going home and killing himself—was a shot of Noiret entering the town house! Although the shot is filmed from a distance, it is impossible to mistake Noiret's silhouette for Piccoli, especially since Noiret walks with a cane throughout the film. So what we finally see is Noiret entering the house, but only at the very end of the shot, at the moment the arm holding the cane is already inside the apartment. Thus, all that appears on the screen is the darkened half-body of a man disappearing behind the door; the image of the house is then frozen and we hear a gunshot, followed by the music and the final credits.

coming aware that he has been discovered. The image of the town house, seen from the exterior, would be frozen for a second, just time enough to insert the sound of a gunshot. In this way, the essential idea would be saved: Piccoli

It is obvious that despite a few scattered beautiful scenes, mainly in the Cuban episode, *Topaz* is not a good picture. The studio didn't like it,

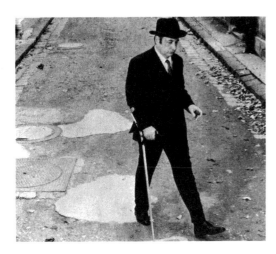

and neither did the public, the critics, nor even the Hitchcockians. The director himself wanted to forget it, and felt an imperative need to make up for it.

According to a letter from Hitchcock, Hollywood was going through a crisis, and was in a state of utter confusion in the summer of 1970. He wrote:

I am looking for a new film project, but it is very difficult. In the film industry here, there are so many taboos: We have to avoid elderly persons and limit ourselves to youthful characters; a film must contain some anti-establishment elements; no picture can cost more than two or three million dollars. On top of this, the story department sends me all kinds of properties which they claim are likely to make a good Hitchcock picture. Naturally, when I read them, they don't measure up to the Hitchcock standards.

How lucky you are not to be categorized and stamped as I am, for this is the root of my difficulties in acquiring a good subject, especially in respect to acceptance by the audience.

Everyone here, and especially the majors, is being very cautious. For instance, Paramount made four big pictures for a global budget of a few hundred million dollars that turned out to be flops. Fox is pretty much in the same situation and the company's fate is dependent on a film no one has seen yet: *Tora, Tora, Tora*, the story of Pearl Harbor, co-produced by the Japanese and the Americans. Several reliable sources have informed me that the picture cost thirty-two million dollars. Universal's *Airport* is a big hit here in the States, and optimistic rumors predict it will net as much as thirty million dollars in American grosses alone.

We also have all kinds of other films which I refer to as "accidental" and which are enormous box-office hits. Filmed for the most part by amateurs, they are apparently very popular with young audiences. Of course, not all these "accidental" films are successful, especially those which include nudity scenes, and it is becoming obvious that nudity in itself is not a guarantee of box-office success.

This is a general picture of the situation that prevails here at the moment. . . .

—excerpt from a letter
dated August 27, 1970

Soon after writing this letter, Hitchcock selected a British novel, *Goodbye Piccadilly, Farewell Leicester Square* by Arthur La Bern. He simplified the plot considerably and named the project with the title of the screenplay he had once rejected—*Frenzy.*

In contemporary London, a sexual maniac strangles women, using neckties. A quarter of an hour after the picture begins, Hitchcock reveals the identity of the killer, who has been introduced in the second scene. We also meet a second character who is going to be accused of the killings; he will be discovered, followed, arrested, and condemned. For an hour and a half we watch him struggling to escape from the trap like a fly caught in a spiderweb.
web.

Frenzy is the combination of two kinds of films: those in which Hitchcock invites us to follow the itinerary of a killer (*Shadow of a Doubt, Stage Fright, Dial M for Murder, Psycho*), and those in which he describes the troubles of an innocent man who is on the run (*The Thirty-nine Steps, I Confess, The Wrong Man, North by Northwest*). *Frenzy* re-creates that nightmarish, stifling Hitchcockian universe in which the characters know each other—the killer, the innocent man, the victims, the witness; that world boiled down to the essential, where each conversation in a shop or in a bar happens to deal with the killings; a world made up of coincidences so systematically organized that they crosscut each other vertically and horizontally. *Frenzy* is the image of a crossword puzzle on the leitmotif of murder.

In May 1972, I met Hitchcock before the

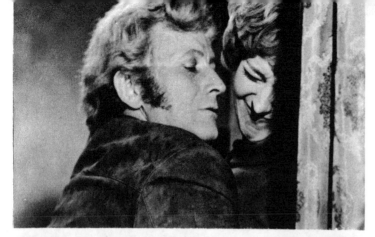

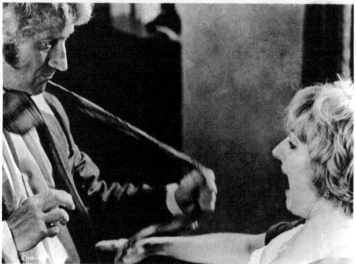

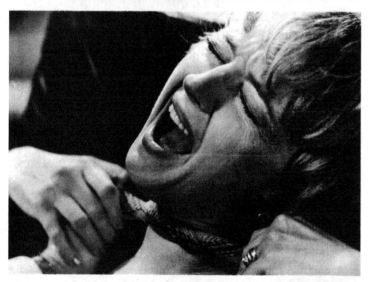

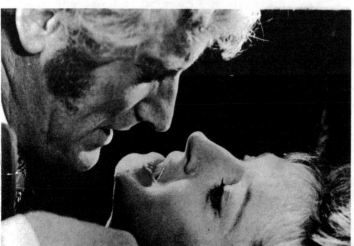

Cannes Festival where he was going to present *Frenzy*. He appeared aged, tired, and tense, for he was always very emotional before introducing a new picture, very much like a young man about to take a school examination. At the request of a television network, I interviewed Hitchcock.

FRANÇOIS TRUFFAUT. You have always made stylized films. Do you miss black-and-white cinema?

ALFRED HITCHCOCK. No, I like color. It's true that I filmed *Psycho* in black and white to avoid showing red blood in the killing of Janet Leigh in the shower. On the other hand, since color pictures, we have problems with the decors. Violent contrast—for instance, extravagant luxury or abject poverty—can be expressed with precision and clarity on the screen. However, if we wish to show an average apartment, it is difficult to create a realistic decor because of the risk of lack of precision.

F.T. A few years back, cinematographic audacity—eroticism, violence, politics—came from European productions. Today, American cinema has gone way beyond Europe in terms of insolence and freedom of expression. What do you think of the situation?

A.H. It reflects the moral climate and the way of life that prevail today in the United States, as well as being a result of national events that have had an impact on the film-makers and on the public. Still, American cinema dealt with social and political themes long ago, without attracting crowds to the box office.

F.T. Are you in favor of the teaching of cinema in universities?

A.H. Only on condition that they teach cinema since the era of Méliès and that the students learn how to make silent films, because there is no better form of training. Talking pictures often served merely to introduce the theater into the studios. The danger is that young people, and even adults, all too often believe that one can become a director without know-

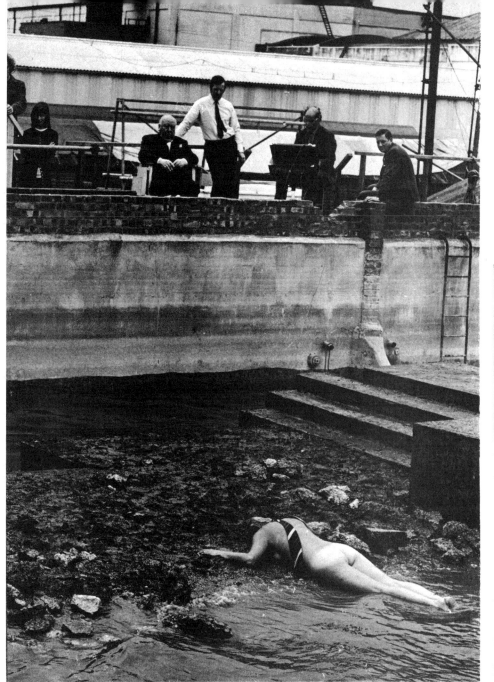

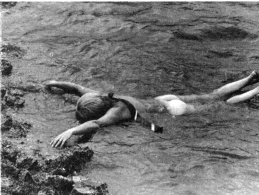

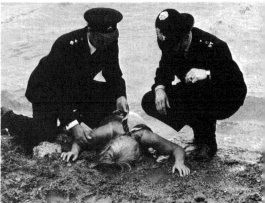

ing how to sketch a decor, or how to edit.

F.T. In your opinion, should a film suggest painting, literature, or music?

A.H. The main objective is to arouse the audience's emotion, and that emotion arises from the way in which the story unfolds, from the way in which sequences are juxtaposed. At times, I have the feeling I'm an orchestra conductor, a trumpet sound corresponding to a close shot and a distant shot suggesting an en-

tire orchestra performing a muted accompaniment. At other times, by using colors and lights in front of beautiful landscapes, I feel I am a painter. On the other hand, I'm wary of literature: A good book does not necessarily make a good film.

F.T. Do you think the old rules still apply, namely that an appealing main character and a happy ending are still valid?

A.H. No. The public has developed.

Un tres Heureux.

ABCDEFGHIJKMN OPQRSTUVWXYZ

Alma Hitch

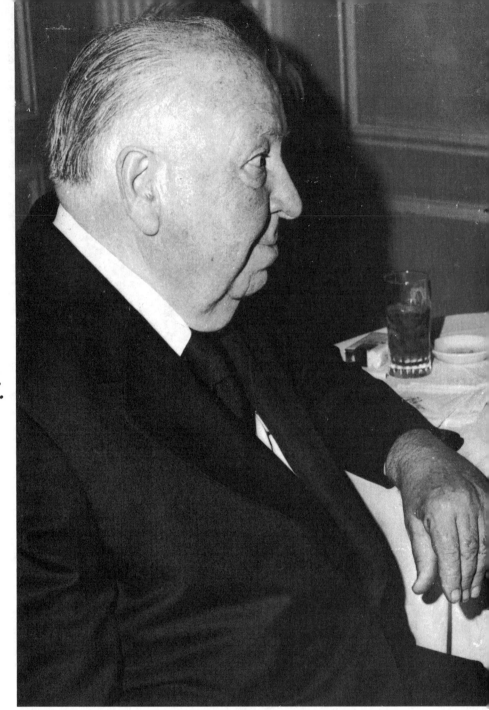

Hitchcock, the practical joker. Upon my arrival in Beverly Hills during the Christmas season in 1973, I found this card, which I understood only after a lengthy examination: Alma and Alfred H. had recopied the alphabet, deliberately dropping the letter L.

Thus, the card can be read: "A VERY HAPPY NO L."

There's no more need for the final kiss.

F.T.   Why don't you film today some of the subjects that interested you in the past, and that producers refused to finance?

A.H.   The need for profit is just as valid today as it was in the past. Even if I wanted to make, write, play, and finance a film on my own, I couldn't do it because I would run into problems with the trade unions.

F.T.   Do you prefer to shoot a screenplay with strong situations and sketchy characters, or the opposite?

A.H.   I prefer the strong situations. It is easier to put them into images. In order to probe a character in depth, you often need too many words. In *Frenzy*, the killer is likable. It's the situation that makes him disturbing.

F.T.   In 1956, the remake of *The Man Who*

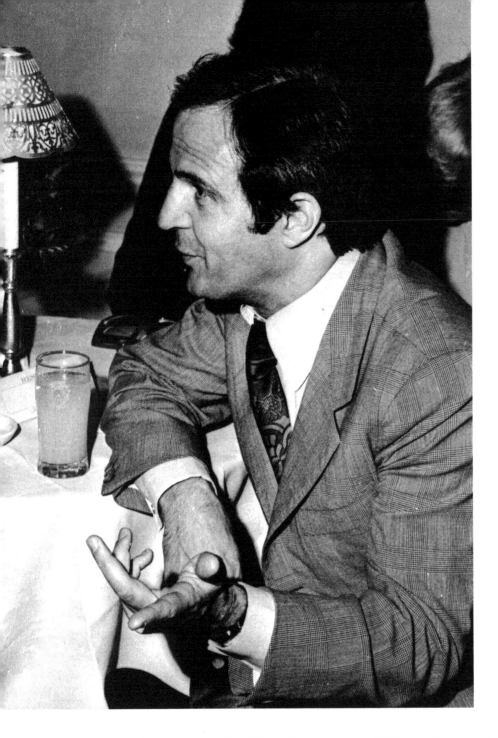

Knew Too Much was a great hit. Your first ver-·
sion of the picture was made twenty-two years
before. If you were to consider another remake
today, which of your former films would you
choose to do over again?

A.H. *The Lodger*, which I made in 1926. A
London family wonders whether their new
roomer is Jack the Ripper—an excellent story
filmed without sound, which was the basis for
two later versions by other directors.

F.T. Do you have any suggestions for re-
forms in respect to the awarding of the Oscars?

A.H. The awards would have to be given
out every three months, which would be difficult. The disadvantage of the present formula is
that the awards invariably go to pictures that
were released between September and December 31st!

F.T. A few years ago, everyday life was

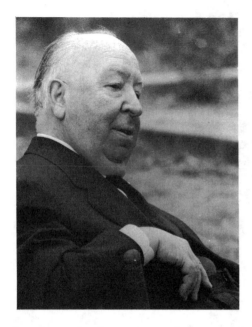

banal, and the extraordinary was in films. Today, the extraordinary is commonplace: political kidnappings, plane hijackings, scandals, and the assassinations of chiefs of state. How can a director of suspense and espionage films compete with everyday life in 1972?

A.H.   The reportage of a news item in a newspaper will never have the impact of a mov-

ing picture. Catastrophes only happen to others, to people we don't know. The screen allows you to meet and to know the killer and his victim, for whom you're going to tremble with fear because you care about him. There are thousands of car accidents every day. If the victim is your brother, you are really interested. If the film is well made, a screen hero will become your brother or your enemy.

F.T.   *Frenzy* is your first European movie in twenty years. What is the difference between your work in Hollywood and your work in England?

A.H.   When I enter the studios—be it in Hollywood or in London—and the heavy doors close behind me, there is no difference. A coal mine is always a coal mine.

———

A week later, when I met Hitchcock on his way back from Cannes, he looked fifteen years younger. *Frenzy* had been enthusiastically hailed at the festival and Hitchcock, beaming with pleasure, admitted that he had been very

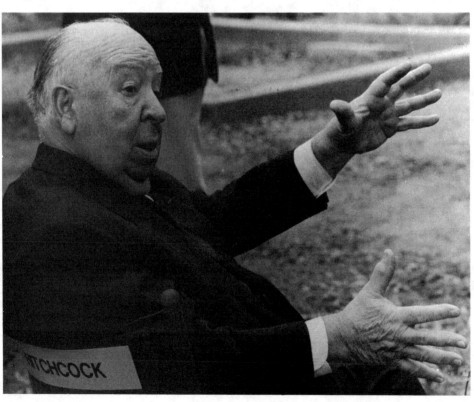

scared. But now, he knew that this "little film," whose budget was slightly less than two million dollars, would be successful, and that the studio would overlook the poor artistic and box-office results of *Topaz*, a picture made against his better judgment.

In casting *Frenzy*, Hitchcock abandoned his long-standing practice of using glamorous and sophisticated stars, à la Grace Kelly, in favor of girl-next-door types—Barbara Leigh-Hunt, Anna Massey, Vivien Merchant, and Billie Whitelaw. They all gave admirable performances, injecting a fresh realism into Hitchcock's work by reinforcing the impression of a commonplace news item, and strengthening the plausibility and raw truth of the gruesome story from which all feeling was excluded.

The male casting was less felicitous. The features of the innocent suspect (Jon Finch) mainly conveyed a self-centered sullenness which kept the public from sympathizing with him. And, as played by Barry Foster, the villain was too lightweight to inspire the viewers with fear.

Even so, *Frenzy* was impregnated with charm,

probably because, following the nightmarish shooting of *Topaz*, Hitchcock made it in a state of euphoria. He was about to celebrate his fifty years of film-making, and with Alma by his side, he set up his camera in Covent Garden, in the popular and lively London of his youth.

Hitchcock had often said, "Some directors film slices of life, I film slices of cake." With its entirely British aspect, *Frenzy* did in fact look like a slice of homemade cake baked by a seventy-year-old gastronome who had turned the clock back and was once again the young boy director of his film debut.

Three months later, Hitchcock acquired the rights to a new British novel, *The Rainbird Pattern* by Victor Canning, with the intention of transposing the action from the English countryside to Los Angeles and San Francisco. It was while working with Ernest Lehman on the screenplay of the film—which became *Deceit*, and, subsequently, *Family Plot*—that Hitchcock underwent heart surgery for the implantation of a pacemaker. I am not being indiscreet in mentioning this, because of all the friends and journalists who saw Hitchcock from 1975 on, rare were those to whom Hitchcock failed

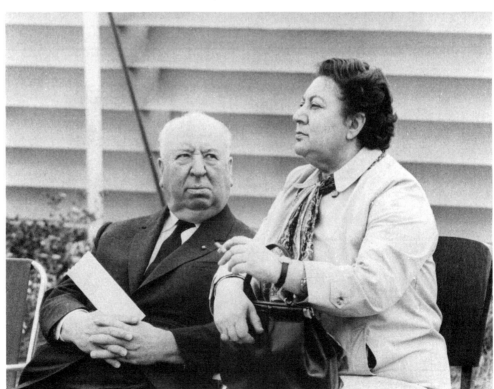

With Helen Scott during the Paris shooting of *Topaz*.

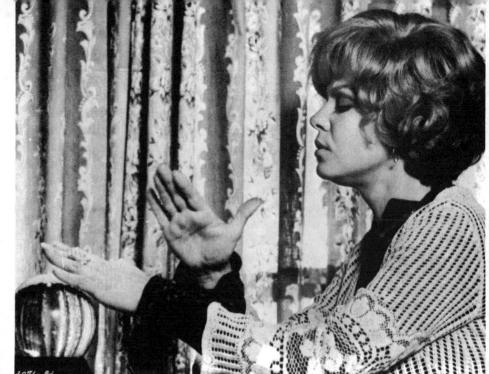

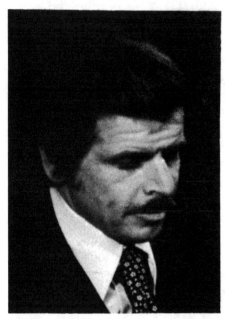

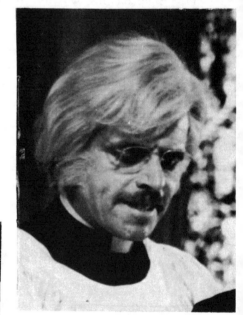

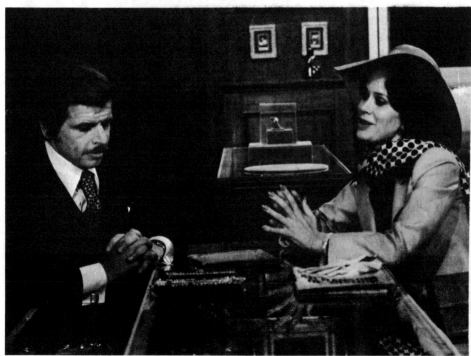

to display this medical gadget, opening his shirt to reveal the rectangular object implanted in his chest. Detaching each syllable and staring at his interlocutor, he would deliberately announce, "It's made to last for ten years." We all know that the pacemaker is made to regularize the heartbeat. Working by battery, the pacemaker ensures seventy heartbeats per minute, and its functioning is verified once a month by phone. This requires dialing the number of the medical center in Seattle (or, in Hitchcock's case, in Chicago), and placing the phone receiver against one's chest.

Once the visitor was fully informed about the use of the pacemaker, Hitchcock would indulge in his favorite pastime: a scene-by-scene description of his forthcoming picture, as if to prove to himself that its construction was solid and that he had mentally worked out its every detail.

What particularly appealed to Hitchcock in *Family Plot* was the passage from one geometric figure to another. First, two parallel stories are introduced, then the gap between them gradually narrows, and finally they mesh, winding up as a single story. This construction stimulated him in that he was about to deal with a difficulty he had never handled before.

In *Family Plot*, we meet two couples who belong to different worlds: The first couple consists of a pseudo fortune-teller (Barbara Harris) and her accomplice (Bruce Dern), a taxi driver who, in the course of his job, discreetly gathers pertinent information which his girlfriend will subsequently pretend to intuit. The other couple consists of an elegant jeweler (William Devane)* and his girlfriend (Karen Black), whose real occupation is kidnapping important personalities and trading them back for valuable diamonds which they conceal in a chandelier in their home.

The stories crisscross when the viewer realizes that the illegitimate son who is sought by the pseudo fortune-teller on behalf of an elderly woman who intends to make him her heir is, in fact, the kidnaping jeweler. It is not until the final reel that a gripping confrontation between the four characters takes place.

Released in the United States and then in Europe during the spring and summer of 1976, *Family Plot* was well received by the press, but the public's response was less enthusiastic. In this all-American film in which, once again, the weakness of the villain was responsible for the weakness of the picture, Hitchcock was renewing the blend of humor and an intriguing kidnaping which had accounted for the success of several of his prewar British pictures.

There was unanimous agreement on the fine performance of Bruce Dern and even more on that of Barbara Harris, who displayed wonderful invention and drollery in the role of Blanche Tyler, the pseudo fortune-teller.

Unfortunately, it soon became apparent that *Family Plot* was not a success. As with *Topaz*, a short suspense segment made American audiences snicker, so it was cut from the prints distributed in the United States. I believe the European prints correspond more closely to the original editing.

Contrary to popular belief, artists who are known to be experts in the art of provoking and controlling the publicity around their reputation and their work are generally candid in their statements to the press. One might even say that the more facetious they sound, the more sincere they actually are. This was true of Salvador Dali when he stated that the two things he loved most were money and his wife.

When *Family Plot* opened in New York, I saw Hitchcock on American television, facing up to some thirty trade journalists. They all manifested friendship and respect, not because they liked his fifty-third film, but because a director who is over seventy years old and still working enjoys what might be defined as critical immunity.

At one point, a journalist raised his hand and asked, "When one is seventy-six years old, and

---

* William Devane was a last-minute choice. Before casting him in the role of the villain, the director had hired Roy Thinnes, whom he fired after two days of shooting. This was the first time this had happened in Hitchcock's career. Simultaneously, Luis Bunuel did the same thing on his shooting of *That Obscure Object of Desire*. There was a difference of only six months in the ages of Hitchcock and Bunuel. Moral: At the age of 75, a director no longer has the patience to deal with a difficult actor who is going to be a pain in the neck.

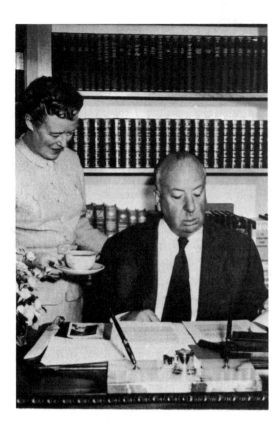

could be made right here in my office with Peggy, Sue and Alma. The only difficulty about that idea would be that one of them would have to be killed off, which I would regret extremely.

—excerpt from a letter
dated October 20, 1976

When I visited Hitchcock two months later, at Christmastime, in the Universal bungalow which had served for twenty years as the office of "Alfred Hitchcock Productions," he was screening Peter Bogdanovich's *Nickelodeon*. He stopped the screening and ushered me into his office, ordered two steaks, and we resumed our conversation in the same place and under the same conditions in which we had left off fourteen years before!

I asked him a question about *Psycho* that had always puzzled me. At the moment Janet Leigh is being stabbed in the shower, I wondered *who* had stepped into the bathroom with knife in hand. Was it Anthony Perkins wearing a wig? A woman? A stand-in? A dancer? Bearing in mind that the killer is filmed in backlighting, conveying the impression of a shadow show, any of these possibilities is plausible. Hitchcock informed me that the attacker was a young woman wearing a wig. He added that the scene was shot twice because, although the only lighting was placed behind the woman, the reverberation of the white bathroom walls was so strong that it revealed her face too clearly. That is why her face was blackened in the second take, so as to create the impression of a dark and unidentifiable silhouette on the screen.

We went on to discuss generalities about Hollywood, among them the rivalry between Paramount and Universal, who were simultaneously working on a remake of *King Kong*, since neither studio wanted to join the other in sharing the risks of this project. Like most genuinely powerful men, Hitchcock concealed his power, claiming that he was merely a producer-director who had to defer to the judgment of Universal's front office. He never referred to the fact that he was one of the five principal stockholders of one of the largest companies in the world, as well as an intimate friend of Lew Wasserman, and therefore an adviser who had considerable influence.

one wakes up in the morning and one is Alfred Hitchcock, what does it feel like?" The question wasn't brilliant, but I loved Hitchcock's response: "When the film is a success, one feels very good, but if it isn't, one feels miserable!"

After *Family Plot*, Hitchcock felt miserable, and I was in Montpellier shooting *The Man Who Loved Women* when I received this letter from him:

. . . At the moment, I am completely desperate for a subject.

Now, as you realize, you are a free person to make whatever you want. I, on the other hand, can only make what is expected of me; that is, a thriller, or a suspense story, and that I find hard to do.

So many stories seem to be about the neo-Nazis, Palestinians fighting Israelis, and all that kind of thing. And, you see, none of these subjects has any human conflict.

How can you have a comedy Arab fighter? There is no such thing: nor can you have an amusing Israeli soldier. I describe these things because they come across my desk for consideration.

Sometimes, I think that the best comedy or drama

A few years earlier, *Airport* had replenished Universal's treasury. The studio had subsequently produced a sequel, and in the neighboring offices, during our talks, a third episode of the aerial adventure was under way. For this version, the screenplay called for a 747 jumbo jet to crash in the water, and apparently the studio approved of the scene. There was no telling whether Hitchcock thought it absurd or valid, but it was obvious that, as an engineer and a narrator, he was fascinated by the problem that the scene raised: "They're going to have the plane crash in the sea with 450 passengers aboard," he said, "but the cockpit will be absolutely watertight, and the oxygen supply will be sufficient for a few hours. Thus, they have to find a way to get the plane back in the air. The studio has assigned two additional young writers to figure out a solution. . . ." I pointed out to Hitchcock that he might have had to cope with similar problems if Selznick had maintained his project of having Hitchcock make *The Titanic* in 1939 instead of *Rebecca*.

Getting back to the current situation, Hitchcock informed me with real satisfaction that he had chosen the subject for his fifty-fourth picture, after having abandoned *Unknown Man: No. 89*, a novel by Elmore Leonard to which he had acquired the rights. He was about to go back to two old projects by adapting two books dealing with the same subject. The first was an investigative reportage titled *The Springing of George Blake* by Sean Bourke; the second was a novel by Ronald Kirkbride, based on the same story and titled *The Short Night*.

It was a spy story between East and West in which a double agent, George Blake, was sentenced to forty-two years of imprisonment for spying on behalf of the USSR. Blake, an Englishman, escaped from the Wormwood Scrubs Prison in October 1966, with the complicity of some of his fellow inmates, but mostly with the help of members of the London underworld recruited by the KGB. Blake and his Irish cellmate, Sean Bourke, escaped from the jail and roamed around London until they were retrieved by the Soviet secret service, which shipped them to Moscow.

But Bourke, who was homesick, returned to Ireland the following year and wrote his adventure, which became the basis for the Kirkbride thriller. The British government demanded his extradition, but their demand was rejected. Meanwhile, Blake was travelling in Eastern Europe. According to the letters he wrote to his mother, it would seem that a sentimental problem was a determining factor in his behavior and his flight. He and his wife had quarreled, and she divorced him shortly after his escape, and remarried.

Hitchcock had been thinking about this story for a long time; as early as 1970 he had approached Catherine Deneuve and Walter Matthau to play the leads. Later on, he decided to locate the action in Finland, and contemplated casting Liv Ullmann and Sean Connery in the picture.

He planned to play up the love story in order to obtain the same balance between espionage and emotion as in *Notorious*, a picture to which he often referred before starting on a new script.

He intended to alter the story of *The Short Night* as follows: A British spy working for the Soviets escapes from a London prison. The U.S. Secret Service knows that he is planning to make his way to Russia after getting his wife and children, who live on the Finnish coast. An American agent is dispatched to the island and assigned to wait there for the escaped spy and to kill him. While he is waiting, the agent and the spy's wife fall in love, but for obvious reasons he cannot tell her about his assignment. As in *Notorious*, the story illustrates the conflict between duty and love, but the last part, consisting of a manhunt on a train on the frontier between Russia and Finland, is more action-packed, and the film was to wind up with a happy ending.

The screenwriter, Ernest Lehman, who was responsible for *North by Northwest* and *Family Plot*, had already created several versions of the scenario, but Hitchcock was not satisfied with any of them.

There was increasing skepticism in Hitchcock's entourage. Alma, who had suffered a first stroke in London at the end of the shooting of *Frenzy*, had become an invalid. She required nursing care around the clock. In the studio, no one could imagine how Hitchcock could abandon his wife for two months to go and shoot the film in Finland. Besides, afflicted with arthritis, his own mobility was becoming increasingly difficult. As the script was written, it seemed highly unlikely that the Finnish part could be shot by a second crew, with Hitchcock directing the interior scenes in the Universal studios. In fact, before shooting *Frenzy*, Hitchcock had travelled to Finland to photograph the locations in which he wanted to shoot.

Toward the end of 1978, he made two decisions to confirm the prospect of an imminent shooting: He dispatched Norman Lloyd, one of his closest collaborators for thirty-five years, on another location tour in Finland and, in an attempt to indicate that the delay was due to Ernest Lehman, he hired a young writer named David Freeman to work out a new version of the screenplay.

I did not see Hitchcock in 1978. That is why the American Film Institute's tribute to him on March 7, 1979, under the glorious and funereal title of "Life Achievement Award," left me and

---

1.

"ALFRED HITCHCOCK'S
THE SHORT NIGHT"

1   EXT. LONDON - ARTILLERY ROAD - 6:45 P.M.

A drizzly London evening in the fall.

Wormwood Scrubs Prison and Hammersmith Hospital sit side by side. Artillery Road, hardly more than a service lane runs between them.

A Humber Hawk sits on the prison side facing Du Cane Road, the main drag that runs past the front of both prison and hospital.

CAMERA is outside the car looking at BRENNAN, who sits in the front holding a bouquet of chrysanthemums. He's in his early thirties, a little paunchy and very Irish. He's listening to a voice we can't quite make out. It could be the car radio, but Brennan's ear is cocked slightly toward the mums.

CAMERA pans off the flowers, toward the prison wall, over the cobble stones and up the rough red bricks toward the top. As CAMERA pans, the voice starts to become clearer.

As CAMERA goes over the top of the wall and starts down the other side, we realize we're going into the prison, toward the source of the voice.

> MAN'S VOICE
> (becoming audible;
> urgent)
> ...I'm here...I'm here...hurry on now...can you hear? I said I'm here...

2   EXT. PRISON YARD - NIGHT

GAVIN BRAND stands huddled against the wall speaking into a walkie-talkie. He's 39, tall and lean, dressed in prison garb, an intense, aristocratic, imperious man who at the moment is taking a very great risk.

> BRAND
> Do you read me?...I'm here, damn it, I'm here. Now move!

3   ARTILLERY ROAD

Brennan, still in the car, speaks into the flowers.

> BRENNAN
> (soothingly)
> I'm here. You'll be fine...you'll be fine...stay calm.

                         CONTINUED

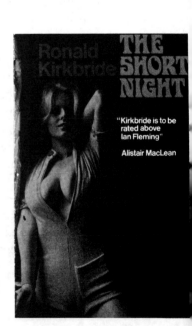

Ronald Kirkbride

THE SHORT NIGHT

"Kirkbride is to be rated above Ian Fleming"

Alistair MacLean

everyone who attended it with a gloomy and gruesome memory, even though CBS, through a series of editing tricks, managed to offer a face-saving version of the ceremony on American television.

Although Ingrid Bergman, who presided over the ceremony, was afflicted with cancer and aware of her own fate, she was deeply disturbed by the obvious deterioration of Hitchcock and his wife. Backstage she whispered, "Why do they always organize this kind of ceremony when it's too late?" Since that was the reason for my presence there, I too was forced to deliver a cheerful tribute: "In America, you call this man Hitch. In France, we call him Monsieur Hitchcock. . . . " But my heart wasn't in it. In front of an all-star Hollywood audience which eulogized them with anecdotes, film excerpts, and toasts, Alfred and Alma Hitchcock appeared to be present, but their souls were missing; they were hardly more alive than Anthony Perkins' stuffed mother in the cellar of the gothic house.

Two weeks later, resigned to the fact that he would never shoot another film, Hitchcock closed his office, dismissed his staff, and went home. The Queen of England bestowed the title of Sir Alfred upon him, thereby settling an old secret rivalry with another London-born genius, Charlie Chaplin. All that was left to Sir Alfred was to await death, a few forbidden vodkas hastening its advent. It came on April 29, 1980.

Whenever I want to forget Hitchcock in his declining years, I think back to a gala homage sponsored by the Film Society of Lincoln Center in New York on April 29, 1974, six years before his death. It was a truly stimulating event.

For some three hours, we were shown a hundred film excerpts displaying his virtuosity and grouped into categories like "The Screen Cameos" (Hitchcock's appearances in his movies), "The Chase" (pursuit sequences), "The Bad Guys" (killings and love scenes), plus two brilliant sequences: the clash of the cymbals in the second version of *The Man Who Knew Too Much,* and the plane attack on Cary Grant in *North by Northwest,* which I had been asked to present. Each series of excerpts was introduced with a short speech by the most beautiful Hitchcockian actresses—Grace Kelly, Joan Fontaine, Teresa Wright, Janet Leigh—and a few friends.

I knew all of these movies by heart, but upon seeing the excerpts isolated from their contexts, I was struck by the sincerity and the savagery of Hitchcock's work. It was impossible not to see that the love scenes were filmed like murder scenes, and the murder scenes like love scenes.

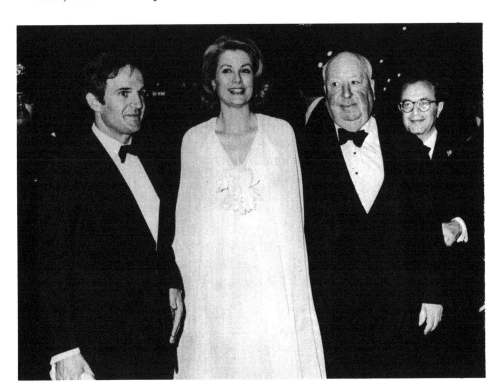

Benefactors and Patrons
will please join

Alfred Hitchcock

for champagne and
"just desserts"
on the Grand Promenade of the
New York State Theater, Lincoln Center
Monday, April 29, 1974
following the
performance at
Avery Fisher Hall
Admit One   Black Tie

I knew his work; in fact I thought I knew it very well. Yet that evening I was awed by what I saw on the screen: splashes of color, fireworks, ejaculations, sighs, death rattles, screams, blood, tears, twisted wrists. It occurred to me that in Hitchcock's cinema, which is definitely more sexual than sensual, to make love and to die are one and the same.

At the end of the evening, in the midst of applause, Hitchcock was supposed to make a short speech from the stage. To everyone's surprise, the lights went out and Hitchcock appeared . . . but on the screen! A few days earlier, he had filmed his final thanks in front of a curtain at the Universal studios.

When the lights went up again, a spot was focused on the loge where Hitchcock and Alma were seated. With the audience urging him to say a few words, he uttered a simple sentence: "As you have seen on the screen, scissors are the best way." It was one of those double entendres that Hitchcock enjoyed using, this time referring to the scene where Grace Kelly stabs the blackmailer with a pair of scissors in *Dial M for Murder*, but also to the film editor's skillful use of scissors in the cutting room.

Today, Hitchcock's work has inspired many disciples, and this is only natural, since he is a master. As always, however, one imitates only that which is imitable: the choice of material, and perhaps even the treatment of the material, but not the spirit with which it is impregnated.

Many people merely admire Hitchcock's science and his skill, overlooking the quality which, with the passage of time, impresses me much more—namely his deep emotivity.

One cannot say Hitchcock was an underrated or misunderstood artist, since he was a public moviemaker, and a popular one at that. At the risk of sounding paradoxical, I would add to Hitchcock's merits that of having been a commercial artist. True, it is not difficult to win the approval of wide audiences when one laughs at the same things they do, when one is sensitive to the same aspects of life and moved by the same dramas. This complicity between certain creators and their audience has resulted in successful careers. In my opinion, Hitchcock does

not belong to this category, since he was a singular man, not only by virtue of his physique, but also by virtue of his spirit, his morality, and his obsessions. Unlike Chaplin, Ford, Rossellini, or Hawks, he was a neurotic, and it could not have been easy for him to impose his neurosis upon the whole world.

When, as an adolescent, he realized that his physique isolated him from others, Hitchcock withdrew from the world to view it with tremendous severity. More than once in the course of our conversations he used the expression "When the heavy doors of the studio closed behind me . . . ," thus indicating that he embraced cinema as one embraces a religion.

It is obviously Hitchcock expressing himself in *Shadow of a Doubt* when Joseph Cotten says "The world is a pigsty. . . ." And in *Notorious*, we recognize Hitchcock when Claude Rains timidly goes into his mother's room in the middle of the night to confess, "Mother, I married an American spy," as if he was a guilty little boy. In *I Confess*, when the sexton tells his wife—whose name is Alma and who is presented as an angel—"We are strangers who have found work in this country. We must not attract attention . . . ," we again recognize Hitchcock speaking.

Finally, in *Marnie*, the last picture to reveal Hitchcock's deepest emotions, can there be any doubt that Sean Connery, in trying to control, dominate, and possess Tippi Hedren by investigating her past, finding her a job, and giving her money, is expressing Hitchcock's own feelings as a frustrated Pygmalion?

In other words, I am less interested in Hitchcock's ritual personal appearances in each of his films than in those passages where I recognize his personal emotions, and the fleeting release of his controlled violence. I believe that all the interesting film-makers—those who were referred to as "auteurs" by the *Cahiers du Cinéma* in 1955, before the term was distorted—concealed themselves behind various characters in their movies. Alfred Hitchcock achieved a real tour de force in inducing the public to identify with the attractive leading man, whereas Hitchcock himself almost always identified with the supporting role—the man who is cuckolded and

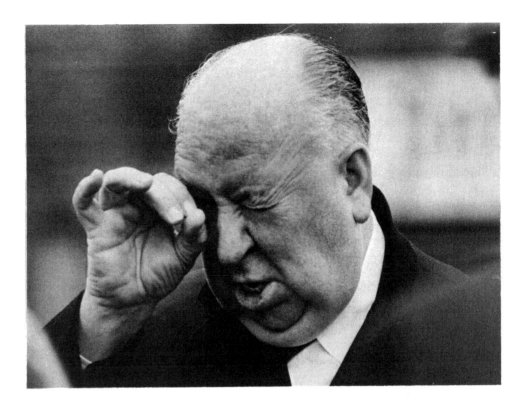

disappointed, the killer or a monster, the man rejected by others, the man who has no right to love, the man who looks on without being able to participate.

André Bazin was not an unconditional admirer of Hitchcock, but I am grateful to him for using the key word *equilibrium* in connection with Hitchcock. The whole world is familiar with Hitchcock's silhouette; it is the silhouette of a man who has always lived in fear of losing his balance. In Los Angeles, I was lucky enough to meet an old Jesuit priest, Professor Hugh Gray, before his death. Hugh Gray was the first translator of André Bazin in the United States, as well as a fellow student of Hitchcock's at Saint Ignatius College of London near the turn of the century. He had vivid memories of Hitchcock as a very plump little schoolboy. In the schoolyard he always stood alone, leaning against a wall, with his hands already folded across his stomach and an expression of disdain on his face, as he watched his schoolmates playing ball.

It is obvious that Hitchcock organized his life in such a way that no one would allow himself the familiar gesture of patting him on the back.

David O. Selznick referred to this detachment when he wrote his wife in 1938, "I finally met Hitchcock. He seems a nice person, but he is hardly the kind of man you would want along on a camping trip."

This is why the Hitchcockian image par excellence is that of an innocent man who is mistaken for another man who is being hunted—a man who finds himself falling from a roof, hanging onto a drainpipe that is about to give way.

This man who was impelled by fear to relate the most terrifying stories; this man who was a virgin when he married at the age of twenty-five and who never had any woman except for his wife; this man was indeed the only one who was able to portray murder and adultery as scandals, the only man who knew how to do so—in fact, the only man who had the *right* to do so.

Hitchcock was never concerned to know exactly what his pictures were saying—and even less to let others know it—but no other film-maker could describe so clearly, in response to the questions that were put to him by Helen Scott and myself, the course he followed in constructing the stories he selected and, in the course of the description, to reveal himself.

When cinema was invented, it was initially used to record life, like an extension of photography. It became an art when it moved away from the documentary. It was at this point that it was acknowledged as no longer a means of mirroring life, but a medium by which to intensify it. The film-makers of the silent era invented everything, and those who were not able to invent were failures. Alfred Hitchcock often regretted the setback that occurred with the advent of talking pictures and the hiring of stage directors who were not concerned with visual-izing stories, but who were content to record them on film.

Hitchcock belonged to a different family, the family of Chaplin, Stroheim, Lubitsch. Like them, he did not merely practice an art, but undertook to delve into its potential, and to work out its rules, rules more demanding than those pertaining to the writing of a novel.

Hitchcock not only intensified life; he intensified cinema.

FRANÇOIS TRUFFAUT, 1983

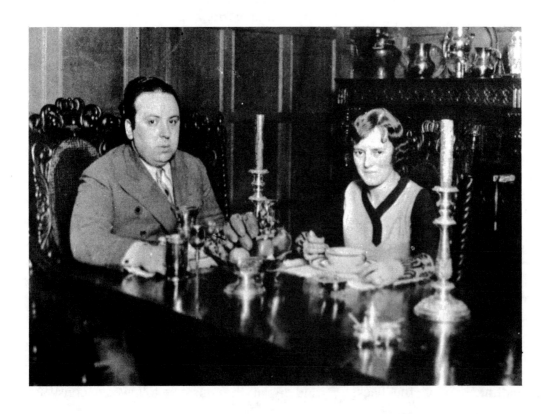

CLOSING PRICES
N.Y. Stocks

Los Angeles Times

TUESDAY
Late Final

CIRCULATION: 1,057,611 DAILY / 1,344,660 SUNDAY — TUESDAY, APRIL 29, 1980 — LF / 108 PAGES / Copyright 1980 Los Angeles Times / DAILY 25c

Alfred Hitchcock Dies

Master of Suspense Dead at 80

By JERRY BELCHER
Times Staff Writer

Sir Alfred Hitchcock, the master director who probably frightened more movie-goers than anyone in history with his 54 suspense-packed movies, died peacefully today at his Bel-Air home. He was 80.

Hitchcock, who began his movie career in London in the 1920s, was one of the few motion picture directors to become a superstar in his own right.

Some of his best known films are "Psycho," "The Birds" and "Dial M for Murder".

In ill health for several years—he suffered from a heart condition and arthritis—Hitchcock had still remained active, visiting his office at Universal Studios almost everyday until quite recently.

He had entered Cedars-Sinai Hospital Medical Center early last month for several days of diagnostic tests, but a hospital spokesman said at the time that the octogenarian "just didn't feel good" and added that the health problem then was not serious.

The cause of death was not immediately announced. A source at Universal Studios said, however, that he died quietly of natural causes about 9 a.m.

Actor Jimmy Stewart, who starred in several of Hitchcock's finest films, was shocked to learn of his old friend's death.

"I've lost a great friend and the world has lost one of its finest directing talents," Stewart said. "Alfred Hitchcock has made a tremendous contribution to the art of motion pictures and has been a source of joy to people all over the world."

Hitchcock was noted as a genius not only as a filmmaker but for his skill in promoting himself as a personality through his cameo appearances in nearly all of his films. He was also well-known for hosting the television series Alfred Hitchcock Presents

The cameo appearances were always ingenious, often humorous, and became his trademark. One famous appearance showed the stout, slow-moving Hitchcock trying to wrestle a cello through a revolving door.

But despite his fame and his penchant for professional self-promotion, the British-born director did not live the limelight life of a celebrity. His personal life revolved about his family—his wife Ama, daughter Patricia and his grandchildren.

Their lives were intensely private.

"My wife and I," he said in an interview, "have never gone into the nightclubs and cafes."

Hitchcock was the son of a London poultry dealer. He began his film career in London in 1925, settled in the United States in 1940 and became an American citizen in 1955.

Among his many films, he once listed his own favorites as "Spellbound," "Lifeboat," "Shadow of a Doubt" and "Psycho."

His first American made film, "Rebecca," won the Academy Award for best picture in 1938.

Oddly, he never won an Oscar in his own name as best director, but was nominated four times.

Some critics consider Hitchcock one of the inventors of the modern motion picture—and certainly the greatest master of the suspense genre in which he specialized.

While often including scenes perceived as gruesome—the "Psycho" stabbing scene is perhaps the most notorious and chilling—the horror was more often implied than directly shown. And always, there was the subtle—sly Hitchcock humor.

In an interview several years ago, Hitchcock was asked to outline his traditional film.

"It encompasses pure horror and comedy at the same time," he said. "If you do a realistic murder story, you should show that life goes on around murder just as in real life. People still laugh and joke in the corridors, as it were. And I've always adhered to the fact that the amusement comes out of the characters as much as anything, not out of the situation."

Hitchcock was knighted by Queen Elizabeth II late last year for his contributions to British culture.

Funeral arrangements are pending.

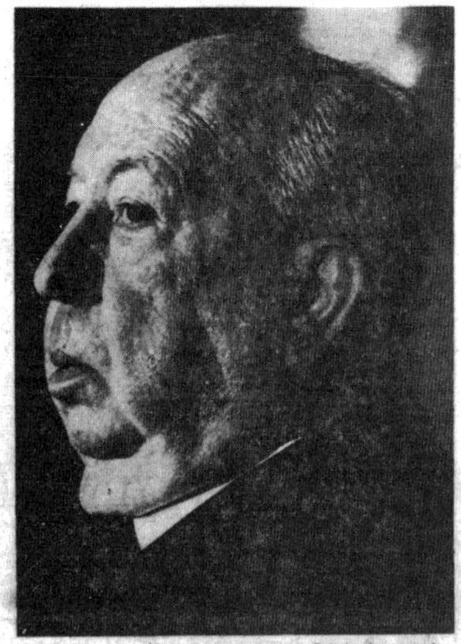

SUCCUMBS—Alfred Hitchcock died at his Bel-Air home today
Times photo by Tony Barnard

Carter Picks Muskie to Be Secretary of State

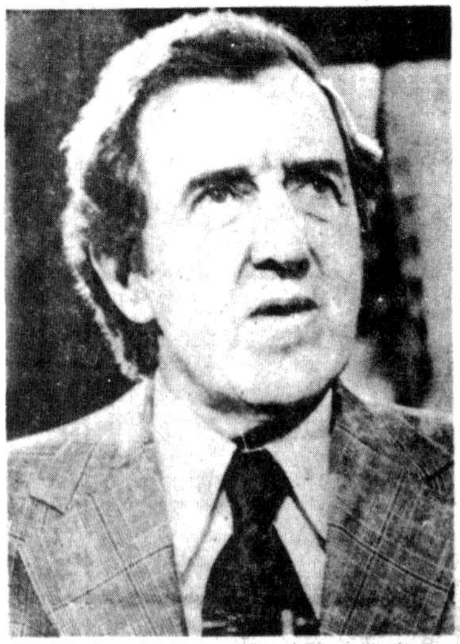

NEW JOB—Edmund S. Muskie will be named secretary of state
Associated Press photo

Maine Senator to Take Post Left by Vance

From Times Wire Services

WASHINGTON—President Carter said today that he will nominate Sen. Edmund S. Muskie (D-Me.) to succeed Cyrus R. Vance as secretary of state, congressional sources said.

Carter notified top congressional leaders of his decision this afternoon. He is expected to make the announcement at a nationally broadcast news conference, scheduled for 6 p.m. PDT.

Muskie, 66, is chairman of the Senate Budget Committee and was Hubert H. Humphrey's Democratic vice presidential running mate in 1968. He lost his own bid for the Democratic nomination in 1972 to George S. McGovern after polls showed him the heavy early favorite.

He replaces Vance, who resigned Monday in a dispute with Carter over the ill-fated Iran rescue effort.

Senate sources said the choice of Muskie, highly respected on Capitol Hill, virtually assures that the nomination will be confirmed. Muskie is a member of the Senate Foreign Relations Committee.

Muskie, a towering 6-foot-6, craggy Down-Easter, is the son of a Polish immigrant tailor who was raised in Rumford, Me.

Muskie has served in the Senate since 1959 and before that served a four-year term as Maine governor, breaking a long dominance there of Republican officeholders.

Muskie's high hopes for the presidency died before the New Hampshire primary in 1972 when he reacted emotionally and with tears to a newspaper article about his wife, Jane.

Muskie also fell victim to what turned out to be a "dirty trick" on the part of Richard M. Nixon's campaign.

The "dirty trick" was a letter planted in the Manchester (N.H.) Union Leader, claiming that Muskie had referred sneeringly to French Canadians as "Canucks" during a visit to Florida.

Heavily favored, he barely defeated McGovern in New Hampshire, and his campaign quickly ran into serious trouble

Muskie has spent most of his Senate career backing legislation to preserve the nation's environment and wilderness areas, and in 1974 became the first and only chairman of the Congressional Budget Committee—a job that has taken on great importance since Congress began drafting its own version of the budget each year.

The Muskies have five children—Stephen, 31; Ellen, 28; Melinda, 23; Martha, 21, and Edmund Jr., 19.

TEXAS DEFENSIVE BACK RAMS' TOP DRAFT PICK

By BOB OATES
Times Staff Writer

This will be remembered as the year when Oklahoma halfback Billy Sims was drafted first (by Detroit), when USC halfback Charles White was drafted 27th (by Cleveland) and when the Rams, as their top choice, went for a defensive back from Texas.

He is All-American safety Johnnie Johnson, who became the 16th athlete selected when the Rams traded a bundle of draft choices to Cleveland.

Johnson continues a local trend. During Dick Steinberg's four years as a chief scout, the Rams have consistently picked one kind of player: one with good size and speed who has been a starter for many years on a big-time college team.

Tall for a defensive back, Johnson, 6-1, 185, has started for Texas since the sixth game of his freshman season. Neutral scouts say he has 4.65 speed for 40 yards. He will play strong safety here. The free safety, Nolan Cromwell, a 1977 draftee, also 6-1, had been a four-year starter at Kansas.

On the first day of the National Football League's first 1980 player-selection meeting, four running backs were named ahead of White, the 1979 Heisman Trophy winner. They are Sims, the 1978 Heisman winner; Curtis Dickey, Texas A&M (Baltimore); Earl Cooper, Rice (San Francisco), and Vegas Ferguson, Notre Dame (New England).

Two other Trojans went ahead of White on the first round: tackle Anthony Munoz, the third player chosen (Cincinnati) and guard Brad Budde, the 11th (Kansas City).

The Oakland/Los Angeles Raiders emerged with the year's top quarterback, Marc Wilson of Brigham Young.

Speculation that the 49ers wanted Wilson proved erroneous when, drafting 13th, they passed him up for running back Cooper. In a draft choice trade earlier, the 49ers had yield the day's second pick to the New York Jets, who named Texas receiver Jonny Lam Jones.

Altogether, three members of the Texas team went on the first round, including two defensive backs, Johnson and Derrick Hatchett (Baltimore).

U.S. Says Jets Chased Off Iran Plane Over Oman Gulf

From Associated Press

Iran claimed that two carrier-based U.S. fighter jets "started to shoot" at an Iranian patrol plane over the Gulf of Oman today in the first U.S.-Iranian military confrontation since the American hostages were seized nearly six months ago. The Pentagon denied that there was any shooting.

In Washington, the Defense Department said: "Two F-14 aircraft from the aircraft carrier Nimitz made a routine intercept of an Iranian C-130 aircraft near the Strait of Hormuz. The U.S. aircraft escorted the Iranian plane back to Iranian airspace. It was a routine intercept. There was no firing of weapons."

Washington officials said the Iranian plane came within about 50 miles of the Nimitz and the two F-14s were launched to chase it off. The Nimitz is one of about 30 U.S. warships stationed in the Indian Ocean after the takeover of the U.S. Embassy in Tehran last Nov. 4 by Iranian militants and the December Soviet thrust into Afghanistan.

The official Iranian news agency Pars quoted the Iranian army joint staff as saying the two American planes started to shoot at the Iranian plane but four Iranian jets were sent up and they "warded off the attack." Pars quoted the army as saying the U.S. planes "changed their direction as the four Iranian jet fighters escorted the patrol plane" back to Iran.

Tehran Radio reported that the Iranian army joint staff has warned the armed forces to "expect extensive action by the U.S. Army" in the wake of last week's abortive attempt to rescue the American hostages in Iran.

Melchite Catholic Archbishop Hilarion Capucci arrived in Tehran today and said he will accompany the bodies of the eight U.S. commandos killed in last week's aborted rescue mission "to another country and hand them over to the International Red Cross for delivery to their families."

"I do not want to have any contact with the United States," he said, and did not name the neutral country he would take the bodies to or give a timetable.

But a Swiss news agency said today in Bern that the bodies will be flown to Zurich.

U.S. Buys Corn

WASHINGTON (AP)—An additional 40.4 million bushels of corn that had been expected to be shipped to the Soviet Union has been bought by the government to help boost farmers' grain prices, Agriculture Secretary Bob Bergland said today.

THE LATEST WEATHER

Decreasing cloudiness and a lingering chance of scattered light showers were forecast by the National Weather Service. The chance of showers today is 30%, decreasing to 20% Wednesday. The expected high today and Wednesday is 67. The low tonight should be in the mid-50s.

LATE NEWS

Dow Rollin' On

From Times Wire Services

NEW YORK—The stock market continued its week-old rally with a moderate advance today.

The Dow Jones average of 30 industrials closed up 5.63 at 811.09.

New York Stock Exchange volume was about 28 million shares compared with 30.6 million Monday.

Tables in Business Section.

Rosie's Victory Voided

BOSTON (AP)—The Boston Athletic Assn. today stripped Rosie Ruiz of New York of her Boston Marathon women's division victory and named Montreal's Jacqueline Gareau official winner.

Race director Will Cloney said the investigation showed "beyond any reasonable doubt" that Ruiz, a 36-year-old Manhattan office worker who said she had run in only one prior marathon, did not cover the entire 26.2-mile Boston footrace.

Executions to Stop

MONROVIA, Liberia (AP)—Liberian leader Master Sgt. Samuel K. Doe, whose regime executed 13 former government officials last week, bowed to domestic and international pressure today and promised there would be no more such executions.

More than 80 officials of the ousted government of assassinated President William Tolbert were still awaiting trial for treason, corruption and violation of human rights.

Plane Crash Kills 7

Seven persons including two children were found dead in the wreckage of a private aircraft in hilly country about 15 miles north of Bakersfield today.

The plane took off at 8:49 p.m. Monday night from Meadows Field for Visalia, Federal Aviation Administration Tower Manager Hank Van Sant reported.

Draft Signup Advances

WASHINGTON (AP)—President Carter's draft registration plan for young men, narrowly approved last week by the House, was passed by a surprisingly wide margin today in a Senate subcommittee.

A Senate appropriations subcommittee voted 8-4 in favor of spending $13.3 million to begin registration this summer of young men, aged 19 and 20. The bill now goes to the full Appropriations Committee, and then to the Senate.

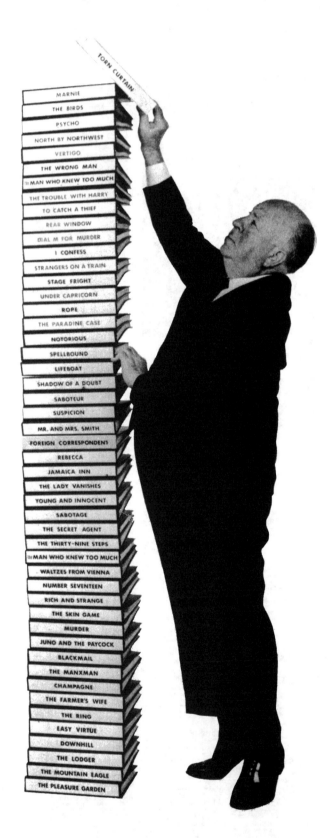

TORN CURTAIN
MARNIE
THE BIRDS
PSYCHO
NORTH BY NORTHWEST
VERTIGO
THE WRONG MAN
³¹ MAN WHO KNEW TOO MUCH
THE TROUBLE WITH HARRY
TO CATCH A THIEF
REAR WINDOW
DIAL M FOR MURDER
I CONFESS
STRANGERS ON A TRAIN
STAGE FRIGHT
UNDER CAPRICORN
ROPE
THE PARADINE CASE
NOTORIOUS
SPELLBOUND
LIFEBOAT
SHADOW OF A DOUBT
SABOTEUR
SUSPICION
MR. AND MRS. SMITH
FOREIGN CORRESPONDENT
REBECCA
JAMAICA INN
THE LADY VANISHES
YOUNG AND INNOCENT
SABOTAGE
THE SECRET AGENT
THE THIRTY-NINE STEPS
³¹ MAN WHO KNEW TOO MUCH
WALTZES FROM VIENNA
NUMBER SEVENTEEN
RICH AND STRANGE
THE SKIN GAME
MURDER
JUNO AND THE PAYCOCK
BLACKMAIL
THE MANXMAN
CHAMPAGNE
THE FARMER'S WIFE
THE RING
EASY VIRTUE
DOWNHILL
THE LODGER
THE MOUNTAIN EAGLE
THE PLEASURE GARDEN

Alfred Hitchcock was born in London on August 13,
1899. He studied at Saint Ignatius College, London.
In 1920 he joined Famous Players-Lasky, an Ameri-
can company that had opened an English studio at
Islington. For two years he wrote and designed the
subtitles for numerous silent "art" films: Hugh Ford's
The Call of Youth and *The Great Day* (1921), Donald
Crisp's *The Princess of New York* and *Tell Your Chil-
dren* (1921), and George Fitzmaurice's *Three Live
Ghosts* (1922).

THE FILMS OF ALFRED HITCHCOCK

(The titles in boldface are those of films directed by Alfred Hitchcock.)

1922

NUMBER THIRTEEN (unfinished)
Production: Wardour & F., 1922. *Producer:* Alfred Hitchcock. *Director:* Alfred Hitchcock. *Director of Photography:* Rosenthal. *Studio:* Islington. *Principal Actors:* Clare Greet, Ernest Thesiger.

ALWAYS TELL YOUR WIFE
After the director fell ill, the film was finished by Alfred Hitchcock and the producer, Seymour Hicks. Famous Players-Lasky stopped production at Islington. Alfred Hitchcock and a small crew were kept on by the studio. When Michael Balcon founded a new independent company with Victor Saville and John Freedman and began to shoot his first film at Islington, A. Hitchcock, hired as Assistant Director, also filled other positions.

WOMAN TO WOMAN
Production: Michael Balcon, Victor Saville, John Freedman, 1922–1923. *Producer:* Michael Balcon. *Director:* Graham Cutts. *Scenario:* Graham Cutts and Alfred Hitchcock, from the play by Michael Morton. *Director of Photography:* Claude L. McDonnell. *Sets:* A. Hitchcock. *Assistant Director:* A. Hitchcock. *Editor:* Alma Reville. *Studio:* Islington. *Distributors:* Wardour & F., 1923, 7 B; France, Gaumont, 1924; U.S.A., Selznick, 1924. *Principal Actors:* Betty Compson (Daloryse); Clive Brook (David Compos and Davis Anson-Pond) and Josephine Earle, Marie Ault, M. Peter.

1923

THE WHITE SHADOW
Production: Michael Balcon, Victor Saville, John Freedman, 1923, G.B. *Producer:* Michael Balcon. *Director:* Graham Cutts. *Scenario:* Alfred Hitchcock and Michael Morton. *Director of Photography:* Claude L. McDonnell. *Sets:* A. Hitchcock. *Editing:* A. Hitchcock. *Studio:* Islington. *Distributors:* Wardour & F., 1923, 6 B.; U.S.A., Selznick, 1924. *Principal Actors:* Betty Compson, Clive Brook, Henry Victor, Daisy Campbell, Olaf Hitton.

1924

THE PASSIONATE ADVENTURE

Production: Michael Balcon, Gainsborough, 1922–1923, G.B. *Director:* Graham Cutts. *Scenario:* Alfred Hitchcock and Michael Morton. *Director of Photography:* Claude McDonnell. *Sets:* A. Hitchcock. *Assistant Director:* A. Hitchcock. *Studio:* Islington. *Distributors:* Gaumont, 1923; France, Excella Films (by agreement with A. C. and R. C. Bromhead), 1928; U.S.A., Selznick, 1924. *Principal Actors:* Alice Joyce, Clive Brook, Lilian Hall-Davies, Marjorie Daw, Victor McLaglen, Mary Brough, John Hamilton, J. R. Tozer.

1925

THE BLACKGUARD

Production: Gainsborough, Michael Balcon, 1925, G.B. *Associate Producer:* Erich Pommer. *Director:* Graham Cutts. *Scenario:* A. Hitchcock, from a novel by Raymond Paton. *Sets:* A. Hitchcock. *Assistant Director:* A. Hitchcock. *Studio:* U.F.A. at Neubabelsberg (Berlin). *Distributor:* Wardour & F., 1925, 6,016 feet. *Principal Actors:* Walter Rilla (the blackguard), Jane Novak, Bernard Goetzke, Frank Stanmore.

THE PRUDE'S FALL

Production: Michael Balcon, Victor Saville, John Freedman, 1925, G.B. *Producer:* Michael Balcon. *Director:* Graham Cutts. *Scenario:* Alfred Hitchcock. *Assistant Director:* A. Hitchcock. *Sets:* A. Hitchcock. *Distributor:* Wardour & F. *Studio:* Islington. *Principal Actress:* Betty Compson.

THE PLEASURE GARDEN

Production: Michael Balcon (Gainsborough), Erich Pommer (Emelka—G.B.A. 1925). *Director:* Alfred Hitchcock. *Scenario:* Eliot Stannard, from the novel by Oliver Sandys. *Director of Photography:* Baron Vintigmilia. *Assistant Director and script-girl:* Alma Reville. *Studio:* Emelka at Munich. *Distributors:* Wardour & F., 1925, 6,458 feet; U.S.A., Aymon Independent, 1926. *Principal Actors:* Virginia Valli (Patsy Brand, the dancer), Carmelita Geraghty (Jill Cheyne), Miles Mander (Levett), John Stuart (Hugh Fielding), Frederic K. Martini, Florence Helminger, George Snell, C. Falkenburg.

1926

THE MOUNTAIN EAGLE (U.S.A.: *Fear O' God*)

Production: Gainsborough, Emelka, 1926. *Producer:* Michael Balcon. *Director:* Alfred Hitchcock. *Scenario:* Eliot Stannard. *Director of Photography:* Baron Vintigmilia. *Studio:* Emelka at Munich. *Location Work:* Austrian Tyrol. *Distributors:* Wardour & F., 1926, 6,000 feet; U.S.A., Artlee Indep. Dist., 1926. *Principal Actors:* Bernard Goetzke (Pettigrew), Nita Naldi (Beatrice, the governess), Malcolm Keen (Fear O' God), John Hamilton (Edward Pettigrew).

THE LODGER (A *Story of the London Fog*)

Production: Gainsborough, Michael Balcon, 1926. *Director:* Alfred Hitchcock. *Scenario:* Alfred Hitchcock and Eliot Stannard, from the novel by Mrs. Belloc-Lowndes. *Director of Photography:* Baron Vintigmilia. *Sets:* C. Wilfred Arnold and Bertram Evans. *Editing and subtitles:* Ivor Montagu. *Assistant Director:* Alma Reville. *Studio:* Islington. *Distributor:* Wardour & F., 1926, 6 reels, 7,685 feet. *Principal Actors:* Ivor Novello (the lodger), June (Daisy Jackson), Marie Ault (Mrs. Jackson, her mother), Arthur Chesney (Mr. Jackson), Malcolm Keen (Joe Betts, the policeman, Daisy's fiancé).

1927

DOWNHILL (U.S.A.: *When Boys Leave Home*)

Production: Michael Balcon, Gainsborough, 1927, G.B. *Director:* Alfred Hitchcock. *Scenario:* Eliot Stannard, from the play by Ivor Novello and Constance Collier, written under the pseudonym of David Lestrange. *Director of Photography:* Claude McDonnell. *Editing:* Ivor Montagu. *Studio:* Islington. *Distributors:* Wardour & F., 1928, 6,500 feet; U.S.A., World Wide Dist., 1928. *Principal Actors:* Ivor Novello (Roddy Berwick), Ben Webster (Doctor Dowson), Robin Irvine (Tim Wakely), Sybil Rhoda (Sybil Wakely), Lillian Braithwaite (Lady Berwick) and Hannah Jones, Violet Farebrother, Isabel Jeans, Norman McKinnel, Jerrold Robertshaw, Annette Benson, Ian Hunter, Barbara Gott, Alfred Goddard.

EASY VIRTUE

Production: Michael Balcon, Gainsborough Prod., 1927. *Director:* Alfred Hitchcock. *Scenario:* Eliot Stannard, from the play by Noel Coward. *Director of Photography:* Claude McDonnell. *Editing:* Ivor Montagu. *Studio:* Islington. *Distributors:* Wardour & F., 1927, 6,500 feet; U.S.A., World Wide Dist., 1928. *Principal Actors:* Isabel Jean (Larita Filton), Franklin Dyall (M. Filton), Eric Bransby Williams (the correspondent), Ian Hunter (Plaintiff's Counsel), Robin Irvine (John Whittaker), Violet Farebrother (his mother, Mrs. Whittaker) and Frank Elliot, Darcia Deane, Dorothy Boyd, Enid Stamp-Taylor.

THE RING

Production: British International Pictures, 1927, G.B. *Producer:* John Maxwell. *Director:* Alfred Hitchcock. *Scenario:* A. Hitchcock. *Adaptation:* Alma Reville. *Director of Photography:* Jack Cox. Assistant *Director:* Frank Mills. *Studio:* Elstree. *Distributors:* Wardour & F., 1927; France, Pathé Consortium Cinéma, 1928. *Principal Actors:* Carl Brisson (Jack Sander called "Round One"), Lillian Hall-Davies (Nelly), Ian Hunter (Bob Corby, the champion), Forrester Harvey (Harry, the traveling showman of the ring) and Harry Terry, Gordon Harker, Billy Wells.

1928
THE FARMER'S WIFE
Production: British International Pictures, 1928, G.B. *Producer:* John Maxwell. *Director:* Alfred Hitchcock. *Scenario:* Alfred Hitchcock, from the play by Eden Philpotts. *Director of Photography:* Jack Cox. *Assistant Director:* Frank Mills. *Editing:* Alfred Booth. *Studio:* Elstree. *Location Work:* Wales. *Distributors:* Wardour & F., 67 minutes; France, Pathé Consortium Cinéma, 1928. *Principal Actors:* Lillian Hall-Davies (Araminta Dench, the young maid), James Thomas (Samuel Sweetland), Maud Gill (Thirza Tapper), Gordon Harker (Cheirdles Ash), and Louise Pounds, Olga Slade, Antonia Brough.

CHAMPAGNE
Production: British International Pictures, 1928, G.B. *Director:* Alfred Hitchcock. *Scenario:* Eliot Stannard. *Director of Photography:* Jack Cox. *Studio:* Elstree. *Distributor:* Wardour & F., 1928. *Principal Actors:* Betty Balfour (Betty), Gordon Harker (her father), Ferdinand Von Alten (the passenger), Jean Bradin (the young man), and Jack Trevor, Marcel Vibert.

CHAMPAGNE (German version)
Production: Sascha Film—British International Pict., 1929. *Director:* Gaza von Bolvary. *Principal Actors:* Betty Balfour, Vivian Gibson, Jack Trevor, Marcel Vibert.

1929
HARMONY HEAVEN
Production: British International Pictures, 1929. *Director:* Alfred Hitchcock. *Musical part:* directed by Eddie Pola. *Lyrical part:* directed by Edward Brandt. *Distributor:* France-Société des Ciné-romans, 1929.

THE MANXMAN
Production: British International Pictures, 1929, G.B. *Producer:* John Maxwell. *Director:* Alfred Hitchcock. *Scenario:* Eliot Stannard, from the novel by Sir Hall Caine. *Director of Photography:* Jack Cox. *Assistant Director:* Frank Mills. *Studio:* Elstree. *Distributors:* Wardour & F., 1929, U.S.A., Ufa Eastman Division, 1929. *Principal Actors:* Carl Brisson (Pete), Malcolm Keen (Philip), Anny Ondra (Kate), Randle

Ayrton (her father) and Clare Greet. *The Manxman* was Alfred Hitchcock's last silent film.

BLACKMAIL
Production: British International Pictures, 1929, G.B. *Producer:* John Maxwell. *Director:* Alfred Hitchcock. *Scenario:* A. Hitchcock, Benn W. Levy and Charles Bennett, from the play by Charles Bennett. *Adaptation:* A. Hitchcock. *Dialogue:* Benn W. Levy. *Director of Photography:* Jack Cox. *Sets:* Wilfred C. Arnold and Norman Arnold. *Music:* Campbell and Connely, finished and arranged by Hubert Bath and Henry Stafford, performed by the British Symphony Orchestra under the direction of John Reynders. *Editing:* Emile de Ruelle. *Studio:* Elstree. *Distributors:* Wardour & F., 1929, 7,136 feet; U.S.A., Sono Art World Wide Pict., 1930. *Principal Actors:* Anny Ondra (Alice White), Sara Allgood (Mrs. White), John Londgen (Frank Webber, the detective), Charles Paton (Mr. White), Donald Calthrop (Tracy), Cyril Ritchard (the artist), and Harvey Braban, Hannah Jones, Phyllis Monkman, ex-detective Sergeant Bishop. (Joan Barry played Anny Ondra's part in the talkie version.)

1930
ELSTREE CALLING
Production: British International Pictures, 1930. *Director:* Alfred Hitchcock, André Charlot, Jack Hulbert, Paul Murray. *Supervision:* Adrian Brunel. *Scenario:* Val Valentine. *Director of Photography:* Claude Freise Greene. *Music:* Reg Casson, Vivian Ellis, Chic Endor. *Lyrics:* Ivor Novello and Jack Strachey Parsons. *Sound engineer:* Alex Murray (Alfred Hitchcock directed Gordon Harker).
There was a burlesque, "The Taming of the Shrew," starring Anna May Wong and Donald Calthrop, which was one of the best scenes in the movie. The reason for this burlesque was the appearance of a film "The Taming of the Shrew," starring Mary Pickford and Douglas Fairbanks.

JUNO AND THE PAYCOCK
Production: British International Pictures, 1930. *Producer:* John Maxwell. *Director:* Alfred Hitchcock. *Scenario:* Alfred Hitchcock and Alma Reville, from the play by Sean O'Casey. *Director of Photography:* Jack Cox. *Sets:* Norman Arnold. *Editing:* Emile de Ruelle. *Studio:* Elstree. *Distributors:* Wardour & F., 1939, 85 minutes; U.S.A., British International by Capt. Harold Auten, 1930. *Principal Actors:* Sara Allgood (Juno), Edward Chapman (Captain Boyle), Sidney Morgan (Joxer), Marie O'Neill (Mrs. Madigan), and John Laurie, Dennis Wyndham, John

Longden, Kathleen O'Regan, Dave Morris, Fred Schwartz.

MURDER
Production: British International Pictures, 1930, G.B. *Producer:* John Maxwell. *Director:* Alfred Hitchcock. *Scenario:* Alma Reville, from the work by Clemence Dane (pseudonym of Winifred Ashton) and Helen Simpson, "Enter Sir John." *Adaptation:* A. Hitchcock and Walter Mycroft. *Director of Photography:* Jack Cox. *Sets:* John Mead. *Editing:* René Harrison. *Supervision:* Emile de Ruelle. *Studio:* Elstree. *Distributor:* Wardour & F., 1930, 92 minutes. *Principal Actors:* Herbert Marshall (Sir John Menier), Nora Baring (Diana Baring), Phyllis Konstam (Dulcie Markham), Edward Chapman (Ted Markham), Miles Mander (Gordon Druce), Esme Percy (Handel Fane), Donald Calthrop (Ion Stewart) and Amy Brandon Thomas, Joynson Powell, Esme V. Chaplin, Marie Wright, S. J. Warmington, Hannah Jones, R. E. Jeffrey, Alan Stainer, Kenneth Kove, Guy Pelham, Matthew Boulton, Violet Farebrother, Ross Jefferson, Clare Greet, Drusilla Vills, Robert Easton, William Fazan, George Smythson.

MARY (German version of **MURDER**)
Production: Sud Film A.G., 1930. *Director:* A. Hitchcock. *Studio:* Elstree. *Director of Photography:* Jack Cox. *Principal Actors:* Alfred Abel, Olga Tchekowa, Paul Graetz, Lotte Stein, E. Arenot, Jack Nylong-Munz, Louis Ralph, Hermine Sterler, Fritz Alberti, Hertha V. Walter, Else Schunzel, Julius Brandt, Rudolph Meinhardt Junger, Fritz Grossmann, Lucie Euler, Harry Hardt, H. Gotho, Eugen Burg.

1931
THE SKIN GAME
Production: British International Pictures, 1931. *Producer:* John Maxwell. *Director:* Alfred Hitchcock. *Scenario:* A. Hitchcock and Alma Reville, from the play by John Galsworthy. *Additional Dialogues:* Alma Reville. *Director of Photography:* Jack Cox, assisted by Charles Martin. *Editing:* René Harrison and A. Gobett. *Studio:* Elstree. *Distributors:* Wardour & F., 1931, 85 minutes; U.S.A., British International, 1931. *Principal Actors:* Edmund Gwenn (Mr. Hornblower), Jill Esmond (Jill), John Longden (Charles), C. V. France (Mr. Hillcrest), Helen Haye (Mrs. Hillcrest), Phyllis Konstam (Chloe), Frank Lawton (Rolfe) and Herbert Ross, Dora Gregory, Edward Chapman, R. E. Jeffrey, George Bancroft, Ronald Frankau.

1932
RICH AND STRANGE (U.S.A.: *East of Shanghai*)
Production: British International Pictures, 1932, G.B. *Producer:* John Maxwell. *Director:* Alfred Hitchcock. *Scenario:* Alma Reville and Val Valentine, from a theme by Dale Collins. *Adaptation:* Alfred Hitchcock. *Directors of Photography:* Jack Cox and Charles Martin. *Sets:* C. Wilfred Arnold. *Music:* Hal Dolphe, directed by John Reynders. *Editing:* Winifred Cooper and René Harrison. *Sound Engineer:* Alec Murray. *Studio:* Elstree. *Location Work:* Marseilles, Port-Said, Colombo, Suez. *Distributors:* Wardour & F., 1932, 83 minutes; U.S.A., Powers Pictures, 1932. *Principal Actors:* Henry Kendall (Fredy Hill), Joan Barry (Emily Hill), Betty Amann (the princess), Percy Marmont (Gordon), Elsie Randolph (the old lady).

NUMBER SEVENTEEN
Production: British International Pictures, 1932. *Producer:* John Maxwell. *Director:* Alfred Hitchcock. *Scenario:* A. Hitchcock, from the play and the novel by Jefferson Farjeon. *Director of Photography:* Jack Cox. *Studio:* Elstree. *Distributor:* Wardour & F., 1932. *Principal Actors:* Léon M. Lion (Ben), Anne Grey (the young girl), John Stuart (the detective), and Donald Calthrop, Barry Jones, Garry Marsh.

LORD CAMBER'S LADIES
Production: Alfred Hitchcock, British International Pictures, 1932, G.B. *Director:* Benn W. Levy. *Scenario:* Benn W. Levy, from the play by Horace Annesley Vachell "The Case of Lady Camber." *Studio:* Elstree. *Distributor:* Wardour & F., 1932. *Principal Actors:* Gertrude Lawrence (Lady Camber), Sir Gerald du Maurier (Lord Camber) and Benita Hume, Nigel Bruce.

1933
WALTZES FROM VIENNA (U.S.A.: *Strauss' Great Waltz*)
Production: Gaumont British, by G.F.D., 1933, G.B. *Director:* Alfred Hitchcock. *Scenario:* Alma Reville and Guy Bolton, from the play by Guy Bolton. *Sets:* Alfred Junge and Peter Proud. *Music:* Johann Strauss the Elder and Strauss the Younger. *Studio:* Lime Grove. *Distributors:* G.F.D., 1933, 80 minutes; U.S.A., Tom Arnold, 1935. *Principal Actors:* Jessie Matthews (Rasi), Esmond Knight (Shani Strauss), Frank Vosper (the prince), Fay Compton (the countess), Edmund Gwenn (Johann Strauss the Elder), Robert Hale (Ebezeder), Hindle Edgar (Leopold), Marcus Barron (Drexter), Charles Heslop, Sybil Grove, Billy Shine Junior, Bertram Dench,

B. M. Lewis, Cyril Smith, Betty Huntley Wright, Berinoff and Charlot.

1934
THE MAN WHO KNEW TOO MUCH
Production: Gaumont British Pictures, Great Britain, 1934. *Director:* Alfred Hitchcock. *Producers:* Michael Balcon; *Associate*, Ivor Montagu. *Scenario:* A. R. Rawlinson, Charles Bennett, D. B. Wyndham Lewis, Edwin Greenwood, from an original theme by Charles Bennett and D. B. Wyndham Lewis. *Additional Dialogue:* Emlyn Williams. *Director of Photography:* Curt Courant. *Sets:* Alfred Junge and Peter Proud. *Music:* Arthur Benjamin, directed by Louis Levy. *Editing:* H. St. C. Stewart. *Studio:* Lime Grove. *Distributors:* G.F.D., 1934, 84 minutes; France, U.S.A., G.B. Prod., 1935. *Principal Actors:* Leslie Banks (Bob Lawrence), Edna Best (Jill Lawrence), Peter Lorre (Abbott), Frank Vosper (Ramon Levine), Hugh Wakefield (Clive), Nova Pilbeam (Betty Lawrence), Pierre Fresnay (Louis Bernard) and Cicely Oates, D. A. Clarke Smith, George Curzon.

1935
THE THIRTY-NINE STEPS
Production: Gaumont British, 1935. *Producers:* Michael Balcon, with Ivor Montagu as Associate Producer. *Director:* Alfred Hitchcock. *Scenario and adaptation:* Charles Bennett and Alma Reville from the novel by John Buchan. *Additional Dialogue:* Ian Hay. *Director of Photography:* Bernard Knowles. *Sets:* Otto Werndorff and Albert Jullion. *Costumes:* J. Strassner. *Music:* Louis Levy. *Editing:* Derek N. Twist. *Sound Engineer:* A. Birch, Full Range Recording System At Shepherd's Bush, London. *Studio:* Lime Grove. *Distributors:* G.F.D., 1935, 81 minutes; France, G.E.C.E., 1935, (excluding F.I.C.). *Principal Actors:* Madeleine Carroll (Pamela), Robert Donat (Richard Hannay), Lucie Mannheim (Miss Smith-Annabella), Godfrey Tearle (Professor Jordan), Peggy Ashcroft (Mrs. Crofter), John Laurie (Crofter, the farmer), Helen Haye (Mrs. Jordan), Frank Cellier (the Sheriff), Wylie Watson (Memory).

1936
THE SECRET AGENT
Production: Gaumont British, 1936. *Producers:* Michael Balcon and Ivor Montagu. *Director:* Alfred Hitchcock. *Scenario:* Charles Bennett, from the play by Campbell Dixon adapted from the novel by Somerset Maugham "Ashenden." *Adaptation:* Alma Reville. *Dialogues:* Ian Hay and Jesse Lasky Jr. *Director of Photography:* Bernard Knowles. *Sets:* Otto Werndorff and Albert Jullion. *Costumes:* J. Strasser. *Music:* Louis Levy. *Editing:* Charles Frend. *Studio:* Lime Grove. *Distributors:* G.F.D., 1936, 83 minutes; U.S.A., G.B. Prod., 1936. *Principal Actors:* Madeleine Carroll (Elsa Carrington), John Gielgud (Richard Ashenden), Peter Lorre (the General), Robert Young (Robert Marvin) and Percy Marmont, Florence Kahn, Lilli Palmer, Charles Carson, Michael Redgrave.

SABOTAGE (U.S.A.: *A Woman Alone*)
Production: Shepherd, Gaumont-British Pictures, 1936. *Producers:* Michael Balcon and Ivor Montagu. *Director:* Alfred Hitchcock. *Scenario:* Charles Bennett, from the novel by Joseph Conrad, "The Secret Agent." *Adaptation:* Alma Reville. *Dialogues:* Ian Hay, Helen Simpson and E. V. H. Emmett. *Director of Photography:* Bernard Knowles. *Sets:* Otto Werndorff and Albert Jullion. *Music:* Louis Levy. *Costumes:* J. Strassner. *Editing:* Charles Frend. *Studio:* Lime Grove. *Cartoon:* Sequence of "Who Killed Cock Robin?" Silly Symphony of Walt Disney, used with his agreement. *Distributors:* G.F.D., 1936, 76 minutes; U.S.A., G.B. Prod., 1937. *Principal Actors:* Sylvia Sidney (Sylvia Verloc), Oscar Homolka (Verloc, her husband), Desmond Tester (Sylvia's brother), John Loder (Ted, the detective), Joyce Barbour (Renée), Matthew Boulton (the Superintendent) and S. J. Barmington, William Dewhurst, Peter Bull, Torin Thatcher, Austin Trevor, Clare Greet, Sam Wilkinson, Sara Allgood, Martita Hunt, Pamela Bevan.

1937
YOUNG AND INNOCENT (U.S.A.: *A Girl Was Young*)
Production: Gainsborough, Gaumont British, 1937. *Producer:* Edward Black. *Director:* Alfred Hitchcock. *Scenario:* Charles Bennett and Alma Reville, from the novel by Josephine Tey "A Shilling for Candles." *Director of Photography:* Bernard Knowles. *Sets:* Alfred Junge. *Music:* Louis Levy. *Editing:* Charles Frend. *Studios:* Lime Grove and Pinewood. *Distributors:* G.F.D., 1937, 80 minutes; U.S.A., G.B. Prod., 1938. *Principal Actors:* Derrick de Marney (Robert Tisdall), Nova Pilbeam (Erica), Percy Marmont (Colonel Burgoyne), Edward Rigby (old Will), Mary Clare (Erica's aunt), John Longden (Kent), George Curzon (Guy), Basil Radford (Uncle Basil), and Pamela Carme, George Merritt, J. H. Roberts, Jerry Verno, H. F. Maltby, John Miller, Torin Thatcher, Peggy Simpson, Anna Konstam, Beatrice Varley, William Fazan, Frank Atkinson, Fred

O'Donovan, Albert Chevalier, Richard George, Jack Vyvian, Clive Baxter, Pamela Bevan, Humberston Wright, Gerry Fitzgerald, Syd Crossley.

1938
THE LADY VANISHES
Production: Gainsborough Pictures, 1938, G.B. *Director:* Alfred Hitchcock. *Producer:* Edward Black. *Scenario:* Sidney Gilliat and Frank Launder, from the novel by Ethel Lina White "The Wheel Spins." *Adaptation:* Alma Reville. *Director of Photography:* Jack Cox. *Sets:* Alec Vetchinsky, Maurice Cater and Albert Jullion. *Music:* Louis Levy. *Editing:* Alfred Roome and R. E. Dearing. *Studio:* Lime Grove. *Sound Engineer:* Sidney Wiles. *Distributors:* G.B., 97 minutes, 8,650 feet; U.S.A., G.B. Productions, 1938. *Principal Actors:* Margaret Lockwood (Iris Henderson), Michael Redgrave (Gilbert), Paul Lukas (Dr. Hartz), Dame May Whitty (Miss Froy), Googie Withers (Blanche), Cecil Parker (Mr. Todhunter), Linden Travers (Mrs. Todhunter), Lary Clare (the Baroness), Naunton Wayne (Caldicott), Basil Radford (Charters) and Emil Boreo, Zelma Vas Dias, Philippe Leaver, Sally Stewart, Catherine Lacey, Josephine Wilson, Charles Oliver, Kathleen Tremaine.

1939
JAMAICA INN
Production: Mayflowers-Productions, 1939, G.B. *Producers:* Erich Pommer and Charles Laughton. *Production Manager:* Hugh Perceval. *Director:* Alfred Hitchcock. *Scenario:* Sidney Gilliat and Joan Harrison, from the novel by Daphne du Maurier. *Dialogues:* Sidney Gilliat and J. B. Priestley. *Adaptation:* Alma Reville. *Directors of Photography:* Harry Stradling and Bernard Knowles. *Special Effects:* Harry Watt. *Sets:* Tom N. Moraham. *Costumes:* Molly McArthur. *Music:* Eric Fenby, directed by Frederic Lewis. *Editing:* Robert Hamer. *Sound Engineer:* Jack Rogerson. *Distributors:* Associated British, 1939, 98 minutes; Paramount, 1939. *Principal Actors:* Charles Laughton (Sir Humphrey Pengaltan), Horace Hodges (Chadwick, his butler), Hay Petrie (his groom), Frederick Piper (his broker), Leslie Banks (Joss Merlyn), Marie Ney (Patience, his wife), Maureen O'Hara (Mary, his niece), and Herbert Lomas, Clare Greet, William Delvin, Jeanne de Casalis, A. Bromley Davenport, Mabel Terry Lewis, George Curzon, Basil Radford, Emlyn Williams, Wylie Watson, Morland Graham, Edwin Greenwood, Stephen Haggard, Robert Newton, Mervyn Johns.
"Jamaica Inn" was Alfred Hitchcock's last English

film. David O. Selznick asked him to come to the United States. Hitchcock left in 1939, but he was to return to England to make certain films.

1940
REBECCA
Production: David O. Selznick, U.S.A., 1940. *Producer:* David O. Selznick. *Director:* Alfred Hitchcock. *Scenario:* Robert E. Sherwood and Joan Harrison from the novel by Daphne du Maurier. *Adaptation:* Philip MacDonald and Michael Hogan. *Director of Photography:* George Barnes. *Sets:* Lyle Wheeler. *Music:* Franz Waxman. *Editing:* Hal C. Kern. *Studio:* Selznick International. *Distributor:* United Artists, 1940, 130 minutes. *Principal Actors:* Laurence Olivier (Maxim de Winter), Joan Fontaine (Mrs. de Winter), George Sanders (Jack Favell), Judith Anderson (Mrs. Danvers), Nigel Bruce (Major Giles Lacey), C. Aubrey-Smith (Colonel Julyan) and Reginald Denny, Gladys Cooper, Philip Winter, Edward Fielding, Florence Bates, Leo G. Carroll, Forrester Harvey, Lumsden Hare, Leonard Carey, Edith Sharpe, Melville Cooper.

FOREIGN CORRESPONDENT
Production: Walter Wanger, United Artists, 1940. *Director:* Alfred Hitchcock. *Scenario:* Charles Bennett and Joan Harrison. *Dialogues:* James Hilton and Robert Benchley. *Director of Photography:* Rudolph Mate. *Special Effects:* Lee Zavitz. *Sets:* William Cameron Menzies and Alexander Golitzen. *Music:* Alfred Newman. *Editing:* Otto Lovering and Dorothy Spencer. *Assistant Director:* Edmond Bernoudy. *Studio:* United Artists, at Hollywood. *Distributor:* United Artists, 1940, 120 minutes. *Principal Actors:* Joel McCrea (Jonny Jones, reporter), Laraine Day (Carol Fisher), Herbert Marshall (Stephen Fisher, her father), George Sanders (Herbert Folliott, reporter), Albert Bassermann (Van Meer), Robert Benchley (Stebbins), Eduardo Ciannelli (Krug), Edmund Gwenn (Rowley), Harry Davenport (Mr. Powers), and Martin Kosleck, Eddie Conrad, Gertrude W. Hoffman, Jane Novak, Ken Christy, Crawford Kent, Joan Brodel-Leslie, Louis Borell.

1941
MR. AND MRS. SMITH
Production: R.K.O., 1941. *Executive Producer:* Harry E. Edington. *Director:* Alfred Hitchcock. *Story and Scenario:* Norman Krasna. *Director of Photography:* Harry Stradling, A.S.C. *Sets:* Van Nest Polglase and L. P. Williams. *Music:* Roy Webb. *Special Effects:* Vernon L. Walker. *Editing:* William Hamilton. *Studio:* R.K.O. *Distributor:* R.K.O., 1941, 95 minutes. *Principal Actors:* Carole Lombard

(Ann Smith and Ann Kransheimer), Robert Montgomery (David Smith), Gene Raymond (Jeff Custer), Jack Carson (Chuck Benson), Philip Merivale (Mr. Custer), Lucile Watson (Mrs. Custer), William Tracy (Sammy) and Charles Halton, Esther Dale, Emma Dunn, Betty Compson, Patricia Farr, Williams Edmunds, Adela Pearce, Murray Alper, D. Johnson, James Flavin, Sam Harris.

SUSPICION

Production: R.K.O., 1941. *Director:* Alfred Hitchcock. *Scenario:* Samson Raphaelson, Joan Harrison and Alma Reville, from the novel by Francis Iles (Anthony Berkeley) "Before the Fact." *Director of Photography:* Harry Stradling, A.S.C. *Special Effects:* Vernon L. Walker. *Sets:* Van Nest Polglase. *Assistant:* Carroll Clark. *Music:* Franz Waxman. *Editing:* William Hamilton. *Sound Engineer:* John E. Tribly. *Assistant Director:* Dewey Starkey. *Studio:* R.K.O. *Distributor:* R.K.O., 1941, 99 minutes. *Principal Actors:* Cary Grant (John Aysgarth: "Johnnie"), Joan Fontaine (Lina MacKinlaw), Sir Cedric Hardwicke (General MacKinlaw), Nigel Bruce (Beaky), Dame May Whitty (Mrs. MacKinlaw), Isabel Jeans (Mrs. Newsham), and Heather Angel, Auriol Lee, Reginald Sheffield, Leo G. Carroll.

1942
SABOTEUR

Production: Universal, 1942. *Producers:* Frank Lloyd and Jack H. Skirball. *Director:* Alfred Hitchcock. *Scenario:* Peter Viertel, Joan Harrison and Dorothy Parker, from an original subject by A. Hitchcock. *Director of Photography:* Joseph Valentine, A.S.C. *Sets:* Jack Otterson. *Music:* Charles Prévin and Frank Skinner. *Editing:* Otto Ludwig. *Studio:* Universal. *Distributor:* Universal, 1942, 108 minutes. *Principal Actors:* Robert Cummings (Barry Kane), Priscilla Lane (Patricia Martin: "Pat"), Otto Kruger (Charles Tobin), Alan Baxter (Mr. Freeman), Alma Kruger (Mrs. Van Sutton), and Vaughan Glazer, Dorothy Peterson, Ian Wolfe, Anita Bolster, Jeanne and Lynn Roher, Norman Lloyd, Oliver Blake, Anita Le Deaux, Pedro de Cordoba, Kathryn · Adams, Murray Alper, Frances Carson, Billy Curtis.

1943
SHADOW OF A DOUBT

Production: Universal, 1943. *Producer:* Jack H. Skirball. *Director:* Alfred Hitchcock. *Scenario:* Thornton Wilder, Alma Reville and Sally Benson, from a story by Gordon McDonnell. *Director of Photography:* Joseph Valentine, A.S.C. *Sets:* John B. Goodman, Robert Boyle, A. Gausman and L. R. Robinson. *Costumes:* Adrian and Vera West. *Music:* Dimitri

Tiomkin; directed by Charles Prévin. *Editing:* Milton Caruth. *Studio:* Universal; also shot at Santa Rosa. *Distributor:* Universal, 1943, 108 minutes. *Principal Actors:* Joseph Cotten (Charlie Oakley, the uncle), Teresa Wright (Charlie Newton), MacDonald Carey (Jack Graham), Patricia Collinge (Emma Newton), Henry Travers (Joseph Newton), Hume Cronyn (Herbie Hawkins), Wallace Ford (Fred Saunders), and Janet Shaw, Estelle Jewell, Eily Malyon, Ethel Griffies, Clarence Muse, Frances Carson, Charlie Bates, Edna May Wonacott.

LIFEBOAT

Production: Kenneth MacGowan, 20th Century-Fox, 1943. *Director:* Alfred Hitchcock. *Scenario:* Jo Swerling, from a story by John Steinbeck. *Director of Photography:* Glen MacWilliams. *Special Effects:* Fred Sersen. *Sets:* James Basevi and Maurice Ransford. *Music:* Hugo Friedhofer; directed by Emil Newman. *Costumes:* René Hubert. *Editing:* Dorothy Spencer. *Sound Engineers:* Bernard Fredericks and Roger Heman. *Studio:* Fox, 1943. *Distributor:* 20th Century-Fox, 1943, 96 minutes. *Principal Actors:* Tallulah Bankhead (Constance Porter: "Connie"), William Bendix (Gus Smith), Walter Slezak (Willy, Captain of the submarine), Mary Anderson (Alice Mackenzie), John Hodiak (John Kovac), Henry Hull (Charles S. Rittenhouse), Heather Angel (Mrs. Higgins), Hume Cronyn (Stanley Garett), Canada Lee (George Spencer: "Joe," the steward).

1944
BON VOYAGE

Production: M.O.I., 1944, G.B., British Ministry of Information. *Director:* Alfred Hitchcock. *Scenario:* J. O. C. Orton, Angus McPhail, from an original subject by Arthur Calder-Marshall. *Director of Photography:* Gunther Krampf. *Sets:* Charles Gilbert. *Studio:* Associated British. *Principal Actors:* John Blythe, The Molière Players (a French company that had fled to England).

AVENTURE MALGACHE

Production: M.O.P., 1944, G.B., British Ministry of Information. *Director:* Alfred Hitchcock. *Director of Photography:* Gunther Krampf. *Sets:* Charles Gilbert. *Studio:* Associated British. *Principal Actors:* The Molière Players.

1945
SPELLBOUND

Production: Selznick International, 1945. *Producer:* David O. Selznick. *Director:* Alfred Hitchcock. *Scenario:* Ben Hecht, from the novel by Francis Beeding

(Hilary St. George Saunders and John Palmer), "The House of Dr. Edwardes." *Adaptation:* Angus MacPhail. *Director of Photography:* George Barnes, A.S.C. *Special Photographic Effects:* Jack Cosgrove. *Sets:* James Basevi and John Ewing. *Music:* Miklos Rozsa. *Costumes:* Howard Greer. *Editing:* William Ziegler and Hal C. Kern. *Dream Sequence:* Salvador Dali. *Psychiatric Consultant:* May E. Romm. *Studio:* Selznick International. *Distributor:* United Artists, 1945, 111 minutes. *Principal Actors:* Ingrid Bergman (Doctor Constance Petersen), Gregory Peck (John Ballantine), Jean Acker (the Directress), Rhonda Fleming (Mary Carmichael), Donald Curtis (Harry), John Emery (Doctor Fleurot), Leo G. Carroll (Doctor Murchison), Norman Lloyd (Garmes), and Steven Geray, Paul Harvey, Erskine Sandford, Janet Scott, Victor Killian, Bill Goodwin, Art Baker, Wallace Ford, Regis Toomey, Teddy Infuhr, Addison Richards, Dave Willock, George Meader, Matt Morre, Harry Brown, Clarence Straight, Joel Davis, Edward Fielding, Richard Bartell, Michael Chekhov.

1946
NOTORIOUS

Production: Alfred Hitchcock, R.K.O., 1946. *Associate Producer:* Barbara Keon. *Director:* Alfred Hitchcock. *Scenario:* Ben Hecht, from a theme by Hitchcock. *Director of Photography:* Ted Tetzlaff, A.S.C. *Special Effects:* Vernon L. Walker and Paul Eagler, A.S.C. *Sets:* Albert S. D'Agostino, Carrol Clark, Darrell Silvera and Claude Carpenter. *Costumes:* Edith Head. *Music:* Roy Webb; conducted by Constantin Balaleinikoff. *Editing:* Theron Warth. *Sound Engineers:* John Tribby and Clem Portman. *Assistant Director:* William Dorfman. *Studio:* R.K.O. *Distributor:* R.K.O., 1946, 101 minutes. *Principal Actors:* Ingrid Bergman (Alicia Huberman), Cary Grant (Devlin), Claude Rains (Alexander Sebastian), Louis Calhern (Paul Prescott), Leopoldine Konstantin (Mrs. Sebastian), Reinhold Schünzel (Doctor Anderson), and Moroni Olsen, Ivan Triesault, Alexis Minotis, Eberhardt Krumschmidt, Fay Baker, Ricardo Costa, Lenore Ulric, Ramon Nomar, Peter von Zerneck, Sir Charles Mandl, Wally Brown.

1947
THE PARADINE CASE

Production: Selznick International, 1947. *Producer:* David O. Selznick. *Director:* Alfred Hitchcock. *Scenario:* David O. Selznick, from the novel by Robert Hichens. *Adaptation:* Alma Reville. *Director of Photography:* Lee Garmes. *Sets:* J. MacMillian Johnson and Thomas Morahan. *Costumes:* Travis Banton.

Music: Franz Waxman. *Editing:* Hal C. Kern and John Faure. *Studio:* Selznick International. *Distributor:* United Artists, 1947, 125 minutes. *Principal Actors:* Gregory Peck (Anthony Keane), Ann Todd (Gay Keane), Charles Laughton (Judge Harnfield), Ethel Barrymore (Lady Sophie Harnfield), Charles Coburn (Sir Simon Flaquer, the lawyer), Louis Jourdan (André Latour), Alida Valli (Maddalena, Anna Paradine), and Leo G. Carroll, John Goldsworthy, Isobel Elsom, Lester Matthews, Pat Aherne, Colin Hunter, John Williams.

1948
ROPE

Production: Transatlantic Pictures, Warner Bros., 1948. *Producers:* Sidney Bernstein and Alfred Hitchcock. *Director:* Alfred Hitchcock. *Scenario:* Arthur Laurents, from the play by Patrick Hamilton. *Adaptation:* Hume Cronyn. *Directors of Photography:* Joseph Valentine and William V. Skall, A.S.C. *Color by Technicolor:* Consultant, Natalie Kalmus. *Sets:* Perry Ferguson. *Music:* Leo F. Forbstein, based on the theme "Perpetual Movement No. 1" by Francis Poulenc. *Costumes:* Adrian. *Editing:* William H. Ziegler. *Studio:* Warner Bros. *Distributor:* Warner Bros., 1948, 80 minutes. *Principal Actors:* James Stewart (Rupert Cadell), John Dall (Shaw Brandon), Joan Chandler (Janet Walker), Sir Cedric Hardwicke (Mr. Kentley, David's father), Constance Collier (Mrs. Atwater), Edith Evanson (Mrs. Wilson, the governess), Douglas Dick (Kenneth Lawrence), Dick Hogan (David Kentley), Farley Granger (Philip).

1949
UNDER CAPRICORN

Production: Transatlantic Pictures, Warner Bros., 1949, G.B. *Producers:* Sidney Bernstein and Alfred Hitchcock. *Managing Producers:* John Palmer and Fred Ahern. *Director:* Alfred Hitchcock. *Scenario:* James Bridie, from the novel by Helen Simpson. *Adaptation:* Hume Cronyn. *Director of Photography:* Jack Cardiff, A.S.C., and Paul Beeson, Ian Craig, David McNeilly, Jack Haste. *Sets:* Tom Morahan. *Music:* Richard Addinsell; conducted by Louis Levy. *Editing:* A. S. Bates. *Costumes:* Roger Furse. *Color by Technicolor:* Consultants, Natalie Kalmus and Joan Bridge. *Studio:* M.G.M. at Elstree. *Distributor:* Warner Bros., 1949, 117 minutes. *Principal Actors:* Ingrid Bergman (Lady Henrietta Flusky), Joseph Cotten (Sam Flusky), Michael Wilding (Charles Adare), Margaret Leighton (Milly), Jack Watting (Winter, Flusky's secretary), Cecil Parker (Sir Richard, the tutor), Dennis O'Dea (Corrigan, the Attorney-General), and Olive Sloan, John Ruddock, Bill Shine, Victor Lucas, Ronald Adam, G. H. Mulcaster, Maureen Delaney, Julia Lang, Betty McDermot, Roderick Lovell, Francis de Wolff.

1950
STAGE FRIGHT

Production: Alfred Hitchcock, Warner Bros., 1950, G.B. *Director:* Alfred Hitchcock. *Scenario:* Whitfield Cook, from two stories by Selwyn Jepson, "Man Running" and "Outrun the Constable." *Adaptation:* Alma Reville. *Additional Dialogue:* James Bridie. *Director of Photography:* Wilkie Cooper. *Sets:* Terence Verity. *Music:* Leighton Lucas, conducted by Louis Levy. *Editing:* Edward Jarvis. *Sound Engineer:* Harold King. *Studio:* Elstree, G.B. *Distributor:* Warner Bros., 1950, 110 minutes. *Principal Actors:* Marlene Dietrich (Charlotte Inwood), Jane Wyman (Eve Gill), Michael Wilding (Inspector Wilfred Smith), Richard Todd (Jonathan Cooper), Alastair Sim (Commodore Gill), Dame Sybil Thorndike (Mrs. Gill) and Kay Walsh, Miles Malleson, André Morell, Patricia Hitchcock, Hector MacGregor, Joyce Grenfell.

1951
STRANGERS ON A TRAIN

Production: Alfred Hitchcock, Warner Bros., 1951, U.S.A. *Director:* Alfred Hitchcock. *Scenario:* Raymond Chandler and Czenzi Ormonde, from the novel by Patricia Highsmith. *Adaptation:* Whitfield Cook. *Director of Photography:* Robert Burks, A.S.C. *Special Photographic Effects:* H. F. Koene Kamp. *Sets:* Ted Hawortt and George James Hopkins. *Music:* Dimitri Tiomkin, conducted by Ray Heindorf. *Costumes:* Leah Rhodes. *Editing:* William H. Ziegler. *Sound Engineer:* Dolph Thomas. *Studio:* Warner Bros. *Distributor:* Warner Bros., 1951, 101 minutes. *Principal Actors:* Farley Granger (Guy Haines), Ruth Roman (Ann Morton), Robert Walker (Bruno Anthony), Leo G. Carroll (Senator Morton), Patricia Hitchcock (Barbara Morton), Laura Elliot (Miriam Haines), Marion Lorne (Mrs. Anthony), Jonathan Hale (Mr. Anthony), and Howard St. John, John Brown, Norma Warden, Robert Gist, John Doucette, Charles Meredith, Murray Alper, Robert B. Williams, Roy Engel.

1952
I CONFESS

Production: Alfred Hitchcock, Warner Bros., 1952. *Associate Producer:* Barbara Keon. *Supervisory Producer:* Sherry Shourdes. *Director:* Alfred Hitchcock. *Scenario:* George Tabori and William Archibald,

from the play by Paul Anthelme, "Our Two Consciences." *Director of Photography:* Robert Burks, A.S.C. *Sets:* Edward S. Haworth and George James Hopkins. *Music:* Dimitri Tiomkin, conducted by Ray Heindorf. *Editing:* Rudi Fehr, A.C.E. *Costumes:* Orry-Kelly. *Sound Engineer:* Oliver S. Garretson. *Technical Consultant:* Father Paul la Couline. *Police Consultant:* Inspector Oscar Tangvay. *Studio:* Warner Bros. *Location Work:* Quebec. *Assistant Director:* Don Page. *Distributor:* Warner Bros., 1952, 95 minutes. *Principal Actors:* Montgomery Clift (Father Michael Logan), Anne Baxter (Ruth Grandfort), Karl Malden (Inspector Larrue), Brian Aherne (the attorney Willy Robertson), O. E. Hasse (Otto Keller), Dolly Haas (Alma Keller, his wife), Roger Dann (Pierre Grandfort), Charles André (Father Millais), Judson Pratt (Murphy, a policeman), Ovila Legare (Vilette, the lawyer), Gilles Pelletier (Father Benoit).

1954
DIAL M FOR MURDER

Production: Alfred Hitchcock, Warner Bros., 1954. *Director:* Alfred Hitchcock. *Scenario:* A. Hitchcock, from the play by Frederick Knott. *Director of Photography:* Robert Burks, A.S.C. *Film:* Naturalvision and 3-D. *Color:* Warner Color. *Sets:* Edward Carrère and George James Hopkins. *Music:* Dimitri Tiomkin, conducted by the composer. *Costumes:* Moss Mabry. *Sound Engineer:* Oliver S. Garretson. *Editing:* Rudi Fehr. *Studio:* Warner Bros. *Distributor:* Warner Bros., 1954, 88 minutes. *Principal Actors:* Ray Milland (Tom Wendice), Grace Kelly (Margot Wendice), Robert Cummings (Mark Halliday), John Williams (Chief Inspector Hubbard), Anthony Dawson (Captain Swan Lesgate), Leo Britt (the narrator), Patrick Allen (Pearson), George Leigh (William), George Alderson (the detective), Robin Hughes (a police sergeant).

REAR WINDOW

Production: Alfred Hitchcock, Paramount, 1954. *Director:* Alfred Hitchcock. *Scenario:* John Michael Hayes, from a novelette by Cornell Woolrich. *Director of Photography:* Robert Burks, A.S.C. *Color:* Technicolor. *Consultant:* Richard Mueller. *Special Effects:* John P. Fulton. *Sets:* Hal Pereira, Joseph McMillan Johnson, Sam Comer and Ray Mayer. *Music:* Franz Waxman. *Editing:* George Tomasini. *Costumes:* Edith Head. *Assistant Director:* Herbert Coleman. *Sound Engineers:* Harry Lindgren and John Cope. *Distributor:* Paramount, 1954, 112 minutes. *Principal Actors:* James Stewart (L. B. Jeffries, called "Jeff"), Grace Kelly (Lisa Fremont), Wendell Corey (Thomas J. Doyle, the detective), Thelma Ritter (Stella, the nurse), Raymond Burr (Lars Thorwald), Judith Evelyn (Miss Lonely Heart), Ross Bagdasarian (the composer), Georgine Darcy (Miss Torse, the dancer), Jesslyn Fax (the lady sculptor), Rand Harper (honeymooner), Irene Winston (Mrs. Thorwald), and Denny Bartlett, Len Hendry, Mike Mahoney, Alan Lee, Anthony Warde, Harry Landers, Dick Simmons, Fred Graham, Edwin Parker, M. English, Kathryn Grandstaff, Havis Davenport, Iphigénie Castiglioni, Sara Berner, Frank Cady.

1955
TO CATCH A THIEF
Production: Alfred Hitchcock, Paramount, 1955. *Director:* Alfred Hitchcock. *Second Unit Direction:* Herbert Coleman. *Scenario:* John Michael Hayes, from the novel by David Dodge. *Director of Photography:* Robert Burks, A.S.C. *Photography Second Unit:* Wallace Kelley. *Color:* Technicolor. *Consultant:* Richard Mueller. *Special Effects:* John P. Fulton. *Process Photo:* Farciot Edouart, A.S.C. *Sets:* Hal Pereira, Joseph MacMillan Johnson, Sam Comer and Arthur Krams. *Music:* Lynn Murray. *Editing:* George Tomasini. *Costumes:* Edith Head. *Assistant Director:* Daniel McCauley. *Sound Engineers:* Lewis and John Cope. *Studio:* Paramount. *Location Work:* Côte d'Azur, France. *Distributor:* Paramount, 1955, 97 minutes. *Principal Actors:* Cary Grant (John Robie, called "The Cat"), Grace Kelly (Frances Stevens), Charles Vanel (Bertrani), Jessie Royce Landis (Mrs. Stevens), Brigitte Auber (Danielle Foussard), René Blancard (Commissioner Lepic), and John Williams, Georgette Anys, Roland Lesaffre, Jean Hebey, Dominique Davray, Russel Gaige, Marie Stoddard, Frank Chellano, Otto F. Schulze, Guy de Vestel, Bela Kovacs, John Alderson, Don McGowan, W. Willie Davis, Edward Manouk, Jean Martinelli, Martha Bamattre, Aimee Torriani, Paul "Tiny" Newlan, Lewis Charles.

1956
THE TROUBLE WITH HARRY
Production: Alfred Hitchcock, Paramount, 1956. *Director:* Alfred Hitchcock. *Scenario:* John Michael Hayes, from the novel by John Trevor Story. *Director of Photography:* Robert Burks, A.S.C. *Special Effects:* John P. Fulton. *Color:* Technicolor. *Consultant:* Richard Mueller. *Sets:* Hal Pereira, John Goodman, Sam Comer and Emile Kuri. *Music:* Bernard Herrmann. *Song:* "Flaggin' the Train to Tuscaloosa." *Lyrics:* Mack David. *Music:* Raymond Scott. *Editing:* Alma Macrorie. *Costumes:* Edith Head. *Studio:* Paramount. *Distributor:* Paramount,

1956, 99 minutes. *Principal Actors:* Edmund Gwenn (Captain Albert Wiles), John Forsythe (Sam Marlowe, the painter), Shirley MacLaine (Jennifer, Harry's wife), Mildred Natwick (Miss Gravely), Jerry Mathers (Tony, Harry's son), Mildred Dunnock (Mrs. Wiggs), Royal Dano (Alfred Wiggs), and Parker Fennelly, Barry Macollum, Dwight Marfield, Leslie Wolff, Philip Truex, Ernest Curt Bach.

THE MAN WHO KNEW TOO MUCH
Production: Alfred Hitchcock, Paramount, Filmwite Prod., 1955. *Associate Producer:* Herbert Coleman. *Director:* Alfred Hitchcock. *Scenario:* John Michael Hayes and Angus MacPhail, from a story by Charles Bennett and D. B. Wyndham-Lewis. *Director of Photography:* Robert Burks, A.S.C. *Color:* Technicolor. *Consultant:* Richard Mueller. *Special Effects:* John P. Fulton, A.S.C. *Sets:* Hal Pereira, Henry Bumstead, Sam Comer and Arthur Krams. *Music:* Bernard Herrmann. *Lyrics:* Jay Livingston and Ray Evans: "Whatever Will Be"; "We'll Love Again"; Cantata "Storm Cloud" by Arthur Benjamin and D. B. Wyndham-Lewis, performed by the London Symphony Orchestra, under the direction of Bernard Herrmann. *Editing:* George Tomasini, A.C.E. *Costumes:* Edith Head. *Sound Engineers:* Franz Paul and Gene Garvin, Western Electric. *Assistant Director:* Howard Joslin. *Studio:* Paramount. *Location Work:* Morocco. *Distributor:* Paramount, 1956, 120 minutes. *Principal Actors:* James Stewart (Doctor Ben MacKenna), Doris Day (Jo, his wife), Daniel Gelin (Louis Bernard), Brenda de Banzie (Mrs. Drayton), Bernard Miles (Mr. Drayton), Ralph Truman (Inspector Buchanan), Mogens Wieth (the ambassador), Alan Mowbray (Val Parnell), Hilary Brooke (Jan Peterson), Christopher Olsen (little Hank MacKenna), Reggie Malder (Rien, the assassin), and Yves Brainville, Richard Wattis, Alix Talton, Noel Willman, Caroline Jones, Leo Gordon, Abdelhaq Chraibi, Betty Baskomb, Patrick Aherne, Louis Mercier, Anthony Warde, Lewis Martin, Richard Wordsworth.

1957
THE WRONG MAN
Production: Alfred Hitchcock, Warner Bros., 1957. *Associate Producer:* Herbert Coleman. *Director:* Alfred Hitchcock. *Scenario:* Maxwell Anderson and Angus MacPhail, from "The True Story of Christopher Emmanuel Balestrero" by Maxwell Anderson. *Director of Photography:* Robert Burks, A.S.C. *Sets:* Paul Sylbert and William L. Kuehl. *Music:* Bernard Herrmann. *Editing:* George Tomasini. *Assistant Director:* Daniel J. McCauley. *Studio:* Warner Bros. *Location Work:* New York. *Technical Consultant:*

Frank O'Connor (Police Magistrate to the District Attorney, Queens County, New York). *Sound Engineer:* Earl Crain, Sr. *Distributor:* Warner Bros., 1957, 105 minutes. *Principal Actors:* Henry Fonda (Christopher Emmanuel Balestrero, called "Manny"), Vera Miles (Rose, his wife), Anthony Quayle (O'Connor), Harold J. Stone (Lieutenant Bowers), Charles Cooper (Matthews, a detective), John Heldabrant (Tomasini), Richard Robbins (Daniel, the guilty man), and Esther Minciotti, Doreen Lang, Laurinda Barrett, Norma Connolly, Nehemiah Persoff, Lola D'Annunzio, Kippy Campbell, Robert Essen, Dayton Lummis, Frances Reid, Peggy Webber.

1958
VERTIGO

Production: Alfred Hitchcock, Paramount, 1958. *Associate Producer:* Herbert Coleman. *Director:* Alfred Hitchcock. *Scenario:* Alec Coppel and Samuel Taylor, from the novel by Pierre Boileau and Thomas Narcejac, *"D'entre les morts."* *Director of Photography:* Robert Burks, A.S.C. *Special Effects:* John Fulton. *Sets:* Hal Pereira, Henry Bumstead, Sam Comer and Frank McKelvey. *Color:* Technicolor. *Consultant:* Richard Mueller. *Music:* Bernard Herrmann; conducted by Muir Mathieson. *Editing:* George Tomasini. *Costumes:* Edith Head. *Assistant Director:* Daniel McCauley. *Sound Engineers:* Harold Lewis and Winston Leverett. *Titles:* Saul Bass. *Special Sequence:* Designed, by John Ferren. *Studio:* Paramount. *Location Work:* San Francisco. *Distribution:* Paramount, 1958, 120 minutes. *Principal Actors:* James Stewart (John "Scottie" Ferguson), Kim Novak (Madeleine Elster and Judy Barton), Barbara Bel Geddes (Midge), Henry Jones (the coroner), Tom Helmore (Gavin Elster), Raymond Bailey (the doctor), and Ellen Corby, Konstantin Shayne, Lee Patrick.

1959
NORTH BY NORTHWEST

Production: Alfred Hitchcock, Metro-Goldwyn-Mayer, 1959. *Associate Producer:* Herbert Coleman. *Director:* Alfred Hitchcock. *Original Scenario:* Ernest Lehman. *Director of Photography:* Robert Burks, A.S.C. *Color:* Technicolor. *Consultant:* Charles K. Hagedon. *Special Photographic Effects:* A. Arnold Gillespie and Lee Le Blanc. *Sets:* Robert Boyle, William A. Horning, Merrill Pyle, Henry Grace and Frank McKelvey. *Music:* Bernard Herrmann. *Editing:* George Tomasini. *Title Design:* Saul Bass. *Sound Engineer:* Frank Milton. *Assistant Director:* Robert Saunders. *Studio:* Metro-Goldwyn-

Mayer. *Location Work:* New York (Long Island), Chicago, Rapid City (Mount Rushmore), South Dakota (National Memorial). *Distributor:* Metro-Goldwyn-Mayer, 1959, 136 minutes. *Principal Actors:* Cary Grant (Roger Thornhill), Eva Marie Saint (Eve Kandall), James Mason (Phillip Vandamm), Jessie Royce Landis (Clara Thornhill), Leo G. Carroll (the Professor), Philip Ober (Lester Townsend), Josephine Hutchinson ("Mrs. Townsend," the housekeeper), Martin Landau (Leonard), Adam Williams (Valerian), and Carleton Young, Edward C. Platt, Philip Coolidge, Doreen Lang, Edward Binns, Robert Ellenstein, Lee Tremayne, Patrick McVey, Ken Lynch, Robert B. Williams, Larry Dobkin, Ned Glass, John Berardino, Malcolm Atterbury.

1960
PSYCHO

Production: Alfred Hitchcock, Paramount, 1960. *Unit Manager:* Lew Leary. *Director:* Alfred Hitchcock. *Scenario:* Joseph Stefano, from the novel by Robert Bloch. *Director of Photography:* John L. Russel, A.S.C. *Special Photographic Effects:* Clarence Champagne. *Sets:* Joseph Hurley, Robert Claworthy and George Milo. *Music:* Bernard Herrmann. *Sound Engineers:* Walden O. Watson and William Russell. *Title Design:* Saul Bass. *Editing:* George Tomasini. *Assistant Director:* Hilton A. Green. *Costumes:* Helen Colvig. *Studio:* Paramount. *Location Work:* Arizona and California. *Distributor:* Paramount, 1960, 109 minutes. *Principal Actors:* Anthony Perkins (Norman Bates), Vera Miles (Lila Crane, Marion's sister), John Gavin (Sam Loomis), Martin Balsam (Milton Arbogast, detective), John McIntire (Chambers, the Sheriff), Simon Oakland (Doctor Richmond), Janet Leigh (Marion Crane), Frank Albertson (the millionaire), Patricia Hitchcock (Caroline), and Vaughn Taylor, Lurene Tuttle, John Anderson, Mort Mills.

1963
THE BIRDS

Production: Universal, 1963. *Producer:* Alfred Hitchcock. *Director:* Alfred Hitchcock. *Scenario:* Evan Hunter, from the work by Daphne du Maurier. *Director of Photography:* Robert Burks, A.S.C. *Color:* Technicolor. *Special Effects:* Lawrence A. Hampton. *Special Photographic Adviser:* Ub Iwerks. *Production Director:* Norman Deming. *Sets:* Robert Boyle and George Milo. *Sound Consultant:* Bernard Herrmann. *Composition and Production of Electronic Sound:* Remi Gassman and Oskar Sala. *Bird Trainer:* Ray Berwick. *Assistant Director:* James H. Brown. *Assistant to Hitchcock:* Peggy Robertson. *Il-*

lustrator: Alfred Whitlock. *Credits:* James A. Pollak. *Editing:* George Tomasini. *Studio:* Universal. *Location Work:* Bodega Bay, California, San Francisco. *Distributor:* Universal, 1963, 120 minutes. *Principal Actors:* Rod Taylor (Mitch Brenner), Tippi Hedren (Melanie Daniels), Jessica Tandy (Mrs. Brenner), Suzanne Pleshette (Annie Hayworth), Veronica Cartwright (Cathy Brenner), Ethel Griffies (Mrs. Bundy), Charles McGraw (Sebastian Sholes), Ruth McDevitt (Mrs. MacGruder), and Joe Mantell, Malcolm Atterbury, Karl Swenson, Elizabeth Wilson, Lonny Chapman, Doodles Weaver, John McGovern, Richard Deacon, Doreen Lang, Bill Quinn.

1964
MARNIE

Production: Alfred Hitchcock, Universal, 1964. *Producer:* Albert Whitlock. *Director:* Alfred Hitchcock. *Scenario:* Jay Presson Allen, from the novel by Winston Graham. *Director of Photography:* Robert Burks, A.S.C. *Color:* Technicolor. *Sets:* Robert Boyle and George Milo. *Music:* Bernard Herrmann. *Editing:* George Tomasini. *Assistant Director:* James H. Brown. *Assistant to Hitchcock:* Peggy Robertson. *Sound Engineers:* Waldon O. Watson, William Green. *Distributor:* Universal, 1964, 120 minutes. *Principal Actors:* Tippi Hedren (Marnie Edgar), Sean Connery (Mark Rutland), Diane Baker (Lil Mainwaring), Martin Gabel (Sidney Strutt), Louise Latham (Bernice Edgar, Marnie's mother), Bob Sweeney (Cousin Bob), Alan Napier (Mr. Rutland), S. John Launer (Sam Ward), Mariette Hartley (Susan Clabon), and Bruce Dern, Henry Beckman, Edith Evanson, Meg Wyllie.

1966
TORN CURTAIN

Director: Alfred Hitchcock. *Scenario:* Brian Moore. *Director of Photography:* John F. Warren, A.S.C. *Sets:* Frank Arrigo. *Sound:* Waldon O. Watson and William Russell. *Music:* John Addison. *Editing:* Bud Hoffman. *Assistant Director:* Donald Baer. *Principal Actors:* Paul Newman (Professor Michael Armstrong), Julie Andrews (Sarah Sherman), Lila Kedrova (Countess Kuchinska), Hans-joerg Felmy (Heinrich Gerhard), Tamara Toumanova (Ballerina), Wolfgang Kieling (Hermann Gromek), Gunter Strack (Professor Karl Manfred), Ludwig Donath (Professor Gustav Lindt), David Opatoshu (Mr. Jacobi), Gisela Fischer (Dr. Koska), Mort Mills (Farmer), Carolyn Conwell (Farmer's wife), Arthur Gould-Porter (Freddy), Gloria Gorvin.

1969
TOPAZ

Production: Universal. *Producer:* Alfred Hitchcock. *Associate Producer:* Herbert Coleman: *Director:* Alfred Hitchcock. *Scenario:* Samuel Taylor, from the novel by Leon Uris. *Director of Photography:* Jack Hildyard. *Color:* Technicolor. *Music:* Maurice Jarre. *Sets:* John Austin and Henry Bumstead. *Costumes:* Edith Head and Pierre Balmain. *Editing:* William Ziegler. *Sound:* Waldon O. Watson and Robert R. Bertrand. *Assistant Directors:* Douglas Green and James Westman. *Assistant to Alfred Hitchcock:* Peggy Robertson. *French Technical Advisers:* J. P. Mathieu and Odette Ferry. *Studio:* Universal. *Location Work:* West Germany, Copenhagen, New York, Washington, Paris. *Distribution:* Universal, 1969, 127 minutes. *Principal Actors:* Frederick Stafford (André Devereaux), Dany Robin (Nicole Devereaux), John Vernon (Rico Parra), Karin Dor (Juanita de Cordoba), Michel Piccoli (Jacques Granville), Philippe Noiret (Henri Jarré), Claude Jade (Michèle Picard), Michel Subor (François Picard), Roscoe Lee Browne (Philippe Dubois), Per-Axel Arosenius (Boris Kusenov), John Forsythe (Michael Nordstrom), Edmond Ryan (McKittreck), Sonja Kolthoff (Mrs. Kusenov), Tina Hedstrom (Tamara Kusenov), John Van Dreelen (Claude Martin), Don Randolph (Luis Uribe), Roberto Contreras (Munoz), Carlos Rivas (Hernandez), Lewis Charles (Mr. Mendoza), Anna Navarro (Mrs. Mendoza), John Roper (Thomas), George Skaff (René d'Arcy), Roger Til (Jean Chabrier), Sandor Szabo (Emile Redon), Lew Brown (an American official).

1972
FRENZY

Production: Universal. *Producer:* Alfred Hitchcock. *Associate Producer:* Bill Hill. *Production Director:* Brian Burgess. *Director:* Alfred Hitchcock. *Scenario:* Anthony Shaffer, from the novel by Arthur La Bern, "Goodbye Piccadilly, Farewell Leicester Square." *Director of Photography:* Gil Taylor. *Color:* Technicolor. *Special Effects:* Albert Whitlock. *Music:* Ron Goodwin. *Sets:* Sydney Cain and Robert Laing. *Costumes:* Dulcie Midwinter. *Editing:* John Jympson. *Sound:* Peter Handford and Gordon K. McCallum. *Assistant Director:* Colin Brewer. *Assistant to Alfred Hitchcock:* Peggy Robertson. *Studio:* Pinewood. *Location Work:* London. *Distribution:* Universal, 1972, 116 minutes. *Principal Actors:* Jon Finch (Richard Blaney), Alec McCowen (Inspector Oxford), Barry Foster (Bob Rusk), Barbara Leigh-Hunt (Brenda Blaney), Bernard Cribbins (Forsythe), Anna Massey

(Barbara "Babs" Milligan), Vivien Merchant (Mrs. Oxford), Billie Whitelaw (Hetty Porter), Elsie Randolph (Gladys, the hotel employee), Rita Webb (Mrs. Rusk), Clive Swift (Johnny Porter), Jean Marsh (Monica Barling, Brenda's secretary), Madge Ryan (Mrs. Davison), George Tovey (Mr. Salt), John Boxer (Sir George), Noel Johnson and Gerald Sim (two men at the bar), June Ellis (the barmaid), Bunny May (the barman), Robert Keegan (the hospital patient), Jimmy Gardner (the hotel porter), Michael Bates (Sergeant Spearman).

1976
FAMILY PLOT

Production: Universal. *Producer:* Alfred Hitchcock. *Production Director:* Ernest Wehmeyer. *Director:* Alfred Hitchcock. *Scenario:* Ernest Lehman, from the novel by Victor Canning, "The Rainbird Pattern." *Director of Photography:* Leonard South. *Color:* Technicolor. *Special Effects:* Albert Whitlock. *Music:* John Williams. *Sets:* Henry Bumstead and James Payne. *Costumes:* Edith Head. *Editing:* Terry Williams. *Sound:* James Alexander and Robert Hoyt. *Assistant Directors:* Howard G. Kazanjian and Wayne Farlow. *Studio:* Universal. *Distribution:* Universal, 1976, 120 minutes. *Principal Actors:* Karen Black (Fran), Bruce Dern (George Lumley), Barbara Harris (Blanche Tyler), William Devane (Arthur Adamson), Cathleen Nesbitt (Julia Rainbird), Ed Lauter (Joseph Maloney), Katherine Helmond (Mrs. Maloney), Warren J. Kemmerling (Grandison), Edith Atwater (Mrs. Clay), William Prince (the bishop), Nicolas Colasanto (Constantine), Marge Redmond (Vera Hannagan), John Lehne (Andy Bush), Charles Tyner (Wheeler), Alexander Lockwood (the pastor), Martin West (Sanger).

SELECTED BIBLIOGRAPHY

AMENGUAL, BARTHÉLÉMY and BORDE, RAYMOND—*Alfred Hitchcock* (Premier Plan, Serdoc, Lyon 1960)

BOGDANOVICH, PETER—*The Cinema of Alfred Hitchcock* (The Museum of Modern Art Film Library/Doubleday & Co. Inc., New York 1962)

Cahiers du Cinéma—No. 39 (Special Issue), Paris, October 1953

Cahiers du Cinéma—No. 62, Paris, August–September 1956

MANZ, HANS-PETER—*Alfred Hitchcock* (Sanssouci Verlag, Zürich, 1962)

NOBLE, PETER—*An Index to the Creative Work of Alfred Hitchcock* (Sight and Sound Supplement: "Index Series," No. 18, London 1949)

PERRY, GEORGE—*The Films of Alfred Hitchcock* (Studio Vista Ltd., London 1965; E. P. Dutton and Co. Inc., New York 1965)

WOOD, ROBIN—*Hitchcock's Films* (A. Zwemmer Ltd., London 1965; A. S. Barnes and Co. Inc., New York 1965)

INDEX OF FILM TITLES

INDEX OF NAMES